The Arnold History of Britain

The Long Eighteenth Century

British Political and Social History
1688–1832

Frank O'Gorman

Professor of History,
University of Manchester

A member of the Hodder Headline Group
LONDON

First published in Great Britain in 1997 by
Arnold, a member of the Hodder Headline Group
338 Euston Road, London NW1 3BH

Co-published in the United States of America by
Oxford University Press Inc.,
198 Madison Avenue, New York NY10016

British Library Cataloguing in Publication Data
A catalogue record for this book is available from the British Library

Library of Congress Cataloging-in-Publication Data
O'Gorman, Frank.
    The long eighteenth century: British political and social
history. 1688–1832 / Frank O'Gorman.
        p. cm. – (The Arnold history of Britain)
    Includes bibliographical references and index.
    ISBN 0-340-56752-X (hb). – ISBN 0-340-56751-1 (pb)
    1. Great Britain – Politics and government – 18th century. 2. Great
Britain – Politics and government – 1800–1837.   3. Great Britain – Politics and
government – 1689–1702.   4. Great Britain – Social conditions – 18th century.
I. Title.   II. Series.
DA480.038   1997
941.07–dc21   97-14187
                                                                     CIP

ISBN 0 340 46752 X (hb)
ISBN 0 340 56751 1 (pb)

3 4 5 6 7 8 9 10

Composition by Saxon Graphics Ltd, Derby
Printed and bound in Great Britain by J W Arrowsmith Ltd, Bristol

To Birgit Kristensen
for incomparable fortitude

Contents

Introduction

Half a lifetime of teaching and research has left me unwilling to apologize for the appearance of a work of synthesis on British history during the 'long eighteenth century'. The steady increase in the number of books and articles on the period pouring from the presses is a sign of great vitality and health. Strangely, no single volume exists which covers the entire period, although there are several excellent volumes on parts of it. This book is offered to the academic public in the belief that the time is ripe for a general synthesis of the fortunes of these islands in this most fascinating period of British history. After all, we need constantly to test and to review received opinions, to explore different approaches and even to construct new 'models', however tentative, of the history of Britain during the long eighteenth century.

The Whig historians used to portray the eighteenth century as a period of unalloyed success. According to the Whig interpretation, it was in this period that Britain set out upon her distinctive and unique quest. Alone among the European powers, Britain combined steady constitutional progress with unparalleled religious toleration and incomparable levels of freedom of thought and expression. On these secure foundations Britain was to expand her economy, undertake an 'industrial revolution' and acquire a worldwide empire. It was a dazzling vision. Its patriotic simplicities, in one version or another, prevailed into the second half of the twentieth century. Even recent social historians like Asa Briggs treated the last 50 years of the long eighteenth century as part of a period of 'improvement' in which the growth of towns, the development of reform movements, the march of industry and the demand for democracy formed the basic themes of a narrative of steady progress.[1]

Now we have abandoned Whig history and the visions that went with it. In the last 50 years eighteenth century history has been rewritten on several occasions and according to different orthodoxies. The triumphalism of Whig history was first overtaken between the two great wars of this century by the 'high' political school of Sir Lewis Namier and his followers which stressed the importance of material and practical influences upon politics in the past.[2] 'Namierite' history emphasized the role played by individuals on the aristocratic political stage yet minimized the importance of ideas and principles in determining behaviour. Although these general approaches were, and remain, controversial there can be no question that Namier placed the political history of the eighteenth century upon sound scholarly foundations. In the process, however, parts of the great narratives of Whig history were found to be unsustainable. According to Namier there was no steady decline in royal power during the eighteenth century, no gradual development of a party system and still less evidence of a liberal public opinion. Since the 1960s a somewhat different approach, typified in the work of E.P. Thompson and George Rudé, has taken a broader view of eighteenth-century society, focusing less on high politics and more on issues in social history, such as class, gender and popular culture.[3] This invigorating approach has widened the appeal of the long eighteenth century and introduced its practitioners to a range of new methodologies and problems, hitherto neglected. Since the mid-1980s a 'revisionist' school of writers has restored the significance of religion to eighteenth century history, arguing that politics was shaped less by economic than by dynastic considerations.[4] They have substituted for the old Whig, and newer, socially based interpretations of the eighteenth century, a much more traditional view of the social and political order. The strength of Britain, according to this interpretation, lay less in its novel entrepreneurial activities than in the elements of stability and continuity which it derived from its status as a rural *ancien regime* society, the monarchy, the church and the aristocracy.

One of the consequences of revisionism has been to change the thinking of many historians. Although many of them may, and do, differ strongly with particular arguments in revisionist history, most of them now study the eighteenth century for its own sake and in its own terms, not as a preparation for the very different mass urban and democratic society which came into existence late in the nineteenth century. Indeed, one of the most prominent non-revisionist historians, Professor John Brewer, has written of Britain as a 'fiscal military state' in the eighteenth century, similar in many respects to the military monarchies of the Continent, far removed from the liberal state of the Whig historians.[5] Where once it was possible to see 'revolutions', industrial, agricultural and cultural, they now see only steady, unspectacular evolution. Where once they perceived the quickening pace of social advance, they now see the pronounced survival of seventeenth-century forms of thought and politics. Where once they had noted the emergence of a secular civilization, they now see only the obdurate survival of a profoundly religious culture. Where once they had seen the origins of the liberal state of the nineteenth century, they now see only a hierarchical society, based firmly upon birth, rank and property.

Historians divide up the past into periods which suit them and which provide a suitable context to their researches. Such divisions are not always easy to justify on wider grounds. However, to argue for a 'long' eighteenth century between 1688 and 1832 makes a good deal of historical sense. Most of the alternative dates, such as 1700 and 1714 at the beginning, and 1783, 1800 and 1815 at the end, are much less defensible. New centuries rarely mark new beginnings and 1714 establishes a new dynasty, not a new order. True, the significance of the Glorious Revolution can be exaggerated, and we can fall into the trap of assuming that an entirely new epoch opened in 1688. However, in many areas of life and in the history of Scotland and Ireland as well as that of England the Glorious Revolution *was* a watershed. Indeed, during the eighteenth century contemporaries were in no doubt that the political structures and the religious order with which they were familiar had their origins in 1688. Furthermore, the period exhibits a certain consistency in its basic concerns and concepts; these shaped a distinctive narrative which, to contemporaries, commenced with the overthrow of the Stuart monarchy in 1688–89 and terminated with a series of legislative reforms after 1828. The main elements of the narrative include the fitful drive towards political centralization, the search for a harmonious relationship between king and parliament, the defence of the Protestant realm against the forces of popery and the expansion of industry, commerce and empire. The year 1815 marks the end of a great era, not the dawn of a new historical era. Few new themes appear in the years immediately after 1815. It is true that the significance of the 1832 Reform Act can be exaggerated: historians are now generally agreed that those who framed it were more intent on conserving as much as they could of the old order. Nevertheless, the Reform Act was a sign that this old order was coming to a close. Contemporaries believed this to be the case and, indeed, many of its structures – political, religious and social – were by then undergoing rapid and decisive transformation.

For all that, it remains abnormally difficult to discern the character of the long eighteenth century in all its complexity. Some of its features – the growth of towns, the demand for political, social and humanitarian reform and the establishment of parliamentary government – seem familiar to us because they anticipate the interests of later generations. Others, however – the huge inequalities of wealth, the exacting formality of manners, the destitution of the masses and the dreadful treatment of children – appear to us to be strange and irrelevant features of a society which have (thankfully?) disappeared. To examine the political and social history of the period is to be struck with the complexity of its values and practices, especially within the four nations and within the heavily localized communities in which people lived their lives. With all this in mind, it may help the reader if I identify a number of central themes which give narrative shape and structural cohesion to the long eighteenth century.

The themes with which I shall be concerned in this book are six in number. The first of these is the development of the internal structure of Britain during the long eighteenth century, a period when a United Kingdom of Scotland and England emerged and a sense of British nationhood became a vital historical force. The Glorious Revolution acted as a powerful catalyst in this process, making for the greatest degree of unity and cohesion which these islands had ever known, although it did so with great violence and at the price of creating powerful religious and national resentments. Wales had been peacefully absorbed in the sixteenth century but the loyalty of Scotland to England was uncertain for at least 40 years after the Act of Union of 1707. Ireland, moreover, was a colony suffering military occupation, dominated by English troops and a small number of English native, and largely non-resident, landowners. During the course of the century these unwilling partners were, to a degree, integrated with England, but in many respects it was an uneasy and incomplete integration. The history of this Britain in the long eighteenth century is introduced in the first part of Chapter 1.

The second theme of the book is the role of religion in the life of the state and the life of the people. After all, religious divisions had been of vital – indeed, of revolutionary importance – during the seventeenth century. Recent attempts to depict England as a 'confessional state', an Anglican state whose essential unifying force was Protestantism, have served the invaluable function of reminding historians that England, to say nothing of Scotland and Ireland, in the eighteenth century remained a profoundly Christian society, one which rested on a nexus of traditional beliefs and practices. Although there can be no denying the importance of secular forces in this period, especially new developments in thought and science, to say nothing of the new opportunities for leisure, prosperity and the massive hunger for new consumer commodities, religious belief adjusted itself to the new realities of social life. Complete loss of faith was a rarity. Towards the end of the eighteenth century, in fact, a powerful religious revival was under way, manifesting itself in, on the one hand, a number of humanitarian reform movements and, on the other, the emergence and rapid development of new churches within the state. Obviously, then, religious sectarianism did not disappear during the 'long eighteenth century'. Although the bitterness of religious divisions was normally controlled and kept in check, they retained their ability to excite people's passions. On numerous occasions, both locally and nationally, religious issues broke the surface of politics, most spectacularly during the Gordon Riots in 1780, when anti-Catholic mobs stormed through the streets of London in a riotous binge of arson and violence. These religious themes will be introduced in the second part of Chapter 1.

Of scarcely less significance is a third theme with which this book will be concerned, the cohesion of the social order. It does not intend to celebrate, nor, indeed, to invent, a 'social consensus' in Hanoverian Britain. Indeed, there was always acute tension between the forces of social control and those of social protest. But, for the most part, acceptable compromises could be negotiated, compromises which safeguarded the social fabric. In the late seventeenth and throughout the eighteenth century Britain remained a society of orders and hierarchies. These she succeeded in maintaining, largely due to the harmony which prevailed between the landed elite and the increasingly wealthy, and numerous, middling orders. This collaboration was to be of the greatest importance, especially in view of the exclusion of so many of the poorer elements in society from the growing affluence of the times and their subsequent social and political alienation. This collaboration, together with the striking ability of the propertied classes, in the end, to maintain the patriotic loyalty of the masses, will provide a recurrent theme. It is first confronted in the fourth part of Chapter 1.

Fourth, and, indeed, one of the most widely remarked themes of the long eighteenth century, was the commercial and imperial expansion which contributed so much to the prosperity of British society. During the eighteenth century the wealth of Britain roughly doubled in real terms. The consequence was a growing domestic market which could only be satisfied through commercial expansion both at home and overseas. Britons were island peoples and they were becoming conscious of themselves as a trading nation. They were mobile, expansive and, not least, enthusiastic consumers of foreign as well as domestic products. Consequently, the defence of her empire, her markets and her raw materials constantly engaged British statesmen. Convinced that political and military power depended upon economic power, Britain sought and won an extensive commercial empire against severe international competition. London was the centre of what became in the eighteenth century one of the great commercial empires in the history of the world, but provincial cities and ports made increasingly significant contributions to Britain's imperial dynamism. It is not too much to claim that the wealth she derived from her commercial and imperial expansion made victory possible in the successive wars in which she was involved after 1688. An introduction to these issues may be found in the fifth part of Chapter 1.

The fifth theme of the book follows naturally from the fourth. It addresses the role of Britain in Europe and considers the status of Britain as a European state. In the eighteenth century the fortunes of Britain were closely bound up with those of her European neighbours. It is scarcely too much to say that the outcomes of the Glorious Revolution, the Jacobite rebellions of 1715 and 1745 and the American War of Independence – to take just three major issues of the period – were determined by the actions of other European states. After a century in which Britain's role in Europe had been modest and even marginal, Britain became a major European power in the early eighteenth century. She was involved in six major European wars during 63 of the 144 years (over 44 per cent) between 1688 and 1832. The consequences of warfare of such frequency were to be considerable, in the end affecting the everyday lives of millions of people. There is, moreover, a further advantage in viewing Britain in her European context. It enables us to establish illuminating comparative views of British society. For example, recent writers, not least Dr J.C.D. Clark, have treated Britain as an *ancien regime* society, similar in her aristocratic, monarchical and religious structures to many of her European neighbours. To what extent is this true? Alternatively, was Britain, as the Whig historians used to argue, unique in her political arrangements and in her social and economic circumstances? In dealing with such issues, we deepen our understanding of Britain in the eighteenth century. These issues are introduced in the fourth part of Chapter 1.

The final theme with which this volume is concerned has been the standard fare of many writers on this period, the development of liberal forms of political thought and action which restricted and limited the power of the state. Perhaps some historians have been more concerned to celebrate this development than to explain it and to analyse it. Even so, it is difficult to avoid the conclusion that already by the end of the eighteenth century royal government had been transformed into government by the King-in-Parliament. The Glorious Revolution ended the prospect of a centralized and absolute monarchy, giving rise to a system based on local political and judicial independence. Consequently, many key activities ranging from law enforcement and tax collection to economic regulation and the raising of armies were placed in the hands of the local gentry and aristocracy. Yet there is far more to 'politics' than the traditional fare of parliaments and parties. It is a distortion of the political structure of the long eighteenth century to erect artificial polarities between 'high' and 'low' politics, with the former imposing itself upon the latter. The political process was led, even commanded, by the landed elite but it depended upon and found room for men from humbler backgrounds. Their contribution to public life was to be immense. It was they who manned the local committees and canvassed the voters at election time, who wrote and distributed political literature, who collected and spent political money and who, in general, organized political events, ranging from processions to petitions. Even lower down the social scale, the world of popular political culture, symbolic, festive and unwritten, could serve as an arena for political conflict between the humble and the great. To those excluded from formal patterns of political power, popular culture provided the stage and the language for protest, whether against the state, the church, the market or the landlord. These issues are introduced in the final part of Chapter 1.

Some of these themes would have been familiar to the Whig historians of earlier generations, but modern historians treat them in a different manner. To historians of our own generation, however, it is less permissible than it was in the days of the Whig historians to use the historical record as an opportunity to celebrate the virtues and victories of any particular social and political regime. We are more genuinely aware of the harsh face of eighteenth-century life than our predecessors were. Polite society rested somewhat precariously upon the tolerance of millions of people for whom life remained hard, uncomfortable and unhealthy. It took little to drive the social leaders of this reputedly strong and stable society into alarmism and panic. Contemporaries may have been agreed about the merits of the British constitution, for example, but they – Whigs and Tories, court and country, government and opposition, Anglican and Dissenter – disagreed deeply about political issues, and sometimes with a terrifying intensity. Contemporaries may have boasted about the stability of the social order, but that order was easily panicked. Furthermore, on many occasions it was clear that there was not much love lost for the upper classes, who protected themselves and their wealth behind the symbolic fencing of the legal system.

We no longer accept the Whig historians' agenda for the long eighteenth century. We no longer see the period as a great patriotic drama, as a continuing story of national success, because we can see the massive evidence of inertia, continuity and reaction. I have attempted in what follows to recognize the complexity of the long eighteenth century while attempting to identify some of its key thematic patterns. From the existing viewpoints available to historians at the end of the twentieth century, the long eighteenth century has no single identity, no single vocabulary and no single characterisation. This is arguably healthy, if sometimes confusing, since overarching interpretations always seem to oversimplify some complex issues and ignore others. I have striven to offer generalizations of national relevance without assuming that national considerations were the only ones that mattered. Finally, I have tried to recognize that social and political history are inextricably intertwined without assuming that one determines the other. In this way the book may illuminate both.

Notes
1. A. Briggs, *The Age of Improvement* (1959).
2. L.B. Namier, *The Structure of Politics at the Accession of George III*, 2nd edn (1982); *England in the Age of the American Revolution*, 2nd edn (1961). The student seeking an easily digestible introduction to Namier's ideas is recommended to try 'Monarchy and the Party System' in Namier's *Personalities and Powers* (1955).

3. E.P. Thompson's work has been of particular importance. See his *The Making of the English Working Class* (1963); *Whigs and Hunters: The Origins of the Black Act* (1975); 'The Moral Economy of the English Crowd in the Eighteenth Century', *Past and Present*, 50 (1971). See also G. Rudé, *The Crowd in History, 1730–1848* (1964); *Paris and London in the Eighteenth Century* (1970); *Wilkes and Liberty* (1965).
4. J.C.D. Clark, *English Society, 1688–1832* (CUP 1985); *Revolution and Rebellion* (CUP 1986); 'A General Theory of Party, Opposition and Government, 1688–1832', *Historical Journal*, 23 (1980).
5. J. Brewer, *The Sinews of Power: War, Money and the English State, 1688–1783* (1989).

Britain in the later seventeenth century

Place

Britain in the early modern period was a decentralized state in which political and social authority were widely delegated. Although Britain, unlike most European states, was blessed with geographical cohesion, her history in the early modern period is not the history of a single political and social entity. Most states in seventeenth century Europe were 'composite states' made up of diverse units acquired either by dynastic union, by military conquest or by political negotiation. Britain was just such a composite state, a dynastic union of the crowns of England and Scotland, to which Ireland was attached by conquest and colonization. Arguably, Britain's problems as a composite state were more serious than those of, for example, Spain, where a common religion prevailed.[1] The three kingdoms were united only by the monarchy; their political institutions, their social systems, their economies and, most importantly, their reformed religious establishments continued largely independently. As a consequence, Britain and Ireland were subjected to serious political, economic and, not least, religious divisions. Yet this composite state survived intact and within a century had become the greatest power in Europe. How this happened is the theme of this book.

At the beginning of our period the islands of Britain were sparsely populated. In rough figures, something under 5 000 000 people lived in England, 2 500 000 in Ireland, something over 1 000 000 in Scotland and around 400 000 in Wales, a total of slightly under 9 000 000. Over one-tenth of the English population lived in and around London, a concentration of population unmatched anywhere in Europe. The capital city far outstripped its challengers. Dublin had perhaps 60 000 people, but only three other towns in Britain had a population of over 20 000: Edinburgh had 40 000, Norwich and Bristol around 30 000 each. Of the population giants of the next century Newcastle had 15 000, Birmingham and Glasgow had perhaps 12 000, Manchester and Leeds only 10 000.

This population was not evenly distributed. Within England there were four principal centres of population: the south east and the south west had about one million people each, East Anglia and the north west about half a million each. In Scotland population was at its densest in the central

Lowlands, including Edinburgh and Glasgow. In Ireland there were two centres of population, one around Dublin, the other around Cork and Limerick in the west of Ireland. In Wales population was more evenly spread, but there were already signs of population density in the vale of Glamorgan.

The pattern of life was overwhelmingly parochial. It was local families, local custom, local institutions and local boundaries that maintained the framework in which people lived their lives. Eighty-five per cent of the inhabitants of England lived either in villages or in small market towns. Over 90 per cent of them were employed in agriculture or in associated trades and crafts. The Midlands area of England was still farmed on the open field system but much of the rest had already been enclosed. Most villages were for some purposes self-contained and self-governing; many were strongly influenced – some even controlled – by the estates of the gentry and aristocracy, which so strongly characterized the English scene. What distinguished the 40 counties of England, the dozens of market towns, the 9000 parishes and the even more numerous villages were their differences. In a society in which the seas and the rivers were the only efficient means of transport, patterns of life and speech remained inherently local and marvellously diverse.

The dynastic union of Scotland with England in 1603 had not led to a merging of their political, ecclesiastical and legal systems. Scotland remained a strongly independent nation with a firm sense of its own identity. This was reinforced by her feudal social organization, which was based on kinship and the clan as much as on lordship. Scottish land law provided for the division of property on death. Consequently the Scottish rural scene was marked by small units and uncertain tenure. Partly for this reason Scottish villages and towns tended to be smaller than they were in England. This does not necessarily imply that Scottish society was backward. In this period the Lowlands were enjoying some prosperity and, under the aegis of a small number of improving landlords, some agricultural improvement and expansion. Yet few benefits trickled down to the mass of the crofters and landless labourers, most of whom endured lives of grinding poverty on inhospitable soil.

Yet it would be a mistake to assume that Scotland enjoyed a fully developed sense of national identity. In many ways Scotland was two nations: about one-third of its population lived in the Gaelic-speaking Highlands, whose feudal culture based on oral tradition and the kinship networks of the clan confronted the more progressive and more commercially orientated print culture of the Scots-speaking Lowlanders. What united Scotland was, first, a common Presbyterian Protestantism and, second, the (largely successful) attempts by Stuart kings to enhance a Scottish identity by uniting Lowlands and Highlands in a common loyalty to the House of Stuart. Last but not least was the unity of national sentiment imparted by an abrasive tendency to attribute Scottish misfortune to the English.

Nevertheless, the prospect of a closer union between the two countries was much discussed during the seventeenth century, not least by James VI of Scotland (James I of England). There are signs that the economies of the two countries were beginning to develop for their mutual benefit: sectors of the Scottish rural economy, especially in the Borders and in the south west, were already geared to supplying food for the English market. More importantly, there were signs that the landed elites of the two countries were beginning to draw together. Although the English landed classes in the later seventeenth century were uninterested in colonizing either the land or the institutions of Scotland, most of the greater landowners (around 1500) of the northern kingdom were speaking English and adopting English patterns of life and leisure.

Nevertheless, serious political and religious differences between the two nations remained which could on occasion undermine relations between them. In 1637 the Scots reacted violently against the introduction of the English Prayer Book, thus contributing enormously to the sequence of events which led to warfare between the two countries in 1639 and to civil war in England in 1642. The Restoration of 1660 restored the political system which had existed before 1637: government by a royal Privy Council at Edinburgh in uncomfortable association with the Scottish Estates. Nevertheless, religion and dynasticism continued with some regularity to plunge relations between the two kingdoms into turmoil, as they did in 1688–92 and as they continued to do long into the eighteenth century.

Ireland did not constitutionally become a part of Britain until the Act of Union of 1800. Nevertheless, the fortunes of England and Ireland were already inseparable. Ireland was governed by a Lord Lieutenant and an executive appointed from England and controlled by a large standing army. She had little effective autonomy. Almost all major posts in church and state were held by Englishmen. Statutes of the English Parliament automatically applied to Ireland while those of the Dublin Parliament required the consent of London before enjoying legal status. Protestant settlers had colonized much of Ireland during the previous century and continued to do so. Indeed, in the second half of the seventeenth century a stream of emigrants from England and Scotland, most of them Presbyterian, were settling in Ulster. By 1700 English settlers and their dependents made up perhaps 20 per cent of the population, but they owned four-fifths of the land. Not surprisingly, this Anglo-Irish ruling elite was deeply unpopular in Ireland. It depended in the last analysis upon British arms to maintain its colonial status; its loyalty to London thus rested upon the strongest of all possible foundations, a sense of survival.

One-quarter of the population of 2 500 000 lived in and around Dublin. Most Irish towns were too small to sustain that rapidly growing middling section of society which was such a feature of English life. In rural areas there was no significant yeoman class of small farmers such as could be found in England. Among the mass of the Catholic Irish the Protestant landowning elite, usually referred to as the Ascendancy, was resented for its high rents and its harsh leases. The peasantry nursed its grievances, past and present, within its own cultural traditions, expressed in the distinctive and, to the English, impenetrable Gaelic tongue. By the end of the century the mass of the people maintained a strong sense of their own identity while the English-speaking Protestant elite looked upon themselves as 'British'.

As in Scotland, religious differences had shaken the foundations of British rule in Ireland in the middle of the seventeenth century. The consequence of earlier policies of settlement and religious discrimination was the Irish rebellion of 1641. During this uprising of the Catholic peasantry the rebel leaders claimed, as they were to claim in 1689, that they were acting in the names of their Stuart kings. The failure of the rebellion was followed by military occupation and savage reprisals. During the Civil Wars in England Charles I looked for military assistance from Ireland. Indeed, the mass of the Irish identified themselves and their religion with the Stuart monarchy and warmly welcomed the Restoration of 1660. Significantly, their Catholicism did not seem to them to be an insurmountable obstacle to their continued inclusion within a 'British' state.

The case of Wales was much more straightforward. Wales had never experienced a national government of her own, knew little of national unity and had never had an agreed capital city. North was separated from south by mountains and by the absence of roads. Wales had been absorbed into England during the reign of Henry VIII. By the terms of the Acts of Union of 1536 and 1543 Wales became a part of England in three ways: *politically* by adopting English forms of administration and by sending 24 Members of Parliament to the Westminster Parliament, *legally* by adopting the English common law and a comparable system of assizes and, finally, *religiously* by accepting Anglican church organization and doctrine. By the early seventeenth century, her landed and urban elites were speaking English and assuming the cultural manners of the English elite, including a vigorous adoption of the hunt, an exaggerated devotion to the London season and a gentlemanly interest in building and architecture. When James VI of Scotland became James I of England in 1603, discussions about a possible Anglo-Scottish Union completely ignored Wales. It was assumed that, like Cornwall in earlier centuries, Wales had become one with England. Her intense loyalty to the royalist cause during the Civil Wars confirmed the fact of her willing obedience. In many ways, too, Wales prospered economically from Union. Certainly, by the second half of the seventeenth century the country's wealth in mineral resources (lead in north Wales, coal and copper in the south) was being exploited by local landowners. It was not quite as simple as that. A distinct Welsh nation survived even if a Welsh state did not. The mass of the Welsh people spoke Welsh, most of her bishops and clergy were Welsh and the Bible was known mainly in Welsh translations. Indeed, the Welsh people continued to regard the English as a separate people. (The English, in return, regarded the Welsh as unruly barbarians.) Furthermore, the anglicization of the Welsh gentry can be exaggerated. In some parts of Wales, notably the south west, it proceeded much more slowly than elsewhere, as ruling families clung to Welsh customs and language. The Welsh ruling class was anglicised but there *was* still a Welsh ruling class.

In the later seventeenth century, then, 'Britain' was made up of a number of nations with distinct past histories and sometimes perplexing present relationships. Furthermore, Britain was a devolved state in which considerable autonomy remained with local families and local interests. Compared to other European countries, however, Britain was a remarkably coherent and unified state. There were at least four principal reasons for this.

First, the economic and political influence of London in particular and of England in general upon Wales, Scotland and Ireland was an immensely powerful agency of cohesion and centralization. The dramatic events of the Civil Wars and of the Interregnum had done much to politicize the country and to involve its outlying areas in matters of state at the highest level. Furthermore, we have already noted the economic pull of London not only upon local hinterlands but even upon areas of Scotland and Wales. In addition, tens of thousands of individuals sought work in London, many of them as apprentices. By the start of this period, moreover, London was the hub of a modest yet growing network of stage-coach services from Chester, Exeter, Newcastle and York. There were no internal restrictions upon the freedom of commerce in this, the largest free trade area in Europe. Such developments promoted a growing awareness of national as opposed to local concerns and tended to broaden horizons which were normally parochial.

Second, the ruling classes of Britain were developing a common political culture alongside common patterns of social behaviour. The growth of literacy and the spread of the printed word opened the door to common cultural and educational standards. The enormous expansion of educational opportunities which had occurred in the previous century had established a national network of grammar schools offering a classical education which shaped the minds and values of the gentry classes and of the urban patriciate and generating the ideal of service to the state. Their political culture acknowledged the leadership of a constitutional monarchy sharing power with ministers and parliaments. This political system celebrated the institution and values not only of the Parliament in London but also those of the subsidiary Parliaments in Edinburgh and Dublin.

Third, the existence of the common law in England, Wales and to a large extent in Ireland stamped a certain level of uniformity upon many areas of life. Whether the law was an instrument for maintaining elite power or whether it was a guarantee of the rights of a free people – or, indeed, whether it was both – cannot be resolved here. What cannot be denied is that it was constantly *used* by large numbers of contemporaries, especially by the propertied sections of the population, who had inflated expectations of the quality of justice which they might receive. The political implications of the common law, its role as the expression of the will of Parliament and its widely perceived historical achievement in imposing limitations upon royal power were widely applauded and rarely questioned.

A fourth element promoting the peaceful coexistence of the nations of the British islands was the common recognition that these nations, whatever their differences, belonged to 'Britain'. By the end of the seventeenth century it was universally assumed that England, Wales, Scotland and Ireland were permanently to constitute a single Union, even though the terms and conditions of that Union, and of the place of the monarchy within it, were to be liable to occasional revision, as in 1660 and 1688–89. Pride in Britishness, most commonly expressed in the figure of Britannia (which first appeared on coins of the realm in 1665), arose out of a popular conviction that the British were a fit and healthy race, enjoying an unmatched standard of living, honest, plain-speaking and, in the end, invincible. In the late seventeenth century Britons enthusiastically followed the fortunes of the British army and, especially, the British navy. They frequently proclaimed the unique virtues of the British constitution and compared her institutions favourably with those of Britain's national enemies, Holland and France. Many Scots and, indeed, some of the Irish, acknowledged their membership of a Britannic state. Many of them pursued their careers and their interests within a British framework: in the armed services, in trade and in the Protestant churches. Within this universe, the English, the Welsh, the Scots and the Irish were able to maintain some elements of their native characteristics while developing their British identities.

Belief

Britain was in formal terms a cluster of Christian societies whose churches claimed a continuity of religious experience and identity stretching back to the Middle Ages. This sense of unbroken tradition was a source of immense strength and confidence to churchmen. Although the mass of the people were casual about church attendance and family prayers – their religion was spasmodic and superstitious rather than devotional and reverent – they believed in the power of religion to give meaning to their existence. Through its universally recognized rituals, religion lent depth and significance to the great transitions in people's lives: birth, marriage, parenthood and death. But Christianity did more than provide an explanation for the trials of this world and the ultimate expectation of happiness in the next. It provided both an explanation and a justification for the existing social order, its hierarchies and its distribution of property and wealth. It provided a religious sanction for the individual's place in the social world. Yet contemporaries were easily frightened into the belief that religious dissent implied an attack upon the social order. Religious belief, therefore, needed to be carefully tempered with discipline and prudence. It was widely believed that if taken to extremes religion could arouse social divisions, excite fanaticism and even provoke civil war. This had occurred in the middle decades of the century and it could occur again.

It was exactly this message of caution and restraint which the established church was preaching towards the end of the seventeenth century. The Anglican church was the most powerful single institution within Britain. Its 26 bishops and two archbishops sat in the House of Lords; its 10 000 parishes ranged across the whole of England and Wales, and parts of Ireland and Scotland. The church, furthermore, had its own system of ecclesiastical courts and, in Convocation, its own representative body. In theory, the church took one-tenth of people's income in tithes. In addition, it was a property-owner on an enormous scale.

The church confidently pursued its religious mission – to minister to the spiritual needs of the people – while maintaining its own discipline and unity. Only thus could its secular objectives – the defence of the social and political order – be achieved. Because the monarch was the head of both church and state it was inevitable that the pulpit would uphold his legitimate authority. Church and state were one, both divinely ordained, the defence of one being the first line of defence for the other.

The Church of England was at the height of its power and influence in the second half of the seventeenth century. The decades immediately following the Restoration witnessed the emergence of a vibrant and self-conscious Anglicanism. The church recovered its lands at the Restoration, repaired the damage to its fabric which had occurred during the Civil Wars and took steps to improve its economic position. Within two decades the church's internal order, discipline and education had reached extremely respectable standards. It was a period of steady consolidation and considerable promise thanks to the quality of the bench of bishops, especially two Archbishops of Canterbury, Gilbert Sheldon and William Sancroft.[2]

The problems facing the Anglican church, however, were much more acute outside England. They were particularly serious in Wales, where a shortage of decently educated clergy weakened the church's ministry, and in Scotland. Here, the Restoration had imposed an Episcopalian but unpopular form of church order. In Ireland the church was top-heavy: four archbishops, 18 bishops and no fewer than 2000 clergymen were at the disposal of no more than 350 000 Anglicans. Some congregations were tiny, reflecting the precarious situation of the Anglican church in that country.

During his long reign from 1660 to 1685 Charles II had not wholly shared the authoritarian beliefs of many members of the Anglican church. For one thing, his scandalous private life seemed to many to make a mockery of the moral teachings of the church of which he was Supreme Governor. He was much more inclined to tolerate Protestant Dissenters and Roman Catholics than was the Anglican church. It was only with reluctance that the King was persuaded to accept and endorse the Clarendon Code of 1661–65 which established the framework within which religious uniformity was to be imposed. It excluded Protestant Nonconformists from any role in central or local government, imposed oaths and subscriptions upon them and levied penalties for attendance at non-Anglican services. It was intended to weaken not only the legal status but the social position and the numerical size of the Protestant Dissenting churches and of the Roman Catholic church. We will take these in turn.

The Protestant Dissenters were the descendants of the Puritans of the reigns of Elizabeth and the early Stuarts. However diverse their churches, they were united on a number of fundamental beliefs: they believed the authority of the Bible to be superior to the authority of tradition; they believed in the legitimacy of the congregation against that of an established, episcopal church; and they believed in their own freedom to practise their faith. In the second half of the seventeenth century the moral strength of Protestant Dissent continued unimpaired. These are, after all, the great years of its literary classics: of Bunyan's *Pilgrim's Progress* (1678), of Milton's *Samson Agonistes* (1671) and of Fox's *Journal* (1694). Their numbers probably remained stable at around one-third of a million in England and Wales in the second half of the seventeenth century. In London, and in the great Dissenting provincial towns such as Norwich and Newcastle upon Tyne, it was impossible either to silence the Dissenters or to close down Dissenting meetings, even in years of stringent persecution. Where Dissenters were less influential, however, their meetings were helpless before the forces of legal repression and illegal violence and intimidation. The greatest cause of desertion from the Dissenting churches, however, was financial impoverishment, the result of fines repeatedly and remorselessly exacted upon individuals.

Of the Dissenting churches, the Presbyterians were the largest (at around 180 000) and the most respectable, drawing their following from the upper sections of the middling orders. The Congregationalists (or Independents) numbered around 60 000 and appear to have drawn their support from slightly lower down the social hierarchy, from artisans, tradesmen and retailers. Only the Baptists (also at around 60 000) seem to have attracted the poor to their services in any numbers. Finally, the Quakers, numbering 40–50 000 in the later seventeenth century, were steadily losing the somewhat sinister and subversive reputation which their distinctive speech, dress and social customs had earned them earlier in the century.

Outside England the fortunes of Dissent varied. Welsh Dissent was organized within 'gathered churches' (structured on a county basis), admission to which was strictly regulated. Presbyterianism, of course, was the national and established religion of Scotland and in spite of its internal divisions enjoyed the loyalty of the great majority of Scots. In Ireland the later seventeenth century witnessed growing divisions between the Anglicans of the Church of Ireland and the Presbyterians of the north of Ireland. These religious divisions, on the whole softening elsewhere, steadily widened in Ireland in the years before the Glorious Revolution.

Fear of Roman Catholicism was the one thing that united the diverse Protestant churches of Britain. It had been consistently fostered since the reign of Mary Tudor, and anti-Catholic prejudices were by now deeply established in the popular mind. Protestants nursed exaggerated legends about Catholic conspiracies against Elizabeth, about Guy Fawkes and the Gunpowder Plot against James I, and, most recently, non-Catholics had experienced something like national paranoia at the prospect of a Catholic succession during the Popish Plot of 1678.[3] By the later seventeenth century, however, Catholics had largely abandoned any lingering expectations they may have retained of converting the country back to the old faith, which by 1680 commanded the allegiance of only 60 000 persons. Its survival depended upon the protection which its own social leaders, some of whom eventually conformed to Anglicanism, could provide and upon the tolerant attitude of their Protestant counterparts. In spite of the fear with which Catholics were viewed in the popular mind, the Recusancy laws were only fitfully enforced. Thanks to the tolerant spirit of Charles II and the sympathetic attitude of his court, the government made serious attempts to enforce them only in the mid-1670s and during the height of the Exclusion Crisis. The pragmatic attitude of Protestant landowners together with the careful dispositions of most Catholics took the sting out of a potentially dangerous situation. It was ironic, indeed, that it was not the actions of Catholics themselves but those of the Catholic James II which renewed ancient fears of popery, even though, as Defoe noted, people 'do not know whether it be a man or a horse'.

Gender

The construction of gender in the later seventeenth century was founded upon apparently timeless social wisdom, justified by a number of familiar biblical texts and confirmed by practical usage. The book of Genesis taught that God had created woman out of man. The Epistles of St Paul preached the Christian doctrine of the natural inferiority of women: wives should submit to their husbands as to the Lord. Most contemporaries, female as well as male, assumed that female inferiority arose naturally, out of the obvious fact that men and women possessed different qualities. The construction of masculinity arose out of the qualities which, it was believed, men possessed. Not only were they physically superior to women; they were also assumed to be rational, decisive and consistent. Women had less positive qualities: they were emotional, their passions uncontrollable and their behaviour, inevitably, inconsistent. Because women were assumed to be of inferior intellectual ability to men it followed that they were ill-suited to public life and responsibilities. Their duties lay in childbearing and in tending the family. The performance of such duties required obedience, submission and modesty.

The central unit of British society was the family. Its importance as the foundation of all social life and order cannot be overstated. All the churches treated marriage as an indissoluble bond: they decreed monogamy and life-long fidelity and forbade adultery, divorce and homosexuality. The health of the family was a barometer of the health of society as a whole. The family was also the basic unit of economic life, in manufacturing and in retailing as well as in farming. It was within a family – their own or someone else's – that most people worked. A son who wished to marry usually left the family home and set up his own household, a new economic as well as social and emotional unit, in order to do so. The family was, in some respects too, the basic unit of political life. It was always assumed that political divisions at court or within the upper orders of society would reverberate down into the middling and lower orders and lead to divisions within as well as between households. Thus the unity of the commonwealth might be endangered. Indeed, the family served as a common metaphor for the state: the king as the father of his people, the kingdom as a confederation of households.

People lived their lives in a nuclear family rather than in an extended family or kinship group. Few households – rarely much more than 5 per cent – contained three generations of co-residing kin; the lower down the social scale, the fewer. The size of household naturally varied with wealth and social status. Some of the great aristocratic households may have contained a score or more individuals; a middling-order household perhaps six to eight, and a household from the labouring masses perhaps three or four. Furthermore, from the (admittedly limited) surveys which have been completed, it appears that kinship relations outside the nuclear family were not of vital significance, even in small rural communities.[4]

Because the health of the social order depended upon the continuing cohesion of the family, the behaviour, especially the sexual behaviour, of women had to be carefully controlled. The ideal of female chastity was a subject to which contemporary writers returned on countless occasions. Female promiscuity was a threat to the stability of the family and, in the event of separation, to the welfare of children and, indirectly, to the smooth, hereditary transmission of family property. Women's place was in the household, the patriarchal household. Women were discouraged, especially by the church, from complaining about or seeking to change their situation. They were, in fact, excluded from holding office in the Anglican church. Women who enjoyed some leisure were not expected to advance their intellects; they were to promote themselves as social adornments, adept at conversation, dancing and music.

Because women were socially inferior, they had fewer legal rights than men. Within the landed classes, the inheritance of an estate passed through all the sons before descending to the daughter. In the household wives were required to accept the authority of their husbands just as their children, especially their daughters, had to do. Women had no rights in common law over their own property once they married, or over matrimonial property acquired after marriage. They had no legal rights over their children and they had few legal rights over their own persons. Husbands were permitted physically to punish their wives and if they ran away they were entitled to force them to return and even permitted to incarcerate them. The legal status of women was akin to that of under-age children: they were regarded by men, and must to an extent have regarded themselves, as goods and chattels to be treated as men thought fit.

Consequently, it was expected that the mass of women would work either in the household or in the basic and most servile of occupations, including labouring work and domestic service. Their sisters in the middling orders contented themselves with running the household and practising their social graces. As families from the middling orders aimed at social improvement and indulged in polite consumption, so these women proceeded to affect the mannerisms of leisure at the expense of the routines of work. For the mass of women, however, life consisted of some combination of work in the household, physical labour and service. These harsh facts, together with their child-bearing obligations, defined the lives of the vast majority of women in Britain.

To what extent was the situation of women really as bleak as the above paragraphs have suggested? Was the inferiority of women as complete and as comprehensive as both the Bible and the law demanded? In real life, practice could be rather different from precept. Although the law favoured the interests of the husband, the wife had some basic safeguards.[5] On marriage, her property became her husband's but she retained possession of her land (if any) and he could not sell it without her consent. Moveable goods, however, became the property of the husband. (Single women and widows could, of course, own property, run businesses and make wills.) Furthermore, the realities of daily life as well as the personalities of countless men and women may have modified the harshness of religious dogma about the inferiority of women. In order to make a living, husband and wife had to work side by side. It is often forgotten that, in addition to giving chapter and verse for the *existence* of patriarchal authority, the Bible also gave detailed guidance about its *exercise*. St Peter had called for husbands to exercise their authority with caution, kindness and understanding. It was love of God and the mutual love of husband and wife which held the family together, not the tyrannical authority of men over women. As Dorothy Leigh had written in 1616 to all husbands: 'If she be thy wife, she is always too good to be thy servant, and worthy to be thy fellow.' Contemporary writers were in no doubt where final authority in the family lay, but they insisted that wives should be treated with honour and consideration; they should neither be belittled nor humiliated. A Christian father had responsibilities towards the members of his family as well as rights over them; these responsibilities included the instruction of the family in the Christian religion, the protection of the lives and persons of its members and the enhancement of their personal growth and welfare. The daily needs of life demanded mutual support and partnership rather than the ruthless tyranny of one individual over others. Whether in the courtly guides to behaviour read by the landed elite, in the conduct books of the middling orders or in the popular literature of the day, relations between the sexes, although unequal and, to our generation, unedifying, were somewhat more complex than a casual reading of legal and biblical texts might indicate.

The age of marriage was late. Men married in their late twenties, women slightly earlier. Most marriages were entered into freely and without the intervention of parents. Only among the upper ranks of society, and when land and other forms of property were at stake, did arranged marriages survive into this period in any number. For those lower down the social scale marriage was a much more casual matter. Many couples married without a church ceremony and its associated formality and expense. Some of them might just as casually terminate their marriage, either by desertion, mutual agreement or by the public ritual of the wife sale.[6]

Children came rapidly; perhaps one-third of newly married couples bore their first child within a year of marriage. Indeed, children were everywhere in seventeenth-century Britain. It has been estimated that around 40 per cent of the population of England were dependent children living in the households of their parents. Parents, then as now, invested most of their social and emotional capital in the upbringing of their children. Although historians have often given the impression that the treatment of children in this period was harsh, formal and even brutal, it may well be the case that such a conclusion is reached by concentrating unduly on selective evidence largely drawn from the experience of the upper classes. Obviously, the enforcement of discipline over children, especially girls, was more rigid than it has come to be in the twentieth century; the sanctions against disobedience in a patriarchal society were intimidating. Furthermore, the practice of sending children out into service or into apprenticeships in other people's households would today be regarded as insensitive, as would the widespread employment of young children in the work of the household, farm or shop. Nevertheless, there is overwhelming evidence that parents in all ranks of society cared for their children with genuine love and affection and did what they could to provide a wholesome, Christian upbringing for them. There is, moreover, evidence to show that children were regarded as a blessing, as a source of pleasure and emotional fulfilment and, of course, as a prospective support in old age.[7] The horrifyingly high death rate – about one-quarter of children failed to survive to their tenth birthday – did not breed indifference or callousness towards the young. Genuine parental grief at the experience of child mortality is suggestive of powerful family bonding. Examples of physical brutality are rare, although beating remained as a last resort. (In the schools, however, it was frequently used as a first resort.) The employment of children in the family economy, moreover, was almost inevitable in a non-mechanized society and, more particularly, one which did not make institutional provision for the education of children. To teach children, even small children, useful skills not only prepared the child for adult life but discouraged begging, idleness and crime. Child labour might be regarded as necessary to the very wellbeing of the family.

The dark side in the treatment of women and children involved orphans and the illegitimate. They had few legal rights and were liable to severe chastisement and beating. The plight of unmarried mothers was particularly distressing: the culpability of women was taken for granted, their resort to abortion and infanticide illegal, tragic and often followed by severe punishment. Thereafter, their prospects of marriage would be minimal; prostitution, begging and poverty were the likely consequences. The birth of a bastard child was regarded as a threat to normal social life because it created a form of family but a family without a head. Such a child was usually pursued with contempt, hostility and, not least, legal disability. Such severity was a reflection of the contemporary belief that sexual promiscuity posed a threat to the status of the family and, it followed, to the stability and order of society. But widows were no such threat. Indeed, widows, especially widows with property, were highly prized in this society. They assumed the vital role of bringing up children without the assistance of a husband and they had the capacity to establish a new family unit.

Gender and family relations were dictated by the prevailing Christian ideology of male superiority. This ideology reduced women and children to a status of near-servility, but in practice a variety of personal, practical and religious influences did something to soften the harshness of its impact. These relationships, however, did not exist in isolation. People did not define their identities solely in terms of their gender and their families; they took very seriously their place on the social ladder. To this aspect of our inquiry we now turn.

Society

In the attitude of men and women towards each other we have observed significant differences between theory and practice. How did people view the society of which they were a part and how did they conceive of their own place within it? To what extent did that mental picture conform to social realities? Most contemporaries believed that Britain was a society of orders, a ladder of social hierarchies. This belief arose from the old Christian cosmology of a 'Great Chain of Being', the idea of God's universe as a hierarchy of superiors and inferiors, stretching down from heaven to earth. Society was ordered in small gradations, like rungs on a ladder. There were no massive, mutually exclusive social chasms between one rung and the next. These gradations were the product of history, convention and custom. It is difficult to define them with any precision. They were made up variously of birth and inherited title, of wealth and property, of occupation and, only in some cases, of legally defined status. Finally, every place on the ladder had its own advantages and its own disadvantages.

Contemporaries were battered with propaganda in catechisms, sermons and the printed word extolling the virtues of this method of social organization. The virtues of obedience and conformity were widely accepted. Inequality was built into the social system; it was natural, inevitable and desirable. The only alternative to it was thought to be anarchy. This conception of society was more than just a theoretical construct: it was confirmed by the everyday experiences of the people. Its inequalities were reflected in dress and deportment, in education, speech and manners and, not least, in leisure and cultural pursuits. These distinctions were also reflected in seating arrangements, especially in church, but also in graded seating at political and social events and in ritual celebrations and processions, whose structure and organization reflected the social hierarchy.

This model of the social order should not be accepted without a little caution. It is, perhaps, an idealized version of a society in which people knew – and were content to stay – where they belonged. Further, economic change constantly threatened the credibility of the model, creating new occupations, new crafts and subdivisions of old ones. At the same time, new developments in science and philosophy were beginning to transform the old Christian cosmology on which this hierarchical theory of the social order rested. Nevertheless, the idea of a society of orders must be treated as the controlling model of the social order which contemporaries employed both to envisage and to make sense of the world around them, and which to a very considerable extent conditioned their behaviour. Indeed, people derived their sense of personal identity, their conception of 'self', less from their own personality than from their place in the social order. Personal identity turned, therefore, on the (often varying) social roles that an individual was called upon to play and, lying beneath them, the only fixed and constant entity, the soul.

The most detailed and the most influential picture of the social structure of England in the later seventeenth century has been Gregory King's famous 'Scheme of the Income and Expense of the Several Families' (see Table 1.1), an attempt to estimate the population and wealth of England in 1688. King's 'Scheme' can be criticized on a number of grounds. Resident domestic servants are not singled out for separate treatment; their inclusion in the households of other groups is not particularly helpful. Even more important, the numbers of 'merchants and shopkeepers' and of 'artisans and handicraftsmen' look suspiciously small. Nevertheless, the Scheme is a detailed contemporary estimate of the social structure, and as such it may be fruitful to use it as a broad guide, especially if we combine some of King's categories into a smaller and more manageable number.[8]

First, we may conveniently single out the first six of King's categories and treat them together. They constitute 2.8 per cent (153 520) of the population who were *landowners*, the aristocratic and gentry families of England. Attempts to describe them encounter problems of definition which are as confusing to us as they were absorbing and engrossing to contemporaries. Peerages were either inherited or created by the crown. The rest are much less straightforward. Baronetcies were bestowed by the crown but differed from knighthoods in that they were hereditable. Esquires (who were the heirs of the younger sons of peers and the heirs of knights), and gentlemen (who were originally the younger sons and brothers of esquires and their heirs) were by the later seventeenth century self-ascribed titles, depending for their legitimacy on social acceptance.

Definitions apart, this rural elite had a significance out of all proportion to its size. It owned perhaps two-thirds of the landed acreage of England. The peerage sat proudly at the top of the social pyramid, the most exclusive of all social groups. The possession of huge landed estates and the hereditary right

Table 1.1 Gregory King's 'Scheme of the Income and Expense of the Several Families of England ... for 1688' compared with Joseph Massie's 'Estimate of the Social Structure and Income, 1759–1760'

King				Massie	
No. of families	Heads per family	No. of persons	Classification	No. of Families	Annual income or expenses (£)
160	40	6400	Temporal lords		
26	20	520	Spiritual lords		
800	16	12800	Baronets		
600	13	7800	Knights		
3000	10	30000	Esquires		
12000	8	96000	Gentlemen*		
				10	20 000
				20	10 000
				40	8000
				80	6000
				160	4000
				320	2000
				640	1000
				800	800
				1600	600
				3200	400
				4800	300
				6400	200
5000	8	40000	Persons in greater offices and places		
5000	6	30000	Persons in lesser offices and places		
			Civil officers	16000	60
2000	8	16000	Eminent merchants		
8000	6	48000	Lesser merchants		
			Merchants	1000	600
				2000	400
				10000	200
			Master manufacturers	2500	200
				5000	100
				10000	70
				62500	40
10000	7	70000	Persons in the law	12000	100
2000	6	12000	Eminent clergymen	2000	100
8000	5	40000	Lesser clergymen	9000	50
40000	7	280000	Freeholders, better sort		
120000	5½	660000	Freeholders, lesser sort		
				30000	100
				60000	50
				120000	25

King				Massie	
No. of families	Heads per family	No. of persons	Classification	No. of Families	Annual income or expenses (£)
150000	5	750000	Farmers	5000	150
				10000	100
				20000	70
				120000	40
15000	5	75000	Persons in liberal arts and sciences	18000	60
50000	4½	225000	Shopkeepers and tradesmen		
			Tradesmen	2500	400
				5000	200
				10000	100
				20000	70
				125000	40
60000	4	240000	Artisans and handicrafts Manufacturers of wood, iron etc., country 9s.		
			per week,	100000	22.5
			London 12s.	14000	30
			Manufacturers of wool, silk etc., country 7s. 6d.	100000	18.75
			London 10s. 6d.	14000	26.25
5000	4	20000	Naval officers	6000	80
4000	4	16000	Military officers	2000	100
50000	3	150000	Common seamen		
			Seamen and fishermen	60000	20
364000	3½	1275000	Labouring people and outservants Husbandmen		
			(6s. per week)	200000	15
			Labourers, country 5s.	200000	12.5
			Labourers, London 9s.	20000	22.5
			Innkeepers, ale-sellers	2000	100
			Ale-sellers, cottagers	20000	40
				20000	20
400000	3¼	1300000	Cottagers and paupers		
35000	2	70000	Common soldiers	18000	14
		30000	Vagrants, as gypsies, thieves, beggars, etc.		
TOTAL		5500520			

*Massie does not distinguish the top ranks by status, but by financial turnover per family per annum.

Source: Reproduced with permission from W. Speck, *Stability and Strife* (London, Edward Arnold, 1977).

to sit in the House of Lords gave the peers enormous economic and political power. The spiritual lords also enjoyed seats in the House of Lords; many of the bishoprics owned extensive land and other forms of property. These rural paternalists ran their estates and interested themselves in the welfare of the local community. The peers, while technically superior to the gentry, had much in common with them. They rented their lands to tenants and involved themselves with the lives of their dependents. As a leisured elite they were able to cultivate a reasonably common lifestyle; they went to the same schools and universities and they exhibited a common code of honour. They indulged in striking displays of conspicuous consumption in, and conspicuous expenditure on, their (often magnificent) country as well as town houses and gardens. Because of their small numerical size it was possible for them to know, or to try to know, everybody of significance within their order. They tended to intermarry and to choose wives and heiresses with the very greatest care in view of their interest in – indeed, intense preoccupation with – estate enlargement and dynastic continuity. These family groupings extended horizontally and vertically through society. Their links with their relations, distant and near, their friends and associates, their servants and, not least, those who depended economically upon their purchasing power, constituted living roots of dependence.

Beneath the aristocracy and gentry came the various segments that made up the middling orders. Freeholders (owner occupiers) and farmers (tenants for lives or years), made up no less than 30.7 per cent of the population (or 1 690 000 out of 5.5 million), according to Gregory King's calculations. Once again, these definitions are vague; some of the better-off freeholders (often termed yeomen) were richer than quite a few of the lesser gentry. At the other end of the scale, the poorer tenants (often called husbandmen) on an income of £30 or £40 per annum might not live much above subsistence level. Some of the freeholders, according to King, had households of seven, while some of the farmers had households of five. The 40s. freeholders enjoyed the right to vote in county elections and the prestige that went with it. At the other extreme, small husbandmen were little distinguishable from day labourers. Whatever their status, these respectable elements among the rural middling orders prided themselves on their independence and the social status that went with it.

The middling orders of late seventeenth-century England are represented in King's table by two further groups. The first of these were professional men, including the clergy, office holders, military and naval officers and 'persons in the liberal arts and sciences'. Many so-called professional activities, however, were not regulated by any official body and represented little more than personal ambition; ideas of professional standards and public service were in their infancy. The second were merchants of one description or another, ranging from 'eminent' down to 'lesser'. Together, according to Gregory King, these two groups made up 6.7 per cent of the population (367 000 out of 5.5 million), almost certainly an underestimate. These may be people of the middling orders but they do not constitute a 'middle class'. Even the first group is sharply divided between the clergy and the rest, while the second includes on the one hand very wealthy metropolitan merchants willing to buy landed estates and, on the other, poor provincial shopkeepers existing on a few hundred a year. These professional and mercantile men did not conceive of themselves separately from the orders immediately above them. Many of them – clergy, attorney, surveyors, bankers, horticulturalists – serviced the gentry and aristocracy and reflected their social values. Many merchants, too, whether wholesalers, dealers or suppliers, also depended upon the custom of the great families of England. Such dependence could create resentment, especially if bills remained unpaid or social snobbery caused offence; nevertheless, they knew where their interests lay. These vertical links between the landed and the middling orders did much, quietly and unspectacularly, to cement these middling and upper ranks of society more firmly together.

Distinctly below the professions and the merchants came two groups quite similar in size and status: the 'shopkeepers and tradesmen' of King's table (225 000 or 4.1 per cent of King's estimated population of 5.5 million) and the 'artisans and handicraftsmen' (4.4 per cent of the population, 240 000 out of 5.5 million). The retailing sector consisted of tens of thousands of small men engaged in selling one product or one small group of products. It included grocers, mercers, book-sellers, drapers, ironmongers, jewellers, tobacconists and hosiers and dozens of others. The latter group were small producers. They included many traditional small crafts such as shoemaking, baking and tailoring as well as newer trades such as printing, instrument-making and various types of manufacturing. Such small concerns were entirely typical of the 'pre-industrial' economy. The average size of the enterprises in which goods were manufactured remained small; the master craftsman might have a couple of apprentices and employ one or more day labourers (journeymen).

Below these groups lay the enormous mass of what King called 'labouring people and outservants', those who worked entirely for other people and not for themselves. This vast and heterodox grouping comprised 1 275 000 people (23.2 per cent of the population). Most labourers were entirely dependent upon wage income and whatever perks and pickings that might come their way. What affected their income and condition of life was a combination of the market value of their skills and the casual nature of their work. A labourer who had acquired a much-needed skill as, for example, a carpenter or as a blacksmith, might enjoy a very decent regular income. An entirely unskilled person might only be able to secure seasonal work at harvest time in the fields. Women were much in evidence in this sector of the market, notably in fruit-picking, milk-selling and fishmongering and, even more widely, working as shop assistants and as non-resident servants. Average income figures for such a diverse group are very difficult to collect, but modern research has tended to confirm Gregory King's estimate that the income of a labouring family towards the end of the seventeenth century might reach £15 per annum, only a pound or two more than an estimate of their expenses and outgoings. As Keith Wrightson has concluded: 'On whatever estimate we employ, the glaring fact is that the life of the labourer was a constant battle for survival.'[9]

Such dismal conclusions need to be qualified. Certain stages of life – the early years of marriage, for example, when both husband and wife might be working and earning – could be relatively comfortable. There were pathways out of poverty, even if it took an unusual combination of personality and circumstance to follow them. To begin as an apprentice might lead to employment as a skilled journeyman; it might even be feasible to consider setting up as a small master. Even a farm labourer might have pretensions to becoming a husbandman. Some trades, moreover, had traditions of collective solidarity which prevented the worst examples of exploitation; some were even protected by statute. The life of the trades had a cultural as well as an economic context. Many had their own job rituals, of initiation and retirement, and their own annual festivities, parades and sports. Some servants may have been poorly paid, but they received their bed and board and often a number of perks and profits which went with the job.

Finally, in this survey of the social structure, we come to the last (and largest) great segment of the population, those whom Gregory King termed 'cottagers and paupers'. He estimated their number at 1 300 000 (or 23.6 per cent of the population). Cottagers, unlike husbandmen, had no land of their own. Their estimated income of £6 10s. per annum was well below subsistence level. For much of the year they were on poor relief. They were casually employed, rarely to be found in steady or in permanent employment. At some times of the year, particularly in the winter, there might well be very little casual work to go round. As for paupers, they could be poor widows, orphaned children, the sick, the old, the insane and the feckless. These were the people with no defences against the cycle of the year, the accidents of the harvest or occasional downswings in employment. Although mass famines were a thing of the past, local food shortages were still common. The existence of these people was bleak, softened only by religion and by occasional acts of philanthropy on the part of their social superiors.

To what extent were the English social forms described by Gregory King to be found in other parts of Britain? Wales was not significantly different. Some of the older Welsh landed dynasties were beginning to die out, to be replaced by English (and in some cases Scottish) families. Even so, at the start of this period there were perhaps 30 landed families in Wales with incomes of over £3000 per annum. Lower down the scale, there would be a score or two families in each county enjoying incomes of between £500 and £1000 per annum; they formed the backbone of the local bench and quarter sessions. As in England, landed families rented out their lands to tenant farmers who, in turn, employed labourers to work the land. As in England, close economic and social links were appearing between the urban middling orders and the rural gentry. At the lower end of the social scale there was possibly less specialization of labour than there was in England, farm labourers in Wales turning their hands to weaving or mining in the winter months.

Partly because of its geographical divisions, Scotland was more complex. In some ways, its social system appeared to be like England's, with over 1000 substantial landowners, hereditary aristocrats and Highland chieftains alike. Around 1500 smaller landlords were perhaps gaining ground against them but they were markedly poorer than the English gentry, most of them on less than £50 per annum. Furthermore, Scotland did not possess anything to compare with the English freeholders. In the Highlands traditional forms of social relationships existed through which land was leased and subleased from the clan chief. Consequently, holdings tended to be small. In the Lowlands, farming households leased their land, as many of their English counterparts did, but they too tended to sublease it in a variety of ways to small families beneath them. As a consequence the size of the holdings of the 8000–9000 'bonnet lairds', small owner occupiers who constituted the broad majority of the Scottish landed class, remained tiny. Furthermore, the Scottish middling orders were much less numerous than their English counterpart. Outside Edinburgh and, to a lesser extent, Glasgow they were few and far between, concentrated in the merchant guilds of the royal burghs. Most Scottish towns were very small and most Scottish industry remained rural.

Ireland displayed some of the worst features of the English social structure. Land was unduly concentrated in a very few hands. Over 80 per cent of the land of Ireland was owned by the Anglo-Irish Protestant aristocracy, many of whom were absentees. As in Scotland, there were few freeholders. When leases were granted on reasonably secure terms (usually to Protestant families of the middle rank), the land was not farmed but usually sublet on stringent terms. Because insufficient capital was available for cultivation and development, farming was left to the efforts of single families on small lots. At this period, therefore, most farming in Ireland remained subsistence farming; in many places a money economy did not exist, most payments being made in kind. Most serious of all, about half the entire population of Ireland was made up of landless labourers (or 'cottiers') who were probably worse off than their English counterparts and who existed precariously at around subsistence level. The poverty of Ireland and the relative absence of opportunities for picking up casual work left large numbers of people dangerously dependent upon the weather and the harvest.

It would be a mistake to imagine that variations in the social structure only coincided with national divisions. Everything depended on local circumstances. Some counties, such as Lincolnshire, were almost gentry-free zones whereas others, notably Cheshire, were packed with gentry families. In general, areas of sheep and corn had larger farms and estates and, to go with them, larger numbers of landless labourers than elsewhere. Areas of dairy farming, by comparison, supported large numbers of small family units with a corresponding variety of casual employment. It would, moreover, be just as misleading to imagine that the social structure was fixed. Some aspects of it, indeed, were changing quite rapidly. In particular, the middling orders, especially in the towns, were increasing in size and importance. In the countryside the small yeoman farmer, unable to sustain a sizeable body of debt, was in a steady decline while in certain parts of the country the size of aristocratic estates and farms was increasing. Contemporaries tended to exaggerate the force of such developments and to anticipate disastrous consequences. Few men and women could grasp the totality of social relations and calmly conceive of their society in an external, objective sense. To them their society remained a society of orders, fixed and unchanging in its essentials. To that there seemed no imaginable alternative.

Economy

In early modern Britain country and town were complementary rather than contrasting social and economic entities. They were natural partners in the business of life. Most towns were simply larger villages; they looked like villages and often contained fields and meadows inside their boundaries. The principal function of many country towns was to market agricultural produce. There were no sharp occupational distinctions between those who lived in the towns and those who lived in the countryside; many of the former worked on the land. Dual occupation was still common in many regions. A miner or a weaver might supplement his income with seasonal work on the land. Most urban occupations, in fact, were directly related to farming. In no sense, then, were rural ways of life incompatible with urban status. Town and country-dwellers would mingle together at inns and theatres and, not least, at the great urban festivals of the year. All the while, migration, seasonal or permanent, from country to town decanted a constant stream of rural people into an urban environment.

The countryside of Britain was dominated by the estates of the aristocracy and gentry. Unlike their French counterparts, the English, Welsh and Scottish (but not Irish) landowners were normally resident and liked to involve themselves closely in the life of the estate and its tenants. Although members of the aristocracy and gentry rented out their estates they continued to exercise a direct and overriding managerial responsibility for them. This included the careful screening of prospective tenants, regular visits to farms thereafter and the careful enforcement of contracts and covenants. They might also be involved in vital strategic decisions concerning improvements in transport and communications, and even in such activities as the patronage of agricultural shows. Indeed, in their capacities as Justice of the Peace, Lord and Deputy Lieutenant of the county and *Custos Rotulorum* many of them displayed a concern for the legal, military and administrative welfare of the community beyond their estates. They never lost this sense of personal involvement, in spite of their tendency to gate and wall off their estates. It was a prosperous and confident landed elite which had been doing well in the later decades of the seventeenth century. The larger estates had tended to prosper at the expense of the smaller. Small owners with less than 300 acres probably still held between 25 per cent and 35 per cent of agricultural land in England but they were being squeezed by the middling gentry (those with between 300 and 3000 acres, who held around 45 per cent to 50 per cent) and the great landed aristocracy (those with over 3000 acres, who held around 15 per cent to 20 per cent).

Agriculture was of the very greatest importance to British society in the later seventeenth century. It supplied most of the country's wealth, moulded the social structure and provided employment and sustenance for the majority of the people. Indeed, English agriculture was in the early stages of what used to be called an 'agricultural revolution'. Historians used to date that 'revolution' from the early and middle decades of the eighteenth century. More recent research has established not only that the chronology of such a 'revolution' is inaccurate – a long period of agricultural improvement may be dated from around the middle of the *seventeenth* century – but that the term 'revolution' gives a misleading impression of what was in practice a series of often unconnected, undramatic and very long-term local developments.[10] We can be confident that agricultural productivity began to improve after the middle years of the seventeenth century. Harvests were good, the population increase of the previous century was slackening and consequently prices, and possibly rents, may even have fallen slightly. These pressures to greater efficiency were increased by localized surges in demand. These were produced by a number of factors. One was urban development, especially the rapid rise in the population of London in this period. Another was attempts by landowners themselves, not least by former royalist families still suffering from the losses of the Interregnum period, to repair their fortunes. More generally, improvements in animal feeding, better methods of fertilization and more intensive and efficient crop-growing methods – many of these popularized and communicated through the activities of the Royal Society – enabled English agriculture to respond to increasing demand. By the end of the century England was feeding herself fairly comfortably and had even begun to export grain. Few reliable statistics exist for the decades before the Glorious Revolution, but the evidence of wills and probates reveals increased wealth, improved machinery and a willingness to invest in new techniques.

The role of the enclosure of common fields in promoting agricultural improvements after 1660 has been much debated by historians in recent years. Currently, they are inclined to scale down its significance.[11] Enclosure had been proceeding steadily for centuries. Its rationale was clear: unenclosed land was uneconomic; its haphazard distribution in huge open fields made it difficult to undertake experiments in crop rotation and even in animal breeding. By 1660 only 50 per cent of English farm land remained to be enclosed. The other half had already either been enclosed or had never been farmed under the open-field system. By the end of the seventeenth century nearly half the remainder was enclosed, almost twice as much as was to be enclosed during the eighteenth century! Here again, we may identify a steady process rather than sudden and abrupt change. What was novel in the later seventeenth century was the complete abandonment of any attempt by the government either to regulate or even to enquire into what was now recognized to be a matter of private agreement among local landowners. Consequently, enclosure by Act of Parliament remained uncommon until the eighteenth century.

Britain was a rural society but one in which industry was rapidly developing, albeit closely related to the servicing of agriculture and agricultural products. In many villages domestic industry was almost as common as agriculture. In some counties, such as Gloucestershire, the number of men engaged full-time in agriculture was less than 50 per cent and over the country as a whole may not have been more than 70 per cent.

The closing decades of the seventeenth century, with stable prices and higher real incomes, saw sustained industrial development based on rising demand: for building materials, household utensils and leather goods and, above all, for clothes and other textile products. The biggest industry was the production of woollen cloth. Like most of industry, it was organized on a domestic basis in small units. Large-scale production units were to be found in the late seventeenth century but these were less likely to be factories than dockyards, paper mills and iron-industry slitting-mills. Important technological breakthroughs occurred, notably in the mining and metallurgical industries, but profits were to be made less through industrial innovation than by the use of traditional techniques and the harnessing of traditional sources of power such as wind and water. Economic growth was also fostered by the negative fact of the declining influence of the guilds. The medieval guilds had traditionally regulated recruitment to a craft and laid down standards of production and had even regulated wages. Few new ones were created in the second half of the seventeenth century, and existing guilds were unable to keep up with new developments. They were often rent by division and weakened by their inability to exert influence over the small shops and small masters of the growing villages and market towns. Their continued demise signalled new opportunities for skilled and unskilled artisans, interlopers, entrepreneurs and others to pursue the path of profit and of self-advancement without social or economic hindrance.

If the day of the guilds was passing, most contemporaries believed that the state had a principal role to play in securing economic prosperity and in generating economic development. After 1660 there are signs that government intervention in the economy was beginning to weaken, but it did so only slowly. The Long Parliament of the 1640s had abolished the old, much-hated monopolies (i.e. the exclusive privilege granted by the crown to an individual, group or company to produce or market a product), but the government still retained the right to issue franchises or privileges (or 'incorporations') to groups and companies like trading, mining and even livery companies. The state could also intervene in the economy by offering bounties to promote a particular commodity, such as that offered to cereal-growers after 1670. Together with restrictions on foreign imports of corn, the bounty did much to stabilize agriculture, to stimulate corn production and, ultimately, to safeguard England from the threat of national famine. Bounties on industrial products were to make their appearance in the eighteenth century. Both before and after the Glorious Revolution, then, economic and financial objectives continued to be legitimate objects of state regulation and intervention, their objective to secure national self-sufficiency and strategic power. In a period when Britain was involved in three wars against the Dutch (1652–54, 1665–67 and 1672–74) this was perfectly understandable.

The later decades of the seventeenth century may not have been of unusual significance in the industrial development of Britain, but they were of outstanding importance in her commercial development. The domestic market was steadily growing as rising demand for consumer products affected not only the gentry and aristocratic classes but also the middling orders and artisan ranks.

> The substitution of regular retail outlets for intermittent fairs, and the fact that by 1650 small-town mercers and even village shopkeepers could supply most if not all the goods available for consumption on the seventeenth century market wrought profound changes in the consumer behaviour of the provincial well-to-do, who had probably learned the new habits from direct or indirect contact with London.[12]

Familiarity with new consumer products was generated locally through the retailing outlets of the great provincial centres such as Bristol, Norwich and York, and, in turn, through the cycle of fashion experienced at county towns and emerging leisure towns like Bath, Tunbridge Wells and the other spa towns. More and more of the population was being drawn into the market for consumer goods, but as yet its extent should not be exaggerated. In the later seventeenth century, at least, few people from the lower ranks of Gregory King's ladder of occupations – those below £20 per annum – could have entered the new market for consumer goods unless more than one person in a household was earning. It is difficult to take seriously the possibility that many members of the labouring masses had access to Delft pottery, pewter, glass, cutlery and worsteds.

It was in international trade that the most staggering developments were experienced; between 1640 and 1700 English exports roughly doubled; re-exports increased twentyfold. The development of new markets in the Eastern Mediterranean and, especially, of new protected markets in North America helped to ensure continued growth. These trends were enhanced by the introduction of new textile products both for domestic but especially for international markets. Even non-cloth manufactures exported to the colonies doubled between 1660 and 1700. How far these trends may be attributed to the Navigation Acts is not clear. The Acts, passed in 1651 and 1660, were directed against the trade of England's greatest commercial rival, the Dutch. They provided that trade between England and her colonies should be carried exclusively in British ships and that the main items exported by the colonists had to be shipped to British destinations. There can be little doubt that the Acts consolidated and enhanced the expansion of British commerce, but they were not the only catalysts. By 1688 Britain had the largest merchant marine fleet in Europe (up from 2 million tons in 1660 to 3.4 million in 1686), some of the best commercial facilities in Europe within the City of London and a metropolitan, mercantile community which was trading with all corners of the globe. If not yet a world power, England was strongly positioned at the centre of a worldwide commercial network.

In all parts of Britain the difficulties in the way of transporting goods and people remained one of the greatest obstacles to her economic development. The cheapest method of moving goods from one place to another was by water, either by river or by coastal shipping. (As late as the 1840s coastal shipping moved three times as much tonnage as shipping to ports overseas.) This was particularly relevant to supplying the needs of London: it was estimated that it was twenty times more expensive to move goods from Newcastle to London by land than it was by sea. The seventeenth and early eighteenth century was a period of improvement to river navigation; by the 1720s over 1000 miles of river navigation had been improved. Not much more could be done with existing technologies to further improve river navigation. At the same time, some much-needed improvements to the state of the highways came in the form of turnpikes. The income from tolls on the users of roads went to the upkeep of the roads; they were administered either by JPs (after the passage of the first Turnpike Act in 1663) or by private citizens (after the passage of an Act in 1706 permitting private turnpikes).

Steady advances in agriculture, commerce and transport were not confined to England. The Welsh economy was being closely bound up with the English market. English towns like Shrewsbury and Bristol commanded their regional hinterlands. Partly because of these pressures, much of the lowland area of Wales had already been enclosed. Here and elsewhere cattle and sheep were raised to satisfy the growing food demands of the English market. Nevertheless, agriculture in Wales remained in some important respects more backward than in England. Farming in strips was still common and sheep farming continued unchanged in many highland regions of Wales.

Estate management was never as advanced in the principality as it was in many parts of England. Land was still regarded in many parts of Wales as a means of subsistence rather than a capital investment. Primogeniture existed only on the larger estates; partible inheritance on the smaller estates restricted the scope for improvement. Even if it had not, the capital required to modernize agricultural methods was not available.

Scotland was less economically advanced than Wales. Most areas were still dominated by subsistence farming; the clan system still predominated in the Highlands and feudal tenures were not abolished until 1746. In many parts of Scotland a version of dispersed strip farming in huge open fields (or 'breaks') predominated within which a wide variety of local tenancy customs prevailed. Nevertheless, in some parts of Scotland, notably the Borders and Galloway, sheep and cattle were reared for the English market and large units were not uncommon. At the same time, the economy of parts of the Highlands was being geared towards supplying the towns of the Lowlands with wool and meat as well as labour. During the 1690s harvest failures led to severe famine. This, together with the Act of Union in 1707, was to stimulate a period of marked agricultural improvement in the form of enclosure for pasture in order to satisfy the Scottish as well as the English demand for food.

In Ireland, the outlook was bleaker. The economy was backward, distorted by religious discrimination and absentee landlordism and dangerously dependent upon the English market. Absentee landlords were content to allow some Protestant tenants something like freeholder status, but they had largely abdicated from the pattern of landlord paternalism towards the lower orders which softened the harshness of social and economic inequality in England. The vast mass of the Catholic peasantry was reduced either to living on very small units of a few acres or, even worse, to the status of landless labourer. Very little agricultural improvement did (or could) proceed in these conditions, and the penetration of consumer goods was considerably more restricted than in England. The Irish rural community remained neglected, poor and in some areas dangerously polarized.

At the end of the seventeenth century Britain was a pre-industrial economy in which the lifestyles, occupations and the products of country and town complemented each other. The period between 1660 and 1688 was one of development in which many sectors of the economy made progress, but economic growth was unevenly distributed across Britain. This was still a rural society, but it was a rural society in which industry was already of acknowledged importance. Although regional variations remained strong – the manufacture and distribution of goods was both specialized and localized – a viable national economy was emerging which, in turn, stood at the centre of a developing international commercial network. A strongly hierarchical society seemed capable of generating a remarkable degree of economic vitality. Whether it could generate a comparable degree of political strength will be the focus of the next section.

Politics

In a rural society landed property was the source of political power and authority. Those with land expected – and were expected – to monopolize political power and influence. 'Dominion follows property,' wrote Mandeville. On the whole, the greater aristocracy reserved the greatest offices in the church, in Parliament, in government, in the law and in the armed services for themselves and their dependants, but thousands of other offices remained to be filled from lower down the propertied hierarchies. Furthermore, although offices were regarded as pieces of property which could be exploited for profit (the great lawyer Blackstone defined office as 'a right to exercise a public or private employment and to take the fees and emoluments thereunto belonging'), people sought offices for a variety of reasons, not just for pecuniary gain. These might include the prestige and honour which office carried with it, the holder's wish to be of service and his ambition to make a career, and even a reputation for himself. Yet it was not land alone but also various forms of urban property which entitled individuals and families to play a role on the political stage, to beg for favours, to petition for offices and promotions in church as well as state, to sit on the bench, to obtain the favour of ministers or the court and, not least, to obtain a seat in Parliament. In this process, the search for a patron to promote a person, a family or a cause was all important: the bigger the patron, the better. As for patrons, they measured their own authority by the extent of their own influence and success in procuring favours and offices. Such influence was known as an 'interest' or 'natural interest'. The greatest patrons of all were the government and the church, with their hundreds of offices to distribute.

Britain was a composite state staffed by only a tiny bureaucracy. She developed the apparatus of 'the state' later than most of her continental neighbours. Her standing army was non-existent before the middle of the century and her bureaucracy – no more than 10 000 office-holders by the late seventeenth century according to Gregory King – very tiny indeed by European standards. The central government had to rely upon the voluntary cooperation of unpaid local amateurs drawn from the landed classes to govern the country effectively. After the Restoration of 1660 the Privy Council lost the will to exercise vigilance over local government and its officials and they were left largely to their own devices. The legislation of the Long Parliament was made permanent. Instruments of prerogative rule such as the Star Chamber, the Court of High Commission, the Council of the North and the Council in the Marches of Wales were all abolished, thus extending both the writ and the reputation of the common law. This was to a large extent why the king and the Privy Council were no longer able to interfere arbitrarily in local affairs against the wishes of local magnates. Local autonomy was the real beneficiary of the Restoration of 1660.

The distribution of local offices reflected the social structure. It seemed natural for the aristocracy to monopolize the most important offices in local government, especially the Lord and Deputy Lieutenancies. In turn, the gentry acted as JPs and as Sheriffs, while lesser offices such as those of coroner, constable and clerk of the peace were manned from the middling ranks. At the bottom of the local office-holding hierarchy, the parish constables were drawn from the respectable ranks of the yeomanry and craftsmen. Britain was thus governed through a mixture of informal patronage and social expectation, its rulers at all levels motivated by a curious mixture of profit-seeking and voluntary service.

The advantages of this arrangement arguably outweighed the disadvantages. If the system invited delay and local obstructionism it was at least cheap, reasonably broadly based and, not least, resistant to the threat of centralized absolutism. The propertied orders felt themselves to be incorporated within the state and had access, or the expectation of access, to patronage and influence. When this system worked well it had all the strength of voluntary cooperation on a national scale. Attempts at centralized direction from above were rarely successful and usually unpopular. The regime worked best when the crown acted in concert with local interests. Only then, for example, would the revenue services, the bench and the militia function harmoniously and efficiently. The efficiency of the state at local level should not be underestimated. After 1660 there are clear signs not only of improved parish administration but of a greater willingness by local elites both to carry out national policies and to oversee local administration of matters such as the Poor Law, crime and migration with some thoroughness.[13]

Just as the father was the head of the family and head of the household and just as the landlord was the paternal head of his estate, so the king was the father of his people. Contemporary beliefs about monarchy arose from the religious conception of the king as a semi-divine being, raised above the lives of normal men and women. While popes claimed to be the vicars of God on earth, Protestant monarchs in early modern Europe retaliated with their own assertions of divinity. Indeed, the legal fictions that were an inevitable part of government bestowed upon the monarchy 'the divine right of kings'. According to this belief, the king owed his throne to God and he could do no wrong. Yet the idea of 'the divine right of kings' has been greatly misunderstood. The idea that kings derived their authority from God does not automatically imply that they should be 'absolute' in the government of their kingdoms. The divine right of kings was a theory about the *origins* of royal authority and a defence of the hereditary foundations of monarchical government. It did not necessarily imply that kings were above the law, nor did it deny that kings should obey the law. However, the divine right theory did expect subjects to obey their king and those who derived their authority or position from the king: active disobedience would be contrary to the will of God. In England, at least, kings used divine right theory to defend themselves against *religious* attacks from Catholics and Presbyterians, but proponents of the theory were usually careful to acknowledge traditional English parliamentary safeguards concerning consent to taxation and demands upon the king to observe the laws. To what extent this theological language of politics continued to dominate public discussion in the eighteenth century is at present the subject of much scholarly discussion;[14] that it set the tone for political debate in the later seventeenth century cannot be seriously doubted.

The government of Britain in the late seventeenth century, then, was still assumed to be the king's government. Contemporaries found it difficult to conceive of the state independently of the person of the monarch. The monarch, or the chief ministers enjoying the favour of the monarch, was responsible for appointments to the major offices of state not only in London but also to the Privy Council in Edinburgh and to the Vice-regal administration in Dublin; the personnel of these governing institutions were responsible to him, not to the parliaments of their respective countries. Government was royal government. Political and administrative action emanated from the king and his court. It was the monarch's responsibility to summon, prorogue and dissolve Parliament, to control the armed forces and to dispose of appointments in both church and state. Royal servants lacked any sense of collective responsibility or awareness; the individuals who composed them owed their allegiance to the crown, not to each other.

Furthermore, as the heads of the first family in the country, as leaders of society, as patrons of the arts and as arbiters of taste and fashion, the monarchs and their courts exercised enormous social influence. The cultural hegemony of the monarchy and of the court can scarcely be exaggerated in the years both before and after the Glorious Revolution. Indeed, the court was a vital political arena, with its own traditions, values and significance. A minister neglected it at his peril. Its sheer size was considerable, amounting perhaps to 2000 individuals, including both those who held offices in the household and those who held offices in the central executive. Membership of the court was regarded as an important barometer of royal favour; the presence of English and Scottish Catholics at the court of James II did much to aggravate prevailing fears both of the old faith and of the King's favourable attitude towards it.

Britain was a composite, monarchical state yet the powers of Parliament had been permanently strengthened at the Restoration. (Indeed, the monarchy was restored at the behest of Parliament, not the other way round.) The lower House continued in some important respects to strengthen its position thereafter. By 1688 the Commons had established their sole right to initiate money bills and to appropriate supplies. Although the House of Lords was restored in 1660, it soon acquiesced in a position of inferiority to the House of Commons. The crown was forced to develop techniques for managing Parliament. These, of course, included the promise, immediate or delayed, of favours, offices and pensions, but there was never enough patronage to go round. This is not to argue that Parliament wished to deprive the crown of its traditional prerogatives. Parliament had a much more modest view of its pretensions. Its members were anxious to defend their interests and those of their constituency, to safeguard traditional privileges of Parliament and, in a general sense, to protect the constitution. It was neither their intention nor their wish to establish parliamentary supremacy.

Consequently, there can be no doubt the most important political reality about politics in Britain towards the end of the seventeenth century was the power and authority of the monarchy. So long as the king governed with the consent of Parliament, and in general maintained the approval of the people, his power would remain unimpaired and unchallenged. For its part, Parliament was normally anxious to cooperate with the monarchy in pursuing an agreed national interest. Indeed, for most of the period 1660 to 1688 Parliament was not able to pose effective resistance to Charles II and James II. The popularity of James II throughout his dominions at the start of his reign is extremely suggestive of powerful monarchist tendencies within Britain. In many ways the reign of William III was to be a remarkable demonstration of the potential strength of the monarchy even after the Glorious Revolution, not an illustration of its weakness after it. Finally, it was not Parliament which challenged the monarchy in 1688 but the monarchy which, through a series of reckless miscalculations, abandoned its own traditions and deserted its own supporters. The reaction of the political nation to this crisis is the starting-point for our discussion of the Glorious Revolution.

Notes

1. For discussion of 'composite states', see e.g. J.E. Elliot, 'Composite Monarchies', *Past and Present*, 137 (1992); A. Williams, 'The Mid-Seventeenth Century British State', *English Historical Review*, 110 (1995); C. Russell, 'Composite Monarchies in Early Modern Europe: The British and Irish Example', in A. Grant and K. Stringer, eds, *Uniting the Kingdom: the Making of British History* (1995).
2. Gilbert Sheldon (1598–1677), Bishop of London, 1660–63, Archbishop of Canterbury, 1663–77; William Sancroft (1617–93), Dean of St Paul's, London, 1664–68, Archbishop of Canterbury, 1678–89.
3. An alleged plot to replace Charles II with his Catholic brother James in 1678. Its instigator was the unprincipled adventurer Titus Oates. The plot generated widespread anti-Catholic feeling and led to several dozen death sentences against those thought to be involved. It provoked an ultimately unsuccessful movement to exclude James from the succession. Not until 1681 did both the judicial murders and the popular frenzy terminate.
4. See R. Houlbrooke, *The English Family, 1450–1700* (1984); P. Laslett, *The World We Have Lost*, 3rd edn (1983).
5. For the ability of quite ordinary women to employ the common law and to use such matters as marriage settlements to maintain their rights, see A.M. Erickson, *Women and Property in Early Modern England* (1993).
6. A wife sale usually occurred at a market when a wife was sold to the highest bidder, often after being led around wearing a halter. The purchase was sometimes prearranged, involving an acceptable partner or even a lover 'buying' the woman. This traditional ritual was regarded by public opinion as an acceptable and legitimate form of divorce.
7. I.K. Ben-Amos, *Adolescence and Youth in Early Modern England* (1994); L.A. Pollock, *Forgotten Children: Parent–Child Relations from 1500 to 1900* (1993); Houlbrooke, *The English Family, 1450–1700*.
8. R. Porter, *English Society in the Eighteenth Century* (1982), pp. 386–87.
9. K. Wrightson, *English Society 1580–1680* (1982), p. 35.
10. See E. Kerridge, *The Agricultural Revolution* (1967); E.L. Jones, *Agriculture and the Industrial Revolution* (1971). The most convenient summary of recent research on the so-called 'Agricultural Revolution' may be found in ch. 3 of J. Rule, *The Vital Century* (1992); See also J.V. Beckett, *The Aristocracy in England 1660–1914* (1986), ch. 5. See also the titles listed in the Bibliography, especially J. Thirsk ed., *The Agrarian History of England and Wales, v: 1640–1750* (Cambridge, 1984–85).
11. On enclosures, see e.g. J.R. Wordie, 'The Chronology of English Enclosure, 1500–1914', *Economic History Review*, 36 (1983); J.A. Yelling, *Common Field and Enclosure in England, 1450–1850* (1977); *Enclosures in Britain, 1750–1830* (1984).
12. B.A. Holderness, *Pre-Industrial England: Economy and Society, 1500–1750* (1976), p. 206.
13. J. Kent, 'The Centre and the Localities: State Formation and Parish Government in England, 1640–1740', *Historical Journal*, 38 (1995), pp. 363–404.
14. See J.C.D. Clark, *English Society, 1688–1832* (1985); pp. 119–98; J.A.W. Gunn, *Beyond Liberty and Property: The Process of Self-Recognition in Eighteenth Century Political Thought* (1983), pp. 120–93.

2

The Glorious Revolution in Britain, 1688–1714

The Glorious Revolution in England, 1688–1689

What came to be known in the early eighteenth century as the Glorious Revolution began with the sudden collapse of the popularity of King James II and the subsequent offer of the throne to William of Orange in 1688. The repercussions of these dramatic events amounted to a real watershed in the history of Britain – even, perhaps, a revolution. Whether they deserve to be described as particularly 'Glorious', as many mid-eighteenth-century commentators were fond of doing, remains a matter of opinion.

When James II succeeded his brother, Charles II, in 1685 the prospects for his reign could not have been better. Although he was a Roman Catholic, he enjoyed widespread popularity, which was confirmed by his promise to respect the established position of the Church of England. The general election which he called soon after his accession resulted in a favourable Parliament dominated by the Tories, who could usually be relied upon to protect and advance the interests of the monarchy. It proceeded to vote supplies for James which were more generous than those enjoyed by any of his Stuart predecessors.

How did James so quickly and so completely dissipate these enormous advantages? The answer is twofold. First he was driven by a sense of religious destiny, a desire to see his country convert back to the Old Faith. This, he believed, might gradually and peacefully occur if the penal laws which discriminated against Catholics, and prevented them from holding office, were abolished. If this happened, Catholics would be able to show that they were loyal citizens. Second, throughout his reign James overestimated the strength of his position. Even in 1685 he was unable to persuade the Tories of the wisdom of his religious policy, and by November 1685 Parliament had demonstrated its reluctance to implement a policy of Catholic toleration. James prorogued it, and it never met again. It is just possible that James might have kept his throne had he been willing to respect the privileged position of the Anglican church, and, at the same time, able to maintain the Tories in office. His refusal to guarantee the first ensured his failure to achieve the second. He used a pliant judiciary to dispense individuals from their obligation to obey the Test Acts and then, in the Declaration of Indulgence of April 1687, suspended all tests and granted full liberty of worship.[1] This threatened to establish a pluralist state, dismantling the privileges of the Anglican church and reducing it to the status of the Catholic and Dissenting churches. Determined to obtain the approval of a new parliament for his actions James dissolved the old one in July 1687. But the King had not realized the inherent contradictions of his actions. Predictably, the Tories and the Anglicans were horrified at what he was trying to do; but even the Dissenters were unenthusiastic, fearing the consequences for the Protestant sects of a policy of toleration for Catholics.

These miscalculations were to have disastrous consequences. The King aroused general anxiety during his preparations for a general election in and after the autumn of 1687, when his supporters ruthlessly purged the borough corporations in attempting to secure a compliant parliament. Recent attempts to justify James's actions have suggested that he was engaged in a serious attempt to establish a new ruling class by creating an alliance between the urban middle classes and the gentry against the aristocracy. These arguments, however, have been unconvincing, and in any case overlook the pro-Catholic intentions of the King.[2] Had James been successful in his schemes Parliament would have ceased to be either a representative of the propertied classes or a check upon royal government; it would have become little more than a rubber stamp for royal wishes. But there is no evidence that James was consciously seeking to erect a royal absolutism either based upon the doctrine of the divine right of kings or modelled upon that of Louis XIV's France. Rather, James was unwittingly exceeding the boundaries of his subjects' tolerance in pursuing his religious objectives so enthusiastically.

In spite of the growing concern aroused by the actions of the King, there is little evidence to suggest that James was facing an imminent rebellion, still less revolution, in the spring or even as late as the summer of 1688. The aristocracy and the gentry had severe reservations about the actions and purposes of their king, but there was no indication that they wished to lift a finger against him. Indeed, the political situation in 1688 was quite different from that of the early 1640s. Parliament was not sitting. It could thus neither focus nor express such sense of national grievances as may have existed. In 1642 Parliament had challenged the royal prerogative, claimed sovereignty in the state and, in the end, raised an army. Parliament in 1688 wished to do none of these things. There was one further, crucial difference. In 1688 Scotland and Ireland were quiet. Disorder in the Celtic kingdoms was a consequence, not a cause, of the Glorious Revolution. Last, and by no means least, James enjoyed not only the support of a large and powerful standing army of around 20 000 men but the security of the biggest navy in Europe. He enjoyed, furthermore, the friendship and the patronage of Louis XIV of France.

The birth of a son to the King on 10 June 1688 added an entirely new dimension to the situation. James had two daughters from his first (Protestant) marriage and until now he had had no children at all from his existing 15-year-old (Catholic) marriage. It had been universally assumed that his controversial political and religious experiments would give way to a more traditional, Protestant regime in the next reign when he would be succeeded by his Protestant daughter, Mary. Now the birth of a Catholic, male heir threatened to postpone indefinitely the prospect of a Protestant succession. Even if James died while his heir was still a child, a regency would inevitably be dominated by his Catholic wife. Tories, fearful for the fate of the Anglican church, were just as alarmed as Whigs. Mary was the wife of William of Orange, Stadtholder of Holland, the most renowned defender of the Protestant faith in Europe, a man who could hardly tolerate passively the prospect of his wife's immense British inheritance drifting into the pro-Catholic orbit of his lifelong rival, Louis XIV. Indeed, ever since 1672, when Louis had invaded the United Provinces, William had assumed the mantle of both Dutch and European champion of Protestantism against the imperialist designs of the Sun King.

Already in the spring of 1688 William had been contemplating the possibility of an invasion of Britain as part of his latest campaign against Louis XIV. He was now able to take advantage of an entirely unofficial invitation issued on 30 June by the 'immortal seven' (five Whigs and two Tory magnates) to William to mount an invasion of England. At this stage William's objective was to secure the Protestant succession for his wife, but not the throne for himself. Indeed, in his 'Declaration' of the reasons for undertaking the impending invasion, which he issued on 30 September, he went no further than to promise to defend the Protestant religion and to guarantee the election of a free Parliament. William could not afford to depict himself as an adventurer threatening to depose a legitimate monarch. On this both Whigs and Tories, Anglicans and Dissenters, could agree.

Not for the first, nor the last time, however, it was events in Europe which were to determine the destiny of Britain. When Louis XIV moved against Habsburg power in Germany by attacking the fort of Phillipsburg on 14 September 1688 with 70 000 troops William was free to move against England. (Only at this point, it seems, did it at last seriously occur to James that an invasion was a real possibility.) With destiny on his side, and remarkably good fortune – notably the 'Protestant wind' that blew the Dutch fleet down the channel also kept James's fleet bottled up in the Thames estuary – William was able to land an army of 14 000 men at Torbay on 5 November 1688. He cautiously occupied Exeter and slowly moved towards London. James advanced his army from London to Salisbury Plain to check the invasion. Astonishingly, however, he failed to engage the invading force with his own considerably larger army. He pulled it back towards the capital, a humiliating and totally demoralizing retreat, but one that was to determine that there would be no civil war in England in 1688. As his own health – and will – failed, so the morale of his army evaporated. James II began to realize that there was little sign of positive support for his wilting cause. Indeed, from the north there were disturbing reports of support for William. Meanwhile, William's progress – words like 'invasion', 'rebellion' or 'assault' seem inappropriate – coincided with reports of secessions from the cause of James. James began to negotiate. Even at this late hour William was prepared to allow James to keep his throne on condition that Catholics were removed from office and a free Parliament summoned. Wishing to avoid such humiliating concessions, James fled London; on 22 December, his nerve at length stretched beyond endurance, he escaped to France.

The precise circumstances of his departure were extremely important. James may not have surrendered the crown, but his flight into the arms of Louis XIV left no practical alternative but to offer it to William. As G.M. Trevelyan put it, he 'dethroned himself'.[3] Even worse, it seemed that James was determined to do as much damage as possible to the political fabric of his own country. He left no formal framework of government behind him. Indeed, he had destroyed the writs authorising the general election and had (it was reported) thrown the Great Seal into the Thames. Even worse, he had ordered the disbandment of his army but without disarming the rank-and-file soldiers. Two days of anti-Catholic rioting in the capital and in a number of provincial centres convinced the propertied classes that the only hope of restoring order lay in surrendering all to William. Informal meetings of peers and commoners invited William to assume the executive government until an elected Convention could meet on 22 January 1689 to provide a legitimate structure for the future government of the country.

When the Convention Parliament met on 7 January 1689 to dispose of the throne it had to decide between a number of alternatives, all of them with their supporters, none of them without serious difficulties. The first alternative was that James might be recalled and reinstated but subject to significant limitations on his power. His recent conduct had, however, eliminated what was left of his support and his popularity, even among the Tory party, the King's most loyal supporters. Furthermore, there were few, even among the Whigs, who really wanted an enfeebled monarchy shorn of its power. It was not the purpose of the men of 1688–89 to establish a seriously limited monarchy. A second alternative was to declare James insane and to appoint a regent during the minority of the newly born baby son. This expedient might have been ingenious but it was also dangerously impracticable. There was no guarantee that it would work. To Tories it might seem like dangerous tampering with the principle of hereditary succession. The third alternative was much to be preferred: to accept the fact that James had, in effect, abdicated the throne by absconding to France and that Mary was therefore the legal heir. James had not, in fact, renounced the throne, but to assert the obvious fact that the throne was vacant might avoid giving distress to Tories. William acted decisively, informing the Convention that he would not agree to be merely a regent. If the throne were offered to Mary it would be he, not his wife, who would exercise the executive powers. With the promise and prospect of firm government, the Convention was content. On 6 February it declared the throne vacant and invited William to become king, subject to the accompanying Declaration – which ultimately became the Bill of Rights. (In Scotland a similar document, the 'Claim of Right' was drawn up and agreed.)

The Bill of Rights was a pragmatic document designed to meet an immediate situation. The throne was empty and legal authority had to be restored as a matter of urgency. The Bill recited the evils of which James had been guilty and provided that they should not be repeated in the future: these included suspending and dispensing subjects from the penalties of the law, establishing a standing army, packing Parliament, levying taxes by force of the royal prerogative and pressuring juries. To these ends Parliament 'ought to be held frequently', elections ought to be free, and not only the male heirs of James but all Roman Catholics were to be barred from the succession.[4]

The significance of the Bill of Rights is that it redesigned the framework within which the monarchy was to function in the future and it defined the limits of royal power. It is important to underscore the fact that the Bill did not envisage a permanently weakened monarchy. Many possible means of emasculating royal authority were discussed in the Convention, but most of them were rejected. Whigs and Tories would have found it difficult to agree on them. More importantly, William would never have accepted them. Indeed, as his reign was to show, there was to be no sudden tilt in the direction of what later generations would recognize as limited or constitutional monarchy. Certainly, William never regarded his throne as being held on a contractual basis, whatever some Whigs in the Convention may have wished. The Bill of Rights was neither contractual in its wording nor conditional in its content. Indeed, the offer of the crown was never even specifically made conditional on William promising to honour the Declaration of Rights. The Glorious Revolution, then, was achieved without any contractual agreement between crown and Parliament, still less between crown and people.

While Whig contract theory was not enshrined in the Glorious Revolution, the Tory principles of divine right, hereditary succession and non-resistance were sorely compromised by the events of 1688–89. Although it was very difficult for Tories to square either those events or the provisions of the Bill of Rights with divine right and hereditary succession, it was just possible to do so: they could argue that it was the *abuse*, not the principle, of hereditary monarchical power which had been responsible for the replacement of James II by William. Most Tories, horrified at the prospect of causing a civil war, were prepared to accept that William was king *de facto* if not *de jure*. Had James stayed to fight for his throne, the political dilemma facing the Tories would have become far more agonizing than it turned out to be. If it could be shown that he had abdicated, there was no purpose in the Tories fighting for him. The fiction that James had 'abdicated' may not have borne much examination but at least it satisfied Tory consciences. In this way, the Glorious Revolution could (just about) be depicted for Tories as confirmation of the principles of divine hereditary right.

Consequently, this was not to be the end of divine right theory. In the 1690s some Tories managed to convince themselves not only that William owed his throne to divine providence but that he continued to occupy it in accordance with the will of God. Once the regime was securely established it, apparently, acquired the divine sanction that upheld the social as well as the religious order. Indeed, the reign of Anne witnessed a resurgence of Tory zeal for divine hereditary right,[5] but the failure of the Queen to bequeath an heir was a fatal blow to such enthusiasm. After the Hanoverian succession in 1714 Tory belief in divine right lingered on more in the realms of political nostalgia and intellectual debate rather than in the sphere of practical politics.[6]

On the whole, the Glorious Revolution may be seen as a victory for a moderate Whiggism which boasted the virtues of a mixed and balanced constitution and the advantages of government by consent. Although much was written by Whig propagandists at this time about the conditional nature of government, about government as a trustee for future generations and, above all, about rights of resistance against tyranny, these arguments were not intended to form a conscious agenda for a revolution. They were used to rebut the authoritarian claims coming from the circles around James. The Convention did contain a small but lively group of radical Whig reformers who sought to implement a thoroughgoing restructuring of the political system during the Glorious Revolution. Indeed, their contributions to the debates of the Convention were vociferous, and may even have had some influence in Scotland and Ireland. Although they largely failed to persuade the Convention to adopt their more ambitious schemes, they were to enjoy greater success in the future, not least with the Toleration Act of 1689 and the Triennial Act of 1694. Even these discussions, however, owed little to the ideas of John Locke. We now know that, far from being a tract for the men of 1688–89, Locke's *Two Treatises on Government* (published in 1690) had been written some years earlier and for very different political circumstances. Indeed, the *Treatises* went far beyond the conventional Whiggism of the day. Locke rehearsed arguments based on abstract reason to outline a thoroughly contractual political philosophy based on natural rights, popular sovereignty and rights of resistance. His conviction that it was legitimate to overthrow a ruler if stability and property were endangered did not fit comfortably with traditional Whiggism and its stress on historic rights and the historic constitution. Such arguments were almost irrelevant not only to the political circumstances following James II's ignominious departure from England and the realities of Convention politics but also to the post-Revolution Whig party. The Whigs of the 1690s were not anxious to popularize Locke's advocacy of rights of resistance. One Revolution, however Glorious, in one political lifetime was quite enough. It was in the sermons of Whig divines and the pamphlets and tracts of the reign of Anne that Locke's ideas were to be more consciously circulated and popularized.[7]

In religious life the Glorious Revolution inaugurated changes of incalculable significance, both immediate and long-term. The Toleration Act, passed by the Convention in May 1689 (although, perhaps significantly, the word 'toleration' does not occur in the Act), removed the obligation to attend Anglican services from the consciences of Protestant Dissenters (but not from those of Catholics). The Act established an extensive licensing system for non-Anglican chapels, a sure sign that the old fear of the Protestant Dissenters as regicide republicans was lifting. By the provisions of the Act, Dissenters were allowed to have their own teachers and schools; it is from this date that the famous Dissenting academies of the eighteenth century have their origin. The Act, furthermore, conceded that the discipline of Anglican church courts did not extend to the whole population, an important preliminary to the abandonment of censorship of theological works which took effect when the Licensing Act was not renewed in 1695. But religious toleration was to go no further than this. The Clarendon Code was not to be repealed. The English universities were still barred to Dissenters and they were still required to pay church rates and tithe to the support of a church of which they were not members. Indeed, even William was unable to persuade an intensely Anglican Parliament to repeal the Test and Corporation Acts,[8] which excluded non-Anglicans from seats in Parliament, from offices and from corporations. Nor were he and his supporters able in 1689 to persuade either the Convention or the Convocation to agree upon a new scheme of comprehension, which would have generously allowed moderate Dissenters to return to the Anglican fold.[9] (By this time, however, most Dissenters, save the Presbyterians, were far more interested in toleration than in comprehension.) Clearly, then, the provisions of the Toleration Act were limited in their scope; they perhaps represented the minimum reward which the Protestant Dissenters would accept for their resistance to James II in the period before and during the Glorious Revolution and the maximum degree of generosity towards them which Anglicans were prepared to permit.

In the decades immediately after the Glorious Revolution, Protestant Dissent prospered. Secure in the protection of William III and (intermittently, at least) reasonably secure in the protection of Whig ministries against Tory attacks, Protestant Dissent thrived. Between 1689 and 1710 no fewer than 3900 meeting-house licences were issued. In London in 1711 there were twice as many Dissenting meeting-houses as Anglican parish churches! By this time the number of Protestant Dissenters in England and Wales was estimated at about 400 000. Pious Anglicans were appalled by the spectacular increase in the growth of Dissent – in this new free market in religion the Dissenters were comfortable winners – by the explosion in the amount of heterodox literature which followed the lifting of censorship in 1695 and, in general, by the emergence of a scientific and sceptical social climate. No wonder Anglican churchmen were so frequently resentful at the behaviour of the Dissenters, especially their practice of Occasional Conformity, by which they attended an Anglican church once a year and thus qualified for municipal office.

Yet, from a different standpoint, it was one of the achievements of the Glorious Revolution to have re-established the dominant theological position and to have safeguarded the commanding social influence which the Church of England had enjoyed before the reign of James II. Indeed, after the worrying flirtations of Charles II and James II with Catholicism, Anglicans might congratulate themselves on having successfully repelled some very dangerous challenges to its position. After all, William was indifferent to Anglican doctrine and the Whigs and Dissenters entertained extensive schemes of religious toleration. The Tories, however, managed to secure the passage of a *de facto* oath of allegiance, on which most of the church could unite, rather than a *de jure* oath of allegiance, on which it almost certainly could not. The Whigs, inspired by hostility to high church clergy, insisted that all clergy should take the oath. About 400 of the lower clergy, together with six bishops, were unable on grounds of conscience to take the oath of allegiance to William and Mary. These Non-jurors, as they came to be known, lost their benefices as a result. Their secession from the church proved to be permanent and, in view of their personal talents and abilities, damaging. The schism of the Non-jurors was the gravest schism in the history of the Church of England in the seventeenth century, especially when, as we shall see, it came to include the whole of the Scottish hierarchy. On the whole, however, over 90 per cent of the Anglican clergy took the oath. Those who resigned were replaced by men who were content to accept the Glorious Revolution. In this manner, therefore, the Church of England was reconstituted at the Glorious Revolution as the established church of England. Its status, however, remained a matter of debate and its prospects in an age of religious pluralism uncertain.

The Glorious Revolution, then, was a real watershed in the history of England. It settled the vexed and urgent issue of the succession, defined the powers of the monarchy and guaranteed, while redefining, the status of the Church of England and its relations with Protestant Dissent. It was not a revolution in the modern sense for it was not, of course, intended to be. It was a revolution in a more traditional sense, a revolution which was not an abrupt break with the past but a revolution which was an alleged return to the past, a past which was ordered and predictable, unlike James II's unconstitutional and illegal innovations. How successful and how permanent the revolution would be none could foresee in 1689.

Crown and Parliament, 1689–1714

It had not been the purpose of the Glorious Revolution to reduce the executive functions of the monarchy. Yet the conservative intentions of the men of 1688–89 were in many ways frustrated by changes which occurred *after* 1689 in the working relationships between the House of Commons and the crown. Consequently the balance of power and authority between crown and Parliament began to tilt a little more in favour of Parliament than the men of 1688–89 could ever have imagined. At the same time, successive monarchs between 1689 and 1714 were confronted with practical problems which made it difficult for them to execute their executive functions.

One of the most vital developments which strengthened the autonomy, and consequently the self-confidence, of Parliament after 1689 was the greater regularity of its sittings. The Stuarts had ignored Parliament whenever it suited them, either by not summoning it or by allowing many years to pass between general elections. Although William retained the prerogatives of summoning and dissolving Parliament, the Declaration of Rights had demanded that Parliament should be 'held frequently' following 'free elections'. In practice, Parliament came to meet annually after 1689 because Britain was at war with France almost continually between 1689 and 1713. It was greatly in William's interest to summon Parliament with some regularity so that he could solicit its agreement to the funds and supplies which he needed and which were raised on the credit of Parliament. Moreover, the sheer quantity of business, especially financial business, which had to be transacted each session rapidly increased during William's reign. Between 1689 and 1702 809 bills were enacted, compared with 533 between 1660 and 1684. This made it much less likely that William III would prorogue Parliament as casually as his Stuart predecessors had occasionally done. Consequently, Parliament met annually throughout the period of the war and thereafter during the period of peace after 1713.

By 1694 the initial infatuation with William was giving way to a growing disenchantment with his high-handed view of his own powers and his willingness to involve England in expensive wars. The ruthless tactics employed by his ministers to maintain themselves in power, including the use of offices, places and pensions to secure support in Parliament, aroused considerable suspicion of the power of the executive. This apparent revival of powerful centralizing tendencies provoked a number of responses from Members of

Parliament of which one of the earliest legislative achievements was the Triennial Act of 1694, which required general elections to be held at least every three years. Such bills had been mooted in 1689, 1693 and earlier in 1694 before the King's resistance could be overcome. The Triennial Act was the first statutory restriction upon the royal prerogative of dissolving Parliament and must be regarded as a significant curtailment of royal power. In practice ten elections were held between 1694 and 1716. In 1716 parliament decided that such frequent elections were not conducive to political harmony and stability, and the Septennial Act lengthened the maximum period between elections to seven years.

The Triennial Act was not the only response to fear of increased executive power. Place bills to restrict the number of office- (or place-) holders who sat in the Commons were introduced in 1692 (unsuccessfully because too sweeping) and in 1694 (successfully, because limited to Land Tax Collectors and Salt Duty Commissioners). Further Place Bills removed Excise Officials (1699) and Customs Officials (1701). A further response to mounting suspicion of the executive was the practice of 'tacking' (or attaching to money bills clauses relating to other issues). Tacking was used only as a last resort and when the Commons were reasonably united, as with the Place Bill legislation of 1694, 1700 and 1701. Even this occasional usage suggests that by the middle of the 1690s Members of Parliament were prepared to use the financial influence over the monarchy which they knew they possessed. Later, tacking was used more widely. On a famous occasion in 1704 some Tories tacked the third Occasional Conformity bill to the Land Tax in a rash and unsuccessful attempt to force it through the House of Lords. Other legislation reflected the growing suspicion of the executive. The Elections Act of 1696 sought to minimize the corruption of electors but concentrated unduly on the malpractices of Sheriffs, neglecting the broader issues of treating, bribery and intimidation. Less spectacular, but rather more effective, was the development of appropriation of supply, a technique which went back to 1665. This meant that money voted for the war had to be used for the specified purposes for which it had been intended rather than the wider schemes of William or his ministers. In the same way, the use of parliamentary committees sought to restrict the government's freedom of action, an expedient that went back to the days of the Commonwealth. These committees reviewed such matters as the conduct of the war and the state of trade. Over the medium term, they did much to establish habits of vigilance over the executive and, indeed, to politicize a wider audience.

Finally, it was suspicion of William, his foreign policy and his political methods which was responsible for the final, great statutory limitation placed on royal power in his reign, the Act of Settlement of 1701. The death of Princess Anne's one surviving child, William Duke of Gloucester, on 30 July 1700 had thrown the political world into uncertainty. The primary aim of the Act was to provide for the Protestant Succession in this new situation. This it did by providing that George, Elector of Hanover, should succeed William's daughter, Anne, and by laying down that no Roman Catholic could inherit the throne. To safeguard England's interests during the reigns of foreign monarchs, furthermore, the Act stated that the agreement of Parliament was to be necessary for any war in defence of the continental possessions of a foreign king of Britain. To safeguard the interests of the English political nation, moreover, the Act of Succession prevented any foreigner from sitting in Parliament or Privy Council, from holding any civil or military office or from receiving any grant of land from the crown. The clause requiring parliamentary consent for the removal of judges was, however, less contentious than it sounds. William had not meddled in the appointment of judges, and the clause merely registered the final defeat of Stuart attempts to control the judiciary. Two important provisions of the Act of Settlement were subject to serious second thoughts: that which eliminated placemen and pensioners from sitting in the House of Commons and that which prohibited future monarchs from leaving the kingdom without the consent of Parliament. Neither of these provisions was ever actually enforced. The complete elimination of placemen might have made the Commons too difficult for the executive to manage. In the Regency Act of 1706 a less comprehensive removal of placemen was promised (though never rigidly enforced). The clause prohibiting a future monarch from leaving the country without parliamentary consent was repealed in 1714. Their passage, however, reflects the willingness even of many Tory MPs to go further towards restricting royal powers than the men of 1688–89 would have done.

A strong and ambitious king like William naturally wished to exercise the traditional prerogatives over foreign policy enjoyed by his predecessors. Much would depend on the extent to which King and Parliament could cooperate. Not every MP could understand why Britain should be dragged into a long and expensive war simply to suit the Prince of Orange. At first, William had to respect the anxieties of his new subjects concerning the vexed subject of the armed services. There was no political problem with the navy, which was steadily expanding throughout the 1690s at a cost of £2.5 million per year. By 1713 Britain had become the greatest naval power in Europe. On the other hand, there was widespread suspicion, even in wartime, of William's attempt to maintain a standing army. In 1699 the Disbanding Act legalized the existence of a peacetime standing army, a significant victory for William. This confirmed the existing suspicions of his subjects. During the partition negotiations with France in 1696–97 an increasingly confident William acted as his own foreign minister. He did little to involve English ministers, preferring to use his Dutch negotiators to deal on their behalf. Parliament was furious. When the news of the Second Partition Treaty of 1700 was revealed in the following year, the Tory majority in the Commons was outraged and threatened to impeach the entire cabinet. A chastened King promised to obtain parliamentary approval for new alliances in the future. The matter did not end there. It led to the inclusion in the Act of Settlement of 1701 of a clause forbidding British soldiers from defending foreign territory for a foreign prince, a significant limitation upon the monarch's freedom of action.

As with so many of the political and constitutional developments of the reign of William III, it was the political necessities of wartime rather than the constitutional provisions of the Glorious Revolution which defined and redefined the acceptable spheres of royal and parliamentary power. Much, in fact, remained unchanged. Nothing in the Revolution Settlement deprived the crown of the right to take the initiative in foreign relations. Nothing in the Revolution Settlement compelled the government either to explain its policy or to release information about it, although it might be tactically sensible for it to do so. Even in the reign of Anne, when parliamentary discussion of foreign affairs became much more common and much more partisan, the crown retained the initiative. Parliament might criticize the Queen and her ministers but it had no wish to seize control of the conduct of foreign policy. There was no great public demand for it to do so. Parliament and public tended to become involved in foreign policy questions mainly when commercial considerations were at stake and when Britain's relations with the Bourbon powers were in dispute. There was much less public interest in Britain's policy towards the rest of Europe.

There is in the politics of the post-Revolution years a certain experimental quality, as King and Parliament strove to accommodate themselves to novel political circumstances in a period of unprecedented warfare. Although there were many areas of friction between them, they were, at bottom, partners rather than enemies in the business of government. At the same time it suited Parliament to place controls upon the crown's financial independence. The financial settlement of 1689 allowed William £200 000 per annum, a sum which fell at least £250 000 short of *peacetime* expenditure and which entirely ignored accumulated debts of around £200 000. The outbreak of war in May 1689 rapidly made a nonsense of such inadequate provision. As early as 1690 Parliament assumed full responsibility for the land forces and voted annual supplies to pay for them. During the 1690s parliamentary approval of detailed estimates, augmented by the investigations of Commissioners of Accounts, became a regular matter. Finally, the Civil List Act of 1698 marked the formal abandonment of the old distinction between ordinary and extraordinary supply in favour of the more modern distinction between civil and military expenditure. By the terms of the Act William was provided with a Civil List of £700 000 per annum for life to cover the costs of the household and of the executive government, including pensions, ministerial salaries and secret service expenditure. All military and naval expenditure became, even in peacetime, the responsibility of Parliament.

These costs were unprecedented. The war (75 per cent of public expenditure under William) swallowed at least £5 million per year, a total of over £40 million by the end of his reign. At the end of the war in 1697 government debt exceeded £14 million; by the end of the War of the Spanish Succession in 1713 the debt had risen to £30 million. To finance debts on this scale required massive tax increases. Under William, customs duties on overseas trade were extended to a wide range of goods and hoisted to 20 per cent and even 25 per cent. Excise duties were imposed upon stamps, salt, malt and leather. Even more important was a revived assessment of the rateable value of landed estates in 1692, resulting in a Land Tax of 4s in the pound. This was to be a particularly successful tax. It brought in about one-third of all tax revenue between 1693 and 1714. Its annual yield of about £2 million was not only predictable, cheap and (because locally assessed and collected) flexible. Its reliability enabled short-term loans to be levied on its security. But even these enhanced yields were not enough to meet the new levels of government expenditure. Something more than a reform of the revenue was needed to fund the enormous sums needed to finance the war.

What was needed was a system of government borrowing which did not suffer from the deficiencies of those adopted under the Stuarts, namely corruption, unpopularity and, not least, their liability to antagonize Parliament. These objectives were in large part achieved by the 'Financial Revolution' of the 1690s. This was, first, the process by which Parliament assumed responsibility for the management of a new system of government debt and, second, a series of technical measures by which government debts were serviced by taxation. Its origins are to be found in the £1 million loan of 1693 which the government raised by offering annuities to investors. For some years the government continued to raise money on a short-term basis. During William's reign long-term debt represented only one-third of all government debt. Only in 1712 did it come to exceed short-term debt. By then, most government debt was floated either through annuities or through loans raised through state lotteries. In this way investment in British government debt became a reliable and regular income for investors. Hundreds of thousands of wealthy citizens with money to invest loaned money to the government, receiving their interest as annuities. Such loans may be usefully regarded as their own personal investments in the political and economic system.[10]

Parliament assumed responsibility for the management of government debt with the establishment of the Bank of England in 1694. The Bank was by statute able to raise money on the capital market and lend it to the government on condition that Parliament guaranteed the repayment of the long-term debt by allocating guaranteed funds to pay interest on the loans. Such a system of borrowing enabled the government to raise loans reliably and cheaply either through the Bank or through the East India Company (and, after its establishment in 1711, the South Sea Company). The governments of William III were able to raise loans at 8 per cent, those of Anne at 5 per cent. (After the Treaty of Utrecht interest rates sank to around 3 per cent.) As a consequence of these financial technicalities, Parliament became in effect the guarantor for the system of government finance in Britain after the Glorious Revolution. By 1714 the Treasury was presenting annual budgets for the approval of Parliament, thus rendering annual meetings of Parliament imperative. In this way, the Financial Revolution arguably had more extensive constitutional consequences than the Bill of Rights.

Yet the consequences of the Financial Revolution went far beyond its constitutional implications. In the long term, this new ability of governments to pay for expensive wars helped to transform the position of Britain on the European stage and enabled her to become a world power. Government finance became more predictable; the 'Stop of the Exchequer' of 1672, in which the government defaulted on its repayments, could never be repeated. The economy, too, in general benefited from the new mechanisms of financial capitalism. Greater confidence in the stability and predictability of financial transactions greatly enhanced the expansion of private as well as public credit and finance. The amount of money in circulation rapidly increased. Cheques became common and promissory notes were legalized in 1705. Consequently, money could safely and swiftly be transmitted over long distances. Even before 1688 marine and other forms of insurance had been gaining in familiarity. Lloyd's of London, in fact, was established in 1688. After 1688 such developments fed upon themselves. Many commercial enterprises came to be organized as joint-stock companies: by 1695 there were 95 of them in England, 44 in Scotland.

Whig apologists have always argued that the events of 1688–89 marked the final failure of continental patterns of absolutism to appear in England. The flight of James II may have given the impression of strengthening the forces of constitutionalism simply because it left peers and parliamentarians to seek their own solutions to the country's problems. But the Convention was not a Parliament, and the solutions that emerged lacked any obvious intellectual ancestry. Most of the participants in the great events of 1688–89 were less consumed with the long-term evolution of the political order than with the immediate problems which James II's erratic and, of course, unprecedented behaviour posed. Even those contemporaries who may have had a longer view of events seem to have been more concerned with the protection of landed property and privilege than with the rights of Parliament. Furthermore, to depict these events as a victory for Whiggism ignores the intrinsic reality that the Glorious Revolution was the achievement of a coalition of Whigs and Tories. As we have seen, doctrinaire Whiggism was not an important driving force in the events of 1688–89. Insofar as a new political direction can be discerned after 1689, it owed much more to King William's war than it did to the Glorious Revolution. Finally, to treat the Glorious Revolution, as many Whig historians did, as a reflection of the genius of the English for moderation and for their ability to resist violent upheaval, is difficult to square with the bloodletting in Scotland and Ireland and the many years of warfare against France into which the Revolution plunged these islands.

More recently, some historians have wished to revise the Whig interpretation of the Glorious Revolution more thoroughly by even questioning its constitutional significance.[11] According to these writers, the Revolution itself did not establish a limited monarchy. The political and (what is not to be underestimated) the social power of the monarchy, and much of its ideological influence, too, survived the Revolution. After all, William III was able to summon and dissolve Parliament, choose his own ministers (in church as well as state), conduct foreign policy (details of which he sometimes concealed from his ministers), declare war and negotiate peace. At the same time, the growing demands of war created a veritable empire of patronage, much of it in the gift of the crown, which could be used to reward the loyalty of the court's friends in both Houses of Parliament. Further, the monarch retained the power to create peers and thus to exert influence over the House of Lords. By the end of William's reign 18 out of 26 incumbent bishops owed their sees to him, while no fewer than 36 of the 112 lay peers owed their peerages to him. When to these are added the household peers, who might normally be expected to support the monarch, well over one-half of the upper chamber might be described as reliable. Insofar as it may have led to the resolution of the key conflicts of religion and taxation, the Glorious Revolution paved the way for a potentially *restrengthened* monarchy. Indeed, the court remained the engine of executive government, with Parliament playing a subsidiary role on the political stage.

On the other hand, in one sense at least, the Glorious Revolution *did* mark the end of an era, with the overthrow of a Catholic monarch and the elimination of any realistic prospect of a Catholic succession. If it was not a total victory for constitutionalism, then the Glorious Revolution *was* a total victory for Protestantism. Their fears may have been illusory, but many contemporaries had been terrified for the survival of Protestantism had James been allowed a free hand in England. After all, in 1686 he ordered that in Scotland the penal laws should be relaxed against the Catholics but enforced against the Covenanters! In 1689, in dramatic contrast, the Scottish Convention declared that it had the constitutional right to dispose of the crown, and proceeded to enact a religious revolution which saw the rejection of episcopacy and the establishment of the Presbyterian Church of Scotland. In the same way, if we view the Glorious Revolution as an event in European rather than as an event solely in British history, it appears as a defeat for the prospect of a Catholic, centralized monarchy on the French pattern and a victory for the prospect of a Protestant, decentralized body politic.

At the same time, it is possible to underestimate the constitutional significance of the Glorious Revolution. Although the Whig historians undoubtedly exaggerated the loss of royal authority in 1688–89, the Convention did disturb the rigid order of hereditary succession in handing the throne to William and Mary. It proceeded to redraw the line of succession while excluding Catholics from the throne in future. Furthermore, the Revolution did lead, and quite rapidly, to exceptionally important changes in the balance of power in the relationship between king and Parliament: in the capacity of Parliament to meet annually, to be elected triennially and to control government expenditure. Since 1660 there had always existed the threat, at least, of royal absolutism exercised through a managed Parliament. After 1689 religious toleration no longer depended on the vagaries of the royal prerogative. In general, a more open civic culture followed the Toleration Act of 1689, just as a more open political culture followed the Triennial Act of 1694 and the abandonment of censorship in 1695. Such vital cultural changes may not have been intended by the men of the Convention, but they proved to be impossible to reverse. With all this in mind, it is difficult to avoid the conclusion that by 1714 Britain had become a multinational parliamentary monarchy. It is true that the monarchy retained formidable prerogative powers and maintained the ability to initiate executive action. These powers and abilities, however, were subjected in practice to a rapidly growing number of statutes and conventions, all operating within a political framework whose essential reality was the annual meeting of Parliament. These pressures became so powerful that the last discretionary royal power, that of vetoing legislation, was used only sparingly. After 1708 it was not used at all.

In the end it is the success of the Glorious Revolution which was to be so striking to posterity. The designs of a Catholic King had been frustrated, the succession altered and foreign policy sensationally reversed without civil war in England or social revolution anywhere in Britain. In the future the independence of the gentry and aristocracy in their localities was to be respected, while the tampering with local borough charters of which James had been guilty was not to be repeated. Whigs and Tories, Presbyterians and Anglicans were united in their support of the political and religious settlement of 1688–89. This guaranteed the privileges of an aristocratic social order but safeguarded the security of property more widely. The settlement eventually obtained the endorsement of the middling, mercantile orders. Contemporaries, naturally, had a different perspective on these experiences, one that did not combine its varied elements into a coherent and continuous narrative, a perspective that was blurred by uncertainties and distorted by confusion. Nevertheless one thing remains beyond dispute. The expansion of the powers of Parliament opened the doors of political debate to a more broadly based political nation than had existed hitherto.

Politics and parties, 1689–1714

There was no guarantee that the political arrangements created by the Glorious Revolution would in practice operate smoothly; the new 'system' of government had to be made to work. In particular, the constant demand for taxation, the frequent sittings of Parliament and, after 1694, the regularity of general elections created partisanship and thus uncertainty. If the king's government were to be respected, if the unprecedented amounts of taxation which he was demanding were to be voted and if armies and navies were to be raised and paid for then the powers of government would have to be utilized as never before. William, however, had learned the lessons of the previous reign. If the powers of government were to be utilized in this manner, it would have to be with the agreement of the parliamentary classes.

The King's ability to conduct business depended in large part upon exploiting the potential for support which existed in both Houses of Parliament. In the Lords, as we have seen, the King enjoyed a built-in majority and one which was steadily growing. In the lower House much would depend upon the distribution of places and pensions. In spite of the rapid expansion in the size of the military and civil administrations there was always a surplus of suitors for the places available. Indeed, the former seemed to expand the latter. As Lord Cheyne remarked to Lord Verney in 1700, 'a place at Court with a seat [in Parliament] there is most people's aim'.[12] By 1702, 132 out of the 513 MPs – just over one-quarter – were placemen. Their influence was greater than this figure suggests because they attended debates more regularly than members of the House as a whole. (The lower House's average attendance at divisions in William's reign was only 238 out of 513, or 46 per cent.) The House's debates and committees, moreover, were dominated by an inner core of some 50–60 MPs, many of whom were placemen. Royal influence over Parliament was not of itself either corrupt or illegitimate. In a mixed system of government it was both inevitable and desirable if the executive were to carry its business through. Both William and Anne resisted the temptation to use patronage to excess. For example, the crown did not directly attempt to bully and corrupt the electorate in the 20 boroughs in which it enjoyed influence, contenting itself with indicating the type of member it wished to see returned.

It was King William's primary motive to promote national unity so that he could prosecute the war against Louis XIV with vigour and energy. This was to be difficult to achieve. 'Fear of Popery has united; when that is over, we shall divide again,' warned a Whig member of the Convention in 1689. He was right. Almost everyone condemned political partisanship, but many members of the political nation indulged in it. William had been horrified at the party feeling displayed in the Convention. He was impatient with the bickering of his subjects and uninterested in their historic vendettas. Rather than become the servant of one party or the other, he preferred to maintain a balance between them in his attempts to manage Parliament. Unfortunately, his dour manner and his impatience with the political arts of concession and compromise weakened his attempts to deal with the political groupings of the day.

Almost all contemporary commentators used the language of party to describe their groupings. This they did apologetically because party divisions aroused profound anxieties in a society racked by fearful recollections of the Civil Wars and the Interregnum of the middle decades of the century. To complicate matters, two kinds of political distinction existed at the time of the Glorious Revolution: that between 'Court' and 'Country' and that between 'Whig' and 'Tory'. The Court–Country axis had first appeared in an organized form during the 1670s, when a standing Country opposition to the supporters of Charles II's Court supporters can be discerned. A few years later party conflict between Whigs and Tories had arisen during the storm over Exclusion between 1679 and 1681, when the Tories had supported, and the Whigs had opposed, the succession to the throne of Charles's brother, the future James II. Such political divisions had rapidly become part of the political order, even though they were widely disliked. Parties generated damaging divisions in the body politic; they created enmities between individuals and, even worse, between families and between localities. They thus threatened the harmony of society and endangered the very stability of the state.

Politicians were defined as Court or Country depending on their attitude towards the executive. Those who supported the king's ministers on a particular issue favoured the Court, those who opposed it favoured the Country position. Most Court politicians were those in power or those who wished to join those in power. Most Country politicians were suspicious of the court and enemies of all governments. They hated the alleged corruption of power, the immorality of the court, the allegedly shady dealings of politicians and, increasingly, the economic power of the state. The issues on which the Country opposed the Court in the 1690s can be whittled down to three. First, they argued that the government's growing administrative and financial weight threatened the independence of Parliament. This explains their attempts to saddle William with a Triennial Act and a number of Place Bills. Second, they believed that innocent taxpayers were being bled dry by speculators and stock-jobbers. They held that land was the legitimate source of wealth, and as the owners of the green acres of England they enjoyed a permanent, vested interest in the nation's welfare. Most of all, they hated the Land Tax. Third, they strenuously opposed William's standing army. At the conclusion of peace in 1697 William's army of 60 000 was three times larger than James II had ever enjoyed. Before the end of his reign, Country politicians had forced him to reduce it to little more than 6000.

It is tempting to dismiss these Country suspicions of the Court as a bundle of negative prejudices rather than a mature political philosophy. Nevertheless, they have to be taken seriously. The Court–Country axis, however nebulous, constituted the principal division between politicians in

William's reign. Moreover, those who professed Country principles were doing more than simply raising issues of political morality; they were raising matters of real public and popular concern. Such concern, moreover, could lead to positive results. The relative success of the Commission of Accounts in investigating the government's management of the huge sums of money being spent on the war owed much to the initiative of its Country members and to their conception of the national interest. Thanks to their efforts, back-benchers developed considerable knowledge and expertise in discussing the financing of the war. Furthermore, the very fact of its existence might have acted as a deterrent against malpractice.

As to Whigs and Tories, they were mainly defined by their stance on three issues: monarchy, religion and foreign policy. After 1689 the parties still differed over the issue of monarchy. The Tories were embarrassed by the disregard of the principle of hereditary succession shown in 1688–89, but their monarchichal tendencies prevented them from plotting against William. Slowly and uncomfortably, they allowed themselves to fall into habits of obedience towards their *de facto* monarch. At the same time, the Whigs, not wishing to set a bad example to supporters of James II, the Jacobites, began to play down their own earlier advocacy of rights of resistance. The death of the Duke of Gloucester, Princess Anne's last remaining heir, in 1700 reopened the succession question. The son of James II (the Old Pretender) unquestionably had a superior claim to that of the Electress of Hanover, but the Act of Settlement of 1701 lodged the succession with the Hanoverians. The Tories found this further violation of the principle of divine, hereditary succession a bitter pill, but most of them swallowed it. Some, however, could not, and adopted Jacobite sympathies. There thus began that identification of Toryism with Jacobitism which was to become a feature of British political life for half a century.

The two parties differed even more bitterly over religion. The Tories were an Anglican party and consistently opposed the Whig party's attempts to promote greater toleration for Protestant Dissenters. The Tories always hated what Richard Baxter termed the 'healing custom' of Occasional Conformity,[13] and in 1702–04 sought unsuccessfully to outlaw the practice. They failed to do so, but public opinion was behind them. The ability of the Tories to mobilize popular Anglican sentiment was further displayed during the Sacheverell case. In 1709 the Reverend Henry Sacheverell had preached a sermon in which he denounced the Glorious Revolution because it had violated the principle of non-resistance to a legitimate monarch. The Whig government sought to impeach him, an action which met with popular hostility. About 100 000 copies of the printed version of the sermon were circulated and within a year no fewer than 600 pamphlets, sermons and books had plunged into the controversy. The impeachment proceedings against Sacheverell at Westminster were accompanied by scenes of horrifying disorder in the capital as religious passions ran to extremes. Although he was found guilty, his sentence – a three-year ban on preaching – was extremely light. Anything more severe, however, might have stoked still higher the flames of religious extremism. Such episodes found Whigs at odds with Tories, renewing and redefining the basic grounds of conflict between them.

Political and religious differences between the parties came together on questions of foreign policy. The Tories opposed the massive civil and military establishment which fought the continental wars of King William and Queen Anne. They preferred the cheaper alternative of naval attacks on France's colonies to the Whigs' preference for long land campaigns in order to safeguard the Low Countries from French occupation. The years of apparently endless warfare provided countless opportunities for Whigs and Tories to debate and to differ. After Marlborough's great victories in the early years of the eighteenth century the Tories became the party of peace and advocated negotiation with France. Their success at the general elections of 1710 and 1713 signified the overwhelming popularity of the religious and foreign policy principles which they advocated.

In the experimental political conditions which existed after the Glorious Revolution, William III had to construct ministries from whatever materials were to hand. At the outset he attempted to weld together a coalition of Whigs and Tories. His personal inclination was to favour Tories as the most instinctive friends to monarchy but they proved to be the loudest critics of his plans for a land campaign against France. He had therefore to indulge the Whigs, his most willing allies in 1688 but usually the most outspoken critics of monarchy. It did not take long for the coalition of Whigs and Tories to fall apart. The general election of 1690 was a bitter affair in which the two parties tried to blame each other for the dark deeds of the previous reign. The Tories were more successful than the Whigs in so doing, and the remaining months of 1690 saw the Whig hold on power weakening. The King's first experiment in two-party government had failed to dilute the partisanship of Whigs and Tories. Between the end of 1690 and March 1693 he proceeded to tilt the balance of the government towards the Tories, much to the disadvantage of the Whigs. This, too, was doomed to disappointment. Perhaps no government could have maintained its reputation amid the military failures and public disquiet of the next few years. In the Parliament of 1690, and particularly after 1692, mounting criticism of the conduct and strategy of the war worked to strengthen the Court–Country axis. Early in 1693 a triennial proposal passed both Houses, to be vetoed by William. The King now gradually withdrew the Tories from his ministry in favour of supporters of the Whig Junto.[14]

After the passage of the Triennial Act in 1694 the ministry became predominantly Whig. Until 1698 William enjoyed perhaps the most settled period of government during his entire reign. Professor Plumb sees in these years the effective termination of the old contractual and constitutional Whiggism of the seventeenth century and the emergence of the managerial Whiggism of the eighteenth century.[15] The Junto was strengthened by the outcome of the general election of 1696 but, more emphatically, by the disclosure of the Assassination Plot against the King. The Junto attempted to capitalize on the Plot by launching an Association to which all office holders had to subscribe, declaring their loyalty to William as 'rightful and lawful King' or face dismissal. This dagger was aimed at the heart of the Tory party. Few Tories lost their offices, but the Junto's firm line at least ensured the loyalty of the magistracy and the militia. Meanwhile, the war was proceeding without particular success, but the government was able to finance it effectively enough and the King was able to make a respectable peace at Ryswick in 1697.

Thereafter the strength of the Whig government began to weaken. The ending of the war reduced the King's dependence on them. Even the unusual organizing abilities of the Junto could not impose order on the unwieldy House of Commons. William made it clear that he desired a renewal of hostilities against France and for that reason wished to retain a large standing army. The country had had enough of war, and its pacific sentiments were reflected in the emergence of the New Country party of Foley and Harley.[16] Nothing could withstand the storm of Country opinion which swept through Parliament and throughout the political nation. For some years the Court–Country axis was to dominate politics, and the King was forced to recognize the fact by including Tories in his governments.

Indeed, between 1698 and 1700 the new Country party even enjoyed a majority in Parliament. These were turbulent and unpredictable years. No fewer than four general elections were held in four years: 1698, 1700, 1701 and 1702. Four years of almost constant electioneering kept the political temperature high and created a huge sense of public involvement in the affairs of the nation. The Country tide carried everything before it. Not only was the standing army savagely reduced in size; William's grants of land in Ireland to friends and supporters were challenged and in the Resumption Act of 1700 they were to be reviewed. The general election of 1701 and the passage of the Act of Settlement, with its constitutional provisions against placemen and foreigners, marked the effective transition of the Tory party from its traditional status as a party of prerogative to its new status as a Country party. Its attacks on the Junto, its attempts to impeach three of its leaders for their alleged role in committing England to the Partition Treaties and its unenthusiastic acceptance of Anne as William's successor (March 1702) all served to stoke the fires of Court–Country partisanship.[17]

Yet during the reign of Anne the conflict of Whig and Tory politics came to predominate over the politics of Court and Country. Tories dominated the early administrations of Anne's reign but they ultimately gave way to the Whigs. The Queen preferred the Tories and mistrusted the Whigs but she was forced to depend on others, notably the non-partisan Sidney Godolphin, for the management of parliament and the prosecution of the war.[18] He was able to work with the lords of the Junto without surrendering to them. The Tories increased their majority at the general election of 1702 and proceeded to flex their muscles by attacking Occasional Conformity. Three times they pushed bills through the Commons which would have subjected the practice to severe penalties, only to be thwarted on each occasion by Junto majorities in the Lords. In 1704 they even sought to tack the third Occasional Conformity bill onto the Land Tax. Divisions within the Tory ranks, not least a revolt of Harley's followers in the Commons against the tack, killed it. These examples of Tory obduracy rebounded against the party. They also offended the Queen and several of her political managers, who were sceptical about the wisdom of agitating religious divisions in the middle of a great war. Two of the leading Tories in the ministry, Nottingham and Seymour, resigned (April 1704), to be replaced by the moderate Tories, Harley – who was rapidly discarding his reputation as a Country Tory – and St John.[19] The ministry was still in theory a Tory ministry but it was led in the Lords by Godolphin and it included Marlborough, both of whom gave the first priority to the prosecution of the war. The great military victories at Blenheim (1705) and Ramillies (1706) vindicated the ministry's right to govern and did much to attract popular and parliamentary support. Further Whig successes discomfited the Tories. Between 1705 and 1708 the Whigs used their strength in both houses to force the Queen to dismiss Tory ministers. Godolphin's successful handling of the Regency Act in 1706, which provided for a Regency between the death of Anne and the accession of the first Hanoverian monarch, offered the prospect of a trouble-free Hanoverian Succession. Furthermore, the negotiation of Union with Scotland in 1707 weakened the strategic position of the Jacobites in their safest retreat. The days of party coalition were numbered. They were ended when Godolphin and Marlborough struck, demanding the resignation of the Tories Harley and St John, who were replaced with loyal Whigs; at the general election of 1708 the Whigs gained about 30 seats.

Thereafter, however, the political pendulum swung back to the Tories. Continued allied victories at a time of economic depression and harvest failure provoked a general demand for an end to the war. By the summer of 1709, they argued, Britain had achieved her military objectives. Peace, patriotism and Anglicanism were conspiring to smile on the Tories. In 1710 Harley engineered the overthrow of Godolphin and brought about the collapse of the Whig cabinet. The general election of 1710 witnessed a Tory landslide. Riding on the crest of a wave, the Tory ministry passed an act against Occasional Conformity in 1711. In the same year they passed a Qualifications bill, which established the qualifications for a Member of Parliament at £600 for county seats and £300 for borough seats, measures intended to maintain the representation of landed gentlemen in the House of Commons. Yet the last years of the reign were dominated by the complexities of Harley's peace negotiations. The Treaty of Utrecht passed Parliament in April 1713, an event which acted as a launching-pad for yet a further Tory election victory in that year. These dramatic events led the Tories to overreach themselves. Some of them, arguing that the Hanoverian claim was much more distant than that of the Stuart, indulged the fantasy that James II's son, the Old Pretender, might renounce his religion and thus qualify for the succession. Partly because this enabled the Whigs to claim that the Tories were a Jacobite, and thus an unpatriotic and unconstitutional party, the beneficiaries of the Hanoverian Succession were to be the Whigs.

By 1714 parties were of considerably greater importance to politics than they had been in 1689. They had improved their organization and developed greater cohesion. Yet party was not the only determining influence we should notice in describing the structure of ministerial politics in the reigns of William III and of Anne.[20] Three others should be recognized. Royal favour was paramount, personality was indispensable and patronage was essential. On its own, the contribution of party was limited. Furthermore, the differences between the parties should not be exaggerated. Whigs may have been sympathetic to the claims of Protestant Dissenters, but the vast majority of Whigs were Anglicans. Similarly, although the Whigs were the great and staunch defenders of the new monied interests almost all Whig politicians were landed men. Finally, not all politicians were party men. Godolphin, Harley and Marlborough were royal managers rather than party politicians.

Yet it is impossible to avoid the use of party labels in describing the ministerial politics of the reign of Anne. Contemporaries themselves used them. Party not only agitated Parliament and the world of high politics. Party divided the electorate, the press, the clubs, the City of London and the corporations of many towns and cities. This was not all. The 'rage of party' divided the churches, the professions, the theatre and even the social life of the nation. There were many times when it truly seemed to contemporaries that it was threatening to rend apart their whole society.[21] The Glorious Revolution, far from providing final solutions to social and political issues, had served rather to generate the most bitter divisions that British society had experienced since the Civil Wars.

Party loyalties were both deeply felt and consistently held. In Parliament, the acid test of division lists reveals that even in the Parliaments of William's reign no fewer than 86 per cent of MPs voted *exclusively* for either the Whig or Tory parties.[22] An occasional dissident vote might be tolerated; regular disobedience to a party was extremely rare. The distinction between Court and Country, on the other hand, was much less well defined. Moreover, the fact that mixed or coalition governments existed in this period does not seriously dilute the significance of party. Coalitions of parties can only be negotiated when the parties concerned have reached at least a minimal state of development, when individuals have identified themselves as Whigs and Tories and when they recognize that in a particular set of circumstances single-party government is not feasible.

The Whig and Tory parties of this period displayed organizational structures of some sophistication. Both parties – particularly the Tories – were prone to internal divisions, but even they normally retained their cohesion. Their awareness of their own party identities did much to frustrate William III's attempts to manipulate them as readily as he would have wished.[23] Both parties used the private influence and patronage of landed magnates as the solid core of their organization, but these were supplemented with a variety of other expedients. Both parties – particularly the Whigs – developed systems of whipping-in their members in both Houses, utilizing the informal resources of the London clubs to maintain the loyalty of their parliamentary supporters. Both parties used the power of religious denominations: the Tories used that of the Church of England, the Whigs the Dissenting congregations. Finally, both parties used the new power of the newspaper and periodical press to publicize and rally support for their cause.

What is even more remarkable than the intensity of party conflict within the political and social elite is the vehemence and consistency of party feeling and behaviour within the electorate.[24] Growing rapidly in the closing decades of the seventeenth century, the electorate numbered around 300 000 by 1700. When allowance is made for the very substantial 'turnover' of voters – many of whom fail to vote from one election to the next – the maximum 'electoral pool' was probably something over 500 000, an astonishingly high figure for an early modern society. Furthermore, between 20 per cent and 25 per cent of adult males enjoyed the right to vote. This is, again, an impressively high figure when it is recalled that at least 50 per cent of the adult male population, many of them servants, paupers, cottagers or simply day labourers, lacked sufficient economic independence to have qualified for the vote on almost any franchise in the pre-democratic era. Indeed, as Professor Holmes has argued, few substantial towns lacked parliamentary representation in the early eighteenth century.[25]

It was within this unique electorate that the party battle was fought. The sheer frequency of elections kept party passions on the boil. Between 1679 and 1716 no fewer than 16 general elections were held, a rate of one election every two-and-a-quarter years. At times, it seemed that the country was in a permanent state of electioneering. However, not every constituency went to a poll at every election. Only about one-third of them did at any single election. Over the same period, however, almost all constituencies were contested at least once. In this situation it was perfectly feasible to maintain party loyalties among electors over time. Almost all constituencies were double-member constituencies in which voters had two votes. The vast majority of them – almost always over 80 per cent and often considerably more – voted a party ticket: two Whig or two Tory votes (it was very rare for candidates of the same party to stand against each other). Furthermore, the number of floating voters was small, somewhere between 10 per cent to 20 per cent in the counties, less in the boroughs. Most electors not only voted a party ticket but continued to do so when they had further opportunities to vote. To some extent, the power of local party managers and patrons must be held responsible for this phenomenon of party voting. In some places the electorate was small and liable to be influenced by social and economic pressures. But in others there were simply too many voters to be influenced in this way; in these places partisanship must have been the consequence of personal preference, political principle and religious conviction.

How important was the electoral power of the parties in the years 1689 to 1714? On some occasions the collective decisions of the electorate *were* national decisions which carried with them political consequences of the greatest significance. Indeed, they frequently determined the complexion of governments. The collapse of the power of the Junto in 1699–1700 was anticipated by the spectacular gains made by the Tories in 1698, itself a striking reflection of opinion out of doors. Further, the spectacular victory of the Whigs at the general election of 1708 cleared the ground for their return to power in the following months. Similarly, the election results of 1705 and 1710 seem clearly to have reflected national opinion.

Party activity was unusually intense in this period. There were many substantial issues for parties to feed on: the problem of the succession, the growing power of the executive, the explosive issue of religious toleration, the question of Britain's place in the world and the conduct of her foreign policy. In this period, in short, there was much to be partisan about. Furthermore, it is surely no accident that this great age of party coincides with the ending of press censorship and the effective beginnings of a national newspaper and periodical press. Nor is it an accident that it also roughly coincides with the period when the Triennial Act was on the statute book, 1694 to 1716. On top of all this, it can hardly be denied that the context of politics in these years was unusual: the astounding occurrences of the Glorious Revolution and their aftermath; the subsequent period of political experiment and improvisation; the continued political uncertainty generated by the strains of war and the possibility of rebellion within Britain; the persistence of religious passions and denominational rivalry. Such a combination of circumstances was unlikely to be repeated.

Britain and Europe, 1689–1713

Of all the long-term consequences of the Glorious Revolution, the reorientation of Britain's place in the world was to be one of the most important. After playing a limited and usually marginal role on the European stage during most periods of the seventeenth century, Britain turned her face towards Europe. She became prominently involved in war against France (1688–97) and then became a major participant in the War of the Spanish Succession (1702–13). These were only the first instalments of a second Hundred Years War against France, one that was to last until 1815.

This reorientation of Britain's diplomatic position met with initial misgivings in England. At first, people were much less interested in the balance of power in Europe than they were in their own domestic preoccupations. They cared less for King William's continental concerns than they did for their own concerns. Yet they were unenthusiastic about a possible restoration of James II, and they certainly did not want a pro-Catholic regime imposed upon them with the aid of France.

Thus Britain's new place in Europe eventually chimed with public opinion, not least because William III's crusade against Louis XIV's attempts to dominate Europe was ultimately seen to promote Britain's political, religious and economic interests. His strategic objectives touched Britain's interests in four major areas of policy, and they did so positively and constructively. First, William inaugurated a commitment to maintaining the balance of power in Europe, to opposing the domination of Europe by any single country. In the century after 1688 this meant France or coalitions dominated by France. In part, at least, this reflected the mounting abhorrence within Britain of the client status to which the Stuarts had persisted in reducing the country. But one further cardinal reason for pursuing this objective was the defence of the Netherlands against French domination, which was an essential part of her military strategy in the Nine Years War. Contentious at first, this commitment became a generally accepted and legitimate objective during the War of the Spanish Succession. Second, a further paramount British objective was to be the maintenance of the Protestant succession. Patriotic enthusiasm for the Protestant succession was never far below the surface in seventeenth-century England, and it was now reinforced by a new wave of Protestant sentiment, unleashed by the Glorious Revolution. The events of 1685–89 gave rise to a dramatic strengthening of the resolution and resolve of large sections of the Protestant ruling establishment, a determination to make sacrifices abroad in order to maintain the safety of the Protestant succession at home. On one crucial occasion, at least, Louis XIV played straight into William's hands. His recognition of Prince James Edward Stuart as rightful King of England in 1701 – just three months after the Act of Settlement had legislated against the possibility of a Catholic monarchy – provoked indignation in England and actually helped William to take a united country into the War of the Spanish Succession. These dynastic themes interacted powerfully with what, in the long term, was to be of even greater significance – the third objective, Britain's commercial prosperity. To a country already accustomed to protecting its commercial interests via the Navigation Acts, it was natural to protect her markets and to seek new ones. When they entered the Nine Years War in 1689 the British, suspicious of Dutch commercial competition, insisted that the Dutch take strong measures against French commerce and demanded that they should not make peace with the French independently. During the war the British closed their markets to French imports, thus permitting native industries to prosper, not least those newly established by the inflow of Huguenot refugees: silk, cutlery, paper and glass. Such issues were important but they remained something of a sideshow during the Nine Years War. They became, however, a principal consideration in the events leading up to the outbreak of the Spanish Succession war. The prospect of the Spanish empire falling under French control threatened Bourbon economic, as well as political, predominance not only in Europe but also in commercial waters outside Europe. Britain could not stand aside and allow the commercial balance of power in Europe to be determined by others. As Professor Jones has pointed out, from this time onwards economic, commercial and imperial matters form a substantial part of all the peace treaties and diplomatic alliances negotiated by Britain.[26] But it was impossible to disentangle the destiny of European from that of extra-European commerce. This leads directly to a fourth aspect of British overseas strategy after the Glorious Revolution: the pursuit of imperial power and possessions. The great wars of these years were not merely wars in and for European objectives. They were fought within an extra-European context of rapidly increasing significance. Consequently, imperial control had to be tightened. Scotland and Ireland had to be drawn more safely into England's orbit. Further afield, the mainland American colonies were brought more firmly under the direction of the Board of Trade, while British policy sought to incorporate them more closely within an Atlantic economy directed from London.

These strategic objectives dominated British foreign policy in the years after the Glorious Revolution and, no less important, British public opinion. This helps to explain why the people and Parliament of Britain were ready to acquiesce in the sacrifices of war on a scale hitherto unimaginable. The land wars in Europe in which England had been engaged over the previous two centuries had been small in scale, had lasted for only short periods and had involved only a few thousand troops. James II's army of 30 000 in 1688 was regarded as a dangerous threat to the liberties of the nation. In 1690, however, William threw 40 000 men into the Irish theatre alone. During the Nine Years War the army in the European theatres averaged 76 000 servicemen and 40 000 sailors every year. During the Spanish Succession war the army averaged no fewer than 90 000 and the navy 43 000 a year. Indeed, by the end of the war combined army and navy personnel exceeded 150 000. This is even more remarkable when it is remembered that the adult male population of England and Wales was less than a million and a half!

More important still, this transformation became irreversible once the power of the press had been unleashed after the lapsing of the Licensing Act in 1695. The genie of Protestant public opinion – especially once it had tasted the blood of military victory – could not be put back into the bottle. Although the Whigs had been very uneasy at several aspects of William's anti-French strategy during the 1690s, the party never actually endangered the implementation of his policy. By 1701 the Whigs were proclaiming the need to oppose France on the grounds of her support for the Pretender as well as her threatened domination of Europe. Tories in opposition might deplore the expense of the policy, and the unprecedented centralization of government which it involved, but there is little sign that they would have acted very differently in office, at least in the early years of the war.[27]

Britain's entry into the Nine Years War was precipitated by William's crusade against France. In the early years most Englishmen would have focused less on long-term commercial and strategic considerations than on the need to prevent a Stuart restoration and on the necessity of bringing Ireland back securely within the English orbit. At first in 1689, indeed, Ireland was the major theatre of war for the British. To contemporaries, the Glorious Revolution must have seemed dangerously insecure until the victory of the Williamite armies at the battle of Limerick in October 1691 and the defeat of the French navy at La Hogue in June 1692. Indeed, while William was in Ireland in 1690 the French enjoyed naval command of the English Channel, a serious threat to British security and a warning that was never to be forgotten. During the rest of the war the deployment of British seapower in order to establish naval supremacy in European waters became a vital strategic priority in the struggle to defend Europe against Louis XIV. The war on land, meanwhile, became something of a deadlock. Louis XIV enjoyed immense military success between 1690 and 1693 in Italy and Spain, but in the Low Countries William's coalition was able to frustrate prospects of a final French victory. The Treaty of Ryswick which ended the war in 1697 was little more than a temporary halt. Most captured territories were restored. Louis XIV gave formal, if insincere, recognition to William and his successors.

The Treaty, however, did not resolve the future of the Spanish empire. British trade with Spain and the Mediterranean had expanded greatly since 1660 and her merchants were already making serious incursions into the Spanish New World. The death of Charles II, King of Spain, in 1700 brought the underlying issues to a head. Louis XIV put his Bourbon grandson on the Spanish throne in 1701 to take over not only the declining power of Spain in Europe but also her extensive commercial and land empire in the New World. In England public opinion, which between 1697 and 1701 had been against a renewal of the war, now accepted the need to defend and, if possible, to enlarge its commercial power and possessions. In May 1702 England and Scotland declared war on Spain. The War of the Spanish Succession had begun.

British objectives in the War were clear: to prevent the union of the French and Spanish thrones,[28] to destroy French support for the Jacobite cause, to maintain the freedom of the Netherlands from French dominion and to challenge Bourbon commercial and imperial power overseas. Indeed, colonial acquisition, in the Mediterranean, in the Caribbean and even further afield, now became one of the principal objectives of the war. When the French struck at the heart of the European alliance by moving on Vienna in 1704 the war in Europe came to a head. Marlborough's army was diverted from the

Austrian Netherlands to link with that of Prince Eugene of Savoy. In the subsequent engagement the French army was destroyed at Blenheim. Marlborough proceeded to make himself master of the north west of Europe with further victories at Ramillies in 1706 and at Oudenarde in 1708. Peace may have come earlier than 1713 had the allied war effort in Spain been as successful as it was elsewhere. Military reverses, especially at Almanza in 1707, prolonged the war. So did the diplomatic blunders of the Whig government. Its excessive demands obliged the French to fight on. After 1710 the Tory government of Harley was anxious for peace; it dismissed Marlborough and, ultimately, 'perfidious Albion' made peace with France at Utrecht in 1713.

As almost all commentators agree, Britain achieved her objectives, and more besides in 1713: the thrones of France and Spain were to remain separate, France renounced her support for the Jacobite cause, the Netherlands remained independent and the balance of power in Europe was preserved. In addition Britain acquired two key naval bases in the Mediterranean, Gibraltar and Minorca. Furthermore, her supremacy in North America was confirmed by gains in the Caribbean (St Kitts, Newfoundland and Nova Scotia) and by the valuable *Asiento*, the right to trade with the Spanish colonies for 30 years, an open door to further commercial penetration of South America. The Treaty of Utrecht thus clearly recognized not only Britain's rise to eminence in Europe but also her new status as a world power.

The Glorious Revolution and the unity of Britain, 1689–1714

The Glorious Revolution, finally, was an event of decisive significance in the internal development of the United Kingdom. Although the violent disruption which it caused in relations between England on the one hand and Scotland and Ireland on the other was of relatively short duration, it was of momentous importance for the future. The Jacobite cause, with its implications of civil uprising and French intervention, acted as a catalyst for a powerful assertion of Scottish national feeling. Jacobitism in Ireland provoked an upsurge of Catholic sentiment and anti-English feeling which could only be dealt with by force of arms. In the long term, however, the Glorious Revolution paved the way for English domination of the British Isles through the military suppression of Irish resistance and the more peaceful negotiation of Union with Scotland in 1707. During the 1720s a united kingdom had emerged which was much more closely united than it had been in the seventeenth century. Indeed, the only alternative to a more united Britain was the fragmentation and disorder which might have accompanied a Jacobite restoration.

The Glorious Revolution in England was followed by a Glorious Revolution in Scotland, but the latter was not masterminded from London. Indeed, Scotland might have chosen to retain James as her king until his flight to France in December 1688 had consequences which were just as damaging for his cause in Scotland as they were for his cause in England. The vacuum of authority created by James's absence was filled by supporters of William. But William was in no position to dictate to the Scottish Presbyterians, his main, indeed his only, supporters there. He summoned the

Convention of Estates which met in Edinburgh in March 1689. The Convention declared William and Mary joint sovereigns; but in the Claim of Right, the Scottish equivalent of the Declaration of Rights, voted in the following month, it asserted the constitutional right of the Estates to depose a monarch. No pretence was made that James had 'abdicated'. With only five dissenting votes, it was decided that he had 'forfaulted' his right to the crown by his misgovernment and by his violations of the laws. William's acceptance of the crown of Scotland in May 1689 implied his agreement to the Claim of Right. Consequently, the monarchy was deemed to be Protestant, its prerogatives dependent upon the rule of law and its resources resting upon the consent of Parliament. In this way, the effect of the Glorious Revolution in Scotland was to leave the Scottish Parliament exceptionally free from royal interference. It could now freely discuss any subject it liked and it could pass any law it wished. It proceeded to enact nothing less than a religious revolution. It disestablished the Episcopal Church, abolished lay patronage and established the Presbyterian Church of Scotland.

Perhaps the Revolution in Scotland would have been less Whiggish, indeed less radical, had it not been accompanied by news of the early and promising success of the Jacobite cause in Ireland and by its early manifestations in Scotland. Enthused by the news from Ireland, James's supporters in Scotland rallied the Jacobites and at the battle of Killiecrankie on 27 July 1689 they won a famous victory. They were incapable, however, of taking advantage of their success, and after their defeat at Dunkeld a month later their cause quickly collapsed. It is possible that a period of good government, stability and prosperity might have reconciled the mass of the Scots to English rule. Sadly, this was not to occur. William offered an indemnity to all those who took the oath of allegiance before 1 January 1692. By that date most of the Highland chiefs had sworn their allegiance to him. William issued a further general order for the execution of vengeance on those who had not sworn. The accidental failure of the MacDonalds of Glencoe to do so led to their massacre at Glencoe on 13 February 1692, an event that was to poison relations between the two countries for decades.

The legends of Glencoe have distracted attention from the fact that the resistance to William's armies was more resolute than English historians are often prepared to acknowledge. After all, the war continued for two years even after Dunkeld. Nor was resistance confined to Jacobites. Many of those involved detested the new Presbyterian church.[29] Even if there remained any possibility that the Scots might have been reconciled to the Williamite regime, the actual machinery of government would have made it difficult to accomplish. The victory of the Revolution in Scotland had weakened the power of the English executive over the Scottish Parliament; indeed, it threatened the union of crowns and created political tensions in Anglo-Scottish relations which – as William concluded before the end of his reign – could only be resolved through a parliamentary Union between the two countries. Preoccupied as he was with the war in Europe, the King was soon frustrated and angry with what he took to be the obstructionism of the Scottish ruling class. He was not able to root out the power of the semi-feudal magnates, who continued to command enormous political influence. Nor was he able to break the loyalty of a large number of Scottish nobles towards James. Reared in the Episcopal Kirk, they still clung to traditions of divine right, passive obedience and, not least, indefeasible hereditary succession. Professor Black has noted 'the massive crisis of confidence in the new regime amongst almost all thinking members of the Scottish ruling class, whether Williamite, moderate, Jacobite or uncommitted'.[30] Even worse, William had not been able to reconcile Scottish public opinion out of doors to the regime. For this failure English political insensitivity and incompetence, together with Scottish resentment at the economic distress occasioned by the Nine Years War, must be held responsible. By the end of William's reign English political failure in Scotland had effectively regenerated the Jacobite cause.

These deep-seated political problems were sharpened by powerful economic differences. The Navigation Acts applied to Scotland and caused serious distress as well as damage to the trade in cattle and linen. Scottish involvement in the Nine Years War was unpopular in the northern kingdom, an unpopularity which became positively xenophobic after the failure of the Darien scheme. In 1695 the Company of Scotland for Trading with Africa and the Indies was established. Its enthusiasm for founding a Scottish colony in Darien in central America endangered William's relations with Spain. There was little enthusiasm in England for the scheme, and it was left to the Scots themselves to raise the money required. In a fine display of national enthusiasm, over 1300 individuals volunteered to finance the scheme. In the end, the Darien scheme failed. By 1700 no fewer than 2000 lives had been lost and perhaps a quarter of all of Scotland's capital resources squandered. Whether English indifference was more to be blamed than Scottish incompetence is not easy to determine. What cannot be doubted is the persisting resentment that the incident aroused between Scotland and England, especially in the concurrent bitter years of harvest failure between 1696 and 1698. Darien became almost as potent a symbol of discord between the two countries as Glencoe!

These tensions were reflected in the proceedings of the Scottish Parliament. In 1701 it declared that the Act of Settlement did not apply to Scotland, thus opening up the possibility that on Anne's death Scotland might determine its own dynastic succession. The prospect of Scotland pursuing an independent foreign policy horrified the English. A Catholic, pro-French succession in Scotland could not be tolerated; the possibility not only of civil war in Scotland but the likelihood of an English invasion of Scotland in the event of a Jacobite succession in the northern kingdom began to loom. Early in the reign of Anne the worst fears of the English were aroused. The new Scottish Parliament which met in May 1703 was even more hostile to rule from London than its predecessor. In the 1703–04 session it passed an Act of 'Security and Succession', which claimed the exclusive right of the Scottish Parliament to determine the succession of Scotland and an Act 'anent Peace and War', which asserted the right of the Scottish Parliament on the death of Anne to resume the power to declare war and to make peace. The prospect of a major crisis in Anglo-Scottish relations in the middle of the War of the Spanish Succession could not be tolerated by the English. The problem of Scottish separatism had to be tackled once and for all. It was at this point that the parties in England began seriously to consider a new structure of political association within Britain, one which would confront Scottish resistance to

English rule but yet satisfy reasonable Scottish aspirations while respecting England's need for external security. As opinion hostile to Scotland was beginning to mount within the English Parliament, Godolphin measured his response and determined to attempt a negotiated settlement. Consequently, the Aliens Act of 1705 required the Queen to appoint Commissioners to negotiate a Treaty of Union with the Scots. In order to persuade the Scots to take the initiative seriously, Godolphin threatened to close English markets to Scottish goods and the property of non-resident Scots in England was to be treated in law as alien property.

The path to Union was smoothed by the recognition in both countries that in a period of almost incessant warfare the two countries could not continue their endless quarrels and disagreements. The Whig Junto in England had seen the necessity for Union in 1704. The seriousness with which they approached the negotiations in 1706 is borne out by the generosity of the concessions held out to the Scots. There was less enthusiasm for Union in Scotland, but in the end no effective alternative was proposed on which Scottish opinion could unite. It is true that the Kirk, horrified at William's reluctance to allow the Presbyterians to take their revenge on the Episcopalians, was hostile to Union. Furthermore, some elements in Scottish public opinion were bitterly xenophobic and a number of hostile petitions was received. Yet resistance to Union, while both vocal and sometimes passionate, was surprisingly limited. Three-quarters of the Scottish burghs and two-thirds of the Scottish shires did not protest. Extra parliamentary public opinion in Scotland appeared to be uninterested and apathetic. The pamphlet war on the subject was fairly evenly divided. Here, indeed, the economic case for Union was powerfully advanced by a number of writers, not least Daniel Defoe. In the end, a mixture of political conviction, political management, a very real anxiety to settle a recurrent problem and, not least, substantial concessions were enough to persuade the Scottish Parliament to vote itself out of existence at the end of 1706 and to agree to Union.[31]

The Act of Union of 1707 provided for the political incorporation of Scotland into England. It created a new unitary state and established the biggest free trade area in Europe. The Scottish negotiators accepted the Hanoverian Succession and abandoned for ever the prospect of an independent Scottish dynasty and an independent Scottish foreign policy. The Act of Union brought the number of MPs up to 558, giving Scotland 45 Members of the House of Commons (30 county members and 15 members to be elected from groups of burghs) and 16 members of the House of Lords, to be elected by an assembly of Scottish peers. It cannot be maintained that the Act established an equal political partnership: although Scotland had one-quarter of the population of England, she was only allowed one-tenth of the representation in Parliament. Furthermore, in 1708 the new Parliament proceeded to abolish the Privy Council of Scotland. There was no immediate protest at the disappearance of the Council, although it amounted to a significant weakening of Scottish influence over the disposal of patronage in Scotland. There was, however, a Scottish Secretary of State appointed from and usually resident in London between 1708 and 1725, and again between 1742 and 1746. In practice, however, it was the aristocracy which was to govern Scotland during the eighteenth century, both in town and country.

The Union had important consequences in religious and legal affairs. Since 1689 the English sovereign had accomplished the difficult feat of being both supreme governor of the Church of England and head of the Presbyterian Kirk of Scotland. After 1707 the independence of the two churches in their government, discipline and worship was to be recognized and respected. This, together with the fact that Presbyterians were now to be allowed to sit in Parliament, seriously weakened the established status of the Church of England. This apparent violation of religious conformity was bound to be used by the Protestant Dissenters in England as an unanswerable argument for permitting them the same privileges. Yet if the Union of Scotland and England were to proceed with reasonable prospects of success, such concessions were vital. This was why the Act of Union preserved both the legal and educational systems of Scotland. There was, in any case, no real need to merge them with their English counterparts. Consequently, the reputation of Scotland's ancient universities, and the place of Edinburgh as the legal capital of Scotland, were sensibly allowed to continue.

The Union had vitally important consequences for the Scottish economy. The trade and navigation of Britain and its commercial empire overseas were to be opened to the Scots within a common customs and excise system. While the Scots accepted the principle of taxation and trade regulation from London, the negotiators were anxious to ensure that the Scots were to be more lightly taxed than the English. The Scottish Land Tax was to yield only one-fortieth of the English assessment; the Salt Tax, after an intermission of seven years, was to be set at a lower level than in England, and Scotland was to be exempt from the Stamp Tax and the Window Tax. Finally, investors in the Darien scheme were to get their money back. Within two decades some beneficial economic effects of Union began to appear. By the 1720s Scottish cattle had become a familiar sight in southern England; Scottish linens were being sold in increasing numbers in England and the grim days of the famines of the late 1690s had become a distant memory.

Within the structures which the Union established, both England and Scotland could begin to create for themselves a new set of relationships and identities within a *British* framework. In the short term, however, Union deprived Scotland of independent means of expressing her national sentiments and underscored her economic and legislative subordination to England. This was evident, for example, in 1709 when the Treason Act replaced the old Scottish law of treason with the more humane English law. Similarly, in 1712 the Toleration Act granted freedom of worship to any clergymen willing to take an oath of loyalty to the government and abjure the Pretender. The established Church of Scotland was appalled. Although most Scots acquiesced in the Union after 1707, many did so unenthusiastically and blamed it for many of their misfortunes. This was the soil in which Jacobitism was to grow during the next half century.

In Ireland the Glorious Revolution was even more violent than it was in Scotland, and it was to have consequences that were to be even more bitter and more long-lasting. To the Catholic majority in Ireland the Glorious Revolution meant neither political freedom nor religious toleration; it meant foreign occupation and military conquest. Ultimately, it was to confirm existing humiliations, not least the legal and social subordination of the Catholic majority, and to endorse the expropriation of Catholic land-owners.

The reign of James II had seen the introduction of policies sympathetic to the majority Catholic population: religious toleration, the opening up of the corporations and the army to Catholics and, not least, the promise of land redistribution. The momentum of events favourable to the Catholics was seriously disrupted by James's failure to maintain his position in England in the winter of 1688–89, but his arrival from France in March 1689 at last promised to establish a pro-Catholic polity in Ireland. He summoned the 'Patriot Parliament' which, like the Convention in England, was an irregular and revolutionary body. Its actions were hasty and thoroughly infected with the spirit of a vengeful Catholicism. This predominantly Catholic Parliament repealed Poynings Law,[32] abolished judicial appeals from Ireland to England and took steps to protect Irish trade and industry. Most provocatively of all, it confiscated without appeal the property of 2400 Protestants. James dared go no further in the direction of establishing a Catholic state for fear of alienating still further the Irish Protestants. Indeed, serious divisions existed within the Parliament and these fatally weakened James's cause. For a while the military situation hung. However, the siege of Londonderry was relieved on 10 August 1689, an enormous moral and military victory for the embattled Protestant population. The English invasion of the same year, however, failed to make much progress. William himself led the invasion of 1690 with an army that included Danish, Dutch and German contingents. He attempted to reach a negotiated settlement, promising religious toleration for Catholics and the retention of Catholic estates, but he received no response. James was over-confident of his military position. However, the shattering defeat of the Catholic forces at William's hands at the Battle of the Boyne (1 July 1690) led ultimately to the collapse of his cause, to his retreat to France and to the Treaty of Limerick.

The Treaty of Limerick of October 1691 marked the surrender of the Jacobite army in Ireland. In his anxiety to concentrate on the European theatres of war William offered conciliatory terms: Irish soldiers were allowed to retreat to France and Roman Catholics were in the future to enjoy a measure of religious toleration. In spite of the relative moderation of its terms, the treaty was to become a symbol of English occupation of Ireland and, like the events that led up to it, the siege of Londonderry and the Battle of the Boyne, part of a historic and – eventually – mythological narrative of victorious and heroic Protestant resistance to Roman Catholicism.

The moderate provisions of the Treaty of Limerick were insufficient to satisfy the Protestant lust for revenge against the Catholics. Thereafter, Protestant landowners, genuinely terrified of the possible combination of Catholicism and Jacobitism, took matters into their own hands. This had not been William's original design, but he was now absolutely dependent upon a Protestant minority which now wished to ensure that the Catholics would never again represent a threat to the Protestant supremacy in Ireland. The years after 1691 erected the structures of the 'Protestant Ascendancy'.

The most characteristic feature of the post-Limerick regime were the penal laws passed by the first Parliament against the Catholics and the dispossession of Catholic land. The major purpose of the penal laws was to entrench the minority Protestant landlord class in power by weakening the civic status of the Catholic majority in a number of ways. Catholics were to be excluded from Parliament (1691); they were to be excluded from the army and prevented from possessing firearms (1692); Catholic children were not to be sent abroad for their education (1695); Catholic bishops were to be banished and missionary priests from abroad were no longer to be tolerated (1697). After the 'Popery Act' of 1703, indeed, Catholics were to be excluded from all public offices. Further, they could not buy land and they could only inherit it on the basis of gavelkind (i.e. partible inheritance), a provision which led to the fragmentation of such Catholic estates as remained. In 1641 Catholics had held 59 per cent of the land of Ireland; in 1688 they still held 22 per cent; by the end of William's reign they held only 14 per cent of the land of Ireland, a figure which steadily declined still further to 5 per cent by 1778. Almost as important as the land grants, however, was an Act of 1695 which weakened most existing tenancies to tenancies-at-will, leaving tenants more easily liable to increased rents and even to eviction. Whatever the possible justification for this treatment of the Catholic population and however inconsistently the legislation might have been enforced, none of it was vetoed by the Westminster Parliament.

If all this were not enough, the English government continued to discriminate against the Irish economy, as it had done throughout the seventeenth century. Ireland was already excluded from the Navigation Acts and she was prevented from sharing in colonial trade except through English ports. Consequently, her shipping industry collapsed. In 1667 the importation of Irish cattle, sheep and swine into England had been prohibited. In 1681 butter and cheese were added to the list, seriously damaging Irish agriculture. Furthermore, the Irish woollen industry was irreparably weakened by an Act of 1698 which restricted Irish woollen exports to England, where they were seriously disadvantaged by high import duties. Linen thereafter replaced wool as the major Irish export industry. Whether the Irish economy would have prospered in the absence of such discrimination is unclear; its ability to compete with the more advanced economy of England, and even that of Scotland, is by no means obvious. What is undeniable, however, is the ability of the Westminster Parliament to determine the economic future of Ireland and its willingness to wield that power in the interests of its own members and their constituents.

Long before then, English politicians and pamphleteers had begun to treat Ireland as a conquered country and had come almost to rejoice at her status as a colony. The establishment of the Protestant Ascendancy and the passage of the penal laws were widely welcomed in England. Many English landowners were happy to see Ireland reduced to client status. In 1720 this status was brutally defined in the Declaratory Act, which stated that Acts of the Irish Parliament could be vetoed by the Westminster Parliament but that the legislation of the latter was automatically to be accepted by the former. Indeed, English treatment of Ireland compared unfavourably with the treatment that Scotland received after the Union. It can hardly be denied that the religion and the laws of Ireland were treated with much less consideration than those of Scotland.

What, if anything, might be said to justify, even to mitigate, the harsh treatment meted out to Ireland in the decades after the Glorious Revolution? For one thing, the penal laws were not enforced uniformly and they were not always enforced harshly. Few, if any, individuals were executed for their religion. Furthermore, the continuing presence of over 1000 priests and over 4000 monks and nuns ensured that the Catholic population was able to maintain the regular practice of its faith. The penal laws were, rather, a guarantee of continued subservience on the part of the Catholic population and, perhaps, a reserve armoury of powers which could be called upon in a crisis. Few things are more revealing than the peace of the Irish countryside in the first half of the eighteenth century. But the fact remains that many sections of the Irish population nursed their grievances without having available the mechanisms of peaceful protest and, consequently, without the expectation of redress. By the early eighteenth century the political and social problems of Ireland had reached an impasse. Just as the Anglo-Irish landowners were dependent on British military support for their existence, so the native peasantry would be dependent upon foreign intervention for the restoration of their religious freedoms. In the end, as the Irish rebellion of 1798 was to reveal, these problems could only be resolved with outside intervention. In 1714, however, this could not be foreseen. In any case, the historian should study the history of Ireland in the eighteenth century for its own sake and on its own terms, not as a preparation for what was to happen in the 1790s.

By the same token, we should not read the history of the British colonies in North America as a prelude to the American Revolution of the 1770s. Throughout the British colonies, in fact, the Glorious Revolution had been greeted with varying degrees of enthusiasm. There had been little affection in the colonies for the Stuart monarchs, who had been more than ready to tamper with local charters and interfere with the rights of local elites. In the West Indies the Revolution was at first greeted warmly. James II had imposed heavy taxes on sugar and tobacco and had limited the bargaining power of local assemblies. The reluctance of William to repeal and reduce these taxes, however, steadily diminished the approval which had been initially displayed. In the mainland American colonies, however, the Glorious Revolution was greeted with rather greater enthusiasm. Here the Stuart monarchs had made wholesale assaults on colonial charters. Indeed, most colonies at least sent some expressions of gratitude to William. Many of them went much further. Seven of the colonial legislatures, in their anxiety to secure formal safeguards of their liberties, attempted to pass their own versions of the Bill of Rights. Enthusiasm for the Glorious Revolution gave rise to social and political upheavals in Massachussetts, New York and Maryland, and took Virginia to the brink of revolution. In the end, however, order was restored and colonial expectations satisfied at least in part. The attack on colonial charters was not revived by William, and during the subsequent decades there was much less interference in the internal politics of the colonies than there had been before 1688. Most important of all, the future of the colonial legislatures never seriously came into question. Yet in other ways, and as in Scotland and Ireland, the Glorious Revolution led to a greater rationalization of control from London. New York, New Jersey, Pennsylvania and Maryland, all formerly private colonies, came under the immediate control of the crown.

Furthermore, a new Navigation Act in 1696 extended metropolitan control over the imperial trade of the colonies. In the following year, in an attempt to obtain convictions in the trials of those accused of breaking the laws, the Vice-Admiralty courts were extended into every colony.

In the early eighteenth century, then, Great Britain may be described as an increasingly centralized body politic but one with powerful local variations in its political, religious and economic life. These, however substantial, were nevertheless contained by a number of unifying influences. These include the pressures making for cultural uniformity created by English educational and social institutions and which powerfully affected the landowning classes of Scotland and Ireland; the enormous social and economic pull of London; the threat – and just occasionally the reality – of the use of military force; and, not least, the emerging sense of pride in belonging to the state of Britain with its armed services (the *British* army and the *British* navy), its rapidly expanding (*British*) empire and, not least, its much vaunted (*British*) constitution.

These were not mere abstractions. The Scottish desire for a close union with England within a larger 'Britannic' framework has its roots in the early seventeenth century, in the court of James VI and I. Already in 1707 Scots held 10 per cent of the regimental colonelcies in the British army (by 1763 this had increased to 20 per cent). Members of the Irish aristocracy, too, were willing to see military service within the empire. Indeed, Ireland in the early eighteenth century shared in many ritual celebrations of British naval and military victories and in the anniversaries of royal birthdays. Furthermore, as we have seen, the enthusiasm generated by the Glorious Revolution reached North America. In a more general sense, British political culture and manners made their mark in many parts of the empire; West Indian planters, the colonial gentry in mainland America and wealthy merchants everywhere identified themselves with the homeland, its aristocratic traditions, its prevailing ideals of the gentleman and, not least, with the continuing influence of 'Country' ideals. Such people conducted their political life and, indeed, expressed their criticisms of colonial rule, in Country terms. The idea of a British nationhood, therefore, was not a theoretical construct but an active and practical catalyst for the creation and definition of people's identities. In the quarter of a century after the Glorious Revolution, indeed, a British national identity, born of tradition, Protestantism, war against France and, increasingly, commercial and colonial achievement, was emerging. A British state, a British empire and a British nation were in the process of construction.

Notes

1. When he reissued the Declaration in May 1688, James demanded that the clergy read it out from the pulpit on two successive Sundays. Ominously, large numbers of them – probably a majority – refused to do so.
2. For these arguments, however, see J.R. Jones, *The Revolution of 1688 in England* (1972), p. 11.
3. G.M. Trevelyan, *The English Revolution* (1938), p. 120.
4. My own slightly dismissive account of the Declaration is different from that of Lois Schwoerer, *The Declaration of Right* (1981). The only completely novel clauses were those relating to the army (see J. Miller, *The Glorious Revolution* (1983), p. 37)

and the right of citizens to bear arms. See J.L. Malcolm, 'The Creation of a "True Antient and Indisputable" Right: the English Bill of Rights and the Right to be Armed', *Journal of British Studies*, 32(3) (1993), pp. 226–49.

5. Indeed, providential elements in Tory thinking remained powerful after 1689. The Tory view of the world still included the belief that civil society and civil government were created by God and that 'the people' did not have the right to dissolve it.

6. The future George I, for example, promised in 1710 that he would assume the throne of Britain 'as a ruler by hereditary right'. See J.C.D. Clark, *English Society, 1688–1832* (Cambridge, 1985), pp. 132–33.

7. H.T. Dickinson, 'The Precursors of Political Radicalism in Augustan Britain', in C. Jones, ed., *Britain in the First Age of Party, 1680–1750* (1987).

8. The Test Act for England had been passed in 1673 and for Scotland in 1681. The Acts compelled holders of civil and military offices and members of corporations to take the Anglican communion, to take the oaths of supremacy and allegiance and to make a declaration against the Catholic doctrines of transubstantiation.

9. Convocation was the representative body of the Church of England and consisted of assemblies of the clergy of the two provinces, Canterbury and York. The bishops sat in the upper house, the clergy in the lower. After this failure, Convocation was not summoned again until 1700.

10. P.G.M. Dickson, *The Financial Revolution in England: A Study in the Development of Public Credit, 1688–1756* (1967). Since Dickson wrote, most historians would emphasize almost as strongly as the growth of the system of public credit the growth in the use of private credit in changing people's attitudes to consumer goods and to many aspects of life itself.

11. Clark, *English Society*, esp. ch. 3.

12. See H. Horwitz, *Parliament, Policy and Politics in the Reign of William III* (1977), p. 316.

13. Occasional Conformity was the practice of Protestant Dissenters who, by receiving communion in Anglican churches on exceptional occasions, escaped the penalties of the Test Act and were thus qualified to serve in the army and navy, to sit in Parliament and to serve on municipal corporations.

14. The Whig Junto was a confederation of aristocratic Whig factions in the reign of William III and Anne, led by Lords Somers, Orford, Wharton, Halifax and Sunderland.

15. '1694 is one of the great watersheds in the development of the party,' J.H. Plumb, *The Growth of Political Stability in England 1675–1725* (1965), pp. 134–35.

16. Robert Harley, 1st Earl of Oxford (1661–1724), one of the great leaders of the Tory party in the reigns of William III and Anne and one of the principal exponents of 'Country' politics. Paul Foley was an ostentatiously incorruptible Country Tory who became Speaker of the House of Commons in 1695.

17. The Partition Treaties of 1698 and 1700 were agreed between England, France and Holland and provided for the partition of the Spanish empire on the death of the current King, Charles II.

18. Sydney Godolphin (1645–1712) accumulated great experience as a politician under Charles II and James II before taking the Treasury on the accession of William III. He served thereafter in a number of capacities. His occasional contacts with the Jacobites infuriated the Whigs, who dismissed him in 1700 and again in 1702.

19. Henry St John, Viscount Bolingbroke (1678–1751), one of the leading Tory politicians of the reign of Anne. St John was the major Tory ideologue of these years. He entered Parliament in 1701, became Secretary for War in 1704 and Foreign Secretary and joint leader of the Tory party in 1710. He became a peer in 1712. On the death of Queen Anne, his Jacobite sympathies led to his flight to France. He returned to England (1725–35), once more retreating to France (1735–42).

20. Few historians today resist the powerful, orthodox view that parties occupied a vital position at the centre of politics in the early eighteenth century. See e.g. J. Plumb, *The Growth of Political Stability*; G. Holmes, *British Politics in the Reign of Anne*, rev. edn (1987); *The Electorate and the National Will in the First Age of Party* (1976); W.A. Speck, *Tory and Whig: the Struggle in the Constituencies, 1701–15* (1970). There is, perhaps, a danger of exaggerating the influence of party – especially in rural areas – to the exclusion of other influences before 1714, and thenceforward of exaggerating the extent of its decline *after* 1714.

21. G. Holmes, *The Making of a Great Power, 1660–1722: Late Stuart and Early Georgian Britain* (1993), p. 334.

22. Horwitz, *Parliament, Policy and Politics*, p. 319.

23. J. Brewer, *The Sinews of Power: War, Money and the English State, 1688–1783* (1989), p. 150.

24. G. Holmes, *The Electorate and the National Will in the First Age of Party* (1976), p. 15.

25. *Op. cit.*

26. J. Jones, *Britain and the World, 1649–1815* (1980), pp. 115–16, 133–35.

27. Historians have tended to exaggerate the foreign-policy differences of William and the Tories. It was William's methods – expensive continental wars and allowance systems which promised to lock Britain into permanent European entanglements – which roused the Tories. They shared his broad strategic objectives of maintaining a European balance of power.

28. Historians have tended to exaggerate the seriousness of the threat which Louis XIV presented to the British, and to the rest of Europe. After 1697 France was not the military threat that it had been earlier. The economy of France was in serious difficulties and the French were soon anxious for peace. As the peace negotiations of 1709 illustrate, Louis was unable to control the actions of his grandson, Philip V, King of Spain.

29. I. B. Cowan, 'Anglo Scottish Relations', *Historical Journal*, 32(1) (1989).

30. J. Black, *The Politics of Britain, 1688–1800* (1993), p. 13.

31. One recent explanation for the readiness of the Scottish Parliament to agree to Union has been the bribery of its members. See C.W. Ferguson, 'The Making of the Treaty of Union in 1707', *Scottish Historical Review*, 43 (1964). More generous treatment may be found in D. Daiches, *Scotland and the Union* (1977) and, most convincing of all in its acknowledgement of a range of factors, T.C. Smout, 'The Road to Union', in G. Holmes, ed., *Britain after the Glorious Revolution* (1969).

32. Poynings Law of 1494 subordinated the Irish Parliament to the English Parliament. The former could not initiate legislation without the approval of the Privy Council in London. Irish Acts, moreover, could not become law without the approval of the Westminster Parliament.

3

Whiggism supreme, 1714–1757

The years between the Hanoverian Succession and the outbreak of the Seven Years War have traditionally been presented as years of peace and calm, sandwiched between eras of upheaval and disruption. In contrast to the era of political revolutions in the seventeenth century and that of the economic and social transformations of the later eighteenth and nineteenth centuries, the first half of the eighteenth century appears to be an ordered and peaceful period in which society was agreed on its fundamentals. According to a traditional historical convention, these years of Whig supremacy represent the dominance of an exclusive landed elite over society and over the political system. According to this view, the ruling classes controlled the political system in order to protect their social and economic privileges, using their wealth and power to command the obedience of their dependents. In this elegant scheme of things the mass of the people had little or no part to play; they were an off-stage chorus whose voices could only intermittently be heard. Indeed, some historians have condemned this regime for its conservatism, its complacency and its corruption.[1]

Few historians today accept this interpretation of early Hanoverian Britain. On the one hand, the Glorious Revolution and the events that followed did not usher Britain down a peaceful path to constitutional progress. The Glorious Revolution, as we have seen, fostered an English domination of the British Isles that was achieved through violent means. This in its turn created powerful tensions, not least in Scotland and Ireland. Both the Presbyterian church establishment in Scotland and the Anglican establishment in Ireland denied civil rights to vast sections of their populations – Episcopalians in Scotland, Catholics in Ireland – which positively fomented the conditions for discord and disunity. Furthermore, how can Britain be treated as an ordered and settled body politic in view of the Jacobite rebellions of 1715 and 1745 and the continuing resentment displayed by a public opinion for many years hostile to the dynasty? As we proceed to examine the nature of Hanoverian politics and the structure of Hanoverian society, these issues need constantly to be borne in mind.

The Hanoverian Succession, 1714–1721

The death of Queen Anne on 1 August 1714 triggered a series of events of some little complexity and which were to have far-reaching consequences. In spite of the fact that no fewer than 58 individuals had a closer kin relationship with the Queen, George Lewis, Elector of Hanover, was immediately proclaimed King. Until he could arrive from Hanover to claim his inheritance, a Regency Council, dominated by Whigs, governed the country.

During this brief period the precarious unity of the Tory party dissolved. Already seriously divided by the terms of the Treaty of Utrecht, the Tories could not agree on its plans for the new reign. Oxford defended the Hanoverian Succession against Bolingbroke's fatuous plans to recognize James Edward, the Old Pretender and son of James II as King.[2] Tory divisions enabled the Whigs to procure the dismissal of Oxford four days before the death of Anne. Worse still, the new King had no love for the Tories. He had been a committed member of the Grand Alliance against Louis XIV and had contributed 12 000 Hanoverian troops. In short, he had been a firm supporter of the policy of William III and he was aghast at the pacific drift of Tory foreign policy after 1710. Even before his arrival in England on 18 September he had dismissed Bolingbroke and challenged the Tories to declare their loyalty. The refusal of several Tory leaders to serve him was little less than a declaration of war against the court and was treated as such. George I and his advisers proceeded to reconstruct the ministry. The new cabinet, in which Townshend and Stanhope were the two Secretaries of State,[3] was almost completely dominated by Whigs and included several Junto lords. This was followed by a purge of office-holders in both local as well as central government. Within a short period, no fewer than 22 of the 42 Lords Lieutenant in England had been removed and their offices placed in loyal, Whig hands. After this purge, the prospects of the Tory party were desperate. Its future hung upon the outcome of the general election of 1715.

The election was a complete disaster for the Tories. In January and February 1715 they campaigned against the new dynasty on the old cry of 'the Church in Danger'. This may have done them some electoral good in the past, but it came a little oddly from a party some sections of which were actively negotiating with a Catholic Pretender who had persistently refused to convert to Anglicanism. The Whigs, not for the last time, tarred the Tories with the brush of Jacobitism and transformed a Tory majority in the House of Commons of 240 into a Whig majority of almost 130. The historical significance of the general election of 1715 is that it gave electoral sanction, and thus a powerful stimulus of legitimacy, to the Hanoverian dynasty. In the open constituencies public opinion was clearly on the side of the Whigs and the Protestant Succession. They doubled the number of the county seats they controlled, traditionally the last redoubts of the Tory party.

The extent of their electoral rout drove a minority of the leading Tories into the arms of the Pretender. Bolingbroke fled to France on 6 April. They were negotiating with the French court for naval and military assistance when on 6 September 1715 the Earl of Mar raised the Jacobite standard at Braemar. Eighteen Lords responded to the call and within three weeks the Jacobite army had swelled to 5000 men. At the end of September Mar had occupied Perth. All of Scotland north of the Tay was in his hands. Had he struck at once against the 1500 regular troops quartered in Scotland the new Hanoverian dynasty might have been sorely pressed. Mar delayed, awaiting reinforcements – by November he had 10 000 men – and the moment was lost. The cause was always going to be decided south of the border, and Mar's delay gave the English government time to strike at its opponents.

The Jacobites had always recognized that a successful rebellion could not be achieved by Scottish forces alone but would require a simultaneous uprising in England. Such a rising was not beyond the realms of possibility. The new dynasty had not been greeted with much enthusiasm. The day of George I's coronation (20 October 1714) had been marked by riots and disturbances in several towns in the south. Matters were not improved by the King's aloofness and the fact that he insensitively chose to surround himself with his own Hanoverian advisers and mistresses. During the general election of 1715, moreover, Jacobite mobs were in evidence in some constituencies. This gave way to more general, desultory rioting in London throughout the spring and early summer. Indeed, the rioting became so serious in the capital and in the Midlands and Welsh Border counties that the ministry had to rush the Riot Act through Parliament in July 1715.[4] This was followed by the suspension of habeas corpus on 21 July. Meanwhile the two Secretaries of State, Stanhope and Townshend, were successful in prising Jacobite secrets out of their spies. Leading Tories, including Bolingbroke and Oxford, were impeached. These were catastrophic blows for the Tory party. Its infuriated supporters retaliated by senseless attacks on Dissenting meeting-houses. It was against this backdrop that Mar raised the Jacobite standard in Scotland.

His fatal hesitations gave the government time to secure England before turning to disaffected Scotland. The standing army was doubled in size and the fleet was sent to watch the Channel ports. Stanhope issued warrants against several of the English Jacobite leaders, placed garrisons around Jacobite centres like Bath and Oxford and sent troops to Bristol and Plymouth, thus stifling all prospects of a rising in the West Country.

When it came, therefore, the English rising was half-hearted, confined to the far north and lacking in popular support. When the Scottish army crossed the border, the English Jacobites raised Northumberland but failed to take Newcastle. The Jacobites advanced as far south as Preston but found the country lukewarm in their support. Most of the 1600 men who rallied to the cause were Roman Catholics. The Protestant majority – including most of the Tories – remained indifferent. The Jacobite advance south was blocked by superior forces and at Preston they surrendered the hopeless cause.

As for the Scottish rebels, they had fought the indecisive battle of Sheriffmuir only the day before the surrender at Preston in November 1715. Their failure to break through into the Lowlands was a severe setback. Their cause was severely hampered by the disunity of the clans and by the difficulty of coordinating their military efforts. Had the Scottish rebels of the south west been able to coordinate their actions with the rising in the north of England, the outcome of the campaign might have been very different. Furthermore, they lacked effective leadership. The Pretender at last came onto the scene, but his landing at Peterhead on 22 December came at least three months too late. After a few fruitless weeks he accepted the inevitable, and on 4 February 1716 he left his cause, and its supporters, to their own devices and took himself off once again for France.

The consequences of the '15 were to be momentous. Although it is often stated that punishments were not unduly severe by the standards of the times, several hundred Jacobites were transported, 26 were hanged and 19 Scottish peerages were forfeited. Of even more significance were the effects on the political balance of power. The '15 confirmed the political supremacy of the Whigs, condemned the Tories to the fringes of politics and established a new one-party ascendancy. Many of the remaining Tory JPs were deprived of their offices – 68 in Middlesex, for example. Of even more far-reaching significance was the passage in May 1716 of the Septennial Act. The Act extended the life of an elected Parliament from three to seven years, and in so doing extended the political supremacy of the Whigs into the next decade. Whether the peace and security of the kingdom would have been seriously endangered had the election due in 1718 taken place is difficult to determine. Tory protests that the measure was unconstitutional were brushed aside. However, Stanhope rewarded Protestant Dissenters for their support both of the Whig party and of the new dynasty by repealing the Occasional Conformity and Schism Acts (December 1718). The ministry's attempts to entrench its supremacy in the House of Lords by passing a Peerage Bill aroused so much opposition in the Commons and in the country that it was abandoned in February 1719. The Bill would have restricted the ability of the crown to create peers and thus have guaranteed the Whigs a permanent majority in the House of Lords. A second attempt to pass the Bill was frustrated in December 1719.

The defeat of the Peerage Bill was the culmination of growing disunity within the ranks of the newly victorious Whig party. Since the Hanoverian Succession the Whig leaders, Sunderland[5] and Stanhope, had been unable to maintain the cohesion and unity of their party. Many of the old generation of Junto leaders departed the political stage at this time through age and infirmity, and Sunderland was bitter at being rewarded in 1714 with only the post of Lord Lieutenant of Ireland. Since then he had become a close confidante of the King, although he ultimately managed to discredit himself by his enthusiastic support for the Peerage Bill. Almost from the beginning of the reign the dominance of Stanhope and Sunderland was resented by Townshend and the rapidly rising Sir Robert Walpole.[6] These political resentments were deepened by divisions within the royal family. They began to come to a head when the Prince of Wales acted as Regent while Stanhope accompanied the King on a visit to Hanover in the summer of 1716. During the King's absence the Prince flaunted his position and, encouraged by Walpole and Townshend, appealed to the public. Differences over foreign policy, especially the prominence accorded to Hanover by Stanhope, sharpened these personal enmities. As a result, Townshend was demoted from his secretaryship and sent to Ireland as Lord Lieutenant in December 1716. In the following April he was dismissed from the government altogether. At this, Walpole and a number of followers resigned their own offices. Stanhope was now raised to the peerage and became First Lord of the Treasury, while Sunderland became the principal Secretary of State. The first of the Whig schisms of the Hanoverian period had begun.

The ruthlessness which underlay these factional differences should not be underestimated. Walpole and Townshend rejoiced in the complete rupture of the relationship between George I and his heir. When the Prince established his reversionary court in December 1717 at Leicester House, they used it as a rallying-point for the opposition, a tactic that was to be used by oppositions throughout the long eighteenth century. Moreover, the new leaders of the Whig opposition shamelessly appealed to the Tories by opposing Stanhope's repeal of the Occasional Conformity and Schism Acts (1718), legislation which Walpole had enthusiastically opposed in Anne's reign. They proceeded, even more shamelessly, to launch parliamentary assaults on placemen and pensioners and then went on to oppose the Peerage Bill of 1719. Their jingoistic attacks on Stanhope's foreign policy for its excessive concern for the interests of the electorate of Hanover were equally designed to capture public support. Their purpose, of course, was to weaken the ministry and to force the leaders of the Whig opposition back into power. The positions of Stanhope and Sunderland steadily weakened. They faced the prospect of continuing parliamentary difficulties after the defeat of the Peerage Bill and they had to manage the serious divisions within the Hanoverian royal family. More urgently, they felt the need to break the power of the cabal of Hanoverian ministers who since the beginning of the reign had surrounded the King, threatening to undermine the position of his ministers. Desperate for security, they opened negotiations with the Tories but these came to nothing. Meanwhile, Townshend and Walpole helped to effect a reconciliation between the Prince of Wales and the King in April 1720. Nothing now stood in the way of a political settlement. Within two months the leaders of the opposition Whigs were back in office. Townshend became Lord President of the Council but Walpole only received the post of Paymaster General.

Whatever its divisions, the Whig party had by 1720 already done much to establish the new dynasty. This could not have been achieved without the far-sighted foreign policy pursued during these years by Stanhope, which preserved peace and national security and thus contributed hugely to settling the new and in many ways unappealing dynasty. Both Britain and France had been exhausted by decades of war, and they negotiated a Dual Alliance in November 1716. This became the Triple Alliance with the adhesion of the Dutch in January 1717. The Alliance committed all three countries to uphold the terms of the Treaty of Utrecht, to protect the Hanoverian Succession and to expel the Jacobite Pretender from French soil. With the ultimate adhesion of Charles VI of Austria in August 1718, the Triple Alliance became a Quadruple Alliance. Stanhope, however, could not persuade the Spanish to adhere to it. The Spanish court had not been signatories to the Treaty of Utrecht and had ambitions to regain Naples, Sardinia and Sicily. In the summer of 1717 Spanish troops invaded Sardinia, which in 1713 had been handed to Austria. In accordance with the terms of the Treaty of Utrecht Britain came to Austria's aid. Together with France, British troops engaged the Spanish army in the Iberian peninsula and independently destroyed the Spanish fleet in the Mediterranean. Early in 1719 two Spanish expeditions were despatched to Scotland in support of the Pretender. The first was dispersed in atrocious weather off Cape Finisterre. The other reached the Isle of Lewis before its military force, supported by a small band of Scottish Jacobites, was defeated. There would be no further attempted invasion of

Britain for many years. The success of Stanhope's policy of peace, through alliances in Europe, did much to create the conditions in which the Hanoverian Succession could continue to establish itself.

Walpole and Townshend found themselves back in office just in time to confront the crisis over the shares of the South Sea Company and the famous episode of the 'South Sea Bubble'. The Company had been founded by Harley in 1711 to counterbalance the influence both of the Whig Bank of England and of the East India Company. His original intention had been to use anticipated commercial revenues to liquidate £9 million of the National Debt (which then stood at £50 million). The favourable terms of the Treaty of Utrecht enabled the Company to prosper, and between 1717 and 1720 it successfully negotiated with the Stanhope–Sunderland ministry to assume no less than £31 million of the National Debt which was in the hands of private investors. In Harley's scheme, these investors would receive 5 per cent per annum until 1727 and 4 per cent thereafter if they transferred their annuities into South Sea stock. The enthusiasm with which the Company tried to persuade investors to convert their holdings created a financial crisis of the first order. The South Sea directors themselves helped to bid up the stock value, generating fictitious stock. They lent over £10 million on the security of their own stock and they issued new stock recklessly. The market for South Sea stock soared from 100 at the start of 1720 to 300 by early April, then to over 700 by the beginning of June. By the end of the month it stood at over 1000. At this point some of the larger investors began to take their profits. By the middle of September the stock had crashed to 400. By the end of the month payments were suspended and the stock stood at 190.

It was Walpole's calm and masterly handling of the crisis which ensured his future political prominence. Although holding only the office of Paymaster General, he showed himself both capable of rising above immediate issues and enmities and willing to take a longer view of events. The first requirement was to quell the financial panic and to restore public confidence. This he did by persuading both the Bank of England and the East India Company to take over £9 million each of South Sea stock, thus ending the free fall in its value. By the end of the year it was up to 200, a sure sign of returning confidence. It remained to clear up the confusion by recompensing those national debt-holders who had mistakenly agreed to convert to South Sea stock. They received between 60 per cent and 80 per cent of the original sums. Many were inclined to grumble but part, at least, of their investments had been recovered. The economy was basically sound, and once the stock-jobbing mania had exhausted itself the affairs of the nation returned to normal. Walpole, moreover, behaved with considerable statesmanlike constraint. To have lambasted the Stanhope–Sunderland ministry for its financial incompetence might have been good politics – it may even have caused the collapse of the government – but it would undoubtedly have alienated the king, it might even have let in the Tories and, conceivably, it might have reawakened the hopes of the Jacobites. And although Walpole earned himself considerable unpopularity by turning a deaf ear to cries for the punishment of directors, ministers and MPs, he at least kept his own hands clean during the 'Bubble' (although we now know that he had, in fact, invested at least £9000 in stock).

All of this, however, may not have been enough to ensure Walpole's ultimate political supremacy had fortune not been on his side. Early in 1721
Stanhope died. At the same time Sunderland, under accusation of seeking
personal gain, was forced to resign from the Treasury. There could only be
one successor. Walpole now commanded the political scene and he took his
prize, in April 1721 becoming First Lord of the Treasury and Chancellor of the
Exchequer. The long years of his political supremacy had begun. If there was
still any question mark about it, his position was confirmed by the result of
the general election of 1722. In spite of the South Sea Bubble the Whigs
increased the number of their seats from 340 to 380, whilst the Tories'
declined from around 220 to 180. Nothing could disguise the extent of
Walpole's triumph. During the middle of the South Sea crisis many observers
had been gloomily predicting a revival of the periodic instability which had
so regularly plagued Britain in the previous century. Within two years these
fears and doubts had been emphatically dispelled. Britain had entered the
age of Walpole.

The Walpolean regime, 1721–1742

In 1721 Sir Robert Walpole was already an experienced and mature politician.
He had entered Parliament in 1701 and, as one of the most ambitious and talented members of the Court wing of the Whig party, he had consistently
sought preferment and power. His experience in administration was extraordinarily wide. Already in 1705–08 he had been appointed to the Council of
the Lord High Admiral; in 1708–10 he was Secretary at War; from 1710 to 1711
he was Secretary of the Navy and from 1714 to 1715 he was Paymaster of the
Forces. Most important of all, he had been First Lord of the Treasury and
Chancellor of the Exchequer from 1715 to 1717. In all of these positions,
especially the last, he had been resoundingly successful. His industry, his
professionalism and his gift for mastering complex practical issues rendered
him a formidable opponent. Indeed, his periods in opposition, especially
between 1711 and 1714 and from 1717 to 1720, added almost as much to his
reputation as his periods in office. His reasonable and persuasive oratory, his
ability to move both the emotions as well as the minds of men and, above all,
his extraordinary self-confidence marked him out as a future leader.

Sir Robert possessed the personal qualities essential to political success in
any age, but he possessed in particular those qualities which most closely met
the needs of the 1720s. A country squire from Norfolk, Walpole was a man of
his class, revelling in its pursuits and ostentatiously wallowing in its fashions.
He was more concerned with the pleasure and pursuits of the countryside
than with those of the capital. It was typical of Walpole that he almost always
seemed able to sense the prejudices and sentiments of the country gentlemen
in the House of Commons upon whom he relied, in the last analysis, for his
majorities. Yet Walpole was much more than a rural squire. Partly through his
marriage to the daughter of a merchant, he was familiar with the London
mercantile classes. Such connections were indispensable in the age of the
Financial Revolution. Never an idealist, he was an exponent of pragmatism,
of caution and of common sense. He was practical, unsentimental and, when

it mattered, ruthless. This is not to claim that Walpole governed wilfully, nor in his own personal interest nor in a narrow and partisan manner. He had a coherent and consistent perception that the national interest demanded international peace, domestic unity, economic prosperity and commercial expansion. These objectives he pursued consistently throughout his long administration. Although he was a practical politician rather than an intellectual in politics, it would be an injustice to accuse him of lacking principle. From his earliest days in politics he had identified himself with the Court wing of the Whig party. He unwaveringly championed the Glorious Revolution, the Revolution Settlement and the Hanoverian Succession. He condemned the Tory peace of Utrecht. He opposed the Tory ideology of passive obedience with assertions of the Whig principles of rights of resistance and religious toleration. Significantly, Walpole was to be a champion of the rights of the Protestant Dissenters throughout his career. On occasion, he could be stubbornly consistent and loyal to his party and to his family. In 1710, for example, he refused Harley's invitation to join his Tory administration. Further, in 1717 he defied George I's summons to him to remain in the ministry and thus to abandon his brother-in-law, Townshend.

In the spring of 1721 Walpole commanded his party, occupied the Treasury, which commanded the bulk of patronage, and enjoyed the respect of a grateful public opinion after the South Sea Bubble. In late 1722 he was fortunate that the revelation of a harebrained Jacobite plot in which Francis Atterbury, the Bishop of Rochester, was closely implicated enabled him to consolidate his power more firmly than anyone would have thought possible. Walpole struck hard. Atterbury was banished, habeas corpus was suspended for a year and Catholics and Non-jurors suffered the humiliation of a special tax of 5s. in the pound. Walpole had given a taste of what his opponents might expect and an indication of the firmness with which he intended to govern the country.

Walpole's supremacy – the longest in British political history – was built upon a number of sound and solid foundations, political, religious, economic and diplomatic. It is by now a platitude to observe that Walpole, like all eighteenth-century first ministers, owed his long tenure of power both to the confidence of successive monarchs and to the support of Parliament. Walpole was always aware of his dependence upon the monarch who had appointed and who could dismiss him. Fortunately for Walpole, the power of George I's Hanoverian advisers had already lapsed. The King had no great love for Walpole, but he respected his abilities and honoured him with his confidence. Indeed, he acquiesced in the single-party rule of the Whigs to an extent that William III and Anne would never have done. Yet although deficient in his mastery of English, the King never entirely surrendered his ultimate independence in politics, especially over questions of foreign policy and military affairs, and his agreement on these matters could never be taken for granted. Nevertheless, his personal limitations disabled him from either exploiting or extending the powers of the crown.

When the King died in 1727, Walpole's dependence was demonstrated by George II's preference for Sir Spencer Compton, an amiable courtier. Walpole had deserted the then Prince of Wales in 1720 and George II was anxious both to punish and to replace him. Walpole could only survive by demonstrating his indispensability to the new King. This he did by obtaining for him the largest Civil List which Parliament had ever voted. Furthermore, Compton's legendary inability to compose the King's speech from the throne together with the influence of Queen Caroline (whom Walpole had been cultivating for some years) over her husband combined to persuade the King to retain Walpole in office. The incident has always been taken to illustrate Walpole's dependence on the monarch, but it equally illustrates the monarch's dependence on the minister. (The smoothness of the succession in 1727, incidentally, also illustrates how firmly the Hanoverian dynasty had established itself in just 13 years.) Even after the death of Queen Caroline in 1737 George II continued to be a loyal supporter of the minister, recognizing his talents and his service to the House of Hanover and, not least, his ability to carry government business smoothly through Parliament. The second Hanoverian King was considerably more assiduous than his predecessor, and evidently more ambitious to extend royal influence over policy. In matters of foreign policy the King usually got his way and, like his father, jealously guarded military patronage.

Walpole's supremacy was no less dependent upon his ability to persuade Parliament to agree to his measures. In the House of Lords he maintained majorities for the government by adopting a number of tactics. During the period 1689 to 1714 the Whig and Tory parties had enjoyed something of a rough equality. Within a few years of his accession to power Walpole had broken the strength of the Tories in the upper House. By the mid-1720s they found it difficult to assemble over 40 peers in a House of just under 200. By then, in comparison, the number of placemen in the Lords had risen to over 80. From the beginning, Walpole was careful only to advance and to promote new peers who were likely to be friendly to his ministry. To this end, he revived the Order of the Bath. Furthermore, the 16 Scottish peers were well disposed towards the dynasty. In addition, many of the bishops were reliable Whigs. In 1723 no fewer than six sees became vacant and Walpole was careful to ensure that only Whigs were appointed. Indeed, in association with Edmund Gibson, Bishop of London, Walpole worked tirelessly to ensure the loyalty of the Church of England through careful and meticulous examination of new appointments. Such political spadework should be noted but its importance should not be exaggerated. It is too easy to attribute Walpole's achievement in the upper House to the exclusive use of patronage. Patronage played a powerful role, but it merely provided the materials from which a Lords majority might subsequently be fashioned. Adherents needed to be carefully managed, and in managing them the Walpole ministry was characteristically thorough.

Within a few years Walpole had succeeded in taming the House of Lords. Although the institutional decline of the upper House was to be a slow and gradual affair, there can be no doubt that such a decline set in during Walpole's tenure of office. As early as 1723 Lord Orrery complained: 'The House of Lords are treated pretty much as an useless body and they seem to acquiesce under that threat for they neither are nor desire to be ... troubled with publick affairs'.[7] It is true that on occasions – a very few occasions – it could still assert itself, as it did during the Excise Crisis and over the Quaker Relief Bill in 1736. Furthermore, defective bills could be remedied and troublesome bills allowed quietly to expire there. Occasionally, the Tory opposition might launch a set-piece debate in the Lords but insofar as political fortunes were decided in the parliamentary arena they were in the future not to be determined in the upper but in the lower House.

It was even more vital, then, that Walpole should establish political mastery over the House of Commons. As in the Lords, the sensible use of patronage was vital. At a time when the state bureaucracy was increasing in size and when the principle of appointment to office on merit had not yet been established, this was absolutely inevitable. Indeed, the number of placemen in the House had been rising from about 120 in Queen Anne's reign to around 180 in that of George II, an increase from less than one-quarter to around one-third of the House. It is utterly characteristic of the man and his methods that under Walpole their reliability signally improved. 'Walpole thus had at his disposal a more solid and reliable phalanx of Court supporters in the Commons than any of his immediate predecessors.'[8] Given the weakening of party ties in this period, such a body of support was of the first importance to the minister.

Yet patronage alone would not have been enough to sustain the Walpole ministry for over 20 years. Three additional political ingredients were needed to establish ministerial control of the House of Commons. First, Walpole needed to identify himself with the Commons chamber. He attended the House assiduously, intervened in debate constantly and patiently, and in simple language explained ministerial policy, and, of course, the dire alternatives, to the Country gentlemen who dominated it. Second, Walpole had to try to conciliate opponents within his own party. The Tories were a lost cause but Whig opponents could be cajoled, convinced and persuaded to support the government. Walpole invested an enormous amount of time and effort in these personal appeals, often to very good effect. Third, the large body of Country gentlemen in Parliament had to be wooed and won. Their support could never be taken for granted. Walpole devoted himself to this objective by playing the country squire, by outrageously indulging in farmyard metaphors with an enhanced Norfolk accent, by keeping the Land Tax low and by a pacific foreign policy. By indulging in such political arts with patience and care Walpole retained a personal respect in the Commons that was one of his greatest political assets.

Above all, it is important to recognize that Sir Robert chose to retain his seat in the Commons. It is possible that he perceived that it was by now advisable for the head of the Treasury and Chancellor of the Exchequer to sit in the lower House in view of that House's influence over financial matters. Alternatively, he may have wished to avoid the upper House where two of his greatest rivals, Carteret and Townshend, might have outshone him in debate. Whatever his motives, it is clear that in uniting the Treasury with the political leadership of the House of Commons he was establishing himself as a prime or first minister in an unprecedented manner. Those of his predecessors, such as Oxford, who had united control of the treasury with leadership of an administration had usually sat in the House of Lords. Walpole's presence in the Commons, together with the sheer length of his tenure of office, established a different set of precedents for future political leaders. Most of the long administrations of the eighteenth century, those of Henry Pelham, Lord North and the Younger Pitt, were led from the House of Commons.

The Walpolean years were not only marked by the government's ability to maintain itself in Parliament. They were years of greater religious tranquillity than had been enjoyed for half a century. In view of the explosive potential of religious issues, indeed, this circumstance may be regarded as one of the keys to Walpole's enduring political success. The first requirement was to confirm and defend the supremacy of the Anglican church. The natural champions of the church, the Tories, were tarred with the brush of Jacobitism and divided by the schism of the Non-jurors. In view of the almost complete lack of interest of the first two Hanoverian monarchs in its organization and traditions, it was left to Walpole and the bench of Whig bishops to uphold the established church and, in upholding it, to subject it to the disciplines of partiality and patronage that accompanied many areas of life under the Whig oligarchy. The Anglican church proved to be one of the most loyal sponsors and supports of the Walpolean regime.

As for the Dissenters, Walpole was anxious to reward them for their fidelity to the throne and to the Whig party. Consequently, his annual Indemnity Acts cushioned them from the force of the Test and Corporation Acts. In addition, after 1723 he quietly set aside a small sum for the relief of widows of Dissenting ministers. This was not enough for some vociferous elements within Dissent. The Committee of Dissenting Deputies (a union of Baptists, Independents and Presbyterians) petitioned Parliament for the outright repeal of the Test and Corporation Acts in 1736 and 1739. On both occasions they were defeated heavily in the House of Commons. It says something for Walpole's political skills that he was able to extricate himself from such an embarrassing position with little or no loss of political face. But on the Quaker Tithes bill he was not so sure-footed. In 1736, after six years of evasion, Walpole agreed to support the Quaker Tithes bill, which would have softened the effects of prosecutions against the Quakers for their non-payment of tithe. The measure slipped easily through the Commons but in the Lords the bishops revolted against Walpole's support of the measure and threw it out. Subsequently, Walpole did not press the matter. However, the episode ended his friendship with Bishop Gibson. The latter's influence over ecclesiastical patronage was subsequently lodged with the Duke of Newcastle.[9] The incident is revealing as one of the few occasions when Walpole managed to alienate one of his natural constituencies of support. In the same session some opposition Whigs made a bid to repeal the Test and Corporation Acts. Although they failed by 251 votes to 123 in the Commons, the issue raised the political temperature. The session of 1736 is interesting because it reminds us that religious sentiments were still potent. Unless they were kept in check they might easily revive to upset the political cohesion so painstakingly fashioned by the minister. Symbolically, the same year saw the publication of William Warburton's *Alliance between Church and State*, the classic justification of the established church and of its close relationship with the state.[10]

Walpole's long ministry rested, then, on structures of support in politics and in religion, but these could neither have been devised nor conserved without the economic stability which was one of his greatest achievements. Britain needed peace and prosperity after the clamour of the South Sea Bubble. Peace would help to nullify the Jacobite threat and to rally the nation behind the dynasty. Walpole stated his economic objectives in October 1721:

to make the exportation of our own manufactures, and the importation of the commodities used in manufacturing them, as practicable and as easy as possible; by this means the balance of trade may be preserved in our favour, our navigation increased, and the greater numbers of our poor employed.

Like his contemporaries he had a (somewhat exaggerated) belief in the importance of exporting manufactured goods in promoting economic growth, the prosperity of the nation and the employment of its people. Walpole was fortunate that his years of power coincided with a fairly strong recovery in trade following the War of the Spanish Succession and with the low price of grain following the good harvests of the period. In the 1720s, moreover, Walpole launched a series of attempts to encourage trade and enhance revenue from customs duties. He stimulated manufacturing industry by removing export duties from over one hundred articles; he issued bounties to encourage the export of selected commodities, including silk, sugar and spirits, and he protected certain domestic industries, including linen, paper and silk, from foreign competition. Furthermore, he abolished duties on agricultural exports, including grain. In a much-needed attempt to reform the outdated and confusing customs system, and to reduce smuggling, he issued a simplified system of import duties, summarized in a revised Book of Rates. Finally, he established a bonded warehouse system for taxing key imported commodities like tea, chocolate, coffee and cocoa.

Care needs to be taken in evaluating Walpole's commercial policies. For one thing, it is not realistic to regard him as an early free-trader, a pioneer looking ahead to the achievements of the younger Pitt, Peel and Gladstone. It is true that he encouraged trade but, by the same token, he was capable not only of protecting domestic industries, as we have seen, but of regulating them by, for example, issuing minimum standards of quality for cloths, linen and serges. If this were not protectionism enough, he pushed through Parliament in 1721 and 1726 Acts to provide for the regulation of wages by JPs and for the prohibition of combinations of workmen.

How effective were Walpole's thoroughgoing attempts to engineer economic recovery and to increase the volume of trade? Perhaps the extent of his achievement should not be exaggerated. Certainly the volume of Britain's trade expanded in the Walpole years, exports from £7 million to £10 million a year between 1721 and 1738, the last year of peace, imports from £6 million to £7.5 million, yielding a significant improvement in the balance of trade from about £1 million to £2.5 million. This was a useful, but hardly astounding, increase. Indeed, exports were to rise even more steeply in the 20 years *following* the fall of Walpole. Many of his attempts to boost individual industries, particularly silk, were unsuccessful. In the absence of reliable statistics it is difficult to be precise, but it may be that the natural operation of an economy during a period of both national and international peace was just as productive of growth as any amount of political intervention.

A peacetime Britain, moreover, could afford to reduce government expenditure and thus cut taxes. Walpole lowered the Land Tax to 2s. in the £ between 1722 and 1726, in 1730 and between 1734 and 1739. In 1731 and 1732, indeed, it stood at only 1s. in the £. To pay for these reductions in the tax bills of the landed classes he increased the revenue from indirect taxes, which fell disproportionately upon the poor, such as those on malt, salt, soap, sugar, leather and candles. Indeed, the yield from these excise duties increased from just over £8 million per annum in the period 1706 to 1710 to just over £14 million between 1731 and 1735. By then, excise duties amounted to around one-half of total government revenue (the Land Tax, by comparison yielded less than one-fifth between 1731 and 1740). The efficiency with which these excise duties were levied by inquisitorial visits from excise officials was the source of much popular resentment. The phenomenon of a minister popular with the landed classes while unpopular with the masses may to some extent be explained by these patterns of taxation.

Furthermore, like most members of the upper and middling orders, Sir Robert Walpole lamented the extent of government indebtedness and abhorred the size of the National Debt. Popularly regarded as a measure of the health of the economy, it had reached the alarming figure of £54 million by 1721 and required £3 million in interest payments each year. Walpole devoted himself to its reduction by the use of a sinking fund. Although he had initially launched the idea, the fund had been established in 1717 by Stanhope and Sir Robert took over the existing fund. By the end of his ministry the National Debt stood at £46 million and the annual interest charge at £2 million. Moreover, he managed to reduce the interest rate from 6 per cent in 1721 to 4 per cent in 1727, which went some way to reducing the financial drain of the debt on the Exchequer. In 1727, indeed, he succeeded in raising a loan of £1 million from the City at only 3 per cent. This contributed economic success, indeed, even if the investing classes may have regretted the falling rates of return on their loans. To what extent it was necessary for political success to rest upon the effective manipulation of capitalist practices and institutions cannot be determined here. What may be suggested is that Walpole was more of an economic manager than an economic reformer. The improvement of the economic condition of the masses was not considered by him, or by most members of the ruling elite, to be a government responsibility. It was that of local government, private agencies and the churches. This was territory where Walpole refused to tread.

The Walpolean period saw continuing English domination of Ireland and Scotland. The general election of 1715 had returned a safe Whig majority to the Dublin Parliament, and because neither the Triennial Act nor the Septennial Act applied to Ireland there was no need to hold another general election during the rest of the reign of George I. The Tories were consigned to a hopeless future in opposition and shortly began to lose their cohesion. Consequently, there seemed no possible political threat to the Whig supremacy in Ireland.

The only significant opposition to that supremacy came not from the Tories, and not from the Catholics but from the Protestants. They had shown signs of dissatisfaction with their political subservience to London even before the Hanoverian Succession. In 1698, indeed, a new strain of Irish Protestant patriotism was announced with the publication of William Molyneaux's *The Case of Ireland Being Bound by Acts of Parliament in England*, in which the author, an Irish MP, argued for the independence of the Irish Parliament. Such sentiments were aroused once again by the Declaratory Act of 1720. To Protestants this final symbol of English dominion over Ireland was humiliating. In 1722 they began to act the part of patriotic Irishmen, defending the rights of their country. The issue on which this unlikely situation arose was trivial enough. The English Treasury had sold the right to issue a new copper coinage for Ireland to the Duchess of Kendal, who in turn had sold the right to an Englishman, William Wood, for £10 000 in 1722. The fact that an Englishman could make a healthy profit out of the Irish coinage, a coinage which, incidentally, turned out to be of mediocre standard, without the slightest consultation either with the Irish government or with the Irish Parliament, provoked a storm of protest. The publication of Dean Swift's *The Drapier's Letters* aroused Anglicans, Presbyterians and Catholics with its clarion call: 'you are, and ought to be as free a people as your Bretheren in England.' Such patriotic language transformed the shoddy dispute into a full-blown discussion of Anglo-Irish relations and the much-resented maltreatment of the subject country.

Walpole defused the situation by recalling the ineffective Lord Lieutenant, the Duke of Grafton, and replacing him in 1724 with Carteret, who had been since 1721 a vocal and troublesome Secretary of State and one who was much too close to George I for Walpole's liking. With one move, Walpole had rid himself of a turbulent and potentially threatening opponent at court and provided the Irish government with much-needed strength and determination. Even this was not enough. The storm of protest showed no sign of subsiding until, at last, Carteret persuaded Walpole to withdraw the patent in 1725. The matter soon lapsed, but its consequences were to be of some importance. The English government determined to take a firmer hold of the Irish Parliament, and placed responsibility for its supervision in the hands of a group of 'undertakers', who demanded, and received, the lion's share of power and patronage as a reward for their continued and reliable management. There was to be little more trouble in Ireland for forty years. Walpole's achievement may best be reflected in the loyalty of Ireland during the '45. 'Until the demise of Jacobitism and the development of a more powerful sense of national identity gave the Ascendancy the confidence seriously to challenge English constitutional and economic paternalism, Anglo-Irish relations would remain fundamentally stable.'[11] The price that was paid for the purchase of this security, however, was weak and inefficient government, the continued subservience of Ireland to England and the identification of English supremacy with a small and ambitious group of political managers.

Although it would be unwise to take the comparisons too far, the situations of Scotland and Ireland were not entirely dissimilar. 'Until at least the 1750s Scotland's rulers were a beleaguered native oligarchy, dependent in the final analysis on English arms to keep them in power.'[12] As in Ireland, London ruled Scotland through a small group of landed families who dispensed patronage and influence to reliable friends and agents. The politics of party, in Scotland as in Ireland, was replaced by the politics of faction. The Scottish Whigs belonged to one of two main factions, the Squadrone and the Argathelians, led by the Duke of Argyll. Even the Scottish Kirk was reduced to submission through the inexorable process of appointing and promoting only reliable friends of the Whig supremacy. As in Ireland, the consequences of partial and exclusive government by place and patronage in the hands of a narrow pro-English clique was subservience purchased at the price of indifference and dissatisfaction.

Tension was never far below the surface of social and political life in Scotland, but it was over the issue of taxation that popular hostility to the Union made itself felt. The Malt Tax of 1725 provoked an outbreak of rioting, most seriously in Glasgow. As with the issue of 'Wood's Halfpence' in Ireland, however, the removal of an independently minded minister, in this case the Secretary of State, the Squadrone's Duke of Roxburgh, a review of the measure and a significant tightening up of political management quelled the unrest. Even so, soldiers had to be called in to restore order. In the following years English rule in Scotland came to depend on the Campbell faction in the persons of the 2nd Duke of Atholl and his brother, the Earl of Islay. For several years the surface of Scottish life remained placid, but the underlying tensions were revealed in the Porteous Riots of 1737, when a crowd of over 4000 broke into Edinburgh prison and lynched Captain Porteous, a guard who was held responsible for the execution of a smuggler. This collapse of law and order was punished by the dismissal of the provost of Edinburgh and a fine of £2000 on the citizens which was to go to Porteous's widow. The government's managers in Scotland disliked the measure. Argyll went into opposition, and although Islay remained in his post the government did badly in the Scottish constituencies at the general election of 1741. Although incidents such as these did not seriously endanger the Union, they indicate not only the existence of repressed hostility to the men and methods used to maintain it but, as was dramatically revealed in 1745, the reluctance of the mass of Scots to spring to its defence.

Like all administrations of the long eighteenth century, that of Walpole generated its own opposition. Because the administration lasted for over two decades, the constitutional competition between the government and the opposition became a settled, and growing, element in the Walpolean political system. After the death of Sunderland, Walpole's only serious remaining rival was Carteret, who had the King's ear, who could speak German and who was noted for his enthusiastic support for the interests of the electorate of Hanover. In 1724 Walpole transferred Carteret to Ireland, as we have seen, and he had no further problems with him. But this was not to be the end of Walpole's internal difficulties. William Pulteney,[13] once a friend and colleague of Walpole, had been affronted when Walpole chose to replace Carteret with the Duke of Newcastle rather than himself in 1724. His accusations of corruption resulted in his dismissal in 1725 and he went into opposition. At just this time Bolingbroke, who had returned to England in 1723, resumed active politics. Bolingbroke and Pulteney together came to enunciate in the pages of *The Craftsman*, founded in December 1726, the classic 'Country' criticisms of Walpole and his system of government. For Bolingbroke and Pulteney the old party distinctions were giving way to a new distinction, that between corruption and liberty. They rejected the ministerial contention that opposition to the ministry meant opposition to the dynasty. They attacked the corruption and influence that allegedly sustained the ministry in Parliament and which reduced its freedom and independence. They sought to root it out by measures such as place bills, shorter Parliaments and a Triennial Act, and they advocated either the disbanding or, at the very least, a drastic reduction in the size of the standing army. In order to confront Walpole's corrupt use of the crown's influence they wished to unite Country Whigs and Country Tories into a powerful new force with which to oppose and bring down the minister and, on the basis of an appeal to public opinion, renew the constitutional functions of Parliament which they believed to have been established at the Glorious Revolution.

In Parliament the burden of opposition was assumed by the Pulteney brothers, William and Daniel, and the Tory Sir William Wyndham.[14] This was the core of the 'patriot' opposition to Walpole and his regime. To their efforts was added the force of the small group of indefatigable Jacobites led by William Shippen.[15] They were joined in 1730 by Carteret on his return from Ireland and by the Secretary of State, Charles Townshend, after his dispute with Walpole over foreign policy. In 1733 the opposition was joined by Chesterfield and the 'boy Patriots' led by Cobham and including his nephews, George and Richard Grenville, and William Pitt.[16] Their constant tirade of criticism may not have unduly disturbed Walpole's peace of mind, but when it coincided with powerful bursts of public sentiment it could unsettle the ministry and force it to change its measures, as it did in 1733–34 during the celebrated Excise Crisis.

To this gathering galaxy of discontented, as well as extremely ambitious, political talent was added the social leadership of some of the great hostesses of the day, Kitty, Duchess of Queensbury, Sarah, Dowager Duchess of Marlborough and Lady Granville, the mother of Carteret. Most of all, the addition of the names of many of the greatest writers of the age – Arbuthnot, Fielding, Gay, Pope and Swift – ensured that the power of the pen and the influence of the stage were alike turned upon the ministry of Sir Robert Walpole. There can be no question that this was one of the most brilliant, most famous, and most talented but, at the same time, most unsuccessful oppositions in modern British history.

We do not have to look far for the reasons for its persistent lack of success. However talented and articulate the opposition may have been, the fact remains that several of its leaders enjoyed somewhat dubious reputations. They were an odd assortment of Whigs, Tories and ex-Jacobites. However persuasive and trenchant their criticisms of the Walpolean system of government may have been, they had no detailed plan for an alternative system. Vapid constitutional generalizations were no real alternative to Walpole's policies of security, stability and low taxation. Furthermore, the opposition was rent with serious divisions, between Pulteney and Bolingbroke, between the Country Whigs and the Country Tories and between the Jacobites and everybody else. Not surprisingly, it did not prove easy to unite opposition Whigs, Tories and Jacobites around the Country programme of *The Craftsman*. Arguably, too, the programme smacked of a perverse distaste for government, especially strong government, which, in view of the recent history of Britain, may have appeared misplaced. Furthermore, the Country programme was economically retrogressive. Its condemnation of financiers and capitalists evinces a reactionary nostalgia for traditional, rural society. No wonder, then, that Bolingbroke wished to restore an ancient constitution more appropriate to a past age.

When *The Craftsman* abandoned the struggle in 1736 Walpole had managed to survive two general elections (1727 and 1734), the accession of a new King and, not least, one of the most damaging political storms to sweep over any administration of the long eighteenth century. The Excise Crisis of 1733–34 bristles with significance for the student of the period. Its origins were simple enough. Encouraged by the success of the excise reforms of the early 1720s, Walpole determined to reduce the Land Tax by extending the range of goods paying excise. He reintroduced the excise on salt in 1732 while lowering the Land Tax from 2s. to 1s. in the £. There was little enthusiasm for these reforms, and the measures passed the Commons by only 39 and 29. Undaunted by these precarious majorities, Walpole next sought to bring tobacco and wine into the scheme. By doing so, he hoped to save between £200 000 and £300 000 per annum and ultimately to abolish the Land Tax in peacetime.

The subsequent uproar took Walpole by surprise. He might have predicted the onslaught of the opposition in Parliament, which based its hostility on the slogan 'Excise, Wooden Shoes and no Jury' and on its scare stories of hordes of excise officers intimidating innocent citizens. Yet what Walpole could not have anticipated were the spontaneous howls of rage from the 54 counties and borough constituencies which voted petitions against the measure. Out of doors, the air was thick with pamphlets, broadsides and squibs. The great commercial interests immediately affected by the scheme, tobacco and wine, launched their own campaigns against the excise.

On 14 March 1733 Walpole won a majority of 61 votes for his Excise Bill. This served only to inflame the forces opposed to it. Although public resistance was certainly stiffening against the excise it was, in truth, other factors which weakened Walpole's position and caused his majority to collapse. A whispering campaign against the measure broke out at court and members of the Court party in both Houses began to waver. On second reading on 4 April 1733 Walpole's majority dropped to 36 and, next day, to an alarmingly thin 16. It was uncertainty in the closet (the small chamber in which the king gave audiences to his ministers) rather than the force of public opinion which was dissolving the minister's majority. He had already offered to drop the bill and to resign, a step which George II refused to consider, when he made one last stand for the excise. On 10 April he fought hard in the Commons against a petition against the bill from the City of London. He prevailed by 17 votes but on the following day, to universal rejoicing, he gave up the bill.

The drama was not yet over. Sensing the possible collapse of the government, the opposition attacked in the Lords. On 24 May, on a motion to enquire into the estates of the South Sea Company directors, the vote was tied by 75–75. Walpole may have occasionally found his majorities in the House of Commons difficult to sustain, but in the Lords he had hitherto been secure. It was only with the greatest difficulty and after dismissals of leading court peers from their offices that the Lords were whipped into line. Thereafter the minister was safe.

In the short term, the Excise Crisis illustrates both Walpole's dependence upon the King and the King's willingness to support his minister. George II used dismissals, promotions and even peerage creations to help his minister through the crisis. Partly, perhaps principally, due to the King's loyalty,

Walpole's reputation with the political nation very quickly revived. On 13 March 1734 the opposition moved up to a formal assault upon the administration by moving the repeal of the Septennial Act. In this great confrontation Walpole won the battle of oratory and argument as well as that of votes. His majority of 247 to 184 was evidence enough that he had re-established his position.

In the longer term, the Excise Crisis unquestionably weakened Walpole's position. The general election of 1734 reduced the number of ministerial Whigs from 342 to 326 and the number of opposition Whigs from 86 to 83, but increased the number of Tories from 130 to 149. Walpole's majority, then, was reduced from 126 to 94. But it was the reverses suffered by the government in the open constituencies which weakened its reputation and its confidence. Voters, horrified at the prospect of excise officers violating their privacy, reacted with fury, taking their revenge on sitting members who had supported the excise. Ministerial Whigs were defeated in counties usually loyal to the government, such as Kent and Hampshire. Even in Walpole's Norfolk, defeat could not be prevented. It required unusual ministerial exertions in the constituencies with small numbers of voters to keep the government's losses to a minimum.

Until 1733 the opposition had had nothing to celebrate. Its victory in 1733 had left Walpole in power, it is true, but weakened and wounded. New elements in the Parliament of 1734, notably 'Cobham's Cubs', strengthened the opposition. Between 1734 and 1741 Walpole's majority in the Commons sank steadily to little more than 40. Carteret and Pulteney had become leaders of a formidable opposition. In 1737 it received the unexpected support of Frederick, Prince of Wales, the heir to the throne. Like all Hanoverian heirs, Frederick quarrelled with his parents over what he claimed to be the inadequacy of his allowance, and he employed the parliamentary opposition to try to force the government to increase it. His enraged father declared Frederick's court at Leicester House out of bounds, whereupon the heir proclaimed his formal opposition to his father and his government. Leicester House was to be the focal point for political and dynastic opposition to the Hanoverian regime for the next decade and a half. It was not so much the 20 MPs, many of them in Cornish seats, who rallied to the Prince's cause and formed a small Prince's party which troubled Walpole. A Prince's court was a much more exciting and respectable focal point for Walpole's disunited band of enemies than the home of any discontented politician could ever have been. It was impossible now to dismiss opposition to Walpole as unpatriotic, because by rallying behind the Prince the minister's opponents could claim that they were defending the interests of the Hanoverian dynasty, as well as hoping for political reward in the reign to come.

Opposition to the ministry was gathering in strength during the 1730s but it was to be foreign policy and foreign war which were to bring Walpole down. The objectives of Walpole's foreign policy had been to maintain peace in Europe and to establish cooperation with France. These straightforward objectives were, however, to be confused by two factors: the presence on the throne of a Hanoverian monarch and the belligerent dispositions of several of the European powers. As to the first, George I was anxious to protect the security of Hanover and willing, therefore, to adopt a much more interventionist diplomacy than English ministers who had to pay for the policy and defend it in the House of Commons. As to the second, Spain, for example, was anxious to seize the Italian duchies of Parma, Piacenza and Tuscany from the Emperor Charles VI, who had his own schemes for the establishment of an Ostend Company, whose purpose was to challenge British and French commercial supremacy.

These objectives were registered in the Treaty of Vienna of 1725 between the Holy Roman Empire and Spain, which fostered the diplomatic and commercial interests of the two countries. Townshend was anxious to resist such initiatives with all possible vigour, and with France and Prussia concluded the Treaty of Hanover in the same year, which provided for the defence of Hanover and Gibraltar and for the protection of British trade against the Ostend Company. The Treaty made expensive demands upon England, including the requirement to provide 12 000 Hesseian troops. Walpole had reservations about such a militant posture, and found it difficult to defend himself in the House of Commons against the opposition's accusations that he was surrendering the country's interests to those of Hanover. Townshend enjoyed the King's support and, for the moment, Walpole was content to watch and wait.

Europe was now dangerously divided into two alliance systems. Walpole was anxious to seek a negotiated settlement and did so by, in effect, buying Spain off. In 1729 Spain and England signed the Treaty of Seville, which confirmed England's *Asiento* rights in return for Anglo-French support for Spanish claims to the Italian duchies of Parma, Piacenza and Tuscany. The Treaty, however, was negotiated behind Townshend's back, the culmination of a long history of personal jealousies between Townshend and Walpole. Townshend's resignation in May 1730 allowed Walpole to assume control of foreign policy and to return to the Imperial alliance. In 1731 he was able to negotiate the second Treaty of Vienna, by which the Emperor suspended the Ostend Company and, at last, allowed Spanish troops into the Italian duchies. In return Britain guaranteed the Pragmatic Sanction by which Emperor Charles VI's daughter, Maria Theresa, was to succeed to the Habsburg throne of Austria.

For some years, Walpole was able to keep Britain clear of foreign entanglements which might have exposed his government to the dangers of war. In spite of George II's willingness to consider a military solution to the problems of the Polish succession in 1733, Walpole opted for a peaceful, diplomatic outcome. To have gone to war in the middle of the Excise Crisis for objectives that were remote from British interests would have been political madness. If Walpole is to be criticized, it is that after the general election of 1734 he began to lose his grip on foreign policy. When the final diplomatic crisis came Britain had no reliable allies in Europe. It was Anglo-Spanish relations which set the course of events leading to Walpole's fall. Relations between the two countries unleashed passions and furies which Walpole could no longer contain and which he may not have entirely understood. A new generation had grown up since the ending of the War of the Spanish Succession, one which took for granted Britain's status as a European power. Many of them were bored with the politics of peace and wished to see some flexing of the national muscle. Spain was to be the object of their antagonism, especially since the Spanish authorities had for many years hindered and obstructed the rights which Britain had won in the Treaty of Utrecht, namely the *Asiento* and the right to send one ship a year to the trade fairs of the Spanish Main. In the Caribbean the Spanish coastguard vessels, the *guardacostas*, customarily seized British ships and cargoes, subjecting British sailors to beatings and imprisonments. A series of bloodthirsty incidents aroused English public opinion to boiling point. The celebrated Captain Jenkins claimed not only to have had his ship captured in 1731 but to have had his ear cut off. His publicity-seeking sympathy for his much-advertised pickled ear contributed to the outbreak of what has sometimes been termed 'the War of Jenkins' Ear'. Negotiations were tried, but failed. In January 1739 Walpole submitted to the House of Commons for ratification the Convention of El Pardo, an Anglo-Spanish attempt to reach a financial settlement of outstanding claims. Against an ugly backcloth of public hostility, Walpole managed to win a majority of only 250–232. The opposition would not have peace, the public was clamouring for war and Walpole's own colleagues succumbed to the hysteria. Spain withdrew the *Asiento*, the fleets of the two countries clashed and in October 1739 war was formally declared. 'It is your war,' Walpole told Newcastle, 'and I wish you well of it.'

Walpole was a peace-minister. His political talents had been forged in a very different theatre from that which was now opening. Early victories in the Spanish Main by the fleet commanded by Admiral Vernon did the ministry no good at all because Vernon was an opposition Whig and a consistent critic of the government. Indeed, his victories made him into something of a national hero. Walpole's stock plummeted further as the War of the Austrian Succession broke out in Europe in October 1740. He was accused of subordinating British interests to those of Hanover when George II, terrified for the safety of his electorate and against the wishes of his ministers, negotiated a convention of neutrality with the French in October 1741. It may have been the Anglo-Spanish conflict which weakened what was left of Walpole's public standing, but the vexed issue of Hanover also contributed to his discomfiture.

The growing weaknesses of Walpole's position were registered at the general election of 1741 when his majority was reduced from 42 to 19. Ironically, it was in Scotland and Cornwall – two of the areas least inclined to register swings in public opinion – that the damage was done. Coincidentally, the consequences of the Porteous Riots and the alienation of the heir to the throne, both traceable back to the year 1737, returned to gloat at Walpole's political funeral. The opposition moved in for the kill. In December 1741 they seized control of the Chairmanship of the Committee of Privileges and Elections, a vital committee which heard and determined election petitions. The decisions of the Committee could make a difference to a government's majority of at least 30 and possibly more. On a petition from Chippenham, Walpole found himself in a minority of 16. With ministerial supporters hanging back and refusing to attend the House, Walpole saw that he could not continue. On 2 February 1742 he tendered his resignation.

The fall of Walpole was only partly the consequence of that weakening in his parliamentary position which may be traced back to 1734. None of this can be laid at the King's door. He supported Walpole to the end. Nor is there any truth in the old idea that Walpole's position with the King weakened after the death of Queen Caroline in 1737. By then George II did not need his wife to remind him of the importance of Walpole to the dynasty. The need thereafter for Walpole to treat directly with the King may even have strengthened his position in the closet. Although the attacks of the opposition in Parliament together with its success in keeping public opinion in a state of continuing excitement were important explanations for the fall of Walpole, it is doubtful if they alone could have brought him down. Down to the general election of 1741 Walpole was rarely in serious trouble in Parliament. In February 1741, indeed, he defeated an opposition motion for his dismissal by no fewer than 184 votes. Even after the general election he had a tenuous, but possibly workable, majority. What hastened the fall of Walpole was the accumulating deterioration in his health and the mounting fragility of his will for political survival. In the years since the Excise Crisis younger politicians had been drifting into the opposition rather than identifying their future careers with Walpole's waning powers. The events of 1741–42 accelerated these processes. It was the battered state of the ministry itself and the declining powers of Sir Robert Walpole which demoralized some of the ministry's own supporters and persuaded them to withdraw their support in those vital weeks early in 1742. Because of their defection, the longest-lived administration in British history came to an end.

Any politician who retains power for over 20 years must possess three qualities in abundance: enormous self-belief, exceptional ability and political good fortune. Of the first two there can be no doubt. Walpole's belief in his own indispensability was matched by remorseless industry and disciplined persistence in the pursuit of his goals. His acute political sensibilities enabled him to balance rival groupings and interests within the vast empire of Whiggism, while his meticulous skill at personal relationships soothed the feelings of the unsuccessful and the neglected. At the same time, there can be no doubt that Walpole was the beneficiary of a number of developments that helped to stabilize his administration: the passing of the Septennial Act, the self-destruction of the Tory party, the failure of the Jacobites and the gradual weakening of the power of religious and dynastic issues to unsettle politics. Certain favourable diplomatic factors, not least the cooperation of France, were by no means initiated by Walpole but they unquestionably promoted the objectives which he was pursuing. It is conceivable that other Whig politicians could have profited from these advantages; whether they would have capitalized upon them to the extent that Walpole did may well be doubted.

Nevertheless, Walpole's achievements were considerable. He consolidated the Protestant Succession. He maintained the peace and stability of the country for over two decades after over 40 years of revolution, war and political upheaval. He steered the country away from religious persecution and sectarian animosities. Personally indifferent to religious pieties, Walpole enabled the Protestant Dissenting churches to practise their religion with little let or hindrance, to establish their own schools and, in many towns, to participate in local government. If the long-term effects of his ministry on the political structures of the country were not entirely wholesome, they were far from being wholly negative. His constant presence in the House of Commons, his excellence as a speaker and debater and his willingness to explain his policies to backbenchers did much to promote the importance of the lower House at the expense of the upper House, where his position was, by comparison, much more secure. His achievement in managing the public finances, in furthering prosperity by promoting trade, industry and agriculture, is no less remarkable; it did much to secure the adhesion of the middling orders to the dynasty and to the regime.

The catalogue of Walpole's deficiencies, on the other hand, was frequently spelled out by his opponents and has often influenced the historical record. These may be distilled into two major charges. The first concerns his deployment of 'corruption' to achieve his political objectives. This has been the subject of grotesque distortion, sometimes amounting to the charge that he raised 'corruption' into a system of government. But Walpole could not have survived as long he did through the use of 'corruption'. It took political and personal qualities of the highest order to dominate Parliament and politics as he did. Inevitable, his central position in the web of patronage cannot be discounted. He deployed not only Treasury patronage but also that of other departments in the interests of his administration. Perhaps understandably in a period of potential rebellion, he saw the creation of stable government almost as an end in itself. It is possible that he employed political loyalty to excess in determining the suitability of individuals for appointment to office, but in doing so he was pursuing party, dynastic and national, not personal, objectives. The second charge concerns his institutional legacy to his country, and this is more damaging to Walpole's reputation. It may be said of Walpole that he used the institutions of his day without taking positive steps to strengthen them. For example, his preference for an inner cabinet or *conciliabulum* of trusted friends over the full cabinet cannot be said to have strengthened the constitutional structures of the country. Furthermore, his ruthless manipulation of the powers and patronage of the Scottish government was not accompanied by any real consideration for the affairs of the northern kingdom, as the events of 1744–45 were to remind the nation. Similarly, it is doubtful if the Church of England emerged from the years of Walpole stronger than it entered them. Indeed, while retaining the Test and Corporation Act Walpole passed the first of the Indemnity Acts in 1727. The minister, of course, used the privileged position of the Church of England as the first line of defence for his own ministry, but he took little interest in the schemes of administrative reform which Edmund Gibson, Bishop of London, was planning. Inevitably, they came to nothing.

Where does the balance lie between these contrasting judgements on the career of Walpole? Coming to power in 1721, Walpole's first concerns were to settle the country by destroying elements of resistance to Whig rule and thereafter to defend and maintain the legacy of the Glorious Revolution and the Hanoverian Succession. Walpole was neither a heroic nor an inspirational figure. He was, as he claimed, 'no Saint, no Spartan, no Reformer'. Perhaps he needs to be judged by other criteria. Walpole was a man of practical concerns who entertained, perhaps, a limited view of the possibilities of political action. He created little that was new but he used to resounding effect the materials that he found at his disposal. He was no ideologue and no demagogue. He was the consummate Whig politician and the indispensable bureaucrat. He was the master of Parliament, the statesman of peace and, if only for two decades, the architect of stability.

The Pelhams and patriotism, 1742–1757

The period following the fall of Walpole is complex and, on the political front, confusing. It is, nevertheless, a period with distinct characteristics. It witnessed the ultimate defeat of challenges to the Whig ascendancy; it was marked by a consolidation of its power and an accompanying general reluctance to seek changes in its political and social structures. The old party distinctions between Whig and Tory continued to exist but they lacked their earlier clarity and agency. The continuing search for ministerial stability was accompanied by a more conciliatory attitude towards opposition groups than Walpole had normally displayed and a greater tendency towards incorporation and conciliation. It was, however, hampered by a noticeable inconstancy in political relationships which lends an unpredictable, sometimes kaleidoscopic, aspect to politics in these years. Most of all, it was a time of warfare, a period in which issues of diplomatic and foreign concern resumed the prominence which they had enjoyed 30 years earlier. Furthermore, as was already becoming apparent in the 1730s, colonial issues were inflaming public opinion and, on occasions, even driving politicians towards war and conquest.

In 1742 Walpole's administration was to be strengthened by reinforcement from its erstwhile opponents. To see how this happened, it is necessary to grasp the structure of political groupings in 1742. Walpole's long ministry had been supported not so much by a Whig *party* as by a coalition of different – sometimes very different – Whig groups. The ministry had been supported by the 'old corps' Whigs. The 'old corps' included some members of the great Whig aristocracy, such as the Pelhams themselves, the permanent placemen (or Court and Treasury party), and a number of independent Country gentlemen who were inclined to support the court and the government of the day. In 1742 the opposition was divided fairly equally between Tories and Country Whigs. The Tories, about 140 of them, divided between crypto-Jacobites and reluctant Hanoverians, were not considered, and did not consider themselves, likely recruits for office. About 80 of the 130 opposition Whigs were independent Country gentlemen who had no ambition for place. But the remaining 50, divided between the Prince of Wales's faction and the followers of Carteret and Pulteney, certainly did and they – the 'new Whigs' as they came to be known – were now taken into the ministry.

The political changes which occurred in 1742 were remarkably limited. Walpole himself was anxious that the unity of the Whig party in general, and of the 'old corps' in particular, should be maintained. He advised against sweeping changes. Indeed, only one Tory received a cabinet post. On the other hand, several powerful members of Walpole's administration continued in office. They included the Duke of Newcastle and his brother, Henry Pelham, together with their close colleagues, the Duke of Devonshire and Lord Hardwicke.[17] Nor were these individuals, and the politics they professed, threatened with punishment. The 'patriots' in opposition to Walpole, notably Pulteney, had for years led the public to expect that the defeat of Walpole would be a prelude to an era of reform and virtue. This was to remain nothing more than a mirage. In the end, the strength of Pulteney's reform credentials was found to be seriously deficient. He accepted a peerage as Lord Bath, retreated to the Lords and did nothing to bring the fallen minister to justice. It was enough that Walpole had been humbled. Pulteney had no intention of rocking the Hanoverian boat which he had for many years denounced but on which he now sought to clamber.

The new ministry was dominated by Carteret. He would stand or fall by his competence in foreign and colonial affairs, which had destroyed Walpole and which were now to dominate the political scene for the rest of the reign of George II. Carteret sought to inject greater vigour into British diplomacy but his flurry of activity, brilliant and bewildering though it may have been, was devoid of positive result. In 1743 George II personally led the English and Hanoverian infantry to victory against the French at the Battle of Dettingen on the river Main. Carteret's failure to capitalize on this remarkable military success was to have damaging consequences. Public opinion, vigorously represented in indignant and intensive press coverage, was hostile at his concern for the electorate of Hanover and for the employment (at British expense) of 16 000 Hanoverian troops. Still worse, Cartaret's diplomacy did not prevent the final breakdown of relations between England and France. In 1744 the French declared war.

Between 1742 and 1744 the opposition lashed the ministry in debate, pressed for the retrospective prosecution of Walpole and moved motions for place and pensions bills and one for the repeal of the Septennial Act. They brought forward over 30 divisions on the conduct of the war. All these initiatives failed as Carteret fell back upon the majorities which had sustained Walpole for so long. Yet his position was still extremely vulnerable. The old corps ministers were unhappy with Carteret's secretiveness, his arrogance and his refusal to cultivate party loyalties. Their position in the ministry was already weighty when in 1743 Henry Pelham became First Lord of the Treasury and Chancellor of the Exchequer. Pelham and his friends were horrified both at Carteret's indulgence of the King's Hanoverian schemes and at the costs of these continental adventures. In the spring of 1744 they forced the King to dismiss Carteret. It was the second time in two years that George II had lost a minister who had his confidence but lacked that of a wider political circle. It was further confirmation of the strength and power of the Whig oligarchy and of the skill and resource of the old corps.

Carteret and most of the 'new Whigs' were replaced in the spring of 1744 with the 'Broad-bottom' administration.[18] The Pelhams wished to enlarge the base of the administration in order to ensure a trouble-free prosecution of the war. Consequently, the new ministry contained some dissident Whigs, including Pitt and his friends, Lyttleton and George Grenville (the 'new allies'), and even a few moderate Tories. (Indeed, a trickle of Tories reinforced the commissions of the peace in the localities.) The experiment in 'Broad-bottom' was not particularly successful. Indeed, the ministry is now best remembered for dealing with the '45 rebellion, which it did with conspicuous success, but it lacked political strength. The old corps had embarked upon it mainly because they felt uncertain of their own positions. There was little enthusiasm for it within the ranks of the Whigs. Within a few months, moreover, all the Tories were back in the familiar routines of opposition. Furthermore, there was little confidence between the King and his ministers. The King insisted on consulting Carteret (now raised to the peerage as Lord Granville) as 'minister behind the curtain' and treated his ministers with little respect. Some of the 'new allies' were in favour of resignation on this issue even during the '45 but members of the old corps preferred a waiting game. This they played to perfection. Once the rising was over they were ready to strike: aware that the King was contemplating the formation of a ministry headed by Granville and Bath, they took the initiative and in February 1746 collectively resigned. Forty junior office-holders resigned with them. George II was forced to recognize that he could not govern without them and he was forced to readmit the old corps at the price of an office (Paymaster General) for Pitt – perhaps the only member of the House of Commons competent to lead a formidable opposition – and the dismissal of several of Granville's friends (the 'new Whigs') who were still in office. It was the end of his role 'behind the curtain' and a signal victory for the old corps. The political crisis of 1746 was an effective demonstration of the power of the old corps and a striking indication of the ability of ministers to impose themselves on the monarch. Its consequence was the re-establishment of the supremacy of the old corps and the effective reunification of the Whigs as the governing party of Britain. The administration which was formed in 1746 lasted until the death of its leader, Henry Pelham, in 1754. Until the middle of the next decade 'Broad-bottom' was to remain under a cloud.

Meanwhile, the Jacobite movement had launched its last serious challenge to the Hanoverian dynasty. Taking advantage of British involvement in the war in Europe and overseas and of the absence of the Highland companies in Germany, the Young Pretender, Charles Edward, raised the Jacobite standard on the island of Eriskay off the west coast of Scotland in July 1745. Landing with only a dozen supporters, the Prince's cause rapidly flourished. By September he had over 2000 troops and he occupied Edinburgh. After the great Jacobite victory at Prestonpans, Scotland was now in rebel hands. In November 1745 an army of over 5000 men invaded England. Their arrival at Derby marked the high point of the Jacobite cause in 1745. It is just possible that had they continued south they might have created panic in London. In the event, the failure of the expected French invasion fleet to arrive and the absence of English support for the Scottish army weakened the latter's confidence and drained its morale. Most significant of all, neither the Tories nor the Catholics moved in its support. By this time, the government had rallied its military strength and at least 30 000 troops were now available to confront the Jacobites. Realising that they had nothing to hope for in England, the Jacobite officers persuaded the Pretender to retreat to Scotland, where in April 1746 their army was destroyed at Culloden by the 9000 troops led by 'Butcher' Cumberland, the King's second son. The remnants of the Jacobite army repaired to Ruthven, still prepared to fight on, but the Prince had fled. The '45 was over.

Henry Pelham took full advantage of the loyalist reaction that swept the country in the wake of the '45 by bringing forward the general election expected under the Septennial Act in 1748. By doing so he hoped to consolidate his parliamentary majority in advance of the impending, and almost certainly controversial, peace treaty to end the war with France. The general election of 1747 confirmed the supremacy of the old corps Whigs over Tories, Jacobites and opposition Whigs alike. The electoral mistakes of 1741 were not repeated. Control of Scotland was tighter than ever before and influence over

Cornwall was re-established. The Duke of Newcastle estimated the ministerial majority after the election at over 120, a figure which was sufficient to pass government measures through the Commons. The King, in spite of his humiliation at their hands, settled down to recognizing the advantages of cooperation with the Pelhams: military security and political tranquillity at home which would allow him to concentrate on foreign affairs.

The ministry of Henry Pelham might have been threatened – as Walpole's had been – by continued war. The signing of the Treaty of Aix-la-Chapelle in 1748 lifted that threat and went some way towards resolving the issues at stake in the European war, but it was little more than a temporary truce in the imperial rivalry between Britain and the Bourbon powers in India, the West Indies and North America. In the domestic arena, however, it enabled Henry Pelham to apply himself, as Walpole had done, to a policy of peace, low taxation and financial reform.

Indeed, the years of Henry Pelham's administration are reminiscent in certain respects of those of Sir Robert Walpole. Secure in the confidence of the King and dominant in the House of Commons, Pelham's was an old corps administration which had nothing to fear from the parliamentary opposition. He was untroubled by the Tories who, as a party, were leaderless and now in terminal decline. Thus they welcomed overtures from Frederick, Prince of Wales, the main focus of opposition in these years. His support in the House of Commons was impressive, steadily increasing from around 20 after the General Election of 1747 to around 60 at the time of the Prince's death in 1751. This alliance between the Prince and the Tories aroused considerable interest among contemporaries. Either in this reign or the next, the Prince promised to end their political proscription and return them to the rewards of political service for which they had yearned for so long. His death destroyed the expectations of the Tory party. After the death of Frederick the importance of the opposition diminished. It was now led by the Duke of Bedford[19] and a few friends who shifted their political allegiance to the King's second son, the hero of Culloden, the Duke of Cumberland. The Duke was a military man with a military reputation, and a faintly militaristic air clung to him. Consequently, for the rest of the administration opposition acquired a threatening and vaguely illegitimate character.

More dangerous to the administration than the antics of the opposition were its own internal divisions. The Duke of Newcastle was obsessively jealous of his fellow Secretaries of State who, one by one, resigned: Harrington in 1746,[20] Chesterfield in 1748 and Bedford in 1751. Even the normally patient Henry Pelham was infuriated by Newcastle's behaviour, and it took all of the conciliatory arts of the Earl of Hardwicke to minimize these antagonisms. William Pitt remained in the administration as Paymaster General, where he quietly devoted himself to reforms within that office. On occasion, however, he could rouse himself to oppose his own government, especially on the reduction of the navy. These problems were annoying, yet little more than minor irritants to one of the most secure and stable administrations of the eighteenth century.

Like Walpole, Henry Pelham and his brother had as their primary diplomatic objective the preservation of peace in Europe rather than the pursuit of a grand imperial strategy. Henry Pelham has been roundly criticized for running down both the army – from over 50 000 to 19 000 men – and the navy – from over 50 000 to 10 000 – after the Treaty of Aix-la-Chapelle. Together with the Duke of Newcastle, he is accused of disregarding France's active preparations for the next round in the worldwide struggle for empire between the two countries, and of underestimating the importance of her provocative actions, such as the fortification of Dunkirk and the erection of a string of forts between Canada and Louisiana. Such criticisms, mostly made with the benefit of hindsight, overlook two factors. First, British public opinion demanded a period of peace after nearly a decade of inconclusive warfare. How would the public have reacted to a belligerent policy? And how sensible would such a policy have been until Britain had completed the negotiation of a system of continental alliances against France? Second, the restoration of the nation's finances could not be achieved overnight. Without it, the victories of the Seven Years War may not have been possible.

Pelham had seen with horror that Britain had become financially overstretched during the War of the Austrian Succession. He brought down annual expenditure from £12 million per year to £7 million, with a reduction in the Land Tax from 4s. to 3s. in the £ by 1749 and to 2s. by 1752. Furthermore, he reduced the capital on the national debt. This had increased from £46 million in 1739 to £77 million in 1748, with an increase in the annual interest charge from £2 million to £3 million. During the war he had started to shift the burden of debt from the City of London to the public. By 1748 no less than £25 million of stock was held by private investors at a rate of 4 per cent. At the expense of some unpopularity with the investing public, Pelham managed to coax the rate down to 3 per cent.

Pelham's administration was also notable for the passage of a number of measures which appeared, perhaps, of more importance to contemporaries than to posterity. Chesterfield's reform of the calendar adopted the Gregorian calendar, thus bringing Britain into line with the rest of Europe at the cost of ignoring the 11-day difference between the two calendars. The measure was carried in the face of much popular hostility. It was not only anxious mobs demanding 'give us back our 11 days' who had their doubts about the measure. Those involved with calculating wages, salaries, leases, rents and, not least, almanacs and calendars had their own reasons for irritation. Hardwicke's Marriage Act of 1753 ended the disgrace of 'fleet' or clandestine marriages. The Act required the consent of guardians for the marriage of minors, imposed residence requirements and stipulated the calling of banns. Perhaps the most significant of these measures was Pelham's Jewish Naturalization Act of 1753. This largely technical measure created a storm of racialist anger and had to be repealed a year later. It was not merely the vitriolic xenophobia aroused by the Tories but the orchestrated propaganda of City interests which caused an anxious Henry Pelham, with one eye on the general election of 1754, to relent. Finally, the government passed a number of minor measures which cumulatively represent something more than the moderate, enlightened reformism with which he is normally credited. A cluster of reforms stimulated the export trade of Ireland (wool) and Scotland (linens), facilitated trade with Africa and India, encouraged the colonization of Nova Scotia and promoted the British fishing industry against Dutch competition. Another series of measures sought to deal with the current crime wave not only by more severe punishments, especially for murder, robbery and prostitution, but by setting the poor to work and by regulating places of public entertainment. Moreover, the Gin Act of 1751 did much to reduce the consumption of cheap spirits. Finally, the founding of the British Museum in 1753 marks a long-term vision of the cultural place of *Britain* in the Europe of the Enlightenment. Few, if any, eighteenth-century administrations can boast a record of reform to match that of Henry Pelham. In such areas of national life he achieved more than Sir Robert Walpole, although he was in power for much less than half the time. Some of these measures, moreover, suggest that Pelham was much more than a spokesman for the forces of oligarchy in Hanoverian society, and that his motives included the protection and enhancement of the interests of large numbers of his fellow-citizens.

Henry Pelham died in March 1754. Not for the first, or the last, time a long and stable administration was succeeded by a period of ministerial confusion. The Duke of Newcastle assumed the leadership of the government which from the start lacked both cohesion and direction. In some respects this was surprising because the general election, which shortly followed Pelham's death, resulted in a majority of around 200. Indeed, Newcastle wrote in May 1754: 'This Parliament is good beyond my expectations, and I believe there are more Whigs in it, and generally well disposed Whigs, than in any Parliament since the revolution.' There were by now only just over 100 Tories and fewer than 50 opposition Whigs, mostly Bedford's group, to confront over 350 supporters of the administration. But who was to lead them in the Commons? The precedents of the Walpole and Pelham ministries suggested very strongly that the First Lord of the Treasury should sit in the Commons, but Newcastle could not bear to cede the leadership either to Fox[21] or to Pitt, who had to be content with relatively inferior offices. Pitt had not allowed his post as Paymaster of the Forces to prevent him from attacking the ministry for its excessive concern for Hanover, its policy of subsidizing European allies (Russia and Hesse-Cassel) and its reluctance to confront France outside the continent of Europe. Together with two other senior members, Legge[22] and George Grenville, he was dismissed from the government in November 1755.

By this time, the diplomatic situation was rapidly deteriorating. Both in India and in North America, hostilities between France and Britain were breaking out. The government seemed incapable of defending British interests with the force and energy which the situation demanded, while Newcastle spent precious time trying to construct alliances with which to defend Hanover. Uncertainty in diplomacy was matched by hesitation and disagreement within the government. Gradually the government's massive majorities began to melt away. When it became clear that Austria had neither the will nor the intention to defend Hanover, Newcastle was forced to reverse the traditional Austrian alliance in favour of an alliance with Frederick the Great of Prussia. This drove Austria into the arms of France. After this 'Diplomatic Revolution' Britain and France declared war in May 1756. The French had already occupied Minorca, but Admiral Byng's failure to defeat the French fleet off the island led at the end of June to its humiliating surrender to the French and to the celebrated court martial of Byng and his subsequent death sentence. A protracted, full-scale war against France could not now be avoided.

None of this met the widespread domestic criticism that Britain appeared to be sacrificing her commercial and colonial interests in favour of continental entanglements designed to safeguard Hanover. Demands for the court martial of Byng thus broadened out into wholesale onslaughts against the government. In October 1756 Fox resigned. A month later Newcastle followed him, declaring that he had no need of numbers in the House of Commons, only 'hands and tongues'. Two days later Pitt became Secretary of State in an administration headed by the Duke of Devonshire, declaring: 'I am sure I can save this country and nobody else can.' For four months the Devonshire–Pitt administration struggled to establish itself in the face not only of the King's dislike of Pitt but also of the suspicion with which the old corps viewed him. Pitt's attempts to save Byng did nothing to enhance his popularity, and in April 1757 the King dismissed him. The outburst of public sympathy for Pitt which followed was never as widespread nor as spontaneous as his followers, and some historians, have believed.[23] Within weeks of taking office, in fact, Pitt had been defending the electorate of Hanover and advocating the virtues of the Prussian alliance, both of which had earlier been the objects of his withering invective. Nevertheless, the 'rain' of golden boxes conferring the freedom of 18 cities, not least that of the City of London, on Pitt was enough to raise him to the status of a patriotic hero in whose person was encapsulated the old Country values of honesty and virtue. It mattered little that most of these boxes came from reliable centres of Toryism and from places in which the opposition Whigs had influence. Pitt's advocacy of naval and colonial warfare against the Bourbon powers caught the imagination of the country in general, of the City and of the Tories. In June 1757 Pitt was back in office as Secretary of State but this time in alliance with Newcastle, who took the Treasury. The Pitt–Newcastle coalition, one of the most glorious administrations in British history, was born. Newcastle and his friends enjoined the loyalty of the old corps Whigs while Pitt rallied the Tories, the independent Country gentlemen and the Country Whigs. Room was found for Fox, who came in as Paymaster General, and for Bedford, who became Lord Lieutenant of Ireland. The new administration was broad-based and commanded the overwhelming majority of political opinion. In this way the pressure of external events had since 1754 broken the political domination of the old corps and created a much broader political structure. How William Pitt would use the political power and the mounting patriotism which underpinned his administration the waiting country would soon discover.

Notes

1. Nineteenth-century radical and Whig writers were particularly critical of the Whig regime, denouncing its repressive and inegalitarian features. Some recent writers have confirmed these criticisms, not least E.P. Thompson, in *Whigs and Hunters: The Origins of the Black Act* (1975) and Roy Porter, in *English Society in the Eighteenth Century* (1982). Others, however, have been much more balanced in their judgements; see W.A. Speck, *Stability and Strife: England 1714–60* (1977).
2. In early 1714 Oxford attempted unsuccessfully to persuade the Pretender to renounce his Catholicism. Meanwhile, Bolingbroke launched his own separate negotiations with him. Even before the death of Anne, the Tories had become fatally divided into two factions.

3. Charles Townshend (1674–1738) was an erstwhile Tory who switched to the Whig Junto. He had been a firm supporter of Occasional Conformity and was one of the negotiators of the Act of Union in 1706–07. On the accession of George I he became secretary for the Northern Department and was closely involved in the suppression of the '15. He refused to accompany the King to Hanover in 1716 and lost his place. He was soon restored, and by 1721 was once again Secretary for the Northern Department. His foreign policy in the 1720s eventually brought him into conflict with Walpole, leading to his resignation in 1730. James, 1st Earl Stanhope (1673–1721), served under Marlborough and became commander of the British forces in Spain in 1708. He was one of the managers of Sacheverell's impeachment (1710) and became a leader of the Whig opposition in the last years of the reign of Anne. He took a leading role in the establishment of the Hanoverian Succession.
4. According to its terms, a capital offence was commited if a crowd of 12 or more failed to disperse within one hour of a magistrate's order.
5. Charles, 3rd Earl of Sunderland (1674–1722), one of the great architects of the Hanoverian Succession. His marriage to Anne Churchill in 1700 won him the support of the Duke of Marlborough. As Secretary of State, 1706–10, he was hated by Tories, who tried to impeach him after his fall from office. Thereafter, he became a close ally of the house of Hanover. His apparently excessive zeal consigned him to the post of Viceroy of Ireland in 1714.
6. In 1714 Walpole (1676–1745) was only 38 years of age and obtained the office of Paymaster General, a tribute to his reputation for financial skill. In the ministerial reshuffle of 1715 he became Chancellor of the Exchequer.
7. See G. Holmes, *Britain in the First Age of Party 1680–1750*, (1987), p. 85.
8. Speck, *Stability and Strife*, p. 212.
9. Thomas Pelham-Holles (1693–1768) was at first a supporter of Townshend but in 1717 went over to Sunderland. He became Secretary of State for the Southern Department in 1724. He was further to become one of the most influential and powerful Whig leaders of the century.
10. For a discussion of church–state relations see below, p. 6–8, 29–30.
11. D. Hayton, 'Walpole and Ireland', in J. Black, ed., *Britain in the Age of Walpole*, (1984), p. 119.
12. G. Holmes and D. Szecki, *The Age of Oligarchy: Pre-Industrial Britain, 1722–83* (1993), p. 216.
13. Sir William Pulteney (1684–1764), MP 1705–42, Secretary of War, 1714–17, was a close ally of Walpole during the resignations of 1717 but was disappointed at not being offered a place.
14. Daniel Pulteney (?1674–1731) had become a Lord of the Admiralty under Walpole in 1721 but was always a loyal supporter of Sunderland. He went into opposition with his brother and remained one of its mainstays until his death in 1731. Sir William Wyndham (1687–1740) had held high office in the Tory ministry of 1710–14 and had been arrested for complicity in the '15. A leader of the Tory opposition to Walpole, he retained strong Jacobite sympathies.
15. Shippen (1673–1743) was the leading Tory-Jacobite in the House of Commons, sitting for various constituencies between 1707 and 1743. He was sent to the Tower in 1718 for his comments about George I, 'a stranger to our language and constitution'. But he kept his hands clean during the Atterbury plot. Almost singlehandedly he opposed the increased Civil List for George II in 1727. He retreated from politics in the 1730s, disliking the questionable consistency of the opposition Whigs.
16. Lord Chesterfield (1694–1773) was one of the foremost wits and letter writers of his day. His stormy relationship with Walpole interrupted his diplomatic career in 1733 and he opposed the Excise Bill. Lord Cobham (1669–1749) served under

Marlborough, but his opposition to the Excise scheme led to his dismissal from his regiment. He joined the 'boy Patriots' but later allied himself with the Pelhams. His real claim to fame was the rebuilding of Stowe and his patronage of the arts. George Lyttleton (1709–73) was MP for Okehampton from 1735 to 1756 and, together with Richard Grenville (1711–79), MP for various constituencies between 1734 and 1752, and William Pitt (1708–78), MP for various constituencies from 1735 to 1766, formed the leadership of Cobham's Cubs, an active and virulent opposition phalanx. The three of them made their maiden speeches on the same day, 22 April 1735, when they spoke in favour of a place bill.

17. Henry Pelham (1695–1754) was the brother of the Duke of Newcastle and, like him, sided with Walpole against Carteret. In the 1730s, when he was Paymaster General, he acted as Walpole's deputy, and became regarded as the minister's heir apparent. In 1742 he took over from Sir Robert the leadership of the old corps in the lower House. William Cavendish, 4th Duke of Devonshire (1720–64) was one of the great aristocrats of the Whig supremacy, known as the Marquis of Hartington until he assumed the peerage in 1751. He was Lord Lieutenant of Ireland in 1755–56 and Prime Minister 1756–57 in the Pitt–Devonshire government. Philip Yorke, 1st Earl of Hardwicke (1690–1764) was the legal expert of the old corps and a distinguished Solicitor-general (1720), Attorney-general (1724) and Lord Chancellor (1737).

18. The political doctrine of 'Broad-bottom' implies the formation of either a government or an opposition upon as broad and wide a basis as possible. 'Broad-bottom' further implies negotiation, consensus and coalition, leading to a government of national union. The purpose of 'Broad-bottom', at least as announced by Bolingbroke's *Letter on the Spirit of Patriotism* (1736), was to establish the dynasty on as broad and solid a foundation as possible, to inaugurate the reign of virtue and to destroy corruption. The idea was further developed by Bolingbroke, in *The Idea of a Patriot King* in 1738, as a manifesto for Prince Frederick's accession to the throne.

19. John, 4th Duke of Bedford (1710–71), had joined the opposition to Walpole and served in Henry Pelham's ministry, resigning in 1751.

20. William Stanhope, 1st Earl of Harrington (?1690–1756), Secretary of State 1730–41, 1744–46.

21. Henry Fox, 1st Lord Holland (1705–74), father of Charles James Fox. Fox had been an MP since 1738 and a loyal supporter of Walpole in his later years. He had been Secretary at War during Henry Pelham's ministry and joined Newcastle's cabinet in December 1754, becoming Secretary of State and leader of the House of Commons a few months later.

22. Henry Legge, 1st Lord Dartmouth (1706–64), an office-holder since the mid-1730s and an MP for various constituencies between 1740 and 1764. He was Treasurer of the Navy (1749–54) and Chancellor of the Exchequer (April 1754–November 1755).

23. Many historians have repeated Horace Walpole's memorable phrase that 'for some weeks it rained gold boxes', but in truth, Pitt and his friends received the freedom of only 18 cities. See P. Langford, 'William Pitt and Public Opinion, 1757', *English Historical Review*, 88 (1973), pp. 54–80.

The social foundations of the early Hanoverian regime, 1714–1757

The identity of Britain

Between 1714 and 1757 the texture of the British state[1] was tightening politically, socially and culturally. This was a European development, as monarchs and ministers centralized their territories and rationalized their administrations. Although British rule was steadily enforced over Scotland and Ireland, these sub-nations retained a strong sense of their own separate identities, valuing highly their own traditions, institutions and privileges. In such a composite state as Britain, sentiments of national identity were bound to be complex. It is too simplistic to think in terms of English dominion over Celtic nations. The Scots and the Welsh did not see themselves as Celtic victims of Anglo-Saxon domination. Their languages were very different indeed, while the Lowland Scots and some sections of the Welsh population were not even Celtic. There were many internal differences and massive regional and local cultural variations. For example, the Lowland Scots and the northern English shared many of the same behavioural patterns, as distinct from those of the Highland Scots. In this sense Scotland was not one nation but two. We should also resist the temptation to assume that English dominion was constantly resented and bitterly resisted. It is surely significant that very few of the Welsh and Irish thought of Wales and Ireland existing apart from England and, to judge from the patchy support for the Jacobite cause in 1715 and 1745, not many Scots.

During these years a sense of British identity was continuing to display itself.[2] There was nothing new in this. Nevertheless, Professor Colley's recent work has memorably charted this development after 1707. What follows is my own reconstruction of the development of a British identity, albeit one which owes much to her work.[3] The following account highlights four elements which, in their very different ways, contributed to the strengthening of a British national identity in this period: warfare, religion, political culture and unity.

First, the years of war against France between 1689 and 1713 and then again between 1740 and 1763 promoted, if intermittently, an intense and widespread British sentiment. France was the national enemy, presenting serious military and political dangers to the cohesion of the unitary state of

Britain. The stakes in these wars were high: the political and military leadership of Europe, the control of trade and, ultimately, the future of empire. The collapse of Jacobitism, followed by the spectacular military successes of the Seven Years War (1756–63), created powerful sentiments of British triumphalism and national euphoria. The armed services became a melting-pot for the peoples of Britain. By the middle of the century one-quarter of the officers in the British army were Scots. Indeed, the English were actually outnumbered in the officer corps. This rearming of the Celtic kingdoms is a development of critical importance in the history of the British state, and one which was unlikely to be reversed. In the case of Scotland, indeed, it enabled the Scots to recapture the heroism of their former martial traditions by superimposing the military valour of the past upon the present. In this sense, Britain was a site in which Scotland and, to a growing extent, Ireland, could recapture, rewrite and even reinvent their former national glories.

Second, although warfare was perhaps the most important single factor in conditioning the sense of Britishness that developed in the first half of the eighteenth century, it was given moral justification through being linked to the force of religion. Early British national feeling was essentially Protestant feeling. Britain was a Protestant nation, favoured by God, a bastion of liberty in a Europe dominated by the Catholic powers of France and Spain, a nation which had pioneered unique political processes and forms, a nation blessed with prosperity and enterprise, to whom famine and dearth were unknown. The history of British Protestantism since the Reformation could be narrated as a continuing struggle against the papacy and the Bourbon powers and, most recently, against James II, Louis XIV and the Jacobites. At the popular level, hatred of Roman Catholicism, stoked continually in the press and from the pulpit and maintained by regular doses of festival and ritual, united the mass of the people. This theme, while illuminating many aspects of popular feeling, should not be pressed too far. After all, what did Protestantism mean? Protestantism was a very broad church indeed, which meant different things in different parts of Britain. In Ireland, for example, it implied the need to safeguard the fruits of the Glorious Revolution against a hostile, Catholic majority. In Scotland, on the other hand, it implied the Presbyterian ideal of rebellious nonconformity. The form that it took varied widely, both between and within the sub-nations of Britain. Furthermore, by the middle of the eighteenth century many members of the educated elite were coming to distance themselves from distasteful displays of religious intolerance. Had not the Irish and English Jacobites proved their loyalty to the dynasty during the '45? Many Britons were coming to pride themselves upon their nation's religious pluralism, its tolerance of different denominations.

This brings us to the third element in the emergence of Britishness in the eighteenth century, the political culture of the propertied politically conscious part of the population. In the eighteenth century the sense of a British political identity was more than a vague cultural tradition; it had real political meaning. It related to the structure of the state and to the circumstances which in the recent past had fashioned it. Indeed, the event that established the context for the long eighteenth century, the Glorious Revolution, had been a seismic event of British proportions. But it, too, meant different things to different people. Groups appropriated one version or another of the

Glorious Revolution for their own use. For Whigs throughout Britain, the Glorious Revolution had achieved constitutional monarchy and safeguarded the rights of Parliament. For Tories, the Glorious Revolution had preserved and guaranteed the Anglican establishment. For Protestant Dissenters in England it had guaranteed their religious freedom. For Ulster Protestants the events of the Revolution, especially the siege of Derry, had highlighted their valour and their collective identity. For radical Whigs the Revolution had represented the victory of liberty over tyranny. In the middle of the eighteenth century the legacy of the Glorious Revolution might be looking a little ragged, contaminated (as many thought it had become) by corrupt politicians, but there remained a powerful consensus which reverenced the *British* (not the English) constitution and worshipped at the shrine of *British* rights and liberties.

At the same time, and fourth, a British elite was beginning to emerge as the landed classes from all parts of Britain began to fuse into a self-conscious, British ruling class. A British or a britannicized elite was emerging, increasingly uniform in its values, lifestyles, educational and marriage patterns and social and political ambitions. The anglicization of the elite in Wales, Scotland and Ireland forged a vital sense of common identity. Rapid turnover in the ownership of estates created a highly mobile market in land. Given the continuing status of landownership and the profits to be made from land, members of the landed classes were prepared to buy estates in any part of Britain. Moreover, as more Irish, Scottish and Welsh members of the landed classes sought and found employment in London and, later, in imperial service, they forged common social and cultural styles and indulged in intermarriage on a massive scale. By the 1770s contemporaries had begun to refer to a 'British' ruling class.

What did 'Britishness' mean? At one level it involved an acceptance of the geographical cohesion of the political units which made up Britain, and a love of their physical characteristics. These qualities were represented in the popularity of maps, atlases and the flood of tourist literature which started to appear during the first half of the eighteenth century. At another it meant an awareness of belonging to Britain and a pride in her cultural traditions, her poetry, literature, and music, whether high- or lowbrow.

Assumptions of British superiority over her neighbours, however, were still at an early stage of development. British art was still regarded as inferior to that of the Continent, and many of the designers, artists, decorators and, especially, sculptors employed in country houses flocked in from Europe. The British elite was not yet culturally britannicized. Its members revelled in Italian opera, imitated continental (especially French) manners and exhibited themselves in dress and hair styles which owed more to Paris than they did to London. Worst of all, the Hanoverian court acted as a conduit for foreign taste and influence. George I, for example, prided himself upon his patronage of Handel. Indeed, the cosmopolitanism of the court and of aristocratic lifestyles in the first half of the eighteenth century provoked satire, ridicule, and considerable amusement among the masses. There a more bullish type of Britishness reigned. The popular self-image which Britons liked to play up to when they prided themselves on being British was of a tough, even a warlike, people, proud and heroic, yet, at the same time, loving freedom and liberty, living life under the law with everyone equal before the law. Above all, Britain was a land of religious freedom where different religious denominations lived in peace.

Much of this strongly resembles English cultural triumphalism, and it is sometimes difficult to detect the differences between the British and the English versions. Against Professor Colley's version of a growing sense of British identity as something distinct from a growing sense of English identity, it is salutary to underline the role of aggressive *English* nationalism in the creation of a great *British* synthesis. On occasion, what may be casually seen as Britishness was little more than a sense of Englishness.[4] Contemporaries were conscious of some of these confusions. Some English people resented the terms 'Britain' and 'British' replacing 'England' and 'English', and begrudged closer relationships with the much-disliked Scots and their associations with Jacobitism. They were, too, contemptuous of the Irish, a people whom they thought to be little better than barbarians. We should not, therefore, simplify a complex process by arguing that a sense of Britishness was superimposed on English, Scottish and Irish identities in the eighteenth century. Nor was Britishness a straightforward blending or merging of these separate identities. A range of Britishness was forged by an assertive English imperialism, political, economic and social, but which yet made space for a continuing assertion of Scottish and Irish national feelings. In my view Professor Colley gives too little attention to English versions of national identity.

In any case, it is dangerous to generalize about a single 'national' opinion, in view of powerful local diversity. For example, the gust of sentiment that did so much to sweep Walpole from power was not uniform. Nor should it be misinterpreted as an early expression of British imperial attitudes.[5] More likely, although such sentiments were sincerely held in some mercantile circles, at the popular level they probably represented a much more traditional expression of anti-Catholic aggression. Popular British imperialism was not to be seen for another generation.

Scotland after the Union maintained her own sense of national identity but within a British framework. The post-Union state included a number of features which safeguarded Scottish uniqueness, the legal and educational systems and, most of all, the Kirk. Yet, although the political incorporation of Scotland worked reasonably well in institutional terms, it failed to safeguard the British state from the ultimate reality of rebellion. The shock of the '15 underlined the dangers of Scottish separatism. After its suppression, Scotland could be persuaded to accept the Hanoverian Succession only through close and judicious management from London together with a careful distribution of offices. The poverty of the Scottish aristocracy enabled England to draw them into its orbit of patronage and influence. By the 1720s many members of the Scottish nobility were physically abandoning their country as they sought residence as well as education, culture and marriage south of the border. At the same time, the Lowlands were being drawn into the economic system of England by the dramatic commercial expansion of the first half of the century which benefited the merchants and gentry. After 1707 Scottish trade was drawn towards England rather than Europe, stimulating the production of cattle for food at first in the border counties and then more widely throughout England.

More importantly for the future of Britain, the English reaction to the '45 led to the restructuring of Anglo-Scottish relations and, indeed, to the restructuring of Highland society. This reaction has often been depicted in harsh terms, and has been severely criticized by many Scottish writers.[6] Coming in the wake of a rebellion, however, the terms are at least understandable. Thus, it was inevitable that the estates of the leaders of the rebellion would be seized (they were restored to their original owners in 1784). It was natural that the Scottish Episcopalian clergy – many of them Jacobite – should be required to take an oath of allegiance to the crown. What is less easy to understand is the attack on the Scottish way of life, such as the suppression of Highland dress. This, perhaps, can best be explained by the desire of the English to render another Jacobite rising impossible. Consequently, two acts were passed in May and June 1747 abolishing the hereditable jurisdictions of the Highland chiefs and their right of claiming military service from their tacksmen, or junior officers. But the safeguarding of Scotland was not simply a military question. It involved issues of Scottish national loyalty, and thus of national identity. The '45 had shown that Jacobitism was not sufficiently strong to form the basis of a permanent and viable sense of Scottish nationality. The only available alternative version was that of maintaining Scottish national identity within a British framework. The Duke of Argyll, the effective Scottish viceroy from 1746 until his death in 1761, ably assisted by Lord Milton, planned to build a peaceful, prosperous Scotland which would be loyal to the British crown of her own free will. The money from the forfeited estates was to be used to stimulate agriculture, commerce and industry. All of this took time and the effects were not seen overnight. By the 1760s, however, the economy of the Highlands was responding to encouragement and competition. This process was greatly assisted by the Turnpike Act of 1751, following which the construction of over 800 miles of road and 1000 bridges did much to break down the isolation of the Highlands.

If in Scotland the clan system enabled Jacobitism to survive long into the eighteenth century, in Ireland such structures of resistance were not available. In Ireland the mass of the peasantry remained sullen and disaffected, but they did not rise in 1745. The requirements for revolt did not exist in early Hanoverian Ireland. Poverty and inertia were not enough. The existence of an Irish Parliament at least permitted the expression of protest and grievance. The penal laws were enforced patchily and tended not to disturb the faith of the majority. Political stability gave rise to modest economic progress. It was not so much the peasant masses that the Anglo-Irish minority feared but the rapidly expanding Catholic middle class and the Presbyterian Scots, who had settled in Ulster in the middle of the seventeenth century. The Irish Catholic landowning class had been reduced to insignificance by the seizure of its land and by penal restrictions placed on them in 1704. Unlike some members of its Scottish counterparts, it had no stomach for rebellion. Before the 1790s, moreover, a Catholic nationalist movement did not exist.[7] Indeed, the modern conception of a Gaelic, Catholic nation is a product of the late eighteenth century. The agencies of nationalism were feeble in the mid-eighteenth century. The Catholic hierarchy was weak and dispersed; furthermore, the Gaelic language was in steep decline. Little more than one-half of the population spoke it in the later eighteenth century. Even the Catholic church abandoned it. English was taught in the schools and English was normally the language of commerce. Traditional Irish culture was only safeguarded by a particularly elitist group of bards and poets; much of it was not available to the masses. It was no accident that the real threat to the peace and stability of Hanoverian Britain in the first half of the eighteenth century came from Scotland, not Ireland.

Moreover, there is some evidence of an emerging British identity in Ireland. There is continuing evidence both that Ireland was benefiting modestly from her participation in British imperial commerce and that she was by contemporary standards a relatively settled and ordered, if junior, partner within a broader British jurisdiction, even if that fragile prosperity remained dependent upon Britain and British trade. At the cultural level, Ireland shared in the festive calendar of royal birthdays and was more than ready to participate in celebrations of British military and naval victories. Eighteenth-century Dublin was a prosperous British as well as Irish city, many of its buildings and statues testaments to an emerging imperial identity. Nevertheless, this theme should not be pressed too far in regard to the first half of the eighteenth century. For example, the term 'British' was rarely used in Ireland; other terms, such as 'Protestant Irish' or 'Ulster Scot', were more familiar. It was the lower clergy of the Church of Ireland who regarded themselves in an imperial sense as 'Irish Protestants'. The bishops were, and were perceived to be, Anglican, and thus English rather than British. Yet even when these reservations have been noted, it is likely that even the Irish Catholics were unable to imagine a political arrangement that did not involve the supremacy of the British crown in Ireland.

By the middle of the century, then, a political experiment of great complexity was proceeding, and with some success. The political, and to some extent economic and social, incorporation by England of her neighbours was being accomplished, and this was accompanied by a growing sense of a collective British identity, albeit still an incomplete one. But this did not occur at the expense of sub-British identities. Indeed, it is possible that both a British sense of identity and a Scots and an Irish sense of identity were all strengthening at the same time. Indeed, it was perfectly possible to retain a sense of Irishness or Scottishness, but to do so within a consciously British context. After all, national identities are never finished or complete, to be thereafter fixed and unchanging. They are much more complex and sensitive, especially in societies with powerful local variations and, not least, persisting religious differences.

The ruling order: oligarchy and deference

Like most regimes in human history, eighteenth-century Britain was an oligarchy (i.e. rule by a few) in which power and wealth were most unevenly distributed. Britain's oligarchy was an *aristocratic* oligarchy and after the defeat of the Tories, increasingly a *Whig, aristocratic* oligarchy. In the subsequent decades, the aristocracy proceeded to confirm its wealth and its power. On any calculation, the aristocratic estates prospered during the eighteenth century. Not many of them were broken up or sold off, even in part. In many cases, the pattern was towards consolidation, as the process of enclosure clearly demonstrates, especially in some southern, eastern and midlands counties of England. Great houses became richer, finer and more opulent. Althorp, Blenheim, Bowood, Castle Howard and Petworth remain towering monuments to the health and wealth of the aristocratic estates of Hanoverian England.

There were many reasons for this. Since about 1680 the proportion of the land held by the aristocracy had been increasing at the expense of the gentry. Indeed, the growth in the size of the great estates is one of the characteristic features of this period. According to Professor Habbakuk,[8] the fall in agricultural prices of the late seventeenth and early eighteenth centuries and the incidence of the Land Tax induced landed proprietors to farm and to administer their estates more profitably. Great estate owners were better able than their smaller neighbours to meet the challenges of falling agricultural prices and declining rent yields. Furthermore, the operation of the strict settlement (which protected the unity of an estate from the attentions of spendthrift heirs) prevented the fragmentation of the great estates. The use of mortgages to purchase further properties and the availability of cheap loans (3–5 per cent) to finance improvements worked to the same end. Moreover, while access to government office, and the profits that went with it, enabled the aristocracy to prosper, high wartime taxation (1689–1713) hit the gentry with devastating effect. Finally, the growing status of Parliament, and of the prestige of owning or representing a county seat, gave a further push towards the consolidation of holdings. Coke of Norfolk represented that county for four decades, and subordinated the administration of his estate to that end.

Support for the 'consolidation' thesis is also to be found in Wales. Although aristocrats were thin on the ground in Wales, the behaviour of the greater gentry – families like the Bulkeleys of Anglesey, the Mostyns of Flint and, most of all, the Wynns of Wynnstay – conformed to the pattern identified by Habbakuk. Such families aped the English aristocracy with the restoration and the enlargement of their country houses and the landscaping of their grounds. They sought to exploit their estates and the resources that lay in them. In Wales, moreover, the smaller gentry seem to have been victims not merely of economic forces favouring consolidation but of a statistically alarming failure of direct male heirs. Estates then passed to females or to distant male heirs, many of them resident in England. The position in the Lowlands, but not the Highlands, of Scotland also confirms the broad outlines of Habbakuk's thesis. There the great landowners increasingly monopolized political and economic leadership. Down to 1747, indeed, they enjoyed their own hereditable jurisdictions. In Ireland the position of the Anglo-Irish aristocracy stabilized during the first half of the eighteenth century. This was a period of prosperity in Irish agriculture, and few demands for significant change were heard. Between 1720 and 1780 rents paid to Irish landlords tripled (those paid to absentee landlords doubled in the same period).

There are, however, a number of important technical difficulties with the theory of the consolidation of the great estates. The strict settlement was applied to only one half of estates in England. Even where it did apply, it was not always the major factor in building up the estate. Furthermore, mortgages were an unlikely source of funding for further property purchases because the interest rate payable on the mortgage was likely to exceed the probable return on the purchased property. Furthermore, although some families did prosper from government office, the vast majority did not. After 1714, indeed, non-Whig families were excluded for political reasons from the really profitable offices.

Although there is much of value in the thesis of the rise of the great estates at the expense of the smaller, it is doubtful if such a general theory could apply everywhere. Where a resident aristocracy existed there was a clear tendency for great estates to grow at the expense of smaller proprietors. This was certainly the case in the Midlands and in the Thames valley, parts of the south-east and some parts of the north-west, but this may not always have been for the reasons advanced by Habbakuk. It may have been the capacity of larger producers to survive the low prices and overproduction of the period 1730–50. It may have been the ability of the larger proprietors to take greater, long-term advantage of the boom years of 1750 to 1780 than their smaller counterparts. Furthermore, we should not ignore the wealth that many aristocratic families derived from sources other than land. Many landlords ('fundlords', as William Cobbett called them) took healthy profits from their holdings in government stock, the Bank of England and the great commercial companies. Many of them profited from the urban property and estates that they owned, especially in London but also in rising provincial centres. If the Westminster family profited enormously from its property in Belgravia, Mayfair and Pimlico, the Duke of Norfolk and the Wentworth-Fitzwilliam family did so on a formidable scale in Sheffield. Others profited from the industrial developments of the time. Many estates contained valuable mineral deposits, such as the coal which inspired the Duke of Bridgwater to create the Manchester Ship Canal. Furthermore, many families profited from skilfully arranged marriages. A well-endowed heiress might bring with her a fortune to rival any that might be made from painfully achieved agricultural improvement. Consequently, we find a very mixed picture. The thesis of a rise of the great estates can, therefore, be applied to particular parts of Britain but sometimes for reasons other than those advanced by Habbakuk.

Were the gentry the victims of the rise of the great estates? There is massive contemporary evidence that they felt the effects of falling prices, rising rents and wartime levels of Land Tax payments. With these trends in mind, Joseph Massie in 1760 calculated that only 480 gentry families had incomes over £2000 per annum, that 640 had around £1000 per annum and that 2400 had £600–£800 per annum, while no fewer than 14 400 had to maintain gentility on a paltry £200–£400 per annum. Massie's figures are impressive, but overlook the possibility that many of these families had income from other sources – from financial investments, from forestry, from industry or from commercial activities. If they did not, then they were likely to find themselves struggling to keep up appearances.

As always in these cases, contemporary evidence is not always reliable and the general situation was not straightforward. First, in some parts of the country, in the north-east of England and the Lindsey area of Lincolnshire, in north Wales, Cheshire and Staffordshire and in Devon it is difficult to see that the gentry declined at all. In such places the smaller landowners and even professional men prospered at least as healthily as the peers. Second, although the gentry may have lamented their declining social and economic standing, there is very little evidence that the middling orders were as yet threatening to challenge, still less to displace them. Some merchants and some professional men prospered sufficiently to purchase small estates, but only at the end of the eighteenth century did they start to purchase landed estates on a significant scale. Third, it was not the gentry who were the victims of aristocratic consolidation but those beneath them in the social and economic scale, the freeholders, most of whom did not identify themselves as gentry. One estimate suggests that between 1688 and 1790 their ownership of cultivable land in England dropped from around one-half to around one-third. As for the gentry themselves, it is doubtful that *as a social group* they suffered any drastic decline in their fortunes and certainly not in their numbers. Gregory King identified 4400 families of baronets, knights and esquires at the end of the seventeenth century. In 1802 Colquhoun calculated their number at 6890 and their incomes as ranging from £1500 to £3000. But we need to add to these a proportion of the ambiguous 'gentlemen' whom both authors identify. If we compare King's 'Gentlemen', admittedly a broad and vague category, with Colquhoun's families of 'Gentlemen and Ladies living on incomes' (some of which, of course, would be non-landed incomes) we find an increase from 12 000 to 20 000. Moreover, Colquhoun estimated the average for these incomes at £700 per annum. Overall, then, there must have been something over 15 000 gentry families at the beginning, rising to perhaps 20 000 by the end of the eighteenth century. Indeed, Professor Rule has concluded that there were at least 15 000 such families, 'less elevated but even more essential components of the rural ruling classes than the aristocracy'.[9]

Britain, then was governed by a landed elite of aristocracy and gentry, both of them robust and wealthy, neither in decline nor in serious difficulty as a social group. Indeed, for most inhabitants of the British Isles the local family of the ruling order was more inclined to be a member of the gentry than a member of the aristocracy. In this sense, then, the 'oligarchy' which governed eighteenth-century Britain extended quite far down into the rural propertied classes. Their awareness of themselves as 'the landed interest' together with the mystique of landed property did much to fuse them together. The eighteenth century was awash with literature, painting, architecture and, not least, landscape gardening which idealized its landed elite. Furthermore, no great social gulfs existed between the gentry and the urban elite of the middling orders. Upward social mobility into the gentry was possible, although in the first half of the eighteenth century it remained comparatively rare. The wealthiest merchants and bankers, whether in London or in the provinces, showed as yet little inclination to sink their fortunes into the purchase of a country seat before the middle of the century. Part of the reason for their hesitation was the high price of land, which increased by 50 per cent between 1680 and 1750, and the relative infrequency with which choice estates came on the market. In any case, they preferred to confine themselves to more modest urban residences and to enjoy the life of the urban patrician class. At the same time the gentry, too, were beginning to discover the pleasures of urban living.[10]

How did this rural elite of aristocracy and gentry command the loyalty of its dependants? The authority of the landlord classes could not be imposed by physical coercion; no police force existed, law enforcement usually resting on the voluntary service of householders in the parishes. The Riot Act, passed in 1715, was unwieldy in operation and absolutely useless for dealing with spontaneous, minor disturbances. If the Riot Act was too cumbersome then it is likely, in the view of some historians, that the increase in capital offences – from 50 in 1689 to 200 by 1800 – shows that the law was used as an instrument of coercion. In a society which lacked an effective police force, harsh laws and, indeed, harsh punishments were deemed to be necessary as a deterrent to the threat of popular disorder. However, the extent to which these draconian statutes were actually enforced was very limited.[11]

If authority was to be respected, then power had to be exercised in ways which commanded respect and elicited consent. To some extent, the sheer grandeur and finery of the great house, the flamboyant carriages and dress of its residents, the vast numbers of servants, the scraping and the bowing, all cultivated an instinctive respect for and acceptance of authority. Hierarchy, and consequently, subordination, was everywhere: in manners, in dress, in speech and even inside parish churches in the shape of reserved pews. The consent that was elicited in this way amounted to more than the consequences of awe and fear. For example, the complex rituals associated with the law, its robes and wigs, its fine and archaic language and the calculated drama of gestures of mercy and clemency, may have had the effect of securing popular acceptance of the legal system, its alleged protection of the rights of the subject and the liberty of the individual. It was not just the law. Many people also experienced the operation of hierarchy at first hand during the rituals associated with parliamentary and civic elections. They plunged into the tumultuous mobbery and clamour of the streets as candidates sought popular endorsement from non-voters and voters alike. They observed, even if they did not participate in, the countless processions and dinners, organized according to status and rank. They watched the canvassing of the candidates and they concluded that favours, petitions and advantages could be wrung out of the upper classes. Through such processes, most people evinced a deference that did much to ensure a general acceptance of inequality and thus a legitimation of the power of the political and social elite in Hanoverian society.

Consequently, the exercise of power was something more than arbitrary. If the landed classes believed that they were entitled to protect their property and their power – and none of them doubted it – they also believed that other sections of society had a right to protect theirs. They were still imbued with ideals of service which cannot simply be dismissed as a cynical posture. At the local level this may be described as the practice of 'paternalism': the protection of the community and of the welfare of its inhabitants. In theory, at least, landowners were expected to treat their tenants with generosity and kindness and to behave with Christian mercy towards them, especially during emergencies or in times of want and difficulty. Although we should avoid sentimentality, we should not underestimate the strength of religious motives in the surviving tradition of Christian benevolence, especially among the provincial gentry in this period. There were many examples of negligence, non-residence and downright indifference among them; but the tradition of paternalism survived not only in the minds of landowners but, just as important, in the expectations of their social inferiors. The close involvement of the aristocracy and gentry in the economic and political life of the community was still taken for granted. So, too, was their participation in the religious, social and sporting activities of their people and, to an extent that cannot be measured, in the lives of individual families. The ubiquity of paternalist obligations thus constituted a set of vital social cements in early Hanoverian society.

Outside England, this settled tradition of paternalism cannot be taken for granted. In Wales, landlords seem to have behaved more arbitrarily than their English counterparts, raising rents with little regard for the ability of the tenants to pay, and even using force to remove tenants opposed to the consolidation of estates. Language and, later in the century, religion played upon the cultural differences between the landowners and their dependents. The Scottish aristocracy had the reputation of being particularly ruthless, its tenants-at-will possessing few legal rights. In Ireland, however, the position was complicated by religion and by national prejudice. Even so, traditions of paternalism were still evident, cooperation between tenants and landlords seemingly healthy. The worst examples of exploitation at the hands of non-resident landowners derive more from nationalist legend than from solid historical research.

The deference which social inferiors showed towards the aristocracy was, of course, an unequal relationship and assumed always to be so. Yet it was at the same time a reciprocal or a two-way process. After all, the aristocracy was dependent in many ways upon its social inferiors. It was dependent upon the toil and exertions of its servants. It was dependent, above all, upon the reliability, the industry and the honesty of its tenants for the profitable exploitation of their farms (it was not uncommon in times of dearth for landlords to write off rent arrears). Social inferiors, moreover, were not above manipulating the potentialities of paternalism for their own benefit, making use of its possibilities in the spheres of employment, benevolence and favours. This deferential order was grounded upon inequality and upon dependence but it was also activated by reciprocal processes which delivered mutual, tangible benefits.

The economic and social features of the Hanoverian oligarchy, then, were characterized by pronounced and continuing aristocratic supremacy. On closer inspection, however, we find a complex set of relationships, linking that oligarchy into a much larger, mainly rural, ruling order of smaller proprietors which sank its roots quite deeply into the social structure. There is no question that these relationships were unequal and authoritarian. They could only be maintained by the adoption of a complex variety of social and legal strategies, through the active participation of this elite in the life of local communities, and through the adoption of paternalist responsibilities.

Interestingly, the *political* characteristics of the Hanoverian oligarchy are reasonably consistent with these social and economic features. By any calculation, it was an exclusive and narrow political oligarchy. On Professor Cannon's definition, the 'peerage' remained remarkably stable in numbers during the first half of the century, tending very slightly to increase from

173 in 1700 to 181 in 1760.[12] The political powers of the upper House may have been declining but its members increasingly influenced the return of members of the House of Commons. Peers had some degree of influence over the return of 105 MPs in 1715, 167 in 1747, 207 in 1784, 221 in 1802 and no fewer than 236 in 1807. Aristocrats not only dominated Parliament; they monopolized the highest political offices. Long into the *nineteenth* century most members of most cabinets were peers. During the eighteenth century the number of commoners who sat in any cabinet could easily be counted on the fingers of one hand. Finally, the aristocracy monopolized offices in the central administration of the state, in the army, in the diplomatic service and in the higher reaches of the professions.

This political elite remained an exclusive oligarchy throughout the century. In spite of the common belief that social mobility enabled members of the bourgeoisie to advance into the peerage, there is very little evidence that this occurred. Of the 257 peers alive in 1800, only seven had had no previous connection with the peerage. Indeed, of the 229 peerage creations made between 1700 and 1800 only 23 had no previous connections with the peerage. Furthermore, the House of Commons remained an exclusive institution. Already in 1715, 224 out of 558 MPs were the sons of MPs. By 1754 the figure had reached 294. By then about 400 MPs were related in some way to other MPs past or present. Parliament was thus becoming a remarkably homogeneous assembly. Legal requirements established a further set of common identities. Only the wealthy could sit in Parliament. The Property Qualifications Act of 1711 obliged county MPs to possess real estate worth at least £600 per annum, borough MPs £300.

These figures are particularly valuable, but they focus only upon the peerage and the personnel of the House of Commons. Yet the influence of the former over the latter should not be exaggerated. Peers may have had some degree of influence over the return to Parliament of a large minority of MPs, but it was not always decisive. Indeed, the influence of the peerage over returns to the House of Commons was, strictly speaking, illegal, and even if the legislation remained a dead letter it was never forgotten.[13] In practice such interference was always deeply resented. In most constituencies, indeed, effective influence was distributed among a number of local, usually gentry, families. Furthermore, it would be a serious mistake to exaggerate the power of the oligarchy over local affairs. As we have seen, the personnel of local government was not exclusively aristocratic.[14] Even more significantly, as Dr Langford has recently revealed, they were willing for reasons of practical necessity to transfer responsibility for extensive spheres of administration to members of the middling orders.[15] This was achieved by dozens of acts of Parliament which appointed commissioners with responsibilities for new administrative functions which were financed out of local rates. Many of these involved the reform of the Poor Law and a variety of other urban improvements such as street paving and lighting. Others were of an essentially commercial character, such as enclosures, canals and turnpike trusts. Yet others were of a charitable character, such as the foundation of hospitals. The point to emphasize is that many of the commissioners established by these acts were individuals with only modest property. For example, the qualification for improvement commissioners was usually between £500 and

£1000 of personal wealth or personal estate; that for Poor Law commissioners was considerably lower. In some towns and in parts of London, the social composition of a parish effectively ensured that responsible officers would be drawn from the lower middling orders of craftsmen, artisans and retailers. But this was not a phenomenon confined to the towns: in rural areas too, commissioners were drawn from the gentry, freeholders of the better or lesser sort and farmers.

There was, therefore, a coherent and exclusive political oligarchy at the very summit of power but which incorporated other interests and groups. Many gentry families identified their interests with those of the aristocracy, and were willing to accept infusions of personnel from the middling orders. There is always a danger in concentrating unduly upon those at the very top of the social and political order. After all, the vast majority of the people of Britain having direct experience of local government experienced 'politics' in their local communities rather than within any national context. Effective local government in the parishes of an increasingly complex society required the cooperation of tens of thousands of willing individuals. Indeed, many members of the landed classes had their own interests and priorities on the national stage and were content to cede local supremacy to others. In the counties and the towns they acknowledged the worthiness and ability of members of the middling orders to govern.

The middling orders: enterprise and docility

It is significant that the term 'middle class' only came into use as late as the 1780s. The middling orders of early Hanoverian Britain were not aware of themselves as an independent and coherent social unit. Their circumstances and their attitudes were immensely varied, ranging from the near-aristocratic fortunes and lifestyles of some of the clergy, lawyers and office-holders, through the moderately prosperous mercantile sections of town and country, down to the humble craftsmen and retailers. They were content to maintain and, where possible, to advance their place within the existing social order. They were not bearers of a new social ethic and they were not the agencies of a new vision of how society should be organized.

Politically, too, they had little in common; they were not to be found acting together during the first half of the eighteenth century. This is not to argue that they were politically inactive. In the early and middle decades of the eighteenth century the middling orders organized their own clubs and societies and published their own newspapers and periodicals. In many ways the political world of the middling orders constituted a structure of politics in many respects distinct from, although still linked into, that of the aristocratic connections and the parliamentary parties which they serviced and supported. At the electoral level, for example, members of the middling orders acted as officers, committee men, writers and canvassers. Such cooperation and mutual identification between the political and social elite, on the one hand, and the middling orders, on the other, prevented conflict between them. After all, the middling orders were content to pursue their own political and occupational interests within the existing structure of politics.

They thus tended to be strong supporters of the existing constitution. They were prepared to mobilize against the government when they thought the constitution was in danger, as some of them did during the 1760s when they believed that the new monarchical regime of George III was a threat to its liberties. But when they believed that it was threatened from below, by colonial rebels after 1775, or by reformers and revolutionaries in the 1790s, then they once again became bulwarks of the existing order.

The growing social and political influence of the middling orders was facilitated by the negligence of the aristocracy and gentry themselves, who erected few obstacles in its way. The middling orders found so much to busy themselves with simply because their landed counterparts left so much for them to do. They were often not inclined to take on the tedious and bureaucratic work involved in estate management, local government and electoral politics, preferring to devolve responsibility to their social inferiors. By the middle of the century voices were being raised against the shortcomings of landowners who preferred the pleasures of the chase, the excitement of the capital city and the leisured routines of the spa and the seaside to the quiet execution of their paternal responsibilities. The duties of the bench, for example, were not always attended to with the dedication which they demanded. For instance, by 1758 only one-third of those appointed to the Commission of the Peace in Kent actually served as magistrates, compared with over one-half at the beginning of the century.[16] This seems to have been fairly typical of the experience of other counties. The reasons for this were varied. Tory JPs did not feel at home among Whig magistrates. New burdens were constantly being heaped upon the magistrates. No wonder that so many of them preferred the pleasures of the social season. But by mid-century the neglect of such paternal duties was being widely condemned.

The fact that the 'middling orders', especially in the towns, remained for so long willing to accept the continuing supremacy of a social and political system dominated by the aristocracy and gentry should occasion no surprise. After all, there was nothing in the Whiggism of the eighteenth century to inhibit the pursuit of wealth nor to diminish the value of commerce. Indeed, the Hanoverian regime was supremely well disposed towards finance, commerce and industry, recognizing their vital importance to the nation, to its security and to its ability to finance the wars in which Britain was from time to time forced to engage. The first half of the eighteenth century witnessed a dramatic expansion in commercial activity. Between 1714 and 1760 shipping increased in tonnage by around 30 per cent, the value of exports by 80 per cent, re-exports by around 50 per cent and imports by 40 per cent. Mercantile capital steadily increased its share of the national wealth of Britain during the first half of the century not only in London but in and around the provincial towns. The expansion of both coastal and of overseas trade encouraged the growth of ports. That of the slave trade lay behind the dramatic expansion of Bristol and Liverpool, that of coal and salt behind that of Newcastle upon Tyne, that of cloth and steel behind that of Hull.

The 'middling orders' were immediate beneficiaries of these commercial developments. They stood in the vanguard of the economic progress of which contemporaries were so triumphantly aware. Observers commented on the vitality and the spirit of enterprise which was everywhere to be found, the rapid diversification and specialization of trades and retailing and the universal interest in science, innovation, and even in gadgets. The religious animosities, the dynastic uncertainty and the party conflicts of previous decades seemed to be dissolving amid the civilizing influences of an age of material prosperity. From the early decades of the eighteenth century, indeed, and urged on by successive governments, Britain became a commercial mecca, dedicated to the pursuit of wealth, consumed with the wish to make a profit and open to innovation and entrepreneurial skill. These economic changes had many cultural consequences, especially in lifestyle, fashion and manners.

Whether these developments were good or bad was a subject of endless debate, but everyone agreed that they could not be confined to the social elite. Britain may have been a hierarchical society but it was also an open house for the pursuit of wealth and ambition and for satisfying the desire for social status. It was, above all, a free market for the purchase of consumer goods.[17] The middling orders of the countryside as well as of the towns were heavily involved in their production, their sale and, not least, in their purchase. Growing incomes, rising expectations and the greater availability of a greater range of products combined to motivate consumer spending on an unprecedented scale. People were willing to purchase almost anything in order to dignify their lives and to add charm and fashion to their surroundings. By the 1730s, indeed, improvements in transport had lowered freight costs and stimulated domestic trade within and between regions. The press familiarized more people than ever before with fashion news and product information from the metropolis and from provincial centres alike. During the first three-quarters of the eighteenth century, in fact, most issues of most newspapers contained far more consumer advertising than political news. The dramatic improvement in the efficiency of retailing, the opening up of tens of thousands of shops (no fewer than 140 000 by 1759) and the perennial power of emulation and imitation all assisted in nothing less than a growing transformation in the material circumstances in the lives of the middling orders.

Some of these consumer items were everyday necessities such as food and drink but now with additional refinement, as coffee houses, inns and taverns sprang up to service the needs of an increasingly numerous, more wealthy and, indeed, more mobile population. Other domestic consumer products included items of discrimination for even humble tradesmen and their families: cheap cotton clothing, tablecloths, china tea services, bowls and coffee pots and medicines of an almost endless variety. Many of these items, although by no means small, were intended for private use and convenience and can have had little to do with either family advancement or social status. Others, however, could have had little other purpose. For much of the century, indeed, the building and rebuilding of houses continued, enhanced by the quality and variety of domestic consumer goods, many of them new to the mass market. These included carpets, glassware, marble hearths, mirrors, mahogany furniture and leather goods together with countless novelties in different ethnic styles, French, Indian and Chinese. Many such items would not even have been found in aristocratic palaces half a century earlier.

For some members of the 'middling orders' status was conferred by a leisured style of life. By the middle of the eighteenth century commercial leisure facilities had become common in many parts of the country. The emergence of spa towns, such as Bath, Scarborough, Shrewsbury and Tunbridge Wells, affected only a minority. However, theatres, concert halls, museums and art galleries sprang up all over the country, while bookshops, print-shops, reading-rooms and libraries marked the presence of a massive reading public hungry for information, entertainment and diversion. This commercialization of leisure, especially in towns large and small, was not confined to the 'middling orders'; but they were its most enthusiastic patrons and its most zealous consumers.

What is the social meaning of the growth of mass consumerism? Cultural and psychological explanations for such a complex phenomenon involving millions of people need to be handled with great care. Two possibilities may, however, be considered. The first is that mass consumerism reflected a changing attitude towards the past, to tradition and thus to the present. In the sixteenth and for much of the seventeenth century old belongings were prized because they identified an individual with continuity and tradition, with established routines and community values. In the eighteenth century the rush to replace old possessions with fashionable new ones perhaps indicates a release of the individual from the past and its influence and a fresh, and arguably more optimistic and self-centred, approach to the present. The second, and more illuminating, explanation suggests that in their purchases and possessions people in the eighteenth century were conveying messages concerning their ideals and their identity. This should not be dismissed merely as social emulation. It is best envisaged not only by purchases of patriotic ephemera, mugs, plaques and prints, but also by the ribbons and colours of political parties, trade societies and the like. More generally, expensive material articles, such as paintings, ceramics and jewellery, might reflect an individual's prosperity, success and, hopefully, his or her social acceptance and status. In particular, the enormous care and consideration devoted to the home may reflect a massive investment of psychological as well as material resources in family life and domestic values. The care with which people exhibited their consumer goods in their homes in particularly visible areas of their houses strongly suggests a determination to present themselves to others in the most favourable light, a determination which was less strongly felt by the gentry than by the professionals and tradespersons of the towns. Furthermore, the rapid development of a secondhand market, particularly for items of clothing, enabled some at least of the poorer elements in society to present a more respectable face to the world.

Contemporaries anxiously observed the new phenomenon of consumerism and wondered where it was all leading.[18] Many clergymen denounced the luxury, the vanity and the indebtedness which consumerism brought in its wake, to say nothing of the arrogance and godlessness. What sort of example, moralists wondered, was this to set before the mass of the population? Others sang to a very different tune, seeing in consumerism a source of economic energy and social utility. Writers as different as Bernard Mandeville and Adam Smith saw consumerism as an engine of continuing economic growth, a constant stimulus to industry and trade and, not least, an incentive and an encouragement to the masses to work and to save.

Many observers, and many historians, too, have linked the social power of the middling orders with individualistic social values. Indeed, it is true that many of them were thrifty and industrious, looking to their own talents to improve their fortunes in this world. Yet most members of the middling orders, far from professing an individualistic ideology, accepted a conventional, Anglican belief in a divinely ordained universe. Very few of them were of a wholly secular, still less of an irreligious, cast of mind. At the same time, it is clear that many of these people were moving away from a purely providentialist view of life, according to which their destiny was in the hands of their Creator. By their actions it is clear that very many of them believed that civil society was moulded by human, not by divine, action. The improvement of civil society was possible, therefore, through human beings taking responsibility for their own lives and for their own fortunes in this world. Paradoxically, then, although their mentality was entirely compatible with that of the traditional social order, their actions emphasized change rather than tradition, initiative rather than authority and human resource rather than passive reliance upon divine providence.

At the most basic level, material wealth was beginning to transform the living conditions and social environments of the upper and middle classes and, in doing so, to enhance their taste and manners. Obsession with social etiquette was a sign of changing social habits. The contemporary rush to imitate the social routines of the upper classes was perhaps a powerful sign of acute status consciousness in a rapidly changing commercial society. So, arguably, was the wide circulation of one of the new art forms of the eighteenth century, the novel, with its concern for the fortunes of individual heroes and, not least, heroines in a Society of Orders. Although the fame of the great metropolitan pleasure gardens of Marylebone, Ranelagh and Vauxhall has stamped an impression of aristocratic exclusiveness upon our perceptions of eighteenth-century high society, they were in fact patronized by a very wide social clientele. Provincial assemblies, indeed, often welcomed members of the trading as well as gentry classes. Similarly, the growth of spa and seaside towns provided further opportunities for the mixing of the upper and middle classes in a common culture of etiquette, courtesy and fashion.

What were the consequences of the growth of the middling orders in the first half of the eighteenth century? Their existence certainly cushioned the impact of aristocratic oligarchy. Although it would be a huge mistake to imagine that the middling orders conceived of themselves as a self-conscious class, their sheer economic power challenged any possibility of aristocratic domination of the economy. Although political power remained with the aristocracy, the exercise of that power was to a great degree dependent upon and shared with the rapidly growing middling orders. The press, for example, never came under aristocratic power. Furthermore, Parliament may have been aristocratic in its personnel but it had to respond to the powerfully and publicly expressed needs of the middling orders. Finally, social values may have been strongly influenced by aristocratic patronage but it was middling order veneration of the family and of domesticity which set the tone for eighteenth century life. Their involvement in civic affairs was no less remarkable. Many of them were ready to play a part, even if it was sometimes a junior part, in helping to organize public affairs in parish, town and county. They were to be found in a wide variety of activities such as sponsoring and organizing charity schools, founding hospitals, schools and academies, supporting the establishment of cultural societies and encouraging humanitarian causes. It may be tempting to view the middling orders as reformist and even radical, but it is unlikely that they regarded themselves in this manner. Indeed, their readiness to wrap themselves in patriotic flags, to rally round the throne and the church and to leap to the defence of property whenever it was threatened, should give cause for hesitation. In the end British society was dominated by an aristocratic elite and its ideals, yet it found a substantial, growing place for the aspirations and the activities of the middling orders.

Urban society: culture and elites

The progress of the middling orders is closely linked to one of the most characteristic features of the period, the development of towns. As we noticed in Chapter 1 the lives of country people and townspeople were closely intertwined. Town and country were mutually supporting economic and social systems. Only in the early nineteenth century, when towns became economically self-supporting, can sharp, qualitative distinctions be made between them. The growth of towns was one of the most characteristic and most remarkable features of the long eighteenth century.

Towns may be grouped in a variety of ways. There were in 1700 up to 500 small market towns with populations of under 2500. In addition there were about 30 regional centres, many of them country towns, some of them also important ecclesiastical centres. These towns had populations of between 2500 and 5000 and incorporated a number of sophisticated social and cultural functions which attracted the local gentry. Finally, we may identify 25–30 provincial centres with populations of over 5000. About half of these were primarily regional centres servicing agricultural hinterlands. The rest, however, included eight industrial towns (among them Manchester, Birmingham and Leeds), three ports (Liverpool, Hull and Sunderland) and three naval dockyard towns (Chatham, Plymouth and Portsmouth).

The towns of Britain had been growing in size, wealth and population since the Restoration. This growth depended upon a combination of local circumstances which collectively generated a demand for urban services. These were usually, but not exclusively, of an economic character. Local specialization of production and sale created an appetite for goods and services. The geographical position of towns on rivers, roads and canals fostered development. Other general factors promoting the growth of towns were population increase, often due to local patterns of migration out of rural areas, and general levels of economic development. In some of the larger towns the catalyst for growth was industry, and the growth of some of them was spectacular, particularly Leeds, Manchester and Sheffield. Most towns, however, grew more slowly. Just as important as the industrial giants were the smaller industrial towns like Barnsley, Dudley, Rotherham and Walsall. Similarly, while the great ports such as Bristol, Glasgow and Liverpool grew spectacularly, the small ones, places like Dover, Poole and Whitby, also prospered. Furthermore, county towns and cathedral cities also advanced in the settled decades of the Whig supremacy as bureaucracy developed and the amount of civil and ecclesiastical business increased.

Towns may be defined by their functions. These could be economic, socio-cultural and political. First, all towns had important economic functions. Towns were the focus of the economic life of their hinterlands. They were important centres of communication and transport, news and information. Towns acted as marketing centres for agricultural goods produced locally. Increasingly, too, they acted as sources of other economic services like banking and credit. Second, towns were also defined by their lifestyles. Many were ecclesiastical, medical and educational centres (even quite small towns had libraries, clubs and theatres). Urban elites were active in their patronage of the arts, their sponsorship of new architectural styles and their role as consumers of fashionable clothing and household products. Through their endeavours towns became centres of fashion and social emulation. But historians should avoid the temptation to glamorize the lifestyle of people in towns. Concentrations of people ensured that towns became centres of poverty, disease and crime. For many people, urban life must have been bleak and depressing. Third, towns were important political and administrative centres. They housed the major professions, the law courts and assizes, and acted as the local agencies of the central government in maintaining law and order and collecting taxes. The 200 corporate towns were independent self-governing entities, with their own councils and their own administration and jurisdiction. Non-corporate towns were governed by whatever was left over from the old manorial system, an unlikely collection of Courts Leet, Lords of the Manor and parish vestries. Both corporate and non-corporate systems shared two features: they were oligarchic and they were corrupt. Their traditional franchises were very narrow, their electorates rarely more than a score or two. In practice they were self-perpetuating oligarchies which enjoyed the spoils and show of office without reference to merit and efficiency. Their budgets – rarely more than a couple of thousand pounds per annum – were remarkably small. The politics of these towns was outwardly, therefore, Whiggish. Opposition, dissent and criticism could come to the surface, and occasionally did so, especially in the 1730s, but this capacity for opposition should not imply systematic and continuous hostility to the Hanoverian regime.

Many of the above themes are well illustrated in the growth of the capital city. In 1700 London had a population of about 500 000 souls, around 8 per cent of the entire population of England and Wales. By 1725 it had risen to 600 000 and by 1750 to about 660 000 out of a total English population of just over 6 000 000. London had all the attractions of a vast capital city, and its population benefited from a continuing stream of immigrants. On one estimate, no less than three-quarters of London's population in the eighteenth century was born outside the capital. London remained an immense market for agricultural products but its economy began to change into that of a clearing house (or entrepôt) for trade. In 1700 around one-quarter of the workforce had some connection with the port and its trades. Even London, however, could not keep up with the national pace of commercial expansion. Its proportion of all of England's overseas trade was starting to fall – from three-quarters in 1700 to two-thirds in 1752. But its commercial importance was underlined by its financial activities, by the steady growth of the Bank of England, by the establishment and development of marine insurance at Lloyd's and by the proliferation of financial services of all kinds. During the course of the century London replaced Amsterdam as the financial centre of Europe. Moreover, the cultural imperialism which London imposed on the rest of the country was almost as marked as its economic influence. Information about London fashion was easily available in the newspapers and reviews. No wonder Defoe called London 'the great centre of England'.

So imposing was the sheer critical, demographic mass of London that some historians are inclined to see 'the making of the middle class' in its huge and rapidly growing middling ranks.[19] It is doubtful, however, if such a wildly heterogeneous mass of occupations, largely unaware of any common interests which they may have had, deserves the description 'class'. The social structure of London was a closely integrated set of hierarchies, ascending and descending in minute gradations, perceptible to contemporaries by quite minor variations of speech, dress and manners which are often too subtle and too varied to be conveyed in documentary evidence. It is these, rather than the vaster and more homogeneous units of 'class', which remain typical of the middling orders even of London society in the middle of the eighteenth century.

The social structure of the other great towns of the country was not dissimilar, although there can be no gainsaying the unique situation of London. Bristol and Norwich, the next two towns, still had populations of only 30 000 in 1700. Bristol then began to pull steadily ahead until by 1750 it stood second to London at 40 000, compared to the 36 000 of Norwich. The other great provincial capitals were smaller. Newcastle upon Tyne had 16 000 in 1700, rising to 30 000 in 1750; Plymouth went from 9000 to 14 000 in 1750, Exeter from 14 000 to 16 000, Chester from 10 000 to 12 000, but York went down from 12 000 to 11 000. Manufacturing towns were by 1750 growing rapidly: Birmingham and Liverpool had shot up from around 10 000 to 20 000; Manchester and Leeds were still slightly under 20 000. Of the remaining towns in England, only Coventry, Ipswich, Nottingham and Yarmouth, and just possibly Bath, Hull and Sheffield, had populations over 10 000. With a very few exceptions, then, the towns of England were small in size. If we accept the figure of 2500, beloved of urban historians, as the minimum population for a town, then in 1700 only one in six of the population lived in a town. Even by 1800 that figure had only reached one in three. In Scotland, Edinburgh had 45 000 inhabitants in 1700 and, in Ireland, Dublin had 60 000. The eighteenth century was a period of unprecedented growth for these two cities. By 1800, indeed, Dublin had a population of no fewer than 200 000 and Cork was approaching 80 000. The growth in the size of other towns in Scotland and Ireland and, indeed, in that of the Welsh towns, was very much slower, at least before the later decades of the eighteenth century.

During urbanization towns became centres for the services provided by the rapidly growing professions. Admission to the army, navy and church was still dominated by the aristocracy and gentry, but the expansion of professional opportunities was beginning to open doors to more humble aspirants, especially in the provinces. In this way, professional status and a common experience of professional life may have done something to integrate the different orders of society both nationally and locally. Admission both to the legal profession and to the growing ranks of surgeons and apothecaries was more broadly based, through an apprenticeship system which permitted upward mobility from the humbler ranks of society. Even so, almost two-thirds of legal clerks came from gentry backgrounds, only one-third from the middling sort of merchants and professionals. The Act of 1731 requiring legal proceedings to be conducted in English boosted the prosperity of the legal profession. The many and varied property transactions of an increasingly prosperous commercial society ensured its continuing health. The medical profession fared no less well. Town-dwellers were extremely health-conscious; this ensured an unceasing trail of visits to physicians and apothecaries. Although surgeons were the princes of the medical profession, the mania for medicine in these decades ensured that physicians, even in country towns, could make a reasonable living. Anxious parents, moreover, sought educational advantages for their children. This bred an enormous market for schoolmasters and mistresses, for day as well as boarding-schools, and for private tutors and governesses as well as a range of commercial needs such as bookkeeping, surveying and modern languages. In general, by the middle of the century most towns of any size boasted an impressive number of professional men and women who were anxious to sell their services both to townspeople and to those from the local rural hinterland. Manchester and Leeds had around 20 attornies to cater for their populations of 20 000 in the 1730s while, with a smaller population, Penzance had no fewer than 11. Overall, it has been estimated by Professor Holmes[20] that the number of professional men in permanent employment increased by no less than 70 per cent between 1680 and 1730, to about 70 000.

There was no cultural schism between the elites of town and country whatever their political and religious differences. Prosperous members of the middling ranks of society used urban environments in order to express both their wealth and their values, but this was an urban culture in which the rural elite might involve itself. Indeed, the invasion of the towns by the rural elite was much more marked than the purchase of landed estates by rich members of the urban, middling classes. The aristocracy and gentry took to patronizing urban centres with some relish. Indeed, the life of an urban patrician elite came to be almost as highly prized as that of a gentleman landowner or farmer. Moreover, different kinds of urban space became arenas for different kinds of social display and competition; the streets, the parks, the gardens, the assembly rooms and the churches. Towns had many practical attractions: the availability of goods, the relatively low cost of living and the convenience of travel and communications. Furthermore, the physical landscape of towns was rapidly improving and architectural standards were rising. Established traditions of vernacular building were discarded in favour of the neoclassical style. Eighteenth-century streets were cleaner and better lit than those of the previous century; parks, walks and boulevards offered a pleasant physical environment. Civic facilities were improving and cultural needs were met by the building of concert halls, museums and schools. This was a polite and fashionable society, one in which gentlemen and gentry could feel at ease, one which catered to their social and leisure needs and which offered a range of cultivated services and refined pleasures. Here, the middling orders of the towns could mingle with members of the propertied elite of the countryside.

The phenomenal number of new town houses gave employment to literally tens of thousands of craftsmen, many of whom used model-books derived from fashionable London designers. This 'urban renaissance'[21] consisted of parks and gardens, terraced houses, neatly laid out squares and side streets, with their shops with massive window frontages and ornate doorways. These were not only tasteful surroundings for the new middle classes. They represented civic status and celebrated a new civic identity, seen in the dozens of town halls, market halls, assembly rooms, bridges, museums and libraries. Such an identity flattered the social sensitivities of the respectable orders, evoked their local loyalties and integrated them into the social and political networks of the towns of Hanoverian Britain.

Yet social distance was beginning to appear between the social elite and its inferiors. In some towns, notably but not exclusively cathedral cities like Gloucester, Hereford, Lincoln and Norwich, parishes in the central parts of town traditionally housed the wealthiest members of the patrician classes. In the decades after the Glorious Revolution new programmes of building were undertaken in many such towns. The adoption of new architectural styles for modern, expensive and socially select residential developments in these places erected huge social, and not infrequently legal, barriers against the mingling of the social orders. Other methods of spatial segregation may be seen in other types of town. Where living conditions in inner-city areas were at their most repulsive, as in the rising manufacturing towns, the wealthy began to retreat to outer suburbs, thus depriving the poorest parishes of much needed rating finance. This residential segregation was most marked in the large industrial towns, Birmingham, Leeds, Manchester and Sheffield. Other forms of social separation may be observed in the 1730s, when the fashionable elite began to fence off their entertainments and leisure pursuits from contamination from lower down the social scale. One way of doing this was to raise the entrance fee for admission to such activities as cricket matches, which might otherwise be attended by the poor and the vulgar. Another was to restrict the provision of cultural pursuits. In the late 1730s a number of Acts of Parliament created licensing systems to regulate the establishment of theatres, gaming-houses and horse racing. By then, popular participation in the leisure pursuits of the social elite was positively not encouraged. Where it could not be prevented it was, at least, kept at a distance by the provision of select and elegant grandstands in an attempt to defend the space of the social elite.

As the century wore on, the distinctiveness of towns attracted more frequent comment. The terms 'town' and 'village' came to have more sharply contrasting meanings, both with their own stereotypical implications. An idyllic, bucolic idea of a timeless 'village' was celebrated in both art and the popular imagination, in contrast to the idea of a dynamic, commercial, bustling 'town'. Even smaller towns were deemed to enjoy these cosmopolitan, urban qualities. Towns were deemed to have qualities and functions distinct from those of villages, but there was no reason to believe that in the nineteenth century towns would come to be regarded as symbols and portents of a new kind of society. In the 1750s, at least, most of them remained extensions of the land.

The common people: assertion, festivity and direct action

The culture of the landed classes and of the middling orders – polite, civilized and formal – coexisted with the culture of the masses – at first sight turbulent, disorderly and unruly. Indeed, popular displays of disrespect towards the middling and upper ranks of society could be so spectacular that they raise the issue of the popularity, or unpopularity, of the regime. At any time in history, the willingness of the mass of the people to accept the prevailing social system is difficult to calculate. In eighteenth-century Britain the difficulty was complicated by problems of communication and by limitations of popular political awareness. When we remind ourselves that the great mass of the people could scarcely conceive of any viable alternative set of social arrangements and when we remember that hardly any of them have confided evidence about their opinions to historians, then in this area of the discipline more than any other the historian needs to exercise caution.

In all this, two points need to be borne in mind. In the first place, people in the eighteenth century may have been poor and ill-educated but they were not automatically victims of oppression or creatures of impersonal forces. They could use their initiative and exhibit assertive patterns of behaviour. In the second place, although popular political behaviour may have been very different from 'high politics', the two intersect in many crucial ways. They fed off each other and interconnected on many occasions, such as parliamentary and local elections and on numerous days of local festive celebration. Indeed, the participation of the masses in the civic life of town and village could be triggered by a wide variety of causes. They might be drawn into the official calendar of national, royal or aristocratic anniversaries and take the opportunity of making their feelings known. This they would do by adopting a variety of strategies, such as making a noise (cheering, singing and jeering), by making music (vocal or instrumental), by the wearing of coloured clothes (clothes of all kinds, particularly hats and ribbons) and by reacting to – or even taking part in – processions and parades. In all this, perpetual references to local community affiliations – families, privileges, institutions, causes and vendettas – did much to register and thus to promote local pride and local consciousness.

The weight of such evidence as we have indicates that many people felt little reverence for the regime under which they lived their lives, and suggests that for many decades they were unable to identify with it. Their lack of enthusiasm for a German monarchy can readily be understood. Indeed, the extent of popular ridicule of the royal family in the first half of the eighteenth century should not be underestimated. It is difficult to measure the extent of anti-Hanoverian feeling because it shades into the vigorous dislike of the aristocracy sometimes displayed by the lower orders and, on occasions in the early years of the regime, this dislike can be confused with displays of genuine pro-Jacobite sentiment. The first few months of the reign witnessed hostile riots all over the country.[22] Even after the suppression of the '15 George I and his entourage remained the object of popular dislike and derision. George II may have been a conscientious monarch and a courageous soldier but public opinion was not impressed. 'In the gutter press he was treated with open contempt. His sexual habits were mocked, his personal foibles, especially his irascibility, derided.'[23] His absorption in military affairs seemed to hint at dangerous absolutist tendencies at a time when people were genuinely afraid of standing armies. His command of a sizeable army of Hanoverian mercenaries pointed in the same direction. Until the extinction of the Jacobite threat Britain lived in some danger of invasion and popular attitudes towards the foreign dynasty remained at best provisional. Only when the threat was removed could a robust and substantial loyalty to the dynasty emerge.

The upper classes, too, had to endure the disrespectful language and boisterous conduct with which the lower orders treated them. The arrogance and pomposity of their manners were greeted with dislike and resentment; their pretension, their fashions and their manners were treated with satire, ridicule and mockery. There was not much that they could do about it. They had to stomach popular displays of protest and resistance which were deeply embedded into popular culture and which went back for centuries. These were normally prompted by the official civic celebrations, sponsored by the largesse of local elites themselves. These parades, processions and meetings were great set-piece occasions. In many places, the routines of party politics had accustomed people to involving themselves in civic affairs. Enhanced by the growing power and influence of the press, the forms of popular, local politics were humorous, assertive and unruly. It was common for these civic events to be used for the expression of a range of grievances, often of a social and economic character. Satirical attacks upon the governing classes were permitted through the popular tradition of social inversion, according to which the normal social order might be inverted as the great men of a community sought the good opinion of the lesser by, for example, serving their food and pouring their drink. The opportunities for personal insult and social humiliation were accepted with relish and with enthusiasm.

The cycle of popular festivity still turned on the traditional calendar of the church, with the feasts and the fairs of saints' days, but these coexisted with secular celebrations deriving from an older, pagan calendar, spiced with local variety, and closely related to the seasons of the agricultural year. After New Year's Day and Twelfth Night, Plough Monday marked the traditional resumption of agricultural work after the Christmas break and saw festive parochial celebrations, including parish feasts and mummers' plays. Thereafter, most communities celebrated Candlemas, Shrovetide (a national holiday for apprentices, marked by sporting events and pancakes), Lady Day, Palm Sunday and then Easter, a period of relaxation and festivity marked by inter-village rivalries and (often quite violent) sporting events. There followed the universally popular May Day and Whitsuntide celebrations, opportunities in the first for maintaining floral, dancing and courtship traditions and, in the second, for indulging culinary and sporting tastes. After Whitsuntide, the middle months of the year were punctuated by Midsummer and Lammas before Michaelmas, Hallowe'en and Guy Fawkes'

Day signified the transition to the autumn months. The years ended in celebration of the greatest Christian festival of them all, but one already heavily secularized, Christmas, with its presents, plays and dancing, and not least its energetic displays of eating and drinking.

In addition to all these the annual parish feast (or wake) provided a familiar and lengthy (usually week-long) means of local, social renewal; friends and relatives who had departed the parish often made an effort to return for the occasion. These wakes were commonly celebrated on the Sunday after the day of the saint to whom the parish church was dedicated. In the early eighteenth century the mass of the people had not yet come to use the formal calendar of days and months, preferring to date events of significance from the nearest saint's or feast-day. These celebrations, whether religious or pagan, did much more than provide entertainment. They brought the different classes and orders of the local community together, affirmed its basic religious and secular purposes, did something to resolve underlying tensions and, to some extent, lent a human face to a society which knew enormous inequalities and very considerable suffering and hardship. They perhaps enabled the individual to locate himself and his family within a broader, communal identity, softened the harsh routines of life and, in some cases, promoted not only personal contact between different social groups but also charity and almsgiving. It is impossible to measure the significance of qualities like 'neighbourliness' and 'friendship' but they are, inevitably, a vital requirement for the humane and stable functioning of social and political mechanisms. At a more mundane level, such events must have done much to encourage the production, judging, marketing and sale of local produce of an almost infinite range and quality while promoting crafts and activities – musical, athletic, cultural and, of course, religious – of all kinds.

Other displays of popular sentiment had a national and patriotic orientation. The birthday of William III on 4 November almost exactly coincided both with his landing at Torbay and with Guy Fawkes' Day (5 November). Furthermore, the accession date of Queen Elizabeth I (17 November) was still celebrated in the first half of the century. Military and naval victories were another opportunity for popular celebration. These became more numerous as the century wore on. Most of these celebrations were harmless enough, but occasionally they acquired political significance. In the early eighteenth century politics was already experiencing the mobilization of public opinion, albeit intermittently. As a number of events illustrated, public opinion could be a powerful and unpredictable force: Sacheverell, the '15, the Excise Crisis, among others. The emergence of Admiral Vernon as a national hero after 1738 in many ways prefigured the emergence in the 1760s of John Wilkes as an anti-government symbol. Popular idolatry of the victor of Porto Bello in March 1740 was seen in numerous consumer artefacts such as prints, pottery, ballads and maps, but more particularly in the numerous celebrations of his birthday (over 50 in 25 counties) in November of the same year. Many of these were spontaneous eruptions of popularity in the sense that they were not organized by local elites and corporations but by local merchants and tradesmen. Standing at the head of massive popular antagonism towards Walpole's government, the figure of Vernon represented a vibrant, largely urban, commercial opinion, common to all classes which was after 1738 hostile to Walpole's government and to its supporters.

On the one hand, these displays of opinion may have encouraged the perpetuation of attitudes hostile towards the social hierarchy. On the other, they may have acted as a safety valve which permitted the expression of dissatisfaction, a periodic release which was absolutely vital to the stable functioning of a hierarchical society. It is difficult for the historian to resolve such an issue because it is impossible to penetrate the opinions of the masses. One key which may open doors to further analysis, however, is provided by the widespread phenomenon of rioting.

Rioting of one kind or another was a customary aspect of eighteenth-century society, a regular manner of expressing protest and dissatisfaction. Crowds rioted for religious, for political but, most commonly, for economic reasons. Crowds rioted about prices, wages, taxes, turnpikes and food shortages. Rioting was normally local, directed at some immediate objective and usually confined to the members of the local community. Most riots were communal, defensive and conservative, directed to preserving and protecting rights, customs and existing practices. In the absence of trades unions, consumer groups and national trades associations people took matters of all kinds into their own hands and used traditions of collective behaviour to protect their interests and to make their feelings known. More effective, and a good deal speedier than peaceful petitioning, riotous behaviour was not only tolerated but acknowledged as a healthy sign that the Free-Born Englishman was alive and kicking. There is, moreover, evidence that in the years after the Glorious Revolution the frequency of rioting was beginning to accelerate quite markedly, especially in London and the larger towns.[24]

The word 'riot' conveys an anarchic picture of the lower orders engaged in mindless violence. The reality of rioting, however, was very different. It is a serious error to imagine either that rioters were usually very poor or that riots represented anything more than the protest of the very poor against the very rich. Those engaged in rioting were only rarely from the poorest classes. Depending on the matter in contention, rioters might be members of a church or a trade or a craft; they might be clients or customers or, not least, housewives responding to changes in prices or the quality of goods and produce. Most rioters had some standing in the community. They were engaged in work or apprenticeships, and they were usually members, often heads, of a household. Very few rioters were vagrants, itinerants or criminals. Frequently, passers-by might spontaneously join the rioters if they sympathized with their objectives, thus rendering the riot a dynamic and changing event in the tumult of street culture.

Crowd action was often triggered by a minor incident. Once triggered, it was direct action designed to secure rough justice. There was nothing haphazard about the pattern of crowd behaviour. It was normally directed at the property rather than the persons of their dislike. Its actions were directed by local self-appointed leaders, sometimes termed 'captains', who, reflecting the innate disciplines of those involved, preferred to threaten and to intimidate rather than to unleash crowd violence. The overwhelming majority of incidents that may be termed 'riots' were peaceful. Crowd actions were grounded on a traditional sense of fairness: the idea of a 'just price', principles of 'fair dealing' and the assumption that traditional liberties and rights protected the interests of the community. If crowds were prepared to break the law when it suited them, it was usually in defence of a more traditional form of 'law'. They normally did not intend to repudiate the existing social order and its principles of hierarchy, obedience and inequality. What they demanded was fair treatment for all within the existing social framework.

By the middle of the eighteenth century rioting over food, its price, quality and availability, had become the most common form of rioting in the parishes of Britain and Ireland. In the two decades following the Glorious Revolution, there had been serious food shortages only in the years 1693–95 and 1708–10. Otherwise these decades were trouble-free. Indeed, government records reveal no food rioting at all between 1660 and 1709 in Wales or in the northern counties of England. Between 1708 and 1709, however, numerous protests against the movement of grain out of local areas swept many parts of the country. Thereafter, food rioting became much more common. In 1727 and again in 1729 the tinminers of Cornwall protested at high food prices, to notably little effect. After the harsh winter of 1739 serious food rioting was to be found over the entire country. It was particularly serious in those areas where it appeared for the first time, the West Riding of Yorkshire, Teesside and Tyneside. From there the rioting swept northwards into the area around Edinburgh. Such rioting was frequently, although by no means universally, influenced by popular attitudes towards a 'just price' for food and, more generally, by a set of ethical standards accompanying food transactions which have been described by E.P. Thompson in terms of a 'moral economy'.[25] Food riots in the 1740s were, however, only partly inspired by such ideals and were accompanied by more direct and more persistent forms of popular action. They were, correspondingly, harshly suppressed. Serious problems of food supply in 1746 were merely a rehearsal for the much more serious shortages of 1756 and the near-famine conditions of 1766–67. At times, indeed, the intensity of food rioting gives the impression of something approaching a regional agitation. Nevertheless, as such riots became more widespread they became, on the whole, more peaceful, less protracted and more firmly characterized by 'moral economy' qualities.

Disputes over land were a further potent source of direct, popular action. In a period in which land was cleared for enclosure at the expense of common right this was not surprising. Most enclosures of the second half of the seventeenth century had proceeded by local agreements and were not publicly contentious. (Indeed, only two enclosure riots have been noted during the period 1660–1714.) Only when enclosure was achieved by statute – and there were to be over 2000 Enclosure Acts during the eighteenth century – did popular action occur on any scale. Even then, it usually required not only the enclosure of common land but also that of wasteland or the threat of eviction to stimulate popular action.[26] Isolated enclosure riots would not unduly trouble the authorities. However, those in the forests of Northamptonshire (1710) and in the Forest of Dean (1688, 1696, 1707 and 1735) were severe. In Galloway in south west Scotland the 'Levellers Revolt' of 1724 represented a regional protest against enclosures and subsequent evictions. Opposed by the landowners, the army, the law and the church, the rising collapsed and the enclosures proceeded. Of equal if not greater intensity were those riots concerned with 'blacking', a response to royal and aristocratic attempts to enlarge deer parks. Such parks were both a practical and a symbolic assault upon traditional means of subsistence. Even the notorious Black Act of 1723 failed to suppress popular resistance, even if it was diverted into such activities as arson, fence-breaking and animal-maiming.[27]

The most dangerous form of rioting was that connected with politics and religion. Every general election threw up a number of examples in which electoral boisterousness got out of hand, even leading to severe injuries and death. The prominence of the Tories in the more open constituencies accustomed them to appeal to a wide audience and probably encouraged them to flirt dangerously with popular agitation, as they did during the Excise riots in 1733–34. National prejudice was another potent source of rioting. The Glasgow Malt Tax riots of 1725 and the Porteous Riots in Edinburgh in 1736 were both motivated by powerful anti-English and anti-Union sentiment. Rioting over religious questions could be even more dangerous. Rioting in defence of the 'church in danger' occurred not only in London in 1688 but in a number of constituencies in 1710, at the accession of George I and during and after the 1745 rising.

The participation of women in rioting has caused considerable interest. Although they were not involved in rioting to the extent of their counterparts in France, women were nevertheless very visible especially, but not only, in food riots. Female participation in rioting accompanied that of men and sometimes dominated it. In London in the early eighteenth century women amounted to one-third of rioters bound over at Quarter Sessions. The market place was, of course, frequented by women, who enjoyed greater knowledge of the price and quality of goods than their menfolk. Women did not act under the instructions of men. They pursued a specific, often less violent tactic in riots. They had their own experience of riots and their own networks of contacts and communication. Their readiness to protest reflects the prominent role they played in popular political and social action in the eighteenth century, and one that should not be underestimated.

How dangerous was popular culture to the Hanoverian regime? Many contemporary observers tended to exaggerate the danger, not least the upper classes themselves, who very frequently convey the impression that outbursts of popular hostility were never far away. Walpole's comments during the Excise debates in 1734 have often been repeated: 'As for faction and sedition, I will grant that in monarchical and aristocratical governments it generally arises from violence and oppression; but in democratical governments it generally arises from the people's having too great a share in the government.' In the age of Jacobite rebellions, the threat of foreign invasion and the absence of a police force, such timidity was perfectly understandable. No doubt the crowd could be touchy and its sensitivities easily offended. On the other hand, as we have seen, much riotous activity occurred in reaction to particular incidents or individual exactions. Most riots were short in duration. Even riots which had a political content did not endanger the regime. They looked to the law or to Parliament to remedy the grievance complained of. Indeed, the very currency of protest and popular defiance acted as a means of informing the regime and warning its officers when they were treading dangerously. On issues such as the Excise and Jewish naturalization the government was prepared to back down. In this way, protest, negotiation and renegotiation were inherent features of the Hanoverian regime. As even Walpole learned to his cost in the 1730s, politics was liable to be heavily influenced by the intervention of the popular voice.

The people of Britain had no great love either for the Hanoverian monarchy between 1714 and 1756 nor, apparently, for the social framework within which they lived their lives. In the last analysis, however, they accepted, albeit grudgingly, the Hanoverian regime. In some ways, the regime had much to be said for it. People were at least allowed to grumble and to complain, unlike – it was widely believed – the state of affairs in continental, Catholic countries. Moreover, in Britain, people were housed and fed. If economic hardship was not uncommon, at least famine on a national scale was unknown. Even in Scotland and Ireland food rioting was rare. More generally, the expectation as well as the practice of paternalism did something to soften the harshness of social inequality. Military victories against France and the noisy trumpetings of patriotism may have done something to stifle, or at least to diminish, popular resentment against a foreign dynasty. By the middle of the century the growing status of Parliament, increasing national pride in the Glorious Revolution and the ostensibly successful establishment of parliamentary monarchy reinforced the popularity of the regime. Fortunately, the vast majority of the English and Welsh, and most of the Scots, had no serious religious grievances which might have given grounds for dangerous discontent. Finally, most people accepted their place in Hanoverian society because no alternative conception of social relationships existed. Popular attitudes in Britain were saturated by hierarchical patterns of life and thought which by the middle of the century were scarcely diminishing in their intensity.

Notes

1. The Act of Union of 1707 created a British state, 'a United Kingdom by the name of Great Britain'. Strictly speaking, then, both 'the United Kingdom' and 'Britain' came into legal existence in 1707. Technically, therefore, Ireland remained outside Britain until the Act of Union of 1800.
2. See above pp.5–6, 59 and 62 for the early eighteenth century character of Britishness.
3. L. Colley, *Britons: Forging the Nation, 1707–1837* (1992). The above account owes much but not everything to this source. My own view is that Professor Colley gives too much emphasis to Protestantism and not enough to some of the more gradual cultural and political developments, to which I would draw greater attention.
4. Englishness arguably rested on two religious assumptions: that the English were a fiercely Protestant race and that they were God's chosen people. It also rested on two secular assumptions: that the English were profoundly conservative, devoted to ancient ways, and that they had a genius for political moderation and freedom.
5. See K. Wilson, *The Sense of the People: Politics, Culture and Imperialism in England, 1715–85* (1995). Although Wilson argues that 'even most humble citizens were drawn into the imperial effort, however distant or immediate that effort may have seemed', much of her evidence relates to the 1750s rather than the 1730s and tends to confirm the existence of imperialist sentiments among the middling orders rather than among the mass of the people. See her 'Empire of Virtue: The Imperial Project and Hanoverian Culture c. 1720–85', in L. Stone, ed., *An Imperial State at War: Britain from 1689 to 1815* (1994), pp. 128–64.

6. B. Lenman, *The Jacobite Risings in Britain* (1980), p. 278; A.J. Youngson, *After the 45: The Economic Impact on the Scottish Highlands* (1973); F. McLynn, *The Jacobites* (1985), pp. 126–29.

7. M. Elliott, *Partners in Revolution* (1982); O. Dann and J. Dinwiddy, eds, *Nationalism in Europe* (1988); M. Elliott, 'The Origins and Transformation of Early Irish Republicanism', *International Review of Social History*, 23 (1978), pp. 405–28.

8. See Bibliography for this section.

9. J. Rule, *Albion's People: English Society, 1714–1815* (1992), pp. 36–50.

10. P. Corfield, *The Impact of English Towns, 1700–1800* (1982), pp. 158–59; A. McInnes, 'The Emergence of a Leisure Town: Shrewsbury 1660–1760', *Past and Present*, 120 (1988).

11. For a more detailed discussion of legal enforcement of capital legislation, see below, pp. 288–900.

12. The figures in the following paragraphs are derived from J.A. Cannon, *Aristocratic Century: the Peerage of Eighteenth Century England* (1984), esp. ch. 4.

13. A standing order of the House of Commons in 1701 forbade the interference of the House of Lords in elections. It was more honoured in the breach than in the observance, but it was continually cited against peers out in the constituencies for over a century.

14. See above, pp. 25–26.

15. P. Langford, *Public Life and the Propertied Englishman, 1689–1798* (1991), esp. ch. 4.

16. N. Landau, *The Justices of the Peace, 1679–1760* (1984), p. 141.

17. The literature on consumerism in the eighteenth century is vast. See particularly N. McKendrick, J. Brewer and J.H. Plumb, eds, *The Birth of a Consumer Society: The Commercialization of Eighteenth Century England* (1982); L. Weatherill, *Consumer Behaviour and Material Culture in Britain, 1660–1760* (1988).

18. 'There is a sense in which politics in this period is about the distribution and representation of this luxury, religion about the attempt to control it, public polemic about generating and regulating it, and social policy about confirming it to those who did not produce it.' P. Langford, *A Polite and Commercial People: England 1727–1783* (1989) pp. 3–4.

19. P. Earle, *The Making of the English Middle Class: Business, Society and Family Life in London, 1660–1730* (1989).

20. G. Holmes, *Augustan England: Professions, State and Society* (1982), p. 16.

21. P. Borsay, *The English Urban Renaissance: Culture and Society in the Provincial Town* (1989). The only serious conceptual fault with Professor Borsay's masterly survey is his comparative neglect of the dark side of eighteenth-century urban life, with the consequent danger of idealizing many of its features.

22. For the widespread, initial unpopularity of the new regime in 1714–15 see above p. 65–71.

23. Langford, *A Polite and Commercial People*, p. 35.

24. See R. Shoemaker, 'The London "Mob" in the Early Eighteenth Century', *Journal of British Studies*, 26(3) (1987), pp. 273–304, and the sources there cited.

25. E.P. Thompson, 'The Moral Economy of the English Crowd in the Eighteenth Century', *Past and Present*, 50 (1971).

26. Enclosure may have delivered many economic gains to landowners and farmers but the social cost should not be underestimated. Dr Keith Snell, for example, has assembled convincing evidence that enclosures boosted winter unemployment and squeezed women out of the rural workforce. It seems difficult to contest the statistical relationship which he has established between enclosure and poor relief. K.D.M. Snell, *Annals of the Labouring Poor: Social Change and Agrarian England, 1660–1900* (1985).

27. E.P. Thompson, *Whigs and Hunters: The Origins of the Black Act* (1975).

5

The political foundations of the early Hanoverian regime, 1714–1757

Politics and print

Historians have focused upon political events and their constitutional significance in the long eighteenth century, but they much less commonly consider the purposes of politics and the origins and processes of political action. They are, perhaps, still influenced by the works of Sir Lewis Namier, who argued that its practitioners were dominated by personal ambition, not least the pursuit of place and profit.[1] In this school of writing, individuals advance their own careers and the material interests of their families; they are for the most part uninfluenced by larger principles and untouched by altruistic motives. To trade instances for or against such a view of history and of human nature is not particularly instructive. To this writer, at least, politics in the eighteenth century was always something much more than the pursuit of place and office. Legitimate ambition and, sometimes, even sheer greed were powerful driving forces, then as now, but to allow these to obscure the more enduring and indeed more human values of service, honour and integrity is to allow cynicism to distort the true motives of men. They sought power but it is often remarkable that they sought it on particular, very specific, conditions and not for its own sake. They sought it for the opportunity it might give them to influence the nation's affairs, to be of service or to promote a cause. The extent of petitioning for place was indeed impressive, but in a society in which power was allocated by connection rather than by merit it was absolutely unavoidable.

Leadership of the political order inevitably issued from a tightly knit social circle dominated by the court and by the great aristocracy. The impetus to political action rarely came from the middling orders, still less from a 'public opinion' that was as yet vague and immature in the early eighteenth century. Public outcries against government were even on occasion the construction of these politically conscious elites rather than the spontaneous demands of extraparliamentary groups. As we have seen, there was a powerful and vibrant popular, and especially provincial, political culture in Hanoverian Britain, but it was only rarely focused upon 'national' as opposed to local concerns. Protests against the Excise in 1733–34 and Jewish naturalization in 1753 were impressive in their extent and force but they were, in the last analysis, short-term gusts of opinion.

Historians are understandably fond of treating politics as a public process, but political action was often generated in situations which were private (dinners, hunts, visits), often formal (levees, drawing rooms) and, frequently, secret (cabinets, closets). Public performances (in Parliament, in Corporations and at elections) were frequently artificial and ceremonial events. In the narratives of historians, events sometimes acquire a logic and a pattern which was not perceived by the actors themselves, who were often ignorant of much that was going on around them and whose actions were consequently motivated by guesswork and subject to rumour and exaggeration.

England did not, of course, have a written constitution. What passed for constitutional theory were disputed renderings of great events (the Glorious Revolution, the Hanoverian Succession, for example), particular legislative acts (such as the Act of Succession or the Septennial Act) and rival traditions of political action (Whig, Tory, Jacobite). On the whole, and in the absence of textbooks of constitutional theory which might have guided action, politics was tentative and experimental. At times – during the ministry of Walpole, for example – the political conflict was clear cut. At other times, however – during the period 1742 to 1746, for example, and then again during 1754 and 1757 – the problem of forming and sustaining both ministries and oppositions taxed contemporaries with difficult and often unprecedented situations which could not be resolved by reference to rival political theories or to repositories of past practice.

Yet political action was vindicated by reference to an agreed set of criteria. The starting-point was the universal reverence for the constitution. Most Englishmen anticipated Edmund Burke's belief that the English enjoyed the most perfect form of government in existence. The constitution, according to Sir William Blackstone in his *Commentaries on the Laws of England*, a series of lectures delivered at Oxford in 1758 but only published in 1765, was in conformity with the laws of nature; it was therefore not only rational and perfect but, it followed, unalterable. This prescriptive idea of the constitution implied that insofar as 'politics' had a purpose it was to protect ancient liberties and historic freedoms. This constitution was envisaged in terms of a balance between King, Lords and Commons. Such a balance of the monarchical, the aristocratic and the popular elements prevented the domination of any single one of them and thus the degeneration of the state into, respectively, a tyranny, an oligarchy or a democracy. Such a balance, indeed, provided for the best features of each of these elements. This formulation was sufficiently vague to permit Whigs, Tories and even Jacobites to participate in the political life of the age. Suggested reforms to the political structure were usually dismissed on the grounds that they might upset the balance of the constitution.

This secretive, traditional and essentially retrospective style of politics was in constant tension with a print culture which was popular, vigilant and often critical of the regime. This print culture – a culture of writers and readers, of authors and editors, of bookshops and printers, of newspapers and periodicals – did not appear in the eighteenth century. No fewer than 320 periodicals had been published between 1641 and 1655, while a London bookseller named George Thomson collected over 23 000 books and pamphlets printed between 1641 and 1660. Thereafter the number diminished, only to increase once again at the end of the seventeenth century.[2] Furthermore, no fewer than 700 newspaper and periodical titles appeared between 1620 and 1700. The ending of licensing in 1695 opened the door to the publication of a greatly increased numbers of titles. Nevertheless, the 900 that appeared between 1700 and 1760 represent a considerable extension of a process already under way and one that now became irreversible.[3] The sudden growth of printing in London after 1695 encouraged the growth of large numbers of printers and publishers. The London market could not absorb them all, so many of them migrated to provincial towns. By 1720 there were no fewer than 70 printers in London and 30 in the provinces. By mid-century most towns had their own printing firm. Although successive administrations tried in vain to stem the tide of personal and political comment by imposing stamp duties (1712, 1725, 1757, 1776), government's more usual response was to use the press itself, paying subsidies to newspapers to follow the approved line and employing its own printers and writers. This was cheaper, and much less contentious, than purchasing printers. By using the press for political purposes, the government was both recognizing its importance and legitimizing its use.

What makes developments in print culture in the eighteenth century so important is the spread of newspaper readership and the growing importance of the press in politics. The first daily paper, the *Courant*, appeared in London in 1702. By 1724 there were three, and by the middle of the century there were no fewer than a dozen papers appearing in the capital either daily, bi-weekly or tri-weekly. The first provincial newspapers followed rapidly. By 1723 there were 24 and by 1753 there were 32. About 20 further provincial papers had appeared during this period but had failed to survive – a significant indication of the precarious finances of newspaper publication. Newspaper circulation rose steadily from about 50 000 per week in the first decade of the century to about 200 000 in the middle. Because they were available in inns, taverns and clubs, because they could be read by countless numbers in print-shop windows, and because of the common practice of passing newspapers from hand to hand, the circulation figure should be multiplied by between 5 and 10. It is likely, therefore, that at least one million people each week were reading a newspaper by the middle of the eighteenth century. Statistics of press circulations, however, tell us little about the ways in which newspapers were read and how an 'audience' was thus created. For most people, reading meant reading aloud or being publicly read to in taverns and clubs. Furthermore, the common practice of indirect transmission of news and opinions should not be overlooked. The role of print-shops, posters, graffiti and even gossip can never be measured, but should not be forgotten.

The quality as well as the quantity of the press deserves special emphasis. Between 1700 and 1760 the newspaper and periodical press was enhanced by a galaxy of writers of the first rank, including Addison, Defoe, Fielding, Goldsmith, Johnson, Steel and Swift. The press was not politically neutral. Most titles, playing to the public gallery, tended to be hostile to the government of the day. No wonder that successive Whig governments were inclined to be hostile to the press. Their inability to prevent its rising circulation, however, is a striking commentary on the growing and insatiable demand for political news and comment. The political dramas of the long eighteenth century were played out before a very vociferous and frequently very hostile audience.

The newspaper press was accompanied by the periodicals. These came with a rush in the first two decades of the century. The *Spectator*, the *Examiner* and the *Tatler* all appeared then, employing the talents of some of the greatest writers of the age. The *Craftsman* in the 1720s was always a stern critic of Walpole. The most popular of them all was the *Gentleman's Magazine*, which appeared in 1731. Both of these latter enjoyed circulations in excess of 10 000.

The development of printed media of communication had a continuing effect on politics throughout the eighteenth century. The press informed and criticized, provoking debate and discussion. It reflected the expansion of the political nation and, to some extent, helped to enlarge it further. Of course, the speed and extent of this process should not be exaggerated. Literacy remained restricted to about half the population, and oral culture persisted in Britain well into the nineteenth century. Nevertheless, the print culture of the eighteenth century was available to everyone who could read and to many who could not. This new print culture affirmed the dominance of the culture of the upper classes, but it at least made space available for the opinions and ideas of its critics. The print culture was not, in the end, friendly to the exclusiveness of aristocratic and government elites. The idea of a public opinion accessible to all in the public realm replaced earlier assumptions about the secrecy that must accompany matters of state. In a very real sense, then, the politics of the elite and a much wider public opinion thus were not hermetically sealed cultural and political worlds. An awareness of the operations of print culture enhances our understanding of the extent of 'politics' and broadens our appreciation of it beyond the parliamentary classes and their interests and into the towns and cities of Hanoverian Britain, the clubs, the debating societies and the inns and taverns. Politics was to be available to all, as William Pitt and John Wilkes were shortly to demonstrate.

Crown and Parliament

Britain in the eighteenth century was a parliamentary *monarchy*. The structures, ideologies and conventions of *parliamentary* government lay in the future. As yet Parliament did not regard itself as a competitor of the crown. Indeed, for much of the eighteenth century it adopted the role of junior partner in politics and administration. Particular political crises, such as those of 1733 and 1742, may give the impression that Parliament had permanently weakened the powers of the monarchy because it could demand a change of measure or of minister, but these were exceptional occasions. (In any case, it was not so much Parliament but threats from discontented ministers which endangered Walpole's position on these two occasions.) Parliament had the right to protest against ministers and their policies. It retained the right to impeach them and in the last analysis it could refuse to support their continuation in office, but these were desperate measures to be used as a last resort. For the most part, it was assumed that Parliament would cooperate with the monarch in the exercise of executive powers. No Parliament in the early Hanoverian period refused to vote a tax or made a tax conditional upon the remedy of grievances. Efficient and stable government depended upon cooperation between king and Parliament, not upon conflict between them.

Standing at the centre of the political stage, the monarch was the dominant figure in the political life of the nation. Responsible for policy and for appointments, he initiated executive action and appointed the ministers who would carry it out. The power to appoint ministers was unquestionably the most important single power enjoyed by the monarch. By appointing the ministers the king could at least influence and at best control both policy and patronage, although the realities of carrying business through Parliament meant that he needed to exercise his prerogative with care. The king retained the right to appoint to, or at least to approve appointments to, a host of lesser offices, in the royal household, in government departments, in the church and, most of all, in the armed services. In practice the monarch's freedom to make such appointments was limited by a number of considerations: life grants, reversions, the freehold rights of office and the traditional rights of major office-holders to appoint their own subordinates. As we have seen, both George I and George II reserved peerage creations exclusively to them-selves; George II, in addition, was extremely careful about appointments to the Order of the Garter.

Foreign policy, in Britain as in other European countries, was still domi-nated by dynastic considerations. The Hanoverian monarchs were particu-larly jealous of their prerogatives in diplomatic affairs in view of their concerns for the electorate of Hanover. In a composite state like Britain in the eighteenth century, moreover, it was perfectly natural that the monarch rather than Parliament should conduct foreign policy, in view of the need for immediate diplomatic response and the overriding necessity for secrecy. After all, war was the ultimate expression of monarchical power and prestige and the epitome of national prestige and unity. It is difficult to exaggerate the influence of the Hanoverian kings on the conduct of British foreign policy in this period. Only once between 1727 and 1757 did a British minister succeed in defying the wishes of the monarch on an important diplomatic matter. This was when Walpole kept Britain out of the War of the Polish Succession in 1733. Normally, royal counsels prevailed. During the early part of his reign George I and his Hanoverian advisers determined foreign policy themselves. For his part, George II was certainly prepared to stand up to Walpole. In 1740 he frustrated Walpole's attempt to detach Frederick the Great from France. In 1741 he signed a treaty to maintain the neutrality of Hanover without con-sulting his ministers, and in the following two years he refused his ministers' entreaties to allow British troops to assume the offensive in Germany in case such initiatives endangered Hanover.

Recent studies have suggested that Britain was well served by her mon-archs after the Glorious Revolution. William III was unusually able and his successors, although dull and unexceptional, were conscientious, assiduous and, on occasion, extremely skilful. Queen Anne may not have been an inspiring monarch but she was intelligent and honest. She was never merely a token presence. If, in the end, the politicians and courtiers could influence her it remains true that her opinions had to be taken into consideration. The first two Hanoverian monarchs had been carefully brought up to prepare for their princely careers. They were alike hard-working and efficient. They had opinions of their own and their agreement could never be taken for granted. Moreover, it is a negative fact, though one of the greatest importance, that Britain did *not* experience a minority and a Council of Regency, and the consequent deterioration in royal power which normally accompanied them. It is not surprising, then, that the court remained the centre of intrigue, the hub of political activity and the cockpit in which the battle for royal favour was won and lost. At the same time, the role of the court as a social and cultural institution was beginning to decline. Anne had been able to maintain the political independence of the monarchy, but the court was too poorly funded either to sustain a court party or to maintain its role as the centre of social and cultural life.

The Whig historians of the nineteenth century were inclined to read the political history of the eighteenth century as a victory for Parliament and as the achievement of a 'constitutional monarchy'. Certainly, politicians after the Glorious Revolution were willing to use their control of the House of Commons to force themselves into office and even to inflict their policies on the monarch. More recently historians have underlined the continuing, *and possibly increasing*, powers of the monarchy and the failure of much of the legislation of the period to restrict royal power. William III's parliaments had been willing to use the threat of withholding revenue as a lever against the King's expensive military policies, but Parliaments after 1714 were much more compliant. The Civil List continued to be immune from regular parliamentary scrutiny. George I obtained a better Civil List than Anne, while George II not only obtained a Civil List of £800 000 per annum but was entitled to keep surplus revenues. This was not all. The Bill of Rights might have established the principle of parliamentary consent to taxation, but the fact remains that after the 'Financial Revolution' successive monarchs enjoyed an income of which any Stuart monarch would have been envious. The Bill of Rights also prohibited the existence of standing armies without parliamentary approval, but it remains true that it was upon massive standing armies, secured by compliant Whig majorities, that the Hanoverian dynasty depended for its survival against enemies without (the Bourbons) and rebels within (the Jacobites). In these and in other ways the eighteenth century saw a remarkable stabilization, and even in some areas a strengthening, of royal power. But it is not at all clear that Parliament was correspondingly weakened. While the powers of *both* Parliament and the monarchy strengthened during the eighteenth century, Parliament remained a subsidiary partner in a relationship that was normally harmonious and thus productive of great benefit to the country.

Consequently, it is easy to understand why theories of divine right continued to be influential, especially in Jacobite and some High Anglican circles. In a society in which the principles of patriarchy, hierarchy and obedience to authority were unquestionably assumed to be valid, it was difficult for contemporaries to conceive of authority in any other manner. The idea that authority might derive from a contract between governors and governed was confined to a small minority of Whig and radical writers. Indeed, many people were concerned at the lingering power of the monarchy and the currency of divine right theories. In this, as in so many other respects, the ideological debates of the years after 1714 were a continuation of those of the years before. Royal absolutism had been defeated in 1688–89 but given the necessities of war, the growth of the royal bureaucracy and the enormous budgets handled by governments, it could conceivably endanger the constitution in the future. Finally, in an age with limited political information, contemporaries found it difficult to distinguish between the powers of the government and the powers of the king. Consequently, many members of the political nation had an inordinate fear of the influence of the crown, which they confused with that of the more general central government.

Still, there can be no denying the fact that while the king's executive responsibilities continued to depend for their enforcement on parliamentary supply some degree of conflict between king and Parliament was unavoidable. In the next century this tension was to be resolved by the emergence of the cabinet, consisting of members of the largest party in the Commons. Before then such a solution would have seemed dangerous. Indeed, the Act of Settlement of 1701 excluded office-holders from the Commons. Fortunately for continuing harmony and cooperation between the executive and the legislative branches of the government, the offending clause was repealed by the Regency Act of 1705. By its clauses office-holders created after 1705 were to seek re-election to parliament, a provision which made possible the establishment and maintenance of harmony between the two branches.

In practice, the huge increase in routine government business after 1689 made it impossible for the monarch to exercise personal control. It required a cabinet of leading ministers to transmit it and to advise the monarch accordingly. However, the composition of the cabinet and its precise functions were nowhere laid down. Everything depended upon personality and circumstance. Walpole, for example, governed through a small group of four or five leading ministers which was called 'the cabinet', but it lacked agreed constitutional functions. When Walpole fell in 1742 his cabinet colleagues remained in office. The idea of cabinet solidarity was scarcely as yet in its infancy. Ministers were responsible individually to the king, not to each other, and not to a party. Cabinets existed to deal with the king's business, and its members were appointed with that objective in mind. They were normally not appointed as a group and they did not come into office on an agreed programme of legislative measures. Indeed, much routine business was done by individual ministers conferring with the king in his closet, the small chamber in which the king gave audiences to his ministers. In theory, the cabinet could not have a leader or a leading ('prime') minister because every minister was appointed by the king and was responsible individually to the king. Indeed, the term 'prime' minister was a term of abuse in the eighteenth century, with its connotations of unjustified royal favouritism. During the reign of William III 'prime' ministers did not emerge because of the King's tight control of business, but in the reign of Anne both Godolphin and Harley were accused of being 'prime' ministers. The term was more consistently used to describe ministers like Sir Robert Walpole and Henry Pelham, who found favour in the closet and who sat in the House of Commons as First Lord of the Treasury and 'Minister for the King in the House of Commons'. Such ministers may with some justice be referred to as 'prime' ministers in the sense that they shouldered responsibility for the performance of the government as a whole, not least defending it in the House of Commons, but it is significant that their position could not be sustained by their successors. Their achievements were largely personal achievements, not those of a party. Indeed, their constitutional position was very different from the prime ministers of the later nineteenth century, who owed their position to electoral victory and to their leadership of a united cabinet and party.

Eighteenth-century governments, lacking such reliable party support, had to create their own majorities. These were fashioned principally from the solid phalanx of 'placemen' or Whig office-holders, who numbered 180 during Walpole's ministry. Under Anne they had been notoriously unreliable. Under Walpole their reliability increased. It was very rare for defectors to number over a dozen on even the most dangerous issue. Even in Walpole's day, however, it is possible to exaggerate their significance, and, indeed, their reliability over the lifetime of a Parliament. Of the 157 place-holders returned to the House of Commons at the general election of 1741 no fewer than 33 turned out to be regular members of the Opposition. Of these 33, 19 held offices under the Prince of Wales and 14 had offices for life. Of the remaining 124, at least 19 voted against the government during the 1741–47 Parliament. We can only conclude that, essential though the systematic support of the placemen must have been to the survival of any administration, it was never enough to ensure any goverment's safety.

A secure ministerial majority required leadership and direction of the placemen by a group who have been described by Sir Lewis Namier[4] as the professional politicians, about 100–120 of whom sat in the eighteenth-century House of Commons. These men fought for, and occupied, the top posts. They were ambitious men, who, in pursuing the spoils of office and the rewards of political service, provided drive, energy and leadership both to government and to opposition. They included the great Whig political families of the eighteenth century with their dependents and retainers, including the Walpoles and Pelhams, the Pitts, Foxes and Devonshires. Whatever their material ambitions, these men exhibited ideals of service to the nation and a self-confidence borne out of generations of self-ascribed political leadership. Their ambitions gave shape and order to a Parliament which otherwise was prone to preoccupy itself with local concerns.

The remaining MPs – around 250 of them – have usually been described as 'Independents'. In the sense that they were 'backbenchers', uninterested, for the most part, in making political careers on the national stage, the description is fairly apt. But many of them were prepared to use their positions to seek favours for family and friends and, it is worth remarking, sometimes for themselves. Many of them were extremely active in parliamentary committees, advancing the interests of their towns and counties. The Independents, whether Whig or, more usually, Tory, hated taxes, wars, contractors and parties. They were suspicious of political connections and their political behaviour was therefore unpredictable. Most Independents prided themselves on the fact that they could not be relied upon, and it was often for this reason that the leading politicians directed their energies and their oratory at them.

Indeed, the use of 'influence' was never enough to ensure the permanent security of even the most accomplished minister. As we have seen, a minister with the king's confidence could be forced out, as Walpole was in 1742 and as Lord North was to be in 1782, but Parliament could not force a minister into office against the wishes of the king. When Henry Pelham died, George II reminded the rest of the cabinet that 'he hoped they would not think of recommending to him any person who had flown in his face'. None of them did. Nevertheless, the wishes of Parliament could be of crucial significance. George II could not save Walpole in 1742 because the minister had lost the confidence of the House of Commons. Nor could George II save Granville in 1744. He did not have a minister in the Commons who had his confidence, and for the same reason he could not prevent Pitt storming his closet both in 1756 and 1757.

Ministerial survival depended not only on majorities in the House of Commons but on effective control of the House of Lords. As we have seen, Walpole had established an overwhelming Whig supremacy in the upper House, although it retained its role as a deliberative and legislative assembly and preserved extensive legal powers as a court of appeal. If the House of Lords had declined in political importance since 1714, there is no sign that the peerage as a social group was losing its political eminence. Most cabinet ministers sat in the Lords; the peers controlled extensive estates, influenced numerous constituencies and manned the senior posts in the armed services, the church, the civil service and local government. Whether elected or not, peers and members of their families effectively represented the localities, lobbied to promote their economic interests in Parliament and, not least, sought favours and promotions at court. In these circumstances, the function of the House of Lords was to incorporate this wealthy and influential upper class within the political order with a constitutional guarantee of its continuing indispensability.

The state: central and local

In its peacetime operations, the Hanoverian regime was sustained less by military and bureaucratic means than by a constant set of interactions between the central government and the localities. The central government won widespread acceptance because it did not threaten the property and the privileges of local elites. Networks of clientage attached the gentry to the aristocracy, and substantial elements within the middling orders to both. Loyalty to the regime was expressed as patriotic pride in the virtues of the regime· constitutional monarchy, religious toleration, representative government and the rule of law.

Consequently, most contemporaries accept the dramatic increase in the size of the central bureaucracy in the first half of the long eighteenth century. At the start of this period the British state was governed by a bureaucracy that was exceptionally small by European standards but which grew quite rapidly: from about 150 to over 900 in the administrative departments and from about 2500 to about 6500 in the revenue departments between the Glorious Revolution and 1755.[5] During this period, the British state became more coherent and many of its institutions more efficient. It was able, for example, to accomplish the demobilization of the great armies which had fought the War of the Spanish Succession with conspicuous success immediately after 1713. Furthermore, it was able to finance astronomical increases in state spending during the wars of the mid-century. Under Walpole, the annual budget had been around £5 million per annum; by 1748 it stood at £10 million and, by the end of the Seven Years War in 1760, at no less than £20 million. But the National Debt, which had stood at £14 million in 1700, had reached what was to contemporaries an unimaginable £130 million in 1763. Such sums could only be sustained by an efficient system of public credit, sponsored by a wealthy, propertied public which had confidence in the institutions of the country.

Yet in peacetime, at least, most of the powers of the state, especially its legal powers, were administered locally. The degree of decentralization of state power was remarkable and, arguably, increasing during the century. The population remained profoundly suspicious of the executive and could be almost paranoid about the possible encroachments of an autocratic state, probably because of its recollection of the threatening precedents of Stuart interference in urban charters. Consequently, when new powers were sought and granted to local agencies, these were usually of a very specific and limited kind, often, as we have seen, to commissioners responsible for nominated purposes. Indeed, the County Rates Act of 1739 actually granted magistrates certain powers of taxation. Thereafter, bridges, highways and prisons came more and more under the influence of the enhanced power and authority of the bench.

Decentralization of the state was emphasized by its differing forms and structures in the sub-nations of Britain. Institutionally, Wales had become absorbed into England and retained no separate bureaucratic identity. The Act of Union, however, had left Scotland with considerable autonomy and little attempt was made to diminish it until the defeat of the '45. Some roads were built after the '15, and a Board of Trustees for the Improvement of the Fisheries and Manufactures was set up in 1727. Such modest centralizing tendencies were accelerated by the '45. Until then, the danger of Jacobitism had dominated Anglo-Scottish relations. Only then, with its passing, was a firmer line taken. Even then, however, Scotland remained largely self-governing.[6] Ireland was even more independent, governed through the Irish executive at Dublin and its accompanying legislature. Since British government depended upon the Protestant Ascendancy, no structural reform of the state was possible. When the Union of Ireland with England occurred at the end of the century, it was in circumstances of war and revolution which could not have been foreseen earlier.

The decentralization of executive action was, therefore, conscious and deliberate. Within a superintending framework, Hanoverian government was devolved government, but this did not mean that the government was incapable, for example, of influencing economic and, to some extent, social policy. The government saw its role not as directing the economy but as creating the conditions in which enterprise might be pursued. In this spirit it effectively abandoned the imposition of export duties after Walpole's revision of the Book of Rates in 1723. In this spirit, too, it attacked monopolies and combinations, whether of merchants concerned to keep prices high or of workers concerned to maintain the value of their wages. Furthermore, the

government was prepared to react to local demands. The government permitted Parliament to pass private bills on a wide variety of topics. Private
bills, in fact, accounted for about half of Parliament's legislative output, many
of them on economic and to some extent on social matters. Some of them
were of an innovative kind – enclosures, turnpikes and canals – thus ensuring that the state was seen to be friendly to commerce and manufacturing.
Commercial and manufacturing leaders on the one hand and MPs on the
other were normally well disposed to each other, and could usually cooperate in order to obtain legislation to promote their interests. In the 1720s
Parliament enacted about 50 bills per session; by the 1760s the number had
increased to around 200. The most commonly recurring subjects of such
legislation included enclosures, workhouses, river navigation and harbour
improvements, turnpikes and schemes for the protection of trade and commodities. The cumulative effect of such legislation could be significant. For
example, the legislative enactments of the period 1736–74 helped to transform fustian into a mechanized, mass production industry. The initiative for
most of these bills came from private interests, but the early Hanoverian state
was remarkably receptive and open to the demands of the propertied classes
from outside the landed elite.

Local government continued to enjoy considerable autonomy from central
control and interference. Local men resented the idea that central government should interfere in their affairs. The government might decide who
should be appointed to a local office, but, once appointed, that official should
be left alone. With the establishment of the Whig supremacy in the 1720s the
wholesale political dismissals from the bench which had disfigured local government in the previous 30 years came to an end. Central government
became less preoccupied with local administration. As a matter of course, the
central government could apply to the Court of King's Bench for a writ of
mandamus to compel local institutions to carry out their functions, over, say,
road and bridge maintenance, but it usually refrained from doing so. Nor, on
the whole, did it trouble to monitor the actions they did take.

Within each county the dominant figure in local government was the Lord
Lieutenant, assisted by Deputy Lieutenants, the number of which depended
on the size of the county. The Lord Lieutenant sat at the top of the social order
in the counties. He was almost always a peer, except in Wales, where aristocrats were at a premium. He was the principal local vehicle of royal patronage.
He commanded the militia, a duty which assumed considerable importance
during wartime. By the eighteenth century the electoral influence which a
Lord Lieutenant formerly enjoyed was in decline. Compensation for this was
found by taking over the office of *Custos Rotulorum*.[7]

It was not, however, this aristocratic elite which did the work of actually
governing Britain in the localities, but the Justices of the Peace, appointed by
the Lords Lieutenant but drawn overwhelmingly from the gentry. In this
sense, the gentry were partners in oligarchy. Sitting alone, a JP could handle
most petty administrative and judicial matters in his part of the county, such
as drunkenness, poaching and vagrancy. He could also issue warrants for
arrest and refer prisoners for trial at Quarter Sessions. With a second justice,
sitting in Petty Sessions, he could try minor offenders such as runaway servants and apprentices and exercise supervision over alehouses. Three justices

could sentence a man to seven years' transportation for rick-burning. However, four justices, sitting in Quarter Sessions four times a year, constituted the real cornerstone of Hanoverian local government, combining both executive and judicial functions. They appointed the overseers of the poor and the surveyors of highways. They dealt with gaming houses, disorderly houses and the suppression of nuisances. They exercised responsibility over the Poor Law and the poor rates, over gaols and houses of correction, over roads and bridges and, with diminishing commitment, over apprenticeships, wages and prices. They were responsible for granting licences to alehouses and, in addition, they tried a wide variety of non-capital criminal cases.

These were substantial responsibilities, not to be undertaken lightly. Naturally, given the increase in population and the great social and economic upheavals of the period, the number of JPs was increasing rapidly during the early Hanoverian period, even though the post was voluntary and unpaid. In 1680 there were only 2560 justices. In 1761 the number had risen to 8400. Yet it was always a problem to find gentlemen willing to sit on the bench. The shortfall had to be made up by the parochial clergy. By the middle of the century contemporaries were noticing that many gentry families were avoiding the office of JP, the deficiency being made good by Anglican clergymen. By the end of the century around one-quarter of justices were clergymen. In these circumstances, entry to the bench was not particularly exclusive. Increasingly, members of the middling orders were to be found quite comfortably rubbing shoulders with the traditional county elite.

The basic units of administration were the 10 000 ecclesiastical parishes (often called townships in some parts of the north of England). Most of them were small; less than one-tenth had a population in excess of 1000. At this level of administration the most important duties were performed by the churchwardens, who were usually drawn from the stratum of local farmers and freeholders. They were assisted by a number of unpaid and voluntary parish officials whose duties are self-evident by their titles: the surveyor of the highways (who had the right to impose six days' unpaid labour on male parishioners for road maintenance), the petty constable (who had to meet the militia quota for his parish) and the overseer of the poor. It is an important fact of eighteenth-century life that for most people the real symbols of authority were neither aristocrats nor gentry but constables, overseers and clergymen. The real social divide in many a parish was that between those who *administered* the system of poor relief and the social groups who *experienced* poor relief at one time or another in their lives. The parishes were not completely independent. Some of their officials (e.g. the constable) were appointed by the justices. Financial control of their activities, notably the Poor Law and the upkeep of roads, also rested with the justices. Final authority in the parishes lay, in theory, with the vestry meeting, an assembly of ratepayers which had the right to elect their officials. In many places their numbers might be few and important decisions thus taken by the squire, parson and a handful of local farmers.

Outside this county structure of local government were about 200 municipal boroughs enjoying the independence bestowed by royal charter. Governed by a mayor, aldermen and common councillors, the powers which JPs enjoyed in the countryside were exercised by corporate officials. Many of these boroughs had originally enjoyed an open franchise for elections to these corporate offices, but by the eighteenth century the franchise was usually restricted to the freemen of the borough and, in some cases, exclusively to the aldermen or councillors. In such places, the corporations had become little better than self-perpetuating oligarchies. Furthermore, the independence of corporate towns was rarely complete. Many of them had fallen in some measure under the influence of local, rural magnates.

London was exceptional in enjoying an open franchise of over 12 000 electors. The Court of Common Council, consisting of 234 freemen, was elected annually by the livery companies. It represented the mercantile, craft and retailing community of the capital. The Court of Aldermen, representing the great monied interests, consisted of 26 aldermen, elected for life. Between 1725 and 1746, however, the Court of Aldermen had the power to veto the activities of the Court of Common Council. The Aldermen were closely tied in to the government's funding requirements while the Common Council flirted with popular Toryism and adamant resistance to the financial oligarchy of the City. In 1746, however, Henry Pelham removed the veto, thus permitting the Common Council to monopolize executive functions, leaving the Aldermen to judicial duties.

The system of local government was remarkable for the independence enjoyed by local officials. In normal times, the central government could try to secure their loyalty and compliance only by the care with which appointments were made in the first place. Lords Lieutenant would carefully sift the names of the justices they would recommend but, once appointed, justices were virtually uncontrollable. At times of crisis, however, supervision could be tightened. During national emergencies like 1715–16 and 1745–46 local officials cooperated closely with central government, reporting incidents or persons which threatened local peace and order.

It is difficult to generalize about the functioning of an entire system of local government and the performance of thousands of different officials carrying out their responsibilities in different places. Because it appears to be a patchwork of local forms and functions, the eighteenth-century system of local government can easily be dismissed as inefficient and, in the view of the method of appointment to office, in which political loyalties could count for more than ability, as corrupt. Measured against the standards of nineteenth-century reformed local government, it may have been so. In a society with severely deficient communications, however, there was much to be said for a system of local government which was locally based and locally manned, varying with local circumstances and, not least, operating according to custom and precedent. Furthermore, many JPs were conscientious in their attention to their duties. While they displayed the prejudices of their class, paying perhaps excessive attention to the protection of property, they tried to be fair, they showed that they could be flexible and they often displayed a conspicuously modern attitude in their treatment of the problems with which they were confronted. There are many examples of JPs calling in specialized assistance, appointing salaried experts and establishing special committees to deal with intractable difficulties.

On the other hand, the deficiencies of the local government system were serious. Local response to local need was, up to a point, admirable, but in important respects a national perspective was wanting. In a rapidly urbaniz-ing country it was not obviously the wisest course to rely upon a system of corporate urban government best fitted for the sixteenth century, which was unpopular and in many cases corrupt. New towns were springing up and expanding for which no modern local government provision was made. Consequently, Manchester – and there are many other examples – was still being run by a manorial Court Leet even at the end of the eighteenth century. In other ways, too, a national, even a regional perspective was badly needed, to maximize, for example, the benefits to be derived from the steadily extend-ing turnpike road and canal networks. Finally, in some cases there can be no doubt at all that some justices acted as judge and jury, using the law to pro-tect their own property and their own privileges. No effective regulatory powers seriously impinged upon their autonomy, and thus upon their own discretionary legal power.

The government of Britain thus took place in the parishes, towns and counties; it was not inspired directly from the capital. In the same way most people had their experiences of parliamentary politics at the local level. Electoral politics, like local government, was remarkably decentralized. Indeed, electoral politics resembled two aspects of local government. First, rural elites may have enjoyed ultimate control, yet effective management was in the hands of large numbers of much humbler people. Second, the electoral system, like the local government system, was socially and politi-cally exclusive in many of its features, but it drew in people from a much wider social catchment, thus ensuring that the roots of oligarchy extended deeply in and fairly widely throughout society.

At first glance, the 'unreformed' electoral system which lasted until the Reform Act of 1832 was narrow and unrepresentative. Most accounts com-pare it unfavourably with the electorate of the period 1694 to 1714.[8] During this 'first age of party' between 1694 and 1714 the electorate had expressed the broad sense of the nation because of the frequency of elections. After 1714 this was the case to a diminishing extent. The passage of the Septennial Act in 1716 gave time for electoral passions to cool. Its extension of the period between elections raised the value – and thus the cost – of seats. Con-sequently, electoral patrons sought to control the electorate more closely in order to render election contests unlikely. They were assisted by the govern-ment of Walpole. The Last Determinations Act of 1729, reinforcing a similar Act of 1696, gave Parliament the right of determining the nature of the fran-chise in a constituency in the event of a disputed election. Walpole and suc-ceeding ministers could now massage electorates to the advantage of friendly Whig candidates, almost always in favour of restriction rather than of enlargement.

At these less frequent elections, the number of constituencies that actually went to a poll declined remarkably. There had been 119 contested elections in 314 constituencies in 1715, and the peak was reached in 1722 with 154. In 1727 there were still 114 contests, but by 1741 this had declined to 94. By 1754 this had become a mere 62 and by 1761 only 53. This suggests that the closing up of the electoral system was a gradual process. The effect of the Septennial Act took time to make itself felt. Indeed, if we count up the number of contested seats at the four general elections of 1705, 1708, 1710 and 1713 we find that the total is only four contests fewer than the total for the four general elections of 1715, 1722, 1727 and 1734. On these figures, the 'first age of party' continued well into the years of Sir Robert Walpole's administration. Furthermore, the absence of a contest does not always imply the absence of electoral competition. The decision not to go to a poll was often only taken after extensive political canvassing and the expenditure of vast amounts of money and effort, when it might be apparent that further expensive effort would be fruitless. In this, as indeed in electoral activity in general, we would be wise to recognize the prominence of political issues. That these were often matters of local rather than national significance does not diminish their importance. Indeed, national issues – especially those involving religious matters – tended to linger longer in the constituencies than they did in Parliament.

The right to vote was one of the more bizarre features of the electoral system. Its oddities were less the consequence of natural, local variation than of political calculation and electoral manoeuvring. They had little or no rational justification. After the Act of Union of 1707 there were 558 MPs elected by 314 constituencies. These consisted of 203 English borough seats, 40 English county seats, two English university seats, 12 Welsh county seats, 12 Welsh borough seats and 45 Scottish seats. Almost all English seats returned two members and voters, correspondingly, had two votes to dispose of. The qualification for the vote in the English county seats was the possession (not necessarily the ownership) of freehold property worth 40s. per year. In the boroughs the situation was extremely complex. There were several different types of qualification. In the 92 freemen boroughs the vote went with the status of being a freeman, which could be obtained by a variety of different methods, including by apprenticeship, by marriage to the daughter of a freeman and by purchase. In the 37 Scot and Lot constituencies the vote went to resident householders or occupiers of household property. In the 27 corporation boroughs the vote went with the status of membership of the corporation (or council). In the 29 burgage boroughs the vote went to the owners of specific pieces of property (burgages). Finally, in the six freeholder boroughs, the vote went to those who owned freehold property. Obviously, much depended on local circumstances, on structures of wealth, property, occupation and ownership. Consequently, the size of the electorate could vary from place to place. In the corporation boroughs and in most of the burgage boroughs it might be limited to a few dozen. The English and Welsh county electorates were normally counted in the thousands; the Scottish county seats in the hundreds. The borough electorate could vary enormously, from single figures to several thousands.

Because of the propertied nature of the franchise, the size of the electorate failed to keep pace with population increase during the first half of the eighteenth century. Between 1689 and 1754 the electorate increased in size from about 240 000 to 340 000, a decrease in the percentage of adult males from about 20.6 per cent to 17.2 per cent – a distinct but not sensational decline. The distribution of electors, however, was seriously uneven. About half the boroughs actually had fewer than 100 voters. Fewer than 30 boroughs had more than 1000 voters. Most seats were under some sort of control or attempted control. In about 20 per cent of the constituencies in 1715 the patron enjoyed such unrestricted power to determine the return as amounted to nomination. The number of nomination boroughs increased steadily to reach around 30 per cent by the end of the century. In a further 25 per cent of seats the patrons made recommendations to the electors (which might not always, of course, be accepted). This figure rose to over one-third by the end of the century. Other features of the electoral system appear to be unrepresentative and anomalous. Because it was considered to be a communal responsibility, voting remained public. There was no secret ballot until 1872. Consequently, the disposal of the elector's two votes could be, and increasingly was, recorded and published. Because many electors were to some extent dependent upon their social superiors for employment, residence or purchase of their goods and produce, it was universally assumed that the latter would attempt to influence the former in the disposal of their votes. In county elections, those electors who lived in or near a great estate would tend to vote *en bloc* for the same candidates. Even in the smaller, and not a few of the larger, borough seats, the enormous economic and social influence of a great patron in the neighbourhood could have a decisive effect upon the outcome of an election.

The electoral system could not remain immune from hierarchy and subordination in a society in which both were rife. Electoral patronage was an inevitable fact of life in a propertied electoral system in a hierarchical society. Even then, however, the influence of electoral patrons was rarely complete. Money changed hands, favours were done and, at times, corrupt practices amounting to intimidation could occur, but in its rough and ready way the electoral system remained open, a market place for personal and political as well as financial transactions. Electioneering was an expensive, insecure and enormously time-consuming business. Consequently, the electoral process may best be viewed as the interaction of patronage and influence on the one hand with the desire of electors to maintain their social, occupational and political independence on the other.

Elections thus have powerful *reciprocal* features. First, patrons and their servants had to respect and promote the needs of the constituency and its inhabitants. The results of elections were determined by the way that the patrons involved themselves in a long-term and often very expensive relationship with the community and its welfare. Elections were opportunities for the non-voters as well as the voters to scrutinize their leaders, to criticize and to hold them to public account. We should not underestimate the alacrity with which people were prepared to *use* the prevailing regime for their own purposes. Second, the oligarchy's ultimate control of the electoral system depended on the work, loyalty and efficiency of thousands of canvassers, committee men, party workers and hundreds of people performing much less elevated tasks. That control was rarely arbitrary and almost always involved mutual responsibilities. Third, the preoccupation of the Hanoverian political elite with, and enormous investment in, the electoral system involved them in a permanent commitment to parliamentary politics and representative processes. All of this did much to render the political system amenable to criticism, responsive to the needs and wishes of local communities and thus, in so many ways, more flexible and open than might have been imagined in the late seventeenth century. Although the electorate in the age of Walpole and Henry Pelham was more placid than its predecessor, it retained many of its open and representative characteristics. For all the restrictive impositions of oligarchy – the Septennial Act, Last Determinations, more infrequent elections and the techniques of electoral manipulation – in spite of all these, many of the open and participative qualities of the electorate of the reign of Anne were never wholly lost and, in the open constituencies, indeed, very largely retained. In London and the great provincial cities like Bristol and Norwich regularly contested elections, high turnouts and tumultuous popular participation indicate that the Hanoverian regime was unable to repress dissent and opposition.[9] These features, indeed, were permanent and integral features of the electoral system of the long eighteenth century.

Whigs and Tories

The Hanoverian Succession marks a major transition in the history of party. Between 1689 and 1714 the Whigs and Tories had engaged in a fairly equal competition for power. They had shared the spoils and, in Anne's reign, alternated in government. After 1714 the victory of the Whig party enabled it to monopolize office and influence. The Tories were consigned to the margins of politics and became a party of permanent opposition. By 1742 there were fewer than 140 Tory MPs and after 1747 fewer than 120, as they fell back upon family boroughs and counties traditionally Tory. (The Tories might have declined still further had it not been for the propertied nature of the electoral system.) In this manner the 'rage of party' subsided, but it did not disappear. The Whigs could not allow it to. Their political domination depended, in part at least, upon their ability to demonize the Tories, to present them as a party of plotters and conspirators, engaged with the Jacobites in treason and rebellion. Only in this way could they convince the political nation in general, and the monarch in particular, that the Whig party alone could maintain legitimate government. In this they were remarkably successful. Only when the political nation ceased to accept these assumptions did Whig supremacy come into question.

So overwhelming was the extent of Whig victory over the Tories that some historians, notably Namier,[10] have wondered whether party continued in any meaningful sense to exist. Certainly, there are countless examples of the continuing hostility which contemporaries displayed towards parties: they were accused of dividing the nation, of spreading sedition and acting merely as the vehicles of individual self-interest. In view of all this, some historians have wondered whether it is more useful to adopt a 'Court v. Country' rather than a party interpretation of politics after 1714.[11] After all, it is argued, the old party issues of the succession, of religion and of foreign policy were largely resolved. After 1714 the old party battles were replaced by a straightforward conflict between the Whigs, who monopolized court favour, and the Tories who, cast adrift on the seas of permanent opposition, were left to represent 'Country' opinion, in alliance with 'opposition' or 'Country' Whigs, hostile to the court.

There is some truth in these arguments. After 1714 the intensity of party conflict was weakening and at certain times Country Tories and Country

Whigs did act together. Detailed analysis of division lists, however, reveals that in Parliament many Country Whigs chose *not* to vote with the Tories. When it came to the point they simply could not trust Tories, too many of whom were thought to be tainted with Jacobitism. In the constituencies there are some interesting examples of electors choosing to vote a Country ticket by dividing their two votes between a Tory and a Country Whig. But this was most unusual. For example, in only seven out of 112 contests in England and Wales were Court Whigs opposed by a Tory and a Country Whig at the general election of 1734.

There *was* a Country platform, but there was no Country party in the early Hanoverian period. During their lengthy proscription from office the Tories maintained a notable cohesion, but both Tories and opposition Whigs retained their separate identities, their distinct social routines, their own party organizations, their own clubs and their own whipping arrangements. They were capable of presenting a unified front on particular occasions, particularly during Walpole's later years, but they were never capable of sustaining such unity. Samuel Sandys, a leading Tory, regarded place and pension bills as 'the flurries of a day', not as long-term political goals. In truth, Country Whigs and Country Tories had always found it difficult to work together. In the years of Whig disunity between 1717 and 1720 Tories and opposition Whigs tried to coalesce in opposing the government's foreign policy, but they were not able to cement a stable alliance. Furthermore, although Tories and Country Whigs could unite against standing armies, their reasons for doing so were very different: Tories hated standing armies on principle; many Whigs accepted the principle but wished to reduce the size of the army. Even more fatal to the thesis of a 'Country party' of Tories and opposition Whigs were the events surrounding the threatened no-confidence motion of February 1741 against the ministry of Walpole. This should have been an ideal opportunity for Tories and Country Whigs to work together, but the Tories refused to vote with the Whigs on the grounds that the motion threatened the royal prerogative of appointing ministers. The Tories were determined not to be pawns in the endgame of the opposition Whigs.

This is not to say that the attitudes and ideas of Court and Country were not at times of the greatest importance both within and without the political nation. But the hypothesis that early Hanoverian politics was dominated by these distinctions cannot be accepted. The basic structural polarity of politics in this period remained that between Whig and Tory. This argument can be developed with reference to four related issues. First, we now know – Namier could not have done – that the Tory party continued to exist as a functioning political entity throughout this period and into the 1760s.[12] We now also know that the Jacobites represented a more considerable danger to the regime than used to be thought. Together, the Jacobites and the Tories constituted a real threat to Whig hegemony. In the end the threat was repulsed but nobody at the time, least of all the Whigs, could be certain that it would be. It is, then, the conflict between the Whigs on the one hand and the Tories and Jacobites on the other which constituted the central agenda of politics in the post-1714 period, not that between Court and Country. Second, although Namier had argued that in the constituencies little more than emotional nostalgia for the old party battles lingered on, we now know that in many places the conflict between Whigs and Tories dominated electoral politics long into the Hanoverian period. Although the survival of party was uneven, and the timing and the pattern of its ultimate decline varied from place to place, there could be no doubt of its currency, especially in the boroughs, many of which remained open to election contests.[13] In these we find that electoral activity was characterized by party issues, a party-conscious electorate, impressive organization and, not least, popular enthusiasm for one side or the other. The election of 1722, for example, was accompanied by noisy demonstrations by Tories, which sometimes had Jacobite overtones. Furthermore, the electoral history of London in the reigns of the first two Hanoverian monarchs can only be understood within a party framework.[14] Third, and, in some degree as a consequence, contemporaries were coming to recognize the constitutional value of party connections and thus to recognize them as thoroughly legitimate political forms. In the 1740s, for example, many writers accepted the abiding reality of party divisions and pointed to their usefulness in preserving parliamentary and personal liberty. In the 1750s, indeed, some of the Whigs who remained outside the charmed circle of the Pelhams were even arguing the virtues of formed and systematic opposition based on party connection. Finally, although Namier declared that 'the political life of the nation could be fully described without ever using a party denomination', there can be no doubt that party terminology was in common usage down to and including the 1750s. For example, after the general election of 1754 Lord Dupplin, a government election manager, classified every single MP in party terms. Party labels were still widely employed during election campaigns and in their reporting. In general, then, we may be satisfied that, although the party battle was by no means as intense as it had once been, the distinctions between Whig and Tory continue to provide the most relevant and intelligible structural framework for understanding early Hanoverian politics. Yet there can be no denying the ineluctable decline of party tensions in the 1740s and 1750s. The old issues of religion, the succession and of foreign policy had lost much of the immediacy they had enjoyed in the earlier decades of the century. Independent country gentlemen in both parties showed increasing signs of adopting Country stances on place bills and the Septennial Act. In the constituencies, there is some evidence that the strictly partisan voting of the reign of Anne and the early years of George I was slightly weakening. From the evidence we have, the *non*-partisan vote roughly doubled in London between 1710–13 and 1727 and in Bristol between 1722 and 1734. Furthermore, while we may recognize the overall continuation of a Whig–Tory duality in Hanoverian politics, there were other sources of support for, and opposition to, the dynasty: political, religious and cultural.

The conflict of parties in the eighteenth century was based on the principle that it was legitimate to oppose the king's government. In strict constitutional theory, political opposition could be, and was, deemed unpatriotic and even treasonable because ministers were appointed by the king; in practice, opposition was a regular feature of eighteenth-century political life. Its value in keeping ministers on their toes, criticizing their actions and thus limiting their pretensions, was widely recognized even by government writers during the 1730s and, after the fall of Walpole, by a flood of pamphlets. Some of them recognized only the right of MPs to oppose measures; others proclaimed the right of the opposition to displace ministers. In the 1750s some writers went so far as to lament the absence of opposition and to deplore the possible dangers to liberties which might follow its disappearance. But none of these writers was prepared to countenance an indiscriminate opposition. For example, a formed or 'systematic' opposition, designed to force the king into a wholesale replacement of his ministers, was considered illegitimate. Opposition leaders like Pulteney and Carteret did not seek to dictate a general removal of Walpole and his ministerial colleagues. What they sought were places for themselves and some of their friends. This was entirely permissible, recalling as it did the seventeenth-century convention that it was a duty to oppose the king's 'evil counsellors'. Such ministerial changes normally amounted to little more than minor adjustments of personnel, and rarely carried with them serious policy implications. This distinction is an extremely important one: it lies at the heart of the political strategies of successive oppositions and it goes far towards explaining the nature of party conflict in the early Hanoverian period.

These inhibitions upon 'systematic' opposition help to explain the currency of the 'heir-apparent' cycle, the tendency of successive heirs of the throne to act as the focus of political groups opposed to the existing administration. Between 1717 and 1720, 1737 and 1742, 1747 and 1751 and 1755 and 1757 the court of the heir to the throne acted as the political and social focal point of the activities of politicians in opposition. For their part, the heirs had much to gain from putting pressure on their fathers. In 1720 the future George II obtained greater social freedom for himself; in 1742 Frederick, Prince of Wales, doubled his personal allowance and in 1756 the future George III gained approval for the appointment of Lord Bute to lead his household. More generally the heirs liked to surround themselves with friendly politicians who would assist them in preparing for the reign to come. Thus, although there had not yet evolved a shadow *cabinet*, Leicester House offered nothing less than a shadow *court* in which those opposed to the existing monarch and his ministers could register their loyalty to the dynasty. Circumstances and conventions, then, both permitted and even facilitated the practice of party politics after 1714. The rest of this section will explore the (very different) experiences of the Whig and Tory parties and try to analyse their respective qualities as parties.

It was the Whig party which dominated both the executive and Parliament during this period, a rare example of political supremacy exercised by one party for such a length of time. Not surprisingly, it was unable to maintain the cohesion which it had enjoyed during the reign of Anne. As the vital constitutional and religious issues which had done so much to nurture parties between 1689 and 1714 lapsed in intensity, so the texture of the Whig party weakened. The first schism appeared within a few years of the Hanoverian Succession, but it was soon repaired and the number of Whigs opposed to the government remained small. Even as late as 1727 there were only 15 of them confronting no fewer than 424 ministerial Whigs. After the election of 1734, however, there were 83 opposition Whigs facing 326 ministerial Whigs. After the general election of 1741 there were no fewer than 131 of the former and only 286 of the latter. Thereafter the numerical importance of opposition

Whigs began to decline. After the election of 1747 there were still 97 Whigs in opposition compared to 338 in ministerial ranks. After the election of 1754, however, only 42 opposition Whigs were left to confront 368 ministerialists. The 'old corps' was reabsorbing other Whig groups, hitherto inclined to oppose successive governments.

What did Whiggism stand for after 1714? Can it be argued that Whiggism became meaningless because everyone who mattered politically was a Whig? Certainly contemporaries found it necessary to insert one or more adjectives before the all-embracing term to render it intelligible. Thus they referred to 'old corps' Whigs, or the Bedford Whigs or the opposition Whigs. But if the term 'Whig' lacked precision it did not lack meaning. Although historians have tended to be cynical about the pragmatism of Whig politicians, it is difficult to believe that the great Whig principles of the defence of the constitution, the protection of Protestantism, the repudiation of Jacobitism and support for religious toleration were little more than figleaves concealing naked human greed. Whigs felt, and cared, deeply about such matters, and their beliefs concerning them were distinct from those of the Tories. Walpole's religious policy in the session of 1736 seriously divided his party but, when contrasted with the high church Anglicanism of many Tories, the anti-clerical stance of Whig MPs falls into sharp relief. On questions of foreign policy, in particular, Whig differences were often debated self-consciously within a common Whig tradition. In the 1740s, for example, the 'new Whigs' justified their inclusion in the post-Walpolean settlement on the grounds that they had revived the interventionist traditions of Marlborough and William III.

This common sense of a historic yet continuing tradition of Whiggism was most strongly manifested by the old corps Whigs. As we saw earlier, this group, emerging from the debris of Walpole's ministry, consisted of the great Whig aristocracy, the court and treasury group and a number of Whig country gentlemen. They were a loose amalgamation of men and groups at the heart of the Whig governments of Walpole and his successors. Many of these men were from traditionally Whig families. Some of their ancestors had even been active in the great events of 1688–89. The old corps were essentially men of aristocratic connection who looked back with pride to the Glorious Revolution and who believed that it was the function of the Whig party to protect the constitutional legacy of the late seventeenth century. The old corps were not a party but an inner core of politicians at the very heart of the confederation of Whig families. Indeed, by the 1740s it is difficult to depict the Whigs as a *party*, except in the most general terms. Although the conflict between Whigs and Tories remained the most important cleavage in mid-eighteenth-century politics, the Whigs had become less a party than a broad-based political establishment with the old corps at its heart. Their presence lent continuity and stability to successive administrations, just as the presence of the solid body of the Tories lent continuity and stability to successive oppositions.

After the fall of Walpole the old corps felt sufficiently insecure in power to reinforce themselves with a number of individuals on the basis of the principles of 'Broad-bottom'. By 1746, however, thanks to the diligence of Henry Pelham and his brother, the Duke of Newcastle, they were able to govern on the principle of a reunion of the Whigs. For the next eleven years the old corps dominated politics. Employing at times a somewhat disdainful attitude to the monarch, they sometimes behaved as though they, and not he, exercised ultimate power. They developed a lofty sense of their own dignity as the King's ministers. They sternly protested that the King should take advice only from his responsible ministers and not from favourites who were not responsible to Parliament. On many of the routine political squabbles between the King and his ministers the King was forced to give way: Pitt did become Secretary of State and Fox was never made chief minister. And, as we have seen, George II bent the knee to the Pelhams in 1746. On the other hand, the old corps had no wish to tilt the balance of the constitution away from the monarchy. They leaned more towards the royal prerogative than towards the rights of Parliament. They saw no contradiction between their basic beliefs in a natural aristocracy and a legitimate, functioning, competent monarchy. It was their business as the former to support the latter. Thus they accepted the King's right to be consulted and to enjoy a general oversight of affairs. They recognized that on most matters the ultimate, formal decision on matters of state rested with him. For his part, the King recognized their philosophy of service. Although he could be irritated by their clannishness he was prepared to accept them as his servants. 'My Lord,' he once told Newcastle, 'I know your faults, but I know also your integrity and zeal for *me.*' After the death of Henry Pelham the King remained aloof from the reconstructed ministry until he could be sure that it was the only ministry that could both manage the general election of 1754 and command the Commons. Only then did he give it his unreserved support. The King may have lost several important political battles with the old corps, but there can be no question that in the end the monarchy remained the essential hub around which ministerial politics revolved.

While Whigs governed, Tories opposed, impotent, hesitant but, in the end, united in their lingering demise. Their political failure is easy to explain. They had through their misjudgments surrendered office to the Whigs in 1714. They were not able to impress either George I or George II that they had the interests of the dynasty at heart, and they were incapable of keeping their distance from the Jacobites. Victims of the Septennial Act, they had been sacrificed upon the altars of successive purges of office-holders in both local as well as central government. Finally, they had to suffer constant Whig propaganda that they were little better than enemies to the throne.

Nevertheless, they continued to exist as a party. Their persistent survival is remarkable, and requires explanation. In one sense, there was nowhere else for them to go but to opposition. Most of them were proud of their (often hereditary) political attachments. There might have occasionally been room in the house of the Whig supremacy for a few of them, but there was never any prospect of the Tories coming in as a party. Furthermore, many of the Tories were staunch Anglicans, and the central ideological pillar of Toryism was the defence of the established church. Although their Anglicanism must have sustained the Tories during their long years of hopeless opposition, it served to underline their differences with the Whigs on religious matters. Tories agreed with Whigs that religious persecution was wrong, but they drew the line at legislative measures which gave aid and encouragement to non-Anglican sects. It was for this reason that they so strongly opposed both the Quaker Tithes Bill of 1736 and the Jewish Naturalization Bill of 1753. On such occasions they demonstrated that slumbering Anglicanism could be roused into a formidable weapon of popular protest. Yet this, their greatest strength, seriously damaged them at court. Both of the first two Hanoverian monarchs were Lutherans and found the staunch Anglicanism of the Tories distasteful. George I, in particular, was keen to promote unity between Protestant sects and disliked the rigidity of the Tories on such matters.

The durability and cohesion of the Tories also owed much to their ideological consistency. They continued to advocate hereditary succession and divine right monarchy, principles of continuing relevance during the dynastic uncertainties of this period. They consistently supported a 'blue water' foreign policy, free of continental entanglements; they advocated place and pension bills and demanded the repeal of the Septennial Act; they opposed the standing army, preferring national defence to be based on a militia in peacetime. This was a distinctive programme and, if ever enacted, would have dismantled many of the foundations of the Whig supremacy. It was, moreover, a Tory not a Country programme, despite the common features which they shared. In 1739, 1740 and 1742 the Tories found it impossible to cooperate with Country Whigs on proposals to repeal the Septennial Act. And in 1758 the Tories opposed to a man the old Country demand for annual Parliaments.

Tory cohesion also owed much to the proprietorial nature of the electoral system. Their ownership of property, especially in the counties, lent them a durability that was almost timeless. Just as important as this, however, as Professor Colley has persuasively argued, was the popularity of the Tory party in the country.[15] To a very considerable extent the Tories were the party of the open boroughs; they were strong in Bristol, Coventry, Nottingham and Westminster. In other sizeable boroughs, such as Exeter, Leicester and Worcester, local Toryism was based on popular Anglicanism. In some cathedral cities and county towns, such as Hereford and Gloucester, it arose from civic and corporate tradition. In rather fewer cases (such as Chester, Monmouth and Newcastle upon Tyne) Toryism rested principally upon the presence and property of powerful local families. The Tories claimed, and with some justification, that they, not the Whigs, were the party of the people. At the general election of 1715, for example, the Tories polled approximately as many votes as the Whigs, although they lost the election. Furthermore, Professor Colley claims that at three of the next four general elections, those of 1722, 1734 and 1741, they actually polled more.[16] Obviously, they were well organized at the electoral level. Although they had not yet developed a central, party election fund, there are examples of regional funds and of measures of regional cooperation. Finally, we should not imagine that the absence of contested elections in a constituency meant an absence of active Toryism. Norwich, for example, did not experience a parliamentary election between 1715 and 1727, but during that period there were over 20 contests for councillors and sheriff, all of them contested on party lines and in all of which the Tories more than matched the efforts of their Whig opponents.

The continuing cohesion of the Tory party also owed much to its effective parliamentary organization. By the 1730s the Tories had developed routines

of consultation and whipping-in which bear comparison with those of the
Junto Whigs. Their attendance rate, between 75 per cent and 80 per cent, was
actually above the rate for the House as a whole. Furthermore, it was rare for
a Tory to vote against his party. Only a handful of such instances occurred in
this period. Such remarkable party loyalty may to some extent be explained
by the effectiveness of the great Tory clubs, the Loyal Brotherhood and the
Cocoa Tree. The clubs facilitated regular meetings, political planning and the
dissemination of information. No less significant was the ability of the Tories
to launch political campaigns of a popular character, such as those in 1733
against the Excise, in 1739–42 at the end of Walpole's ministry and in 1753
against Jewish Naturalization. By the 1750s, indeed, some Tory pamphleteers
were trembling on the verge of what later generations were to term 'radicalism', with their demands for the repeal of the Riot Act and the widening of
the electoral franchise.

To what extent may the Tories be regarded as a potential and feasible party
of government-in-waiting? After the '15 and their original proscription, the
prospect of an exclusively Tory administration was poor. There was always a
number of Hanoverian Tories who would have accepted office and there
were sometimes rumours and, conceivably, some possibility of Tories being
brought into a mixed administration, such as happened in 1717, 1721, 1725
and 1727, but nothing materialized. Even when the adhesion of a few individual Tories was negotiated in 1744 the arrangement collapsed. Indeed, so
long as the monarch was firmly opposed to a Tory administration, or even a
mixed administration in which the Tories played a substantial role, then the
Tories were likely to remain a party of opposition.

Whatever their own wishes about office may have been, the Tories had no
alternative but to provide the numerical ballast for successive oppositions.
Their numbers drifted steadily downwards. After the general election of 1715
there were 217 Tories; after that of 1722 there were 178; after that of 1727 there
were 130. For about a decade and a half their numbers stabilized; 149 after the
election of 1734; 136 after that of 1741. Thereafter their numbers drifted down
once more: 117 after the election of 1747 and 106 after that of 1754.

Ironically for a party wasting in opposition for so long, the great ideological
and emotional centrepiece of Toryism remained its reverence for the institution and person of the monarch. Many of them found the Hanoverian
Succession a regrettable departure from the pattern of strict hereditary succession; this explains the recurrent Jacobite tendencies of a recalcitrant
minority of Tories. Recent historians have made much of such tendencies.
They led one eminent authority to conclude that 'the Tories were a predominantly Jacobite party, engaged in attempts to restore the Stuarts by a rising
with foreign assistance'.[17] Given the nature of the evidence which the
Jacobites generated – rumour, secretiveness, exaggeration and report – it is
doubtful if the detailed evidence on this matter will ever be settled. Some
leading Tories undoubtedly had Jacobite connections, some of them very
dangerous ones, but this does not commit the whole party to the cause of the
Pretender. Although Jacobite agents liked to talk up the Jacobite attachments
of members of the Tory party, especially when seeking foreign assistance,
such exaggerations should not mislead historians. Judged by the acid test of
how they behaved in the '15 and the '45 most Tories showed themselves to be

Hanoverian and not Jacobite. The reluctance of Tories to lift a finger for the Young Pretender in the '45 is particularly suggestive.

To judge by their *behaviour* in Parliament, and their readiness to play by the rules of the eighteenth-century political game, the Tories appear as a constitutional political party, willing to accept the Hanoverian dynasty. Most Tory MPs stoically accepted their political proscription, but sought to remove it less by rebellion than by patient parliamentary effort. Their prospects of office were slight but – by utilizing popular appeals in the open constituencies and, when opportunities presented themselves, by attaching themselves to successive heirs apparent – not entirely negligible. If we remember that the unifying sentiment of the parliamentary Tory party was its attachment to Anglicanism, it is difficult to see how it could enthusiastically embrace the cause of a Catholic dynasty which steadfastly and publicly refused to renounce its Catholicism.

At the same time, we cannot simply dismiss the issue of the Jacobitism of the Tory party as though it were not a serious problem for contemporaries. Walpole certainly thought they were a Jacobite party and believed them to be implicated in plots for the restoration of the Stuarts. Detailed research on the 136 Tory MPs returned to Parliament at the general election of 1741 has revealed that 20 were actively involved in the plots which led to the '45, another 20 were strongly sympathetic to the cause, while at least a further 20, probably more, would have passively accepted a Jacobite restoration.[18] These figures suggest that even at this late date Jacobitism was alive and well among a large minority of Tory MPs. If these men had believed that the Young Pretender had stood a reasonable chance of success in the '45 then they may well have declared for him. As it became clear that it was a hopeless cause, there seemed no purpose in their risking themselves, their families, their property and their fortunes.

If many Tories, albeit a minority, were Jacobite, it was a nebulous sort of Jacobitism which would not seriously trouble the dynasty unless foreign invasion or defeat in war precipitated a major political and military crisis which removed the old corps from office. Even if such a catastrophe occurred, a Jacobite restoration, sponsored and supported by the Tories, was one of its least likely consequences. Much more feasible was a reconstructed ministry based upon an alliance between the old corps and the opposition Whigs which might or might not include the Tories. Another alternative was a coalition between the patriot Whigs and the Tories which did not include the old corps. Before 1751, at least, it is likely that such a reconstructed administration would have included Frederick, Prince of Wales, and in such an arrangement Tory participation would have been almost certain. In all these cases, the Jacobite option took a low priority. Much of this is speculation, but it does at least suggest that a Jacobite restoration sponsored by the Tories, albeit a possibility, was a somewhat remote possibility.

The failure of the '45 and the subsequent disappearance of the Jacobite route for a Tory return to power seriously weakened the party. Its ultimate decline and disappearance, however, owed more to purely domestic matters. There are signs that in the 1750s the cohesion of the Tory party was beginning to weaken. In the long run the stream of constant failure was wearying a new generation of Tories, who found it difficult to rouse themselves in the 1750s on account of the great constitutional issues of Anne's reign. The death of Prince Frederick in 1751 removed their great prospect of power either in this reign or in the next. There were still isolated bursts of Tory party activity, especially in the constituencies. At a by-election in 1750, for example, the party unexpectedly regained a seat it had formerly held in Middlesex. Yet in the second half of the decade the overriding need for wartime unity began to dissolve Whig mistrust of the Tories. The disappearance of the Jacobite threat removed the last barrier to Tory cooperation with the government. For their part, the Tories needed little persuasion that the need for patriotic unity during the Seven Years War demanded the ending of old party vendettas. Consequently, they began to play down the high-Anglican, populist and anti-executive attitudes which they had nursed during the long years of opposition. Moreover, in the Elder Pitt they at last found a minister who both took them seriously and treated them with consideration. The Tories could not help but notice that in the summer of 1755 Pitt established himself high in the affections of Leicester House, where the future George III was receiving his political education. They also noticed that the Princess Dowager refused to allow the court of the Prince to be used for political purposes. Here, perhaps, could be the agency of the ending of their proscription in the reign to come. The Tory party in Parliament began to curtail its attacks on the government's foreign policy and on its conduct of the war. In return, William Pitt began to coax them away from opposition. The implementation of the Militia Act of 1757 once more gave the Tories an important military function in the localities and began the process of reintegrating them with their Whig neighbours.[19] They rallied around the Pitt–Newcastle ministry, revelling in its patriotic victories, approving its concentration on naval warfare and enjoying the new ministerial concern for Tory susceptibilities. The formal ending of their proscription came when George III succeeded to the throne in 1760. As soon as the proscription was ended the old Tory party disintegrated. Some of its members came to court, others joined one of the various Whig groupings, while a few lingered in their traditional and familiar world of opposition. The Tories did not fight the general election of 1761 as a party. By 1763 it is not even meaningful to refer to a 'Tory' party at all.

By then, too, the Whig party had lost both its unity and its *raison d'être*. By the 1750s the dynasty was secure and the fruits of the Glorious Revolution confirmed. By then, too, the Whigs were abandoning the two assumptions upon which their supremacy had been predicated: that the Jacobites were a constant and dangerous threat to the throne and that the Tories were a Jacobite party. Furthermore, the death of Henry Pelham in 1754 removed the one man who might have held together the sprawling confederations of the Whigs. It took several years of painful reconstruction before a stable coalition, the Pitt–Newcastle ministry of 1757–61, could be established. Although Pitt was a Whig he was not a member of the old corps and he did not share its morbid fear of Toryism. His rise to power weakened the tenure of the old corps and prepared the ground for the more general fragmentation of the Whigs in the following decade.

By the later 1750s, then, the structure of party politics which had dominated British public life since the Glorious Revolution was slowly crumbling. The years of party, however, had stamped their effects on British life. Party competition had permanently opened up the political process to public scrutiny and some measure of popular involvement. The country platforms of both parties had compelled court politicians to debate and to justify their measures both in local as well as in central government. The need for politicians to obtain support not only at but also between general elections had prevented the ruling order from ossifying into a brittle and narrow oligarchy. The competition of the parties had thus contributed to the permanent establishment of parliamentary habits and conventions with the British public. If the labels of the old parties did not survive into the following decade, there can be no doubt that their precedents, their habits and their languages had exerted a salutary effect upon British public life.

The Jacobites

The Jacobite movement has been of considerable interest to historians in recent years. Once regarded as an eccentric symptom of an irretrievably lost cause, Jacobitism has now been restored to the very centre of historiographical attention. The persistence of its diplomatic support abroad, the impressive size of its popular support in Britain and the continuing relevance of its ideological challenge place it alongside Whiggism and Toryism as one of the central features in the political and social history of the early Hanoverian period. How dangerous a threat to the Hanoverian regime were the Jacobites? How did Jacobitism survive for so long as a dynastic and political alternative? How much support did it really have? The lack of evidence in so many areas of the subject, the doubtful nature of the evidence where it does survive and thus the mystery in which the subject is shrouded helps to explain its attractiveness both to contemporaries and to recent historians. But it is also difficult to grasp the dimensions of the topic because of the many-sidedness of Jacobitism. It was a political movement, yet its ultimate weapon was violent, military uprising. It had an international context, while its followers were fiercely patriotic. The culture of Jacobitism was to be found equally in polite society and in rioting election crowds. It is a topic of unusual fascination, to some extent because the nature of the evidence precludes the possibility of ever finding conclusive answers to the most important of our questions.

Jacobitism was a revolutionary conspiracy whose objective was to topple the Hanoverian dynasty with foreign diplomatic and military assistance. In the long periods when such assistance was not forthcoming the faith had to be preserved and the banners of loyalty and optimism kept flying. During these long periods, then, Jacobitism can only be described as a faith, a set of convictions which generated a sense of mission and of martyrdom, an ideology which touched religious and patriotic chords in the hearts of thousands of men and women. People were prepared to die on the scaffold for this faith. Over 200 of them actually did so between 1689 and 1752, and every execution became yet another heroic episode in the folklore of Jacobitism. All of this kept alive the burning conviction – in defiance of the harsh realities of the present – that at some time in the future the Messiah would come. Had the Jacobite option, however shadowy, not seemed so urgent and so relevant to many contemporaries it would not have lasted as long as it did nor would it have appealed to so many. That it did so is a reflection of the hundreds of songs, poems and stories that carried the Jacobite message, not merely about a future restoration, a future golden age, but about the need to accept misfortune in a harsh and unyielding world. In short, Jacobitism crystallized popular resentment against the regime, not least in Ireland and in Scotland.

We should remember that modern labels of 'left' and 'right' do not neatly apply to eighteenth-century political groups. Some Jacobites may indeed be dismissed as courtly reactionaries, entranced by the culture of the clan, but Jacobitism was to be found among almost all sections of society, including the middling orders and, not least, the lower orders of society. What may be termed the programme of Jacobitism, indeed, proved to be remarkably flexible. As time went on it became much less rigid until it acquired some features of radical reform. In the early years of his exile James II uncompromisingly aimed for a military restoration of his throne. But the key to a Stuart restoration lay in England. By 1693, under pressure from Louis XIV, he was promising to respect the constitutional position of Parliament, to preserve the established church and to agree to an indemnity for supporters of the Glorious Revolution. In patent attempts to capitalize on the unpopularity of the Whig oligarchy after 1714, the Jacobite leaders began to adopt a position almost indistinguishable from that of 'Country' politicians. In 1753 Charles Edward wrote a memorandum in which he proposed annual Parliaments, the abolition of placemen and severe reductions in the standing army in the (by then unlikely) event of his restoration.

To which groups did Jacobitism particularly appeal? In answering this question we need to remember the religious foundations of the movement. Jacobitism, in fact, depended on religious adherents from three churches. In England and to some extent Lowland Scotland, old Roman Catholic families and their dependents constituted the inner core of Jacobitism. After almost 200 years of underground existence the old faith was an ideal breeding-ground for the cause of Jacobitism, and its adherents were conspicuously well represented in every area of Jacobite activity. Catholics were prominent in the '15, although they held themselves aloof from the '45. (Irish Catholics did not move during either rebellion.) In Scotland, however, the overwhelming majority of Jacobites were Scots Episcopalians. Members of this church had seen themselves as victims of the Presbyterian Church of Scotland ever since 1690, and wore their Jacobitism as a political and dynastic mark of their spiritual alienation. Finally, in some parts of England the descendants of the Non-jurors tended to support Jacobitism. Their numbers, and thus their influence, diminished considerably after 1715.

Indeed, loyalty to the Jacobite cause had distinctly political as well as religious overtones. As we have seen, Jacobitism profited for many years through its association with, or rather infiltration of, the Tory party in England. The links between Jacobitism and Toryism were particularly strong between 1714 and 1722. Though weaker thereafter, they remained the subject of a degree of political speculation which was never really justified. Although they shared a common hostility to the Whig oligarchy after 1714 and a belief in divine right monarchy, Jacobites and Tories yet differed profoundly on religion. The Tories were a party of the Church of England, and the Catholicism of the Pretenders stood in the way of their enthusiastic cooperation. The Young Pretender, indeed, was remarkably cavalier about the Tories both before and during the '45: he did little to cultivate them, he failed to consult them before landing in Scotland, and had no safe channel of communication with them. If the Pretender did not take them seriously in 1744–45, it is perhaps difficult to see why the historian should.

In attempting to identify the composition of the Jacobites, it would be unwise to ignore the noticeably large number of 'economic Jacobites' who were involved in the movement. Such people were Jacobites because they yearned for high office, for profits and for favours when the restoration came. They included a large number of debtors and bankrupts who were convinced that their debts would be liquidated under the new regime. Three members of the Pretender's council in 1745 were bankrupts. One of them, Lord Kilmarnock, openly admitted: 'For the two Kings and their rights I cared not a farthing which prevailed; but I was starving, and by God if Mahommed had set up his standard in the Highlands, I had been a good Muslim for bread and stuck close to the party for I must eat'.[20]

On the other hand, a real or pretended loyalty to the Stuart dynasty could justify all manner of opposition to the Whig regime. We should not discount the number of people who would never have dreamed of taking any actions to aid a Jacobite rebellion, but who nevertheless manifested some degree of support for the cause. Rioters, pamphleteers, protesters and even illegal groups which generated their own commercial culture, such as smugglers, adopted Jacobite slogans and language, particularly in the years 1714 to 1720. They did so, presumably, because no other prominent discourse of protest was so readily available to them. Thereafter the currency of Jacobitism at the popular level declined, but it did not disappear. In the later 1730s there is still evidence of Jacobite rioting among the tinminers of Cornwall, the clothiers of the West Country and the keelmen of Newcastle. All of this strongly suggests that at times Jacobitism could be as much a convenient cloak for lower-class social protest against an inequitable social and legal system as a genuine wish to see the restoration of a Roman Catholic dynasty.

The home of Jacobitism lay, of course, in Scotland. Scottish Jacobitism was an amalgamation of three distinct forces: dynastic nationalism, religious sentiment and clan rivalry. As to the first, the Jacobite cause might have quickly subsided but for the short-term reaction in Scotland to the Act of Union of 1707. Jacobites were able to exploit bruised national feelings on several different levels. After 1707 the old Presbyterian form of nationalism disappeared as that church made its peace with the Whigs. The Jacobites now became the standard-bearers of popular nationalism, and continually promised to repeal the Act of Union. Not surprisingly, Jacobitism had a wide appeal in Scotland. It was not just confined to the Highlands and the less economically developed areas of the country. For example, the Scottish cultural renaissance of the early eighteenth century may be traced in part to Jacobite sources. Most printers and booksellers in Edinburgh were Jacobites, as were many members of the polite societies of the age, and most members of the legal profession. As to the second, there was always a powerful religious basis to Scottish Jacobitism. It appealed naturally to the Scottish Catholics but, more importantly, to the Scottish Episcopalians, who were especially strong in the north east of the country. Since the establishment of the Presbyterian form of Kirk government in 1690 almost one half of all the ministers in Scotland were left disaffected and resentful, a prime breeding-ground for Jacobitism. As to the third, the Jacobitism of many of the clans represented a defensive reaction against the expansionist designs of the most powerful clan of all, the Whig Campbells (Dukes of Argyll), in the south west of the Highlands. The 2nd Duke abandoned the old patterns of clanship by letting land directly to his tenants, a social and economic regime which, had it continued to spread unchecked, would have threatened the destruction of the traditional patriarchy of kinship rights. The clan leaders depended on traditional, hereditary right for their authority and looked to the Stuarts as the bulwarks of their power. Not all the clans were Jacobite by any means, and those that supported the cause were often chronically divided; but the dependence of the Stuarts upon the military power of the clans was an indispensable element in their endless plots and plans for over 60 years.

It would be a serious underestimation of Scottish Jacobitism to dismiss it merely as the political and military offspring of a declining Highland culture. Similarly, it would be a grotesque caricature to treat either the '15 or the '45 as a cultural clash between a backward-looking Highland civilization on the one hand and a more progressive, modern society on the other. In the '15, in fact, James Edward had drawn his support from Lowland burghs and the economically developed north east of Scotland. In 1745 the larger towns remained loyal to the government, but many lowland areas were remarkably sympathetic to the rebels. Interestingly, Charles Edward found the most northerly and north-westerly clans of the Highlands against him.

In England Jacobitism was an umbrella phenomenon, a cloak for all manner of dissatisfaction with the status quo, but it was a much less positive alternative to the Hanoverian regime than it was in Scotland. Obviously, it lacked the patriotic momentum which was such a force in Scotland: the Protestantism of so many English Jacobites diluted their support for a Catholic Pretender. The growth of English Jacobitism from the initial aftermath of the Glorious Revolution, when its following was negligible, to 1715, when it conspired to topple the new dynasty, was remarkable. Its appeal first to Catholics, then to Non-jurors and Tories, and then to wider sections of the population made it a force to be reckoned with. It also went far towards absorbing disappointed former radical Whigs who, having failed to achieve major changes in the political and social order at the time of the Glorious Revolution, now hoped to have more success in the event of a (preferably insecure) Stuart restoration. Yet the best hope for Jacobitism in England remained the Tory party. Sadly for the Jacobites, the Tories only adopted the Jacobite option with any relish when their political situation was at its nadir. They did so on two occasions, during the great proscription of 1715–22 and after the defection of the opposition Whigs and the failure of 'Broad-bottom' in 1744. On both of these occasions some of the Tory leaders allowed themselves to fish in the ponds of Jacobite intrigue, but little came of it. This Jacobite tendency within the Tory party was constantly challenged and, on the whole, weakened by the party's habits of constitutional behaviour during normal times and by its distaste for French intervention in the affairs of Britain. In the end, Jacobitism in England after 1722 turned out to be less of a threat to the Revolution settlement than a stick with which the Whigs could beat the Tories and thus confirm the power of the oligarchy.

How did people experience Jacobitism? In the first place we may identify a culture of Jacobitism which was secretive and conspiratorial. At a time when it was dangerous openly to express opinions which might have been judged to be treasonable, an underground culture of loyalty to the exiled dynasty spread throughout Britain. This amounted to something more than a superficial dislike for the Whig regime. Individuals chose to adopt some positive indications of support for the Stuart cause, perhaps by drinking the health of the Pretender, by wearing tartan waistcoats, by collecting Jacobite souvenirs or by observing one or more of the Jacobite anniversaries. Just as compelling was the writing and dissemination of Jacobite propaganda, the circulation of songs and stories and the meetings of Jacobite clubs and societies. This culture of Jacobitism depended on regional, national and even international communication networks. The existence of such a Jacobite 'underground' was extremely worrying to the authorities. Its success in preserving and, after the military catastrophes of the early 1690s, rebuilding Jacobite support should not be underestimated.

In the second place, we may discern a tradition of plots and conspiracies which preoccupied the leaders of Jacobitism especially during periods of acute international tension. Most of these came to nothing, but several of them have come to the notice of the historian. Three of them occurred within 20 years of the Glorious Revolution. It is only with the benefit of hindsight that they can be dismissed as harmless. In the Ailesbury Plot of 1691–92 a group of mainly Catholic peers and gentlemen in the south of England hoped to coordinate a raising of their tenants with the landing of a French army. The failure of the army to materialize led to the rounding-up of the conspirators. In the Fenwick Plot of 1695–96 a French army was to combine with a local force of Kentish Jacobites as a preliminary to a march on London. A dilemma which was to become very familiar in the history of Jacobitism was then confronted: the army would not sail until the plotters had risen and the plotters would not rise until the army had arrived. In the event, the invasion plan was still-born. The plotters then diverted themselves with a plan to assassinate William III which was frustrated by timely government action. Finally, in 1708 the French, reeling from Marlborough's victories, were anxious to pin down the British at home by sending a small force to the north east of Scotland which would link up with a Jacobite rising in the northern kingdom. A naval squadron prevented the French fleet from landing the troops and the domestic rising was aborted. On all three occasions the causes of the lack of success were identical: the failure of the French to land, the inability of the Jacobites to take the government by surprise and their failure to nurture domestic support for their cause.

After 1714 the Jacobite cause was a pawn in the European diplomatic game, one that was kept on the board by the French court and one which was for many years checkmated by Walpole's policy of peace at any price. It was only when the circumstances of European diplomacy permitted that the Jacobites had any real expectation of the military support which was necessary for the victory of their cause. In 1719 a Spanish invasion fleet set sail, but much of it was dashed to pieces in the Bay of Biscay. A few ships managed to reach Scotland, but the soldiers were joined by only a few hundred Highlanders, and at Glenshiel in mid-June they were easily mopped up by loyal government forces. The 'Atterbury Plot', of such great significance in the history of the Tory party, was much less menacing. The usual Jacobite conspiracy had no effective foreign support and was easily foiled. So effectively did Walpole exploit the incident that the only further Jacobite 'plot' that managed to break the tranquil surface of politics until the rebellion of 1745, if such a term can be given to the Cornbury Plot of 1733–35, was even less substantial.

In the third place we must identify the great risings of 1715 and 1745, the two culminations of Jacobite activity in their respective periods. On the first of these occasions, the rebellion was a consequence of profound political and social tensions in both Scotland and England. A steady accumulation of Scottish grievances after the Act of Union of 1707 coincided with the dynastic insecurity of George I and the willingness of France to fish in British waters. It is unlikely that the rebellion would have got off the ground had the Tories not been driven into the arms of the Pretender by the Whigs seeking to impeach Tory leaders. In England, it was only where local, usually Catholic, gentry of the north of England decided to support the cause that Jacobitism enjoyed any degree of popular support. Indeed, the powerful representation of Roman Catholics in the English Jacobite army – somewhere between one-half and two-thirds – did much to discredit the cause among a largely Protestant population. In Scotland, on the other hand, the rising met with at least passive support. Very few Scots were prepared to fight for the Hanoverian dynasty. It is surely significant that the Jacobites recruited over three times the number of soldiers into their ranks as the government. They mobilized, furthermore, between 5 per cent and 10 per cent of the adult male population of Scotland. What destroyed Jacobite prospects in the '15 – much brighter prospects than those enjoyed by William III in 1688 – was the dismal military strategy of the Earl of Mar. Had he and the other Jacobite leaders behaved more competently the '15 might have given rise to a prolonged civil war in the two countries.

The '15 occurred at a time of great domestic unrest. The '45 occurred in the middle of a major war. Much of the impetus for the '45 arose out of the sheer personal magnetism generated by the Young Pretender and his wild gambles, and by the willingness of the French court to play the Jacobite card. Indeed, the rising came astonishingly close to success even though the political climate was unfavourable. Fatally, the inability of the Jacobites to synchronize their rising with French support in the end destroyed its prospects. The reluctance of the English, in particular that of the Roman Catholics, to move doomed the rebellion to failure. No wonder that the failure of the Jacobite march into England to attract respectable and propertied support on any scale demoralized its leaders. Although there is much evidence of apathy and indifference towards the regime in England, there is scarcely any evidence of a desire to do anything to change it. It is true that many English landed families held back from declaring for the government until the outcome of the Jacobite advance into England was clear. It is even more revealing that the towns that fell to the Jacobites without resistance – Edinburgh, Carlisle, Lancaster, Manchester, Preston and Derby – was a long and ominous one. But it was up to the Jacobites to force the issue. In the absence of a French invasion force in the south of England, they were unable to do so. The only circumstance in which it is possible to imagine a rebel victory in 1745 is if the Jacobite army had continued on to London and either taken the capital or seriously challenged it, thus creating the conditions for a French invasion into the south of England which might have sorely embarrassed the regime. As it was, the English ruling class kept its nerve and maintained its morale. In the end, the '45 resembled a civil war of some seriousness in Scotland, but it entirely failed to arouse effective support in England.

The failure of the '45 marked the final resolution of a major international, political and religious issue which had bedevilled politics since 1688: that of the dynastic succession to the throne of Britain. The Jacobites could only look back to disastrous political and military failure between 1688 and 1692, to the disappointment of a French invasion scare in 1708, to the sad end of a serious rebellion in 1715, to the frustration of a Spanish invasion attempt in 1719, to the revelation of a plot in 1722 and to ultimate disaster in the great gamble of 1745. Until Hawke's victory over the French fleet at Quiberon Bay in 1759 permanently established British naval supremacy there was still a lingering prospect that the Jacobites might try again, but little enthusiasm could be found for it anywhere.

The significance of the Jacobite movement can be variously assessed. In the light of recent discoveries that Jacobitism was more widespread in both Scotland and England than had been previously imagined, we can never return to the days when the movement could be dismissed as irrelevant and archaic. Yet it is difficult to see that Jacobitism, however extensive its support, represented a mortal threat to the Hanoverian regime. Many individuals and groups had some interest in the Jacobite cause but most of them were unwilling to use violent means to effect a Stuart restoration. Neither the English nor the Scots showed any enthusiasm for the prospect of a Catholic monarch restored by force of arms, backed by a French invasion. The Jacobite option unquestionably existed, but it was not an option that many were prepared to back. In a dynastic society it is not surprising that a dynastic alternative to the Hanoverian regime was available. What is surprising is how unattractive it was to the majority.

Indeed, what is remarkable is the degree of anti-Jacobite sentiment which had sprung up in both countries by 1745 and which acted as the vehicle of a vociferous British patriotism. The failure of Jacobitism was a fatal blow to the development of a viable Scottish patriotism as it had developed after 1707. After all, Jacobitism implied absolutism, Catholicism and French imperialism – all of them totally unacceptable to the mass of the people in both countries. In this sense Jacobitism may have helped to promote the acceptance of parliamentary government, the unity of the Protestant faiths, and even the cohesion of the United Kingdom, all of which were threatened by a Jacobite restoration. Had Jacobitism led to an independent state in either Ireland or Scotland, that state would have looked to Europe for support and resources to use against the English. Such a challenge to English rule within the British Isles might have weakened England's ability to overcome France and Spain. In this sense, then, the defeat of Jacobitism was an essential preliminary to Britain's emergence as a European and world power.

Notes

1. L.B. Namier, *England in the Age of the American Revolution*, 2nd edn (1961); *The Structure of Politics at the Accession of George III*, 2nd edn (1982).
2. P. Backscheider, *Spectacular Politics: Threatened Power and Mass Culture in Early Modern England* (1993), p. 60.
3. R.P. Bond, ed., *Studies in the English Periodical* (1957), pp. 3–4.
4. L.B. Namier, *Crossroads of Power* (1962).
5. J. Brewer, *Sinews of Power: War, Money and the English State 1688–1783* (1989), pp. 66–67.
6. For the reaction of the government to the '45, see p. 89.
7. The *Custos Rotulorum* was historically the principal local civilian officer who recommended the men to serve as justices.
8. G. Holmes, *The Electorate and the National Will* (1976), pp. 30–39; J.A.Cannon, *Parliamentary Reform* (1972) pp. 36–46.
9. N. Rogers, *Whigs and Cities* (1989), chs. 4 and 9.
10. L.B. Namier, 'Monarchy and the Party System', in *Crossroads of Power* (1962).
11. W.A. Speck, 'Whigs and Tories Dim Their Glories', in J.A. Cannon, ed., *The Whig Ascendancy: Colloquies on Hanoverian England* (1981).
12. See L. Colley, *In Defiance of Oligarchy: The Tory Party, 1714–60* (1982). For doubts about Colley's arguments, see P.D.G. Thomas, 'Party Politics in Eighteenth Century Britain: Some Myths and a Touch of Reality', *British Journal for Eighteenth Century Studies*, 10(2) (1987), pp. 201–10. I believe that Professor Thomas both underestimates the survival of Toryism in the constituencies and understates its parliamentary continuity. He is right to query the extent of its organizational coherence but not, I think, to repudiate it entirely.
13. Rogers, *Whigs and Cities*, especially chs. 8 and 9; F. O'Gorman, *Voters, Patrons and Parties: The Unreformed Electorate of Hanoverian England, 1734–1832* (1989), especially ch. 6; R.R. Sedgwick, *The House of Commons, 1715–54* (2 vols, 1970), I, pp. 19–78.
14. Rogers, *Whigs and Cities*, pp. 133–220.
15. Colley, *In Defiance of Oligarchy*, ch. 5.
16. *Op. cit.*, pp. 121–23.
17. Sedgwick, *The House of Commons, 1715–54*, I, p. ix.
18. I.R. Christie, 'The Tory Party, Jacobitism and the '45', *Historical Journal*, 30(4), (1987).
19. The Militia Acts of 1757 provided for the training of militia levies to take over the burden of home defence. The existence of a national militia enabled the country to defend itself against invasion and rebellion much more safely, thus enabling the authorities to dispense with foreign auxiliaries.
20. B. Lenman, *The Jacobite Risings in Britain* (1980), pp. 256–57.

6

What kind of regime?
(1714–1757)

A stable regime?

From a vantage point in 1714, the history of Britain during the Stuart period must have seemed bleak and unpromising. The country had experienced two major revolutions, three civil wars, one major rebellion (Monmouth's), several minor, local risings and an unhealthily large number of conspiracies since the Gunpowder Plot. Although the Glorious Revolution had removed the threat of autocratic monarchy it actually inaugurated a period of further instability, seen in the intense bitterness of party competition and the numerous ministerial changes of the time. If all this were not enough, the '15 seemed an ominous reminder that the age of revolutions and rebellions had not passed. But then, within a decade the clouds of disruption had parted and in the years of Walpole and the Whig supremacy a new age of stability dawned.

How was this astonishing change to be explained? What exactly had happened? In his influential *The Growth of Political Stability in England 1675–1725*, published in 1967, J.H. Plumb set out a series of answers to these questions. There were, he announced, three major factors: 'single party government; the legislature firmly under executive control; and a sense of common identity' in those who wielded economic, social and political power'.[1] Defining stability as 'the acceptance by society of its political institutions, and of those classes of men and officials who control them', Plumb enlarged his account of its achievement by pointing to additional causes: the victory of the Court over the Country, the control of the electoral system by a small oligarchy of patrons, the pacification of Scotland and Ireland and the establishment of government influence over the City of London. This interpretation had much to commend it. Not least, it enabled the student of the period to identify many of the underlying developments which conditioned early Hanoverian politics, to clarify the achievement of Walpole and the Whigs and to place that achievement in a general historical perspective.

But no general interpretation can endure for almost three decades without attracting a number of serious criticisms. First, a number of scholars have remarked upon Plumb's omission of religious considerations. It is, with the benefit of hindsight, astounding that such a powerful and ubiquitous force should have been ignored. Obviously, it needs to be incorporated within any viable theory of 'stability', if only to suggest that religious issues were no longer as potent in the era of 'stability' as they had been earlier. Second, some historians have wondered just how politically stable the period after 1725 actually was. The Jacobite option remained a profoundly unsettling issue until Culloden, at least. In addition, how could a period of two major wars (1739–48 and 1756–63), with their concomitant threats of French invasions, be accommodated within the 'stability' hypothesis? Indeed, how stable was a society which was still subject to acute religious divisions, as was seen in 1753? How stable *was* a political order which could be brought to its knees on a relatively minor matter of taxation, such as the Excise Crisis of 1733–34, when rioting was alarmingly widespread and in which the regime was shown to be bitterly unpopular? How 'stable' was a society in which the accession of a new king in 1760 could throw the political world into confusion? (As late as 1788–89, indeed, the simple issue of the health of the monarch could divide the political nation with extraordinary intensity.) Third, many contemporaries did not believe that they lived in a particularly settled and ordered society. It was not just the aristocracy but the propertied classes in general during the eighteenth century who were persistently anxious about the possibility of disorder. Sir Robert Walpole constantly worried about enemies within and without, and fretted about losing his parliamentary majorities. The political confusion and ministerial instability which characterized the periods 1714–21, 1739–46 and 1754–57 dismayed many contemporaries who looked back upon half a century of recurring political disruption, lamenting that the British could be so wild and ungovernable in their politics. The 'liberty' on which the British prided themselves seemed too frequently to tend to anarchy rather than to stability. Some observers even wondered (rather extravagantly) whether such licence might have to be tempered by royal despotism. Fourth, there are difficulties with some of the detail of the explanations for 'the growth of political stability' which Plumb adopted. For example, he attributed 'stability' in part to the rapid growth in the size of the executive, but between 1689 and 1727 that expansion was really quite modest. Dramatic reductions in the size of the army from 42 000 to 18 000 and the navy from 50 000 to 10 000 at the end of the Spanish War of Succession and, indeed, reductions in the diplomatic and navy boards, offset increases in the bureaucratic machine occurring elsewhere. Furthermore, significant increases in the excise and salt offices only occurred in the 1730s.

To what extent does the 'stability' thesis apply to Scotland and Ireland? Perhaps it is significant that Plumb regarded Scotland and Ireland merely as managerial problems requiring little more than containment. Indeed, he actually dismissed the government of Scotland and Ireland as 'minor matters'.[2] For Plumb, all that was needed in Scotland was sensible management of policy and patronage to allow time for the beneficial economic effects of the Act of Union to show themselves. No wonder that he credits Walpole with solving the Scottish problem. As for Ireland, the problem was successfully 'contained' early in the century. But later, with the consequences of economic prosperity, a growing number of Irish families were left dangerously outside the Irish establishment. Furthermore, Plumb's peremptory account of political 'stability' in the Celtic kingdoms characteristically ignores the underlying religious problem. The existence of a Presbyterian religious establishment in Scotland alienated the mass of Episcopalians. Even worse, the existence of an Anglican establishment in Ireland offended the mass of the Roman Catholic population. On any definition, 'stability' could not be achieved in these circumstances. All that could be done was to use political patronage together with immediate security measures to keep the lid on potentially explosive situations. In Ireland this was achieved for several decades without much difficulty. So long as Jacobitism remained a threat to English supremacy in Ireland then the Ascendancy would make few serious difficulties for the British government. But, even on Plumb's definition, this hardly amounted to a satisfactory and 'stable' situation. Even worse, in Scotland the idea of 'stability' surely cannot be maintained in view of the reaction against the Act of Union and the rebellions of 1715 and 1745.

On a more general chronology it is difficult to accept the case that political stability had come to Britain by the middle of the eighteenth century. After all, the political convulsions of the early years of the reign of George III, the great political and military crisis of 1779–84, the Irish rebellion of 1798 and the attendant economic and political disruption, to say nothing of the great radical challenge to the political order between 1815 and 1821, do not suggest any long-term and settled stability. As we shall see in later chapters of this work, they suggest rather a recurrent tendency for Hanoverian politics to collapse into renewed, arguably worsening *instability*. The achievement of stability in the first half of the eighteenth century may have been a notable achievement, but it was only a temporary one. That it represented any sort of enduring legacy is difficult to demonstrate.

Plumb's optimistic treatment of the 'stability' of the period after 1725 may be reviewed and its validity questioned, but in the end, whether that period is to be described as 'stable' or 'unstable' can only be decided by reference to an agreed set of criteria. Strictly speaking, on Plumb's own criteria – 'the acceptance by society of its political institutions, and of those classes of men and officials who control them' – we must conclude that stability did *not* prevail at all times because of the '45 rebellion, unless its ultimate failure is to be construed as 'acceptance'. Elsewhere in his book, as we have seen, Plumb adopts different criteria of 'stability'. For example, he demands 'a sense of common identity' among those who wield political, social and economic power, but unless 'a sense of common identity' is more closely defined it is difficult to take the discussion much further.

One way out of this impasse may be found in the reformulation of the stability thesis undertaken by Geoffrey Holmes in 1981.[3] What Holmes sought to do was to investigate the social and economic foundations of Plumb's alleged political stability. In doing so, he in effect changed the terms in which the argument was being conducted. In demonstrating that the foundations of stability were strong and healthy, he showed how political conflict could be managed and contained. In a sense, he scaled down the significance of such political instability as might be found because the social and economic groundwork of the regime was so secure. In this way, the 'stability' thesis could be broadened out into the social and economic arenas and, in this way, salvaged and strengthened.

Holmes argued that three major developments impinged upon the issue of political stability. The first was a modest increase in population. From the mid-seventeenth century down to 1736 the population of England and Wales increased by only a gentle 3–4 per cent per annum. As a result there was little pressure upon either economic or political resources. Indeed, the standard of living of the mass of the people almost certainly improved. Second, there is some evidence that real wages may have been increasing in some industries by as much as 25 per cent between 1680 and 1720. Certainly, agricultural prices remained stable between 1660 and 1750 and England became a grain-exporting country after 1670. For these reasons, popular protest was rarely tinged with political radicalism. Indeed, the lower orders seemed uninterested in popular agitation, and in dangerous years like 1688–89, 1715 and 1745 they remained strikingly docile. Third, a significant increase in the amount of employment available in the professions met the needs of the younger sons of the gentry, whether in the church, in the law or in the armed services, which increased in size so rapidly after 1689. Such career decisions amounted to family commitments to and personal investments in the regime. Moreover, the dramatic expansion in foreign and colonial trade opened up further prospects of employment and profit to the rural and urban elites. Had these opportunities not existed, such people might have become disenchanted with the regime and might even have had a motive for undermining it, for giving covert or overt support to the Jacobites or for resuming the rage of party with its attendant bitterness and mistrust. Certainly many Tory families, shut out for decades from political power, were yet able to console themselves with reasonable economic prosperity and the possibility of professional advancement.

One of the great merits of Holmes's treatment of 'stability' is its readiness to show the capacity of social factors to take the sting out of such problems as had proved incapable of political solution. An additional advantage of Holmes's arguments is that they draw attention to dynamic elements in Hanoverian society. Too frequently, it has been assumed that the achievement of political stability was accompanied by oligarchical tendencies in political and social history whose consequence was to maintain the status quo. The concept of stability, whether political or social, should not emphasize the absence of change and challenge but should rather incorporate them. Holmes's thesis does this, as well as building valuable bridges between political and social developments. However, the stability debate, valuable though it has been in illuminating many of the political issues concerning the Hanoverian regime, has not even now succeeded in giving due weight to religious considerations. Only when we have reviewed the interpretation of Britain as a 'confessional state' is a more rounded view of the Hanoverian regime likely to be forthcoming.

A confessional regime?

England in the early eighteenth century was a confessional state, a state in which one official confession of faith, Anglicanism, was established by statute and enforced through the law – a faith, moreover, in theory accepted and practised by the vast majority of the population. A confessional state was thus characterized by uniformity and conformity in religion. Most contemporaries believed that adherence to the Anglican communion was necessary for the enjoyment of the full rights of a citizen. A confessional state did not only service the religious needs of its people but intervened widely in many areas of social life, such as education, the treatment of the poor and the care of the sick and hungry.

At the end of the seventeenth century the Church of England had survived the attacks of its enemies and had managed to maintain its established status. In the reign of Charles II the position of the church had been guaranteed by Test and Corporation Acts and by the Licensing Act. During the revolutionary period the protection provided by these guarantees was removed. The ending of censorship in 1695 was particularly serious, opening the doors to an avalanche of anti-Anglican propaganda. Attempts to reinforce the position of the church, for example by Tory bills to outlaw Occasional Conformity, all failed at the hands of the Whigs. The Whig supremacy in the state after 1714 was matched by the supremacy of the low-church party in the church. In the famous Bangorian controversy of 1717 the lower House of Convocation attacked the extreme low-church views of Benjamin Hoadly, the Bishop of Bangor.[4] To prevent a prolonged and damaging dispute the Whigs suppressed Convocation, the national representative body of the Anglican church. This deprived the church of its independent means of expression and its main focus of discussion. Without Convocation, the church was incapable of evolving measured policy responses to its own internal problems, still less to the challenge of its enemies. After 1717, the low-church party was in the ascendancy. Walpole and Edmund Gibson, Bishop of London, were careful to promote only safe low-church men to the highest offices in the church after 1723, a policy which was largely continued by the Duke of Newcastle, who assumed the control of ecclesiastical patronage after the quarrel between Walpole and Gibson in 1736.[5]

Such developments have helped to convince generations of the Church of England's enemies – whether Methodists, Evangelicals, Oxford Movement, high-church Tories, radical reformers, Protestant Dissenters or Roman Catholics – as well as historians that the eighteenth-century church was little better than an instrument of state, a mouthpiece for the Whig supremacy. There is much to support this view. After all, the supremacy of the state over the Church of England was in practice demonstrated by the willingness of the bench of bishops in the House of Lords to defend successive Whig administrations, by the enthusiasm with which ecclesiastical patrons supported Whig candidates at parliamentary elections and by the waves of sermons, pamphlets and treatises giving ecclesiastical blessing to the Whig supremacy. It was demonstrated more widely by the phenomenon of lay patronage, the legal and historical right of lay patrons to appoint to clerical livings: by the middle of the eighteenth century lay patrons were appointing to slightly over half of them. The domination of the church by the state could not be more starkly illustrated.

More recently, a revisionist approach to the issue of the extent to which England was a confessional state in the eighteenth century has attracted considerable attention. To revisionist scholars, the church was the dominant social force in the eighteenth century. 'The ubiquitous agency of the state was the church, quartering the land not into a few hundred constituencies but into ten thousand parishes, impinging on the daily lives of the great majority, supporting its black-coated intelligentsia, bidding for a monopoly of education, piety and political acceptability.' Anglicanism was much more than a 'political theology'; it was a pervasive social cement binding all orders of society. 'The ideology of the Confessional State thus legitimised social hierarchy, underpinned social relationships and inculcated humility, submission and obedience.'[6] According to this interpretation, Britain was governed not so much by a Whig supremacy as an Anglican supremacy, in which an Anglican elite retained control of the most powerful positions not only in the church and in politics but in the universities, the public schools, the armed services and the other professions. Challenges to the confessional state might occur, but such challenges simply provided opportunities for the reassertion and reiteration of the principles and assumptions upon which it was based. During the crises associated with Jacobitism and, later, in the crises occasioned by first the American Revolution and then by the French Revolution, many Anglican clergy preached sermons reminding their congregations of their place in the confessional state. Through obedience and submission to the church the state would be strengthened and preserved.

Such a revisionist interpretation of English society presents a conservative view of a stable and continuing church-state, one which emphasizes the importance of traditional institutions and attitudes at the expense of modern and 'progressive' forces such as secularism, radicalism and reform. In many ways, revisionism has been a healthy corrective to an established historiography which, for several decades, had played down the influence of Anglicanism upon public as well as private life in the eighteenth century.[7] It is, moreover, in line with the results of recent research which has reasserted the central significance of religion in political and social thought. If the early eighteenth century was not a golden age of Anglican culture it was, nevertheless, a buoyant one. Religious themes continued to be powerful in painting, literature and music and much excellent religious verse was published. Concerts of church music became very popular and the sale of religious artefacts became something of a vital sub-theme in the development of consumer markets. In the middle of the century, the sacred oratorios of Handel epitomized this society's continuing preoccupation with religious themes. Furthermore, when contemporaries discussed the relationship between the state and the church they did so in theological terms, in terms which owed more to Hooker and Filmer than to Locke and natural rights.[8] This was of great political as well as theological significance. It did much to ensure the loyalty of Tories to the regime. The Tories of the early eighteenth century may have been defeated politically, but the strength of their attachment to the Anglican church guaranteed their allegiance to the regime. They did not need to be told that the continuing strength of the church was absolutely necessary to the preservation of social order. Most people, not just high-church writers, accepted the interdependence of church and state as both natural and desirable.

But to what extent has this revisionist approach to the Church of England succeeded in refuting the old allegations which had been so devastatingly critical of that church? To what extent can the extensive claims for the

Anglican church contained within the revisionist thesis of a confessional state be justified? These, for convenience, may be separated into four distinct issues. To what extent was the church in the confessional state controlled by the political authorities? To what extent was the church corrupted by its association with the state? How successfully did the church maintain religious practice and belief among the mass of the people? Finally, in what degree was the church able to maintain the confessional state by maintaining religious conformity?

On the first of these, it is very difficult to avoid the conclusion that the Church of England came under stringent political control after 1714. Its bishops were required to reside in London, in order to attend Parliament, rather than their dioceses during the (normally lengthy) annual sessions. The highest posts in the church were treated as political appointments. Many of the lowest, including those subject to lay patronage, were outside the church's control (the church itself had the right to appoint to little more than a quarter of all livings). Politicians and administrators may have paid their respects to the ideals of a confessional state, but when we peruse their private correspondence we rarely find Anglican principles among the explained motives of their actions.

Yet we should not rush to condemn the church. Its religious and administrative standards remained high and exhibited little sign of decline or degeneration, at least during the period covered by this chapter. Walpole, Gibson and Newcastle tended to promote to the bench of bishops reliable and competent men who had both pastoral as well as administrative ability. Their relationships with the state were marked more by cooperation than by servility. On occasion they had the temerity to oppose government measures, such as a proposal to reduce the duties on spirits in 1743. The early Hanoverian bench included some distinguished names such as Wake of Lincoln and Canterbury and Nicolson of Carlisle. Others may have had lesser reputations, but there were few sinners among them. Recent research has discredited anecdotal evidence about the fabulous wealthy and aristocratic lifestyles of the Hanoverian bishops, although many of them were from aristocratic backgrounds. On the whole, although the bishops may not have been men of great religious passion, they were something more than the political time-servers of historical legend.

The bishops were, of course, fond of proclaiming the Christian purposes of the confessional state in their sermons and in their speeches, but to what extent were their principles borne out by their practice? It is difficult to generalize about such matters; but there are indications that to a large extent they made honest attempts to live up to their precepts. There was certainly no decline in ordinations and visitations after 1714. Indeed, there is some evidence that there was, after the upheavals of 1689–1714, some improvement. When Nicolson was translated to Carlisle in 1702 he found that nobody had been confirmed in his diocese since 1684. During his first visitation he confirmed no fewer than 5449 individuals. Nicolson may have been exceptional, but under the guidance of Walpole and Gibson the leaders of the church were chosen with great care – indeed, it was not in their interest to promote unpopular and incompetent bishops. After 1736 these responsibilities passed to the Duke of Newcastle, a devout Anglican. By then, although the quality of the bench as a whole remained high, there were signs of deterioration in the quality of the very highest appointments. Already, the tenure of Archbishop Blackburn at York between 1726 and 1743 was having distinctly unfortunate consequences. Moreover, the succession of two weak Archbishops of Canterbury between 1737 and 1757, Potter and Herring, was to lead to a noticeable decline in episcopal standards in the second half of the century.

On the second issue, to what extent was the Anglican church guilty of the catalogue of abuses repeated by generations of historians? These include the charges that many parishes had no resident priest and that the quality, and thus the reputation, of the clergy damaged the status of the confessional state. Precise statistics covering the church as a whole are difficult to collect. At the beginning of the century about one half of Anglican livings were worth less than £50 per year. The operation of Queen Anne's Bounty[9] did something to improve the position in just over 1000 parishes, but with uneven consequences: the Midlands and East Anglia benefited more than Wales and the north of England. Indeed, in the dioceses of York, Chester and St David's, nearly 70 per cent of livings were shown in the returns of 1736 to have stipends of less than £50, many of them much lower. Such miserable stipends bred pluralism and non-residence. Figures for a slightly later period (1780) suggest that only 38 per cent of parishes had resident incumbents while no fewer than 36 per cent of the clergy held more than one living. The comparable figures for the middle of the century are likely to be lower but, even so, still serious. In 1743 only half the parishes in Nottinghamshire and Yorkshire had a resident priest. It has been suggested that the poverty of the clergy accounts for holdings of more than one living, but it is most unlikely that this covers more than a part of the problem. The English clergy tended to be wealthier than their Welsh counterparts, but they were just as likely to be pluralist. 'The fact of the matter is that neither wealthy laymen nor bishops had any great desire to alter a system from which they benefited.'[10] The most scandalous aspect remained the dire poverty of assistant and stipendiary curates, especially in the more remote areas of the north of England and parts of Wales, just those areas of the country that were to face intensive ecclesiastical competition from Methodism in the second half of the century. It was here, in the backwardness of its parochial organization, that the church remained vulnerable to future demographic change and religious competition.

Third, how seriously did these structural problems affect religious observance? Common sense would suggest that absence of a resident clergyman must have bred negligence and indifference among the congregations. Nevertheless, the basic pattern of worship seems to have been maintained without much change for some decades. In the north and the west of the country and in most market towns two services were provided on Sunday. In the south and east one service was more common. A similar pattern of regional observance is discernible with respect to weekday services. By the 1720s, however, contemporaries were noticing a drop in attendance at weekday services. Little is known about the frequency with which communion was celebrated in the eighteenth century and local evidence varies enormously, a reflection of the willingness of individual clergymen to keep reliable records. Few places celebrated weekly communion, although there are remarkable exceptions, particularly in some of the larger towns. Perhaps a rough average for the country as a whole would be three to four times per year. Such evidence as we have, moreover, suggests a decline in the celebration of communion over the century, small and gradual in the first half of the century, thereafter accelerating rapidly.

By some measures, therefore, the church exhibited worsening patterns of religious observance, although – it can hardly be stated too often – statistics on these matters need to be treated with great caution. On the other hand, local studies reveal the continuing vitality of the parochial structure of the Church of England and the extent to which it was interwoven with the rhythms and routines of local life. Moreover, we should not ignore the extent to which Anglicanism retained its late-seventeenth-century sense of mission. The schism of the Non-juror bishops and clergy left the leadership of the church in the hands of latitudinarians who were appointed in their place. Under Tenison at Canterbury (1695–1715), Stillingfleet at Worcester (1689–99) and Patrick at Chichester and Ely (1689–1707) the low-church party ousted its rivals. Such men wished to work for a broad and comprehensive church, but they were much less willing than their high-church rivals to do so by using the power of the state. They wished, on the contrary, to mobilize the life of the spirit. The Church of England actively sought to spread the word of God to all the people and, in so doing, to transform itself into a genuinely popular, as well as prescribed, faith. Surviving manuals, catechisms and tracts demonstrate the very real attempts that were made to christianize the poor. It was this energy which lay behind the establishment and proliferation of the Society for the Reformation of Manners in the 1690s, whose prosecutions of immoral actions ranged from drunkenness to violations of the Sabbath; of the Society for Promoting Christian Knowledge, founded in 1698 to spread the Christian message through the circulation of cheap religious literature; and, more generally, of the Society for the Propagation of the Gospel, founded in 1701–02 to promote the work of overseas missions. It also provided much of the stimulus for the charity school movement. Established in the early eighteenth century, the movement swept the country, founding 600 schools by 1712 and more than double that number by 1725. The Church of England was closely involved in the activities of these societies in countless localities. Indeed, without its sponsorship of charity schools the education of the poor would have been nonexistent. However, by the middle decades of the century the crusade to transform Anglicanism into a popular creed was beginning to lose momentum. Some of the clergy, at least, were beginning to lose their earlier confidence and enthusiasm. They complained about the immorality and irreligion of the people. They noticed, helplessly, the reluctance of the lower orders to attend services and even their continuing addiction to paganism, superstition and magic. As late as 1789 Hannah More complained of whole village populations estranged from the church.

What explains this inability of the Church of England to launch an ultimately effective ministry to the masses and to sustain the energy of the late seventeenth and early eighteenth centuries? It was not just the limitations of its archbishops and bishops, the extent of lay control of the church and the poverty of so many of its clergy, with its damaging consequences of pluralism and non-residence. Nor was it simply the inability of the church to make effective provision for the new urban populations. What took the missionary edge off the early eighteenth-century Anglicanism and diffused its mission-ary zeal was also the prominence in ecclesiastical circles of rational religion or deism. Few of the bishops of the middle and later decades of the century were unaffected by it. Deism weakened the expansionary, missionizing Anglicanism of the later seventeenth century and promoted an acceptance of the world as it was to be found. Deism was undogmatic, reasonable, willing to leave as much latitude (hence latitudinarianism) as possible to the con-science of the individual. Reacting against seventeenth-century extremism and enthusiasm, and profoundly influenced by the science of Newton and the philosophy of John Locke, deists stressed the virtues of toleration and moderation. Such qualities, admirable in so many ways, were not likely to maintain the missionary attitudes which would have been necessary to carry the Anglican message effectively to the masses.

Fourth, to what extent was a confessional state actually maintained in the first half of the eighteenth century? How thoroughly could the proposition be sustained that it was only through Anglicanism that citizenship and loy-alty to the state could be promoted? The answer must be that, although prodigious attempts were made to sustain the uniformity which under-pinned the confessional state, by the middle of the eighteenth century they were showing signs of failure. This outcome could not have been predicted. The Test and Corporation Acts survived the Glorious Revolution and the Hanoverian Succession, and gave Anglicans a monopoly of national and local office. Consequently, the Whig state of the eighteenth century was embellished with Anglican privilege. Yet, in spite of protestations to the con-trary, the ramparts of the confessional state were breached on a number of occasions during this period, and many contemporaries recognized that they lived in a society which in religious terms was becoming pluralist. It is true that the Toleration Act of 1689, while permitting certain categories of Protestant Dissenters to worship outside the church, retained civil penalties for their nonconformity. But the fact remains that the Act introduced a dan-gerous element of voluntarism into religion, even if it did not recognize any denomination as a rival, still less as an equal, to the Anglican church. The Occasional Conformity Act of 1711 and the Schism Act of 1714 were intended to be the structural pillars of a confessional state, but both were repealed by the Whigs in 1718. Both of these Acts, however, were party mea-sures designed to strengthen the Tory party rather than the Church of England. The first, in particular, was intended to place local government in the hands of loyal Tories and to exclude Whigs. The second would have excluded non-Anglicans from keeping a school. Furthermore, the enforce-ment after 1714 of the Test and Corporation Acts was undermined by the practice of Occasional Conformity, whereby Dissenters outwardly con-formed by taking communion once a year. Few ambitious Nonconformists found Occasional Conformity a problem. Those who did, the Quakers and the Baptists, formed self-sufficient communities and professed little desire to enter Anglican public life. In this manner, the half-century after the Toleration Act witnessed a notable increase in religious pluralism, volun-tarism and, by the middle of the century, even signs of religious apathy. To have imposed Anglican uniformity by greater legislative force would have taken a superhuman act of political will and would surely have risked a religious reaction. At a time of potential Jacobite rebellion, such an initiative would have been dangerous, even foolhardy. The low-church party which was in the ascendant did not even contemplate it. Thus a Whig political establishment was willing to accept voluntarism and even irreligion as a means of defeating high-church Toryism.

The use of the idea of a confessional state as an organizing principle for the political and religious history of the first half of the eighteenth century has been facilitated by the outward continuity in the forms of church establishment, In fact, the position of the Anglican church may have appeared stronger to contemporaries than it really was. The maintenance of its privileges depended upon a variety of factors, not least its own self-confidence. This magnificent exercise in self-belief and self-projection beguiled contemporaries as, to some extent, it has beguiled some recent historians. After all, the church in a confessional state cannot afford to admit or to anatomize its own weaknesses. If it does so, its status at once comes into question. Furthermore, it is possible to exaggerate the extent to which Anglicanism was the dominant intellectual force of the time. To many of those in positions of power in church and state the official legitimacy of the regime might have been an Anglican one, but the perceptions of those outside were very different. Many contemporaries viewed the society of which they were a part less in terms of Anglican belief than in terms of their secular concern for their lives and careers, their security, their families and their property. Moreover, commercial values had widely penetrated British society by the middle of the eighteenth century, intersecting with values from other sources, such as law and politics. Popular culture, moreover, was imbued with secular elements which left little room, and often little sympathy, for Anglicanism. Even when individuals affirmed the role of theology and morality in their lives, it was not always in terms of a corporate theology but as a matter of individual conscience and personal responsibility.

Finally, even when we have exonerated the Anglican church from the worst of the criticisms of its enemies, some elements of the old interpretation refuse to go away. The Anglican church *was* in political thrall to Whig politicians who had every interest in preserving a decent and respectable church as the first support to their power, but little or no interest in the much-needed structural reform of that Church. Although the abuses have been seriously exaggerated, the fact remains that they did discredit the church and seriously weaken clerical initiative. Indeed, by the middle of the century – just when it was safe and secure from the (however distant) possibility of a Catholic restoration – the Anglican church was beginning to lose some of its earlier vitality. The biggest enemies of the confessional state were not the enemies without, secularism, science, urbanization and radical reform, but the enemies within: deism, lay control, complacency and, as we shall see later, Methodism and Evangelicalism. In the end, these occupied the attention of the church, drained the vitality of its missionary endeavour and weakened its will to undertake the vitally needed structural reform of its practices and institutions.

An *ancien régime*?

The concept of a confessional state is a helpful means of understanding the place of the Anglican church within Britain in the first half of the eighteenth century. But it will not deliver a comprehensive view of the Hanoverian regime more broadly. This may, however, be realized by adopting the notion of Britain as an *ancien régime* society. According to J.C.D. Clark, the structural foundations of eighteenth-century society were the monarchy and the aristocracy as well as the Church. 'Gentlemen, the Church of England, and the Crown commanded an intellectual and social hegemony.'[11] To recognize these realities, according to Clark, liberates us from the idea of Britain in the long eighteenth century as a preparation for Britain in the nineteenth. To do so allows us to conceive of this period in British history in its own right, as an age of hierarchy and patriarchalism, not an age of liberalism and individualism, as an age of faith, not of secularism, and as a monarchical and aristocratic age, not as an age of reform, protest and modernization. To conceive of Britain in this way offers a yet further advantage: it allows us to emphasize the common features which Britain shared with her European neighbours and enables us to avoid the mythology of Britain's 'exceptionalism', the idea that Britain pursued a unique and independent path to constitutional government, economic revolution and imperial greatness. According to this revisionist interpretation, therefore, Britain was an *ancien régime* society, in many ways like those of the European Continent.

In many ways Britain *was* like eighteenth-century European states. Her society was hierarchical and rural and her ruling class was a small and privileged aristocracy. Many aspects of British politics resembled those of a European state such as France. Her monarchy remained the central hub around which politics revolved. The crown in Parliament was all powerful. Indeed, the elimination of the powers of the Highland chiefs after the '45 could not have happened in France, where the government lacked the power to override local separatism in this manner. Furthermore, the British fiscal-military state, characterized by its growing bureaucracy, was as powerful as any in Europe. The idea that Britain was treading the path to constitutional government while her European neighbours were stumbling along the road to absolutism can no longer be accepted unthinkingly. Traditional assumptions that the British ruling order willingly taxed itself in the cause of constitutionalism have had to be revised. It was her ability to raise loans, not to impose taxes, which underpinned British capacity to wage war so effectively. Furthermore, there were many practical limitations upon the practice of absolutism in Europe. Strong central government everywhere required cooperation, not compulsion. Britain was like many European states in her 'composite' character, her union of crowns and the existence of different nations under the same monarch.

However, there was no single *European* standard of an *ancien régime* state. France differed from Spain, from the Scandinavian countries, from Holland, from Prussia, from Poland and from Russia. The massive variations in the power enjoyed by monarchs and the number of large and important states in which monarchs were self-evidently *not* absolute – Britain, Sweden, Poland, Holland – and the irrelevance of the label of 'absolutism' to so many parts of central and eastern Europe – all weaken the force of the *ancien régime* argument. There were broad similarities between them – they were hierarchical, they were Christian, they were monarchical – but these characteristics were shared by most societies in Europe from the tenth to the nineteenth centuries. Indeed, it is the differences between them which need emphasizing, because it is the differences which explain varying patterns of political change and development. Even Dr Clark has noted that 'in respect of their ideological structure, there were at least three equally viable forms of the *ancien regime*: Roman Catholic, non-Calvinist Protestant, Russian Orthodox'.[12] No doubt Britain shared some features with her neighbours, but it was arguably the differences that mattered.

It cannot be irrelevant that eighteenth-century Britons *felt* themselves to be distinct and different from their neighbours. The eighteenth-century version of the Glorious Revolution flattered Britons by emphasizing the Whiggish virtues of toleration, restraint and constitutionalism which underpinned their political system. There was some justification for this. After all, in some ways Britain was unlike European states. She was an island perched on the north-western periphery of Europe; she was a naval rather than a military power, and her geographical position determined particular types of strategy in warfare. For long periods she was able to achieve an unusual degree of political stability, which was the foundation of her commercial growth and prosperity. Her common law system retained its distinctiveness and her version of Protestantism its character. The established, Anglican church was, of course, unique. During the eighteenth century Britain achieved European economic pre-eminence, acquired a global maritime superiority and established a (largely non-white) empire. No other country achieved all these things.

To recognize these achievements is not to exaggerate Britain's uniqueness nor to create damaging myths about her distinctiveness. Yet British economic life *was* different in many respects from that of her neighbours, notably France. The French economy was so backward that it was subject to structural crises of food production of unusual severity, perfectly exemplified by the decade of the 1780s, and France's vulnerability to famine continued into the nineteenth century. That was not the case in Britain, where famine was a thing of the past. The productivity of French agriculture was only half that of Britain. As a consequence, Britain had a surplus rural population which flocked into the towns. After the Act of Union with Scotland in 1707, Britain constituted the largest free-trade area in Europe, while the French economy was still held back by internal tolls. These and other differences may be explained by reference to the comparative historical development of Britain and her European neighbours. Britain was late to develop her central administrative institutions; in the late seventeenth and early eighteenth centuries they were not overburdened with debt or weakened by corruption. The government was thus relatively free to innovate and to establish efficient systems of tax collection and state borrowing. As for taxation, there were few countries in Europe which could boast that government taxation was collected by centrally appointed state officials.

There were, moreover, important political differences. In Britain the position of Parliament in the political system was guaranteed through its role in public finance, which reinforced the power of the state. By comparison, there was nothing in France to compare with the power and reputation of the House of Commons. There were after 1707 no local estates or assemblies in Britain and, with the exception of the corporate towns, few privileged bodies of any kind. Detailed comparisons are lacking, but it is likely that the British aristocracy retained some idiosyncratic features compared with its French counterpart. Its involvement in agrarian and industrial capitalism and its strong sense of political service distinguished the British aristocracy from European aristocracies in general.

There were, then, serious differences between the two countries. Contemporaries, at least, would have been astonished to learn that Britain and France closely resembled each other as *ancien régime* societies – the term was not coined until the French Revolution – since they spent so much time at war with each other. Contemporaries were much more inclined to compare Britain with Sweden or Holland than with France. Furthermore, when describing their own society, Britons utilized such organizing concepts as the Glorious Revolution, limited monarchy, parliamentary government and Protestant nationhood, not that of an *ancien régime* social order. Contemporaries may have been blinded through prejudice to the similarities between French and British social and political systems which historians may now recognize. But contemporaries certainly did not consider Britain to be an *ancien régime* society.

There are other weaknesses with the *ancien régime* thesis, not least the tendency to underestimate the importance of change and innovation. The *ancien régime* is pictured as a set of institutions and a system of attitudes which hardly seemed to change in outline as the eighteenth century advanced. But there was no reason why rapid social and economic change should not have been an integral feature of a monarchical and aristocratic regime. Too much emphasis upon traditional elements in British society can minimize the significance of those social currents within the Whig polity which were helping to fashion commercial and industrial developments in the first half of the eighteenth century. In this, of course, the contribution of the 'polite and commercial people' of the middling orders, as Paul Langford has termed them, was outstanding. Their importance, as well as their number, was increasing. Not only this. The regime itself welcomed their participation and approved their involvement, especially at the local level. Furthermore, it was the economic and political demands of the government itself which acted as a catalyst for many aspects of that involvement. For example, the credit demands of eighteenth-century governments rendered their own securities an admirable vehicle for middle-class investment. Down to the early nineteenth century, at least, the middling orders were prepared to pay for the 'fiscal-military state' and to enjoy the economic and political benefits which flowed from it. There was no obvious reason why forces of change should threaten the established order. It was not only the *ancien régime* engines of monarchy, aristocracy and church which preserved and strengthened the old order in Britain, but the newer forces of commerce and the ability of the regime to broaden its base. Indeed, the very revenues of the monarchy and the power of the *ancien régime* depended on the taxes of the middling orders, the customs dues of commerce, the trade of the empire, the strength of the navy and the wealth of the City of London.

Yet Jonathan Clark finds 'no room ... for bourgeois modernity'. 'Until the evolution of class,' he writes, 'hierarchical subordination was scarcely dissolved.'[13] It may not have been 'dissolved' and it certainly continued to exist, as it had in almost all societies in the past; but it was not unaffected by the new demands of commerce and consumerism. The traditional elite had to make concession after concession to the values of commerce and trade. It was the very nature of the Hanoverian elite to adapt and change with the times. Aristocratic superiors would legitimately seek to exercise their supremacy within a social framework which recognized mutual dependence. Aristocratic domination was always less than complete and it always depended upon careful patterns of negotiation and compromise. As we have seen, aristocratic 'control' of the electoral system, for example, so complete and 'hegemonic' when viewed from afar, looks very different when examined more closely.[14] The values which regulated the electoral system were not handed down by the aristocracy but were the product of decades of negotiation between the needs of the community and those of local patrons. In such ways, the leadership of the ruling order was conditional upon the fulfilment of widely accepted needs. It could only be maintained by negotiation, concession and accommodation. The seeds of the ultimate transformation of the Hanoverian regime lay not merely in the forces to which it was exposed during the long eighteenth century but in the essential, reciprocal features of the regime itself.

What, then, were the distinctive features of the Hanoverian regime at mid-century? The continued prominence of church, aristocracy and monarchy provided some, but only some, elements of social stability, other elements of which stemmed from the social and economic developments noted by Professor Holmes. The influence of the church had peaked by mid-century, while aristocratic power was more deeply embedded in the social structure and more limited and conditional in its exercise than is normally appreciated. The one-party rule of the Whigs was triumphant, but the vitality of its party cohesion was weakening. Mid-eighteenth-century Britain derived enormous strength and stability from her monarchy, but she derived no little strength, too, from her ability to discipline and limit the powers of the monarchy and what remained of its pretensions. Furthermore, while Britain did derive strength from her aristocracy and church she derived increasing strength too from commerce and consumption, from the fiscal-military state, from the new bureaucratic and financial structures and from the incorporation of the middling orders into the political and social structures of the age. Furthermore, Britain was an imperial state and becoming an imperial nation in the eighteenth century. To ignore and to neglect that dimension in favour of a 'little Englander' conception of an unchanging *ancien régime* would be unfortunate.

Notes

1. J.H. Plumb, *The Growth of Political Stability in England, 1675–1725* (1967), p. xviii.
2. *Op. cit.*, pp. 18, 23, 179–82.
3. G. Holmes, 'The Achievement of Stability: The Social Context of Politics from the 1680s to the Age of Walpole', in J.A. Cannon, ed., *The Whig Ascendancy: Colloquies on Hanoverian England* (1981).

4. Benjamin Hoadly (1676–1761), Bishop of Bangor, was made a royal chaplain on the accession of George I as a reward for his services to the Whig cause. His sermon of March 1717, 'A Preservative against Non-jurors', was a remarkably low-church statement which came close to stripping the church of its doctrinal and disciplinary authority. Not surprisingly, the sermon threw the church into turmoil and provoked a full-scale pamphlet war which attracted over 200 titles.
5. Here, as elsewhere, Newcastle's importance has been exaggerated. He did not appoint over the heads of the bishops; he did not even monopolize recommendations to George II, who was more active in ecclesiastical appointments than has been assumed. See S. Taylor, 'The Duke of Newcastle and the Crown's Ecclesiastical Patronage', *Albion*, 24(3) (1992), pp. 409–33.
6. J.C.D. Clark, *English Society, 1688–1832* (1985), p. 277; see also pp. 417–18.
7. The works of Lewis Namier found little room for the Anglican church, and Plumb, Thompson, Porter and other writers of the 1960s and 1970s treat the church with hostility as a secularized arm of the state, reinforcing privilege and defending property.
8. Clark, *English Society*, pp. 55–56, 141–60, 199–204; J.A.W. Gunn, *Beyond Liberty and Prosperity: The Process of Self-Recognition in Eighteenth Century Political Thought* (1983), pp. 141–64.
9. Queen Anne's Bounty (1704) was an attempt to overcome the problems of clerical poverty. The Queen surrendered her right to take First Fruits and Tenths, taxes on the clergy inherited from the papacy in the sixteenth century. The money went into a fund, separately administered, and was used to raise the stipends of poor clerics.
10. D. Hempton, 'Religion in British Society, 1740–90', in J. Black, ed., *British Society and Politics from Walpole to Pitt, 1742–89* (1990), p. 205.
11. Clark, *English Society*, p. 7.
12. J.C.D. Clark, *Revolution and Rebellion: State and Society in England in the Seventeenth and Eighteenth Centuries* (1986), p.79.
13. Clark, *English Society*, pp. 118, 94.
14. See above, pp. 141–2.

7

Patriotism and empire, 1756–1789

Commerce and empire

The development of the British empire in the eighteenth century was a logical extension of a regime which was assertive, expansionist and, on occasion, even belligerent. This in its turn was the consequence of England's growing domination of her neighbours within Britain, seen in the Act of Union with Scotland (1707) and the Declaratory Act of 1720, which defined the subordinate relationship of Ireland. The political hegemony of England within Britain was a partial consequence of her economic supremacy. The 'backwardness' of the Celtic countries has been grotesquely exaggerated, but it remains true that England was economically in advance of her neighbours and sought to maintain that position by using their economies to service her own. In this sense England adopted a 'colonial' policy within Britain, just as much as she did in her relations with her overseas possessions. Many of the attitudes, as well as some of the practices, of empire grew out of English dominance of Britain.

Commerce and empire inescapably became prominent issues of the very greatest importance in Hanoverian Britain – and not just England. Whig ministers may have been willing to allow the internal government of the country to be devolved down to local landed families, but they were determined to take direct responsibility for commercial and imperial matters. In this scheme of things, it was the first duty of the state to promote the national economy by protecting sources of raw materials and by expanding its international markets. Building upon the experiences of the period 1689–1713 and the peacetime lessons of commercial expansion following the Treaty of Utrecht, the ruling elite at mid-century was building a British state whose strength derived not from territorial expansion but from commerce, from the growth of a commercially orientated empire and the existence of powerful marine as well as territorial forces.[1] Britain was becoming a trading nation. There was nothing anomalous in a dynastic state flexing its commercial muscle. The landed interest had consciously promoted modernization and entrepreneurial values within a hierarchical social order. Furthermore, commercial expansion was a means of expressing Britain's identity as a Protestant state. Until the 1740s, however, there was relatively little public support for imperial expansion. Popular fury could be aroused by alleged atrocities committed by the Bourbon powers, but that reaction should not be mistaken for a settled national commitment. The state still preferred to rule many parts of the empire through chartered companies. Britain successfully upheld a protected trading system in North America, Africa and parts of Asia, and one which even penetrated the Mediterranean and the Spanish empire in South America. The ability of the British navy to retain command of the seas not only protected her trade routes but also maintained the confidence, and protected the investments, of the landed and commercial classes. Commerce also made a massive contribution to the state's finances in the shape of customs duties and harbour and shipping dues. In some years, such sources were responsible for up to two-thirds of government revenue. Consequently, eighteenth-century governments could not be indifferent to trade. Ministers were usually receptive to commercial opinion and to the complaints and petitions of the mercantile lobby. Commercial pressure groups, such as the East India and West India interests, had the ear of ministers and were active, often successfully in lobbying for favourable legislation. It was no accident that every war in which Britain was engaged in the long eighteenth century was a commercial war in which colonial issues loomed large. 'The overwhelming preoccupation of the Hanoverian state was with funding and directing the kingdom's foreign, strategic and commercial policies.'[2] Consequently, over 80 per cent of all public money spent on goods and services between 1689 and 1815 was spent on these, and related, items. These enormous expenditures of money were profitable investments for the economic development of Britain and her empire.

The commercial and colonial policies of successive Whig governments did much to further the expansion of trade. Consequently, the first half of the eighteenth century was a period of spectacular, and quickening, commercial growth. The average annual value of overseas trade increased from £10.4 million in the decade 1700–09 to no less than £26.8 million in 1765–74, an increase of 250 per cent. The average annual rate of growth for the period 1700–09 to 1745 was around 0.5 per cent but between 1745 and 1771 the rate accelerated to 2.8 per cent. Between 1745 and 1763 it almost reached 4 per cent per annum. The tripling of the tonnage of the merchant marine from 3300 vessels (260 000 tons) in 1702 to 9400 vessels (695 000 tons) in 1776 reflects the spectacular commercial growth of the period.

Within this overall increase, British trade with her colonies was increasing much more quickly than her trade with established markets in Europe – by 250 per cent compared to 25 per cent between 1700–09 and 1760. Although the phenomenon can be traced back to the 1720s, it is in the middle decades of the century that the rising importance of the North American market to a number of rapidly growing industries, especially the metal and textile industries, becomes evident. However, it still only accounted for 20 per cent of British exports (£2.5 million per annum) compared with Europe's 60 per cent (£7.5 million). A rather more dramatic trend is revealed in the import figures. Imports from Europe between 1715 and 1724 had been 53 per cent of all British imports (£3.39 million). By the 1750s they had declined to 43 per cent (£3.87 million). Set against this percentage decline, imports from British colonies in the New World had risen by 75 per cent during the same period, from £1.49 million to £2.6 million. By the 1750s, indeed, British re-exports of goods from the American colonies represented no less than 40 per cent of all

Britain's exports. This reorientation of British commerce reflected changes in domestic consumer taste, for tea, coffee, sugar and tobacco. It probably also reflects the near-saturation of the European market for British manufactured goods and the need to seek markets elsewhere, especially the North American colonies with their rapidly growing population and purchasing power. (The population of the North American colonies increased tenfold between 1700–09 and 1776, from 300 000 to almost 3 million.) Such a lucrative trade bound the mother country to her North American empire with the steel bands of economic interest.

The British empire in the middle of the century was scattered across the globe in four principal groupings, in all of which it came into conflict with France. First, in the North Americas Britain occupied a number of Caribbean islands. From these small, tropical islands staple goods that could not be produced in Europe were exported, notably tobacco, cotton, coffee, sugar and indigo. Islands like Jamaica, Barbados and Bermuda were thought to be ideal colonies because they depended upon the mother country for the supply of basic commodities like meat, timber and most manufactured products, and for the purchase of local products. However, the British possessions in the West Indies suffered from the competition of the French islands Dominica, Martinique and Guadeloupe. Successive governments were, moreover, incensed at the willingness of the North American colonies to trade with the French and Spanish islands rather than with the British islands. Second, the 13 mainland American colonies, settled and governed by Britain, were wealthy and industrious, capable of fostering a rapidly growing trade with the mother country. They were characterized by an enterprising spirit and by a hunger for land which brought them up against the French in Quebec to the north and in Louisiana to the south, in a wilderness where boundaries were disputed and frontiers unclear. Third, there were a number of forts and trading posts on the West African coast from which trade, especially in slaves, was conducted with African rulers and merchants. Fourth, and further east, British trading-posts in the Persian Gulf, in India and in China were bases for further transactions, especially in luxury commodities. In India, French influence in the Deccan peninsula and in the Carnatic threatened to surround the British base at Madras.

Only in the second of these groupings was the empire an empire of settlement. Indeed, from the 1670s to the 1740s there are few examples of Britain actually seizing territories in wartime for permanent possession, however commercially desirable, that were not returned at the peace table. Territorial acquisitions were thought to be expensive hostages to fortune which involved problems of political control. Where settlements did exist, as in North America, they were deemed to be British colonies, entitled to be governed under British laws and in accordance with British political principles. One of these principles, to which the North American colonists heartily subscribed, was that of political autonomy. By the 1740s, indeed, the Board of Trade, which in theory was responsible for coordinating imperial administration, was expressing the anxiety that such tendencies had gone too far. Nevertheless, before the middle of the century the empire remained secure, easily and cheaply governed and relatively small, if widely dispersed.

Contemporaries agreed that the colonies existed for the commercial benefit of Britain. The economic philosophy of the British empire was expressed in the Navigation Acts. Their purpose was to ensure that Britain would not become dependent upon her European neighbours for vital economic supplies. They also ensured a first call for Britain upon colonial products while denying them to other countries. Indeed, whatever their political status, colonies were believed to be indispensable to the economic health and prosperity of Britain, acting both as vital sources of raw materials and as stable markets for British goods. However, colonial goods should not compete with British goods in case such competition led to domestic unemployment. The southern colonies of North America and the Caribbean fitted happily into this scheme of things because their products did not, on the whole, compete with those of Britain. But this was not the case with those of the northern colonies, especially iron products and shipbuilding. Britain attempted to persuade the colonists to switch production out of such staples and into the production of those raw materials which Britain lacked, especially naval supplies such as timber, hemp and iron, for which Britain was dangerously dependent on the Baltic countries. These attempts, whether through bounties or other official policies, were usually unsuccessful. They highlight an inherent contradiction in the prevailing British attitudes towards commerce and empire, between her wish to promote trade within the empire on the one hand and her wish to regulate it in the interests of the mother country on the other. This contradiction was particularly evident in the passage of the Molasses Act in 1733. The objective of the Act was to restrain the trade of the American colonies with the French West Indies in order to exclude non-British sugar from the imperial market. In the short term, the contradiction could be managed by turning a blind eye to violations of the Act. In the longer term, this was to be an issue that would return to haunt British ministers.

By the late 1730s there were signs that opinions in the country towards commerce and empire were becoming more aggressive. Commercial opinion, especially in the towns, was already highly sensitive to commercial issues and tended, if anything, to exaggerate the importance of extra-European trade. By the end of the 1730s such opinion was expressing itself in patriotic demands for war against Spain. During the War of the Austrian Succession Britain was still principally concerned to fight a war in Europe, to which end in 1742 she despatched troops to the Austrian Netherlands, in 1743 to the western parts of the Holy Roman Empire and between 1744 to 1748 to the unsuccessful defence of the Low Countries. During the Seven Years War, however, it was to North America that Britain dispatched her ships, leaving to others the business of protecting the Low Countries. The naval victories towards the end of that war vindicated the value of an extra-European commercial strategy and prepared the way for the intoxicating vision of a global commercial empire, articulated by and epitomized in the figure of William Pitt the Elder.

Until the middle of the century the British government had shown little interest in the internal affairs of the American colonies. The Board of Trade, which managed colonial affairs, lacked a cabinet seat. Such central direction of imperial affairs as there was came from successive Secretaries of State. Not until the energetic administration of Lord Halifax between 1748 and 1761 was there much evidence of administrative reform, and even then the fruits of his work only came after his retirement. Until then, a policy of 'salutary neglect' prevailed, according to which the colonies were left alone to administer their own affairs while the British government interested itself largely in commercial issues.

Within each colony a governor, aided by a council, represented the interests of the British crown. In making colonial laws, the governor was helped, in practice often hindered, by an assembly. The colonial elites who made up the assemblies were heavily Anglicized groups which were thoroughly influenced by the political rhetoric of English opposition parties in England and their Country opinions. As a consequence, they vigorously championed local interests against the centralizing and allegedly corrupt politics of London. In the North American mainland colonies, moreover, the assemblies were elected by fairly large electorates which were fiercely sensitive to local needs and local rights. In Massachussetts elections were held annually, in South Carolina and New Hampshire triennially. By the early decades of the century the assemblies had already established their right to initiate as well as to give their assent to legislation. Not surprisingly, it was difficult for the governors to retain intact their prerogatives as local representatives of the monarch. Deprived of adequate funding by the Treasury in London, governors were thrown back upon the goodwill of their assemblies. If they refused to vote supplies, then the governor's room for executive action was almost extinguished because none of them had the resources with which to organize an effective Court party. Enjoying the power of the purse, some of the assemblies had even won the right to appoint to important offices.

Nevertheless, during the first half of the century there were few signs of serious conflict between the colonial legislatures and the mother country. The British Parliament legislated as a matter of course upon commercial matters affecting the colonists but only rarely on internal questions. When it did legislate on the domestic concerns of the colonists it was, again, usually on economic and commercial concerns. In theory at least, the principle of parliamentary sovereignty entitled the British Parliament to legislate on any matter, including the right to levy internal taxes. In practice, the principle was never tested. Many colonists denied the right of Parliament to tax them, and would have refused to acknowledge the sovereignty of the King-in-Parliament. Whenever a scheme of internal imperial taxation was under discussion, as it was, for example, in 1726, or whenever Britain brought forward any other economic measure which threatened their prosperity, such as the Molasses Act of 1733, the slogan 'No taxation without representation', which was to become one of the cardinal precepts of the American Revolution, was soon on the lips of colonial protesters.

William Pitt and the Seven Years War, 1756–1763

Few periods in British history have been so decisive as the middle decades of the eighteenth century. Britain fought one of the most important wars in her history; her victory in it enabled her to become the leading imperial power in Europe. Furthermore, the British nation achieved a unity which was not to be seen again for almost half a century. It is no accident that all of these changes were bound up with the political career of William, the Elder, Pitt.

Few eighteenth-century personalities made as great an impression upon their contemporaries as Pitt the Elder. Unlike Walpole and Newcastle, Pitt had not been born into one of the traditional governing families. Indeed, his grandfather, 'Diamond' Pitt, had been a buccaneering East India merchant who rose to become Governor of Fort St George in Madras. He entered politics in 1735 for the rotten borough of Old Sarum – like most young men of his generation, in opposition to Walpole. His spellbinding oratory, his patriotic integrity and his lofty view of the importance of commerce and empire to Britain's future marked him out as a rising man, albeit an independent force, an outspoken outsider. It would be unwise to credit William Pitt with a comprehensive imperial strategy in this early part of his career. His speeches were more conspicuous for their patriotism, their concern for the strength and security of Britain and their passionate dislike of France and Spain than they are for any early intimations of imperial destiny. Yet there are signs of his firm belief that the future of Britain lay with her trade, her markets and her manufactures, that French military and economic power would stand in her way and that the key to military conflict between them would lie in North America. If Britain could wrest Canada and the sugar islands from France, then their enormous wealth would be denied to the enemy and would supplement Britain's already rapidly growing strength. This does not amount to a comprehensive imperial strategy but it shows in which direction Pitt was beginning to turn. Pitt obtained the office of Paymaster of the Forces in 1746. During the Pelham ministry he worked patiently to improve conditions in the army, but he received little credit for it and lost his post in the reshuffle following Henry Pelham's death. Only in 1755, when Newcastle showed his preference for working with Henry Fox, did Pitt begin to articulate the gospel of commerce and empire, the sense of imperial destiny with which his biographers and admirers have usually, and wrongly, credited him.[3]

We saw in a previous section how Pitt the Elder eventually rose to the highest offices in the land, first in the Devonshire–Pitt administration in October 1756 and, more permanently, in the Pitt–Newcastle ministry from June 1757.[4] At that date, Pitt's reputation with the public was still uncertain. The Pitt–Newcastle ministry represented a victory not for any 'Pittite' principles but for the principles of 'Broad-bottom'. Almost all politicians rallied behind the throne, sick of faction and anxious to unite in the patriotic cause of war against France. The cry of patriotism, indeed, had been neglected by the Whig regime in recent decades. Pulteney had raised the standard of patriotism against Walpole only, in the early 1740s, to disappoint the hopes he had raised. Thereafter, patriotism had been an oppositionist and indeed a popular cry. In the years after Henry Pelham's death, Pitt made it his own. As Paymaster he had ostentatiously demonstrated his virtue by refusing to make money out of the office. His lavish support for the Militia Bill was little more than playing to the patriotic gallery. The militia issue was a happy combination of popularity and patriotism, and Pitt did well to identify himself with a cause that was overwhelmingly more popular than the hated standing army. After initial acute unpopularity, in which 50 000 troops were required to suppress over 50 riots in different parts of the country, Pitt's support of the militia was to pay rich political dividends.

Yet it was less the rise to power of the Elder Pitt than events outside Europe which created the momentum for political change, forcing political leaders to focus directly upon imperial concerns and to develop strategies for dealing with them. Events in Canada, and to a much lesser extent in India, where hostilities in the south had continued almost uninterrupted since 1748, dragged the European powers into military conflict. (Indeed, the war is sometimes termed the 'Nine Years War' for empire between France and Britain (1754–63).) The peace of Aix-la-Chapelle of 1748 had settled once and for all the troublesome issue of the Protestant Succession, with the French promise at last to abandon the Jacobites. The treaty, however, left unresolved most of the outstanding colonial problems, especially in North America, where British and French interests clashed. The treaty had left frontier disputes to be settled by commissioners of the two countries, but they made little progress. The French sought to link up their colonies of Canada and Louisiana in order to restrict British expansion to the west, and to this end looked to strengthen their position in the Ohio valley. But British land companies from the colony of Virginia were already planning to settle the fertile regions of the Ohio valley. The largest company was the Ohio Company, founded in 1748 and awarded half a million acres by the crown. In retaliation, the French built Fort Duquesne on this territory. The situation steadily worsened until in 1755 the French defeated a joint British and colonial force at Fort Duquesne. Worse was to come. Admiral Boscawen failed to stop French naval reinforcements from reaching the American colonies.

Meanwhile events in Europe were leading to the declaration of war between England and France in May 1756. Newcastle, moreover, now found that the old diplomatic certainties of his earliest days in politics, an active policy of military intervention in Europe in the 'old alliance' with Austria and the United Provinces, were dissolving. Austria was no longer prepared to fulfil her customary role as defender of Hanover, and she had no wish to go to war against France. What she wanted was to take her revenge on Frederick the Great for the loss of Silesia.[5] Newcastle in desperation negotiated an alliance with Russia in 1755 for the defence of Hanover, an alliance which in its turn persuaded Frederick the Great to ally with Britain in January 1756. This 'Diplomatic Revolution' was completed when France, hitherto the ally of Prussia, negotiated an alliance with Austria in May 1757.

The French seizure of Minorca in May 1756 drew Britain into hostilities. The early years of the war were clouded by news of the 'Black Hole of Calcutta', in which the officers of the young Nawab of Bengal, Surajah-Dowlah, confined 146 Europeans in a badly ventilated room. In 1757 a British naval attack on the French naval base at Rochefort failed dismally. If this were not enough, in the same year the Duke of Cumberland and his newly formed Army of Observation of Hanoverian, Hessian and Prussian troops was defeated at the battle of Klosterzeven. Hanover was now at the mercy of France. In spite of his earlier tirades against the electorate, Pitt saw that the German front was of vital significance for the outcome of the war. He proceeded to throw money and men at Frederick the Great.

This strategy quickly paid dividends. It may not have helped Frederick to defeat the French at Rossbach as early as November 1757, but it did much to assist the reconstruction of the Army of Observation on the Rhine under Ferdinand of Brunswick, one of Frederick's own generals. By the summer of 1758 he was pushing the French back to the River Weser. While keeping the central European military front secure in 1758, Pitt sent several raids to the French coast which inflicted some damage on the enemy while failing to take the ports against which they were directed, principally St Malo and Cherbourg. More successful was the tactic of blockading the French navy in its home ports in order to prevent the transport of enemy reinforcements to North America.

The turning-point in the war was rapidly approaching. There was to be seemingly no end to French disasters in Britain's *annus mirabilis*, 1759. Throughout the year the French were planning to invade England. To frustrate the expected invasion, Pitt summoned the militia and stationed it along the south and east coasts, but it was even more important to prevent the fleet sailing in the first place. To this end the British navy blockaded both the Toulon and Brest fleets. Desperate to beat the blockade, the French fleets engaged the English. In the end Britain secured the great victories at Lagos and Quiberon Bay, which practically ensured British command of the seas for the rest of the war. Elsewhere in Europe, Britain was fortunate in her alliance with the military genius of Frederick the Great. Although suffering the calamitous defeat at Kunersdorf in August 1759, endangering even more seriously an already threatened Hanover, the Prussian army won the momentous victory of Minden.

The fortunes of Britain soared as much in the colonies in *annus mirabilis* as in Europe. In the American campaign of 1758–59 Pitt followed a threefold strategy. One British army was to clear French forces out of the Ohio valley while another was to advance via Lake Champlain into the heart of Canada. A third army would attack Louisburg before advancing on Quebec. In September 1759 Quebec fell to Wolfe, and within a year Canada had submitted to the British. Pitt did not stop there, but transferred his attentions to the Caribbean. Guadeloupe had already fallen in early 1759; in May 1759 the rich prize of Martinique was taken by the British, and during the final years of the war most of the important French sugar islands capitulated. Other colonial victories followed in Africa and India. French trading stations had already suffered serious defeats on the coast of West Africa in 1758, and the loss of the gum and slave trades. On this was now heaped defeat in India. Already in 1757 Robert Clive had defeated Suraj-ud-Dowla at the historic Battle of Plassey and proceeded to take Chandernagore from the French and then to overrun Bengal, India's richest province. In January 1760 the French defeat at Wandiwash at the hands of Eyre Coote, a protégé of Pitt, was the turning-point in the battle for India. A year later, the final French base at Pondicherry fell. Britain was now the dominant power in both the north east as well as the south east of India.

Britain was saturated in military victories and was beginning to anticipate the problems of peace. The war was proving unprecedentedly expensive. Normal peacetime expenditure was about £2 million per annum. The Land Tax was raised to 4s. in the £, excise duties on a wide range of goods were

steeply increased and the sinking fund was raided. These expedients succeeded in doubling government income to £4 million, but this still left an
enormous deficit against an estimated expenditure of several times that
amount. The chosen remedy was to borrow money from the City of London
and this Newcastle did on an extraordinary scale: in 1761 and 1762 the sum
borrowed reached £12 million per annum.

The years of the supremacy of the Elder Pitt during the Seven Years War
were years of unprecedented political tranquillity at home. Opposition had
gone out of fashion. The old corps Whigs were united with Pitt, the apostle of
patriotism. Even the heir to the throne, the future George III, supported the
war. Yet Pitt's position was in some ways not as strong as it looked. The government was a coalition of disparate parts.

> The old guard had lost its nerve with the fall of Minorca, but it had not mislaid its
> malice. The King grudged and grumbled, Cumberland sulked in his disgrace, Fox
> was temporarily content to count the profits to be made by a Paymaster-General in
> wartime ... Everything depended on the success or failure of British arms.[6]

For William Pitt to strengthen his independence from the old corps and to
maintain his reputation with the public, it was essential that he should stand
on his own base, cultivate the image of a patriot, appeal to the Tories and
speak to the middling orders over the heads of the political classes. For the
moment, however, he was the hero of the nation.

By this time public opinion was turning strongly towards peace. The publication of Israel Maudit's pamphlet *Considerations on the Present German War*
(November 1760) reflected this shift. Maudit's message that Britain should
abandon the continental war touched a chord in public opinion. The pamphlet quickly ran through five editions. Even more important, the death of
George II in October 1760 and the accession of the young George III weakened
the position of Pitt. The new King, and his principal friend and adviser, Lord
Bute, disliked the war, mistrusted the old corps and envied the power of
William Pitt. These changing domestic circumstances happened to coincide
with the early consequences of another new reign, that of Charles III of Spain,
who had inherited his throne in 1759. In August 1761 he signed a family com-
pact with France. Scenting trouble, Pitt advocated a pre-emptive strike against
the Spanish colonies in the new world. George III, Lord Bute and almost all
members of the cabinet were horrified at the prospect of extending the war,
and refused to accede to Pitt's demands. In October 1761 Pitt resigned. In the
end, Britain was forced to declare war against Spain in January 1762. Within a
few months both Havana and, on the other side of the world, Manila had
fallen to British arms. In May 1762 Newcastle resigned, too, manfully but
unsuccessfully defending the continuation of the subsidy to Frederick the
Great.

British naval victories against Spain were to be little more than negotiating
counters in the protracted peace process which was completed by the Treaty
of Paris in February 1763. Britain made overwhelming gains, whose effect
was to make her the leading power in Europe and, indeed, a world power of
the first rank. In North America Britain took Canada and Louisiana from
France and Florida from Spain. In the Caribbean, she won Grenada,
Dominica and Tobago and thus became the greatest power in that region. In

Africa, she reinforced her position as the dominant power over the slave trade with the acquisition of Senegal. In the Mediterranean, Minorca was restored. These were massive gains but they were not enough to satisfy Pitt, who became the most trenchant critic of the peace terms. He deplored the abandonment of Frederick the Great and the eventual decision to end the subsidy to Prussia. He condemned the British negotiators for restoring too many of France's conquests, particularly Guadeloupe, Martinique and St Lucia in the Caribbean. With these, argued Pitt, France would be in a position to rebuild her wealth and to redevelop her naval power. He also condemned other clauses of the treaty. France received back Belle Isle, Gorée in West Africa and her trading-posts in India; Spain received back Manila and Havana. Pitt's denunciations of such generosity knew no bounds. Yet it is likely that he overlooked the probable consequences of too great a victory. Had the British negotiators extracted every drop of blood that they could have done from their French and Spanish counterparts, they would have done little more than prepare the groundwork for another war against the Bourbon powers as soon as the latter had recovered. Britain was already the superior power in North America, Africa and India. To adopt a conciliatory approach at least made it possible that in the years to come peace might be preserved.

Historians have for over two centuries debated the status of Pitt's achievement. There has, thankfully, been a revision of the old imperialist and triumphalist accounts which idolized Pitt's heroism and foresight and attributed victory in the war principally to his genius. British victory in the Seven Years War, in fact, owed more to external factors than to those within Pitt's control. The fact that Spain remained neutral for most of the war years was a vital advantage to Britain. The military genius of Frederick the Great, furthermore, tied up hundreds of thousands of French troops in Europe for the duration of the war and created gaping holes in French resources. Moreover, the French army and navy had been allowed to run down in the previous decade. By contrast, British naval strength in the Seven Years War was a result of decades of careful expansion which owed nothing to the Great Commoner. It was ludicrous for Pitt to claim all the credit for the war's successes: 'Every action of government had been a collective one, from the ministers in Whitehall to the men on the battlefield'.[7]

Pitt was no innovator, no reformer. He advocated no new political or imperial theories. He was a patriot before he was an imperialist. The idea that he brought a master imperial design to the government in 1756 which he then proceeded to implement is not borne out by the facts. This imperial design was a rationalization voiced by Pitt and his admirers *after* he left office in 1761. During his years in office between 1756 and 1761 he learned to appreciate the value of commerce, and there is no doubt that he came to understand the importance of empire. But others showed a clearer appreciation of the value of colonies and a greater sensitivity to domestic imperial interests. Pitt's intentions in 1756 were to safeguard the interests of his country and to destroy the power of France. How that might be done, in which theatres of conflict the war might proceed, under which commanders and with what strategy had to be determined pragmatically and pursued with the materials to hand. He was forced to use existing political and administrative machinery, but he was to a large extent constrained, and indeed frustrated, by existing departmental boundaries.

Victory in the war was not the achievement of one man. Naval victories owed more to Anson[8] and his colleagues at the Admiralty than they did to Pitt. The naval strategy that was so successful after 1758 had been planned for over a decade. Furthermore, Pitt owed just as much, although historians have been slow to recognize this, to the Duke of Newcastle. Newcastle did far more than distribute patronage while William Pitt ran the war. 'He was not indispensable – only Pitt bears that distinction – but he was performing indispensable tasks.'[9] Newcastle was closely involved not merely with the essential business of financing the war through his contacts in the City of London but also with supplying British armies in Germany and North America. His skills, furthermore, in managing Parliament were absolutely indispensable. The almost complete absence of parliamentary opposition to the government during the Seven Years War was most unusual, compared to the political experiences of the other wars of the eighteenth century. The careful management of men and issues, to say nothing of the management of King George II, during the war was one of Newcastle's greatest achievements.

What Pitt did bring to government was a burning sense of patriotism, an overwhelming desire to defeat the Bourbon enemies of Britain and a clear-sighted view of the value of trade to British national strength and security. His contributions to the war effort were threefold. First, he was an important influence in the promotion on their merits of a group of outstandingly talented commanders. After Klosterzeven, Cumberland was replaced as Commander-in-Chief by the aged Ligonier. It was he, rather than Pitt, who was responsible for the rapid promotion of the young Amherst (40), Howe (28) and Wolfe (31). Pitt's chosen First Lord of the Admiralty was Anson, under whom exceptional officers like Hawke, Rodney and Saunders served. Indeed, the promotions of Boscawen, Hawke and Rodney probably owed more to Anson than to Pitt. But to deprive Pitt of any credit for presiding over this extraordinary flowering of talent would be unwise and unfair. Second, Pitt made a decisive impact upon the strategy of the war. He enjoyed the gift of global vision in the execution of his strategy, seeing the interconnectedness of European and maritime operations. For example, he conceived the policy of blockading the French fleet in its home ports as a necessary preliminary to maritime exploits in the far corners of the globe. If it is dangerous to credit him with a prepared strategy before the war he was, nevertheless, capable of evolving one during it. He was prepared to adapt his earlier views, and quite rapidly came to the conclusion that a war in Germany was justified only insofar as it facilitated British success in the global naval and colonial struggle and, in particular, in the North American theatre, which for Pitt was the centrepiece of the overall strategy. Third, and whatever the limitations of his influence on events, William Pitt had the courage, the energy and the self-belief to conduct the war with savage energy, at whatever cost to his political and personal relationships and even to his own health. Furthermore, the extraordinary willingness of the House of Commons to accept his leadership owed much to the force of his personality. With the benefit of hindsight, there is something almost inevitable about the great military victories of 1758–63. That is not how they appeared to most contemporaries, many of whom were fearful of being committed to warfare against at first two, later three, of the greatest powers in Europe. Most of all, Pitt appeared to epitomize simple, timeless values: patriotism, courage, honesty. Pitt had the great virtue of believing in himself. He lacked the capacity for self-doubt. To the contemporaries whom he inspired, he conveyed the excitement of greatness.

The origins of the American Revolution, 1756–1776

The American Revolution was one of the most important events of the eighteenth century. Its significance can hardly be exaggerated. It established the independence of a nation state of huge potential wealth and political power; it served as a symbol of national independence and political and economic freedom in the age of the Enlightenment; it exhausted France, diverted her energies and left her with problems so complex and so deep-seated as to be almost insoluble; it created immense political and economic problems for Britain which, although they were ultimately surmounted and resolved, nevertheless taxed her resources to the limits.

Historians seek comfort in generalizations, including generalizations about the 'American colonies' but until a very late date the American colonies remained remarkably diverse. There was no American nation and very little American national feeling before the Revolution. It is true that most of the colonists were of British descent, spoke English and retained many of their former cultural characteristics. By the middle of the eighteenth century, however, these original cultural forms, already subjected to the influence of emigration and of the new physical environments in which the colonists lived, were rapidly changing. Insofar as an 'American' identity was emerging it was shaped by the interaction between English and colonial values, and the varied, localized character of American life. Although communications of all kinds, pamphlets, press, post and sail, were rapidly improving, it is simplistic to talk about an 'Atlantic community' stretching well over 3000 miles. No doubt the Atlantic as a thoroughfare united many of the peoples of the North American empire in a set of shared experiences, but it could lead to division and disunity as much as to community and cohesion. Colonists had inherited the Country mentality of early eighteenth-century British politics and the rabid anti-Catholicism of the mother country, but they blended into it their own elements of populism, nonconformity and self-help.

One of the most remarkable aspects of the culture of the colonies was its pronounced Dissenting character. The four New England colonies – Connecticut, Massachusetts, New Hampshire and Rhode Island – were strongly Puritan in character. In two of the five middle colonies, New York and Pennsylvania, in particular, the steady emigration of Scotch-Irish Presbyterians from Ulster during the eighteenth century reinforced an already strong Puritan tradition. More generally throughout the colonies, the overall effect of 'the great awakening' of evangelical religious groups reinforced these non-Anglican tendencies. From the late seventeenth century down to about 1720, a number of colonial rebellions against British rule had been inspired as much by religion as by the political example of the Glorious

Revolution. When we recall the close relationship between the Anglican church and the Whig regime of the first half of the century, the potential danger of the cultural cleavage between the mother country and the colonists can be understood. Yet serious conflict was as yet in the future, and the government of the empire, whatever its shortcomings, was untroubled by serious colonial problems on the eve of the Seven Years War.

There was a general assumption on the British side that the King-in-Parliament at Westminster was sovereign over the colonies and that it therefore enjoyed the right of taxing them. When the government came to reorganize the finances and administration of the empire after the heady victories of the Seven Years War, it believed that it was entitled to impose taxation on them. The government regarded this reorganization as a specific exercise of power, a once-and-for-all correction in the balance of imperial relationships. However the colonists regarded themselves as having the rights of Englishmen, and free-born Englishmen at that. They had for decades enjoyed a large measure of both political and economic, to say nothing of religious, freedom and they were not now prepared to accept without protest British schemes of imperial reorganization. Quoting English political theories of the seventeenth century back at the mother country, they stood their ground on the principle of 'No taxation without representation'. Between these two positions there appeared to be little common ground.

The Seven Years War inflicted serious damage upon relations between Britain and her colonies. British politicians believed that the colonists had done little to contribute to their own self-defence; the legislatures had been uncooperative and, in trading with the enemy during the war, the colonies had done much to prolong it. Such convictions bred attitudes of patronizing contempt for the colonists in England, summed up in Wolfe's view of them as 'the most contemptible cowardly dogs you can conceive'. The decisions of the British government to retain the whole of Canada and to maintain a powerful commercial and military presence in the West Indies placed the American colonies right at the centre of British imperial concerns. The government believed that the North American colonies had to be disciplined and their administration placed on a new footing. Not least, an army was to be quartered in North America and the colonists were to pay for it. On the other side, the colonists believed that the British had ridden roughshod over their rights and privileges during the war and had treated their assemblies with disdain. Now, with the threat of France removed from their northern borders, at least one of the most basic reasons for their loyalty to Britain – security – had been removed. They were not likely to look favourably upon the British demand to pay for an army of occupation.

At the end of the Seven Years War the two most urgent problems facing the British government were those of settlement and taxation. The territorial gains made in the war obviously needed to be protected and consolidated and some provision made for the vast wilderness west of the Allegheny mountains. Those in the south, especially Florida, were easily accessible from the sea. Those to the north presented further problems. The presence of 80 000 French settlers in Quebec required the presence of a military force. If this were not enough, the great Indian uprising known as Pontiac's Rebellion in the summer of 1763 lent urgency to these problems. The British response to the uprising was to establish the area around the Great Lakes and the Ohio basin as a massive Indian reserve. Furthermore, in October 1763 a royal proclamation prohibited the colonists from further settlement west of the Alleghenies in order to prevent Indian unrest. The legal claims to westward expansion were not disallowed; for the present, however, the administration of the frontier areas was lodged with the commander-in-chief of the British army in America, a restriction which was offensive to the land-hungry colonists, who regarded it as an unnecessary surrender to the primitive red-skins. From the very first it was ignored. Furthermore, the Quartering Act of 1764 placed an obligation upon magistrates in the colonies to find billets and to fund barrack supplies for British troops. This appears to breach the principles of internal taxation, according to which the colonists believed that they ought to be taxed by their own assemblies. Taken with the proclamation, the resentment of the colonists can be readily understood.

When George Grenville came to office in 1763, he found that the National Debt had doubled during the war to almost £140 million and that the estimated expense of defending America and Canada amounted to at least £300 000 per annum. To meet these costs the Grenville government (1763–65) imposed a range of taxes which were to have devastating consequences. The new policy was announced in 1764 and 1765. It received only slight opposition in the press and commanded massive support in both Houses of Parliament. The first component of the Grenville policy was the Plantation Act, usually known as the Sugar Act, of 1764. This Act defined the list of enumerated goods, imposed duties on certain heavy goods imported into the colonies and, more importantly, established a system of enforcement which was drastically different from the traditional lax habits of control. The Molasses Act of 1733 had set the duty at *6d.* but it had never been rigidly enforced. The Sugar Act lowered the duty on Molasses from *6d.* to *3d.* in an attempt to weaken the prosperity of the French sugar trade as well as to provide a substantial revenue. The new rate was agreed only after considerable lobbying between mercantile and West India interests. It was not prohibitive, but the government's determination to enforce it was controversial, not least because it threatened the future of the trade in rum. A second financial measure was the Currency Act of 1764 which attempted to regulate colonial currencies. The depreciation of colonial currency had embarrassed many British debtors. The Act of 1764 actually forbade the issue of colonial bills of credit as full legal tender. The third great financial measure of these years was the Stamp Act of 1765, which imposed taxes on newspapers, legal documents and on a variety of other such items. The Act was intended to yield a revenue, although Grenville made it clear that the revenue was intended to defray military expenses, and not to reduce the importance of the colonial assemblies. The extension of Stamp Duties to the colonies had been mooted on several occasions in the century, most recently during the Pitt–Newcastle coalition in 1757. The time to grasp this particular nettle now appeared to be right. To the British government the great virtue of the tax was that it was cheap to collect and difficult to evade. Furthermore, the government certainly wished to establish the right of Parliament to tax the colonies. To the colonial objection that the tax violated the principle of 'No taxation without representation' Grenville responded that many people in Britain did not vote but still paid their taxes. Furthermore, there was nothing new about internal taxation. For example, the establishment of the American post office in the reign of Queen Anne had subjected the colonists to internal taxation, as indeed had the Molasses Act of 1733.

The imperial strategy of the Grenville ministry was a clear departure from the 'salutary neglect' of earlier decades. To what extent was it a reasonable response to imperial problems, and what were its chances of success? The military objectives of the policy are not entirely clear. The colonies were in no immediate military danger. There was little prospect of retaliatory attacks from France and Spain in North America. (The only harbour possessed by France was in distant New Orleans.) Furthermore, the revenues which were to cause so much damage to imperial relations would never have amounted to more than one-third of the costs of military defence. The Stamp Act, for all the opposition it aroused, would only have yielded £60 000 per annum, according to Grenville himself. Furthermore, the colonists may have had some justification for some of their deepest fears. Grenville's strategy was not directed only at revenue. The stated purpose of the Sugar Act also included, 'extending and securing the navigation and commerce between Great Britain' and America, in practice enforcing to the letter the provisions of the Navigation Acts. With some justice, the colonists believed that their trade and prosperity were threatened by the measures contained in the Sugar Act. Far more serious, however, were the political and constitutional implications of Grenville's measures. They breached the principle of internal taxation. The colonists regarded as unwarranted and illegitimate any taxes imposed by Parliament with the purpose of raising revenues which would render Governors independent of their assemblies. To the British government and to most MPs, however, this viewpoint was unacceptable. If Parliament was sovereign then it must have the power to tax. If it did not have the power to tax and if, as the colonists were arguing, that right rested with colonial assemblies, then there could be no coherent imperial financial or commercial policy. How, then, could imperial defence be financed? How could the colonists themselves be protected from the French and Spanish? How, above all, could the empire have a secure future if it had no coherent government?

The colonial reaction to these measures took the British government by surprise. The colonial assemblies denounced the constitutional status of the measures, affirming their own entitlement to the privileges and legal rights of Englishmen. Nine of the assemblies sent delegates to a congress at New York which outlined the grounds of their objection to the legislation. If this were not enough, colonial merchants launched a boycott of trade with Britain and declared a moratorium on repayment of debt to British suppliers. In most of the colonial seaport towns, royal governors were unable to staunch the incidence of organized violence. Most of it was directed against the Stamp Act and the hapless officials who were trying to collect it.

Faced with extensive hostility and disorder the British government had only two alternatives. One, supported by George Grenville and his party and, almost certainly, by the court was the physical suppression of what amounted to a rebellion. Those who advocated such a solution were seriously disunited, especially when Grenville fell from power in the summer of 1765. Such a policy would have found little support in a country that was just beginning to recover from the last war and would have given little support to a major land and sea campaign 3000 miles away. If nothing else, the expense of such a war would have been impossibly daunting. The only alternative was to climb down with as much grace as possible. This was achieved with commendable dignity by the first Rockingham administration (1765–66), the successor to Grenville's. Rockingham repealed the Stamp Act on economic grounds: the interruption to commerce and the damage to the British economy which resulted. He accompanied the repeal with a Declaratory Act which reaffirmed the supremacy of Parliament and its right to legislate for the colonies 'in all cases whatsoever'. Not only was the Stamp Act swept away; the Rockingham ministry repealed the Sugar Act, substituting for the 3d. duty on molasses a duty of 1d. on all imports entering the American colonies. Such measures were, in the last analysis, acceptable to the colonists because they were external revenue measures, taxes upon trade, not internal taxes. An accompanying measure established a free port in Dominica which was authorized to trade with foreign colonies, and thus to regulate and tax sugar, coffee and indigo coming from the West Indies to the colonies.

These measures took the sting out of colonial resistance but they did not end it. Whilst resentment was still simmering, the British government aggravated colonial feeling by a measure associated with the Chancellor of the Exchequer in the Chatham administration (1766–68), Charles Townshend. In a further attempt to meet the spiralling costs of colonial defence, Townshend proposed to raise a revenue through imposing customs duties on a wide variety of goods including paper, glass, paints, lead and – with the benefit of hindsight, most provocatively – tea. It was not merely the raising of a revenue which offended the colonists but the specific use to which it was to be applied. Unlike Grenville's Stamp Act, Townshend intended the revenue to fund the colonial Civil Lists. Townshend believed that he was learning the lessons of the Stamp Act crisis, namely that imperial officials needed to have a source of revenue independent of the colonial assemblies, otherwise government could be brought to a stop whenever the assemblies or the colonists desired. At the same time, he tightened up anti-smuggling measures by facilitating searches for smuggled goods in on-shore premises. Another measure established a commission of customs in America to give drive and direction to this vitally important service. That it was established in Boston reflects the central role of that city in the unravelling pattern of colonial resistance. John Dickinson's *Letters from a Farmer in Pennsylvania to the Inhabitants of the British Colonies*, published between December 1767 and February 1768, spelled out the constitutional and political issues and reaffirmed the principle of 'No taxation without representation'. In the *Letters*, as well as in the *Massachusetts Circular*, which went round the colonies in 1768–69, objection was voiced to the purposes for which the revenue derived from the Townshend duties was to be put. Yet so long as the supreme legislative authority of the imperial Parliament was still acknowledged there remained some prospect of compromise and accommodation. This was, however, dashed when Boston and parts of Virginia erupted into violent demonstrations against the duties in July 1768. The British government dispatched troops in order to quell the disturbances. The colonists reacted by joining non-importation agreements, which by early 1769 had spread throughout every colony except New

Hampshire. London stepped back from the brink. Some ministers had never been happy about the duties. The death of Townshend late in 1767 removed the author of the controversial measures, but it was not until May 1769 that the cabinet voted (by five votes to four) to abolish the duties, except – as a symbolic demonstration of the continuing legislative sovereignty of Parliament over the colonists – that on tea. Legislation to this effect was passed in 1770.

There, for some time, the situation hung. The British government was satisfied that it had not only retained its constitutional rights but, in the hugely important case of tea, shown its determination to stand by the principle of the duties and to establish independent civil lists. Normal trade was to a large degree restored and the non-importation and non-consumption agreements within the colonies ended. But the bitter conflict, and the memories it evoked, would not go away. During the next few years the situation steadily deteriorated because of a series of incidents which was interpreted by each side as evidence of the bad faith of the other. Constitutional disputes in a number of colonies, especially Georgia, South Carolina and North Carolina, kept the pot simmering. In 1770–71 demands among the Anglican clergy in America for the appointment of an American bishop caused a storm of protest among Protestant denominational groups, especially the Congregationalists. Meanwhile resistance to revenue officers had become something of a mark of colonial resistance. In 1772 violence among smugglers led to the destruction of the revenue ship, HMS *Gaspee*, by groups from Rhode Island while she was aground on a sand bank. The British decision to institute a commission of inquiry aroused the deepest misgivings about her constitutional authority to do so. The culmination of these conflicts came in 1772–73. The tea duties had financed the salaries of the governors of New York and Massachusetts and those of the lieutenant-governor and judges of the latter. Massachusetts patriots and protesters objected to the constitutional basis of these provisions and brought the dispute to a head. They were now denying the authority of Britain to tax without consent, her right to mobilize troops within the colony without the approval of the assembly and the power to try revenue offences in the admiralty courts, where trial by jury would not apply. The campaign against the tea duties was resumed. The destruction of £10 000 of tea in Boston harbour in December 1773 raised the twin issues of law and order and of parliamentary sovereignty. The colonists believed that, faced with the Boston Tea Party, as on previous occasions, the British would back down. British ministers believed that a small group of conspirators was threatening to disrupt law and order in Boston and in the colony of Massachusetts, and that if their efforts were not confronted then the spirit of disorder might spread throughout all 13 colonies. The government of Lord North (1770–82) decided that the Boston Tea Party deserved exemplary punishment so that, once and for all, the sovereignty of Parliament would be asserted and the rule of law maintained. There is no doubt that ministers reflected public and parliamentary opinion in taking such a strong line against those responsible for the Boston Tea Party. However, the four 'coercive' or 'intolerable' Acts of 1774 probably went further than most observers in Britain expected.

The first of the 'coercive' acts was the Boston Port Act, which effectively closed the port of Boston and moved the customs house to Salem, where it would be free from the attentions of the town mob. The Massachusetts Charter Act was much more far-reaching. It strengthened the powers of the governor of the colony over judicial appointments. It also allowed the governor to appoint the upper chamber of the assembly, in place of the annual election of its members by the lower house. The Administration of Justice Act allowed trials of Massachusetts citizens accused of law and order offences to take place outside the colony. Finally, the Quartering Act reinforced the powers of the governor and magistrates to billet troops wherever they thought necessary. This policy met with overwhelming support in Parliament, but the government wished to temper its firmness with conciliation. Although additional troops were to be sent to Massachusetts, it was at pains to reassure the colonists that troops were only to be used as an aid to the civil power. And, in replacing the existing governor of the colony, Thomas Hutchinson, with General Thomas Gage, the government had chosen a man who had great experience of America and who was well known and, to a degree, well liked there.

It is one of the ironies in the history of the American Revolution that at just this juncture the British government at last produced its long-awaited policy for Canada. The Quebec Act placed the province under the rule of a governor and of a nominated council. The Act imposed English criminal law but left French civil law in existence for the indefinite future. Many aspects of the Act were anathema to the American colonists: the authoritarian nature of the political regime thus proposed, its concession of full rights to the Roman Catholic church and, not least, its definition of the boundaries of Quebec to include vast areas north of the Ohio and as far west as the Mississippi. It was impossible for the colonists to regard the Quebec Act of 1774 as anything other than a further coercive measure. They ignored the humane and progressive features of the Quebec Act. Most of the inhabitants of Quebec were Roman Catholic and it satisfied their aspirations; it brought under one political regime a vast area which was linked by the river system of the great lakes and the St Lawrence River; it did something to conserve and protect the Indian people of the wilderness. In practice, however, on political, religious and territorial grounds the Americans regarded the Quebec Act as the last straw.

A wave of anger swept through the colonies; meeting after meeting denounced the legislation of 1774, refused to acquiesce in it and called for its repeal. Even before the texts of the Acts had been received, plans were being made for a continental congress, which met in September 1774 in Philadelphia. By then, American public opinion had converted the complex constitutional disputes over taxation and law and order into a simple issue of freedom versus slavery. It was quickly evident that the coercive acts were unenforceable. In Boston there were even calls for the militia to be embodied and trained. The Congress decided in favour of the renewal of non-importation and non-consumption agreements, called for a national association of local committees to enforce them, demanded the repeal of the coercive acts and of the Quebec Act and denounced as illegal the maintenance of a military force in any colony against the wishes of that colony's assembly. What the colonies were now seeking was an empire founded on voluntary attachment to the monarchy. To the government of Lord North, such a conception rendered imperial government impossible and endangered the stability of the commerce on which the prosperity of the British economy was increasingly dependent.

The British government could not tolerate such colonial defiance, and instructed governors to suppress the local committees. Gage asserted that what looked increasingly like a state of rebellion in Massachusetts could only be suppressed by at least 20 000 troops. The government offered to send 4000. It also passed the Non-Intercourse Act in March 1775, which excluded the New England colonies from trade with any area outside Britain, Ireland and the West Indies. As the other colonies came to endorse the protest of Massachusetts and the other New England colonies, so the Act also applied to them.

The political response of the British government came in February 1775 with North's Conciliatory Proposition, an interesting indication of the minimum degree of imperial central direction which Britain would accept. North insisted on the retention of Parliament's legislative sovereignty and its right to tax but allowed the colonial assemblies to pass their own financial legislation, subject only to the final approval of the British government. Moreover, the colonies would be responsible for their own civil lists. More importantly, they would have responsibility for their own military expenditure, once each colony's proportion had been agreed with London.

This was a significant set of concessions which deserved detailed consideration and negotiation. It was, however, overtaken by the outbreak of war at Lexington and Concord on 19 April 1775. These engagements were unsuccessful attempts by General Gage to suppress the rebellion but, heavily outnumbered and in hostile territory, he found himself in an impossible situation. Now that blood had been spilt, the rebellion spread throughout the colonies as opinion hardened and the more radical elements swept moderates aside. The writ of British government disintegrated as the effective power of its representatives, the colonial governors, dissolved. At the same time, the room for compromise was rapidly diminishing. In July 1775 the Congress rejected the Conciliatory Proposition and sent the 'Olive Branch' petition to George III. This affirmed the colonists' wish to remain within the British empire but only on the terms which the Philadelphia Congress had spelled out a year earlier. If these were not conceded then the colonists would use force to obtain them. That this was not an empty threat was shown by the dispatch of colonial expeditionary forces which took Montreal and approached Quebec. In the winter of 1775–76 the government recruited 17 000 German mercenary troops to put down the rebellion. By then, moreover, the whole of the Atlantic coast had been blockaded by Sir Guy Carleton, the governor of Canada, and in December 1775 Parliament prohibited all intercourse with the rebellious colonies. In early 1776 Gage's heavily outnumbered army was withdrawn from Boston. By that time Congress was acting as an independent government, sending negotiators to France and opening American ports to foreign shipping. The Declaration of Independence, adopted by Congress on 4 July 1776, was the logical conclusion.

The American War of Independence, 1776–1783

The war for America was now joined. British strategy was to isolate the New England rebels by taking New York and controlling the Hudson valley, thus cutting the rebel territory into two. At the start of the war the only British army was encircled in Boston, and it was not until March 1776 that it was able to break out. During these precious months most of the colonies were lost by default; the American colonial leaders won valuable time, trained their militia army and organized and established a revolutionary government. Nevertheless, the 1776 campaign did not go well for the rebels. Strengthened by reinforcements from England, the new commander, Howe, evacuated Boston and during the summer campaign of 1776 took New York, Rhode Island and New Jersey. By the end of the year the British had a decided advantage but the rebel army, led by George Washington, having avoided direct conflict with the superior British forces, was still in the field, and had even retaken New Jersey. Indeed, a minor victory by Washington on Christmas Day 1776 boosted American morale. The strategy for the 1777 campaign was for Burgoyne to march south from Canada and, by taking Albany and linking up with Howe's army, to cut off the New England colonies. The British overestimated the difficulty of the latter operation and Howe even launched a successful attack on Philadelphia, the largest colonial city and the centre for meetings of the Congress. Had Howe moved to coordinate his tactics with Burgoyne by a thrust up the Hudson river the New England colonies would have been encircled, and probably doomed. However, Burgoyne's army, sweeping down from Canada, found itself surrounded at Saratoga. The surrender of his army was a major turning-point in the war. The British realized that only a long and hard campaign, possibly stretching over several years, could suppress the rebellion. In view of the extensive distances involved in fighting the war, the irregular and unfamiliar nature of the terrain and the superior numbers of their colonial adversaries, the British were disconcerted at the men and materials that would be needed. Although George III shrugged off the reverse as 'serious but not without remedy' Lord North laid peace proposals before Parliament in February 1778 which would have repealed the Declaratory Act and appointed Commissioners to discuss peace. This might just have satisfied the Americans in 1775, but they would now settle for nothing less than independence. Far more important, however, than unavailing peace proposals was the alliance between France and America signed in the same month. By its terms, France abandoned any claim to territory east of the Mississippi and promised not to make peace with England until American independence was achieved. At once the colonial rebellion became a world war with potential implications for Europe, the West Indies and India. In June 1779 Spain joined the alliance.

With the benefit of hindsight, the recovery of the colonies was now almost impossible. Confronted in theatres across the globe and with no allies to assist them, the plight of the British was desperate. The colonies were now not prepared to compromise. The Carlisle peace commission, an initiative by Lord North to draw the Americans into discussion of his peace proposals, was a dismal failure. The commissioners arrived in America in June 1778 but this last opportunity to preserve some political link between Britain and

America came to nothing. In spite of some military successes British military and diplomatic prospects worsened. Quite simply, Britain's resources were overstretched. In 1778 the British withdrew from Philadelphia and Rhode Island so that West Indian theatres could be reinforced. Furthermore, the English channel had to be protected from a Franco-Spanish invasion, threatened in 1778 and attempted, without success, in 1779. In the same year the French seized Grenada and St Vincent. French naval power was beginning to have its effects on the British military effort in America and by the second half of 1779 was stifling British movement in the southern colonies, especially in South Carolina and Georgia. Still worse for Britain, in 1780 the Baltic powers, including Russia, established the Armed Neutrality, whose purpose was to resist and oppose the British action of searching neutral shipping. In order to prevent Holland from associating itself too closely with the Armed Neutrality, Britain declared war on her before the end of the year. The British were in an impossible situation and by 1781 had lost command of the American waters to France and Spain. The French took Tobago; the Spanish took West Florida. The balance of the war was tilting ominously against Britain. Within the colonies, Cornwallis had raised British hopes in the south with his victory at Charleston in May 1780 and by the recovery of South Carolina and Georgia. He attempted to follow up these successes by marching into Virginia, where he expected the loyalists to flock to his support. Encamped in Yorktown and surrounded by American and French troops, Cornwallis was cut off, the navy unable to reinforce his army. His surrender at Yorktown on 17 October 1781 marked the effective end of the war, and of British control of the American colonies. 'Oh God: it is all over,' cried Lord North.

The result of the American war was a disastrous defeat for Britain. It is impossible to contest the point. Yet the ultimate outcome of the war could have been much worse. The military defeat has overshadowed the fact that Britain escaped to a large extent without suffering excessive damage to her economy and to her empire. Indeed, after Yorktown Britain recovered much of her naval, and thus diplomatic, influence. In April 1782 Admiral Rodney won a glorious victory in the West Indies at the Battle of the Saints. By then both the French and the Spanish were ready for peace. France, in particular, had found the war a crippling financial burden. The British were fully aware of French exhaustion and intended to exploit it. The British minister who concluded the peace terms signed at Versailles in 1783, Shelburne, insisted that France and Spain should not frustrate America's ambition to expand west to the Mississippi. Influenced by the new free-trade theories associated with Adam Smith, Shelburne saw that if Americans settled and developed the west then they would become a valuable market for British manufactured goods. To Shelburne, commercial intercourse with North America could still continue even though Britain had lost a territorial empire. In this he was to be proved right. Within a decade, Anglo-American trade was once again one of the cornerstones of British prosperity, later to become one of the foundations of her credit during the Napoleonic wars. Furthermore, and possibly owing to divisions between Britain's enemies, the peace terms of 1783 were not nearly so bad for Britain as they might have been. France gained Tobago and fishing rights off the west coast of Newfoundland. In India, however, she only procured some territory near Pondicherry. In Africa she recovered

Senegal. Spain, it is true, recovered Minorca and Florida, but the fabric and structure of the British empire remained substantially intact. America had been lost but almost everything else had been retained. The united power of the Bourbon nations had helped to prise America out of Britain's grasp, but it had not been enough to overwhelm British naval power. Finally, America had indeed become an independent nation; it did not become a client state of the Bourbons.

Could the British have won the American War of Independence? At a distance of 3000 miles it would have been extremely difficult but it need not have been impossible. The significance of the 3000-mile separation between Britain and America was that it took three months – at certain times of the year much longer – to communicate messages, instructions, supplies and reinforcements. By the time any of these arrived in America the situation with which they were intended to deal might have changed out of all recognition. Indeed, to avoid the hazards of winter sailings, reinforcements usually set sail in spring, arriving in summer, when the campaigns were already well advanced. Within North America geographical distances were enormous, the terrain unfriendly and an invitation to forms of guerrilla warfare to which the British had no answer. But if geographical factors weakened the prospects of a British victory, we need to remember that they were almost as damaging to the colonists. It was not easy for the fragile American government to raise armies and keep them in the field. Colonies which were bitterly resentful of the centralizing policies of the British were not likely to accept those imposed by Washington without reluctance. There was no overwhelming reason why the British should not have defeated the colonists in the first year of the war had they been better prepared and ready to exploit from the outset the fact that the war for American independence was also, in part, a civil war. Furthermore, in 1775 there still existed in the colonies a strong fund of goodwill towards the mother country and the monarchy. At the outset, perhaps as many as a quarter of the colonists were British loyalists rather than colonial patriots. Many of them served in militia units, provincial regiments or merely as recruits and volunteers in the regular army. They did so, moreover, with energy and passion, but their talents were never really mobilized. The British were seriously unprepared for the war and, as we have seen, allowed many months to pass in which they lost the initiative both militarily and politically.

Recent research has gone some way towards exculpating the North ministry from many of the charges levelled against it by earlier historians looking for a scapegoat for the loss of the colonies.[10] North himself was not an inspired leader but he had many excellent qualities, not all of them unsuited to the conduct of the American war. He was a born conciliator, a man of peace, a politician who believed in political solutions achieved through negotiation, although he was inclined to play for time if no immediate solution to a problem was in sight. He was a skilful politician, combining influence in the closet with (until the later stages of the war) unrivalled parliamentary supremacy. Like Newcastle between 1757 and 1762, he was successful in raising the loans on which the prosecution of the war depended. His great weakness was his inability to breathe energy and unity into the imperial cause, to exploit the collective abilities of ministers to the benefit of the war effort as the Elder Pitt had done during the Seven Years War. Most damaging of all, he lacked the personal resources to respond positively to military defeat. His collapse of morale after Saratoga was striking: he yearned to resign and dreamed of ministerial reshuffles.[11] He was not capable either of remedying the deficiencies or of exploiting the abilities of his colleagues. The First Lord of the Admiralty, Lord Sandwich, is now credited with considerable ability and drive.[12] Between 1770 and 1779 he increased the size of the fleet from 15 to 100. But for the government's penny-pinching stringency in the middle of the decade he might have raised it still further. Even so, his building programme was prodigious and it bore fruit at the Battle of the Saints. His problem was that the navy was hopelessly overstretched; it had to defend the English Channel, the West Indies and the North American coast as well as sustaining active service in the Mediterranean, Africa and India. Lord George Germain, Secretary of State for the Colonies, had energy and spirit but less talent than Sandwich.[13] He suffered from two serious weaknesses. He exaggerated the fund of loyalist support that existed in America and he quarrelled with almost every commander-in-chief of the army in America. He disliked Carleton and, significantly, both Burgoyne and Howe blamed him for their military failures.

It was one of the tragedies of the American War of Independence that Lord North was unable to impose himself on the ministers and the commanders. Had he been able to do so, a more decisive strategy might have been devised. Furthermore, there were at least two serious errors in the strategy that was pursued. They failed to coordinate their tactics on a number of occasions; the failure to do so before Saratoga was an error of epic proportions. They failed, moreover, to draw Washington's army into open battle. Consequently it survived, and with it the American cause, long enough to profit from favourable, if contingent, circumstances. Of these, the most important was unquestionably the entry of the Bourbon powers into the war. Once Britain was faced with the prospect of fighting a global war the likelihood of defeating the American rebels was sharply reduced. Even then, however, we should not lose sight of the (very respectable) British military successes in the war. Every American invasion of Canada was repulsed; Philadelphia and Charleston were captured; New York was held; the Battle of the Saints was a historic victory. The war was far from being a series of unmitigated failures.

In the end, it is unjust to place the responsibility for the loss of the American colonies solely upon the government of Lord North. The problems of distance are impossible to imagine, the logistics of timing, transport and supply almost insoluble. It was certainly not the fault of the North administration that Britain was diplomatically isolated in these years. The damage had been done much earlier. During the Chatham administration (1766–68), in fact, Britain had tried and failed to entice Prussia back into an alliance. Like Russia and Austria, Prussia had no interest in an alliance with Britain, which was left to look to its own destiny against France and Spain. Spain might have been conciliated by the surrender of Gibraltar, but it is doubtful if British public opinion would have tolerated such a concession. In the end, the loss of the American colonies was a British national responsibility. The monarch, both Houses of Parliament and the great bulk of public opinion adhered until a late date to a belief in parliamentary sovereignty on which it was not possible to find common ground with the American colonists. The only compromises which the British monarch, government and Parliament would have accepted were those which would not have commended themselves to the Americans. Once the war had begun, it was always likely to be a war to the finish.

As Professor Colley has noted, Britain learned at least one lesson from the war: the need for a less permissive, more centralized imperial structure.[14] The conflict had arisen out of ambiguous views of what was, and what was not, constitutionally legal and legitimate. The war had arisen not, as the Americans argued, from a settled plan to establish tyranny but, on the contrary, after successive sets of concessions made by ministers of the crown following on from continued demonstrations of their reluctance to use military force. More certainty and a more settled basis to imperial affairs was to be preferred in the future. It is surely no accident that the loss of the American colonies was followed by the India Act of 1784, the Canada Act of 1791 and the Act of Union with Ireland (1800), which, in their different ways, redefined a closer relationship between Britain and her colonies.[15] On the whole, moreover, the empire's centre of gravity in the future was to lie in the east rather than in the west, with peoples who were not Christian and the vast majority of whom did not speak English.

If the American War of Independence was a negative event in the history of the British empire, there are grounds for treating it as a rather more positive event in the emergence of Britain as a political and cultural unit. The Scots had identified themselves closely with the colonies since the early eighteenth century, as another provincial people within the empire; such identification had been strengthened by commerce, by their common Presbyterianism, by cultural interchange and by emigration. In the 1760s, however, the Scots, became even more determined than the English to maintain parliamentary sovereignty over the colonies. The American War served as an ideal opportunity for Scotland to affirm its loyalty to the Union and many Scotsmen flooded into the British armed services. The war thus marks an important stage in the continued incorporation of Scotland into Britain. In this empire the Scots and, of course, the Irish were to play a role – in its conquest, settlement and government – out of all proportion to their demographic and economic significance at home. Simply by virtue of governing an empire of alien peoples and religions the British were coming to see themselves as one people, distinct and unique.

Notes

1. D. Baugh, 'Maritime Strength and Atlantic Commerce: The Uses of a "Grand Marine Empire" ', in L. Stone, ed., *An Imperial State at War: Britain from 1689 to 1815* (1994), pp. 185–214.
2. P. O'Brien, *Power with Profit: The State and the Economy, 1688–1815* (1991), p. 12.
3. The best guide to, and critique of, the myth-laden historical writing on Pitt is M. Peters, 'The Myth of William Pitt, Earl of Chatham, Great Imperialist: Parts 1 and 2', *Journal of Imperial and Commonwealth History* 21(1) (Jan. 1993), pp. 31–74; 22(3), (Sept. 1994), pp. 393–431.
4. See above, pp. 92–3.
5. On 1 December 1740 Frederick the Great invaded the rich Austrian province of Silesia, and kept it after years of warfare in 1763. The acquisition of Silesia marked

the rise of Prussia to great power status in Europe. More immediately, it provoked the War of the Austrian Succession.

6. P. Langford, *A Polite and Commercial People: England 1727–1783* (1989), p. 334.

7. R. Middleton, *The Bells of Victory: The Pitt–Newcastle Ministry and the Conduct of the Seven Years War, 1757–62* (1985) p. 196.

8. Lord George Anson (1697–1762), one of the most experienced and most successful admirals in the British navy since the closing years of the War of the Spanish Succession. Anson became a celebrated hero with his voyage around the world in 1744. He was Vice-Admiral of the Channel Fleet in 1746 and was made a peer after his victory against the French off Finisterre in 1747. He was First Lord of the Admiralty in 1751–56 and 1757–62.

9. R. Browning, *The Duke of Newcastle* (1975), p. 261.

10. See P.D.G. Thomas, *Lord North* (1976); K. Perry, *British Politics and the American Revolution* (1990); J. Derry, *English Politics and the American Revolution* (1976).

11. On 6 May 1778 he wrote to the King : 'Every hour convinces me more of the necessity your Majesty is under of putting some other person than myself at the Head of your affairs ... a man of great abilities, who can chuse decisively, one capable of forming wise plans, and of combining and connecting the whole force and operations of government.'

12. John, 4th Earl of Sandwich (1718–92). First Lord of the Admiralty after 1771 and usually blamed for the navy's unreadiness at the start of the war in 1775. In reality, his lengthy experience of naval affairs stretched back to the 1740s.

13. Lord George Germain (1716–85), 1st Viscount Sackville and until 1770 known as Lord George Sackville. Wounded and captured at Fontenoy in 1745, he was dismissed the service after neglecting to lead the British forces in pursuit of the French at Minden in 1759. He was restored to favour by George III. He was Secretary of State for the Colonies between 1775 and 1782.

14. L. Colley, *Britons: Forging the Nation, 1707–1837* (1992), p. 145.

15. For this legislation, see below, pp. 313–14 and 325–6.

8

The age of George III, 1760–1789

George III and the politicians, 1760–1770

The reign of George III had been awaited with keen anticipation, and the accession of the King in October 1760 did not disappoint those who expected great changes. One of the first actions of the new King was to signify to the Tories that their proscription was over. Although the number who received office was small – six Bedchamber appointments in the immediate aftermath of the accession – it was nevertheless a symbolic political move, and it was not long before Tories returned in some numbers to the county benches. The old Whig–Tory polarity had been weakening for nearly two decades. Now it was shattered. In the absence of the Whig–Tory framework which had given shape to politics for so many decades, politics became factionalized. The Tory party disintegrated and the texture of the Whig party loosened, leaving effective political control of Whig MPs in the hands of a group of great political leaders – Bute, Pitt, Bedford, Grenville and, not least, Newcastle, who in 1765 allowed the leadership of his connection to pass to the Marquis of Rockingham. This was not all. A further familiar landmark of the last two reigns was absent. The King was only 22 years old, and was not to have an heir to the throne who might meddle in politics for over two decades. Politicians in opposition could no longer look to Leicester House for their social unity and their political direction. The King to come was now on the throne. Furthermore, the steady disappearance from this scene by death or by ill health of many of the stalwarts of the old party battles – George II, Newcastle and Hardwicke, amongst others – and the appearance of a new generation of political leaders, including Bute, Rockingham and Grenville, lends a fresh and in many ways uncertain appearance to the politics of the 1760s. Clearly, the new King was to enjoy rather more freedom of manoeuvre than his grandfather had normally experienced, and much would therefore depend upon his personal preference for one set of politicians over others. Whether this would lead to stable government or to short-lived, unstable ministries, however, could not be predicted. Much would depend on the King's choice of minister and the ability of that minister to earn the confidence of Parliament. Finally, the prominence of a new set of political issues, those arising from the conquests of the Seven Years War and others concerning the status of Parliament and the role of public opinion, were to create serious divisions in the body politic. Now that criticism of and opposition to the regime could by no stretch of the imagination be dismissed as treasonable, these divisions would reverberate beyond Parliament.

George III came to the throne smarting from the isolation which he had experienced and the neglect he had suffered at the hands of the leading politicians of the age. Since 1757 the union of Pitt, Newcastle and most of the other political leaders had left him powerless and resentful. Only the Prince's 'dearest friend', John Stuart, 3rd Earl of Bute, had stood by him during these dark years. In 1754 Bute had become the heir's most trusted adviser, and in 1756 his tutor. Bute was in many ways an ideal courtier, dignified, loyal and accomplished. Yet as a politician he was unapproachable, his judgement was faulty and he lacked the courage of his convictions. These faults would not have mattered had he remained of no political significance; but in the person of the friend and adviser of a young and inexperienced King they had damaging consequences. There is no evidence that Bute infected the future King with authoritarian, still less unconstitutional, intentions. By the time he came to the throne, however, George III, under Bute's influence, had formulated a number of objectives for the new reign which were, to say the least, singular. His primary objective was to free the monarchy from what he imagined to be its humiliating subjection to the great Whig ministers. By 1760 the new King was thoroughly convinced of the evil intent of Pitt, Newcastle and the old corps. In his view, their use of patronage and corruption had enslaved the monarchy and threatened the constitution. Far from planning to reduce the powers of Parliament, George III actually wished to protect the constitution from the Whigs and the corruption which he imagined that they employed to reinforce their power. In one of his first public announcements he 'gloried in the name of Briton', a signal that he intended to be a 'Patriot King', by which he meant that it was time to admit men of talent to office whatever their earlier party loyalties. Finally, he wanted to bring to an end the dangerously expensive war in which the ministers had entrammelled the country. None of this was unconstitutional; some of it, such as his concern to negotiate peace, was likely to be popular; all of it was bound to be controversial in execution and, quite possibly, disruptive in its consequences. Within little more than 18 months Pitt and Newcastle were out of office, a gloriously triumphant war was being wound up and Lord Bute had attained the highest office in the land. There can be no doubt that a change in the role of the monarch in politics was intended in 1760 and, to a considerable extent, achieved, even if there was no intention of establishing an unconstitutional and arbitrary monarchy.[1]

In October 1760 Lord Bute, then Groom of the Stole, was appointed by the King to the cabinet, and it was at once made clear that it was he, rather than Pitt and Newcastle, who had the King's ear, and thus his confidence. In March 1761 Bute became Secretary of State for the Northern Department, an appointment which terrified Newcastle that his own services, and those of his friends, might be dispensed with. Pitt was equally concerned. He was already annoyed at Bute's pretensions; he disapproved of the court's desire to bring the war to a conclusion, and deplored its willingness to abandon Frederick the Great to his European enemies. When Pitt and his brother-in-law, Temple, advocated a pre-emptive strike against Spain in the summer of 1761 they were outvoted in cabinet, and resigned. The Duke of Newcastle was now at the mercy of the court. The Duke was distressed to find that he had no voice in the appointments of Lord Egremont and the Duke of Bedford to replace Pitt and Temple. The reconstruction of Newcastle's ministry was completed when George Grenville became leader of the House of Commons. The loan from the City for 1762 had only been forthcoming on the general understanding that war against Spain would not occur, but on 2 January 1762 the cabinet declared war. Worse still for Newcastle, the government now wished to reduce the subsidy to Frederick the Great. The architect and spokesman of European alliances for almost 40 years could not accept this and in May Newcastle resigned, for the moment leaving most of his followers in their offices. Lord Bute became First Lord of the Treasury.

The dissolution of the administration which had won the greatest war in the history of Britain now gave way to a succession of five short-lived, weak and divided governments in an almost unprecedented display of ministerial instability. To this instability George III and, of course, his 'dearest friend', Lord Bute, undoubtedly contributed. While they had no sinister designs on the constitution, their inexperience and their miscalculations aggravated the structural changes in the political situation which we have already noticed. At the end of 1762 the Bute ministry presented the Peace Preliminaries to Parliament. On this critical test of confidence Newcastle's friends opposed the government. In the 'Massacre of the Pelhamite Innocents' in the months following December 1762 many of the old corps were purged from office. This action was to be almost fatal to the prospects of maintaining stable government. For several decades these civil servants and office-holders, or 'King's Friends' as they were commonly termed in these decades, had usually, and willingly, followed the political line of the first minister who also had the confidence of the King: Walpole, Pelham and Pitt. Now they had been dispersed and broken. A ministerial majority in Parliament would now require unusual exertions. Bute lacked the experience and the political will. His successors lacked the confidence of the King and the King's Friends, and therefore became much less reliable. George III was constantly suspicious of George Grenville (1763–65); he had little liking for the friends of Newcastle when they returned to office in the first Rockingham ministry (1765–66); his early enthusiasm for Pitt (promoted to the peerage as Lord Chatham) did not survive more than a few months of the Chatham administration (1766–68); and it was difficult for the King to warm to the hapless, weak and unfortunate leader of the Grafton administration (1768–70). Only with the coming to power of Lord North in 1770 did the King once again find a minister in whom he could trust, and only then could the loyalty of the King's Friends to the ministers once more be relied upon.

For the moment, however, Bute was in office, Pitt was sulking in opposition to the peace and Newcastle's old corps had been overthrown. The King appeared to have destroyed his opponents. And just when he had attained the summit of success, Bute's nerve cracked. He had been wilting under public criticism of the peace treaty and at the widespread popular ridicule of him, his nationality and his status as a royal favourite. In April 1763 he resigned, negotiating on his departure from office the personnel of the Grenville administration.

Bute's status thereafter became – to the friends of Newcastle at least – more rather than less alarming. He retained the king's confidence and friendship but without public office and public responsibility. He was, in the terminology of the time, 'minister behind the curtain', dispensing his 'secret influence'. By the end of 1763 the friends of Newcastle had embroidered this myth of Lord Bute's influence into a more general charge against the court that the humiliation of the old corps had been part of a settled plan since the start of the reign to destroy Whiggism, reduce the aristocracy to subservience and elevate the standard of prerogative. This was a deliberate and dangerous attack on the constitution. Government by royal favourite would diminish the independence of Parliament which, packed with royal sycophants, would be incapable of fulfilling its historic role as a check upon the power of the executive. This set of misguided accusations amounted to a retrospective, and very partial, explanation for the dismal political fortunes of the Newcastle Whigs in the early 1760s. The great merit of the myth of Lord Bute's secret influence, however, was that it was marvellously flexible: it could explain any failure which might beset the friends of Newcastle, any set-back, any reverse. It could even explain any abuse of government, any misuse of power.

Meanwhile, the administration of George Grenville (1763–65) was wrestling with the great issues of colonial taxation to general domestic approval. Indeed, the ministry had much in its favour, not least the great administrative and financial competence of its leading minister. The Grenville Whigs had spent much of the previous decade in opposition, and Grenville had kept his distance from the Pelhams. His undoubted financial ability and his wish to reform and reduce government expenditure made him popular with the Country gentlemen in Parliament. These assets, together with his political weight and his stature in the House of Commons, might have raised the prospect of many years in power. His ministry, however, suffered from two serious weaknesses, one of which he overcame, the other to which he succumbed.

The first was his government's attitude towards John Wilkes; the second was his relationship with the King. His ministry's high-handed use of general warrants to silence the journalist and critic John Wilkes aroused a fury of opposition and tested its majorities in Parliament to the limit.[2] Grenville, however, rode out the storm of protest and on the decisive division on 17 February 1764 enjoyed a majority of 14. It was enough to vindicate his policy. Subsequently the tide of opposition receded and Grenville was safe in parliament. The real danger to Grenville came less from Parliament than from the court. To ensure that Bute would not meddle further in politics, Grenville insisted that the King should no longer consult the favourite, and he demanded control of all appointments to offices. He was determined to establish his own position in the opinion of the political nation and he had no intention of becoming a creature of the court. He was appalled at the King's decision to award Stuart Mackenzie, Bute's brother, the office of Scottish Privy Seal for life, and with it considerable influence in Scottish patronage. Grenville was determined that such an event would never recur. Now Grenville watched the King's every move with suspicion. The King, quite understandably, resented these restrictions upon his freedom of action and, in spite of his minister's feelings, continued to consult Bute. Early in 1765 the King fell ill with porphyria, the illness which was later to engulf him entirely. Porphyria is a physical, hereditary condition which inflicts such pain that the sufferer endures symptoms which can sometimes be taken for insanity. On his recovery he was determined to rid himself of Grenville and to provide for the succession with a Regency Bill. Insisting that he reserve to himself the right to name the head of a regency council in the event of his own indisposition, he was reluctant to name a regent in the event of his death. His preference for the Queen over the Duke of York, his brother and the obvious candidate in the male hereditary line, as regent in the event of his death was more contentious. The King, however, wished to conceal these embarrassing stipulations from his minister and, indeed, from the public lest they cause a major and divisive dynastic conflict as well as an even bigger political sensation. The minister thought the worst. Grenville's suspicions that Bute was behind these proceedings knew no bounds. He tried to make the King promise to take advice only from his ministers, but such an understanding could not possibly provide the basis for a stable administration. In desperation the King put out feelers to Pitt. These met with no response, and the King was driven into the arms of the friends of the Duke of Newcastle.

The families of the Whig connections which had ruled Hanoverian Britain in the previous two reigns were back in office in the summer of 1765. The great achievement of the Rockingham ministry (1765–66) was its solution, albeit temporary, of the colonial problem. The repeal of the Stamp Act together with the Declaratory Act composed, at least for a time, the worst of the controversies surrounding taxation and sovereignty, but did so at the cost of severely weakening the administration. Rockingham's policy was opposed on the one side by the Grenville and Bedford faction, who had been responsible for the Stamp Act, and on the other by William Pitt. Pitt clung to a belief in Parliament's right to impose indirect taxation, but he opposed the Stamp Act because it violated the principle of 'No taxation without representation'. To complicate matters further the King's Friends, who had originally supported the Stamp Act, were divided. Some of them looked to Bute and the policies towards America upheld by Bute and Grenville; others looked to Rockingham and Newcastle. On the great parliamentary tests of opinion on the Stamp Act early in 1766, therefore, some voted with but some voted against the government. The Rockingham Whigs, as they had now become, were as suspicious of the influence of Bute as George Grenville had been, and demanded that offending office-holders be punished. George III was unwilling to discipline recalcitrant placemen for voting in accordance with their consciences on a policy which they had only recently adopted. Rockingham was furious with the King and pessimistic about the prospects of his administration. Believing that the ministry could survive only with Pitt's support, he had little alternative but to resign in the summer of 1766 when Pitt refused to come to his aid.

The Chatham administration (1766–68) was a further attempt by George III to establish a stable administration, one which enjoyed both the confidence of the King and the support of Parliament and public. George III expected much of the new ministry and started to recycle some of his earlier opinions about destroying party. By now he was desperate, confiding to Bute in May that 'if I am to continue the life of agitation I have these three years there will be a Council of Regency to assist in that undertaking'. Pitt by now was anxious to oblige the King, assuring him that he too wished to destroy faction and see the best men of all parties in office. It would be necessary to take the Rockingham administration as the basis of the new one, but in time he would transform it into an instrument of virtue and efficiency. Pitt of all people, however, lacked the conciliatory arts which such a lofty enterprise demanded, and he quite failed to soften existing political resentments and personal differences. He was determined to play an olympian role, to use others as the instruments of the great enterprise and to govern through remote control. This is why he accepted only the office of Lord Privy Seal, without executive responsibilities. The details of government he delegated to the Duke of Grafton, who became First Lord of the Treasury, and to the two secretaries, Shelburne and Townshend.[3] Worst of all, his decision to go to the Lords and accept the earldom of Chatham lost him much of that patriotic, public support on which his reputation had rested for a decade. His decision to take a peerage caused a sensation at the time and is still difficult to justify. If he had enjoyed the services of a Duke of Newcastle, as he had during the great wartime ministry, it is just possible that his ill-thought-out scheme would have worked. But his decision to go the Lords had two serious consequences. It left the ministry exposed in the Commons – Townshend was brilliant but unreliable and Conway lacked both debating strength and personal confidence – and it left the King's Friends there desperate for strong leadership.[4] Almost as soon as it was established, therefore, the ministry was drained of the strength and momentum which it so badly needed. Much was said about making war on party – indeed, some attempt was made to include men of all parties – but the ministry to end party was soon looking to the parties for support.

From the beginning, then, there was little prospect that the plans of the court might succeed. That prospect soon diminished further. From January 1767 Chatham was ill with nervous exhaustion, perhaps even a form of nervous collapse. He was absent from London for long periods and incapable of imparting order and discipline to his broad-based administration. He plunged into depression, deepened by Frederick the Great's refusal to revive the Anglo-Prussian alliance. A sample of what was to come was the ambush that the government walked into when it moved to keep the Land Tax at the wartime level of 4s. in the £. The opposition parties, those of Rockingham, Grenville and Bedford, ganged together and on 27 February, by a majority of 206 to 188, voted to reduce the tax to 3s. in the £. This was sheer opportunism. More important were the two other great issues of the 1767 session: America and India. On these Chatham had little to contribute. He was deeply concerned about Charles Townshend's policy towards America but did little to dissuade him. On the problems of the East India Company, moreover, his wishes were to a large degree thwarted. After the conquests of the Seven Years War, it was by now urgently necessary to establish an effective structure for the government of India and for the regulation of the East India Company. A financial crisis in the affairs of the company in 1766 had brought the matter to a head. Chatham's solution to the Indian problem, characteristically, was to bring all Indian territory under royal sovereignty; it could then be leased out to the company as a preliminary to resolving its financial problems. Rockingham and Grenville, unusually in alliance, were horrified at this apparent attack on the chartered rights of the company. The eventual solution, reached in 1767, was for the company to continue to enjoy its commercial and territorial privileges on condition that it restrict speculative investments in its stock and pay £400 000 per annum to the Exchequer. This solution patched up the problem but it hardly amounted to the resounding imperial gesture which Lord Chatham had envisaged. He now became totally indifferent to the fate of his ministry, leaving responsibility in the hands of the weak and increasingly desperate Grafton. In an attempt to strengthen the government, therefore, the King unenthusiastically approved negotiations with the opposition parties in the summer of 1767. The discussions proved to be fruitless. Both Grenville and Rockingham demanded the leadership of a future ministry for themselves. The King would not even acknowledge that the existing administration was at an end. Although these negotiations failed, the Bedford Whigs entered the ministry before the end of the year, a sure and symbolic sign that the ministry to end party could now only continue with the aid of one of the parties. The Bedfords were small in numbers but disciplined and talented. Moreover, on America and on reform issues their opinions coincided with those of the King. They were to be a valuable acquisition. Furthermore, the inability of Rockingham and Grenville to unite or even to combine, especially on the American policy of Charles Townshend, was a negative source of strength to the paralysed ministry.

By this time the Duke of Grafton was in effective charge of the administration, although Chatham's formal decision to retire did not come until the summer of 1768. By bringing in the Bedfords Grafton had broadened the basis of the government, but it remained an uneasy coalition of Chathamites, old Rockinghamites and (now) of the Bedford Whigs. The death of Charles Townshend in September 1767, however, enabled him to attach the rapidly rising star of Lord North to the ministry, as Chancellor of the Exchequer. It was to be tragic for the ministry's prospects that it had to encounter the public hostility aroused by the issue of John Wilkes and the Middlesex election, his expulsion from the House of Commons in February 1769 and his subsequent re-elections. The ministry's decision to seat Wilkes's defeated opponent for the constituency aroused popular fury. Could a government be allowed to overturn the expressed wishes of electors and thus make a nonsense of the representative principle? A nationwide petitioning campaign in 1769 demanded the dissolution of Parliament and fresh elections. Chatham came out of retirement to line up with the Rockinghams and the Grenvilles. At this the Chathamites in the government wavered and began to resign. In January 1770 Grafton was succeeded by Lord North.

The first ten years of the reign had been years of acute ministerial instability. The accession of a new King, the effects of a great war and the ending of Tory proscription were bound to have extensive political consequences. Furthermore, with the disappearance of the old party distinctions politics had entered a new era in which established political routines were no longer useful guides to conduct. The structure of politics was more complicated, and thus potentially more unstable, than in the previous reign. But these were not the only reasons for the failure of the ministries of the 1760s to repeat the success of Walpole and Henry Pelham. George Grenville was the only first minister between Henry Pelham and Lord North both to lead the Treasury and to sit in the House of Commons, an inestimable political advantage. Nevertheless, the King must accept part of the responsibility for the ministerial instability of the decade. His own political prejudices and his predilection for his own opinions and preferences had much to do with the end of the Pitt–Newcastle ministry and with the fall of the Grenville and Rockingham ministries. He had a wider choice of ministers than his grandfather, but he completely failed to exploit this advantage. He did little to cement the unity of any of the administrations of the 1760s. There were new issues in politics, to be sure, those of colonial rights and radical reform, but these did not impinge greatly upon the survival of governments until the end of the decade.

The only individual who comes near to the monarch in culpability for the ministerial instability of the decade is William Pitt, Earl of Chatham. Pitt had been a patriot politician throughout his career, eschewing the rewards of office and the blandishments of party. He had never been easy with the politicians of the old corps. He was no party man, preferring to cultivate his pride in self-imposed, splendid isolation. Finding his imperial strategies repudiated by his cabinet colleagues in 1761, and finding no support at court, he was content to resign and to leave his reputation to public opinion and to posterity. With a patriot king on the throne there seemed much less room for a patriot minister. However, when the plans of the court began to disintegrate Pitt began to manoeuvre himself back into the political mainstream, and in doing so did much to unsettle both the Grenville and Rockingham ministries. In the summer of 1763 and again in June 1765 he was prepared to negotiate with the court and when, as in June–July 1766, the terms were acceptable he was prepared once more to form a government. The dramatic failure of his administration deprived both the monarch and the political world of a major talent, one high in public esteem which, had it been directed differently, might have strengthened rather than weakened the political fabric.

While Chatham's political career was demonstrating the redundancy of his habits of independent patriotism, the Marquis of Rockingham and his party were looking to the rehabilitation of party politics in the confusing and unstable politics of the 1760s. In the early years of the decade what was left of the Whig party was tending to fragment into its constituent connections, but some continuity and cohesion at least were retained. The old corps following of Newcastle represented the main body of the Whigs, but it was seriously weakened by the 'Massacre of the Pelhamite Innocents'. Only about a third of former supporters of Newcastle, about 75 MPs in all, remained loyal to him thereafter. Many of the others remained in office. The magnetism of monarchy, especially at the dawn of a new reign, proved to be more powerful than the strength of loyalty to the old corps, many of whom, of course, had developed habits of loyalty to the court over years of office-holding. From this disarray, however, the core of a revived Whig party was to emerge. By the end of the session of 1763 the number of Newcastle's friends had increased to slightly over 100. In the winter of 1763–64 Newcastle's younger friends began to organize themselves at Wildman's Club in London. Between 1764 and 1766 the size of the Rockingham party stabilized at around 100. The Rockingham Whigs were thus not a new party in 1765; they grew out of the old Newcastle connection. They accepted the Pelhamite assumptions that they represented the tradition of the Glorious Revolution and that they embodied the historic achievements of Whiggism. After all, the old Whigs had defended the constitution against a series of threats, from the Stuarts, from the Bourbons, from the Jacobites and from the Tories; they were in a very real sense its sponsors and guardians. Although the monarch was entitled to respect it was responsible ministers, not royal favourites, who should manage the King's government. Rockingham shared the Duke's obsession with Bute's influence and accepted most of the political assumptions of the old corps. Yet Rockingham was not just another old corps aristocrat. He was a Yorkshire magnate, who brought to a connection hitherto dominated by the southern aristocracy and its traditions of court service an invigorating blast of provincial country opinion. During the ministry of 1765–66, indeed, Rockingham moved close to provincial mercantile opinion in the process of repealing the Stamp Act.

The next few years of his leadership of the Rockingham party were disastrous. On his resignation in July 1766 Rockingham advised his followers to stay in their places rather than to resign with him. He really had little alternative. He was convinced that he could exert more influence upon the fortunes of the Chatham administration if they did stay in their places. Had he called on his men to resign they might not have responded. Even if they had done, their places might have been filled with friends of Bute and Chatham. For the time being, then, they stayed where they were. But when Lord Edgecumbe, a leading Rockinghamite, was dismissed in humiliating circumstances in November 1766 Rockingham at last called his men out. Between 40 and 50 of his followers, preferring the fruits of office to the cold winds of opposition, refused to answer Rockingham's call. This was a major disaster for his party. Perhaps Rockingham underestimated the attraction of Chatham, now in alliance with the monarch. Many of these men were now lost irretrievably. By the time of the general election of 1768 the size of the party, once over 100, had halved. Before the election there were 54 MPs in the Rockingham party; after it there were perhaps 57.

The circumstances following the dismissal of Edgecumbe may have been unfortunate for the Rockingham party, but in losing so many men to Chatham they at least left themselves with a narrower and better defined ideological base. That so many old Pelhamites should have returned to the court, especially during the Chatham administration, should not occasion surprise. Now, the Rockingham party in opposition continued to nurse its Pelhamite principles of dedication to the legacy of the Glorious Revolution, strengthened by its conviction that the new regime of Lord Bute was subversive of the constitution. Its principles were outlined by Edmund Burke[5] in his *Observations on a Late Publication intituled The Present State of the Nation* (1769) and, more memorably, in *Thoughts on the Causes of the Present Discontents* (1770). Burke gathered together the ideological inheritance of the Pelhams and linked it with the anti-Bute prejudices of the Rockingham party to fashion a new brand of Whiggism. Burke did not invent these ideas. He came to the party in 1765 as Rockingham's secretary and entered the House of Commons a year later. His writings expressed in memorable prose the principles and prejudices of his new party, its conviction that in the reign of George III a new and unconstitutional system of government had been established. In these writings Burke expressed a version of Whiggism suitable for a party in opposition. According to Burke, Lord Bute's personal involvement in politics was no longer the issue: it was the system of secret influence which the Rockinghams opposed. This may have had its origins in the early years of the decade but it had now fallen into more sinister hands and had, indeed, been elevated into a system of government. Only the exertions of a dedicated Whig party could protect the rights of Parliament from the sinister purposes of the executive. Constant reiteration of these ideas lent to the activities of the Rockingham party an identity and a consistency, whether on colonial policy, issues of domestic reform or of constitutional right, which was to be their hallmark. Although the Rockinghams had an exaggerated sense of their own moral superiority, Burke had no exclusive concept of party; he believed that the Rockinghams must be prepared to participate in 'healing coalitions' (though not with those involved in secret influence) but that the Marquis should always demand, and receive, the first place.

The Rockingham Whigs were not the only political party to exist in the 1760s. Of the others, however, the Bedford Whigs were an office-storming faction who had enjoyed a spell of office in 1763–65. They came back into office in 1767, after which they lost their cohesion and ceased to act as a party. Those who gathered around Chatham behaved as that near self-contradiction, a non-party party. As for the Grenville Whigs, when Grenville left office in 1765 they numbered over 70. But the party faded quite rapidly, as his erstwhile followers attached themselves to the court and to other groups. By 1768 there were only about 30 Grenville Whigs, and the party failed to survive what was always an eighteenth-century party's greatest crisis, the death of its leader, in 1770. In this way what had always been an essentially personal party disappeared. But the Rockingham party survived the 1760s and proceeded to survive the death of Rockingham in 1782. That party was the only political, as opposed to personal, party in the politics of the 1760s. Its distinctive ideological antipathy to Bute, to the new court regime and, ultimately, to George III enabled it to survive the treacherous factional politics of the 1760s and to furnish the materials for the only opposition party to the government of Lord North.

Politics and party, 1770–1789

The ministry of Lord North (1770–82) represented a return to the ministerial politics of the reign of George II. It was in very few senses a victory for the more idiosyncratic ambitions of George III. North himself had been an orthodox career politician within the old corps, and a junior Lord of the Treasury between 1759 and 1766. If he had steered his career towards the court since then, he had been in very good company in so doing. His uncle was Lord Halifax, who had been President of the Board of Trade during the 1750s and a Secretary of State during Grenville's ministry (1763–65). In the Chatham administration (1766–68) North became joint Paymaster of the Forces and, on Charles Townshend's death in 1767, Chancellor of the Exchequer. At this juncture, North had two assets: the fact that he had kept himself clear of the factions during the first seven years of the reign, and his very considerable political ability. His economic competence, his parliamentary presence, his skilful deployment of humour in debate and his ability to arouse trust and loyalty marked him as a rising man. North did not play the great man, preferring a mixture of common sense, good humour and honesty. The manner of his succession to Grafton in 1770 endowed him with two more advantages. The first was the confidence of the King. Lord North made no conditions with George III. He insisted on the inclusion or exclusion of no man. His wish devoutly to serve his country commended him to the weary and harassed King, who rewarded him with trust, loyalty and, on occasion, something approaching friendship. This does not mean that North was a cipher in the hands of an autocratic monarch. Having found a minister who had constructed a durable administration and who was capable of governing, George III wanted nothing other than to let him get on with it. Political and administrative decisions, in any case, were taken not by the monarch but by ministers at departmental and cabinet level; royal approval was a formality that was normally taken for granted. The second advantage that North enjoyed, in addition, was that he led the ministry from the House of Commons. Indeed, from 1771 to 1775 North was the only cabinet minister in the House of Commons. From there he could lead his team of ministers, appeal to the Country gentlemen and defend himself from the charges of the opposition. North thoroughly exploited his advantages, and he remained in power for 12 years.

Within weeks his ministry had established itself and repulsed the attacks of the opposition. On 31 January, on the Middlesex election issue, North won a majority of 40 votes and his majorities on subsequent divisions on the issue increased. On non-party issues he showed that he was prepared to accept the occasional reverse. He accepted defeat on George Grenville's bill to transfer the hearing of election petitions from the whole House (where party considerations usually overrode those of electoral fairness). On 30 March 1770 North's motion for the adjournment was lost by 52 votes, a defeat which he acknowledged and accepted.

The safety of North's ministry was further enhanced by the collapse of the unity of the opposition groups. Burke's pamphlet, *Thoughts on the Causes of the Present Discontents*, appeared in April 1770. Its public declaration of the principle of party offended Chatham, who prided himself on his independence of conduct. The two groups led by Chatham and Rockingham had been cooperating closely since the beginning of their campaign against the Grafton ministry's policy on the Middlesex election. Their ultimate failure left them divided. In the summer of 1770 Chatham, influenced by the radical mercantile elements in the capital, began to advocate the reform of the electoral system, a step that the propertied aristocracy of the Rockingham party could never accept. They were horrified when Chatham began to advocate war with Spain in the summer and autumn of 1770 in a dispute over the Falkland Islands. Among the public there was absolutely no stomach for a war for a few islands 8000 miles away from Britain. Chatham's extravagant attacks upon the settlement which North eventually negotiated embarrassed the Rockinghams and only served to emphasize North's good diplomatic sense. In November the opposition was further damaged by the death of George Grenville and the subsequent acquisition of most of his supporters by the government. What was left of the unity of the opposition disappeared during the parliamentary session of 1771 on the issue of the law of libel. Lord Mansfield, the Chief Justice, in recent trials had laid down the principle that the only function of juries in libel trials was to determine the fact of publication, leaving the judge to determine the issue of libel. Chatham and Rockingham were united in their wish to empower juries to determine the matter of libel, but Chatham wished to go further and to advocate an inquiry into the administration of the law. This direct and personal attack upon Mansfield, an old corps man through and through, offended Rockingham and caused personal difficulties. The Rockinghams proposed a bill that would simply change the law, but public differences with the Chathamites when the bill came before the Commons on 7 March 1771 marked the ending of the united opposition. It was not even able to take any political advantage of the Printers' Case in 1771, perhaps the one issue during his early years on which North blundered. North's government attempted to restrain the publication of parliamentary debates, summoning and subsequently imprisoning certain of the printers concerned. It was the enthusiastic defence of the printers by their supporters in the capital rather than the political efforts of the parliamentary opposition which freed them. For the foreseeable future, North was safe. Indeed, it was to be another eight years before his ministry faced a serious threat from a united opposition.

North settled down to several years of quiet administration during which he demonstrated considerable financial acumen. He was able to take full political advantage of the vigorous economic recovery of the early 1770s. In 1772 and 1773 he kept the Land Tax down to 3s. in the £, to the delight of the Country gentlemen in Parliament. He aimed for small surpluses on the budget which he devoted to reductions of the national debt. By 1776 he had trimmed £3.5 million from the total. To fund this reduction he imposed a number of taxes on luxuries, simplified some of the more arcane features of the existing taxation system and paved the way for the more ambitious reforms of the Younger Pitt in the next decade. In the same way, the government's handling of the latest instalment of the affairs of the East India Company commended itself to large parliamentary majorities and considerable public approval. The settlement of the company's affairs in 1767 had never worked well; its revenues were in decline because of a trade recession and rising military costs. These problems were exacerbated by the great Bengal famine of 1769–70, and by increasing instability among the native states in India, which made possible the revival of French influence. These problems were compounded by a credit crisis in Europe which reduced the company's affairs to confusion, inducing it to petition the government for a loan and to request that it postpone its customs payments. These territorial and financial complexities were thoroughly reviewed by the government, and a comprehensive package of measures received parliamentary approval in 1773. As North proudly announced, 'I have endeavoured to make myself a master of the subject.' The Loan Act issued a loan of £1.4 million to the company and limited its (hitherto over-generous) dividends. The Tea Act allowed the levy of a duty on tea and permitted its export to America. Most importantly, the Regulating Act provided for less regular elections to the court of directors (every four years in place of the annual elections which had imparted such a sense of uncertainty to Indian government) and laid down a new set of voting qualifications. These provisions required regular government involvement in the affairs of the company to prevent them from falling prey to hostile influences. The government of India was remodelled. Bengal was placed under the control of a governor-general and four councillors, who were also to regulate the subsidiary presidencies of Bombay and Madras. In addition, a supreme court of justice was established in Bengal. With the benefit of hindsight it is possible to criticize these measures as allowing the company and its officers too much freedom of action. Within its own time, however, the policy was a major step towards state regulation and superintendence, and probably represented the greatest degree of state intervention that contemporaries would tolerate.

In 1774, as we have seen, the American issue disrupted the steady and quiet purpose of the North administration, and it remained to curse and to overwhelm the minister. The outbreak of war in the colonies, the involvement of France and Spain and the threatened invasion of 1779 were enough to shake the foundations of the ministry. As early as 1778 North was begging the King to release him and when he refused North plunged into depression, indecision and inactivity. By 1779 departmental heads were being left to their own devices. The government was moribund.

By the same token, the American crisis had reinvigorated the Rockingham party, added to its numbers (about 80 after the general election of 1780) and effected bitter confrontations in Parliament such as had not been seen since the last years of Walpole. The death of Chatham in 1778 removed the great rival to Rockingham's ambition to lead the opposition. His successor as leader of the tiny, if talented, band of Chathamites was Shelburne. The 'Jesuit of Berkeley Square' was as brilliant as he was deemed untrustworthy by his contemporaries for his seemingly inconsistent attitudes. For Shelburne had politically advanced opinions; he was a radical reformer with an advanced belief in free-market economics, yet he strongly believed in monarchy and its prerogatives. He was an early advocate of American independence once the military battle had been lost, but dreamed of maintaining close economic ties. It was, therefore, with rising confidence that the opposition challenged North on the American War. Both Chathamites and Rockinghamites were dismayed at the war, appalled at the slaughter of fellow Englishmen and terrified of the consequences of a victorious war and the prospect of a restrengthened monarchy. As the architects of the Declaratory Act, the Rockingham Whigs found it difficult to oppose the war, and one which had the support of a clear majority of public opinion in its early stages. They therefore attacked the persecuting spirit which, in their opinion, had led to the war and condemned the inefficiency and corruption with which it was being conducted. For some years they advocated a policy of reconciliation but during 1778, as the consequences of Saratoga began to sink in, they began to advocate the independence of the American colonies. In February 1778 Charles James Fox, one of the party's brightest recruits and a future leader, secured no fewer than 165 votes for a motion which opposed sending additional troops to America. By the end of the session of 1779, indeed, ministers were fending off opposition attacks with majorities that had dropped below 30. In the summer of 1780, therefore, North tried to buy off some members of the opposition, especially the old friends of Chatham, such as Grafton and Camden, and some of the Rockinghams. By now, however, the Rockingham party had demands of its own. These amounted to a recognition of American independence, economical reform and a substantial redistribution of offices, with Rockingham taking the lead.[6] The Rockingham leaders were standing firm on Burke's theory of party, advocating substantial changes of policy and personnel. They would only come in as a party. The King was prepared to make a few concessions in minor places but he would not hear of changes of policy. As for surrendering his prerogative of appointment to Rockingham, he would have none of it. North had to continue to shoulder the burdens of office.

Even before Yorktown, however, the war was becoming politically unsustainable. In May 1781 a Rockinghamite motion to end the war was defeated by 106 to 72. When Fox followed this up with a further motion on 12 June he was defeated by 172 to 99. North cannot have been comforted, however, by the fact that he was opposed in the division by some independents and former ministerialists. The defeat at Yorktown destroyed the ministry. In February 1782 Conway's motion for an end to the war was defeated by only one vote, 194 to 193. Within three weeks North had resigned.

North and the King had been defeated but who had won? North, indeed, had advised the King on 28 February that 'it may be feasible to divide the Opposition, and to take in only a part'. Desperate to maintain some freedom of action, George III, declaring that 'my language went to a broad bottom, not the delivering myself up to a party', appointed both Rockingham and Shelburne and their respective supporters to cabinet offices. The changes were more extensive than they had been at the fall of Walpole; only Thurlow survived from North's cabinet. Rockingham took the Treasury but the two dominant personalities were the two secretaries, Shelburne and Fox. The Rockingham–Shelburne ministry proceeded to enact a programme of economical reform and, in an attempt to prevent Ireland going the way of America, granted legislative independence to the Irish Parliament. On the issue of peace with America, however, serious divisions within the ministry soon appeared between Shelburne and Fox, the former unwilling to concede total independence. Fox was on the point of resignation when Rockingham's death on 1 July threw the political scene into confusion.

The King seized his opportunity, appointing Shelburne to the Treasury and bringing Chatham's son, William Pitt the Younger, into the cabinet as Chancellor of the Exchequer. Rockingham's men resigned, unwilling to accept – and by accepting to vindicate – the King's action. Rockingham's successor, they argued, should have been chosen by the cabinet, not by George III. This drastic extension of the claims of the Rockingham party against the royal prerogative was treated with contempt by the King. The parliamentary recess intervened, permitting Shelburne to turn his attention to the peace negotiations. Meanwhile, the Duke of Portland had succeeded to the leadership of Rockingham's party. The Portland party, in which Fox was the effective leader, regarded their latest political misfortune at the hands of the King and Shelburne as yet further evidence of the existence of a system of secret influence and court favouritism. Only by continuing the party's struggle against the system of government which had lost the American colonies could they continue to carry the mantle of Rockingham. When Shelburne's peace terms came before the Commons in February 1783 they were defeated by 224 to 208 and by 207 to 190. Like North in 1782, Shelburne took defeat by a Commons majority as sufficient cause for resignation. Like Chatham in 1766, he had an exaggerated belief in the ability of the monarchy alone to sustain his administration. Like Chatham's, his was collapsing around him before he resigned. Thereupon Fox and Portland stiffened their terms: the King must appoint Portland to the Treasury and allow him, not the King, to appoint the cabinet and the junior ministers. The King was aghast at this public, open assault on his prerogatives. For six weeks Britain was without a government as George III twisted in every direction to avoid surrender to the politicians of party. In the most serious constitutional crisis since the Glorious Revolution, the future of the monarchy, of the Portland party and, indeed, the future shape of British politics appeared to be at stake.

The King would not have Fox and his men at any price. It was not merely their dogma which he detested. George III always tended to think the worst of his enemies; he regarded Fox and Portland as evil and ambitious men hungry for office. There was some personal justification for his attitude. He had come to hate the leaders of the opposition who had during the past year struck up a relationship with his son George, the Prince of Wales, who had established his court at Carlton House, playing on his weaknesses and cultivating his friendship as political insurance for the reign to come. Furthermore, Fox and his friends did not conceal the fact that they were engaged in a deadly serious political war against the King. The coalition between Fox and North, which was negotiated in March 1783, threatened the independence of the monarchy. Fox calculated that only by uniting his own force of approximately 90 supporters to North's 120 could Shelburne (who had about 140 followers in all) and the King be defeated. The coalition between Fox and North caused a political sensation. They had been bitter political enemies for years. But there were arguments in favour of the coalition. Was Fox to stand back and allow Shelburne and North to unite? The American war had been the great issue which had divided Fox and North but it now lay in the past. Some sort of coalition was necessary to carry on government. A Fox–Shelburne coalition was unthinkable in view of the events of the previous 12 months, and the Younger Pitt had ruled out a North–Shelburne coalition because of the way North had governed during his 12 years in power. Yet the Fox–North coalition has gone down in British history as an 'infamous coalition', and many contemporaries were shocked at the sight of Fox and the Rockinghams uniting with the man whose war and whose regime they had consistently denounced for many years.

In the end, the King realized that there was no alternative to the coalition, and he admitted them to office with great reluctance and with public indications that they lacked his confidence. The most that can be said for the coalition ministry (April–December 1783) is that the King tolerated it. It is just possible, although unlikely, that the King might have reconciled himself to the coalition had its leaders treated him with respect and settled down to a period of quiet, efficient and unselfish administration. The King's prejudices against it, however, were confirmed by the unpleasant and public need not only to obtain a large annual sum (£50 000 per annum) for the Prince of Wales but also to pay his huge debts (£60 000) in the summer of 1783. We now know that the King was biding his time and awaiting the right opportunity to dismiss the coalition.[7] This was to come on Fox's India Bill, a yet further measure to regulate the government of the subcontinent. Fox proposed that the government of India should become subject to a board of seven commissioners which would run the administration and, more to the point, control all the patronage of India. These commissioners would be appointed not, as hitherto in such cases, by the crown but by the ministers for four years at a time. Since it was widely believed that the account of Indian patronage exceeded that of domestic patronage, it was clear that under Foxite commissioners the India Bill would have gone far towards installing Fox and his friends in office for an indefinite period. The East India Company was horrified, and turned its engines of propaganda against the government. In December the Bill received majorities in the House of Commons by a ratio of 2 to 1. As it was proceeding through the Lords, however, the King sent a message with Pitt's cousin, Lord Temple, that 'he should consider them as his enemies' who voted for the Bill. On 17 December 1783 the Bill was defeated in the Lords and the coalition government was dismissed. The next day, William Pitt was appointed First Lord of the Treasury at the age of 24, a place he was to retain until 1801.

We now know that Pitt was implicated in these proceedings, and that he had in fact persuaded George III to dismiss the coalition ministry in the manner that he did. Whether Pitt had thought out the implications of his action is less clear. His government (aptly but, in the end, inaccurately termed 'the mince pie administration', because it was not expected to last beyond Christmas) was in a minority in the House of Commons. It was now up to the House to decide between the conflicting claims of crown and party. Was the royal prerogative of appointing ministers to be sustained, or was Fox's belief in the right of a majority in Parliament to determine the composition of a ministry to prevail? In one of the most exciting parliamentary battles in British history the organization and patience of the forces of the Fox–North coalition held for no less than three months, but Fox's majority eventually shrank until on 8 March 1784 it was down to one. This was the signal for the King to dissolve a Parliament which still had three years to run. At the historic general election of 1784 Pitt obtained a workable majority of over 100. Before the election the combined forces of Fox and North had slightly exceeded 200; after it they numbered slightly over 130. Although the influence of the crown and the government was actively employed against the coalition, there can be no doubt that Pitt had public opinion on his side, and he won seats in some of the larger boroughs and in the counties.

Yet Pitt's victory over Fox in 1783–84 did not only depend on ministerial propaganda. In what was still a traditional society most of the political nation retained enormous respect for the King and deeply disliked the prospect of the closet being stormed and the monarchy shorn of its traditional powers. Although the actions of the Rockingham and Portland Whigs had done much to re-establish the idea and practice of party in the two decades after the 'Massacre of the Pelhamite Innocents', their efforts did not meet with the seal of public approval in 1784. Fox and his friends were widely criticized for their part in seducing the Prince of Wales from his family attachments and princely duties. Furthermore, the coalition with North was universally condemned. For his part, the King preserved his dignity and won considerable sympathy and respect. It was extremely fortunate for him that his champion was the son of the Great Commoner, William Pitt, and not, as had been the case in the 1760s, an unpopular Scottish nobleman. Pitt's courage, his oratorical skill and, not least, his deployment of patronage and propaganda consolidated and strengthened his position and carried his message out of doors.

The victory of William Pitt ended the ministerial instability of the previous two years. The King now had a minister in whom he had confidence and who had a comfortable majority in Parliament. George III could now retreat from the central position on the political stage which he had for several years been forced to occupy. Disputes about royal powers in relation to those of Parliament and party had been settled for the foreseeable future and politics could return to normal. Pitt acknowledged his place as the King's servant and resisted any temptation he may have felt to build up his own party. Even at the height of his power, however, he never had more than 50 'friends', and probably rather fewer. Although on routine matters his majority was secure, it was not automatic. Everything depended on the votes of the independents. To the support of the King's Friends (around 200) could be added Pitt's 50 supporters. Against these the opposition would deploy about 130 MPs. The 150 independents in the House could therefore ultimately determine whether the government won or lost a division. Pitt's claims on parliamentary support were those of merit and service. Many MPs preferred Pitt's virtues of patriotism, methodical industry and integrity compared with Charles James Fox's pursuit of personal and party advantage, in active and well-publicized association with the Prince of Wales.

The first year of Pitt's administration saw the government defeated on a number of occasions. For nine months Pitt ostentatiously supported a scrutiny of the votes cast in the recent election in the constituency of Westminster, Charles James Fox's seat. This petty and unpleasant attempt to unseat his great opponent from one of the most prestigious parliamentary constituencies did Pitt no good, and he appears to have realized it. After a series of defeats in the spring of 1785 he dropped the matter. Similarly, in the same year he acquiesced in the defeat of a ministerial proposal to fortify the dockyards at Plymouth and Portsmouth. Although it was only lost on the casting vote of the Speaker, Pitt had sensed that he did not have the support of the independent Country gentlemen. Further defeats in the same year on parliamentary reform and on a plan to liberalize trade with Ireland chastened him and warned him off future schemes of ambitious reform. In the future he was to recognize the limits to his authority. He came to see that he might not be able to carry either his cabinet or the Commons on a number of issues: these included parliamentary reform, the abolition of the slave trade and the repeal of the Test and Corporation Acts. Throughout the remaining years of peace he preferred to improve the political structure less by flamboyant gestures of reform than by the quiet abolition of places and sinecures. Indeed, it has been calculated that in this way Pitt did more to reduce the influence of both the crown and the government than any politician of his generation. Nevertheless, his India Bill of 1784 restored to the crown the appointment of members of the board of control, and Indian patronage was left with the East India Company. Not unnaturally, both the crown and the company were satisfied with this arrangement. Pitt had learned the lessons of Fox's India Bill very thoroughly. Whatever its weaknesses – and Fox and Burke claimed that corruption in India continued unabated – Pitt's act was to provide the basis of Indian government for three-quarters of a century.

Like Walpole, Pitt believed that the strength of the country derived from its economic prosperity which, in turn, depended upon peace. In the years 1783–93 Pitt did much to restore the economy by promoting sound national finance and by presiding over a veritable explosion in commercial activity. The first need was to balance the budget and raise revenue, which in 1783 lagged behind income by over £10 million per annum. This was done in two ways. First, the yield from existing taxes was raised by preventing fraud and smuggling, which saved £1 million a year for the Exchequer. Second, new taxes raised another £1 million a year. Pitt's taxes were a curious assortment which included taxes on luxuries like hackney coaches, everyday items like ribbons, linens and candles and fixtures like windows and, in 1785, shops. Not all of Pitt's taxes were wise. Indeed, he recognized as much by withdrawing the unpopular shop and window taxes and the tax on linen, and by dropping a projected tax on coal. More successful was the increase in revenue derived simply from increased consumption, a further £2 million. By 1792, as Pitt boasted in his famous budget speech of that year, total government income was 47 per cent higher than it had been nine years earlier. However, Pitt did not merely increase revenue. He attacked the national debt, which in 1783 stood at what contemporaries thought was the ruinous level of £238 million. He re-established the sinking fund in 1786 and by 1793 had managed to liquidate a modest but useful £10 million of debt.

Sound national finance and the maintenance of peace were two essential prerequisites for commercial confidence. During the years of peace British commercial activity roughly doubled. Imports rose from £10 million to £20 million between 1783 and 1790, while the value of exports increased from £12 million to £20 million. In this development the European and American markets were vital. The value of British exports to Europe almost doubled between 1783 and 1792, helping to convert an annual trade deficit of £2.5 million into a surplus of almost £2 million. As for the trade with America, it very quickly recovered from the impact of the war. As early as 1785 the value of British trade with the ex-colonies had attained its prewar level. As with taxation, however, Pitt's record was not one of unalloyed success. His proposed free-trade treaty with Ireland in 1785 caused an outcry in England, had to be modified and even then was thrown out by the Irish Parliament. A commercial treaty with France, negotiated in 1786, provided for the reduction of duties of between 10 per cent and 15 per cent on trade between the two nations. Industrial opinion was divided. Old-established manufacturers, especially of silk, paper and leather, wanted protection, while Manchester textile manufacturers and Midlands metal traders yearned for free trade.

In 1783 Britain had been defeated in a major war and stood isolated in Europe. Pitt was careful to keep out of continental entanglements during the first few years of his ministry. Although he was anxious to involve Britain in commercial competition with France he had no illusions about that country.

Like his father he was profoundly suspicious of French colonial and naval objectives and concerned about her ambitions in the Low Countries. These latter he was keen to resist, and to that end in 1788 negotiated the triple alliance with Prussia and Holland. Pitt, moreover, kept his head when a minor dispute with Spain over an attack on a small British settlement off Vancouver island in the Pacific, Nootka Sound, in 1790 aroused demands in the cabinet and in the Commons for war. British interests were not seriously at stake, and Pitt was able to press the Spaniards to negotiate a peaceful settlement which was wholly to Britain's advantage. In a rather more dangerous dispute arising out of the Eastern question Pitt almost overreached himself in 1791, threatening Catherine the Great of Russia to restore to Turkey territory conquered in the recent Russo-Turkish war. In the end he was forced to climb down, even at the cost of losing his Foreign Secretary, the Duke of Leeds. The best that can be said is that Pitt realized his mistake, saw that it was not in Britain's interest to pursue a war in the Turkish empire and ultimately kept the peace.

If these were the great years of William Pitt then they were harsh and bitter years for the opposition of Charles James Fox, the Duke of Portland and Lord North. Having gambled heavily – and lost – during the political crisis of 1782–84 they were now licking their wounds. Their prospects for the rest of the present reign seemed hopeless; they were marking time, hoping for the King to die and for the Prince of Wales to succeed. What was the point of the harsh and punishing round of constitutional opposition if failure was inevitable? Past reverses and the hopelessness of their future prospects gnawed away both at their confidence and at their sense of responsibility. They continued to indulge the Prince of Wales and to be identified with him in the public mind. This was to be most damaging. Not only was the Prince widely disliked; he used the opposition for his own purposes – usually to help him extort money out of Pitt and George III – and involved them in his private dealings. These were not only unwholesome; when he married Mrs Fitzherbert, a Catholic, in 1785, they became unconstitutional, for the marriage violated not only the Royal Marriages Act of 1772 (which required the consent of the monarch to the marriage of a royal) but nothing less than the Act of Succession of 1701 as well (which forbade the marriage of a monarch to a Catholic). Although Fox and the Whig leaders denied the rumours, such associations were politically damaging and compared badly with Pitt's loyal service to his King and his country.

The opposition was also plagued with problems of leadership. The Duke of Portland deferred to Charles James Fox in most things. Fox was a charismatic figure, whose talent for friendship and loyalty combined with great oratorical gifts. Although Fox was a towering public figure it was clear that he could neither control nor discipline the rising young men in the party, such as R.B. Sheridan, the playwright, and Charles Grey, the future Reform Bill prime minister. During these years, too, Edmund Burke drifted away from a central position in the everyday concerns of the opposition, applying himself to causes which transcended party, not least that of the reform of the government of India. Pitt was careful, after 1785 at least, to present the fewest possible targets for the opposition to aim at. Fox was frustrated and restless in the placid political climate, yearning for great events and dreaming of major issues. Opposition attendance at Parliament became casual and policy was sometimes treated lightly. On many issues, especially those touching taxation and tariffs, for example, the opposition agreed with Pitt and did little to oppose him.

Yet these years were not entirely without marks of positive achievement for the opposition. Its attendance may have been less than regular, but so was that of oppositions throughout the century. Indeed, a policy of occasional but wounding attacks could be more successful than months of solid toil. The defeat of Pitt on the Westminster Scrutiny, Irish Trade and Fortifications in 1785–86 owed much to the ability of the opposition to attack where Pitt was weakest and to rally the independents. Furthermore, the opposition maintained its cohesion and its identity. It stabilized its numbers and suffered few defections during the 1784–90 Parliament. It began to organize more effectively than it had done in the past, raising and spending money in a more systematic manner, preparing for elections and using propaganda in a more professional and bureaucratic manner than hitherto. In William Adam it had an efficient and willing party manager. Adam was a Scottish MP and former Northite who since 1782 had been close to Fox. He did much to weld the two wings of the coalition into a working unit, acting as a party whip. By 1790 the opposition controlled five London papers, had established three funds and employed a string of agents to help with the work of appealing for extra-parliamentary support. As the Regency Crisis of 1788–89 was to demonstrate, this opposition could sustain for several months a major organizational challenge to one of the most successful administrations of the century, dividing around 200 time and time again. Few oppositions of the century could claim as much.

At the ideological level the coalition marked time, its two wings, Rockinghamite and Northite, incapable of sharing, and thus of shaping, a common political tradition. The Northites had never adequately been incorporated into the party of Portland and Fox, and by the end of the decade their adhesion was much less strong than it had been. The old Rockinghamites believed that the King's intervention in the House of Lords over the India Bill in 1783 had been simply a further manifestation of the system of secret influence which had existed since the beginning of the reign; the Northites, who made up 40 per cent of the foot soldiers in opposition and who had spent their political lives operating the system, found such language mystifying.[8] Outwardly, at least, most of them went along with it. They would not have done so if they had been fed a diet of stale charges about Lord Bute. In the 1780s tirades against secret influence gave way to criticism of an overweening first minister and to defence of the independence of the House of Commons. The other serious division between the two wings was on the subject of parliamentary reform, but Fox had agreed to abandon his support for the measure when the coalition had first been negotiated. It cannot be regarded as a major bone of contention in the opposition between 1784 and 1790, but it remained a potentially serious problem which would in time return to torment the opposition.

The only threat to Pitt's political supremacy in these years occurred during the Regency Crisis of 1788–89. In November 1788 the King was once again afflicted with an attack of porphyria. On this occasion the attack was so serious as to raise the possibility of his permanent incapacity. In October 1788 Pitt introduced a Regency Bill which would have installed the Prince of Wales, albeit with reduced powers, on the throne as Regent. Unwisely, Fox and his friends opposed and delayed the passage of the bill, arguing that the limitations placed upon his power, including that which prevented him from making peers, unfairly derogated from royal power. They would have been better advised to have accepted the limitations, and passed the Bill. Had they done so, the prince would almost certainly have removed Pitt's government and replaced it with one fashioned from the opposition. As it was, the opposition was left to argue an unconvincing case and one which emphasized the absolute hereditary right of the Prince to succeed to the throne without the need for parliamentary sanction. This was scarcely good Whig doctrine. Burke was horrified; Rockingham would have turned in his grave. Moreover, they argued the case badly; Pitt was far more at home in the tricky world of historical precedents and constitutional theory than Fox. After bitter political exchanges lasting for several months, the Bill passed the Commons. The King recovered in February 1789, just in time to prevent the passage of the Bill through the Lords. Once more Pitt had repulsed the attacks of Fox and the opposition, safeguarded his ministry and won the gratitude of the King and most sections of public opinion.

Reform politics, 1763–1789

This reform movement has customarily been seen as the ancestor and origin of the reform movements of the early nineteenth century and thus of the Reform Act of 1832. Its critical place in the emergence of a modern, reformed and more democratic political system gives it particular significance. So compelling has it seemed that many historians have actually adopted the perspectives of the reformers themselves and claimed that Hanoverian politics were corrupt, its electoral system ludicrously unrepresentative and its management autocratic and intimidating. On this reading, Britain badly needed a new electoral system to keep abreast of the remarkable changes in population, in society and in the economy.

In the face of such an emotive, thematic interpretation, a few warnings need to be issued. Most contemporaries were in fact content with their parliamentary system and the electoral structure which underpinned it. To the modern mind the distribution of seats, the varied nature of the franchise and the rumbustious method of electoral campaigning seem anomalous and unfamiliar. The old electoral system, however, lasted as long as it did because it worked in a rough and ready fashion to meet contemporary requirements. The output of private bill legislation demonstrated Parliament's readiness to provide for local needs. Moreover, the fact that the electoral system may not have been representative did not unduly trouble contemporaries. It was not intended to reflect population. It is true that new towns sprang up and old ones increased in size, but it is important to recognize that some of their residents could vote in county elections even if the town lacked *separate* representation. At the same time, we should not be too ready to assume that the eighteenth-century reform movement was simply a byproduct of social and economic changes. Radical reform was not simply a response to the increase in population: reform opinion was to be found in some areas of the country least affected by it. The demand for reform was not merely a consequence of rapid industrialization: in the 1760s industrialization had hardly begun. Similarly, the demand for reform cannot simply be linked to urbanization because reform activity, especially in 1779–85, was to be found in many rural areas. Least of all was it a reflection of the rise of the middle class: many sections of the middling orders were notably unsympathetic to reform. In any case, the key reform demand was less for the enlargement of borough electorates than for their transference to county constituencies.

More plausible is the view that the origins of many aspects of the radical reform movement of the later eighteenth century are to be found with the Tory party, and, to a more limited extent, with the opposition Whigs, of the first half of the century. There is some similarity, for example, between the open boroughs in which the Tories enjoyed strong popular support (Bristol, Coventry, London, Newcastle, Norwich, Westminster), those unrepresented towns which might in the middle of the eighteenth century more realistically be labelled Tory than Whig (Birmingham, Leeds, Manchester) and those towns which were later to be identified with reform. It was the opposition to Walpole which commanded the great urban centres and the Tories who were the 'popular' party. Tories wished to remodel the electoral system in order to improve their prospects of power. Chronically incapable of persuading the Commons to pass their place and pensions bills, they moved on to adopt a platform of measures which would later be included within the label of parliamentary reform. These included a variety of expedients whose purpose was to increase the influence of electors over their MPs, not least campaigns for 'instructions' which would bind MPs. As early as 1722 several constituencies were demanding undertakings from their members that they would support a triennial act. During the Excise Crisis of 1733–34, indeed, over 50 constituencies instructed their members against the excise, and on subsequent issues between 1733 and 1756 no fewer than 21 constituencies instructed their MPs on at least three occasions. By then the Tories had come to embrace the principle of the redistribution of seats, especially the abolition of rotten boroughs and their redistribution to the counties. After the demise of the Tory party in the early 1760s its traditions of extra-parliamentary political action and its programme of parliamentary reform were available for any political group that wished to protest against the men and measures of the governments of George III.

All that was needed to mobilize discontents was a political crisis and a popular figure who could work on the materials of protest. The first was provided by the accession of George III and the ending of the Seven Years War; the second was furnished by the astonishing figure of John Wilkes. The social and economic background – postwar depression, declining trade and lower wages, rising unemployment and higher prices – did not create the Wilkite agitation, but did much to provide an audience and not a few participants.

Wilkes had been in Parliament as MP for Aylesbury since 1757. Although he had moved on the fringes of Pitt's circle, he had made little mark in the House. In June 1762, however, he founded the *North Briton*, an opposition newspaper which was intended to be a counterblast to the pro-Bute *Briton*.

The paper quickly became notorious for its outspoken attitude to the royal family, even alleging a sexual relationship between Bute and the Princess Dowager. Then, in the famous issue 45 on 23 April 1763, Wilkes attacked not only the Treaty of Paris but the ministry and the person of the King in offensive terms. The King, according to No. 45, was either a liar or the instrument of lying ministers. Such language almost invited retaliation. George Grenville's response was to issue on 30 April a general warrant for the arrest of those responsible for the offending issue, and Wilkes was imprisoned. General warrants did not name an accused individual but merely specified the crime of which he was accused. They were capable of an alarmingly wide interpretation: the accused's person, home and possessions were at the mercy of the authorities. Wilkes made a flamboyant public protest against the unconstitutionality of general warrants, even though they had been used throughout the century. Lord Chief Justice Pratt freed him on the grounds that his imprisonment had violated his privileges as an MP. Wilkes, however, asserted that he owed his liberty not to his status as an MP but to the common-law tradition of English freedom. Determined to keep the issue alive, Wilkes sued the government for trespass. He was successful, the judge declaring general warrants 'unconstitutional, illegal and absolutely void' – a verdict which established the precedent for the later legal processes which put an end to the warrants. After these embarrassments the government decided to make an example of John Wilkes. On 15 November 1763 the House of Commons voted by 237 to 111 that No. 45 was a 'false, scandalous and seditious libel'. At the same time, the cabinet denounced Wilkes for his part in the composition of the *Essay on Women*, a semi-pornographic parody of Pope's *Essay on Man*.

At this point Wilkes, fearing arrest, left for Paris, and he was absent when Parliament returned to the matter of general warrants. His expulsion from the House was voted on 19 January 1764 by 225 to 64; and, after one of the most famous debates (and narrowest divisions) of the century on 17/18 February 1764, Parliament approved the conduct of the ministry by 232 to 218. It was one thing for the government to make use of its majorities and of the courts against the absent Wilkes, but it earned little public credit for doing so. Not surprisingly, however, the rising tide of sympathy for Wilkes ebbed in his absence.

Wilkes returned to England for the general election of 1768, hoping that his election to a seat would save him from the sentence of outlawry which had been passed against him. Furthermore, he hoped for better treatment from the Chatham administration. His victory at Middlesex, however, led only to his imprisonment on outstanding charges of blasphemy and libel. Rioting in his favour led to the 'Massacre of St George's Field' in May 1768, in which seven people died and 15 were injured. However, Chatham's government was no more sympathetic to Wilkes than Grenville's had been. Its majority in parliament expelled Wilkes from the House for his attack on the government for the 'Massacre', and a new election for Middlesex was ordered. At the subsequent election Wilkes was again returned and duly expelled. At a further election he was elected yet again, and not only expelled but replaced by his defeated opponent, Colonel Luttrell, who had obtained only a quarter of Wilkes's votes. It was one thing to expel a Member for his personal behaviour, and even for his political opinions, but it was quite another to seat his defeated opponent. In the opinion of many, the rights of the Middlesex electors were being seemingly ignored and, indeed, overridden by an autocratic government.

By now, Wilkes had become something of a popular hero. His continuing imprisonment only emphasized his popularity and invited a popular response. It came in the shape of an avalanche of gifts and of money. His release early in 1770 set off rejoicing on an unprecedented national scale. Wilkes's extraordinary career now assumed new directions. He became a hero in America as a symbol of liberty. He was elected as an Alderman of the City of London in 1769, Sheriff in 1771 and in 1774 Lord Mayor. He defended the freedom of the press during the Printers' Case in 1771 and with the help of the London mob safeguarded the publication of parliamentary debates. Elected to Parliament once more in 1774 Wilkes advocated popular causes, spoke for the American colonists, defended the principle of 'No taxation without representation', championed the reform of Parliament and advocated greater toleration for Catholics and Dissenters. Later in life, with the experiences of the Gordon Riots and the French Revolution behind him, Wilkes became a conservative pillar of the establishment, but his earlier extraordinary career as a 'man of the people' deserves further analysis.

The importance of John Wilkes is that he became not merely a national figure but the first 'popular' politician to create a distinctive political movement. He appealed directly to the mass of the people, not just the political nation, in a campaign which he was to sustain over many years and on a succession of issues. There was little that was particularly modern or progressive about John Wilkes. He was no orator, or thinker – not even a competent administrator. But he played to the gallery, casting himself as an anti-hero, a joker, a lord of misrule. He masterfully worked upon some of the principal elements in popular culture, appealing to popular traditions of self-expression, of resistance to power, identifying himself with English liberties and English rights. His use of mockery and satire to draw attention to himself and to the injuries he suffered at the hands of those in authority was inspired. But he had a fund of moral courage, he was untroubled by self-doubt and he was a genius at self-publicity. Through his outrageous behaviour and his willingness to challenge the authorities he cultivated an enormous following, which accepted his identification of his own personal cause with that of English liberty in general. His career was a succession of crises, of instances of victimization at the hands of governments, sometimes goaded beyond endurance by Wilkes himself. He could thus present himself as the champion of the people and as a martyr for liberty. In doing so Wilkes willingly kept the searchlight of publicity on himself, his figure, his life, his cause. Wilkes employed the press to marvellous effect, using printed addresses to encourage his followers and to impose upon events his own sense of drama and crisis. Above all, he kept his supporters constantly informed, tailoring his material – pamphlet, paragraph, print, handbill, cartoon, ballad and verse – to vastly different audiences, geographical and social. Much of this material was passed around by hand, displayed on walls and windows and, not least, reproduced in the local press, thus projecting the man and his cause throughout the country. The press was ready and more than willing to report the extravagant career of

John Wilkes. Given this inspiration, Wilkite clubs and groups sprang up in many major, and some minor, towns.

Its home, of course, was London but it would be a mistake to regard the Wilkite movement as overwhelmingly metropolitan. It prospered in a number of seaport towns which enjoyed both good communications and strong political traditions, such as Portsmouth, Liverpool, Bristol and Newcastle upon Tyne. It flourished in a number of industrial regions: the west Midlands, the West Riding of Yorkshire and some of the small towns of the south west. It was particularly strong in a number of market towns and cathedral cities, especially Worcester and King's Lynn. It is dangerous, however, to leap to broad conclusions from a number of instances. There are traces of Wilkite activity in many places of diverse character.

Who were the people who supported the 'man of the people', brandishing 'No. 45' placards and shouting 'Wilkes and Liberty'? The membership of Wilkite clubs seems to have been drawn from sections of the middle ranks of settled, urban society, and included small merchants, small manufacturers, wholesalers, publishers, innkeepers, retailers and craftsmen. As Dr Langford has remarked: 'Men of very small property rarely found their way on to the political stage'. But in 1763–64 and in 1768–70 they did.[9] There seem, furthermore, to have been few denominational tendencies in Wilkes's followers. Dissenters as a body were not involved in the movement to any great extent. If it is possible to hazard any sort of generalization about Wilkes's following it may be that they were drawn from generally literate sections of the middling and lower middling orders who were removed from, and in many cases dissatisfied with, local power structures (such as corporations and patronage networks) and located in or near well-politicized communities. Wilkes's message, however, in places penetrated much further down the social scale than the middling orders. In the metropolis the Wilkite crowds included Spitalfields weavers, rural freeholders, coal-heavers and many day-labourers from the East End.

One of the most interesting achievements of Wilkes and those around him was to use his personal experiences as triggers for huge exhibitions of popular enthusiasm. These employed many features of an active, traditional popular culture. The Wilkites utilized popular habits of taking to the streets by mobilizing (surprisingly peaceful) crowds, by organizing celebrations and processions and, not least, by using the calendar to commemorate recent events in politics in general and in Wilkes's career in particular. There was an explosion of national celebration when Wilkes was released from the King's Bench prison in April 1770. On such occasions Wilkite managers exploited the popular love of display by distributing cockades, ribbons and colours. They deployed Wilkite consumables, almost all of them – badges, pictures, cartoons, porcelain, rings, buttons – embellished with the No. 45 symbol in order to generate enthusiasm and to manifest loyalty. This aspect of Wilkite organization can be seen as 'a commercialization of politics', the publicization of Wilkes and his career through the techniques of the market. By using commercial techniques he was able to open up a national market for his propaganda, and to make his cause a national issue.[10] But the culture of the middling orders was utilized, too. Many of the old clubs and lodges, such as the Albions, the Bucks and the Robin Hood debating societies, were to be found supporting Wilkes by the later 1760s. Regular political meetings, debates and discussions were held, even the occasional large public meeting. In 1769 the movement organized a nationwide petitioning campaign which yielded over 20 petitions with over 50 000 signatures.

The ideological significance of the Wilkite movement is not readily apparent. In some ways, it is not strictly accurate to regard the Wilkes phenomenon as a 'radical' movement. Wilkes himself had no political programme. The movement that takes his name was mobilized in order to support and protect him in his disputes with successive governments; it was not intended either to profess to or prosecute a programme of reform. Only as late as 1769 did the reform of Parliament seriously enter into Wilkite politics, when a number of London merchants, lawyers and other professional groups formed the Society for the Supporters of the Bill of Rights. The Society aimed to mount a nationwide petitioning campaign in defence of Wilkes's election for Middlesex. With the funds it collected and with the propaganda at its disposal it made considerable headway in organizing support not only in London and Middlesex but even as far afield as Yorkshire and the West Country. At this point, the Wilkite agitation may be said to be moving beyond the boundaries of a personal protest movement. The SSBR began to advocate shorter Parliaments and a redistribution of seats. Most significantly, the friends of Wilkes were unhappy at this development. Conflict ensued, and in April 1771 a group of radicals including Horne Tooke and Alderman Sawbridge detached themselves from Wilkes and formed the rival Constitutional Society in London. The Wilkite movement, thus fractured, was profoundly weakened and was thereafter incapable of maintaining its earlier momentum. By the date of Wilkes's election as Lord Mayor of London, it was to all intents and purposes over.

Yet these conflicts should not be allowed to conceal the very robust ideological foundations upon which 'Wilkes and Liberty' was built. It derived its ideological inspiration from the Country party principles of the first half of the century. These Wilkes magnified and enlivened with entertaining dashes of Little Englander patriotism. His attack on Bute and the Scots touched a popular nerve, enabling him to pose as the epitome and, at this vital point in history, as the guardian of English liberties. Both in his willing self-characterization as a John Bull figure, in the frequency of patriotic allusions in his writings and in the incessant singing of patriotic songs at Wilkite events there can be little doubt that the Wilkite movement was patriotic, loyalist, even conservative in its ideological stance. Professor Colley has even deemed it 'traditional ... offering reassurance ... administering comfort' that England would retain her primacy within Great Britain.[11] But there was far more to the Wilkite movement than English nationalism. Both in its tone and in its content, in the issues which Wilkes raised and the manner in which he treated them, the movement was intensely anti-oligarchical, taking its stand on the assumption that those in power were accountable to the people. Indeed, some Wilkite pamphlets even adopted a markedly Lockeian interpretation of the Glorious Revolution, emphasizing rights of resistance and placing Wilkes in a long line of Whig heroes, including Hampden, Sydney and Russell. The construction of a radical tradition, alongside the popularization of a radical view of the Glorious Revolution, is one of the more positive, if indirect, aspects of the Wilkite phenomenon.

How successful was the Wilkite movement? In the short term it achieved its immediate objectives of having general warrants declared illegal (in 1765), of having the Middlesex election resolutions expunged from the record (in 1782) and, ultimately, of seeing John Wilkes returned to Parliament (in 1774). The Printers' Case was won, thus vindicating the principle of public access to knowledge of parliamentary proceedings. At the electoral level, a handful of independent radicals won parliamentary seats between 1768 and 1774. At the general election of 1774 about one dozen radical MPs were returned, most of whom retained their seats at the general election of 1780. At the municipal level, radicals penetrated every layer of the government of the City of London for over a decade. Elsewhere they were much less successful in prising open existing corporations. Nevertheless, the establishment of permanent oppositions to local elites was a significant development in many places. Less measurable than electoral success, but in the long run just as important was the politicizing effect of the Wilkite phenomenon. Although it is true that John Wilkes, unlike his rivals in the Constitutional Association, was uninterested in perpetuating the political organizations which he created once they had served his immediate purposes, their true significance was very much greater. The best tribute to the organizational techniques of the early radicals is that they were imitated by most extra-parliamentary groups in the late eighteenth and early nineteenth century, not least the movement for the abolition of the slave trade and the campaign by Protestant Dissenters for the repeal of the Test and Corporation Acts in the 1780s. The long-term effect of John Wilkes's campaigns is difficult to measure, but large numbers of people were drawn into both national and local politics, many of them for the first time. Whether as participants in crowds and processions or simply as readers of Wilkite newspapers, pamphlets and broadsides, a wide public, sympathetic to Wilkes, was mobilized, entertained and deployed. More specifically, vitriolic criticism of successive governments poured off the presses in the 1760s and 1770s, stimulated partly by the controversial stance of the monarchy in politics, partly by the American problem but principally by John Wilkes and the causes which he made his own.

In the end the movement ran out of steam when the man who was essential to it lost interest, when serious divisions weakened its momentum and when events overtook it. The support of the radicals for the American colonists ensured that they were among the most prominent victims of the popular mood of loyalty to crown and Parliament which swept over Britain in the early years of the American war.

The war in America ultimately gave rise to a further instalment of extra-parliamentary agitation albeit one less focused on the career of a single individual. The Petitioning movement associated with the name of Christopher Wyvill was the product of two wartime forces. First, the serious economic consequences of the war steadily intensified in the late 1770s, causing interruption to trade with consequent unemployment, low wages and high prices. Many of the counties and towns which participated in this next phase of radical reform had been badly hit by the war. Second, the issue of the responsibility for the ill success of British arms revived the old accusations of secret influence, ministerial corruption and plain executive incompetence. What the American crisis did was to highlight the old fears about court conspiracies and secret influence. Irrespective of the constitutional rights and wrongs of American taxation, somebody must have been responsible for the fact that Britain was locked in a thankless and uphill military struggle 3000 miles away whilst at war with half of Europe, and with a first-rate economic crisis threatening to ruin the country. Wyvill's movement was a popular attempt to weaken and destroy the secret influence which was at the root of the disasters afflicting the country.

Significantly, the Petitioning movement was a provincial movement. It had its origins in Yorkshire where in December 1779 the Reverend Christopher Wyvill summoned the gentry to a county meeting to protest against high wartime expenditure and excessive taxation. For Wyvill and the gentry of Yorkshire the ultimate cure for corruption in government was to restore the independence of the House of Commons from executive influence by making MPs more accountable to those who elected them. This could be achieved by a programme of economical (or administrative) reform as a prelude to a cautious restructuring of the electoral system: triennial parliaments, the abolition of rotten boroughs and the addition of more country members. Wyvill determined to set about these objectives by organizing a series of petitions to present to parliament. He directed the operation from Yorkshire, appealing to the entire nation and obtaining in the early months of 1780 no fewer than 26 petitions from the counties and another dozen from some of the larger boroughs. He proceeded to hold a meeting of delegates of the petitioning bodies in London in early 1780.

The Petitioning movement did not maintain the early cohesion imparted by the energy and efficiency of Wyvill. The movement in London and the south east of England was markedly more radical than Wyvill's cautious programme. It was inspired by the radical ideology which had its origins with the Society of the Supporters of the Bill of Rights in 1769, by the radical theory of the American Revolution and by the enormous attention generated by the publication of Major John Cartwright's *Take Your Choice* in 1776, which had argued the case for universal suffrage, annual parliaments, secret ballots and equal member constituencies. This was to be the programme of the metropolitan radicals, who worked through their own radical bodies such as Major Cartwright's Society for Constitutional Information. This body, founded in April 1780 by Major Cartwright, John Jebb, Brand Hollis and the playwright R.B. Sheridan, adopted Cartwright's programme and decided to achieve it by adopting Jebb's idea of a permanent association. The association, a standing, unofficial 'parliament', would be elected by local bodies based on the principle of universal suffrage, and it would be supported by a national network of corresponding societies. Such a body, enlivened by popular election, would challenge Parliament and, it was hoped, by its example peacefully compel that body to reform itself. Not surprisingly, such ambitious objectives aroused real fears among many moderate supporters of Economical Reform.

For the moment, however, the parliamentary opposition led by Rockingham and Shelburne sought to use the public support aroused by Wyvill's Petitioning movement to strengthen their own campaign against secret influence, aimed at diminishing the influence of the executive over Parliament. The purpose of their Economical Reform was not to make Parliament more efficient, still less more representative. It was to restore the independence of Parliament from the executive and thus restore the balance of the constitution. Although the influence of the crown (although not that of the executive) over Parliament was diminishing in this period, many contemporaries continued to believe the opposite. Given the Rockingham party's prejudices against Lord Bute and secret influence, its sponsorship of Economical Reform legislation was both natural and reasonable. Indeed, its support for it goes back to 1770 when one of its leaders, William Dowdeswell – significantly, an ex-Tory – moved in 1768 to disfranchise revenue officers.[12] The Rockinghams rediscovered the issue in 1778 when Sir Philip Jennings Clerke moved a Contractors Bill. It narrowly failed, encouraging Clerke to reintroduce it in February 1779, when it was easily thrown out. In the session of 1780 the centrepiece of the Rockinghams' attack was Burke's plan of Economical Reform. In order to minimize government waste and extravagance, Burke sought to eliminate offices which served no useful function. To achieve this he proposed to reduce expenditure on pensions and to cut down the number of hereditary offices. More boldly, he wished to abolish the separate administrations of Chester, Lancaster, Wales and Cornwall as well as the third secretaryship of state. Although Dunning's famous resolution 'that the influence of the crown has increased, is increasing and ought to be diminished' passed the Commons by 233 to 215 the string of Economical Reform bills introduced by the opposition in the spring of 1780 all fell victim to Lord North's majorities. Burke ran the ministry close on several divisions, but he was unable to overcome the independent country gentlemen's reluctance to interfere with the monarch's customary freedom to appoint to the household.

During the summer of 1780 the prospects for reform suddenly worsened. In May 1780 the capture of Charleston by Cornwallis temporarily revived ministerial morale. More importantly, the Gordon Riots, which ravaged London in early June, terrified propertied opinion, giving a terrible warning of what might happen if concessions were made to the popular voice.[13] The Gordon Riots reminded contemporaries of the frailty of social order and of the ease with which social disciplines could disintegrate. The Economical Reform movement was temporarily under a cloud as Lord North dissolved Parliament and the political classes concentrated on the general election of 1780.

The political scene was dominated during late 1780 and 1781 by the final acts in the drama in America. Wyvill summoned a second meeting of his congress for the spring of 1781, but the turnout was disappointing: only nine counties and two boroughs were represented. The fall of North's ministry, however, revived the prospects for reform. The Rockingham–Shelburne ministry proceeded to pass some of the Economical Reform legislation which had been proposed in 1780. Crewe's Act to disfranchise revenue officers achieved what it set out to achieve, but excessive expectations had always accompanied it: the number of revenue officers had always been exaggerated and the Act cost the Treasury little more than the control of a couple of seats. Clerke's Bill against contractors likewise passed easily, but it could be evaded by technically transferring the contract in question to a friend or relative. Burke's Civil Establishment Bill was much more extensive, directed, as it was, to the elimination of secret influence, but compared to his grand scheme of 1780 it was notably more moderate. Burke conceded that it would save only one-third of the £200 000 per annum of which he had then boasted. Nevertheless,

Burke removed 134 household offices, 22 of them tenable with a seat in Parliament, the third secretaryship and the Board of Trade, as well as a number of other offices. Yet he was able to effect few savings on pensions and he did not undertake the abolition of the separate jurisdictions. Finally, the Bill sought to enforce economy on the King by restricting the Civil List to £900 000 per annum. Although the bill did not satisfy the overoptimistic expectations which it aroused, it was a major achievement to carry it in the face of the court's hostility. If it did not transform the balance of the constitution in favour of the House of Commons, it kept up pressure in that direction. Taken together with the Younger Pitt's administrative reform, Burke's Bill did much to weaken the financial basis of the eighteenth-century monarchy.

These seemed to be famous victories, but to supporters of parliamentary reform they were little more than appetizers. The cabinet had three prominent supporters of parliamentary reform (Fox, Shelburne and Richmond) and the election of 1780 had brought into Parliament two significant, younger spokesmen, Pitt the Younger and R.B. Sheridan. Wyvill decided to summon another congress for 1783, and in the meantime he put pressure on Pitt to keep the issue before the public. This he did in May 1782 by moving for a committee on the subject of parliamentary reform. Pitt adopted a moderate tone, arguing that he was not engaged in innovation but in restoring the constitution to its original purity. His motion was lost, but by the intoxicatingly close division of 161 to 141. This encouraged Wyvill's new petitioning campaign in which 12 counties and, perhaps surprisingly, 23 boroughs submitted petitions. However, Pitt's second reform motion on 7 May 1783 met with much less success. He denied that he was aiming at universal suffrage. What he was proposing was the gradual elimination of corrupt boroughs and their replacement by at least 100 county members. On this occasion, however, the opponents of reform, especially Lord North, shone in debate. Surely, argued North, the fact that his own ministry had been overthrown was proof, if proof were needed, that Parliament was susceptible to public opinion. A motion for the order of the day was carried against Pitt by the overwhelming majority of 144 on division figures of 293 to 149.

The great political struggle between Pitt and Fox distracted attention from the issue of reform for over a year, but in 1785 Wyvill and Pitt decided to make one last effort. Wyvill attempted to rouse the country, but in 1785 only two counties and ten boroughs petitioned. On 18 April 1785 Pitt proposed to disfranchise 36 rotten boroughs and redistribute their representation to the counties and the metropolis, leaving open the prospect that large, unrepresented towns might benefit from further redistributions. It was a moderate, once-for-all package but Pitt's motion was lost by 248 to 174.

The reasons for Pitt's defeat were fourfold. They bear examination because they throw light on his earlier failures and, more generally, upon the strategic problems faced by the reform movement. First, the disfranchisement of rotten boroughs represented an attack on property which thoroughly alarmed many sections of the political nation. Second, although couched in moderate terms the effect of Pitt's proposals would have been really quite radical, adding, on Wyvill's estimate, about 100 000 electors, 30 per cent of the existing total. Third, Wyvill had committed a tactical error in identifying his fortunes so closely with those of Pitt, thus excluding and discouraging Foxites and radicals. Fox, indeed, had agreed as a condition of the coalition with North in 1783 to drop reform, and the Petitioning movement suffered from the failure of several counties which had petitioned in 1780 to do so in 1783 and 1785. Fourth, the fact that only two counties petitioned in 1785 is telling comment on the lack of support for reform in the country. Furthermore, several of the ten boroughs were relatively small places: Launceston, Scarborough, Lyme Regis, King's Lynn and Morpeth. Public support for reform had evaporated. In short, the conditions which had given rise to the Petitioning movement – high taxation, military defeat and economic recession – had now passed.

With Pitt's defeat the parliamentary reform movement lapsed although movements for moral and religious reform did not. The Petitioning movement had been a remarkable and sustained mobilization of respectable opinion, owing much to Wyvill's personal assets of diplomacy and patience, and depending above all on his organizational genius. The canvassing of opinion from house to house in many counties of England required organizational exertions which were extraordinary for the times. Wyvill's movement represents the first institutionalized extension of radicalism into the provinces. Building on the example of the Wilkites, Wyvill and his friends used the press and the printed word to good effect but relied to a much lesser degree on festive celebration and carnivalesque tradition. Although the movement for parliamentary reform waned in the second half of the 1780s, the accumulated experience, personnel and ideology which it had gathered were to be of immense importance in Britain in the age of the French Revolution.

Notes

1. Down to the work of Lewis Namier, the Whig interpretation of the reign of George III affirmed that Bute and the King wished to destroy the existing administration, raise the standard of prerogative and force Parliament, via bribery and corruption, to submit to the royal will. For the standard refutations of these discredited conspiracy theories, see L.B. Namier, *England in the Age of the American Revolution*, 2nd edn (1961), ch. 1; H. Butterfield, *George III and the Historians* (1957) ch. 6; R.R. Sedgwick, *Letters of George III to Lord Bute* (1939), Introduction; J. Brooke, *George III* (1972), chs. 2, 3.
2. For the Wilkes controversy, see below, pp. 222–7.
3. For Townshend see above, pp. 191–2. Augustus Henry, 3rd Duke of Grafton (1735–1811) was MP for Bury St Edmunds in 1756, he succeeded to the peerage a year later. He was one of Newcastle's strongest supporters in the early 1760s, but gravitated to Chatham after the fall of the Rockingham ministry, in which he was Secretary of State for the Northern Department. He was outvoted in his own cabinet on the repeal of the Tea Duty and was immortalized in the venomous *Letters of Junius*. Later served under North and Rockingham. William, 2nd Earl Shelburne and 1st Marquis of Lansdowne (1737–1805), served in Grenville's cabinet but quite quickly attached himself to Chatham; between 1766 and 1768 he was a Secretary of State. Between 1768 and 1782 he was in opposition, becoming the leader of Chatham's group on that statesman's death in 1778.
4. Henry Seymour Conway (1721–95), a nephew of Sir Robert Walpole, saw active service in the War of the Austrian Succession and in the Seven Years War. His

support for Wilkes led to his dismissal from the service. He was Secretary of State under both Rockingham and Chatham, and became a fervent critic of the American war.

5. Edmund Burke, the great philosopher-statesman (1729–97), was an Irish lawyer who came to England in 1750 to advance his fortunes. He published on philosophy and aesthetics in the second half of the decade, and in 1758 he started the *Annual Register*. After minor political office he became private secretary to Rockingham, entering Parliament in 1766. He made an immediate impact in Parliament and defended his party staunchly against the court, against North and against Chatham.

6. Economical Reform was the elimination of corruption by administrative reform, including the abolition of offices and pensions and the reduction of fees and perquisites.

7. J.A. Cannon, *The Fox–North Coalition Crisis of the Constitution 1782–84* (1969), pp. 128–32.

8. I.R. Christie, 'Party in Politics in the Age of Lord North's Administration', *Parliamentary History*, 6 (1987).

9. P. Langford, *A Polite and Commercial People: England 1727–1783* (1989), p. 379.

10. J. Brewer, *Party Ideology and Popular Politics at the Accession of George III* (1976), p. 174.

11. L. Colley, *Britons: Forging the Nation, 1707–1837* (1992), pp. 112–17.

12. Indeed, Dowdeswell's early endeavours achieved respectable support. His motion of 17 February 1768 was lost by 263 to 188.

13. The Gordon Riots arose out of protests made by Lord George Gordon and his Protestant Association against the Catholic Relief Act of 1778. That Act had been passed in order to permit Catholics to serve in British regiments during the War of American Independence, and it allowed them to do so by taking an oath of fidelity to the crown. What stoked the fires of religious intolerance in England was the panic aroused by the invasion scare of 1779 and, more seriously, by a march on Parliament led by Lord George Gordon and his Protestant Association in early June 1780. Attacks on Catholic premises gave rise to more indiscriminate violence, some of it directed against the rich and famous. After several days and nights of constant rioting, order was restored with the use of the army, but only after some 300 deaths and many thousands injured.

9

The crisis of the Hanoverian regime, 1789–1820

The Revolutionary and Napoleonic Wars, 1789–1820

The French Revolution presented Britain with the most serious challenge to her social and political structure since the Glorious Revolution. The challenge existed at the military level: the danger not merely of invasion by the French Revolutionary and Napoleonic armies but of the possibility of exhaustion and surrender. It existed at the political level: the proliferation of new reform movements and ideologies and the countervailing emergence of organized loyalist and patriotic groups. It existed at the social level: the threat to social cohesion posed by over two decades of warfare, accompanied by rapid economic change and by occasional, and extremely potent, crises of subsistence. It says something for the speed of her political and economic, and perhaps of her psychological, recovery after the disasters of the American war that Britain in the early 1790s was confident of her ability to chart her own future and to maintain her place in Europe. Nevertheless, her newly recovered confidence was to be severely tested in the following three decades.

Most Britons reacted with approval to the early events of the French Revolution in the summer and autumn of 1789: the fall of the Bastille, the abolition of feudalism and the establishment of constitutional government. There was a widespread feeling that the French had set out on the same path that the British had been travelling since the Glorious Revolution. Everyone could rejoice in the collapse of tyranny and the liberation of the people of one of the greatest countries in Europe. George III may have reflected a wider view that France was now reaping what she had sown when she had supported the American rebels. The government rejoiced that one of Britain's major competitors was likely to be weakened for some time. It now seemed possible that the limited *rapprochement* which the Anglo-French treaty of 1786 had created might be strengthened. Reformers, both secular reformers who were seeking to reform Parliament or religious reformers who were seeking the repeal of the Test and Corporation Acts, were particularly excited. They convinced themselves that the French Revolution had inaugurated a new era of reform, enlightenment and benevolence, claiming that Britain ought to follow that example. Poets and intellectuals were no less ecstatic, Wordsworth glorying in 'human nature seeming born again', Southey believing that 'Old things seemed passing away, and nothing was dreamt of but the regeneration of the human race'.

By 1792, however, this early euphoria had given way to alarm and fear. Although Pitt, in his budget speech of February 1792, was still expecting 15 years of peace in the new Europe, events were taking a worrying turn. In April France declared war on Austria and invaded the Austrian Netherlands. Assuming that a country in the chaos of an internal revolution could offer little real threat to the peace of Europe, Pitt remained aloof from the war, a decision of possibly vital significance. In the summer, however, everything changed. In July Prussia came into the war against France. In August France abolished the monarchy. Worse, the September massacres were horrifying evidence that the Revolution had become a revolution of blood. In September French armies threw the allied Austro-Prussian armies back towards the boundaries of France. In November the French invaded the Austrian Netherlands and crossed the Rhine at Mainz. At the same time the French government issued a decree inviting the peoples of Europe to rise up against their oppressors, offering them encouragement and assistance. On 21 January 1793 they executed Louis XVI and on 1 February 1793 declared war on Britain.

What were to be Britain's objectives in the war? Pitt, like his predecessors, was motivated by very practical concerns for Britain's security and trade. He was much less concerned with issues concerning the internal state of France, such as the restoration of the Bourbon monarchy and the restitution of aristocratic estates. What preoccupied Pitt was the need to keep the Netherlands out of French hands. French occupation of the Austrian Netherlands and, above all, the opening of the River Scheldt to traffic was watched with horror in Britain. The closure of the Scheldt had been guaranteed since 1648 and confirmed as recently as 1785 (by France) and 1788 (by Britain). The French decision to tear up international guarantees and treaties, according to Pitt, threatened British commerce and, indirectly, her security. As Lord Grenville,[1] the Foreign Secretary, put it in December 1792: 'England never will consent that France shall arrogate the power of annulling at her pleasure ... the political system of Europe, established by solemn treaties, and guaranteed by the consent of all the powers'.

Believing France to be in ruinous chaos, Pitt did not anticipate a long military campaign. He underestimated the strength and stamina of France's new ideological convictions. As the war continued, however, British war aims tended to become identified with her military strategy. Pitt fought the war as his father would have fought it, concentrating upon imperial conquests, keeping control of the seas and subsidizing her allies to fight on the mainland of Europe. Thus disengaged from Europe, Britain would be free to make conquests in the French colonial empire, especially in the West Indies, and to make occasional attacks upon the French coastline. Consequently, possession of the French West Indian islands and the establishment of British maritime security through the destruction of the French navy became legitimate war aims.

As at the start of most major wars of the long eighteenth century, Britain was cruelly unprepared. Although the seriousness of the situation can be exaggerated, in 1793 the government had only 13 000 troops at its immediate disposal, and found it difficult at first to scrape together enough soldiers for service in the Netherlands. Furthermore, Britain only had 16 000 sailors in 1793 (compared with 110 000 in 1783), although over 110 ships of the line were in tolerable condition. It took some years to strengthen the armed services. Meanwhile, the early campaigns had limited success. In a desperate effort to save Holland Britain sent a force of 7000 to hold the River Maas, but it was too late to save the Dutch and the force had to retreat. Other theatres were more promising but hardly more successful. Admiral Hood had captured Toulon in August 1793 with the aid of French royalists, but a British attempt to lift the French siege of the town towards the end of the year failed dismally. Naval manoeuvres in the West Indies in 1793–94 ended in the capture of most of the French West Indies, but St Lucia and Guadeloupe were surrendered to the French by the end of the year; the island of Haiti, wealthy through its sugar, cotton and coffee, was not adequately secured and ultimately had to be ceded as well. The actions in the West Indies cost 40 000 dead and 40 000 sick, more even than Wellington was to lose in the Peninsular War after 1808. Valuable though the colonial acquisitions were, they did not immediately affect the course of the war in Europe. Nor did Admiral Howe's great naval victory on the 'Glorious First of June' 1794, when he overcame the French Brest fleet.

On the mainland of Europe, indeed, the years 1793–96 were a succession of victories for the French *levée en masse* against the First Coalition of Prussia, Austria, Britain, the Netherlands, Russia and Spain. The French occupied Holland and Italy and swept the British navy from the Mediterranean. It was scant comfort that Britain proceeded to occupy the Dutch empire in the east: the Cape of Good Hope, Ceylon, Pondicherry and Trincomalee. By then the First Coalition was fast disintegrating. In April 1795 the Prussians sued for peace, surrendering their territories on the left bank of the Rhine. Austria abandoned Belgium, compensating herself with land in Poland, and negotiating the treaty of Campo Formio with France in 1797, which left the French in the Netherlands, in occupation of the left bank of the Rhine and in possession of Napoleon's Italian conquests.[2] Even worse, the old Franco-Spanish axis was restored when Spain negotiated an alliance with France in 1796. By 1797 Britain was the only power left in the field against the French Revolutionary armies.

The French plan was now for the French, Dutch and Spanish fleets to engage the British navy while an invasion fleet landed in Ireland. Admiral Jervis's great victory off Cape St Vincent in February 1797 thwarted the serious prospect of a combined invasion by destroying the Spanish fleet. In October of the same year the Dutch fleet was destroyed at Camperdown. Nevertheless, British security was still seriously imperilled by mutinies in the fleet at Spithead and the Nore in April and May 1797. Meanwhile, Napoleon had returned from his victorious campaigns in Italy to dominate the Directory.[3] He was to impose his will and his personality upon Europe for the next two decades. Working on the premiss that Britain could best be weakened by putting pressure upon her empire and her commerce, he occupied Malta. From there he proceeded to Egypt, where he rapidly subdued the Mameluke's armies. British historians have traditionally argued that Napoleon had India in his sights;[4] contemporaries, however, believed that his intention was to partition the Ottoman empire, of which Egypt was a part. The possibility that Napoleon might be aiming at acquisitions outside Europe, however, began to disturb the chancelleries of Europe. Before he could proceed further, however, the British fleet blockaded the French fleet and, at the battle of Aboukir Bay (the Battle of the Nile) in 1798, won one of its greatest victories against the French. Napoleon had to abandon his plan of moving into Syria and, leaving his army in Egypt, returned to France, where he became First Consul in 1799.

With the Mediterranean once more in British hands, the Second Coalition was formed, including Britain, Austria and Russia. A joint Anglo-Russian invasion to recapture Holland followed which soon collapsed into confusion. More importantly, Napoleon smashed the Austrians on the plains of Marengo in northern Italy in June 1800, and defeated them again at Hohenlinden six months later. Austria left the Coalition at the Treaty of Luneville (1801), recognizing the French satellite republics in Italy, the Netherlands, the Rhineland and Switzerland. The Russians had at first cleared the French out of parts of northern Italy, but they had suffered reverses since then and they too sued for peace. Russia then organized an armed neutrality of northern countries against Britain and the British navy's insistence upon searching neutral shipping. Britain had clung onto control of the Mediterranean and, indeed, had overwhelmed France's allies, the Danes, at the Battle of Copenhagen (1801). By now both Britain and France were exhausted enough to negotiate the Treaty of Amiens in October 1801. By its terms Britain retained her conquests of Trinidad and Ceylon but returned the Cape to Holland, restored Egypt to the Ottoman empire and surrendered Malta to the Knights of St John. France withdrew her armies from Naples and the papal states while evacuating Egypt. This was little more than a truce, recognized on both sides as such. The pretext for the renewal of hostilities was Britain's eventual refusal to give up Malta, but this was in its turn a response to French expansionism in annexing Piedmont to France and in acquiring Louisiana and Parma from Spain. Significantly, the British government, now led by Addington after Pitt's fall from power in 1801, was careful to keep its army up to a strength of 130 000 during the peace.

War resumed in May 1803. Napoleon's immediate strategy now was to invade Britain. Pitt was back in office in 1804, just in time to preside over an unprecedented display of British patriotic resistance. In the summer of 1804 a French force of 100 000 men and 2000 transports waited off Boulogne for the order to sail. To prepare for this threat, the government mobilized a force of over 800 000 men, no less than one in five adult males. However, the invasion threat did not materialize. By his arrogance in having himself crowned King of Italy Napoleon enraged Austria, which now joined Russia, Britain and Sweden in a Third Coalition. Napoleon thus had to turn his attention east and north, and the threatened invasion of 1804–05 came to nothing. Moreover, Nelson's great victory at Trafalgar in October 1805 destroyed the Franco-Spanish fleet and ended the possibility of a naval invasion during the rest of the war. However, if Napoleon could not invade Britain he could at least attempt to ruin her economy. The Berlin decrees of November 1806 and the Milan decrees of 1807 established the Continental System, which placed a ban on France and its dependencies from trading with Britain and closed the ports controlled by France to ships from Britain and her colonies. Britain retaliated in March by forcing neutral ships trading with Europe to proceed via Britain to pay customs dues and licence fees. On the mainland of Europe, meanwhile, the Third Coalition was being destroyed by the armies of Napoleon. The Austrians were defeated at Ulm in October 1805, Vienna was occupied in November and in December the epic French victory at Austerlitz over the Austro-Russian armies drove Austria to sue for peace. Defeats at Jena (1806) and Friedland (1807) took Prussia and Russia out of the war in turn. The Treaty of Tilsit of June 1807 between Russia and France marked Russia's acceptance of all of France's conquests, and raised the prospect of these powers jointly dominating the continent of Europe. Britain, once again, stood alone.

Pitt had died in January 1806, but his successors continued the dogged strategy which he had pursued. The arrival of George Canning at the Foreign Office marked a more aggressive British approach. Naval retaliation against the Treaty of Tilsit came with the bombardment of Copenhagen. Economic retaliation against Napoleon's Continental System came with the 'Orders in Council' of 1807, forbidding neutrals to trade with France and her allies on pain of confiscation of the ship and the cargo, and providing for the blockade of ports attempting to exclude British ships. Their objective was to unsettle the Napoleonic regime in Europe by disrupting its economic base. In this they had significant but limited success. At the same time, the Continental System had failed to bring Britain to its knees. Parts of Europe – the Baltic, Portugal (and, after 1810, Russia) – remained open to British ships. France was damaged much more than Britain by the Continental System; between 1807 and 1809 her customs receipts plummeted by almost 80 per cent. Meanwhile, British trade with the rest of the world was increasing.

Unexpectedly, however, commercial conflict in Europe dragged Britain into war with the newly independent American Republic. In denying merchant ships of the USA access to the European mainland, the Orders provoked outrage and retaliation in the North American continent. In 1811 the American government passed a Non-importation Act. This caused the collapse of Britain's largest single market and led to the futile Anglo-American war of 1812–14. Most of the military action was confined to the Canadian frontier, with isolated engagements elsewhere. The damage to the trade of the two countries was so great that they negotiated the Treaty of Ghent in 1814, which largely restored the *status quo ante bellum*. Ultimately, Britain abandoned the Orders in Council in 1812 after a vigorous campaign of opposition from mercantile groups. As for the Continental System, it expired in 1813 when the Russians and the Prussians invaded northern Germany and when Sweden declared war on France and Denmark.

In 1808 Napoleon's ambition, and his wish to deny European trade outlets to the British, spread to the Iberian peninsula. French troops invaded Portugal and Napoleon installed his brother Joseph on the Spanish throne. Britain could not ignore this latest example of French expansionism and, encouraged by nationalist risings in Spain and massive anti-French feeling in Portugal, poured in 15 000 troops immediately, increasing their numbers to 60 000 within two years. Canning was aware that the stirring force of peasant nationalism might be a powerful ally against Napoleon, and indeed the presence of native troops and guerrilla brigades was to be a valuable asset to the British. During the next five years British troops, led by Arthur Wellesley, later Duke of Wellington, fought a courageous, if tactically complicated, war. Although British intervention in the peninsula in 1808 was not successful, it at least diverted huge numbers of French troops that might have been put to more damaging use elsewhere in Europe. Slowly the fortunes of war turned in the peninsula, until in 1812 Wellington was able to march into Spain, and in 1813 into France.

The peninsular war, however, was a sideshow to one of the great events of modern history – Napoleon's march into Russia with an army of over half a million men in June 1812. To occupy Russia would enable Napoleon to dominate Europe, command routes to the East and thus control the commercial lifelines of Britain's empire. By September he was at the gates of Moscow but, finding the city in flames and winter approaching, he ordered the famous retreat. By December he had lost almost half a million men, his disintegrating army the victim of Russian weather and his own arrogance. The allies pounced: in February 1813 Russia allied with Prussia, and a month later war broke out. The Prussians were hammered by Napoleon's armies at Lutzen and Bautzen and the French armies occupied Dresden. Prussia was at the feet of France but Napoleon agreed to an armistice. This gave the allies a breathing space before inflicting one of the great defeats of the war on the French at the Battle of the Nations at Leipzig in October 1813, which broke French predominance in Germany. This was a real turning-point. For the first time since 1795 the allies had presented a united front and had acquired at last some hope of breaking Napoleon's grip on Europe. The French retreated to the boundaries of France. At about the same time, Wellington cleared the French out of southern Spain at the battle of Vittoria in June 1813, and by the end of the year had invaded France from the south west.

The diplomats were now beginning to look forward to the shape of Europe after the war. At the Treaty of Chaumont in March 1814 the four allied powers, Britain, Austria, Prussia and Russia, formed the Grand Alliance. Pledging to retain 150 000 men in the field until France was finally defeated, they defined the aims of the war as independence for Holland and Switzerland, a free Spain under the Bourbon dynasty and a confederated Germany. Remarkably, they also pledged to remain in alliance for 20 years after the war. A few weeks after the treaty was published the allies entered Paris and Napoleon abdicated to Elba. In May 1814 the dominant statesmen, Castlereagh for Britain and Metternich for Austria, led the peace negotiations at Paris to a successful conclusion. France had to accept the boundaries of 1792 and the restoration of the Bourbon dynasty. French claims to the Low Countries, Germany, Italy, Malta and Switzerland were withdrawn and Britain took Mauritius, St Lucia and Tobago. Finally, further meetings of the great powers would seek to establish a 'system of real and permanent balance of power', a reference to the future Congress system. The wider settlement of Europe was deferred to a meeting at Vienna which convened in September 1814.

It was during the Congress of Vienna that Napoleon escaped from Elba and received a hero's welcome on the roads to Paris. On his arrival there he promised to rule as a constitutional monarch, but Europe was now weary of

Bonaparte. In the dramatic final act, Britain and Prussia defeated the French armies at Waterloo on 18 June. The peace terms were correspondingly stiffened against France. Castlereagh's broad strategy was to ensure European stability by strengthening Austria and Prussia as bulwarks against the possibility of a revived France, by merging Holland and Belgium into a new kingdom of the Netherlands and, as a further buffer against French power, to merge the republic of Genoa into Piedmont. As is always remarked, the treaty of Vienna took little account of national feeling. Hence Venetia was given to Austria in compensation for Belgium, while Denmark, which had remained loyal to Bonaparte, surrendered Norway to Sweden, which lost Finland to Russia. The states of Germany were aggregated into a confederation of 38 states under the presidency of Austria. The peace terms were particularly satisfying for Britain, although she was careful not to go too far and take too much. Widespread resentment had already been aroused by the Orders in Council and by British reluctance to commit mass armies to European soil. Consequently Java, a rich and potentially matchless colony, and only recently conquered by Sir Stamford Raffles, was returned to Holland, and Martinique and Guadeloupe were returned to France. Indeed, Britain retained Tobago and Dutch Guiana for purely commercial reasons. Other gains were made for a mixture of strategic and commercial reasons. Britain took Malta, thus greatly facilitating her naval control of the Mediterranean. She retained the harbour in St Lucia, to facilitate her control of the West Indies. Most vitally, she retained the Cape of Good Hope and Mauritius, which gave her command of the sea route to the east. When to all this is added the existing British settlements in Canada, Australia and her political and commercial predominance in India, Britain's status as a world power was indisputable.

For another seven years the experience of the Revolutionary and Napoleonic wars continued to dominate European – and, indeed, British – diplomacy. In wishing to reinforce the power of the great empires of Europe Castlereagh revealed his traditional caste of mind. It was never his intention to sympathize with liberal movements nor to give any encouragement to revolutionary groups. He maintained the customary British abhorrence of a single power dominating Europe and he was anxious to restrict both French and Russian ambitions in the postwar years. His object was to maintain peace in Europe after a generation of war, a peace in which Britain could trade and prosper. He was anxious for the Vienna settlement to be strengthened by peaceful collaboration and consultation. The Holy Alliance of 1815 between Russia, Austria and Prussia worried Castlereagh because the three monarchs who conceived the alliance, and the succession of European congresses to which it gave rise, clearly intended it to be a vehicle for suppressing nationalist and revolutionary movements. The Congress of Aix-la-Chapelle in 1818 performed useful work in ending the allied occupation of France and restoring that country to the concert of Europe. At the Congress of Troppeau in 1820, however, he strongly opposed Tsar Alexander I's policy of collective interventions against democratic movements in Spain, Portugal and Naples. These were 'domestic upsets' which did not endanger the security of Europe. A further Congress at Laibach in 1821 stumbled over the same difficulty. The outbreak of a revolt in Greece raised the dangerous prospect of Russian intervention in the ailing Turkish empire. Before the next Congress began at

Verona in 1822 Castlereagh was dead. His successor, Canning, was even more suspicious of European entanglements, and bitter in his condemnation of the principle of collective intervention in the internal affairs of European states. By this time the Congress system was in terminal decline. Britain retreated from European involvements and into her more familiar position as a detached, imperial power. By now, however, she was noticeably stronger than she had been at the beginning of the Revolutionary period, emerging from the ordeal of the Revolutionary wars covered in success.

To what did Britain owe her success? It was hardly the quality of her political leadership, still less the virtues of her grand strategy that had achieved such a satisfactory outcome. She owed her success to other factors: her ability to deploy large numbers of men, the consistent performance of her navy, the economic expansion which characterized most of the revolutionary period and, perhaps most of all, the almost unbelievable financial resources which she was able to muster.

During peacetime the number of men in the army and navy was usually under 100 000. By 1812 the figure had leaped to almost one million. In 1814 the army stood at a quarter of a million men, the navy at 150 000. On top of this, there were by 1804 about half a million part-time and volunteer units of various categories, public and private, defending the home front. With a population only half that of France, Britain was able to mobilize almost equivalent numbers. Indeed, if the militia is included, Britain had a bigger percentage (over 10 per cent of men in the 18–45 age group) of its population under arms than any other major power.

The achievement of the navy in defending British security and protecting British trade was a remarkable one. Recruitment to the navy was still through the press gang; there is thus little to suggest that British sailors were superior to their French counterparts. It was the quality of the officer corps that made the difference. Furthermore, the strategic deployment of the fleets was of an invariably high standard. Moreover, the British navy was simply too big for the French. The size of the French navy declined by more than a half between 1793 and 1801 while the number of British naval personnel increased from 15 000 to 133 000 men, from 135 to 202 ships of the line and from 133 to 277 frigates.

Such an increase in the power of the navy rested on strong economic foundations. In this crucial early period of the so-called 'industrial revolution' most industries expanded their production. The invention of the cotton gin in the USA in 1793 caused an explosion of cotton imports into Britain, from half a million pounds in that year to over 20 million in 1801. British looms clothed the soldiers on all sides in the European war. The iron trade boomed with the demand for metallurgical products while the coal mines could scarcely keep up with the demand from the iron foundries. Indeed, iron output actually doubled between 1796 and 1806. Shipbuilding also flourished, increasing production by perhaps one half in the same period. Many dockyards were built, too, in these years, especially the huge complexes in London: the East India, the West India, the London and the Surrey docks. Industry, however, was badly hit by the Orders in Council between 1806 and 1811 and by the collapse of the American market. By 1810–11 a full scale economic crisis threatened to undermine the war effort. An unprecedented campaign by the merchants and by the manufacturing towns succeeded in persuading the new government of Lord Liverpool to repeal the Orders in 1812. During the last three years of the war, business and industry once more boomed. Meanwhile, agriculture was experiencing one of its golden ages. The Board of Agriculture, established by Pitt in 1793, had familiarized the farming community with new trends and techniques. Of more significance in expanding production, however, were the high prices received by farmers for their agricultural products in most years and the high rents which landlords could charge, as well as the low rates of interest which were required to fund improvements. Partly because of these factors, no fewer than 43 per cent of all English enclosure acts were passed between 1793 and 1815, affecting almost 3 million acres, roughly 9 per cent of the surface of the country.

Such a protracted war was frighteningly expensive. In 1793 government spending was 6 per cent of GDP. By 1815 it was over 25 per cent. It must be remembered that an integral part of Britain's strategy was to pay European powers to do the bulk of the mainland fighting. Britain spent £66 million on this alone, half of it in the last five years of the war. But this was only a trivial portion of war expenditure, which totalled around £1650 million, nearly four times as much as war expenditure under William III. In the early years of the war Pitt used loans to finance British campaigns: £11 million in 1794, shooting up to £32 million in 1797. Between 1793 and 1798 only 11 per cent of the extra revenue required to pay for the war was raised through increasing taxation. Because 80 per cent of total public revenue came from customs and excise duties, which fell disproportionately upon the poor, Pitt was forced to expand the tax base. This he did by introducing the income tax in 1799. Between 1806 and 1816, the date of its abolition, it yielded no less than £172 million, which was 28 per cent of all revenue derived from new taxes in the period. Additionally, after 1806 the yield of taxation was sufficient to pay the costs of the war but not the interest charges on the debt. By 1815 these charges amounted to more than half government expenditure. Between 1793 and 1815 the National Debt expanded from £228 million to £876 million.[5]

Material resources made possible Britain's outstanding contribution to the victory of the allies over the French. But this does not mean that victory had been inevitable. It owed much to the military dispositions of the last few years of the war, especially Napoleon's suicidal march on Moscow. It also owed much to the diplomatic tactics of Castlereagh and the coordinated response of the allies. Yet money and resources do not win wars unless they are applied to clear strategic objectives. In the end British strategy was vindicated, but it has not been without its critics. Pitt's reliance on extra-European naval strategy against France is understandable but, however successful this may have been, it did not bring about the defeat of Napoleon. The seizure of French sugar islands may have contributed to Britain's long-term economic prosperity but, in the end, France would have to be – and was – defeated within Europe. Britain is often charged with wasting resources on subsidies to allies and, by adopting such a cautious approach to the war in Europe, may have helped to prolong it. Pitt can, in part at least, be defended from this accusation. Allies had to be sustained in the war if there were to be any prospect of defeating France. It was not entirely Pitt's fault if successive coalitions proved to be unreliable and short-lived. The Prussian army in the west, for example, rarely exceeded 40 000 men, the King of Prussia preferring to help himself to territory in Poland. Similarly, the Austrians were also happy to compensate themselves for the loss of the Netherlands by joining in the Partitions of Poland in 1793 and 1795.[6] Pitt and Grenville had to deal with the realities of their situation. In the end, victory against France may have come but, so far as military strategy is concerned, it perhaps owed more to the mistakes of Napoleon and the contingencies of the later stages of the war than it did to the inherent virtues of British strategy.

Radicalism and patriotism, 1789–1820

Historians have traditionally treated the reform movements of the 1790s as the product of the French Revolution and of its impact upon British society, placing them in a line of development which connects them with the great working-class reform movements of the nineteenth century.[7] They are assumed to have attracted considerable popular support, thus apparently justifying their role as catalysts of mass protest. Yet many features of the reform movements of the 1790s had already appeared before the French Revolution, their class content was very limited and their social constituency very traditional. Far from being typical of public opinion, reform societies were heavily outnumbered by loyalist and patriotic groups all over the country and in all walks of life. It was, rather, the continuing competition between radical and patriotic societies which was to dominate popular politics for over 30 years after 1789.

The revival of popular support for parliamentary reform appears to date from the centenary celebrations of the Glorious Revolution of 1788. Although these festivities were seriously inhibited by the onset of the Regency Crisis, Revolution Societies sprang up all over the country to mark the anniversary. There is no doubt that reforming groups, especially the Protestant Dissenters and even some elements within the Whig opposition, colonized these celebrations and used them for their own purposes. Indeed, it was in towns in which either the Whig opposition or the Protestant Dissenters, or both, were strong that the French Revolution found the most enthusiastic welcome in the spring and summer of 1789. Such towns included Birmingham, Derby, Newcastle upon Tyne, Norwich and Sheffield. But the Revolution was warmly greeted everywhere. In 1789 the Revolution Societies sent a message to the French urging that the two countries should promote the cause of liberty, their correspondence receiving wide publicity. In such ways the French Revolution may be said to have quickened the existing recovery of the old, if moribund, reform societies. The Society for Constitutional Information was reactivated in 1791 and began to hold regular meetings. Some of its branches enjoyed immediate success. The Sheffield Society for Constitutional Information boasted over 2000 members after little more than a year, and acquired a missionary enthusiasm which carried its message to neighbouring towns and villages. In September 1792 the society put over 5000 people on to the streets of the town to celebrate the French military victory at Valmy. Norwich rivalled Sheffield as the Jacobin city of the 1790s, but its tradition of reform was longer established among a powerful Dissenting elite. By the end

of 1792 there were over 40 tavern clubs in the city with a collective membership of over 2000. Their influence was felt over much of East Anglia. Sheffield
and Norwich led the way but other towns were willing to follow. The French
Revolution even revived the flagging enthusiasm for reform among the
Whig opposition. The Association of the Friends of the People was founded
in April 1792. The society was the creation of a section of the opposition
Whigs, led by the young aristocrat Charles Grey; its purpose was to guide the
public clamour for reform into constitutional channels under the careful
supervision of the Whig aristocracy.

There is every indication that this revival of reforming activity had caught
the public mood, but by the spring of 1792 the initial optimistic and popular
phase of the reform movement was coming to an end. It was not just that the
French Revolution seemed to be moving into a menacing and violent direction now that war had broken out in Europe. Tom Paine's *The Rights of Man*
gave to the reform movement an angry philosophical text which was to be of
immense influence. The first part of the book had appeared in February 1791,
affirming the right of every generation to renew its social and political order.
The second part appeared in March 1792 and seemed shocking to many contemporaries in its attack on hereditary property and its sneering mockery of
the principle of monarchy. Paine's influence on the reform movement is seen
in the establishment in January 1792 of the London Corresponding Society.
This society, led by a humble shoemaker, Thomas Hardy, is usually taken to
be the most innovative and, in its lower-class membership and audience,
most popular of the reforming societies. In its *Address to the People* in August
the LCS demanded lower taxes, cheaper food, better education, legal reform
and provision for old age, much of which was derived from Paine. It believed
that politics should be available to all, hence their rule that 'the number of our
members be unlimited'. But what type of members were they to be? Their
supporters, far from being representatives of a proletarian working class,
ranged from small independent retailers and publishers to fairly wealthy
skilled craftsmen such as watchmakers and cabinet makers, and even
included some doctors and lawyers. In spite of its popularity with historians,[8]
the LCS only had a limited appeal to contemporaries. At the height of its success it could boast little more than 2000 members in London, perhaps 10 000
members nationally and, at its height in 1795, perhaps 90 'branches'. Their
targets were privilege, unearned wealth and corruption. They wished to
inspire others to improve and to educate and to think for themselves. They
had a cause and, in *The Rights of Man*, they had a bible. Indeed, nothing is
more significant than the anxiety of many of the societies, not just the LCS, to
publish and to sell cheap editions of Paine.

They may have been naïve in their belief in the power of the printed word
and they may have overestimated the extent to which others in the population did, or could, share their ideals. Nevertheless, to the relatively humble
people attending its meetings and hearing the radical gospel according to
Paine and other writers, the society was of vital importance. However important economic and occupational factors may have been in the progress of radical reform in the 1790s, it is essential to grasp that a comprehensive
critique of existing political and social arrangements was being developed
and circulated. It was this critique which was to form the intellectual core of a

self-conscious, popular radical movement for the rest of the 1790s. Paine was not the only architect of this critique. Indeed, the drift of recent scholarship has been to downplay the influence of Paine and to emphasize the fact that there was no single model or language of radicalism but a variety of them. The message of Thomas Spence was to nationalize the land; that of William Frend was to question the status of the established church; that of Mary Wollstonecraft was to advance the equality of women; that of John Thelwall was to equalize the ownership of property; that of William Godwin was to weaken the power of the state and establish a democratic body politic; that of Daniel Eaton was to bring the poor man into the national community. These writers and their messages were taught, discussed, popularized, and then incorporated into the radical tradition. Not surprisingly there came a revival of contract theory and a further great change in radical thinking: 'less was heard about the merits of the Anglo-Saxon constitution and more about the living conditions of the poor.'[9] At the same time, radical writers strove to find popular styles of argument and expression with which to appeal to a wide audience. It is the rich variety of popular radicalism rather than the dominance of Paine which deserves emphasis.

This revival of reform was not confined to England. Scotland had experienced a reform movement of her own in the 1780s, that for the reform of the Scottish burghs. Led somewhat unenthusiastically by the Whig politician R.B. Sheridan, the cause of burgh reform in 1788 attracted no fewer than 46 petitions, but it created little interest in Parliament. Further attempts to reform the Scottish burghs were made in 1789, 1791 and 1792. By then, however, the influence of the French Revolution had overtaken the cause of burgh reform. The Society of the Friends of the People spread rapidly in Scotland, although many of the Scottish societies calling themselves 'Friends' had more in common with the LCS than with the English 'Friends'. Nevertheless, by the end of 1792 there were perhaps 80 reform societies of one kind or another in Scotland. It was no accident that the first great demonstrations of radical strength were the anti-government protests of June 1792, when Henry Dundas was burned in effigy not only in Edinburgh but in a number of other cities as well. Nor was it accidental that the first radical convention was held in Scotland in December 1792. By the end of the year, 'Trees of Liberty' were planted in many towns and cities of Scotland to celebrate French military victories. As for Wales, although radical ideas penetrated even into some of the smaller towns organized radicalism was not common. In north Wales, however, branches of the SCI and the LCS were formed. The latter also had branches in the south, in Cardiff and in Brecon and possibly even in Bala. On the whole, however, meetings were few: Welsh radicalism was not to be a powerful force until the next century.

Although the overwhelming majority of reformers were peaceful and constitutional men, the progress of the radical reformers was beginning to cause serious alarm by the end of 1792. Already in November 1790 Edmund Burke, in *Reflections on the Revolution in France*, had articulated what later generations would come to recognize as the fundamentals of Conservative social theory: that society was a complex organism that steadily grows and matures over the centuries; that radical reformers wished to uproot traditions and institutions that had been found serviceable to successive generations and which had proved their capacity to adapt and change. Burke condemned the French Revolution for proceeding on the atheistical principles of the rights of man rather than on the historical principles of Christianity. If they were ever to be put into practice in Britain, as they had been in France, the principles of the rights of man would destroy the basis of a propertied political and social order and throw political power into the hands of the envious masses, guided by radical demagogues. At first Burke was regarded as a fanatic, but his ideas gradually won acceptance. As the continental situation darkened, as the prospects of the French monarchy and aristocracy deteriorated and as the possibility of war against France approached, radicals who supported the French Revolution became tainted by its excesses. Indeed, the Dissenters' campaign for the repeal of the Test and Corporation Acts had already begun to worry Anglicans, to sow the first seeds of disunion between different groups of reformers and to give rise to expressions of a nervous, reactionary loyalism. In Manchester, for example, a Church and King Club appeared as early as 1790. In July 1791 the eminent dissenting minister, scientist and philosopher Joseph Priestley was the victim of a mob attack on his home in Birmingham in the so-called 'Priestley Riots'. The cry of 'Church and King' became increasingly common during the second half of 1792. In November John Reeves, a lawyer with connections in governing circles, founded the Association for Preserving Liberty and Property against Republicans and Levellers. During the next six months, at least 2000 local patriotic clubs sprang up, modelled on John Reeves's parent body. As one observer reported, 'the whole country is forming itself into an Association'. The influence of these loyal associations in inoculating England against revolution cannot be overstated. With the local ruling elite providing the example, and not infrequently the money, with which to finance their activities, they distributed propaganda, particularly the homilistic stories of Hannah More,[10] harassed and prosecuted radicals, suppressed seditious publications and mobilized public opinion through a variety of local agencies. While it may be an exaggeration to conclude that loyalist propaganda actually changed people's minds, it may well have helped to undermine the reformers' case by confirming many patriotic assumptions about Britain and her monarchy, about the perfection of her constitution and about the prosperity of her people and the fairness of her institutions. At the same time, loyalist propaganda did much to undermine radical arguments concerning the possibility, even the desirability, of achieving equality, and raised serious concerns about the likely consequences of intemperate and untimely reform. The propaganda of the loyal associations, combined with that of the government, in particular the circulation of the pro-government newspapers *The Oracle, The Sun* and *The True Briton*, and, later, influential periodicals such as *The Anti-Jacobin*, did much to marginalize radical ideas.

All this was achieved with government connivance but without direct intervention. During the next few years, however, the government was to become more active in the campaign against reform. Already in May 1792 a proclamation had been issued bidding magistrates to be on their guard against seditious writings. In December a further proclamation called out the militia to safeguard the country from internal disruption. In 1793 the government began to use its massive legal resources against the reformers. In

August 1793 a series of state trials in Scotland led to the imprisonment of a number of reformers. In May 1794 the government had suspended habeas corpus, but the reformers were not silenced. The holding of a British national reform convention in Edinburgh in October 1793 caused a good deal of alarm in loyalist circles that reformers might be seeking to establish a rival Parliament. Consequently, conservative opinion greeted the State Trials of 1794 with approval. The leaders of the convention, Thomas Hardy, Horne Tooke[11] and John Thelwall, and ten other leading reformers were tried for treason. Amidst scenes of tumultuous rejoicing in London, the great Whig lawyer Thomas Erskine[12] secured verdicts of 'not guilty' for his radical clients. This was a historic victory, but it did not dissuade the government from taking further measures against reformers. Their cause was aided by the economic deprivations caused by the war and by harvest failure. That of 1794 resulted in a steady rise in prices and a serious food shortage in many regions. In 1795 these problems were aggravated by yet further harvest failure. The price of wheat rose by a third over the 1794 price. Real distress combined with war weariness to produce serious rioting. At the opening of Parliament in October 1795 violent demonstrations against the King and Pitt horrified the government. These threatening scenes, coming so soon after the great radical demonstrations of St George's Field on 29 June and the Copenhagen Fields meetings on 26 October, persuaded the government to strike. It passed the Two Acts, the Seditious Meetings Bill, which closely regulated the holding of public meetings, and the Treasonable Practices Bill, which extended the definition of treason to include any criticism of king or government. The pressure on radicals was remorseless. It matters little that the legislation was not much used. The Two Acts set an example and alerted the propertied classes to the potential danger in which the country stood. They increased the pressure on the radical societies which by the summer of 1796 were in serious decline.

These legal restrictions coalesced with the continuing force of loyalist action and example to inhibit radicalism. Many loyal associations mobilized their resources to assist the war effort by raising money for the recruitment of troops and for the relief of the dependants of men killed or wounded in the war. They even became an active source of volunteers. In March 1794 Pitt's government authorized the establishment of Volunteer regiments, and they quickly became objects of local and civic pride. By the end of the century there were almost 300 000 Volunteers. During the invasion crisis of 1804, there were no fewer than 450 000.

After 1795, in fact, radicalism was forced underground. The continuing suspension of habeas corpus enabled the government to keep suspects under lock and key, and it availed itself of the privilege. The societies fell into crisis. Indeed, the SCI had never managed to recover from the seizure of its papers during the period of the State Trials in 1794. The Friends of the People ceased to meet in 1796. In 1797 the government raised stamp duties on newspapers from 2d. to 3s. 5d. The naval mutinies of 1797 reminded an alarmed population that constant vigilance was needed against the radical threat from within. In April 1798 the papers of the LCS were seized, and the society was banned in July 1799. Many radical leaders emigrated or, like Francis Place,[13] withdrew from active agitation for some years. Everywhere, the public organization of radicalism was snuffed out. But in private it survived and in many ways even prospered. In London a radical underground had become by the end of the decade a cluster of groupings, some with links into the worlds of popular religion, of petty crime, of unconventional science and of other marginalized groups. Such radicalism was popular, plebeian and theatrical, thriving on mockery and abuse. If such a broad and amorphous 'movement' had a core, it was perhaps provided by the Spencean radicals, followers of the agrarian reformer Thomas Spence. These men kept the radical flag flying and created a seedbed from which the shoots of conspiracy, or even revolution, could spring.

The radicals went underground at the same time as the nerve-centre of the radical movement was shifting away from London and to the north of England. In defiance of the Two Acts, a Manchester Corresponding Society was formed in 1796. It was one of the few largely proletarian bodies of the decade and it developed cells in cotton factories as well as spawning further branches outwards from Manchester. Echoes of similar groups were heard in the West Riding, in the Midlands and in the Glasgow area. It is not clear whether a national conspiracy was being organized, but many of these groups contained revolutionary elements. As its public influence declined, the LCS was penetrated by plotters and revolutionaries, including a number of members of the United Irishmen, who dreamed of a united Anglo-Irish movement. An unlikely revolutionary conspiracy to organize simultaneous Irish and English risings in 1798 with French assistance was unearthed by British spies and one of its leaders, Father James O'Coigly, went to the gallows. The Irish rebellion of 1798 had no English counterpart, but its failure caused many members of the United Irishmen to flee to England. The Combination Acts of 1799 and 1800 banned workers' combinations, driving protest even more emphatically underground. By 1800 there were still perhaps 20 divisions of the LCS active in London. The failure of the harvest in 1800 created a threatening situation which both alarmed the government and provided an ugly context in which plots and conspiracies could thrive. When the Two Acts expired in 1801 the revolutionary organization of the radical movement quickly revived. The government did not hesitate to revive the Acts. There were some disturbances and a certain amount of nocturnal plotting in Yorkshire, but London was now back at the forefront of this phase of the movement. A handful of arrests was sufficient to break the back of the conspiracy. This did not deter Colonel Despard's plot of 1802, which planned to seize key points in London with the aid of disaffected elements in the army. Riddled with government spies and without a French invasion force to support it, the plot had no chance of success, and Despard's was hanged in 1803. Thereafter underground radical activity continued, but without much coordination or confidence, and for almost a decade the cause of extra-parliamentary reform is almost entirely lost to the historian.

Pitt has been roundly condemned for his repressive attitude towards reformers, but there is little doubt that public opinion, hostile to France in the middle of a great war and fearful of popular agitation, supported his measures. Furthermore, these conspiracies cannot be dismissed as the actions of a lunatic fringe. They have to be treated as a serious and considered response of one section of the reformers. Furthermore, loyalist sentiments were not entirely comforting to the government. The immediate upsurge of loyalist opinion in 1792–93 had been impressive but it soon petered out. Further surges of patriotic activity came later in the decade with the establishment of the Volunteer regiments but these, too, had only partial success. In 1796 a supplementary militia had to be raised by compulsory ballot. Even though many towns proudly raised their own militia regiments in 1797–98, there were still dangerous, albeit patchy, signs of popular support for the cause of reform. With the benefit of hindsight historians have the luxury of knowing that this phase of conspiratorial radicalism was to be unsuccessful. Pitt's government, fighting a dangerous and, to that point, largely unsuccessful war, could take no chances and had no way of knowing that victory would ultimately come. The years 1796–98 witnessed military defeat, naval mutinies, rebellion in Ireland and continued economic crisis. In the early years of the new century, however, the situation entirely changed. The Treaty of Amiens brought a blessed respite from the privations of war. When it resumed, loyalism seemed to be a natural patriotic duty against the threat of Napoleon's schemes of personal aggrandisement and imperial ambition. Radical reform did not revive until after the invasion scare of 1804–05. The heavy hand of repression which had driven radicalism underground in the 1790s was, with the death of Pitt in 1806, removed. The Ministry of All the Talents of 1806–07 brought the Whigs back to power, and if the ministry accomplished little to please parliamentary reformers, its greatest achievement, the abolition of the slave trade, was both a testament to humane government action and an indication that the mood of the country was changing after the repressive days of the 1790s. In the period 1789–92 it had been the euphoria created by the French Revolution which had given reformers their audience. In 1795–96 and 1800–01 it had been the pitiful conditions created by famine and want. Now it was the unemployment and interruption to trade – what contemporaries termed 'distress' – created by the Continental System and the Orders in Council which drove merchants, manufacturers, artisans (skilled and unskilled), and now factory workers into the arms of the radical leaders. Much of the moral and ideological force of this phase of radicalism was very traditional: distaste for corruption, suspicion of government and a reverence for the ancient constitution. It was no accident that several senior figures in the radical pantheon had been active a generation earlier in radical politics, including Major Cartwright, John Horne Tooke, Christopher Wyvill and Capel Lofft.[14]

In the period 1807–12 four distinctive strands of radicalism appeared and interacted: a revived metropolitan radicalism principally linked with the figure of Sir Francis Burdett;[15] a provincial 'Hampden Club' movement among the working-class communities of the new, and many of the old, industrial towns; a provincial, largely middle-class movement protesting against the war and the Orders in Council; and a wave of machine-breaking in 1811–12, popularly known as Luddism.

The first significant catalyst in the revival of metropolitan radicalism was the general election of 1806, at which a number of notable radical personalities fought noisy but unsuccessful campaigns. The ex-Tory William Cobbett[16] stood at Honiton, Major Cartwright at Boston and Sir Francis Burdett at Middlesex. Burdett was an old-fashioned paternalist, believing in the ancient constitution and the gentry's right to rule and advocating a moderate brand of parliamentary reform. He believed in the free-born Englishman, not the rights of man. At the general election of 1807 Burdett won Middlesex thanks to the energetic and populist campaigning of a revived Westminster committee, organized by Francis Place. The next few years witnessed continuing, if not always well coordinated, radical attacks on the governments of Portland (1807–09) and Perceval (1809–12), supported by new journalistic talents, William Cobbett and his *Political Register*, the Whig *Edinburgh Review* (1806) and the radical *Examiner* edited by Leigh Hunt. Such journalism was able to feed off a succession of minor wartime scandals, and one major one – that of the mistress of the Duke of York, Mrs Anne Clark, who had apparently used her position to sell army commissions. In effective alliance with the journalism of Cobbett and his *Political Register*, Burdett made a conspicuous success of drawing attention to himself and to his cause. In 1809 he moved for a householder franchise and the division of county constituencies, arguing significantly that only in this way would the ancient constitution be restored and recent abuses removed. His motion was defeated by 74 votes to 15. In 1810 he was thrown into the tower for denouncing a decision of the House of Commons to imprison a fellow London radical, John Gale Jones. This was a signal for mob activity and popular idolization of Burdett in the capital reminiscent of the days of John Wilkes. Floods of petitions demanded reform of Parliament. In June 1811 radicals of all persuasions, including not only Burdett and Cobbett but also Christopher Wyvill and a dynamic new force, Henry Hunt,[17] came together in a new society, the Society of Friends to Parliamentary Reform. It was by then too late to effect anything before the cause of metropolitan radicalism suffered yet another of its periodic collapses.

Radicalism appeared once again in the provinces through the agency of the Hampden Clubs. The original Hampden Club was formed in 1812 with the purpose of enabling radical leaders to keep open their contacts with hesitant Whig politicians, who were at this time beginning to interest themselves once again in parliamentary reform. The Hampden was an extraordinarily exclusive club, restricted to people worth £300 a year and with a subscription of two guineas. Cartwright had by now reached the conclusion that parliamentary reform could only be achieved through mass support for a radical platform of universal suffrage. Believing that the exclusiveness of the Hampden was entirely the wrong strategy, he resigned in June 1812, formed the Union society and proceeded in 1812–13 to visit many of the industrial towns of the country, politicizing local leaders and spreading the gospel of universal suffrage. It is difficult to measure exactly the effectiveness of Cartwright's missionary tours, but the 1813 tour covered 900 miles in 29 days, visiting 34 towns and, ultimately, generating 130 000 signatures on 430 petitions. No immediate benefit to the radical cause was forthcoming, but it would be difficult to deny that Cartwright had laid some at least of the foundations for the wave of radical activity that flooded the country after the war.

Meanwhile, it was not perhaps surprising that the unprecedented length and cost of the war, together with the unusual sacrifices to which it gave rise, should generate a peace movement, especially among provincial, middle-class Dissenters. In one of the earliest popular Nonconformist pressure groups, moral revulsion against war combined with solid economic discontent. Leading Dissenting manufacturers like William Roscoe of Liverpool, Josiah Wedgewood in the Potteries and William Strutt of Derby coordinated provincial opposition to the war which merged, in 1807, into a strongly organized protest against the Orders in Council. Its initial failure to change government policy did not daunt the organizers. An extra-parliamentary campaign, led by the Whig politician Henry Brougham[18] and backed by 150 000 petitioners, ultimately achieved its objective in 1812. These agitations of the 'Friends of Peace' acted as a powerful vehicle for a thoroughgoing critique and condemnation not only of the war but also of the government and the social and political establishment. Certainly, middle-class Dissenters, unlike lower-class radicals, were not daunted by the repressive apparatus of the state. Possibly reacting against the revived Anglicanism of the 1790s, the peace movement marks a revival in the political self-confidence of Protestant Dissenters. Furthermore, this alliance of Whig politicians, middle-class Dissenters and lower-class political agitation was a foretaste of the alliance which was to force Parliament to reform itself in 1831–32.

The pressures of war were also largely responsible for the Luddite movement. In 1811 and 1812 a wave of machine-breaking swept three industrializing areas of the country, beginning in the east Midlands, then moving on to the West Riding of Yorkshire and then to parts of Lancashire. Machine-breaking was a traditional means of lower-class protest. In 1811–12 it became a last resort when orderly protest had failed to persuade Parliament either to enact new or to utilize existing legislation affecting working and living conditions. The Luddism of the early nineteenth century was a reaction to industrialization, to mechanization and to exploitation. It was a protest not only against low wages but also against the high rents of the frames of the Nottinghamshire framework knitters and the looms of the handloom weavers of Lancashire. In Yorkshire Luddism was a protest of the skilled croppers against the introduction of new machinery such as the gig mill and the shearing frame. More generally Luddism was a protest, especially in the lace trades of Nottinghamshire, against the declining status of old crafts and the inferior quality of goods now mass produced. The scale of Luddism should not be underestimated. In Nottinghamshire well over 1000 frames were destroyed in over 100 raids. There was also a powerful political element in Luddism, especially in Yorkshire and Lancashire. Luddism only appeared in Yorkshire after the croppers had failed to persuade the authorities to enforce Tudor legislation against both the use of machinery in their industry and against the use of unapprenticed labour. Although it is impossible to distinguish fact from rumour and exaggeration, there is evidence of political activity in the industrial towns of the West Riding. The old clandestine organization of the radical underground reappeared there and, to a lesser extent, in south east Lancashire, where food rioting was often confused with Luddism. In some places there are traces of quasi-military oath-taking and drilling, and there were a few attacks on militia depots, but these were unusual. Luddism, however, was not a revolutionary movement. Had it been so it would have remained tiny and ineffective. Luddism had widespread popular support; it was embedded in local communities and rooted in local problems. Parliament was sufficiently alarmed to make machine-breaking a capital offence in 1812 but it took more than that to suppress Luddism. It took considerable military force. Two thousand soldiers were stationed in Nottinghamshire to break Luddism in the county, and at one time there were 15 000 troops in Yorkshire. Even then, Luddism was a long time disappearing. In Nottingham a committee of framework knitters promoted a parliamentary bill to regulate the trade. When it failed to pass the House of Lords in July 1814, frame-breaking resumed, and continued intermittently in the county until 1816.

This wartime phase of radicalism perhaps lacks the ideological freshness of the radicalism of the 1790s. Nevertheless, it confirmed many of the reformers' suspicions concerning the corruption of the regime, and it did something to stir the middling orders out of their unthinking loyalism. Furthermore, it unquestionably acted as a stimulant to the cautious MPs of the Whig party. After 1812, however, the excitement generated by the reformers, Dissenters and Luddites slowly subsided. The murder of the Prime Minister, Spencer Perceval, in 1812 horrified moderate opinion, while the recurrence of Luddite disturbances continued to arouse fears for the preservation of social stability. However, the repeal of the Orders in Council and the improved business prosperity of the last three years of the war did much to lower the political temperature. As the climax of the Napoleonic wars approached, patriotic opinion once more rallied behind the throne.

The return to peace in 1815 created severe economic dislocation which found expression both in political and in economic protest. The demobilization of regular and volunteer forces, the immediate decline in government orders and the resulting rapid rise in unemployment created scenes of pitiful distress. For example, the great iron works of Shropshire, south Wales and Scotland lost their armaments orders and threw surplus labour on the markets. The industrial recession coincided with a poor harvest in 1816. According to one tradition, one in five of the population was on poor relief in Birmingham. If this were not enough, the passage of the Corn Law of 1815 aroused fury among the labouring classes. This act, by which no foreign corn could be sold in Britain until the domestic price had attained 80s. a quarter, had as its object to protect the landed interest against falling prices. (By the new year of 1817 the price had reached 100s. a quarter.) Its consequence was to keep the price of bread unnecessarily high. It showed that there was one law for the rich, landed classes – protection, and thus, security – and another for the poor – the free market, and thus poverty and insecurity. The Corn Law aroused bitter resentment in London, which in March 1815 was hit by a series of riots which came near to paralysing the city. As a consequence of all these economic problems, the extent of postwar radical agitation was entirely unprecedented, fuelled as it was by the sharpness of class antagonism. In the north of England in particular, the growth of factories was producing a huge social as well as economic chasm between the labouring classes and their masters. In Lancashire and Yorkshire particularly, political agitation for reform was difficult to distinguish from economic agitation for shorter hours or for better wages. Interestingly, in harsher times it tended to be the political objective that was uppermost; in better times, the labouring classes tended to concentrate on their economic objectives.

These were not merely years of economic distress and political resentment. These were years of intense politicization affecting the masses as well as the middle classes. These were the great years of the radical press. Newspapers such as the *Leeds Mercury*, edited by the Dissenter Edward Baines, rallied the merchants and manufacturers against the Corn Law of 1815 in particular and against 'old corruption' in general. Similar though less distinguished papers included the Sheffield *Independent* (founded in 1819) and the *Manchester Guardian* (1821). Even more striking was the mass circulation of working-class journals. Cobbett's *Political Register* attained a circulation of 40 000–50 000 per issue, no doubt in part because of its price reduction from 5*d*. to 1*d*. in 1816. Thomas Wooler's *Black Dwarf* (1817–24) was possibly even more savage in its condemnation of the establishment (or 'The Thing' as Cobbett liked to describe it) than Cobbett himself was. Similarly, William Sherwin's *Weekly Political Register* (1817–19) was widely read in the London area. When it was taken over by Richard Carlile in 1819 it became a more powerful, and more distinguished, radical journal.

In the summer of 1816 Burdett appealed to the Hampden Club to organize reform petitions to present to Parliament. He was concerned lest machine-breaking frightened the middle classes and thus set back the cause of reform, and hoped to yoke working-class radicals to his peaceful parliamentary strategy. His appeal did not go unanswered: union clubs sprang up everywhere, in towns and villages, in pubs and chapels, in homes and workplaces throughout the country. The radical leaders even found it possible to work together. In January 1817 a conference of 70 radical leaders met at the Crown and Anchor tavern in London. In spite of their differences, they agreed upon a campaign of mass petitioning. It was an outstanding success. No fewer than 700 petitions to Parliament were forthcoming from over 350 places in support of Burdett's motion of 20 May 1817 for a select committee on parliamentary reform. Although the motion was lost, and lost badly by 77 votes against 265, it had been the most spectacular radical mobilization of public opinion for over two decades. The geographical distribution of the petitions reflects that of radical opinion in general. Although Wales and Ireland were not involved, Scotland was in the vanguard of the movement. Again, although East Anglia and the West Country made a paltry showing, the north west of England, Yorkshire and the east Midlands, with some support from London, were more solid for reform.

The same tactics were repeated in 1818 and with very similar consequences. Although no fewer than 1570 petitions were raised, many of them had only a score or more of signatures on them. In May, Sir Robert Heron's motion for triennial parliaments was lost by 117 to 42. Petitions alone would not be sufficient to overcome the resistance of Parliament. So in 1819 the radicals devised one of their happiest initiatives, the holding of 'elections' in the great industrial towns for their 'legislative attorneys', a tactic that kept the reform pot boiling throughout the first half of the year. On 12 July a meeting to elect a 'legislative attorney' was held in Birmingham, and another was planned for Manchester. On 16 August tens of thousands of workers from Manchester and the surrounding areas gathered in St Peter's Fields to listen to 'Orator' Hunt. The magistrates, anxious for the preservation of peace, instructed the local yeomanry to arrest him. This led to still greater disorder and the intervention of the cavalry in which 11 people were killed and over 400 injured. In some ways, the aftermath of 'Peterloo' was almost as important as the 'massacre' itself. There was an immediate national outcry among radicals and a flurry of mass meetings throughout the country to protest against the government. But what did such meetings actually achieve? What were the radicals to do after Peterloo? It was impossible for them to challenge the government further without resorting to direct revolutionary action and, for all his wildness in words at times, Hunt was not prepared do so. As the reformers considered their strategy after Peterloo, the momentum slowly evaporated and the energies of radicals were deflected in to other directions.

The years after 1815 were marked by other forms of direct action spawned by the hardship of the times. Luddism sprang up again in the east Midlands in 1816. No sooner had that begun to disappear than rural areas of eastern England were racked with food rioting. In March 1817 the Manchester workers organized their 'Blanketeers' march. It took the unity of the local magistracy as well as a force of cavalry to ensure that most of them got no further than Stockport. The march of the Blanketeers was a genuine attempt, however poorly organized, to draw the attention of the nation to the distress of the masses. The 'Pentrich rising' of June 1817 could have been more dangerous had 'Oliver the Spy', W.J. Richards, not given advance warning of the rising to the authorities. The eventual rising of 300 stockingers and ironworkers from a handful of villages in north east Derbyshire came to nothing, save the execution of Jeremiah Brandreth and two of his fellow leaders. Other manifestations of direct action had overly political overtones. In November and December 1816 three great radical meetings, seething with class resentment, were held at Spa Fields in London. Nothing like these had been seen in the capital since the great meetings of the London Corresponding Society in 1795 and the government was alarmed, particularly so after one of them when a group of extremists looted gunsmiths' shops and tried to storm the Tower of London. This conspiracy was led by Arthur Thistlewood and James Watson, who were motivated by the ideas of Thomas Spence. Freed on a technicality from these charges they continued to plot, and in 1820 formulated a plan to assassinate the cabinet. This, the 'Cato Street Conspiracy' of February 1820, had already been infiltrated by spies and was easily frustrated. Thistlewood and four others were hanged and five others transported.

Surprisingly, however, the great climax of the radical agitations of the postwar years came neither with Peterloo nor with Cato Street but with the affairs of Queen Caroline. With the death of George III in January 1820 and the accession of his son, George IV, the status of the King's unwanted and discarded wife, Queen Caroline, became a matter of immediate public concern.[19] The King's hostile attitude towards his wife, from whom he had been separated for many years and who had been living on the Continent, rendered her an object of public sympathy. Caroline was treated instantly as a victim of the establishment, a martyr of the corrupt executive. On her arrival in London in June 1820 she took up residence in the home of Alderman Wood, a prominent London radical. Immense public rallies in favour of the humiliated Queen were held all over the country, which watched with fascination as the drama unfolded. The Queen demanded that she be declared Queen Consort; the ministry instituted a public scrutiny of her conduct with a view to proving grounds for divorce. As the sordid spectacle continued, the ministry's case began to run into difficulties and the bill was abandoned. On the other side, however, the opposition's cause began to weaken when the Queen accepted an annual pension of £50 000. At a time of widespread distress, such an action was bound to cause offence, and support for the Queen's cause began to subside. However, only her death in August 1821 put an end to the episode. The economic situation was already beginning to ease and the confidence of merchants to recover. As employment and wages rose and as the stock market boomed, discontent melted away.

The radical challenge to the government of Lord Liverpool had been unprecedented. It had involved hundreds of thousands of people in many parts of Britain, and had launched a popular agitation that was quite unequalled; it had alarmed the government, terrified property-holders and politicized the lower classes. So impressive is this achievement that its ultimate failure demands explanation. Two factors stand out. The divisions in the postwar radical movement were crippling. The new working-class radicalism of Henry Hunt, with its appeal to factory workers, stood in direct contrast to the more traditional radicalism of Burdett, who appealed more strongly to small shopkeepers and tradesmen. Such differences were aggravated by the bitter antagonisms between the sturdy personalities of Burdett, Hunt, Cartwright and Cobbett. The movement was seriously weakened by physical and geographical differences; moreover, regional and provincial loyalties remained strong and communications still difficult in this pre-railway age. Although Cartwright's tours and the journalism of Cobbett had done something to give a national orientation to postwar radicalism, the movement remained seriously fragmented and, thus, weakened. Nevertheless, the postwar radical movement had achieved the mass platform it had hitherto lacked. It had acquired the moral force and the popular backing with which to confront the forces of government, and to do so with confidence. Its ultimate tactic of conspicuous confrontation with the authorities created expectation, tension and, not least, drama and excitement in which all could participate. Such a confrontation did not only occur at the political and legal levels; it occurred also at the level of language, with radicals seeking to broaden the meaning of terms like 'freedom', 'the people' and 'the constitution', loyalists to limit them. In the battle for the minds of men and women, such strategies were of great importance. What historians are coming to understand, moreover, is the extent to which radical leaders and organizers were able not only to create an attractive radical platform but also to produce compelling radical theatre. Radical leaders played upon the rich traditions of popular culture to make elaborate appeals to the people through the careful utilization of civic and national celebrations, through dinners and toasts, through the dazzling deployment of light and colour and the accompanying recitation of music, rhyme and stories. Radicalism was shot through with traditional practices such as burning in effigy (of opponents), chairing and hero-worship (of radical leaders) and, not least, by the use of symbols (such as the cap of liberty and the white hats of reform). One of the many explanations for the *mass* radicalism of these years is the ability of radical leaders to convey their messages in a lively and compelling manner to their potential supporters, and thus to expand the arenas in which political power was contested. In the end, however, the nerve of the government held, partly because it saw that it retained the confidence of the majority of property-holders and partly because its political and parliamentary position, although embarrassed on some occasions, was never seriously threatened. For the moment the castle had been saved, but a further siege was almost certain to occur in time.

The politics of wartime and after, 1789–1820

After the Regency Crisis of 1788–89 the government of William Pitt was secure in the affections of the King, respected, if not loved, in the country and seemingly in a comfortable majority in Parliament. The general election of 1790 quietly confirmed Pitt's supremacy, renewing his majority of over 150. Yet that supremacy was not without its weakness. One, usually underestimated, was the possibility that if his brother, Lord Chatham, were to die then Pitt would go to the Lords, from where his control of the administration would be much more tenuous than from the Commons.[20] Pitt enjoyed a comfortable majority in the Lords but it belonged to the King rather than to the minister – about half the peers were amenable to George III rather than to William Pitt – and the ministry was weak in debating talent there. Pitt, furthermore, had only a limited personal following, usually estimated at about 50. The source of his power was the support of the court and administration group of around 200. Even this was not always enough to give him a reliable majority, faced as he was with an opposition of over 130 which on certain issues could hope to recruit the support of a majority of the independent members. Pitt was not always sure of the independents; he was not a sociable man, rarely mixed with MPs and did not always know their opinions. It was his talents rather than his personality that kept him in office. Ultimately, however, his very vulnerability was his best security so long as the only real alternatives to him were Fox and the Prince of Wales. By 1789 Pitt had been in office for six years and had demonstrated his very real talents. He was also blessed with the support of two political heavyweights, Henry Dundas, the 'King of Scotland', and his cousin Lord Grenville, then Speaker of the House of Commons and after 1791 Foreign Secretary. Pitt's cabinet was not a particularly distinguished one. Without Dundas and Grenville it would have been notably lightweight.[21]

Between 1789 and 1794 Pitt's ministry was gradually remodelled. The Whig opposition was seriously divided by the French Revolution, a development which worked strongly to Pitt's advantage. The publication of Burke's *Reflections on the Revolution in France* in November 1790 marked his public challenge to the enthusiasm with which Fox had greeted the Revolution. For some time, however, such differences remained differences of opinion and had little or no effect on political conduct. When in May 1791 Fox and Burke formally ended their political friendship during a tearful scene in the House of Commons, it was a parting of friends and had little immediate impact in the cohesion of the Whig party. Indeed, during these early years of the decade the French Revolution seemed of less political importance than the expansionism of Russia in the Black Sea region. Indeed, the debates of May 1791 which saw the ending of the friendship of Burke and Fox coincided with crucial debates on this issue. The opposition cheerfully trounced Pitt in debate, especially in view of the resignation of his foreign secretary, the Duke of Leeds.[22] At a time when the government was in serious disarray, divisions in the Whig party seemed of trivial importance.

In 1792, however, those division began not only to intensify but also to affect the daily conduct of politics. The formation of the Association of the Friends of the People in April was a public repudiation of Burke's alarmist opinions. Although Fox did not join the Association, men like Portland and Fitzwilliam,[23] senior figures on the conservative wing of the party and men much influenced by Burke's views, began to worry lest Fox lose control of the reformers in the party. Indeed, as the radical tide flowed ever more strongly in 1792, they began to show concern lest the old Whig party itself might start to act as a vehicle for the circulation of radical, and even revolutionary, opinions. Charles James Fox's reiterated belief – that Britain had more to fear from the influence of George III than from the French Revolution – seemed to many to be irresponsible and self-indulgent. Seeing what was happening to the Whig party, William Pitt did not hesitate to drive his knife into the wounds of his opponents. He consulted the Portland group on the proclamation of May 1792 and began to tantalize senior members in opposition with hints of office and preferment. Yet so long as Fox continued to have the will to keep his party united there was still a chance that the Whig party might survive intact. When Pitt called out the militia in December 1792 it was too much for Fox. Incensed by what he took to be Pitt's willingness to play party politics with the nation's defences, he at last came off the fence, declared for reform and the reformers and proceeded to defend the French Revolution. Although Fox did not publicly support parliamentary reform until May 1793, his historic decision had been made. Slowly, the old Whig party was being prised apart by the pressure of events. In January 1793 Lord Loughborough[24] deserted the opposition to accept the office of Lord Chancellor. It was the first serious breach, and a sign of what was to come. In the same month about 30 MPs, led by Burke and William Windham,[25] deserted the opposition to form a 'third party', uneasily positioned between government and opposition. Even now, however, party loyalty and abiding suspicion of Pitt kept the bulk of Whig party members from uniting with the ministry; indeed, the main body of the party still remained loyal to Fox. But this situation could not possibly last. Fox opposed the war against France. To advocate peace with a regicide republic which was proclaiming the cause of revolution throughout Europe was too much even for Fox's closest friends. If this were not enough, he at last threw in his lot with the Friends of the People. On Charles Grey's motion for reform on 7 May 1793, to the horror of the conservative wing of his party, Fox came out for reform. The split within the Whig party was humiliatingly reflected in the division of 282 votes against Grey's motion and the paltry 41 in favour.

As the military crisis that Britain faced in Europe deepened so the need to strengthen Pitt's administration became more apparent. Fox's motion on 17 June for peace with France only served to underline the impossibility of keeping his party together. By the end of the year the conservative Whigs had separated from Fox. Pitt set himself to win them over to his government. When he decided in May 1794 to establish a Committee of Secrecy to consider further measures to be taken against the radicals, he consulted them and sought their assistance. In July 1794 they negotiated a coalition with Pitt in which they took five out of 13 cabinet posts.[26] Amidst much talk of the Whig party's new role in cleansing the government from within, they won assurances from Pitt on the objectives of the war and the restoration of the Bourbon dynasty, and they were promised the government of Ireland with vague hints that they might introduce measures of reform there. Pitt, however, retained overall control of the government and kept direction of the war in the hands of the triumvirate of himself, Dundas and Grenville. Reconstructed in this manner, Pitt's government, in coalition with the Portland Whigs, continued until 1801.

The Foxite Whigs now stood apart from the political consensus created by the coalition. They managed to stabilize their numbers at around 60 and even, eventually, to increase them slightly to around 80 in the early years of the new century. They began to outline a coherent set of political objectives of their own which has often been credited with the ideological title of 'Foxite Whiggism'. During the next three years they were to demonstrate their commitment to peace and reform on a variety of issues. Fox was a savage critic of Pitt's war aims, believing that he was going much further than the security of Britain demanded in seeking to dictate to France the form of her government. Fox suspected that Pitt was using patronage and influence, swollen by the demands of war, to build up a power base for himself. Furthermore, Fox had always been a keen supporter of civil and religious freedom and he had been opposed to religious tests for civil offices. He was moving steadily in the direction of Catholic emancipation, a position which he was to adopt in the early years of the new century. Like two-thirds of his party, Fox was now an open advocate of parliamentary reform, but that, in the circumstances of the 1790s, was a long-term aim. Meanwhile, he distinguished himself by his commitment to free speech. He was a stern critic of the government's prosecution of Scottish and English radicals in 1793 and 1794, and in 1795 the Foxites attacked the Two Acts with magnificent oratory and commendable persistence, dividing Parliament repeatedly but in vain. Indeed, these liberal attitudes, together with Fox's Libel Act of 1792 (which gave juries the right to decide whether material was libellous instead of, as previously, whether the person accused had actually written the disputed matter), have led some historians to depict the Foxite Whigs as the ancestors of the nineteenth-century Liberal party. To what extent can this claim be justified?

For all his faults, his personal resentments and his distorted exaggerations, Charles James Fox remains a towering figure, especially in the great years of 1794–96, professing a consistent and idiosyncratic, if sometimes misguided, version of Whiggism which was to have a long life ahead of it. The Foxite Whigs, furthermore, kept aloft the mantle of party and proclaimed the need for unity and principle in politics. They related their own struggles to those of earlier generations of Whigs and imagined themselves in an ancestry which stretched back to the Glorious Revolution. In this Whig Interpretation of British history the Foxite Whig party, like its predecessors, was fighting the battle for freedom against a repressive government and an authoritarian monarch.

However, not all nineteenth-century liberals took their inspiration from Foxite Whiggism. They may have found some anticipations of their political and religious radicalism (although Foxite Whiggism is essentially a secular philosophy) but not their economic radicalism. Furthermore, Fox was a man of his time and in 1794 had been active in politics for over two decades. His mind-set was securely rooted in the opposition politics of the later eighteenth century. Although his philosophy had in many respects advanced far ahead of them, Fox remained in many ways a prisoner of the Whig legends of the Rockingham party. Although he instinctively welcomed the French Revolution as a blessing to humanity, his initial postulate was the Rockinghamite belief that the influence of the crown lay at the root of the nation's ills. In this sense, and in the aristocratic origins of almost half of their members, the Foxites were much closer to Rockingham than they were to Gladstone. Indeed, a sustained comparison of the Foxite and Rockingham Whigs is most instructive: both were aristocratic Whig parties, advocated the principle and practice of party and opposed popular wars; both spent most of their lives in opposition, hostile to George III's men and measures; both achieved office for only brief periods, unable to sustain themselves in the unfriendly courts and cabinets of George III. Fox was no democrat. He was an eighteenth-century Whig; his was the classic Whig objective of maintaining the balance of the constitution between the twin evils of royal absolutism and popular licence. He had the political limitations, too, of the eighteenth-century Whig. After the failure of Charles Grey's reform motion in 1797 he and his party seceded from Parliament.[27] There seemed no other practical plan of action. They had stated their case on the war, on reform, on freedom of speech, on royal influence. They could do no more. The Rockingham Whigs had practised secession in 1776 when they, too, had been consigned to the margins of politics, opposing a popular war and having exhausted the legitimate political expedients available to them. All that could be done in such circumstances was to wait on events. In fact the Foxites waited a long time, until the fall of Pitt in 1801 raised both the political temperature and their own political expectations.

It was not through the activities of the Foxite Whigs, however, that the government which had ruled Britain since 1783 finally came to its end. The fall of Pitt in 1801 occurred on an issue of constitutional principle. Pitt had let it be understood even before the Union with Ireland in 1800 that he would pursue the issue of Catholic emancipation.[28] To this, however, the King would not agree and Pitt, although he promised never to raise the issue again in the King's lifetime, felt that he had no alternative but to resign. He may have done so because of internal disputes within the government on the conduct of the war, Pitt being incapable of resolving the alternative claims of continental, land war and maritime and commercial war. There is in addition evidence of Pitt's mental and physical decline after nearly two decades of office and eight years of largely unsuccessful warfare. On Catholic emancipation, moreover, it is often forgotten that George III reflected majority opinion within the cabinet as well as within the political nation. There may also have been another reason for the King's willingness to part with the minister. Pitt was nothing if not high-handed: he had in recent years treated the cabinet as his own and he had taken the King's consent to measures for granted. Indeed, only Dundas, Grenville and Windham came out with Pitt in 1801. The ministerial crisis may just have been the King's way of restoring a measure of royal influence over cabinet decisions. The political crisis of 1801 thus marks the continuing importance of the monarch in politics, and starkly demonstrates the need for ministers to have his confidence. It was not just Pitt, however, who was sacrificed upon the altar of the King's conscience but – although no one could know it in 1801 – ministerial stability. A succession of five weak ministries in the next eleven years was the unintended consequence of the fall of Pitt.

The reasons for ministerial instability in these years were partly personal and partly structural. The coalition which had governed Britain in the 1790s was fragmenting. The old Pittite coalition of the 1790s was now divided into three groups: those led by Pitt, Grenville and Addington. The permutations were complicated. Pitt still had 50–60 followers after his resignation, Addington 30–40, Grenville 20–30 (later in the decade a fourth group, led by Canning, appeared which consisted of 10–15 MPs). It took 11 years for three of these groups to unite their forces under Lord Liverpool. Pitt disapproved of Addington's policy of disarmament and was a lukewarm supporter of Catholic emancipation. Like Pitt, Grenville opposed disarmament but was a strong supporter of emancipation. Fox, however, supported both the policy of disarmament and that of emancipation. Numbers, as well as policy, hindered unity. In a House of Commons of 658 after the Act of Union, the Court and Treasury group of slightly over 200 was not a sufficient basis for government. To achieve a reliable majority several of the political groups needed to unite together and then proceed to give firm leadership to the Court and Treasury group. They also needed to rally the independents, around 70–80 of whom could still be identified in the House of Commons.

Pitt was replaced by the King's first choice, Henry Addington, the Speaker of the House of Commons. Addington patched up a cabinet which included prominent anti-Catholics like Chatham, Eldon, Hawkesbury and Portland and a number of rising politicians, including Castlereagh after 1802, but the ministry stood in awe of Pitt, on whose sufferance it existed for three years.[29] The ministry was not without its achievements. It successfully negotiated the quiet general election of 1802. It passed the Army of Reserve Act of 1803, which produced a modest increase in the number of regular troops, and the Militia Acts of 1802 and 1803, which provided for the raising of 70 000 men for home defence by ballot. Addington had further positive achievements in the sphere of finance, including a 'property tax', really an income tax of 5 per cent on annual incomes of over £150. By the spring of 1804, however, the renewal of war was endangering the government. Addington was no war minister and was already faced with the 'New Opposition' led by Grenville, Pitt's erstwhile foreign minister, and two of Fox's earlier friends, Fitzwilliam and Spencer, all united by their hostility to the Treaty of Amiens. Grenville, in particular, was emerging from Pitt's shadow and advocating the prosecution of the war by a national coalition. Even Fox supported renewing the war against France. He had been sympathetic to the cause of the French Revolution in the 1790s because he imagined its cause to be the cause of liberty. But Napoleon was a bullying imperialist, more interested in conquest than in freedom. In 1804 Fox and Grenville, agreed on their hostility to Addington's peace policy and united by a common belief in Catholic emancipation, negotiated a coalition. At the same time, Pitt withdrew his support for Addington's government. On its collapse in 1804 he returned to office.

Pitt's second and last ministry was to be a tragic disappointment. It coincided with the great invasion scare of 1804–05 and was thus accompanied by a wave of patriotic sentiment. But it had serious political weaknesses. Deprived of Grenville's support, his ministry was no more secure than Addington's had been. Pitt managed to bring Addington back into office in early 1805 as Lord Sidmouth, but this was a doubtful benefit. Indeed, it was Sidmouth's own investigation which revealed the corruption and financial irregularities of which Dundas, now Lord Melville, had been guilty when he had been Treasurer of the Navy. Amidst mounting rumours in 1805, Melville was forced to resign. Pitt was sorely distressed by his loyal colleague's embarrassment. By the end of the year his health was in ruins, and in January 1806 he died. Ill will between the followers of Pitt and those of Addington crippled the prospects of shoring up the government and George III had perforce to find another.

Pitt was succeeded by the 'Ministry of All the Talents', a coalition of Grenville and his group, Fox and his followers and Sidmouth and his friends in which Grenville held the Treasury. The ministry represented a reunion of the older, aristocratic Whigs, such as Spencer and Windham, with Fox and with the newer generation of Foxite Whigs such as Grey and Erskine. The Pittites sat on the opposition benches. The only feasible alternative to the 'Talents', a coalition ministry of the old Pittites and old Addingtonions, was ruled out by Sidmouth himself. The King had no stomach for a repeat of the great constitutional battles of 1783–84 and he quietly allowed Fox to take office. He had no need to worry about the possibility of great political and constitutional changes; the politicians were too divided. The one great reform achieved during the lifetime of the 'Talents', the abolition of the slave trade, was not a government measure. Indeed, the 'Talents' was not a reforming administration at all. The power of Grenville and Sidmouth prevented Fox from actually taking any measures to reduce the influence of the crown, the source of all the nation's ills (as he had been telling the country for over two decades). Fox's promise to make the peace with Napoleon which he had been promising for years stumbled on the obstacle of Napoleon's indifference. William Windham's proposals to recruit soldiers for seven-year periods and to reduce expenditure on the Volunteer regiments were controversial but hardly the stuff of which political reputations were made. In general, the ministry was a great disappointment to the reformers. The 'Talents' were perhaps fortunate that the old Pittite party could not bring itself to go into systematic opposition. Lacking unified leadership – Canning, Castlereagh, Hawkesbury and Perceval all had a claim to Pitt's mantle of leadership – the opposition to the 'Talents' cut a sorry figure. Fox's death in September 1806 was a terrible blow, and weakened the ministry in the Commons. More seriously, the government's decision to make some concessions to the newly formed Catholic Association in Ireland was an understandable attempt to head off serious discontent in Ireland, but it fell foul of the King. At first, the government gave the impression that only the lower appointments in the army would be opened to Catholics, but then it appeared to extend the privilege up to the rank of general. This the King could just about stomach. But when he realized that the government wished to extend these provisions to the navy he was implacable. Concerned that the ministers were threatening his freedom to act consistently with the promise in his Coronation Oath to maintain the Protestant Religion, and strengthened in his views by the opinions of Sidmouth, he demanded that the ministers promise not to raise the Catholic issue in the future. On their refusal he removed them from office.

The new ministry was led by the Duke of Portland, who had been the victim of the King's advice to the House of Lords in 1783, who had negotiated the coalition with Pitt in 1794 but who had recently conspired with the King to remove the 'Talents'. The new ministry was very similar in its structure to Pitt's second administration: a coalition of groups which looked to Pitt and regarded themselves as his heirs. Its functions were to wage the war with vigour at a time of relentless French success and to unite against the friends of Catholic emancipation. With this latter object in mind, the government dissolved Parliament and at the general election of 1807 were able to win perhaps 50 seats. In the new Parliament, indeed, it carried the Address of Thanks by 350 to 155. Yet the standing of Portland's government was weakened by the revival of radical campaigning in the country and, in particular, was dogged by the disrepute attaching to the Duke of York, who was forced to resign his post of Commander-in-Chief after a scandal involving the sale of military commissions by his mistress. It was also disrupted by the mutual detestation of Canning and Castlereagh, Foreign Secretary and War Secretary respectively, the former constantly scheming for the removal of the latter from the cabinet.

The fatal illness of Portland in September 1809 led to the patching up of a new administration led by Spencer Perceval, but it lacked the support of Canning and Castlereagh, whose bitter feuding had led to a duel between the two.[30] Perceval had been Chancellor of the Exchequer since 1807 and was a leading Commons spokesman for the government. His experience, good sense and personal integrity rendered him an effective, if not an outstanding, leader of the post-Pittite Tory factions. He was nimble enough to accept the principle of J.C. Curwen's bill of 1809 to outlaw the sale of parliamentary seats, and after suffering heavy amendments it became law. Moreover, after the onset of George III's final illness towards the end of 1810, Perceval managed to negotiate the conditional regency which the future George IV was to occupy without bringing the Whigs into office. Imitating Pitt's tactics of 1788–89, he restricted the Regent's right to create peers, to bestow offices in reversion or to grant pensions for at least a year. The Queen, furthermore, was to have custody of the person of the King. Taking advantage of fatal differences between the Prince of Wales on the one hand and Grenville and Grey on the other, Perceval managed to strengthen the ministry by bringing in the groups led by Castlereagh and Sidmouth. In its last months Perceval's government had become the strongest since 1801 and had gone far towards absorbing the Pittite factions into a true Tory ministry, opposed to parliamentary reform and Catholic emancipation. At just that moment, the assassination of Spencer Perceval (in May 1812) precipitated its collapse.

After three weeks of negotiation, essentially the same structure was taken over by Lord Liverpool, who maintained it in power for 15 years. One of its first actions was to repeal the Orders in Council. In 1812 Liverpool dissolved Parliament and strengthened the government's majority by up to 60 at one of the quietest general elections to the unreformed Parliament. Indeed, with military success enhancing its reputation and forging its unity, the government went from strength to strength. In 1814 the government absorbed what was left of Canning's group and, with the solitary exception of Grenville's group, now completed the re-establishment of the old Pittite coalition. Even Grenville, who did not join the ministry until 1821, abandoned the Whigs in 1817.

Secure in the Regent's confidence and enjoying considerable administrative and managerial skills, Liverpool enjoyed a Commons majority of over 100. His dogged pursuit of victory in the war and, later, his hard line towards popular movements attracted the support of the Independent members. That support could not always be taken for granted and Liverpool was often anxious about, not to say obsessed with, the possibility that it might be withheld. In 1816, for example, the House threw out the hated property tax by 238 to 201, a defeat caused by the desertion of 80 government supporters and the abstention of a similar number. Too much should not be made of the political context of this upset. It was a crushing defeat on a particular measure but by no stretch of the imagination a call for a new government. The real significance of the event, however, lies in the mounting role of public opinion, in the shape of over 400 petitions against the tax. Coming so shortly after the repeal of the Orders in Council, the failure of the Liverpool government to renew the property tax stands as a remarkable indication of the increasing attention that politicians were having to give to extra-parliamentary opinion. Liverpool tried thereafter to protect his majority and his policies more carefully, but he suffered no fewer than twenty defeats between 1816 and 1826, three-quarters of them on major issues.

There was talent aplenty in Liverpool's cabinet, especially in the later years, when the early promise of talented individuals like Peel was beginning to mature.[31] Liverpool kept the government together and managed its (often prickly) individuals with tact and patience, but it cannot really be said that he welded it into a coherent force. In the earlier years there was also considerable dead wood in Liverpool's cabinet. Many of the heavyweights of the ministry, like Sidmouth, Wellington and, of course, Liverpool himself, sat in the House of Lords. The government was in somewhat less reliable hands in the Commons, where the responsibility of defending the ministry fell on Castlereagh, who was leader of the House of Commons as well as Foreign Secretary. Neither a popular nor a charismatic individual, Castlereagh at least had the weight to impress the Commons and convey the impression of solid, responsible government. Liverpool was neither an inventive nor an original politician but he certainly did not deserve Disraeli's description of him as an 'arch mediocrity' nor of his government as a 'government of departments'. No 'arch mediocrity' can stay in power for 15 of the most convulsive years in modern British history. Indeed, Liverpool was fully aware of his place in the Pittite tradition. He was unsympathetic to popular agitation, he was the opponent of radical reform and the defender of Britain's institutions, and he looked to market forces to improve the condition of the masses. Further, he consciously modelled his government's policy towards the radicals on that of Pitt in the 1790s. He was prepared to allow, even to encourage, local propertied men to pursue radicals in the name of loyalism as Pitt had in 1792–93; he was willing to appoint Committees of Secrecy to pursue their one-sided 'inquiries' into the existence. of treasonable plots as Pitt had in 1794; in the end, he was ready to use the powers of statute against radicals and to enable magistrates to license public meetings, as Pitt had done in 1795. The Six Acts of November 1819 regulated the holding of public meetings, encouraged magistrates to search for arms, increased the stamp duty on newspapers and tightened the law against seditious publications.

In economic policy, too, Liverpool consciously modelled himself on Pittite precedents, adopting his policy of encouraging commerce and industry whilst protecting the landed interest. There is little evidence that the ministry entered a 'liberal' phase in the early 1820s. It had always been a liberal government in its pursuit of commerce and free markets, but the financial consequences of the war dominated everything in the early years of the ministry. In the early years, no less than 80 per cent of government income was swallowed by national debt repayments and a further 11 per cent in other fixed charges (such as war pensions). Liverpool had very little room for manoeuvre with expenditure when the government controlled only 9 per cent of the monies available to it. Worse, government *expenditure* was running at £13 million a year over its income. The 1819 budget announced a plan for a staged return to the gold standard while interim deficits were to be mainly financed out of the sinking fund. In the long term, increased yield from indirect taxes like the excise would have to bridge the gap between income and expenditure. Such increased yields could only result from a higher level of economic growth which, in turn, could best be achieved by the stimulation of commerce and consumption and thus the lowering of tariffs. His great 'free trade' speech of 1820 outlined Liverpool's economic ambitions. Like Pitt, he looked to a greater liberalization of trade but not to free trade as an end in itself. Indeed, there was little general demand for free trade in the mercantile community at this time and Liverpool was willing to raise tariffs when necessary, as he did that on wool in the years 1815–22.

The government's repressive policy towards popular agitation has received massive condemnation from historians in the past, touched by the pitiful plight of many sections of the labouring poor. More recent historians, however, have been struck less by the callousness of the Liverpool government's approach than by its uncertainty and by the fact that it was motivated by a mixture of considerations.[32] Like Pitt in the 1790s, Liverpool wished to uphold strong government, not to establish a legal tyranny. He was very much aware of the need to set an example to the propertied classes and to respond to their fears and anxieties. He wished to act with firmness but did not wish to make martyrs out of the reformers. The Six Acts were intended to deter reformers from agitation, but the legislation was enforced with some restraint. Indeed, it was very little used. Its real function was to rally the propertied classes, to encourage local justices to exercise vigilance and to satisfy parliamentary opinion. Furthermore, it would be a mistake to draw too many comparisons with the repressive legislation of the 1790s, because there were at least three notable differences. The first, obviously, is that the country was no longer at war, and it follows that the tactic of labelling all reformers as traitors was no longer credible. The second is that while conservative opinion was, of course, horrified at the mass rallies organized by the reformers in the years after 1815 there was nothing equivalent to the witch-hunting hysteria of, say, the winter of 1792–93. The Seditious Meetings Act of 1817 was not the action of a panic-stricken government; it was that of a government which naturally wished to uphold the traditional social hierarchies and to defend them against the attacks of popular agitators. Third, Liverpool had fewer resources with which to maintain law and order than Pitt had enjoyed. The armed forces and the Volunteer regiments had been hugely reduced. It was simply not in the power of central government to patrol the country. Peterloo, after all, had occurred because of the miscalculations of the *local* yeomanry.

If the reaction of Liverpool's government to the challenge of popular unrest vividly illustrates both its social objectives and its political limitations, then the same issue reveals the dilemmas and confusions in the Whig party, which was led by Grey after the death of Fox. Most of the party followed Grey's cautious lead in opposing the suspension of habeas corpus while accepting the principle of the Seditious Meetings Bill of 1817. The opposition was anxious to support legitimate public complaints against the high-handedness of the executive while opposing violent and revolutionary activity. Even this moderate position was too much for Grenville, who abandoned his coalition with Grey in the same year. It was just as well that he did, for he would have been horrified at the Whigs' response to Peterloo and its aftermath. They leapt to the defence of popular liberties in their savage denunciations of the Six Acts. Buoyed up with the support of public opinion, they continued to play the popular card during the Caroline agitation in 1820. Initially, the Whigs took up her case with some reluctance, finding the matter distasteful. Yet, Brougham, who had done so much to nail the party's colours to the mast of the Queen's cause, vividly hinted at the party's ultimate motive by noting that she was 'a Constitutional means of making head against a revenue of 105 millions, an army of half a million, and 800 millions of debt'.[33] In short, Caroline became a sort of reversionary interest which the Whig party was prepared to use against the King, as they had used him against his father many years before. Here, as elsewhere, eighteenth-century patterns of politics were recurring amidst social and political conditions, not least the rising power of the press and of public opinion, that belonged to a different age. The Whig opposition was capable, on certain carefully chosen occasions, of energetic and effective action in carrying the political battle beyond Westminster, as it had done in helping to secure the repeal of the Orders in Council in 1812 and in creating the climate of opinion in which the property tax was abandoned in 1816. It was not, however, willing to adopt parliamentary reform as an immediate objective. The principle that Grey pursued was that the party should not bring the issue forward until public opinion had become favourable to the measure. In many respects the aristocratic leaders of the party were suspicious of extra-parliamentary opinion which they could neither effectively control nor easily influence. Furthermore, sheer indolence played its part. Grey, in particular, preferred the sheltered life of his own estate to the invigorating and boisterous world of extra-parliamentary politics. Finally, deference to Grenville and his friends and their reluctance to offend an increasingly reactionary heir to the throne for many years inhibited their handling of the reform issue. It did not, however, stop their followers from raising it. In March 1809 Samuel Whitbread tried to commit his party to a policy of reform, and in May 1810 Thomas Brand's motion for a moderate reform attracted a fairly respectable 115 votes, against a majority of 234.[34] This was all very well, but it effectively gave the Whig party the worst of both worlds. Such motions horrified conservative opinion while failing to impress extra-parliamentary radicals.

While the Whig party was uneasy and sometimes unconvincing on such issues, it could be frivolous and even irresponsible on others. Constant criticism of the war policy of the ministry lent a factious appearance, while continued attachment to the old Foxite policy of peace on the part of several of its members did them no good with the public whatsoever. In February 1808 Whitbread lost a motion for peace by 253 to 108. Grenville was aghast at these pacific tendencies within the Whig party. His group wanted the overthrow of Napoleon and war to the death against France. Grey and his friends preferred the old Foxite formula of non-intervention in the internal political arrangements of other states. Somehow, they managed to stumble on to the end of the war without making their differences the subject of excessive public embarrassment.

It was during these years that the party and the heir to the throne began to drift apart. The watershed was the 'Talents' ministry, when the Prince resented what he took to be the ministers' neglect of him. Grenville, in particular, disliked and distrusted him and was unwilling to fawn over him. After the death of Fox relations between the Whig party and the heir were never the same. Consequently, the Whigs were unable to take advantage of no fewer than four opportunities to enter governments between 1809 and 1812. The events of 1782, 1783, 1792–94 and 1806–07, and the mythology to which they had given rise, had taught the Whigs that they should never again be victims of the court; that, therefore, they should only serve in a completely new administration; that the old one must be declared to be at an end; and that they should have ultimate control over men and measures in the new one. Thus, on the fall of Portland's ministry in 1809 the Whigs were invited to participate in 'an extended and combined administration'. Grey was unwilling to shore up the existing ministerial structure, refusing to have anything to do with men who, in his opinion, had ruined the country in recent years. The second occasion came early in 1811 with the final illness of George III and the establishment of the Regency. The Whig leaders were concerned at the influence of Lord Moira and Sheridan[35] in the counsels of the Prince, and demanded assurances about their position in a future government. On this rock the negotiations foundered, and the Prince decided against a change of administration. A further attempt to bring the Whigs into the ministry in 1812 arose out of the Regent's detestation of Perceval and his desire for a broad-bottom administration. This, too, came to nothing because the Whigs resented the prospect of being junior partners in the new arrangement and because they advocated measures, particularly in Ireland, with which the Regent could not agree. Finally, in the political vacuum which followed the assassination of Perceval the Whigs, yet again, had an opportunity to play a part in a new administration, but they were offered only four cabinet places out of 12, the others going to men over whom they had no influence and whose measures they might not approve. Believing that it was better to enjoy freedom of movement than to compromise themselves, as they had in the past, by entering arrangements with which they were in less than total sympathy, they decided to remain in opposition.

The Whig party, then, stranded in a semi-permanent opposition partly of its own making, occupied a political ground separate from that of the radicals in Parliament but distinct also from that of the government. Members of the Whig party shared many of the social and economic assumptions of the Liverpool ministry – Grey, for example, supported the Corn Law of 1815 – but their hostility to its repressive policy, their belief in Catholic emancipation and their (admittedly unenthusiastic) support for parliamentary reform gave them a coherent identity as the heirs of the Foxite Whigs. Their numbers held steady between 1807 and 1818 at about 150, until the general election of 1818 brought them about 30 gains. Like all oppositions in the unreformed Parliament, however, they had little chance of defeating the existing administration. They were capable of appealing to the people, embarrassing the ministry in debate and even, occasionally, defeating a ministerial measure. Even if they had been able to overthrow the government, there existed no legitimate constitutional mechanism by which they might have forced themselves on the King. They had perforce to wait on events outside their own control to bring about their return to office: for the succession of a new monarch, perhaps for disastrous military defeat in some undeclared war or, conceivably, for some distant convulsion in public opinion.

The avoidance of revolution, 1789–1820

Just before the fall of the Bastille an English aristocrat in France mused upon the confusing scene before him, which included 'the poor's need to plunder because not provided for, ladies not daring to live in the country, evasion of taxes, enclosure of common land, venal corporations, trade and manufacturing overstrained, bankruptcies in every town, laws unenforceable being multiplied beyond comprehension'.[36] He was not talking about France; he was talking about England. To what extent did Britain come close to revolution during the long and dangerous period from the outbreak of the French Revolution to that of Peterloo? After all, many regimes in Europe were overthrown, numerous ruling houses were expelled and the map of the Continent was drastically redrawn in these years. We tend to forget that in 1789 a revolution seemed just as likely to break out in England, where the bitter political battles of 1782–84 and 1788–89 had indicated something approaching constitutional breakdown, as in France, which seemed to be well on the way to achieving some measure of peaceful reform of its finances and institutions. There was nothing inevitable about Britain's avoidance of revolution. Indeed, Britain did come very close to revolution, as the Irish uprising of 1798 reminds us.

In what precisely did the threat of revolution consist? Simply stated, the threat lay in the strains of over two decades of war, which coincided with unsettling and sometimes dangerous political situations and economic crisis. Chronologically, there were a number of occasions when the regime found itself in difficulties. First in 1792–93 the expansionism of France, the execution of Louis XVI and the approach of war created a security crisis and an atmosphere of something near panic. Second, in 1794–96 a subsistence crisis coincided with an upsurge in popular radicalism, with military defeat and with widespread hardship and popular rioting. Third, in 1797–98 naval mutinies were a precursor to further military defeat, attempted French invasions and, finally, the Irish uprising of 1798. Fourth, in 1799–1801 yet further military defeat coincided with a serious crisis of subsistence, precipitated by the harvest failure of 1799, and with the political crisis of the fall of Pitt. Fifth, in 1811–12 the Orders in Council and the Continental System caused an economic crisis, accompanied by an upsurge of machine-breaking known as Luddism. Finally, the return to peace in 1815 inaugurated a period of almost constant uncertainty, economic hardship, radical mobilization and popular unrest which lasted down to 1821. Three basic issues intersect at the above junctures of crisis: the strains of war, the pain of widespread economic hardship and the challenge of popular reform.

For many periods in the years of its long duration, the war against France was dramatically unsuccessful and thus bitterly hated, most spectacularly in 1793–94, 1795–96, during the invasion scare of 1797 and in 1799–1801. At such periods Pitt's government plumbed the depths of unpopularity and public contempt. His military failures and the severe taxation which was necessary for the continued prosecution of the war hit the middling as well as the lower orders. If the French Revolutionary and Napoleonic wars were not total wars as the twentieth century has come to experience them, they penetrated more deeply and more comprehensively into the experiences of the nation than any previous wars had done.

Moreover, Britain had to endure economic hardship on a scale that had not been known during the eighteenth century. The grain crisis of 1795 led to a 70 per cent increase in the price of wheat compared to 1791, to trade depression, to unemployment and to a rash of strikes which raised the temperature of radical agitation and fed the huge outdoor meetings of that year. The ugly public mood which was seen in the mobbing of the King in October 1795 led to the passing of the Two Acts. The grain crisis of 1800 was even more threatening in its consequences. Extensive food shortages and a severe trade depression led to unemployment, riots and strikes. It was noticeable that the authorities were reluctant to enforce maximum price regulations, a failure which led to disorder in London, Nottingham and Oxford. It was against this dangerous background that the Despard conspiracy was played out. Finally, any prospect that the return of peace in 1815 would remove the threat of revolution was dashed by the speed with which the artificial stimulus to the economy lent by the war was removed. Although the worrying possibility of international conspiracy did not exist after 1815 there remained, nevertheless, massive distress and unemployment allied to popular radical agitation, sometimes of a republican and revolutionary character.

On top of all this, the country was faced with an ideologically advanced radical challenge to the regime which derived in part from the French Revolution and in part from British philosophical and religious traditions. This radical movement was well organized, well patronized, articulate and capable of appealing to all classes of society. The writings of Paine aroused enormous excitement among the lower and middle classes and consequently created apprehensions for the security of property and the possibility of social upheaval. Interacting with the results of military failure and the social and economic hardship caused by harvest failure in the middle of the decade, the movement was driven underground. It could not, however, be eradicated. There followed after 1797 an extra-parliamentary radical challenge of unprecedented danger, as both Marianne Elliott and Roger Wells have recently shown, through an Anglo-Irish revolutionary conspiracy which in the later 1790s was closely linked into French invasion plans.[37]

How might a revolutionary situation have emerged from these conditions? There can be no question of the vulnerability of the regime. It did not possess national policing agencies, and the deference and respect which protected it came under severe strain on many occasions. As always, London, in particular, was potentially a weakness, as had been shown during the Wilkite disturbances and again during the Gordon Riots. A mounting sense of vulnerability was responsible both for that apocalyptic mood which occasionally swept over some sections of the reform movement in the 1790s and for that sense of impending panic which spread among the propertied classes, and which continued among them until the 1820s. That there were good reasons for their fears can be shown by the naval mutinies of 1797 and the Irish uprising of 1798. But it can also be seen in the occasional unreliability of the Volunteers at moments of local crisis and even, on some occasions, by instances of disloyalty among the militia and the regular army. Militiamen and soldiers were reluctant to turn their rifles on the people, and there are examples of desertion from and disobedience in their ranks. The vulnerability of the regime was further emphasized by the countless demonstrations of little less than hatred of the authorities, of the war and, on occasion, of the King, by the willingness of so many reformers to take to the streets and by the need to shore up ephemeral loyalist sentiment with the power of statute. Everything suggests that the mass of British public opinion was volatile, capable of being aroused and stirred by one side or the other.

A revolution might have occurred in Britain as a result of external or of internal forces or some combination of the two. At its simplest, could the regime defend itself against a domestic insurrection at the same time as it was conducting the war against France in theatres in Europe and all over the globe and, perhaps, while Ireland was unreliable and diverting yet more British troops from home defence? The crucial issue was the likelihood of a French invasion. Had the French launched a successful invasion, a number of serious possibilities would have opened up: divisions within the ruling order, the emergence of collaborationism, the disintegration of the army, the dissolution of the militia and, conceivably, a run on the banks – any of these would have had devastating consequences for the Hanoverian regime. However, a successful invasion was most unlikely. Britain had command of the seas. Even if an invasion force had landed successfully in this period it would probably have received even less support than the Jacobite invasions of 1715 and 1745 had done, in England, at least. There was one further crucial difference. George I and George II had not dared to arm their peoples because of their dynastic insecurity. In the 1790s George III and his government were quite prepared to arm the Volunteers. At the very least, a French invasion in the 1790s would have had a very different military reception from that of the leisurely Dutch invasion of 1688–89.

What were the prospects of a purely internal collapse? Some of the sources for mass protest and a mass rising undoubtedly existed: serious economic distress, outspoken public criticism of the regime and organized street demonstrations. Yet an uprising would have been unlikely to occur without united political leadership. There was never much concord among the different radical groups at any time and the 'liberal' aristocracy, under Fox, had no stomach for a *coup d'état*. Fox, of course, was no democrat and boasted that he had not even read the second – and more notoriously radical – part of *The Rights of Man*. Moreover, there is no sign that the armed forces were likely to defect. The naval mutinies of 1797 were an alarming glimpse of what could happen when political disaffection (in the shape of the United Irishmen) combined with inadequate pay and economic grievances. However, as events showed, the elimination of the latter liquidated the threat of the former. The Despard conspiracy revealed only a handful of disaffected soldiers in one Guards regiment. Furthermore, all the military plots from Despard to Cato Street had the objective of a sudden strike on the capital. If their first strike had been successful, what would the rebels have done next? Would they have had the resources actually to take over the government, to say nothing of the physical agencies of the state?

Indeed, no revolutionary conspiracy worth the name existed in the first half of the 1790s. The government and the propertied orders were too vigilant, being particularly alarmed at the rather eccentric behaviour which became popular among some radicals in the early 1790s, who revelled in French names, habits and manners. Yet they need not have worried. Almost all the reforming societies hated violence and renounced revolution. Indeed, French revolutionary ideology was of much less relevance to reform in the 1790s than traditions of native reformism. English reformers wished to restore the virtues of their old constitution, not establish a new one. Many of them had found the work of Paine inspirational in 1791 and 1792, but thereafter Painite influence is much more difficult to trace in the broad mainstream of radical reform. To some extent this was a consequence of the demonization of Paine in 1792–93, when something resembling a witch-hunt for Painite opinions was launched. More likely, however, it was a consequence of the inherent moderation of the native reform movement itself, its non-insurrectionary traditions and its ultimate repudiation of republican influences.

In the second half of the 1790s there was a revolutionary fringe to the reform movement, particularly that associated with the United Irishmen, but it was not numerically extensive (nor could it be if the secrecy necessary for its effectiveness were to be maintained and if it relied for its success upon collaboration with France). Those involved in the plots of 1797–1802 were preoccupied with their own manoeuvres; they lacked any understanding of the broader organizational means by which different regions of the country might be synchronized into common support of the plots. This was painfully apparent in Ireland during the 1798 uprising. Just when the threat of revolution did appear, the radical movement had lost the bulk of such mass appeal as it had ever had. Popular hostility to Pitt, to the war and, indeed, to the regime existed in the 1790s. Such hostility did not, however, coincide with, and could not be drawn into, support for conspiracy with the United Irishmen and plots of a French invasion.

After the ending of the war radical protest assumed momentous proportions and was far more extensive than anything that had been seen hitherto.
Not only were the sheer numbers mobilized infinitely greater than had been
the case in the 1790s. Protestors evinced a greater readiness to take to the
streets and to indulge in direct action. The number of conspiracies, marches
and risings speaks for itself. Nevertheless, the mainstream reformers like
Cartwright, Cobbett and even Hunt did not advocate political violence.
Those who did, men like Thistlewood, remained on the fringes. They lacked
any sort of national organization and the resources with which to develop it.
The real threat of revolution in these years appears to have existed chiefly in
the mind of the governing classes. The reports of the Committees of Secrecy
presented to Parliament in February 1817 (like those of 1794, 1799, 1801 and
1812) lumped together every conceivable expression of discontent into a
gigantic radical conspiracy to organize a revolution. But it remained nothing
more than an alarmist's nightmare. The carelessness of some radicals and the
ability of some reformers to drift into the radical underworld of secret meetings and assemblies should not be taken as a commitment to the systematic
and violent overthrow of the existing social order.

On none of these occasions did the governments of Pitt and Liverpool
either lose their nerve or fail to take measured action in support of their
authority. Although their actions, whether the imprisonment of radicals, the
passing of 'repressive' legislation, the encouragement of extra-parliamentary
loyalism or the establishment of spy networks, can be, and were, criticized as
being either too harsh or too lenient, the fact remains that there was never a
vacuum of authority. The regime was neither too weak to permit the unrestricted advance of popular hostility to the regime, its representatives and its
institutions, nor too authoritarian to drive reformers to arms. Both the forms
and the practices of parliamentary government were maintained. Even when
the legal system was drawn into service on behalf of the government, it
quickly became apparent that there were legal and political limits to what the
government could do.

The mobilization of patriotic opinion in these years is just as important as
the essential moderation of radical groups in explaining how Britain avoided
revolution. Patriotism, hatred of the French, fear of the French Revolution –
all of these sentiments created a rising tide of loyalty which served to inocu-
late people's minds against the wilder assertions of radical spokesmen.
Particularly, but not only, in 1792–94, in 1804–5 and in 1817–18, the country
was swept by recurrent outbursts of loyalist sentiment. As historians have
pointed out, the number of loyalists far exceeded the membership of the
reforming societies. This may have been the case, but the membership of
patriotic societies in the 1790s does seem to have been particularly unstable
and, arguably, unreliable. (The Pitt clubs that proliferated rapidly after the
death of the great statesman in 1806 were much more permanent structures
than the earlier loyal associations.) Nevertheless, the importance of such bodies lies not merely in their numerical strength but in the fact that they acted as
triggers for latent patriotic sentiment, acting both to support the government
of the day and to rally loyal opinion around the monarchy and the church.

In Britain, unlike France, the ruling elite did not lose its unity either before
or after 1789. In France an 'aristocratic revolt' (1787–89) acted as a precursor to

the French Revolution. In Britain this did not happen. This achievement is frequently underestimated. In view of the great political divisions within the landed classes in the 1760s, between 1782–84 and in 1788–89 there was certainly nothing inevitable about it. Pitt was always anxious to maintain political cohesion among the ruling class. His anxiety to conclude a coalition with the Portland Whigs can be interpreted in narrow terms of party competition and partisan advantage, but it may also have proceeded from his desire to maintain social and political unity. It is at this point that the positioning of the Foxite Whigs within the regime becomes of crucial significance. As Ian Christie has perceptively noted, 'the Opposition could not give whole-hearted loyalty to the system within which they were operating'[38] because the strength of their belief in secret influence disabled them from admitting the legitimacy of the regime. No wonder there were doubts about Fox's loyalty. Did the Foxite Whigs secede from Parliament in 1797 in order to keep their distance from the Pittite regime? It is an intriguing speculation, albeit one that cannot be verified by the existing evidence. On the other hand, the reluctance of the Foxite Whigs to rally to the ranks of the poor and the under-privileged is a negative fact of some significance. Although they opposed Pitt's repressive policy the Foxites in the end were unable to resist it. The power of the state that was mobilized in the 1790s was unprecedented. The attacks on habeas corpus, freedom of speech and freedom of assembly were merely the official set themes to a counterpoint of informal aggression directed against reformers, dissenters and radicals at local level by the local magistracy. The Foxite Whigs were, and wished to be, involved in as little of this as possible.

Political consolidation was matched by social consolidation. The social and propertied elite closed its ranks, in the loyal associations, in the army and navy, in the Volunteer regiments, on the bench, in the professions, in local and national voluntary and charitable bodies and, of course, in the church. E.P. Thompson has argued that the aristocracy were likely to have been confronted by a bourgeois challenge had the war not strengthened their position.[39] Nothing could be further from the truth. As I shall argue in Chapter 10, until the second decade of the nineteenth century there was little sign of any desire among the middling orders to displace the aristocracy, every sign of their wish to join them. Political unity and social consolidation were accompanied by forms of economic response to the problems of the masses which served to safeguard the regime. The doubling of some food prices within less than two years in the middle of the 1790s created enormous pressure on resources, giving rise to terrible human distress. It was the operation of the Poor Law which did much to stabilize and perhaps to save the situation. In 1795 the Berkshire magistrates sitting at Newbury, following precedents elsewhere, laid down that a labourer's wages should be supplemented out of the parish rate to an extent depending upon the price of bread. Furthermore, he should receive an allowance for his wife and each child. This humane set of decisions was furiously denounced by conservatives. Burke, in his flinty *Thoughts and Details on Scarcity* (1797) somehow managed to convince himself that magistrates should not interfere with the operations of the free market, whose principles were equivalent to 'the laws of God'. Had people listened to Burke it is likely that the countryside and towns might have been terrorized by roaming bands of starving vagrants. What saved the situation, however, was not merely the Poor Law – in 1802–03, according to one return to Parliament, no less than 90 per cent of those dependent on the Poor Law were also in receipt of outdoor relief – but, what is not to be underestimated, an immense expansion in private charity and relief. In 1795–96 the poor received more money in charitable gifts than they did from the Poor Law. In 1796, indeed, some evangelicals even founded the Society for Bettering the Condition and Increasing the Comforts of the Poor, a body which proceeded to distribute cheap food and handy recipes while founding soup kitchens and subsidizing village shops.

The avoidance of revolution in Britain has been recently attributed to the fact that the conservatives had the best of the political argument.[40] It is true that the writings of Paley, Burke and Hannah More laid out the conservative case with clarity, weight and wit, but it is not obvious that their writings were superior to some of the greatest reforming literature in British history. Unless there exists a set of agreed external criteria by which it can be rationally demonstrated that, for example, Burke had the better of the argument against Price or Paine or Thelwall or Wollstonecraft or Godwin or Spence, it does not seem that superiority on either side can be established beyond dispute. Nevertheless, the ready availability of conservative literature may have helped to steady the intellectual support of the regime. Long before Burke pronounced his classic vindication of the regime in *Reflections on the Revolution in France* other writers had ventured their own defences of the existing system. The arguments in favour of the status quo were already in place by 1790. A natural process of simplification encouraged an enormous outpouring of popular literature designed to safeguard the labouring orders from sedition. Hannah More's twopenny 'Repository Tracts' had a wide circulation: in 1795, at their height, 300 000 copies were sold or distributed free. How much notice was taken of such literature is impossible to measure but it may have had some effect, convincing humble people that, whatever their deficiencies, the institutions with which they were familiar worked reasonably well and had weighty justifications. They may have been persuaded that to imitate the French Revolution would have been dangerous as well as ungodly, and that deference brought its own blessings. Indeed, the loyalists may have been more adept than their radical counterparts at speaking and writing simply and clearly to humble people. Much radical literature went over the heads of the masses. Much of it was intellectually demanding; little of it is strikingly popular. Even Paine, about whose popularity with the lower orders much is often assumed, is likely to have been too taxing for them. Furthermore, few radical writers – Paine and Thelwall are among the exceptions – actually had anything in the slightest degree realistic to suggest about the cure for poverty. Most radicals, of course, wanted to weaken rather than to strengthen the state. Most would have been horrified at the suggestion of a welfare state funded through taxation and manned by a benevolent bureaucracy.

Such propaganda was underwritten by renewed religious pressures towards social discipline and conformity. These were years not only of Anglican recovery and revitalization but of Methodist revival in places as far apart as Lancashire and Cornwall. The Anglican church played a prominent part in promoting discipline and patriotic loyalty during the difficult years of war and poverty. But it would be unwise to exaggerate the influence of a church whose hold on the mass of the people was by no means complete. The Methodists actively rivalled the Anglicans in their anxiety to tranquillize the masses. Although it used to be suggested that Methodism was a catalyst of protest and a vehicle of class formation, historians as distinct as Halevy and E.P. Thompson, however, have seen in Methodism a mechanism of social control.[41] In the 1790s, at least, it was official Methodism that denounced agitation. In 1792 the statutes of the Methodist body identified respect for the monarchy and support for the government with the law of God. In the early nineteenth century the issue is much less clear-cut. During the Caroline agitation, however, official Methodism was on the side of the government. To summarize, then, this discussion of Britain's avoidance of revolution between 1789 and 1815: the extent of hardship was very great, the materials for revolution very limited. Support for a revolution, both external and internal, was marginal. The mass of reformers were moderate, the radical leadership divided and the forces of unity strong, and arguably getting stronger. Governments kept their nerve and did not fall into the error of relying upon force alone. In 1820 Britain emerged from the threat of revolution in many ways stronger than she had been in 1789. She had endured the ordeals to which she had been subjected without endorsing reforming ideologies of any sort, without parliamentary reform and, in Ireland, without Catholic emancipation. Indeed, the only change to the structure of the state was the Act of Union with Ireland of 1800. The crisis had been weathered with the existing political and social system intact. Indeed, it could then be argued that the crisis had been weathered *because* Britain had made no great structural changes and because she had maintained the existing political and social system. The avoidance of revolution thus reinforced the legitimacy of the *status quo*.

Notes

1. William Wyndham, Lord Grenville, (1759–1834), youngest son of George Grenville, Speaker of the House of Commons 1789, Home Secretary, 1789–90, Foreign Secretary, 1791–1801; leader of the war party in the government and its leading spokesman in the House of Lords.
2. Napoleon Bonaparte (1769–1821) entered the French army in 1785, and through his great victories in the north of Italy in 1796 established his reputation as the first great general of the French republican armies. He took a prominent role in dictating peace terms to the Austrians at Campo Formio.
3. The Directory was the name given to the executive power in France, 1795–99. There were five directors jointly responsible for the conduct of affairs.
4. See the accounts in A. Bryant, *The Age of Endurance, 1793–1802* (1944), pp.256–7; J. Holland Rose, *William Pitt and the Great War* (1911).
5. P. O'Brien, 'Public Finance in the Wars with France, 1793–1815', in H. Dickinson, ed., *Britain and the French Revolution* (1989); 'The Political Economy of British Taxation, 1660–1815', *Economic History Review*, 41 (1988).
6. In the first Partition in 1772 Poland lost half of its population and 30 per cent of its territory to Austria, Prussia and Russia. The second Partition (1793) was mostly to the advantage of Russia. In 1794 a Polish rebellion led to the final share-out of the spoils in the third Partition (October 1795), which removed Poland from the map altogether.

7. It is often assumed that this tradition owes much to E.P. Thompson, *The Making of the English Working Class* (1963), G. Williams, *Artisans and Sans-Culottes* (1968) and H. Perkins, *The Origins of Modern English Society* (1969). It is, of course, much older, going back to P.A. Brown, *The French Revolution in English History* (1918) and W. Laprade, *England and the French Revolution* (1909). It was effectively repopularized in S. Maccoby, *English Radicalism, 1762–85* (1955) and A. Briggs, *The Age of Improvement* (1959) in the decade before the publication of Thompson's great work.

8. Edward Thompson remarked that 'they resemble less the Jacobins than the sans-culotte of the Paris "sections", whose zealous egalitarianism underpinned Robespierre's revolutionary war dictatorship of 1793–4'; *The Making of the English Working Class*, pp. 171–2.

9. J.A. Cannon, *Parliamentary Reform: 1640–1832* (1972), p. 121.

10. Hannah More (1745–1833) was perhaps the most influential loyalist writer both before and after the 1790s. Her 'Cheap Repository Tracts' (1795–98) are reputed to have enjoyed a circulation of 2 million.

11. John Horne Tooke (1736–1812) had begun his radical career in the Wilkite groups in London, continued it in opposing the American war and was a founder member of the SCI in 1781. Like Cartwright, Tooke believed in an idealized ancient constitution, now enfeebled through corruption. John Thelwall (1764–1834) began his radical career in close alliance with Tooke and was involved in the founding of the London Corresponding Society.

12. Thomas Erskine (1750–1823) was a close friend of Fox and Sheridan and a regular defender of radicals. He was frequently on good terms with the Prince of Wales and manifested an intense dislike of Pitt.

13. Francis Place (1771–1854) was the 'radical tailor of Charing Cross' who joined the LCS in 1794 and served as chairman of its general committee until 1797.

14. Major John Cartwright (1740–1824), the 'Father of Reform', had an incredibly long radical career in which he never wavered from the principles expressed in his greatest work, *Take Your Choice* (1776): manhood suffrage, annual Parliaments and secret ballots. His radicalism was narrowly political, overwhelmingly patriotic and much less populist than that of Paine and others. Capel Lofft (1751–1824) moved in the same radical and Whig circles, opposed the American war and called for the repeal of the Test and Corporation Acts.

15. Sir Francis Burdett (1770–1844) was an eminent landowner but represented Westminster from 1807 to 1837. Like Cartwright and Tooke, he looked back to a golden age of popular freedom, and he was a somewhat unlikely leader of the small radical group in Parliament in the early nineteenth century.

16. William Cobbett (1763–1835) was a romantic radical, an ex-Tory who looked back with nostalgia to a pre-industrial utopia. His *Political Register* (1802–35) appealed to popular audiences, clamoured for parliamentary reform and denounced the corruption of the establishment.

17. Henry 'Orator' Hunt (1773–1835), a patriotic landed gentleman who became the greatest agitator of the early decades of the nineteenth century. He drifted into the circle around Place, Tooke and Hardy. Eccentric and egotistical, he nevertheless achieved national eminence in the years after 1815.

18. Henry, Lord Brougham (1778–1868), an eminent lawyer who was accepted into the Prince Regent's circle. A great opponent of slavery and a champion of public education, he led the cause of Queen Caroline in 1820.

19. Ten years after his illegal marriage with Mrs Fitzherbert, the Prince of Wales had married Princess Caroline of Brunswick Wolfenbüttel. Their relationship did not prosper, the Queen went abroad and the Prince wished to divorce her. In 1806 he persuaded the government to launch an inquiry into her much-publicized personal life while abroad, but the case against her was not proven. After 1815, when

the Regent's health was not good, there was some possibility that his daughter Princess Charlotte might succeed to the throne. The Whigs, Brougham in particular, adopted the Queen's cause. The death of Charlotte in 1817 reduced Caroline's value to them, but it did not eliminate it altogether.

20. Sir John Pitt, 2nd Earl of Chatham (1756–1835), First Lord of the Admiralty, 1788–94, Lord Privy seal 1794–96 and President of the Council, 1796–1801.

21. Henry Dundas, 1st Viscount Melville (1742–1811) had been Treasurer of the Navy since 1783 and was a Commissioner of the Board of Control after 1786. He was, in effect, minister for Scotland and had, in addition, control of Indian affairs.

22. Francis Osborne, 5th Duke of Leeds, had been ambassador to Paris under Rockingham in 1782 and became Foreign Secretary under Pitt in 1783.

23. The 2nd Earl Fitzwilliam (1748–1833) was Rockingham's nephew and heir, and he strongly embodied Rockingham's principles. He became Lord Lieutenant of Ireland after the Pitt–Portland Coalition of 1794, with tragic and disastrous consequences.

24. Alexander Wedderburn, 1st Baron Loughborough (1733–1805). He had been close to Bute but supported Wilkes before joining North's government in 1771 as Solicitor-general. He became Attorney-general in 1778, and eventually attained his ambition to be Lord Chancellor in 1793.

25. William Windham (1750–1810), a friend of Samuel Johnson and Edmund Burke. MP for Norwich, 1784–1802, he was a conservative Whig who sided strongly with Burke against Fox in 1792–3. He was Secretary at War, 1794–1801.

26. Portland became Home Secretary; Fitzwilliam became Lord President of the Council with a promise of the Irish Vice-Royalty; Lord Spencer became Lord Privy Seal; Lord Mansfield entered the cabinet without portfolio while Windham became Secretary at War.

27. Grey's motion advocated household suffrage, triennial Parliaments, abolition of rotten boroughs and the establishment of more county seats. The motion was lost by 256 to 91.

28. 'Catholic emancipation' was the term given to the policy of freeing Catholics from the disabilities which prevented them from holding offices, voting and serving in Parliament. It was not achieved until 1829.

29. John Scott, 1st Lord Eldon (1751–1839) was an outstanding lawyer but a reactionary conservative. He became Solicitor-general in 1788 and Lord Chancellor in 1801–06 and 1807–27. Robert Banks Jenkinson, 2nd Lord Liverpool (1770–1828), Foreign Secretary under Addington, Home Secretary and leader of the House of Lords in Pitt's second ministry, 1804–06; leader of the opposition to the 'Talents' ministry (1806–07). Robert Stewart Castlereagh (1769–1822), Secretary for Ireland, 1798–1801, Secretary for War and the Colonies, 1805–06, 1807–09; Foreign Secretary, 1812–22.

30. George Canning (1770–1827) came into Parliament in 1794, was Under-Secretary for Foreign Affairs 1796–99, Paymaster 1800–01 and Treasurer of the Navy 1804–06. Canning was Foreign Secretary in Portland's ministry but resigned in 1809. Spencer Perceval (1762–1812) was MP for Northampton, 1796–1812. He was a Pittite but, as Attorney-general under Addington, he defended the government in the Commons against Pitt, Fox and Windham. Chancellor of the Exchequer under Portland. He had difficulty forming his own administration in 1809 because of the enmity between Canning and Castlereagh. Kept in office by the Prince Regent, Spencer Perceval is the only British prime minister to be assassinated.

31. Sir Robert Peel (1788–1850) came into Parliament in 1809; he was Under-Secretary for War and the Colonies, 1810–12, and Chief Secretary for Ireland, 1812–18. He was later to be Home Secretary and Prime Minister.

32. J.E. Cookson, *Lord Liverpool's Administration* (1975), ch. 2; M. Bentley, *Politics Without Democracy, 1815–1914* (1984), pp. 31–46.

33. See F. O'Gorman, *The Emergence of the British Two-Party System* (1982), p. 91.
34. Samuel Whitbread (1758–1815). Whig MP for Bedford (1790–1815) and a Foxite Whig of radical tendencies, he took the lead in the impeachment of Melville. He took a popular line on most issues but was disappointed at not receiving office under the 'Talents' and in not becoming leader of the opposition when Grey went to the Lords in 1807. A moderate parliamentary reformer, Whitbread also took a leading interest in social issues. Thomas Brand (1774–1851), MP for Helston, 1807 and Hertfordshire (1807–19). was an independent Whig and leading reformer.
35. Francis Rawdon-Hastings (1754–1826), 2nd Earl Moira, was a soldier who distinguished himself in the American war. He joined the opposition in 1789 and became a friend of the Prince of Wales. He saw service in Europe in the 1790s but drifted into politics, serving as Master General of the Ordnance in the 'Talents' ministry and defending the interests of the Prince Regent. He was Governor-General of Bengal, 1813–22.
36. I. Gilmour, *Riot, Rising and Revolution: Governance and Violence in Eighteenth Century England* (1992), p. 433.
37. R. Wells, *Insurrection: The British Experience, 1795–1803* (1983); M. Elliot, *Partners in Revolution: The United Irishmen and France* (1982).
38. I.R. Christie, *Stress and Stability in Late Eighteenth Century England: Reflections on the British Avoidance of Revolution* (1984), p. 42.
39. Thompson, *The Making of the English Working Class*.
40. Christie, *Stress and Stability* (1982) pp. 156 ff; H. Dickinson, *Liberty and Property: Political Ideology in Eighteenth-Century Britain* (1979), pp. 270 ff.
41. Thompson, *The Making of the English Working Class*, pp. 40–53, 381–400; E. Halevy, *England in 1815*, 2nd edn (1949), pp. 410–28.

10

State and church in later Hanoverian Britain, 1757–1832

Monarchy and the party system, 1780–1832

During the later Hanoverian period Britain still remained a strongly monarchical state, although the power of particular monarchs went into a serious decline. Government remained the king's government and executive action was an extension of the royal prerogative. Ministers were still responsible to the king rather than to Parliament, party or each other, and executive powers were legally vested in the monarch. In practice, too, the monarchy retained considerable powers. Monarchs could veto policy, as George III did in 1801 and again in 1807, and they could veto ministers, as George IV did in keeping Canning out of the cabinet until 1822. Furthermore, the personal popularity of the monarchy was at its height during the years 1784–1810. George III had achieved levels of popularity during the second half of his reign which would have been the envy of most of his predecessors. It owed much to his standing among the middling orders, his simplicity of mind and manner and the projection of his 'Farmer George' image. Furthermore, he was not identified with any one party. His two predecessors had been closely identified with the Whigs, to the evident distress of Tory opinion. Consequently, during the 1780s the monarchy became a powerful social symbol, a focus of national unity and the object of celebration and festivity.[1]

Yet such arguments should not be taken too far. With the disappearance of George III from view after 1811 and his replacement by the obnoxious Prince Regent, the reputation of the monarchy began to suffer. The pro-Pittite press treated the King with respect but it was Pitt who was idolized, both before and after his death, not the monarch. 'There is very little evidence of any cult of royalty or cult of George III in the eighteenth century right-wing press.'[2] Even the loyalist press could be critical of the monarch, especially at the time of the Caroline scandal in 1820–21. Furthermore, the language of prerogative was in steep decline. As J.J. Sack has concluded: 'It is rare, though not impossible, to find an unqualified assertion of passive obedience and non-resistance in later Georgian England.'[3] There could be no doubt about the indefeasible right of George III and his successors to inherit the throne, but divine right theory was being diluted into a vague assertion of the broader rights of society binding individuals into a commitment to its preservation. In a vague sense it was taken up by later reformers. 'The indefeasible hereditary right of the sovereign was not abandoned by late eighteenth century radicals, but atomised into a possession of all individuals which became known as the rights of man.'[4]

By the early nineteenth century the monarchy no longer occupied the pivotal position in politics which it had formerly enjoyed. The delicacy of George III's health in the last two decades of his reign was responsible for a continuing decline in the political position of the monarch. The King had already shown himself unable to save the ministries of North (1782), Shelburne (1783) and Addington (1804). After the Regency Crisis of 1788–89 he could on some occasions remind the political world that the monarchy could still be a force to be reckoned with, but he could no longer keep continuously abreast of political and military affairs. This deterioration in the political influence of the monarch was emphasized by the indifference to politics of his successor as well as by his great unpopularity in the country. George IV was incapable of reversing this drift of power and influence away from the monarchy. Ministers preoccupied themselves with the business of government, taking for granted the approval of the King on many routine matters, thus continuing to oust him from any involvement in the day-to-day activities of government. George IV shouted and blustered at his ministers and was fond of boasting that he ruled them, but he normally gave way to their inflexible sense of political service.

Furthermore, the long years of war after 1793 diminished royal influence over events. Ministers took the initiative over the complexities of military logistics. Unlike his grandfather, George III was not a military man; the crown increasingly adopted a passive rather than a proactive role. The great decisions taken during the war were those of a small group of ministers, Pitt, Dundas and Grenville, not the King. Even though Pitt the Younger had no party in the 1790s, he was behaving like a prime minister in his determination to centralize power in his own person and to reserve to himself key decisions about the personnel of his cabinet, as he did in 1794 over the Portland coalition. Indeed, by around 1800 it had become an established practice for the crown normally to accept unanimous advice tended by the cabinet. By then, significantly, George III had been complaining for some years that Pitt did not keep him adequately informed, a sure sign of the transfer of power and influence. Even so, the cabinet still lacked a collective sense of responsibility. It was still not customary for ministries to resign *en bloc*. They did so in 1782, 1783, 1806 and 1807, but not in 1801, 1804, 1809, 1812 and 1827. By 1812, however, some sense of collective cabinet responsibility had appeared, and it was to be further developed during Liverpool's long ministry.

Moreover, the patronage and influence once available to the monarch had considerably diminished. On his accession, George III surrendered his hereditary revenues in return for a fixed annual Civil List of £800 000, which inevitably failed to keep its real value. In spite of opposition taunts to the contrary, the value of the resources available to the monarch tended steadily to fall thereafter. Pitt's Civil List Act of 1804 marked the end of the old idea of an independent provision for the crown. Thereafter, the Civil List was funded by and accountable to Parliament. At the same time, the economical reform legislation of 1782 and the steady stream of reforms to the administrative and

fiscal system undertaken by Pitt and later by Liverpool had a slow but cumulative effect. By 1815 the amount of influence available to monarchs and their
ministers was very limited. It was not only the influence of the monarchy
itself but that of the Court and Treasury party which was diminishing.
Ministers found it increasingly difficult to maintain their majorities in
Parliament. In the 1780s it had still been possible to identify about 180 office-
holders in the Commons. By Liverpool's time the number had shrunk to
60–70. Even more serious was the deteriorating position of the crown in the
House of Lords. In spite of occasional reverses there, ministers normally used
the influence of the crown over the peers to support themselves. Yet the party
of the crown in the House of Lords still looked to the monarch for their lead,
as the events of 1783 demonstrated, when George III used his influence to
bring about the defeat of Fox's India Bill. Pitt's peerage creations and the
addition of Irish peers after 1800, however, swamped the party of the crown.
From constituting almost half of the upper chamber in 1800, the party of the
crown accounted for little more than 20 per cent in 1830.[5] Consequently,
Liverpool's government found Parliament difficult to control because it could
no longer depend for its strength upon the distribution of patronage and it
had not yet built up the reliable party majorities of later decades.

By the later eighteenth century the pattern of politics was being fashioned
by party influences; by the decade immediately before the Reform Act it was
being dominated by them. The history of party in this period is particularly
contentious. This was a confusing, sometimes bewildering, period of political, not merely party, development. Contemporaries themselves found it difficult to agree among themselves exactly what the terms 'Whig' and 'Tory'
meant, what the differences between the parties were and what the common
ground was, especially when both parties were changing with some rapidity
and both were capable of multiple identities. It may simplify the discussion
and highlight the relevant issues to approach the problem of party through
the conflicting interpretations of recent historians.[6]

One group of historians argues that in the half-century before the 1832
Reform Bill parties played an insignificant role because the structure of politics did not change markedly between the 1770s and the 1820s.[7] Pitt's government of 1783–1801 did not rest on a party basis any more than North's had.
Like most eighteenth-century governments, Pitt's was chosen by the
monarch and Pitt himself governed on inclusive, national (as opposed to
exclusive, party) grounds. When both monarch and minister were united in
this endeavour, stable government was possible. It was not parties that gave
governments their majorities but the legitimacy that came with royal support, the deployment of royal patronage, the claim of ministerial ability and
the backing of the independent members. In the same way, according to this
version, Fox's opposition was not based on party considerations. It was pragmatic, dependent (as oppositions traditionally were) on the support of the
Prince of Wales. In the Parliaments of 1784 and 1790, moreover, Fox depended
heavily for numerical support upon the non-party Northites, whose political
principles and conduct had been denounced by the Rockingham Whigs for
over a decade. It was the personal rivalry between Pitt and Fox which gave a
superficial resemblance to a two-party system. After 1801, moreover, even
this degree of duality collapsed with the disintegration of Pitt's following.

Furthermore, the parties were not separated by great political issues in the early nineteenth century. The war, the abolition of the slave trade, Catholic emancipation and parliamentary reform cut across government and opposition alike. There was, on this reading, no clear ideological divide between them. The supporters of Pitt's administration, and of those of its immediate successors, did not accept the description 'Tory'. They were Whigs. Pitt may have differed with Fox on certain issues, not least on the role of the monarch in appointing ministers, but he was just as good a Whig as Fox was.

Furthermore, Pitt the Younger did not believe in party. After he fell from power in 1801 he fastidiously refused to organize his friends into a systematic opposition. Pitt never doubted the right of the King to dismiss him in 1801; nor did the vast majority of MPs. He was perfectly relaxed when some of his friends accepted office under Addington; he did not expect them to waste their careers in opposition. It was up to them to seek service with the crown, not to band together in an organized party in order to force themselves upon the monarch. Only after his death in 1806 could Pitt's followers even begin to contemplate behaving as a party. Charles James Fox, on the other hand, had for years been proclaiming the value of acting in a party united in its principles; but it is difficult to see just what united a party that included on the one hand Grenville's supporters and on the other reforming Whigs like Samuel Whitbread. Furthermore, Fox's party remained dangerously dependent for its return to office upon the goodwill of the heir to the throne. Its inability to reach an understanding with him in 1811–12 damned its political prospects for two decades. When the Whigs did return to office in a party ministry in 1830, it was the consequence less of their own initiatives than of the political self-destruction of their opponents.

Finally, a large proportion of MPs did not take a party whip. The Act of Union with Ireland had added 64 more county members, most of whom had little liking for party, to the existing 80–90 independent, English county members. When to these are added the 60–70 court and administration members, who would support any government, it is clear that at least a third of the 658 members of the House of Commons were indifferent to party in the years of Lord Liverpool. Furthermore, so long as most MPs brought themselves into Parliament and did not owe their return to centralized party institutions, they cannot in any valid organizational sense be regarded as party men. Governments in the early nineteenth century were constructed from the pool of Pitt's supporters, together with those acquired by the Portland coalition of 1794. Oppositions were based on the heirs of the old Rockingham party, reinforced by Northites, by Prince of Wales men on some occasions and, for much of the period, by the Grenvilles. There was, then, a consistent duality in politics, but it was not a duality arising from the conflict of two political parties.

We may summarize this sceptical interpretation of the role of party in the second half of the long eighteenth century by concluding that while parties in some vague sense may have existed, there was no party system. Politics was not dominated and determined by parties as it was to be later in the nineteenth century, one of them in office, marked by its own organization and its self-consciousness as a party, the other in opposition, seeking through its own endeavours to displace the governing party. This interpretation has the particular merit of reminding us of the continuing importance of the power of the crown and of emphasizing traditional political ideas and ideals. It also warns us not to mistake political loyalty for party. It is true that the long years of the ministries of North, Pitt and Liverpool lent a certain polarity to politics in which habits of association and common feeling were forged. In view of the failure of these loyalties to endure in the political confusion of 1782–84, of 1801–12 and even of 1828–30, this should not be confused with the enduring loyalties of a modern party system.

This interpretation of early nineteenth-century politics has been challenged by a number of historians[8] who, while accepting the general view that the ultimate conquest of Parliament and politics by two parties still lay in the future, are still inclined to lay the major emphasis on the tendencies towards two-party politics which they discern in the decades before the Reform Act of 1832. Acknowledging the formal survival of the monarch's prerogative of appointing ministers, they argue that after the first decade of the century the effective power of the monarchy went into a rapid decline. The actions of George III in 1801 and 1807 were not to be repeated. Liverpool tolerated George IV's prejudices and was prepared to humour them. As is often pointed out, the King kept Canning out of the cabinet until 1822 and left Sidmouth in until 1824. But that was as far as Liverpool would go, and George IV had little influence over the cabinet changes of 1827–28. In the routine of politics, moreover, the increasing power of the cabinet was formalizing relations between the monarch and his government. His assent was now being taken to be a formality. When the king was no longer the hub of executive government then a Tory, as opposed to a king's, government could come into existence.

As we saw earlier in this chapter, the old supports of royal power in Parliament were eroding with the steady decline in the number of independents and of the court and administration party and the corresponding increase in the number of party men. By 1812, if not earlier, party MPs were in a clear majority. Furthermore, in the early nineteenth century most MPs were remarkably consistent in their support of either government or opposition on the big issues. Party defined loyalties. On a series of great national issues, on constitutional and foreign policy questions and on many reform issues, government and opposition thought and voted differently. During Liverpool's long administration, only about 10–15 per cent of MPs wavered in their loyalty to government or opposition by voting for both. In a single session of Parliament only about 5 per cent of MPs would vote on both sides. Attendance at Parliament could be patchy, and some division lists distinguish carefully between solid supporters of government or opposition and their 'fringe' supporters; but front-bench decisions about policy and procedure were now being normally accepted by backbenchers. On most social and economic questions party did not determine policy positions, but on certain very important occasions it did, such as on the Orders in Council and on the property tax. Even on issues usually regarded as crossing party lines, party was still an important influence. Catholic emancipation is always regarded as an issue that transcended party, but almost all Whigs supported it while a majority of Tories opposed it. By this time, too, the number of party divisions was beginning to overhaul the number of non-party divisions in any one session.

In such ways, then, party was exerting an increasing influence over the proceedings of Parliament, although the cohesion of parties was much less complete than it later became. Admittedly, early nineteenth-century writers and speakers tended to use a number of almost interchangeable terms to define political conflict: king versus Parliament, ministry versus Parliament, king versus people, government versus opposition and, of course, Tory versus Whig. In the end, however, they all came down to the same thing. The routine of regular support for either government or opposition was replacing the mid-eighteenth-century ideal of political independence.

During the mid-eighteenth century formed opposition had been frowned upon and the formation of parties regarded as illegitimate. The Foxite Whigs, however, positively revelled in the language and rhetoric of opposition, while Fox flamboyantly draped himself in the mantle of party. By the early nineteenth century the existence of party in opposition needed little justification. Even during the French Revolutionary war it was generally recognized that a responsible opposition was an integral part of the political order; its disappearance during the secession of 1797–1801 was noted and condemned. By then the old Rockinghamite arguments in favour of parties had been commonly accepted. Even those on the other side of the House of Commons were coming to accept the legitimacy of party. In 1830 the Tory John Wilson Croker remarked that 'party attachments and consistency are in the *first* class of a statesman's duties'.[9] Even on the Tory side of the House party had arrived.

Party rivalry may be seen to most dramatic effect in the personality cults which sprang up after the deaths of Fox and Pitt. Within a few years at least 20 Fox clubs appeared in the major provincial towns, bodies extravagantly dedicated to the greatness of a man who in his lifetime had been a political failure but who could nevertheless be seen to have professed great principles. The speeches and toasts at Fox club dinners were widely reported in the press. Together with other Whig party propaganda, they served to identify Fox and his party with the cause of the Glorious Revolution and to fuse the sacred flame of the Whiggery of the past with the urgent claims of civic reform and religious freedom in the present. As for Pitt, a grateful nation raised monuments to 'the pilot who weathered the storm', not least in the shape of the dozens of Pitt clubs, which far outnumbered those dedicated to his great rival. In this way, those who wished to commemorate the two men were perpetuating their struggles whilst alive into an indefinite future beyond their graves.

Involvement in party competition was not restricted to the wining and dining classes. Party was a vital element in parliamentary elections. During the first three decades of the nineteenth century the rate of elections suddenly accelerated, nine in 29 years, a rate that was continued after – it was not initiated by – the 1832 Reform Act, with four elections in nine years.[10] This return to the electoral rhythms of Queen Anne's reign kept the political temperature on the boil. It allowed the competition of parties at Westminster to be filtered down into the constituencies. It is not too much to say that party competition in the constituencies structured political participation. There was already a local Toryism and a local Whiggism in many parts of the country, vestigial remnants of the first age of party. The party conflict at

Westminster was now transmitted into the constituencies through a number of agencies, particularly the political activities of MPs and candidates and, where relevant, of local patrons and the more frequent discussion of national issues in the press. Furthermore, the proliferation of Fox and Pitt clubs and the growth of Loyalist, Protestant and Constitutional societies all served the same function. In some of the larger boroughs, indeed, especially those with considerable numbers of Protestant Dissenting electors, the identification of local activists with the parties and traditions of Fox and Pitt was quite marked. Especially in those places with strong Anglican corporations and powerful opposing parties of Dissenters, such as Exeter, Lincoln, Worcester and Norwich, such identifications were strong and underpinned local politics. In about 40 places in all, Protestant Dissenters were in the vanguard of local party rivalry.

Party divisions were also reflected in the organizational expedients upon which both government and opposition depended. Both sides had fairly well developed whipping procedures in both Houses. On the government side the position of leader of the House was rapidly developing. In the 1780s he had been responsible for organizing ministerial supporters. By the early nineteenth century he had become the representative and spokesman of the ministry, especially when the first minister (Liverpool) sat in the Lords. Indeed, Lord Liverpool was forced to adopt party methods. He employed Tory whips, Charles Arbuthnot and William Holmes, and demanded 'a generally favourably disposition' from his followers. By the 1820s the government whips had become salaried officials. Charles Arbuthnot was Joint Secretary to the Treasury; his work as patronage secretary did much to weld the government's majorities together. Without its growing organizational apparatus the government could not have survived. As for the opposition, the bureaucratic structures pioneered by William Adam in the 1780s survived the Portland schism of 1794 and Adam continued to organize the Foxite party after 1794. There was, however, little further development. Although the work of William Adam was not repeated after his retirement from the House in 1812, the opposition could not blame organizational deficiencies for its weaknesses. They held, for example, far more party meetings than the governing side thought fit, at least two in each session during Liverpool's administration. Outside Parliament, at least, the old Whig club, with a membership of about 1000, had spawned about 20 provincial equivalents as early as 1800. These coexisted with the metropolitan and provincial Fox clubs which sprang up after 1806. Together, these societies constituted a real and substantial, if untidy and informal, infrastructure. The organizational advances of the post-1832 period were both impressive and widespread. That they were founded upon well-developed precedents is equally clear.

Those who wish to argue the case for party in this period like to emphasize three points. First, parties influenced proceedings in Parliament, defining the allegiance of Members, determining the arguments marshalled for and against particular measures and mobilizing support for and against government within Parliament. Second, parties powerfully influenced elections at a number of points: in the selection of candidates, the character of election campaigns, the quality of the ideas and arguments held out to the public and, not least, the result and outcome of those campaigns. Third, parties contributed to the politicization not only of the electorate but of a much wider audience, bringing to the awareness of the public their respective principles and ideologies, programmes and policies and, indeed, their contrasting party histories and mythologies.

The reader must reach an independent decision on the precise status to be allocated to party influences in the early nineteenth century. While there were important structural and ideological differences between government and opposition, it has to be remembered that they shared many common features. Both were tentatively organized political forces with large and sometimes vague fringe memberships. Both were difficult to lead and to coordinate. As the Tory party began to distance itself from the monarch, so the Whig opposition began to distance itself from the heir apparent. Both were adept at appealing to the nation through the use of press and propaganda. Both were intervening regularly in the constituencies at election time, beginning to break down the isolation of local patronage structures. Furthermore, their mutual perceptions forced both parties to define themselves. Whigs disliked the policies of Tory governments; Tory governments feared what the Whigs might do in government, how much ground they might concede to public opinion, how much damage they might do to the royal prerogative. It was these interactions between the parties which created the tension which underpinned the rivalry of Whigs and Tories.[11]

Furthermore, it surely cannot be denied that government and opposition represented contrasting ideological positions in the age of George IV. Liverpool was running his own, a Tory ministry committed to Tory measures in response to Tory opinion, a Tory ministry one of whose principal objectives was to keep the Whigs out. Indeed, the epithet 'Tory' was regularly applied to Liverpool's ministry, in order to distinguish its supporters from those of the indubitably named 'Whig' opposition of Fox and his successors. If the 'Toryism' of the early nineteenth century was less clearly delineated than that of its 'Whig' counterpart, it does not follow that it did not exist. Indeed, the policies pursued by Pitt in the 1790s had occasionally had the epithet 'Tory' attached to them: the government's repression of radical reformers, its patriotic defence of the country during the recent war and the maintenance of order at home. In the 1790s, moreover, some of its defenders were beginning to adopt distinctly un-Whiggish sentiments. The *Anti-Jacobin Magazine* contrasted 'our High Church and Tory principles' with 'the modern Whigs, and their associates, who see nothing praiseworthy in our present constitution'. In the 1790s some Pittite writers were even arguing that the British constitution was not in essence a balanced constitution but a monarchical constitution since the monarchy was the most ancient element within it, more ancient even than Parliament, the stock from which the other branches of the constitution had sprung. By the early nineteenth century the ministerial press was regularly defending its actions in terms that can only be described as Tory. It maintained a running justification of the actions of successive 'Tory' governments in the pages of the *Courier* between 1807 and 1830 and, more cerebrally, in *the Quarterly Review* after 1809 and the high-Tory *Blackwood's Edinburgh Magazine* after 1824. By the end of the second decade of the nineteenth century the term 'Tory' was back in regular usage to denote the supporters of the government, and was used by those supporters themselves. By the end of the 1820s the Tories had provided themselves with a (quite illegitimate) pedigree which quietly dropped the old Tory infatuation with divine right and passive obedience in favour of the loyalism of the 1790s, the ideology of Burke, the wartime sacrifice of the revolutionary and Napoleonic period, the defence of Protestantism and, not least, nostalgia for the towering figure of William Pitt. The continuity of personnel, the long survival of Pitt's government and the continuation of Pittite policies under his successors meant that it was not necessary to mark the point where loyalty to the king's government could be distinguished from loyalty to a Tory government. Only when the Tories entered the unfamiliar world of opposition in 1830 was it necessary to redefine themselves more openly and more avowedly as a political party, now that they could no longer rely on the almost automatic support of the crown.

On the other side of the House of Commons, the Whig party had carved out for itself a position of semi-permanent opposition to successive Tory ministries. The failure of the 'Talents' administration and the death of Fox left the Whig party in the hands of men who were prepared only to mark time. Fox was succeeded by Grey, who for many years had to be watchful of the reactions of the Grenvilles to any initiative which he might make. The party, moreover, was deprived of his considerable oratorical talent when the death of his father in November 1807 consigned him to the upper House. With Grey and Grenville in the Lords, who would lead the party in the Commons? Grenville vetoed the obvious candidate, Whitbread, and the affable but incompetent George Ponsonby led the Whig troops in the Commons until 1817. The only realistic alternative, Lord Henry Petty, was removed, like Grey, to the Lords on the death of his father in November 1809. On Ponsonby's death in 1817 George Tierney became leader of the opposition in the lower House and, at once, a more positive note was struck. Indeed, for three years the opposition was at its liveliest and most threatening. However, his failure to topple the government weakened both Tierney's authority and his health. The momentum which he had generated could not be sustained in the calmer political climate after 1821.

The Whig opposition, then, existed as a government-in-waiting, acting as a semi-permanent opposition, convinced that on Catholic emancipation and parliamentary reform their time would come and public opinion would swing in their direction. Weakened by years of failure, demoralized by internal divisions and crippled with indecisive leadership, the Whig party limped on from year to year. They consoled themselves for their political misfortunes by reiterating all the old Rockingham/Foxite Whig prejudices concerning the secret influence of the crown and the evils of the ministerial system of government. To the Whigs, Pitt and Liverpool were the allies of royal tyranny, just as Lord Bute had been. It was irksome, therefore, for the leading Whigs, splendidly assembled at Holland House, the home of Fox's heir and nephew, to be kicking their heels and awaiting the summons of the public. Their very aloofness concealed from them how outdated was their view of public affairs, how inaccurate their picture of the well-meaning and totally unautocratic Lord Liverpool, how ridiculously conspiratorial their general reading of politics. Everyone was to blame but themselves. Their political horizons were frozen in the 1760s. Even their supposedly 'popular' opinions were the product of Whig prejudice rather than social observation and political principle. Their case for parliamentary reform, for example, arose not from the need to represent the literate, talented and propertied middle class but from the need to strengthen the House of Commons against the Hanoverian monarchy. Their inability to move on the issue without upsetting the Grenvilles cut them off from middle-class opinion. It was left to Whitbread and the more radical Whigs in the party, collectively known as 'the Mountain', to keep the flag of reform flying, but they did so without the support of the leadership.

No wonder these narrow and sullen aristocrats failed to capture the imagination and sympathy of the public. They might enjoy harassing ministers and occasionally disrupting their parliamentary business, but to the public this seemed factious and irresponsible conduct. Their justification for their behaviour would have been that it was not for Whig aristocrats to go around stirring up a dangerously unpredictable public opinion. The art of responsible government was to wait for public opinion to turn, as one day it surely would, and then to go to meet it half-way. In this manner, the Whig party never abandoned its historic belief in aristocratic and party government, pledging itself to defend the propertied public from ministerial despotism and popular anarchy alike. Consequently, there can be no doubting the party credentials of the Whig party of the age of Grey; but if their convictions were the ultimate source of their consistency in unhappy and unpromising times, it has to be conceded that these party convictions were at the same time a source of weakness, complacency and self-congratulation.

The state and the law

The principal features of the fiscal-military state continued with little structural change down to the end of this period. The size of military establishments grew to extraordinary proportions during periods of warfare, while the revenue-raising departments of state had a staff of over 20 000 officials by the end of it. By comparison, the civilian bureaucracy remained very small. In the early nineteenth century the Foreign Office had a staff of just over 30, the Board of Trade 20, the Home Office 17 and the Colonial Office 14. The central bureaucracies simply lacked the means to develop coordinated national policies. Consequently, they lacked the will to do so.

Britain remained a politically decentralized state in which the sources of political and legal action remained parochial. The regulation of political and social action remained in local hands, supplemented powerfully by a large and varied number of bodies, some statutory, some voluntary. It was not the state but the churches and bodies like the Society for Promoting Christian Knowledge which founded schools, including hundreds of charity schools. Moreover, local government was left to powerful local families who enjoyed discretionary authority over remarkably wide areas of life. By the later eighteenth century the demands made on local government were intensifying as social and economic change accelerated. The period of the French Revolutionary and Napoleonic wars was something of a golden age for the independence of the local magistrates. It was the local mobilization of forces which repelled the radicals and manned the militia and the Volunteer regiments. It was the magistrates of Berkshire who evolved the Speenhamland system, not Parliament and not the central government. As the burden of work falling upon Quarter Sessions increased, so the informal arrangements of earlier decades gave way to more formal procedures. By the end of the century most counties had developed separate committees for distinct areas of their work: for the management of prisons, for the supervision of workhouses, for the maintenance of roads and bridges, for the work of the police, for the approval and collection of parish rates. Unelected and unaccountable, Quarter Sessions remained, however, a valuable and flexible instrument but responsive to central direction when needed.

In the corporate towns a similar pattern may be discerned. Although conditions varied enormously, ranging from corrupt corporations, in which self-perpetuating groups practised corruption and even peculation, to others, where a decent, accountable and economical administration prevailed, the corporations were not particularly successful in meeting the complex challenges of rapidly changing social and economic conditions. When new demands arose they frequently could not be answered by the corporations because they lacked both money and specialized experience. The needs of the new urban communities were often met by new agencies established either by voluntary action or by parliamentary statute. These included watch committees, street commissioners, water boards and harbour boards. Sometimes several such activities might be collectively entrusted to improvement commissioners, over 200 of which existed in 1830.

The existence of such bodies reveals that in the towns the corporations were in serious need of reform. Indeed, the absence of any sort of rational governing structures for the rapidly growing industrial centres like Leeds, Manchester and Sheffield was striking. The haphazard collection of magistrates sitting in quarter sessions, medieval officials sitting in Courts Leet and parish officials vainly striving to keep the peace and look after the poor was almost a standing invitation to disorder. Even in the counties the need for reform was being felt. There was a serious shortage of magistrates, a shortage that was worsening as the demands made upon the magistracy increased in size and complexity. By the end of the eighteenth century it was proving increasingly difficult to find enough gentlemen willing to sit as magistrates. In 1792 Parliament passed an Act empowering the appointment of stipendiary (i.e paid, professional) magistrates. The passing of this Act does not only imply that the older system of administering justice was becoming harder to sustain. It also suggests that the old ideal of a local, amateur, unpaid gentleman-landowner who was the natural leader of the community was beginning to pass away. An official return in 1831 stated that there were 4500 magistrates qualified to act in the English counties, many of whom had sat on the bench only infrequently.[12] In the north of England, in particular, there was a serious shortage of magistrates. One of the reasons for this was a noticeable reluctance to appoint magistrates from the industrial and mercantile middle classes. Increasingly, it was left to the Anglican clergy to act as JPs. After 1815 no less than a quarter of all magistrates in England and Wales were clergymen, a fact which reinforced radical criticisms that the church was little more than a prop for the state.

Together with religion, law was one of the principal anchors of society during the long eighteenth century. Politics was dominated by conflicts *over* and discussions *of* the law, and many parliamentary debates were conducted with legal precedents principally in mind. Social conflicts were mediated by the law, whether landlord quarrelled with tenant, master with man or rioter with wholesaler. Public order rested on legal foundations. The reading of the Riot Act and the summoning of the militia were themselves legal acts, enacted with precision and ceremony. Last, and certainly not least, property of all types rested on a legal basis.

It is a truism that the Glorious Revolution made the world safe for property – especially, but by no means exclusively, aristocratic property. Indeed, the Glorious Revolution had been the achievement of men with very considerable amounts of property. Moreover, in the British state during the long eighteenth century full citizenship was conveyed by the possession of property. At least two of the outcomes of the Glorious Revolution – the independence of the judiciary from royal control and the regular meeting of Parliament – were intended, in part at least, to act as continuing protections for the rights of property-owners. No wonder that upper-class commentators vied with each other in their admiration of the superiority of English law and the excellence of the British constitution. Furthermore, the legal system did have much to commend it. Torture was not used, legal proceedings were public, trial by jury was common and habeas corpus acted as a safeguard for personal liberties. On top of everything, the judges were not subject to political intimidation. So valuable was this inheritance that its preservation was just as much a concern of the masses as of the propertied groups in society. According to Blackstone, the law guaranteed 'those equitable rules of action, by which the meanest individual is protected from the insults and oppression of the greatest'.[13] Although there was considerable sympathy for those who defied the law – men like highwaymen and smugglers – most Britons believed that the law was the ultimate guarantor of the order and stability of their society, a belief carefully cultivated by the propertied classes. The only alternative to the rule of law was the awful prospect of a return to the anarchy of the mid-seventeenth century.

This fear of anarchy was the prime motivation for what most historians have identified as the most striking feature of eighteenth-century legal life: the rapidly increasing number of statutes that carried the death penalty for minor offences. The governing classes of Hanoverian Britain had to cope with the problems of unprecedented social and economic change, poverty, vagrancy and violence which, they were convinced, were not only rapidly increasing but also threatening to endanger their lives and their property. With no standing army and no national police force at their disposal, they were driven to use the law to protect themselves. In 1688 there had been about 50 crimes for which the death penalty could be invoked; by 1800 the number had increased to 200. The Black Act of 1723 alone created 50 such offences. Some of them were of a singular character. In 1698 the theft of goods worth 25*d.* or more was made a capital offence. These statutes remained on the statute book until the early nineteenth century. Most of them passed in empty Houses and with little debate, and even less opposition. The first repeal of a capital statute did not come until 1808, and most of them remained in force until the 1820s.[14]

What is to be concluded from this avalanche of statutes? Although historians usually assume that they were the legal expression of a hardening, authoritarian attitude on the part of the ruling classes, we should examine not only the statutes that were passed but also the way in which they were enforced. Most of them were extremely specific and referred to one place or offence. Separate acts legislated against damaging Fulham Bridge (1725), and Westminster Bridge (1736), and even forging an entry in a North Riding of Yorkshire Land Register (1735). Clearly, such legislation was passed because particular institutions and groups decided to avail themselves of the greater opportunities for legislation that the annual sittings of Parliament offered to them. Although much is made of the fact that the statutes protected new forms of property, in fact it was only for certain types of very traditional offence that people were actually executed – for forgery, sheep-stealing and theft from shops and warehouses. Although more capital offences existed in the eighteenth century, there were in fact fewer executions than there had been in the seventeenth. In this way, it can be argued, the terrifying penalties that existed were there simply to deter and to impress the masses. They were rarely enforced.

Nevertheless, many people *were* executed for crimes against property. By the end of the century, about 200 people each year were being executed in England and Wales alone. The number *sentenced* to death was far higher. Between 1770 and 1830 no fewer than 7000 men, women and children were executed out of 35 000 sentenced. The authorities were reluctant to execute people indiscriminately. However, such summary figures need careful analysis. They varied wildly from year to year and from place to place. In London and Middlesex in 1759, for example, six people were executed, while in 1785 there were as many as 97 executions. Only a small proportion of those hanged had committed murder; in London and Middlesex only one-tenth of those executed between 1749 and 1771 had done so. (Of the 97 hung in 1785 only one was a murderer. Of the rest, 43 had been convicted of burglary and 31 of highway robbery.) In London by the end of the century only one in three people sentenced to death was actually hanged. Overall, the number of those condemned to die who were pardoned increased from around 50–60 per cent in the early to middle part of the eighteenth century to around 90 per cent in the early nineteenth.[15] What explains this growing reluctance actually to enforce the capital legislation so recently enacted?

The explanation may be sought in the need which the governing establishment felt to use the law and the legal system to reinforce their authority. Lacking physical, coercive powers they stood behind the terrifying majesty of the law, ostentatiously using the prerogatives of mercy and moderation in order to humanize their power. The authorities did not need to hang every criminal guilty of a capital offence. They needed to be seen to have the power to do so and the power, where appropriate, to pardon. After all, the purpose of the legislation was to deter acts of violence, to make examples of individuals, not to inflict as much cruelty as possible upon unfortunate men and women. By the end of the century, indeed, many educated people had reached the conclusion that the lurid spectacle of public execution might be less effective in deterring crime than other methods of punishment. The major alternative to public execution for most of the century had been transportation. In the half-century following the passage of the Transportation Act of 1718 some 50 000 convicts suffered transportation to the American colonies alone. The loss of the colonies led to the popularization of an established yet relatively little-used method of punishment, imprisonment. As late as 1776, according to John Howard's survey, only 653 persons were imprisoned in gaols, and of those almost 60 per cent were debtors. Thereafter, lengthy periods of imprisonment found their place in the range of punishments available to judges. By the 1780s imprisonment, sometimes accompanied by hard labour, was coming to seem a more rational and reasonable punishment for crimes against property. By then, for example, slightly over 50 per cent of men convicted on non-capital offences in Surrey had received terms of imprisonment, in about one-quarter of cases accompanied by whipping.[16] Finally, one thing was never in doubt: the idea that it was the responsibility of the state to deal with criminals and thus to uphold, and to be seen to be upholding, the law. The Gaols Act of 1823 embodied the principle not only of imposing discipline in prisons up and down the country but also of standardizing that discipline.

To what extent, then, was the law an instrument of class rule, an agency of social control? In the sixteenth and seventeenth centuries the law had been an arena of severe conflict which had divided communities and the state. In the eighteenth century, however, according to Douglas Hay, the governing elite used the law to maintain its own power in at least three ways.[17] First, the authority of the elite was expressed through symbolic behaviour and performances, through the terrifying rituals of public execution, through the pomp and swagger of quarter sessions, through the more informal courtesies of the JP's study and, not least, the (to the majority) almost unintelligible niceties of courtroom formality. Second, the authority of the elite was expressed through the capacity of the legal system to treat people with clemency and with mercy. It was the unusually potent ritual of the pardon of a poor offender which demonstrated the terrifying majesty and power of the law at the same time as its incorruptibility and its humanity. The prospect of harsh punishments might be softened at the moment of sentencing by the clemency of merciful judges. Transportation or some other alternative to execution might thus be publicly seen to be fair and adequate punishment. Finally, according to Hay, the law could be and was used as an ideology of control. Through the recycling of justifications for the law, most Englishmen, even reformers and radicals, came to believe that all were equal before the law and that no man or woman was exempt from its penalties. Such sentiments were universal in Hanoverian Britain. The function of the ideology of the law, then, was to render the entire social and economic system acceptable to the mass of the people, to endow it with qualities with which they could identify and of which they might even be proud.

On the other hand, this sort of approach, with its simplistic dualism of 'governors' and 'governed' and, what is implied, 'elite' and 'popular', has important limitations. The thesis that the law was an agency of social control rests on a partial misunderstanding of the new capital legislation of the eighteenth century. It is not always clear that it was actually enacted for purposes of social control. The Black Acts have been viewed as a government measure enacted to overawe the masses, but it can also be maintained that they were a response to the Jacobitism of the early 1720s, not a response to fears for the security of property.[18] Furthermore, most of the historians who argue this case do so with very specific types of crime in mind. It is, however, surely misleading to concentrate exclusively upon criminal activities which have connotations of social division. Poaching, rioting and smuggling embrace elements of social tension, but to view them as evidence of a class war in the villages and the towns of Hanoverian Britain is to do violence to the subtlety and complexity of crime and its meanings. Smuggling in fact was a big commercial business, rather than a defiant act by small men against repressive superiors. Poaching, too, could be an organized affair rather than the reaction of a poor man trying to pot his family's Sunday dinner. Many landowners took organized poaching extremely seriously, and even grouped themselves into joint prosecution societies both to suppress it and to prosecute offenders. Most litigation, indeed, was instigated not by the government nor by the governing classes against their social inferiors but by private individuals against people of roughly the same social standing. A very large number of those bringing cases to court were men with small amounts of property. Most prosecutions were brought privately by individuals, anxious to use the law in their own interests and service at a time when little attempt was made (by the courts) to detect crime. Thus the law was used overwhelmingly by the broad middling orders of society against each other, rather than being used by the propertied elite against the rest. Indeed, at the Essex Quarter Sessions between 1760 and 1800 over 20 per cent of prosecutions for felony were brought by labouring men, and the lesser middling orders like tradesmen and artisans contributed 30–40 per cent more. In Essex, at least, more than half the cases of felony were brought by quite humble people.

Indeed, we should not accept the assumption that people were passive recipients of legal and ideological control from above. People knew the law and they were determined to secure their own rights. In all this there was a traditional, customary awareness of what 'law and order' might mean. Law was not a fixed and static commodity. What was legal and what was not legal was not always clear and unquestioned. What was legal often needed to be defined, even to be fought over. There was no blind and fearful acceptance of the law of the elite. At the same time, trial by jury meant that verdicts in many cases were delivered not by the elite but by men of the middling orders. By the end of the eighteenth century the modern notion that the accused is innocent until proven guilty had made its appearance. Consequently, a broad constituency was involved in the administration and execution of the law, and public opinion was a force that could not be discounted. The rhetoric of the law could be taken very seriously by the poorer classes. The crowds in the streets of London that awaited the verdict on Thomas Hardy and his colleagues in the London Corresponding Society in 1794 shows how legal processes could become an object of public concern. Law was not something handed down from above and passively and obediently received. In a rough and ready way, it belonged to everybody.

There is a variation in the thesis of the law as an extension of state power. This is the theory of the law as a protection for the emergence of capitalism. According to this theory[19] many customary practices, such as access to common land, rights of wood-gathering and the killing of game, became criminal offences as enclosures proceeded and land became the object of capitalist exploitation. Furthermore, the case law built up by Lord Mansfield at the Court of King's Bench between 1756 and 1788 is regarded as a landmark in the history of commercial practice, and amounted to a substantial revision of commercial law. Moreover, during the eighteenth century capital punishment was extended to newer forms of commercial property, such as the protection of turnpikes (1735) or of coal mines (1737). In this vein, too, laws were passed against embezzlement and forgery and, in 1740, against the pilfering of materials entrusted to a worker. Yet it is not easy to detect direct relationships between the law, its enforcement and new forms of capitalist property and practice. Crime was much more complex than an undifferentiated protest against alleged loss of customary rights. Most of those charged with property offences were charged with offences against statutes which actually pre-dated the eighteenth century. Few were charged with offences against new codes of economic practice. Lord Mansfield's verdicts on a host of commercial matters including contract, credit and debts were, however, highly technical and would have had little direct effect upon everyday routines of economic activity. Indeed, a leading authority has recently come round to criticizing the eighteenth century legal system because it did *not* adequately facilitate the development of capitalism.

> Parliament's failure to sweep away a penumbra of obsolete statutes and to push the courts towards an assertion of free market principles maintained a climate of uncertainty surrounding businessmen and traders and gave a semblance of legality to the actions of disorderly crowds and combinations of workers seeking to use collective forms of organization, intimidation and violence, to change prices and wages in their favour.[20]

Apparently the law did not adequately cater for cases of breach of contract nor for the speedy settlement of debtors' claims and disputes. There are, furthermore, many instances in which magistrates and judges *defended* customary practices such as wood-collecting and gleaning. Here, as elsewhere, the law was available to the poor petitioner as well as to the landed and propertied gentlemen.

This argument may be developed by considering the way that alleged criminals were prosecuted. There was no clear relationship between the seriousness of an offence and the degree of punishment which it would attract. A complex assortment of variables was responsible for the rate – and vigour – of prosecution. Two require particular attention. First, those who administered the law were local, unpaid amateurs. Parish constables were either appointed or elected annually. These people had to live in the community, and tended to treat trivial offences quite lightly, influenced as they were by community opinion and community values. They might not share the opinions of the upper classes of the seriousness of an offence. Consequently, no fewer than a third of those prosecuted for crimes against property in Surrey between 1736 and 1753 were acquitted.[21] Second, the punishment of crime was an informal matter, depending upon personality and circumstance. It was the eagerness of individual JPs to prosecute, the view they took of the offence and the offender and the prosecution strategy they intended to adopt that determined the rate of prosecution rather than the seriousness of the offence.

Indeed, in cases that did not involve victims, such as prostitution, the energy of informers and parish officers was the principal factor. Certainly, JPs sought strenuously to utilize a variety of devices, including mediation and negotiation, and did not automatically reach for the most severe punishment. The influence of magistrates could be decisive. The influence of the two Fielding brothers, Henry and John, on patterns of crime enforcement in London was considerable. Henry was a Westminster magistrate between 1749 and 1754, John from 1751 to 1780. Their constant energy in the apprehension and sentencing of criminals, in the use of 'runners' and informers and in the professional marshalling of scarce resources set a standard that was not to be matched until the following century.

None of this means that we cannot make some kind of estimate of the pattern of crime in the eighteenth century. During the first half of the century the incidence of crime appears to have been fairly stable, perhaps slightly diminishing in rural areas, slightly increasing in urban areas. In the second half of the century, probably because of population pressures, it began to increase, particularly in the towns. Contemporaries believed that they were living in the middle of a crime wave, influenced perhaps by the extraordinary contemporary media interest in crime and criminals. The poverty of large numbers of the population and their sheer vulnerability to economic recession meant that there was no rigid separation between a presumed criminal 'class' and the mass of the population. In time of dearth, crime, especially crime against property, would inevitably increase as a consequence of unemployment, low wages and high prices. Furthermore, it has been suggested that there was a link between the incidence of crime and warfare.[22] According to this argument, the recruitment of tens of thousands of young men may have artificially reduced the rate of crime during the years of war. Correspondingly, the demobilization of large numbers of soldiers at the end of the war would give rise to the severe increase in the rate of crime which occurred at the end of every war in which Britain took part during the long eighteenth century. Although doubts have been expressed about this phenomenon – especially on account of the small size of samples taken, the low levels of crime and the capacity of a relatively small number of cases to bias the figures – it does not seem possible to eliminate it entirely.

What was the significance of the law and the legal system in this period? Goldsmith's aphorism, 'Laws grind the poor, and rich men rule the law', makes the obvious point about inequality but, as we have seen, the argument only begins there. To depict the law as the exclusive agent of class power is a grotesque simplification. Even when every account has been taken of cynicism and abuse, it remains true that the political and social elite was expected to observe and to administer the law; that the law was available to everyone; that although the rich were bound to have advantages over the poor, even they expected – and were expected – to obey the law. If the law was used by the elite to protect its own position and its own property, it was also used by the middling orders to protect their own position and their own property and, as we have seen, by some members of the poorer classes, too. The operation of the legal system, moreover, served to involve many men of small property in the official arrangements of a legally minded society. In this sense, the law acted to integrate individuals and communities. The legal system also did much to reconcile divergent interests and groups, thus serving important stabilizing functions. Insofar as the legal system may have enjoyed the confidence of the broad mass of the people it may have facilitated some general degree of acceptance of the social structure of Hanoverian Britain. Whether it was more or less important in doing so when compared to some of the other great integrative forces – such as patriotism and Protestantism – is a matter for discussion. But the law, surely, did not replace these established forces or overwhelm them in significance. What a study of the law and crime reveals and reminds us of are the limitations of central government, the autonomy of the localities and the constant process of negotiation and accommodation between the localities and the centre. In this way, the tentacles of the law extended throughout Britain, strengthening and uniting a diverse and decentralized body politic.

The retreat from the confessional state, 1756–1820

Anglicans and Evangelicals

During the second half of the long eighteenth century the British confessional state began to weaken under the pressure of internal divisions and external challenges. During this period the Church of England experienced two serious internal divisions. It had to cope with the rapidly growing strength of the Methodists, their schism from the Church of England and the subsequent competition between the established church and its new rival. It also experienced the Evangelical revival, a movement which initially attracted and involved notable members of the ruling establishment, such as Hannah More and William Wilberforce. For decades the struggle for the soul of the Church of England weakened and dissipated its unity. During this period, too, the confessional state was forced to withstand two serious challenges from without: from the Protestant Dissenters and from the rapidly reviving forces of Roman Catholicism. Before turning to these challenges, however, we need to examine more closely the situation in which the church found itself in late Georgian Britain. Why was it not able to meet more successfully the challenges to which it was exposed? Why was it not better able to maintain its status as an established church? The traditional explanation has emphasized that the church steadily weakened from within, its organizational structure outdated, its vigour wilting because of its subjection to the political establishment and its vitality sapped by secularization.[23] An alternative case, recently propounded by Jonathan Clark, has argued that there was little seriously wrong with the church. What destroyed the confessional state was the sudden and dramatic events of the 1820s, culminating in the legislation of 1828–29. 'What changed was not the theoretical validity or potential success of Anglicanism in an urban or industrial society, but the emergence of that society very largely beyond the pale of the traditional Anglican parochial structure.'[24]

The argument I shall present here is that these assaults, challenges and problems would not have worn down the Church of England had it not already been weakening from within *because of its status as an established church*. In other words, the Church of England was responsible for its own decline. Its complacency in the face of mounting problems resulted from its continuing inability to initiate its own solutions to its problems, which in turn resulted from its willingness to allow the state to defend it and to safeguard it. It was surely not beyond the wit of the late-eighteenth-century church establishment to have developed the parochial structure in a manner more suited to the new urban and industrial populations. As Clark concedes, 'the Church did not act swiftly to extend her parochial ministrations to such areas' and only responded 'after the problem had become acute ... and on an insufficient scale'.[25] That was indeed the case. Between 1810 and 1820 152 new Anglican churches were built; in the same period no fewer than 15 601 non-Anglican places of worship were either built, adapted or licensed. In the next two decades the respective figures were 943 Anglican churches compared to 18 007 non-Anglican places of worship. The comparison is devastating. Furthermore, such Anglican churches as did exist were distributed according to the population patterns of earlier centuries. There were 10 000 parishes in the archdiocese of Canterbury but only 2000 in that of York. At the end of the eighteenth century some of the parishes, especially in the north of England, were huge, stretching over many townships. Prescot, near Liverpool, contained 15 townships, Manchester 19, Leeds 13. Churches in such places were hopelessly inadequate to deal with the needs of their populations. However, it was very fortunate that the populations in such towns did not go to their local Anglican church, because the available seating would have accommodated less than half of them, sometimes much less. In London the situation was spectacularly worse. The parish of St Pancras had 50 000 inhabitants in 1815, but its church could have accommodated only 200 of them. We need to be clear that it was the established status of the church which was in large part responsible for this state of affairs. To create a new parish, to amend parochial boundaries or to build a new parish church required legislation. On the other hand, to found a new Dissenting chapel all that was needed was the hire of a hall and a magistrate's licence.

Furthermore, the church was a prisoner of several features of its own established status that made it almost impossible to reform itself. Political recommendation to ecclesiastical office may have been almost inevitable in a society in which church and state were so closely bound up with each other, but some worrying features remained. As we saw earlier, no fewer than half of church livings were under lay patronage (the number of livings under aristocratic patronage actually increased from 1200 to 1400 between 1780 and 1830), one-tenth were with the crown and only the remaining 40 per cent under the direct control of the church itself. This does not imply that large numbers of priests were inadequate; it does mean that it was difficult for the church to confront its own economic problems. Pluralism, moreover, was inevitable where clerical incomes were low and where the state of rural parsonages was often deplorable, many of them verging on the uninhabitable. A large minority of incumbents saw very little of their benefices. In Derbyshire, for example, between 1772 and 1832 one-third of clerical incumbents had either none, or very little, contact with the benefices to which they had been appointed. In the early nineteenth century, indeed, over half of Anglican benefices had no resident priest. The church simply did not have enough priests. Peter Virgin has shown that of every 100 ordained priests only about 50 actually held a benefice in England. The others drifted into other professions, especially teaching, or emigrated, or suffered early death. Only one-fifth found a benefice within five years of ordination.[26] One immediate solution to this crisis was the employment of stipendiary and assistant curates. These men 'lived a life of peripatetic poverty with few incentives, little supervision, an absence of like-minded company and an element of rural boredom'.[27] They were indispensable to the church and, until the Stipendiary Curates Act of 1813, miserably paid for their efforts.

Improvements were slowly coming. The operation of Queen Anne's Bounty was beginning to increase the incomes of some of the poorest benefices. Those concerned, however, were located principally in the east of England and in Wales rather than in the Midlands and the north. Other benefices, especially in the Midlands and eastern counties, benefited from the enclosure of common land, as a consequence of which the tithe was normally commuted into land. Thereafter, some clerics became small or medium-size farmers. In this way the social position of some sections of the clergy did improve a little during the second half of the eighteenth century. The church, therefore, tended to become a more rather than less desirable career for younger sons. As we have already noticed, the number of clerics who acted as magistrates rose very steeply after 1760. Such developments, however, did nothing for popular piety. Indeed, by the early nineteenth century the church was becoming increasingly identified with the secular establishment, and with some of its most unpopular features; enclosures, the Poor Law and the courts.[28]

Parallel developments could be seen in Scotland. The Act of Union of 1707 had confirmed the Presbyterian Church as the established church of Scotland, but it had been racked by disputes over lay patronage throughout the eighteenth century. The consequence was a series of splits and secessions, that of the Sandemanians in the 1720s, the Secession Church in the 1730s and of the Relief Presbytery in the 1750s. Nevertheless, under the 'Moderate' party the Presbyterian Church survived, diluting the fiery Calvinism of the previous century and thus rendering the church acceptable to the Scottish middling and upper classes. The price that was paid, however, was an aloofness to popular piety that was to be disastrous to the Scottish Presbyterian Church.

By the early nineteenth century the theory of a confessional state – the theory that, as Burke put it in 1792, 'In a Christian Commonwealth the church and the state are one and the same thing, being different integral parts of the same whole' – no longer corresponded with reality. In the early nineteenth century the number of practising Anglicans began to fall behind the number of practising non-Anglicans in England and Wales. In 1750 the demographic basis of a confessional state could still be maintained. About 90 per cent of all churchgoers worshipped in the established churches. (The established church in England and Ireland was Episcopal. In Scotland it was Presbyterian.) By the early nineteenth century the base was shrinking. Many millions of British people existed outside the boundaries of the confessional state. Already in 1801, merely half a million people took communion in the Anglican churches of England and Wales, less than 10 per cent of the population aged 15 and over. Indeed, as early as 1811, according to a return made by Anglican bishops, there were already more Dissenting chapels than Anglican places of worship by a ratio of 7 to 5. In 1810, indeed, Lord Harrowby confessed to the House of Lords that the country was drifting towards 'the most alarming of all situations, in which the religion of the Established Church would not be the religion of the majority of the people'.[29] In 1815 only one-sixth of the Irish people were Anglicans. By 1851 the established church in Scotland attracted only one-third of worshippers, in England and Wales slightly less than half. One survey has shown a decline of 25 per cent in the numbers of those taking communion between 1738 and 1802 in 30 Oxfordshire parishes. On the most optimistic reckoning, the numbers of practising Anglicans may have increased very slightly between 1740 and 1831, a period, however, when the population of England and Wales rose from 5.5 to over 13 million.[30]

Moreover, the theoretical justifications of the confessional state were beginning to alter even before the middle of the eighteenth century. For example, one of the most popular Anglican writers of the century, William Warburton, published his *The Alliance between Church and State* in 1736. Warburton's classic eighteenth-century defence of the church establishment was one of the most influential expressions of church–state relations. He argued that the church was a separate institution, with its own social contract, as a consequence of which every person had the right to express his or her religion freely. The church was connected to the state through a further contract for their mutual advantage in their very different spheres of life, the church receiving the benefits of the protection of the state, including public provision for its clergy and the further protection of religious tests. This was a much more individualistic, indeed, utilitarian, view of religion than would have been acceptable in 1688–89. Ironically, it may have been the case that the only acceptable defences of the confessional state were those which in the long run were to weaken it. Towards the end of the century, moreover, Anglican apologists began to turn away from their former preoccupation with ecclesiastical and political authority, their origins and character, towards a concern for social theory and an investigation of the roots of social order, discipline and restraint. In particular, Josiah Tucker and William Paley can be seen to shift their arguments away from the theological towards secular justifications of the confessional state.[31] By the middle of the 1790s, probably because of the impact of the war against France, Anglican political theory was preoccupying itself with the social rather than theological legitimations of power. Such a shift undermined the specific and unique qualities of *Anglican* supremacy. As Dr Hole remarks, the theoretical direction taken by these Anglican writers of the 1790s 'fatally undermined the case for an Anglican monopoly of state power'.[32]

The Anglican church may have found itself incapable of maintaining its status as a confessional church, but it nevertheless continued to foster powerful currents of religious health and even elements of religious revival. As early as 1760 it is possible to distinguish a score or more of Evangelical ministers who launched local evangelical revivals within their own parishes. Henry Venn (1725–97), curate of Clapham and later the vicar of Huddersfield, had already spread the Evangelical message throughout the West Riding in the 1750s. John Newton, an ex-slaving-ship master, was similarly influential in London. These ministers operated within the parochial framework, most – but not all of them – in quiet country districts, usually independently and without the benefit of collective action. Like the Methodists, these early Evangelicals placed their trust in a vital, personal faith, in the individual's communion with God and in the Bible as a source of wisdom and everyday inspiration.

By the end of the eighteenth century Evangelicalism was established as an important, if minority, movement within the Anglican church. In the 1780s, however, it was taken up by a number of individuals of considerable public importance who were to have a disproportionate influence on British society in the early nineteenth century. A cell of Evangelicals in Cambridge, notably Charles Simeon (1759–1836), who was converted in 1779, and Isaac Milner (1750–1820), influenced the minds of a younger generation of upper-class men. However, it was a group of Evangelicals in south London, the 'Clapham Sect', who made Evangelicalism a major force not only within the Church of England but more widely in public life. It was led by the son of Henry Venn, John (1759–1813), who was rector of Clapham after 1792. Among the most prominent members of the Clapham Sect were William Wilberforce (1759–1833), the MP for Yorkshire, who was converted to Evangelical Christianity in 1785, Henry Thornton (1760–1815), MP for Surrey and John Shore (1751–1834), governor-general of India, 1793–98. Zachary Macaulay (1768–1838), the father of the great Whig politician and historian Thomas Babington Macaulay, had been governor of the non-slave colony of Sierra Leone in 1796, and he proceeded to edit the Evangelical *Christian Observer* after 1802. His strength of character and moral energies were essential to the abolition of the slave trade, which passed Parliament in 1807.

The objective of the Clapham Sect was to encourage positive Christian action in order to achieve redemption for sinners. The Evangelicals were pious but they were not doctrinaire. Most of their leaders were uninterested in theological wrangling, professing instead a form of practical Calvinism which sought to do good in this world. The Evangelicals were reformers, advocating the freeing of the slaves, the reform of the penal system, the abolition of duelling, the improvement of the manners and morals of the upper classes and the keeping holy of the Sabbath day. In 1787, under the influence of Wilberforce, they established the Proclamation Society, which advocated the moral regeneration of the ruling elite and the restoration of its sense of responsibility. This society was similar in many ways to the much older Society for the Reformation of Manners (1692) but it was to be more successful and more effective. Its influence was to be felt long into the next century in its hostility towards popular entertainments, in the establishment of proper observance of the Sabbath (the Prime Minister, Spencer Perceval, in fact, refused to call parliamentary sittings on a Monday so that MPs from distant constituencies would not have to travel on the Sabbath) and in the censorship of plays and books which offended against modesty and political conformity. Such projects had an added urgency on account of the long years of war against France after 1793. It was widely believed that the French Revolution had occurred because of the atheism and immorality which had penetrated French society in the last decades of the life of the *ancien régime*. If

Britain were not to go the way of France, then her social leaders ought to look to the example they were setting. One of the most famous and influential members of the Clapham Sect was Hannah More. She admonished the rich to set an example to the poor in her *Thoughts on the Importance of the Manners of the Great to General Society* (1787). In *An Estimate of the Religion of the Fashionable World* (1790) she went further, protesting against the conventional religion of taste, fashion and urbanity, advocating 'a turning of the whole mind to God, a concentration of all the powers and affections of the soul into one steady point, a uniform desire to please him'. In the 1790s she sought to promote Evangelical Christianity as a counterweight to radical doctrines. Her collection of 'Cheap Repository Tracts' in 1795 was enormously influential, selling around 2 million copies. (Significantly, the Society for the Reformation of Manners proceeded against Paine's anti-Christian *Age of Reason* in 1797.) In the same year Wilberforce himself published his inelegantly titled *A Practical View of the Prevailing Religious System of Professed Christians in the Higher and Middle Classes of this Country contrasted with real Christianity* in which, in true Evangelical style, he called on the upper classes to set a decent, Christian example to the lower. In this vein, in 1802 the Proclamation Society changed its name to the Society for the Suppression of Vice, a reflection of the strength of the conviction that vice, especially the vice displayed by the upper classes, might be productive of social disorder.

Within a few decades, observers were commenting on the improvement on the styles of life of the upper classes and the middling classes, especially in the provinces. They noted the greater stress on family life, family prayers and family reading of the Bible in middle-class households. After the war ended, many habits and practices which had once been accepted unquestioningly were regarded more critically. Drunkenness and ostentation in dress were now much less acceptable. In polite society, respectable behaviour, self-discipline and orderliness were expected. Some, at least, of the famous values of the Victorians were making their appearance long before Victoria came to the throne.

It was not for want of trying that the Society for the Suppression of Vice was unable to achieve a similar influence among the lower classes of society. The boisterousness, licence and disorder which accompanied popular festivity disgusted serious men and women who were motivated by a severe puritanism in their personal lives. To the Evangelicals, innocent amusement could be a deadly moral trap for the unwary. Yet moral exhortation and personal example could not persuade the labouring masses to abandon their festive culture. Nevertheless, there are signs that they had some influence and that they may have slowly mellowed the worst excesses of popular culture. For example, although the Evangelicals failed in 1809 to pass a bill outlawing bull-baitings, the sport was already declining, and popular habits thus changing, due in part at least to their efforts.

The spread of the Evangelical movement within the Church of England was slow but steady. It was assisted partly by the energies of prominent individuals. Spencer Perceval, Prime Minister between 1809 and 1812, was sympathetic to the cause. Lord Harrowby, a cabinet minister, was an Evangelical. In 1812 he steered a bill through Parliament to establish minimum stipends in poor livings, graduated according to the size of the parish. In 1815 the first

Evangelical bishop, Henry Ryder, was appointed to Gloucester, partly through Harrowby's influence. By then the Evangelicals were at the centre of public networks of patronage which made them a formidable national force. Furthermore, the spread of the influence of the Evangelical movement also owed much to its ingenious organizational tactics. After 1815 Simeon began the practice of buying advowsons from a central fund to enable talented ministers to take livings in specified areas of the country. In this way, for example, Birmingham became a strongly Evangelical town. Yet the numbers of Evangelicals remained small. Many parishes remained unaffected and the movement had a limited organizational impact upon the church. Evangelicals were not able to remedy its serious structural weaknesses. On the whole, their analysis of the faults of the church was excessively spiritual, even if their faith and their energies did inject much-needed moral energy.

Evangelicals were particularly active in spreading the word of God to the pagan peoples of the British empire. In 1776 they founded the Society for Missions in Africa and the East (later better known as the Church Missionary Society). Simeon, John Venn and Henry Thornton were all closely involved. In 1795 they founded a London Missionary Society, based on united action by all the churches. Other Evangelicals founded the African Association (1806) for the welfare of West Africans. The British and Foreign Bible Society (1804) also depended on Evangelical energies; it was also powerfully supported by Methodist and Nonconformist groups. In the first 15 years of its existence, it distributed no fewer than two and a half million copies of the Bible. By 1815 every county in the land had its branch of the Bible Society. High Anglicans were furious, and continued to compete in the market of Bible distribution by continuing the work of the Society for Promoting Christian Knowledge. Evangelicals even dreamed of a Christian India. In 1813 they were involved in the appointment of a bishop and three archdeacons for the subcontinent. They even managed to secure the insertion into the new East India Charter of 1813 of a clause enabling the Board of Control in London to overrule East India Company decisions which withheld licences to missionaries.

If missionary work was a characteristic expression of the redemptionist Christianity of the Evangelicals, then the movement for the abolition of the slave trade enabled them to cooperate with other Protestant churchmen in one of most numerous and best-organized reform movements of these decades. Indeed, many abolitionists defined their work in missionary terms, slavery being but one manifestation of the barbarism against which they were crusading. The abolitionist movement arose out of the womb of the Quaker movement in 1783, before the establishment in 1787 of the London Abolition Committee. Corresponding committees sprang up in most counties and towns. In 1788 100 abolitionist petitions were presented to Parliament. They met with some modest, immediate success: an Act of that year limited the number of slaves carried by each ship. The abolitionists moved up to a major attempt to abolish the slave trade, but within a few years any prospect of passing a major reform such as abolition fell victim to the loyalist reaction. However, Wilberforce and his friends continued to struggle to obtain at least a partial or gradual abolition. Between 1800 and 1804, however, they suspended their parliamentary endeavours, knowing that they stood little chance of success. Thereafter, opinion began to shift. A few months before his death Pitt forbade the importation of slaves into newly conquered colonies. By then the abolitionists had added to their humanitarian case a direct appeal to British national self-interest. Their argument – that slavery hampered economic expansion and that abolition would foster economic development – carried the day, and persuaded a majority of MPs during the Talents ministry to pass a bill abolishing the slave trade.

Even more impressive was the popular mobilization whipped up against the institution of slavery itself within the British empire. In 1823 the Anti-Slavery Society was formed. In May of that year a motion for abolition was deflected by the Tories, who inserted the word 'gradual' into the motion, as their predecessors had done in 1792. Steadily the pressure for abolition mounted. By 1830 the Anti-Slavery Society was demanding immediate and total abolition. The extent of its agitation is impressive. Compared to the few score of abolitionist societies existing in the 1780s and 1790s, there were over 200 of them in 1814, 800 in the mid-1820s and no fewer than 1300 in 1832–33. Indeed, over 4000 anti-slavery petitions were received by Parliament between 1830 and 1833, compared with about 50 in favour. A clearer expression of national opinion would have been difficult to imagine. (Significantly, too, women took a prominent role. In 1833 a single 'ladies' petition' was signed by no fewer than 187 000.) The few parliamentary candidates at the elections of 1831 and 1832 who were lukewarm about emancipation almost invariably failed to win their seat. At the general election of 1832 the abolition of slavery became part of the Whigs' general programme of civil and religious liberty. Carried along by the reforming momentum created by the Reform Act of 1832, the bill to abolish slavery passed in 1833.

In spite of their achievements, the Evangelicals were unpopular in many quarters. Their arrogance and their determination to interfere in the lives of other people caused great offence. Their alleged hypocrisy came in for much criticism, particularly their seemingly greater concern for some of the harmless entertainments of the masses rather than real social abuses such as poverty, industrial exploitation and the employment of children. They were, it was widely believed, prepared to exert themselves for the benefit of slaves and of heathen peoples in foreign countries while ignoring the sufferings of the underprivileged at home. Furthermore, their distaste for radical reformers and their support for successive governments failed to commend them to a growing army of converts to reform after 1815.

Although their political ideology is often dismissed as Tory, the Evangelicals in their own way posed a potential threat to the establishment in the 1790s. Their values were a powerful critical commentary on the life styles of the aristocracy, the status of the Church of England, the beliefs, manners and morals of the country's elite and the manner of the performance of its paternalist responsibilities. Moreover, the Evangelicals should not be dismissed as either reactionary or irrational. Many of them welcomed progressive developments in science and on social issues. Indeed, they accepted the Enlightenment theory that people were the product of their environment and could be changed and improved by the reform of public institutions, such as prisons, hospitals and work-houses. Evangelicals certainly accepted their own responsibilities for their own actions. Thrift and hard work would thus bring their own rewards. This amounted to a form of 'spiritual capitalism', as Boyd Hilton has put it,[33] which nurtured the individualism which was frequently the dynamic of economic development. In this way, the personal morality of Evangelicalism fitted comfortably into the world of consumerism and capitalism.

Methodists and Dissenters

One of the major features of religious history in the second half of the long eighteenth century was the process by which Britain became a pluralist society, as the new Methodist and established Protestant Dissenting denominations came to rival the appeal of the Anglican church. These developments constitute one of the great religious epics in the history of modern Britain, and one which is full of significance for our understanding of Hanoverian society. The rise of Methodism may be approached at three levels. At the first it may be seen as part of a European and Atlantic religious dynamic beginning in the 1730s and 1740s which expressed itself in a revival of religious enthusiasm, taking the form of evangelical patterns of thought and worship. Many of the characteristic features of Methodism, for example, including class meetings and itinerant preaching, could be found in other countries. At the second level, it may be explained as a consequence of powerful social forces: the dramatic growth in population and drastic changes in people's living and working environments in country and in town. Yet religious revivals have an internal dynamic of their own and cannot be reduced to political or economic explanations. At the third level, indeed, changes in religious practice were triggered by changes within religious structures and cultures. In this case, a changing pattern of religiosity can be treated not merely as a growing dissatisfaction with traditional Anglican patterns of religious provision but as the revival of older patterns of high-church Anglicanism. Indeed, immediate pointers to the timing of the rise of Methodism came with the climate of ideas and sentiment generated by the publication of William Law's influential work, *Practical Treaties on Christian Perfection* (1729). Law's message – that communion with Christ was to be sought through faith and not through reason – generated ripples of commitment, especially among young Anglicans.

On his way to attend a recently founded Anglican religious group in London in May 1738, John Wesley experienced a profound religious conversion. A Church of England priest, a missionary and an Oxford don, Wesley himself traced the origins of Methodism to the 'Holy Club' formed by his brother Charles in 1729, while they were both at Oxford. But the significance of the Holy Club would have remained confined to the cloisters of Oxford had it not been for further developments. Wesley himself seems to have recognized as much when he went on a missionary journey to Georgia in the American colonies from 1736 to 1738, but he returned to England still uncertain of his future religious direction. At this time he came under the influence of the Moravians, familiarizing himself with their organization into classes and bands, their attempts to educate the poorest members of society and, most vital of all, the indispensability of faith to salvation. About this time, too, the influence of George Whitefield, one of the members of the Holy Club, who had already established himself as the most effective, popular preacher of the day, made itself felt. Whitefield brought together American missionary methods and a charismatic preaching personality. Inspired, in turn, by the open-air preaching of the Reverend Griffith Jones in Wales as early as 1714, Whitefield began to preach to huge open-air meetings in the Bristol area in 1739. Within a few weeks John Wesley followed his example and, in a series of over 150 outdoor meetings in a 10-week period from April to June 1739, addressed huge audiences. It was during these weeks that he discovered his power to move crowds and to inspire faith even among the poorest and most wretched elements in society. Within this short time, his national reputation was made. The rest of his life was to be spent on missionary tours, using his talents to move the godless to salvation by faith. Sometimes, indeed, his appeal was so overwhelming that he drew under the wing of his church small groups and connections of revivalists which already existed, especially in Yorkshire.

The numerical growth of Methodism was steady rather than spectacular. Down to his death in 1791, John Wesley covered a quarter of a million miles on horseback, preaching the word of God in no fewer than 40 000 sermons. By 1767 there were about 22 000 Wesleyan Methodists in England alone, by 1791 around 56 000, and perhaps 72 000 in the whole of Britain. By 1816 there were no fewer than 180 000 Methodists in Britain. Although in some places the growth was patchy, especially during the war years after 1793, by 1832 there were a quarter of million, in addition to perhaps another 50 000 in the various Methodist schismatic groups. These figures, however, understate the real numbers, as they include only those class members who were formally enrolled; attendance at Methodist services was considerably higher. By this time, moreover, Methodists were beginning to outnumber Anglicans in some towns.

Although the rise of Methodism owes everything to John Wesley, to his brother Charles's hymn-writing abilities and to Whitefield's own activities, a further cluster of reasons for the solid growth of Methodism lay in its organizational ingenuity. Wherever Wesley went, he left behind him small groups of people, usually fewer than 20, organized at first into 'bands', later into classes. These classes met once a week for discussion, self-confession, reading and instruction. Their members, women as well as men, were encouraged to preach. They paid a subscription of one penny a week and elected a leader who acted as their delegate to a district meeting which, in turn, elected delegates to a larger district, and thence, after 1744, to the annual conference. Methodist unity and momentum were generally maintained through a mixture of services, class meetings, band meetings, quarterly meetings and the distinctive Methodist 'love feasts'. In 1746 the societies were grouped into seven circuits. By the early nineteenth century, the 19 districts and 300 circuits delivered the word of God and gave institutional permanence to Wesley's message. Methodism is sometimes dismissed as an emotional and irrational faith; but a more productive view would be to regard it as bringing vigour, discipline and rationality to the fragmented and sometimes chaotic experiences of thousands of individuals, enabling them to find peace and security after religious torment and suffering.

One subsidiary reason for the steady expansion of Methodism and the fervent commitment of Methodists was the constant and intensive use of the press. Pamphlets and books, Bibles and lives of the saints, hymn-books and worthy literature poured from the printing presses. Indeed, the Methodist movement was to prove an excellent vehicle for the rapid and cheap circulation of print, as well as oral, culture throughout Britain and the wider world. In the *Arminian Magazine* of John Wesley, after 1778, in the *Methodist Magazine*, edited by Joseph Benson, which succeeded it, and in the large number of other Methodist periodicals and pamphlets which appeared during the reign of George III, the Methodists had constant communication with their leaders and enjoyed the benefit of their advice and influence on affairs, political as well as religious, as they arose.

Who were the Methodists? Which social and occupational groups tended to adopt Methodism? Skilled and semi-skilled artisans can account for almost half of Methodist congregations in some places. Female servants also figure prominently. Women frequently outnumbered men, especially the widowed and the unmarried, who in some Methodist communities outnumbered married women. Certain occupations recur throughout the early history of Methodism, especially clothworkers, weavers, coalminers, tinminers and seamen. However, there is often not much difference between the profile of Methodists and that of the communities in which they lived. In other words, the type of community and its geographical location are of no less importance than the occupation of individual Methodists.

Not surprisingly, Methodism was primarily to be found where the Anglican church and its hierarchical patterns of paternal and social control were weak. It tended to prosper where the Church of England was particularly unpopular, such as Lincolnshire and Caernarvonshire, where clerical magistrates had not endeared themselves to the population. It also made converts where Evangelicals made an impression and where Old Dissent was faltering. In view of the greater difficulty of seeking conversions in small, rural parishes already covered by the Anglican church, it is not surprising that Methodism tended to struggle in many country districts. In urban areas Methodists did best where economic change and population growth found the Anglican authorities unable to respond with a positive religious appeal. It prospered in many of the new industrial villages and rapidly growing towns. It also occurred in many market towns, but it was also to be found in more dispersed rural settlements which lacked unity and integration and in which Methodism could provide a solid structural core to a community. But much always depended on local factors and, above all, on the moral strength and personal charisma of particular Methodist leaders.

Methodism was much more pronounced in some districts than in others. It prospered in London, the north (Lancashire and Yorkshire), north east (Durham and Northumberland), the north Midlands (particularly Staffordshire, Derbyshire and Nottinghamshire) and parts of the west and south west of England. Other parts of the country did not prove to be attractive to Methodists: East Anglia and the counties of southern England from Wiltshire to Surrey. Methodism flourished in Wales and Ireland but not in Scotland. Calvinistic Methodism in Wales had its origins in the 1730s and remained somewhat independent of the English movement. Largely the achievement of Howell Harris, the Welsh evangelical revival had its own momentum and organization.[34] Yet Wesley made over 40 visits to Wales, and in 1746 reached an agreement with Harris to avoid duplication of effort and competition. Wesley made 21 visits to Ireland and by 1789 there were 14 000 Irish Methodists, many of them in Ulster in areas already attuned to Protestantism. By the early nineteenth century Irish Methodists were 23 per cent of the total, springing up rapidly in those parts of Ulster with the out-work system in the linen industry. Few converts to Methodism were made among the Catholic peasantry.

The first generation of Methodists saw themselves as loyal Anglicans, working within the Church of England to promulgate the message of Christ. Until his death in 1791 John Wesley regarded his movement as an agency for strengthening and revitalizing the Church of England, not as a means of weakening it. Wesley always urged his followers to attend their local parish churches, and he was always careful to ensure that his meetings did not clash with Anglican services. As we have seen, however, Methodist church organization was quite distinct from that of the Anglican church. Methodist ministers were itinerants, operating within their own national structure. In practice, moreover, the appearance of a Methodist society could draw members from the local Anglican congregation and, to all intents and purposes, weaken the established church. The culture of Methodism, and especially the emotionalism engendered by its meetings and occasional displays of religious extremism, seemed incompatible with the stately ritual and order of Anglican services. Methodists themselves seemed instinctively to see their society as an immediate and preferable alternative to that of the Anglican church. By the 1750s, indeed, the annual conference was already debating the issue of secession. Since 1739 Wesley had found it necessary to appoint lay preachers, and in the early 1750s he had to resist pressure from his followers to ordain his own ministers. The independence of the American colonies forced the issue; the reluctant Wesley was forced by the pressure of events to appoint his own American church officers. After Wesley's death a series of secessions split the movement. In 1797 the 'Kilhamite Secession' of Alexander Kilham, a 'Methodist Jacobin' who preached the virtues of simplicity, led to the establishment of the New Methodist Connection, which differed from the Methodist church in its desire to enhance still further the power of the laity. In 1806 the Independent Methodists left and, more seriously, in 1811–12 the Primitive Methodists split off from the main branch of Methodism. The Primitives represented an intensely revivalist and emotional form of popular Methodism, imported from America by the preacher Lorenzo Dow in 1805, which proceeded to sweep through the north of England and the Midlands. The Methodist leaders refused to countenance popular religious excess.

As the decades advanced Methodism became increasingly respectable. Methodists began to impose their values of sobriety and discipline upon the rowdy and ill-disciplined world of popular culture. There had always been an enormous gulf between the admonitions of the Church of England and the vigour and exuberance of popular leisure and sports, a vigour which Anglican parsons and curates had long since reluctantly steeled themselves to accept. Now, Methodists came out against wakes and parish feasts, against sports which caused cruelty to animals (including badger-, bull- and bear-baiting, cock-fighting) and even disorderly sports like village football. Most of all, however, Methodists made a stand against drink, dancing, swearing and Sabbath breaking. Their denunciation of the popular leisure activities open to the masses in a bleak and harsh society had the merit of courage, but it also explains the hostility, and sometimes the violence, with which their self-right-eousness was greeted in some quarters. Within their own communities, Methodists were anxious to replace the existing pattern of popular culture with a new popular culture of their own, a culture of hymn-singing, love feasts, and night watches. Insofar as Methodists promoted values of disci-pline and sobriety, it might be argued that they were seeking to undermine the old values of festivity and celebration with a new, perhaps recognizably 'modern' culture of restraint, work and self-discipline. In a very real sense, then, Methodists were serious in their attempts to improve the quality of daily life even if, in so doing, they made themselves less welcoming.

In such ways, Methodism bred sober, respectable and conformist personal qualities. This is not necessarily to argue that Wesley was a political reac-tionary. Like so many of his contemporaries he believed in the *divine* origins of monarchy, but he also believed that the king was bound by the laws and conventions of the nation. During the last two decades of his life he defended George III, condemned the Wilkites and in the 1790s threw his support behind the loyalist defenders of the regime against its opponents. Nevertheless, by the early years of the nineteenth century Methodist influ-ence in some communities in the north and Midlands was awakening some sections of the labouring poor from their torpor and arousing them to polit-ical activity. Indeed, Methodism gave humble men the opportunity to express themselves in public while schooling them in the arts of organization, group activity, and even financial management. In many areas of Yorkshire in 1811–12, for example, Methodists were sympathetic to Luddism. This, and the presence of Methodists in areas of radical strength like Bradford and Huddersfield, cannot have been a coincidence; it is short-sighted simply to argue that Methodism was nothing more than a conservative force which acted as a controlling agent upon radical and revolutionary tendencies.

What, then, were the consequences of Methodism? Although it is haz-ardous to attribute too much to a single cause, Methodism did much to awaken the established church from its apathy, to pave the way for the Evangelical revival and, at the personal level, to heighten and intensify reli-gious experience. Significantly, many Methodists had had prior religious involvements and, sometimes, an intense personal religious life before their conversion. There can be little doubt that Methodism injected moral strength and stamina, enabling people to withstand the harsh routines of contem-porary life. Indeed, it fostered sociability and participation, self-improvement and even a modest degree of social mobility. Through the preaching of spiri-tual regeneration in this world and its divine reward in the next, Methodists emphasized individual and moral reform rather than collective or class action. Methodism instilled discipline, sobriety and, perhaps, regularity and thrift, thus contributing to the acceptance of society's ills and burdens and the assumption of responsibility for one's own life and destiny. At the level of charity, Methodists contributed to many causes to help the suffering and the underprivileged. They were active in a wide variety of philanthropic move-ments, educational, penal and medical, and were to be found in such groups as the movement for the abolition of the slave trade and the Society for the Reformation of Manners.

Religious revivalism was not confined to Methodists and Evangelicals. It contributed markedly to the revitalization of the Protestant Dissenters. In the first part of the eighteenth century the Dissenters had declined in numbers as well as in spiritual enthusiasm. In 1715 there had been perhaps 300 000 of them out of a population of 5.5 million, but by the middle of the century that number had been at least halved. Like the Anglican church, the Dissenting churches were failing to meet the spiritual and social needs of the lower orders of society. Within Old Dissent the fortunes of the Presbyterian church were the most serious. In 1715–16 there were over 900 Presbyterian congregations; 60 years later over 100 of them no longer existed. By then they were fast becoming Unitarian in their views and drifting away from the more rigid Calvinism of the Congregationalists and Baptists. Their liberal and tolerant Christianity may appeal to the modern mind but it was not particularly conducive to their numerical health. In the early eighteenth century, Presbyterians had made up about two-thirds of all Dissenters. By 1800, however, they accounted for less than half. Similarly, the Quakers were steadily declining. At the end of the seventeenth century there had been about 40 000 of them. A century later this number had declined to 20 000 and was continuing to shrink.

It was the churches of New Dissent which prospered after the middle of the eighteenth century, and whose numbers increased spectacularly in the early nineteenth century. There were only 15 000 Congregationalists in 1750 but their numbers increased steadily thereafter, to 26 000 by 1790, 35 000 by 1800 and, remarkably, to 127 000 by 1838. A corresponding increase was experienced by the Particular Baptists, who had numbered only 10 000 in 1750. Their number had grown to 17 000 by 1790, 24 000 by 1800 and 86 000 by 1838.

One of the principal reasons for the expansion of New Dissent in the second half of the eighteenth century was the competition between Dissent and Methodism which encouraged the former to revitalize its organization. This initially took the form of itinerant preaching, often on the part of students of the Dissenting academies. Where a minister was the agent and representative of his congregation, as he usually was in the congregations of Old Dissent, itinerant preaching was not encouraged and the minister came under pressure to remain at his post. But the Congregationalists enthusiastically adopted itinerant preaching, establishing in Lancashire in 1786 a county association within which it could take place. Within a few years most counties were copying the Lancashire model. In 1796 the Baptists began to follow in their footsteps and to organize itinerant preaching tours. Significantly, in 1784 the Baptists had established a central committee to assist the construction of chapels. Furthermore, in 1816 they founded a central body to assist needy ministers. More importantly, in 1812 60 churches united to establish the Baptist Union. In 1830 even the Congregationalists decided to follow this example.

There was little significant difference in the social and occupational strata from which Old and New Dissent drew their congregations. Perhaps half of them were skilled artisans, particularly carpenters, masons, shoemakers, spinners and weavers. On the whole Old Dissent tended to draw upon a somewhat more affluent section of society than Methodism. It was less their social distinctions than their geographical locations which set them apart. Old Dissent was strongest in the London area, the south and west and, in general, other areas where Anglicanism was strong and where they had competed for religious support in the previous century. Methodism and New Dissent, on the other hand, flourished where both Anglicanism and Old Dissent failed to establish a popular and permanent presence. Within the dissenting tradition, New Dissent was a phenomenon analogous to that of Methodism within the Anglican tradition'.[35]

By the second half of the eighteenth century the intensity of religious rivalry was no longer a threat to social stability as it had been in the seventeenth. Consequently, the prospect of relieving the Protestant Dissenters of some, at least, of their disabilities was not viewed unsympathetically by Parliament. In the early 1770s the Dissenters had attempted to obtain the release of Dissenting ministers from the need to subscribe to the 39 articles. In 1779 Parliament at last agreed, demanding only that the ministers accept the Bible as the basis of Christianity, a sure sign that Britain was becoming a religiously pluralist society. Further reforms were now a distinct possibility. Parliament might have been sympathetic but extra-parliamentary opinion was less obliging. Even before their support of the American revolutionaries had rendered the Dissenters a suspect body, pro-government newspapers had already been whipping up religious prejudice against them, anticipating the sharp anti-Dissenting sentiment of the 1790s. In the late 1780s the Dissenters, led by the Presbyterians, launched a campaign to secure the repeal of the Test and Corporation Acts. This, together with the rapturous reception they gave to the French Revolution, created a massive swell of opinion against Old Dissent, one of the manifestations of which were the Birmingham riots of 1791, directed against Joseph Priestley. Not until the early years of the new century did prejudice of this type begin to subside. In many ways this was unfair to the mass of Protestant Dissenters, many of whom did not identify themselves with the advanced political views of their more radical spokesmen, such as Price and Priestley. Although, as Professor Bradley has demonstrated, Dissenters had been prominent in the petitioning campaigns against the American war,[36] many Dissenters remained neutral in their politics. Historians have perhaps tended to exaggerate the political consequences of the Dissenters' rational and scientific educational theories and practices.

Yet there can be no escaping the extraordinary renaissance that the great Dissenting academies were undergoing during the second half of the eighteenth century. Those at Findern, Hackney and Warrington were simply the most famous of a much larger number of academies which led the way in curriculum innovation and teaching methods. Most of all, they disseminated current philosophies of science and, in particular, experimental science. By the end of the century they were providing a high standard of intellectual and scientific training. Their progressive curriculum, their commitment to scientific knowledge and their doctrine of self-improvement stood in harsh contrast to the catechisms and Christian pieties of the Sunday schools of the Anglicans and Methodists. Nevertheless, the achievement of the academies should not be exaggerated. Much depended upon the abilities, reputation and personality of a gifted master. After his death the quality of education available at an academy might decline sharply. Furthermore, the number of places at these academies was always so small that they cannot have directly touched the lives of more than a small minority of boys from the families of Protestant Dissenters.

Notes

1. This case has been argued with considerable energy by L. Colley, 'The Apotheosis of George III: Loyalty, Royalty and the British Nation, 1760–1820', *Past and Present*, 102 (1984).
2. J.J. Sack, *From Jacobite to Conservative: Reaction and Orthodoxy in Britain, c. 1760–1832* (1993), p. 131.
3. *Op. cit.*, p. 124.
4. J.C.D. Clark, *English Society, 1688–1832* (1985), p. 185.
5. D. Large, 'The Decline of the Party of the Crown and the Rise of Parties in the House of Lords, 1783–1837', *English Historical Review*, 78 (1963). Yet it is dangerously easy to exaggerate the ease with which governments controlled the upper House. The attendance of the party of the crown was often very poor. That of Scots peers between 1765 and 1775 was below 10 per cent. See W.C. Lowe, 'Bishops and Scottish Representative Peers in the House of Lords', *Journal of British Studies*, 17(3) (1978).
6. Although the writer is an active participant in these discussions, he will attempt to present both sides of the case as fairly as possible. The discussion on pp. 279–84 gives both sides of the case. The subsequent comments reflect his own opinions.
7. See e.g. I.R. Christie, *Wars and Revolutions: Britain 1750–1815* (1982); J. Derry, *Politics in the Age of Fox, Pitt and Liverpool* (1990); J.C.D. Clark, 'A General Theory of Party, Opposition and Government, 1688–1832', *Historical Journal*, 23 (1980).
8. See B.W. Hill, *British Parliamentary Parties, 1742–1832* (1985); J.A. Cannon, *The Fox–North Coalition: Crisis of the Constitution* (1969); F. O'Gorman, *The Evolution of the British Two-Party System, 1760–1832* (1982); *Voters, Patrons and Parties: The Unreformed Electorate of Hanoverian England, 1734–1832* (1989).
9. See R. Stewart, *British Politics, 1830–32* (1989), p. 4.
10. 1802, 1806, 1807, 1812, 1818, 1820, 1826, 1830, 1831, 1835, 1839, 1841, 1847.
11. It is this ideological dimension to politics which makes a simple 'government v. opposition' view of early-nineteenth-century politics so inadequate. By reducing politics to office-seeking, it entirely neglects the historical dimension to the politics of the time and much of its emotional content. It also fails to take account of the ties of loyalty and sentiment between politicians in Parliament and those in the constituencies.
12. D. Eastwood, *Governing Rural England: Tradition and Transformation in Local Government, 1780–1840* (1994), p. 77.
13. See W.A. Speck, *Stability and Strife: England 1714–60* (1977), p. 20.
14. Some of them extended the capital penalty to the protection of new forms of commercial property, e.g. malicious damage to industrial land and commercial property such as factories, coalmines and turnpikes.
15. J. Rule, *Albion's People: English Society, 1714–1815* (1992), pp. 236–44; V.C. Gatrell, *The Hanging Tree: Execution and the English People, 1770–1868* (1994), pp. 18–29, 30–32, 616–18.
16. J. Beattie, *Crime and the Courts in England* (1986), p. 507. There is simply inadequate research to vindicate the view of Michael Ignatieff that the move towards incarceration revealed the development of a 'disciplinary state'. One study, of the crucially important county of Lancashire, concludes that Lancashire's prisons were

not particularly regimented and were still characterized by 'relatively humane administration'; M. de Lacy, *Prison Reform in Lancashire, 1700–1850: A Study in Local Administration* (1986), p. 55; M. Ignatieff, *A Just Measure of Pain: The Penitentiary in the Industrial Revolution, 1750–1850* (1978).

17. D. Hay, 'Property, Authority and the Criminal Law', in D. Hay, P. Linebaugh *et al.*, eds, *Albion's Fatal Tree: Crime and Society in Eighteenth Century England* (1977).
18. E.P. Thompson, *Whigs and Hunters: The Origin of the Black Act* (1975); E. Cruickshanks and H. Erskine-Hill, 'The Waltham Black Act and Jacobitism', *Journal of British Studies*, 24(3) (1985), pp. 358–65; J. Styles, 'Criminal Records', *Historical Journal*, 20 (1977), pp. 977–81.
19. D. Hay, 'Property, Authority and the Criminal Law', in Hay et al., *Albion's Fatal Tree*.
20. P.K. O'Brien, *Power without Profit: The State and the Economy, 1688–1815* (1991), p. 9.
21. J. Beattie, 'Crime and the Courts in Surrey 1736–53', in J.S. Cockburn, ed., *Crime in England* (1977).
22. D. Hay, 'War, Dearth and Theft in the Eighteenth Century', *Past and Present*, 95 (1982).
23. See above, pp. 164–8, for an extended discussion of this view.
24. Clark, *English Society* pp. 372–73.
25. *Op. cit.*, p. 373.
26. P. Virgin, *The Church in the Age of Negligence: Ecclesiastical Structure and Problems of Church Reform, 1700–1840* (1989).
27. D. Hempton, 'Religion in British Society', in J. Black, ed., *British Politics and Society from Walpole to Pitt* (1990), p. 207.
28. E. Evans, 'Some Reasons for the Growth of Rural Anti-Clericalism, c. 1750–1830', *Past and Present*, 66 (1975), pp. 84–109.
29. N. Gash, *Aristocracy and People: Britain 1815–65* (1979), p. 63.
30. A.D. Gilbert, *Religion and Society in Industrial England* (1976), pp. 27–8.
31. William Paley (1743–1805), one of the most influential and widely read Anglican publicists of the period, a passionate anti-deist and in many respects a utilitarian. Josiah Tucker (1712–99), a staunch defender of clerical subscription to the 39 articles yet an advocate of American independence. Dean of Gloucester from 1758, he was a renowned economic theorist, anticipating several of Adam Smith's arguments against monopolies.
32. R. Hole, *Pulpits, Politics and Public Order in England, 1760–1832* (1989), p. 269.
33. B. Hilton, *The Age of Atonement: The Influence of Evangelicalism on Social and Economic Thought, 1795–1865* (1988).
34. Howell Harris (1743–1805), the great pioneer of Welsh Methodists and advocate of 'family' and religious communities.
35. Gilbert, *Religion and Society in Industrial England*, p. 36.
36. J. Bradley, *Popular Politics and the American Revolution* (1986), ch. 6.

11

The social foundations of the later Hanoverian regime, 1757–1832

The United Kingdom

During the second half of the long eighteenth century the unity of the United Kingdom and Ireland endured and even strengthened, despite momentous challenges. The deployment of huge armies defended Britain from her enemies abroad. At home, however, massive standing armies and militia regiments maintained the Revolution Settlement, and thus the supremacy of England within Britain. By 1815 a coherent and a powerful British body politic was emerging. Military force, however, played only a limited part in its emergence. It was underpinned by a developing sense of a British identity. Indeed, as Professor Colley has remarked, the half-century following the Declaration of Independence was 'one of the most formative periods in the forging of British identity'.[1] I argued earlier that the growth of this identity was a consequence of four distinct yet related developments.[2] All four of them continued to function in this period.

The first of these was warfare. The American war had rallied the nation around the flag and the throne, but it was the long years of the Revolutionary and Napoleonic wars which sealed the unity of Britain. By 1815 around half a million men were serving in the army and navy combined, and another 400 000 in the Volunteers – amounting to nothing less than one in four to one in five adult British males. Having recruited so many men from so many walks of life and from so many parts of the country, the authorities proceeded to treat them undifferentiatingly as patriots. Armed service did much to dissolve national loyalties. Furthermore, from the 1813 inspection returns we can calculate that the army had become one half English, one third Irish and one sixth Scots.[3] Indeed, in the officer corps the English were already decisively outnumbered by the Scots and Irish.

This process was likely to be permanent. Moreover, once local defence had been conceded to local forces it would have been very difficult to reverse it. Already in 1794 Catholics in Ireland were being openly recruited, a conscious policy of assimilation which applied to officers and rank and file alike. By 1815 over one in six Catholic males in Ireland had seen military service with the British army; indeed, by the early nineteenth century probably three-quarters of the British soldiers in Ireland were Catholic. The loyalty which the army in Ireland displayed during the rising of 1798 was even more strongly exhibited after the Union of Ireland with England in 1800, in particular at the great king's birthday reviews which began in 1804. Such symbolic events, together with generous award of battle honours, represented the growing military incorporation of Ireland within Britain. Indeed, Irish attachment to Britain may be witnessed in the great memorial to Nelson that was erected in Dublin three years after Trafalgar, as well as in the construction of the great monument to Wellington in Phoenix Park. These developments were matched for Scotland by the creation of exclusively Scottish regiments, which became a source and a focus of Scottish pride. Over 70 per cent of Scottish soldiers were concentrated into ten, most of them Highland, regiments (the Irish, by contrast, were spread much more widely). The Revolutionary and Napoleonic wars enabled the Scots as well as the Irish to engage in present, whilst perhaps reliving ancient, military glories.

The second development which facilitated the expression of a British identity was, as it had been earlier, religion. The years of war generated a feeling of Protestant imperialism which cannot be denied. Nevertheless, there are clear signs that the polite classes were beginning to abandon the rabid Protestantism of earlier decades. The internal Catholic threat had waned with the defeat of Jacobitism. The Catholics had exhibited their loyalty to the Hanoverian dynasty in 1745 when they had furnished troops and money. They were declining in numbers, too, from 115 000 out of a population of 5.7 million in 1720 to only 70 000 out of 7.5 million in 1780, a percentage decline from a tiny 2 per cent to 1 per cent of the population. Moreover, Whig politicians had no wish to make martyrs on the business of the previous century. They had to live up to their much-vaunted boasts about the virtues of public life in Britain, one of which was religious toleration. The passage of the Catholic Relief Act of 1778 has to be seen in this context. The Act enabled Catholics to serve in the British army and legally to purchase and inherit land. Indirectly, the Act led to the Gordon Riots of 1780, a terrifying reminder that among the lower classes more brutal sentiments still persisted. This was hardly surprising: anti-Catholicism was built into the fabric of the Hanoverian body politic. Indeed, what else could be expected of a society whose national enemy had been Catholic Spain and then Catholic France, and whose commercial and imperial future depended upon almost constant commercial competition with and warfare against the Bourbon powers? However, the Gordon Riots were unable to stop the march of toleration. In 1791 Pitt passed another Catholic Relief measure which permitted the building of Catholic churches and chapels and opened up the legal profession to Catholics. The Act provoked very little opposition and, most significantly, played no part in the loyalist hysteria of 1792–93.

The political culture of the elite continued to act as a focal point of British unity. The abolition of the Irish Parliament in 1800 completed the legislative centralization of British political life and emphasized the claim of the Westminster Parliament to speak for the realm of Britain. At just this moment, the social prestige of the monarchy attained unprecedented heights. In the closing decades of the century the monarchy became the object of loyalty and, indeed, veneration not only in England but also in Wales, Ireland and even Scotland. George III gloried in the name of Britain and after his victory over Fox in 1783–84 attained huge popularity. The general sympathy for his indisposition in 1788–89 seems to have been genuine, highlighted as it was by the disgraceful and unseemly behaviour of his son. The years of war and patriotic sacrifice did much to rally the nations of Britain behind him. 'Royal visits to every part of the kingdom, carefully choreographed and synchronised royal celebrations in which all classes and both sexes were encouraged to participate, an ostentatious royal patronage of British culture' elicited approval, generated loyalty and encouraged the involvement of a wider audience.[4] (George I and George II, in contrast, had never visited Scotland, Wales, the north of England or even the Midlands.) The launching of ambitious schemes of royal building and a growing demand for royal splendour converted the monarchy into a popular focus of loyalty and emulation. The royal jubilee of 1809 was celebrated in 650 different locations in England but it was also celebrated throughout Wales, Scotland and Ireland and also throughout the empire. Affection for the royal family was expressed by the purchase of a wide variety of consumer goods, pictures, books, medals and mugs and was represented in an incessant stream of monarchical poetry, much of it written in Scotland and Ireland.

Finally, the integration of the elites of Britain continued in this period to act as a strongly unifying influence. Obviously, it was the political and social elite which was 'britannicized' first because they – merchants, bureaucrats, military adventurers – found that Britain and the British empire served their interests. 'The growing need to raise taxes and cannon fodder from the island as a whole (and from that other island across the Irish Sea) forced those elite Englishmen who initially monopolised civilian power in London to accept a quota of Scots, Anglo-Irish and Welshmen into their ranks.'[5] On the other hand, the Scottish and Irish elites set out to ingratiate themselves with the English elite during the second half of the eighteenth century, and no insuperable barriers were placed in their way. The English ruling classes of the mid-eighteenth century probably felt more comfortable with their counterparts in Ireland than with their more touchy and Jacobite counterparts in Scotland. Yet Scots flooded over the border to seek office and employment, especially in London. Furthermore, in an expanding economy there was employment aplenty for talent from the north, whether political, military, mercantile, architectural, intellectual or, above all, medical. Over 200 students a year graduated from the University of Edinburgh, far more than from all of the educational institutions of England put together. No fewer than 47 per cent of the 249 men appointed as writers (clerks) in Bengal and 60 per cent of the 371 men allowed to settle in Bengal as free merchants were Scots in the decade after 1775.[6] The resentment that Little Englanders like Wilkes felt for the Scots reflects the extent of the invasion. There are even some signs of the emergence of a British peerage at the end of the century. Of the 113 peerages created between 1780 and 1800, seven were promotions from the Scottish peerage and 17 promotions from the Irish peerage.[7]

Earlier in the eighteenth century the cosmopolitanism of the ruling classes had caused offence and even attracted ridicule. While many cosmopolitan habits persisted, not least the Grand Tour, it is possible to detect a more patriotic element in the cultural life of the second half of the eighteenth century. The founding of the Royal Academy in 1768 to advance the cause of British art unquestionably struck a note of cultural patriotism. This is also seen in the tendency to combine patriotic themes with classical motifs in landscape gardening which appears as early as the 1780s. Furthermore, in the second half of the century the ruling elite came to employ culture for patriotic purposes, commissioning native art with relish. The 2nd Earl of Egremont had been a notable collector, especially of Italian art. His son, the 3rd Earl, however, collected British painting, especially the work of Gainsborough, Reynolds and Constable. In a very different way Britain began to pay court to its own literary masters. In the middle decades of the century Shakespeare, Spenser, Dryden and Bacon came into their own. In 1765 Johnson's edition of Shakespeare elevated the bard to a new status in British history.

The British empire, furthermore, had its economic and occupational attractions for the upper and middle classes throughout Britain. The strength of the burgeoning imperial loyalties thus created should not be underestimated. Already in the first half of the century awareness of and pride in empire were spreading throughout British society. In the second half of the century, however, Britain became an imperial nation, many of its people flocking to make their lives, their futures and their fortunes in the empire. The loss of the empire in North America in some ways actually facilitated the emergence of a British imperial identity. The mere fact of empire reinforced assumptions about British superiority. Images of overseas empire, naval dominion and limitless oceanic wealth began to infect British consciousness with jingoistic militarism and expansionism. Possession of a worldwide empire, especially one which after 1783 was based in the East among dark-skinned Asiatics, enabled Britons to assume a variety of roles: military conqueror, civilizing gentlemen and gentlewomen, enterprising merchant, Christian missionary, educational reformer, scientific collector and geographical explorer. British *imperial* identity was many-sided rather than monolithic, inclusive rather than exclusive.

The significance of these influences moulding one or more British identities are important, but they should not be exaggerated. First, they run the risk of exaggerating the cohesion and stability of the British body politic, which was not infrequently in serious danger, as in 1715–16, 1745–46, 1779–84 and, as we shall shortly see, 1798. There was nothing inevitable about the success of the project to create a British state out of the composite state of the early eighteenth century. Second, there was no significant countervailing decline in Scottish, Welsh or Irish consciousness. A sense of British national identity developed alongside, not at the expense of, sentiments of Englishness, Welshness, Scottishness and Irishness. There was a complex interaction between national cultures within the broader framework of Britain. All nations within the British state, Wales, Scotland, Ireland and, not least, England, experienced a dramatic revival of interest in their own cultural traditions, in their art, their history and their literature.[8] Wales, for example, maintaining her own language and less addicted to participating in imperial adventures than the Scots and Irish, remained more distinct than either. Seen from London, Wales appeared to be stable and quiescent; Welsh Jacobitism was never very strong, and signs of positive resentment at Welsh incorporation into Britain were never very visible. But such perceptions should not allow us to underestimate the powerful evidence of residual Welsh self-awareness. Wales had an expanding middle class, aware of its own capacities and which was capable of taking the appropriate cultural and educational pathways to self-improvement. It was increasingly indignant at the linguistic hegemony of the English language in a Welsh-speaking society. For this the Welsh gentry had been at least partly to blame, because in the early eighteenth century they had begun to abandon their role as patrons and preservers of their own language and culture. Although poverty and local isolation were further inhibitions upon the continuing process of Welsh self-consciousness, the spread of the printed word, the growth of tourism and an enhanced nostalgia for a lost Welsh culture were beginning to exert a discernible influence by the 1770s. The Wilkite and Wyvillite movements did not set Wales alight but they planted the seeds of politicization. From its lowest ebb in 1700, Welsh culture now began to experience a general revival, particularly in the fields of poetry and antiquarianism. In this way the Welsh used the power of the printing press to enhance their own identity within a British political and social framework.

In Scotland in the second half of the eighteenth century the complex processes of assimilation were continuing. The military disaster of 1745–46 marked the passing of the Jacobite option. Road-building in the Highlands and the subsequent restructuring of traditional Scottish society in the years after 1745 took the sting out of Scottish national feeling. Scotland was politically quiescent in the second half of the eighteenth century. There was now nothing to prevent the emergence of a powerful loyalty towards the Hanoverian dynasty in the northern kingdom, not least among the old Jacobite aristocracy. Even the son of the Lord Lovat who was executed for treason in 1746 had the family estates restored to him three decades later out of gratitude for his part in the conquest of Canada. Emigration out of the Highlands and the service of many Highlanders in the armies of the crown acted as a safety valve against any revival of militant nationalism.

As the long eighteenth century neared its end, the tactical options of any sort of *national* or, still more, *nationalist* insurrection were steadily receding. Scotland was noticeably loyal during the American War of Independence, a stance which contrasted strongly with dissident stirrings in Ireland.[9] By the end of the century there was emerging a powerful *British* sentiment, manifested in the great rebuilding of Edinburgh. As Linda Colley has remarked: 'Scottish towns were now far more affluent places, secure in post-Jacobite stability, made fat on imperial trade, elegant private houses and imposing public building.'[10] The showpiece was Edinburgh New Town, designed in 1767 as a celebration of British patriotism, and the most famous but by no means the only such example of imperial consciousness in Scotland. The rebuilding of Glasgow at the same time was triggered by the colonial trade, interests which were reflected in the names of some of the more prominent of the streets of the town.[11] Such tendencies were enhanced by the unprecedented flow of Scottish professional and artistic talent into England. These people brought with them some of the older patriarchal and authoritarian attitudes which in Scotland, at least, were becoming increasingly redundant, but which were becoming increasingly typical of English society in the second half of the eighteenth century.

By 1800 Scotland still retained many of the characteristics of a distinct nation, but it was a nation that was fairly comfortably contained within the wider unit of Britain. This was deliberate state policy. London began to look carefully to the stability of the Scottish economy by subsidizing basic industries like tanning and paper-making, by offering bounties to improve the manufacture of linen and by training skilled workers. Prosperity and patriotism were never far apart. The assimilation of Scotland into Britain had always been facilitated by access to imperial wealth and trade. After 1750 the Scottish economy grew at an accelerating rate, especially in the Glasgow region, faster even than that of England. Between 1750 and 1800 its overseas trade tripled in volume while that of England doubled. As the bitter legacies of Jacobitism receded further into the past a new Scotland was fast emerging. With it came a new sense of Scottish national identity within a larger, Britannic framework.

But what was to be this new identity? At least two variants became available in the later eighteenth century. The first involved an exaggerated and nostalgic vision of Scotland. 'Scots tried to balance out their loss of political independence by exaggerating their special characteristics – literature, education, religion and general "moral fibre".'[12] Furthermore, the writings of authors from Robert Burns to Sir Walter Scott served to present the history of the Scottish past as a romantic tale of cultural loss and a catalogue of military heroism against the English. This idealized view of Scottish society in the past, founded upon the clan system, was being propagated during the years in which that society was being dismantled after 1745.[13] This romantic view of Scottish history and culture did much to shape nineteenth- and twentieth-century perceptions of Scottish national identity, but it is largely a wistful and fabricated version. An alternative version of Scottish identity was asserted during the Scottish Enlightenment of the second half of the eighteenth century. This was the ideal of a cosmopolitan and highly cultured and progressive Scotland occupying a proud place within a 'British' body politic. Building on the foundation of Scotland's universities and schools, Scots writers and artists took advantage of this period of peace and moderate prosperity to experience an Enlightenment which even Voltaire celebrated, claiming that 'at the present time it is from Scotland we receive rules of taste in all the arts – from the epic poem to gardening'. The Scottish Enlightenment was an extraordinary flowering of talent – Adam Smith in economics, Dugdale Stewart in moral philosophy, David Hume and William Robertson in history, James Boswell in biography, James Watt in engineering, Tobias Smollett in fiction – which announced the arrival of a new cultural power in Europe, artistic, humane, scientific and progressive.

In political terms, the assimilation of Scotland to England was starkly illustrated in the political imperialism of Henry Dundas. As Lord Advocate of Scotland in 1775, Dundas began to erect a huge empire of Scottish patronage, controlled from London. By the time of the general election of 1780 Dundas was the most powerful political figure in Scotland, enjoying the support of many of the 45 Scottish MPs. At the general election of 1784 he influenced the return of half their number. Through the extensive deployment of patronage, thus procuring the loyalty of local and regional magnates, he was able to increase this support to well over 30 at the election of 1790. As Home Secretary in 1791 and as Secretary for War in 1794 he used this enormous influence to sustain the ministry of Pitt, to strengthen English control of Scotland and thus to enhance the integration of Scotland into the English body politic. In so doing he raised Scotland from its somewhat peripheral and subordinate status and brought Scottish interests squarely before the locus of power in London.

Down to the 1760s Ireland was more securely under the control of the British government than was Scotland. In political terms, the *'ancien régime'* in Ireland continued comfortably enough into the second half of the eighteenth century. The power of the Protestant Ascendancy was unimpaired. The alliance of the British administration of the Lord Lieutenant at Dublin Castle with the Anglo-Irish Protestant landed interest provided stability, and a tolerable degree of prosperity, even if it did not seek to cure the fundamental religious and economic problems of the island. In the Irish Parliament an opposition party of 'Patriots' emerged under Henry Grattan and Henry Flood.[14] They advocated greater political autonomy for Ireland within the British empire and demanded greater commercial equality. The concession of an Octennial Act in 1768, which provided for regular elections at least every eight years, did little to satisfy Patriot opinion.

Meanwhile, the economy of Ireland was experiencing a period of steady growth. Although she remained little more than an economic dependency of England – between 1720 and 1800 the percentage of Irish exports shipped to England rose from 44 per cent to over 80 per cent – some sectors of the Irish economy prospered. Agricultural prices doubled and rents quadrupled in the last third of the century as Irish landlords struggled to cope not only with English demand for grain but, more importantly, with the social and economic consequences of the rapid growth in the population of Ireland during the eighteenth century, from about 2.5 million in 1701 to about 4.57 million in 1791. Although English regulations had weakened the ability of the Irish woollen and cattle industries to export, the Irish developed alternative export trades in butter, linen and hides. Indeed, in 1758–59 concessions permitting the freer export of Irish dairy produce to European markets reinvigorated Irish dairy farming in some areas. These signs of economic development were reflected in the continued growth of market towns like Cork and Limerick, in the remarkable development of Dublin and in the growth of the great mansions of the landlords of the Ascendancy. A small middle class, much of it Catholic, was expanding. Increasingly well informed and self-conscious, it began to press for the repeal of the Penal Laws.

These promising economic developments were damagingly affected by the interruption to trade with the American colonies caused by the war. The resulting economic problems – unemployment, high prices and shortages – created unsettled conditions in which protest against English rule, often in conscious imitation of American precedents, became widespread. Indeed, the Patriots within the Irish Parliament now came out in support of the American rebels. In these conditions, religious resentment revived. Some Irish peasants, angry at having to pay tithes to the Church of Ireland, joined the secret society of Whiteboys, which carried out physical attacks on landlords, tenants, cattle and ricks. Such actions were imitated by other religious groups, notably the Steelboys, a group of Ulster Presbyterians.

Economic crisis was matched by a vacuum of security. British troops were required for service in America and Ireland was left almost defenceless. This military vacuum became an imminent crisis in 1778 when the prospect of a Franco-Spanish invasion of Ireland became a real possibility. The vacuum was filled by the emergence of the Volunteers in Ulster in 1778, officered by the Irish Protestant gentry. The Volunteers began to act as a political as well as a military force and, appealing to Protestant and Catholic alike, demanded economic and political reform. Their influence spread rapidly; by 1780 there were about 40 000 Volunteers. At war with half of Europe in 1779–80, and facing a repetition of American techniques of popular agitation, the British government had no alternative but to make sizeable economic concessions. In 1780 a series of statutes enabled Ireland to export glass and wool, to import gold and silver and to trade with the empire on the same terms as the English themselves. This bought off protest for a time. As in England, however, the defeat of British troops at Yorktown created political earthquakes in Ireland. At the great Convention of Dungannon in February 1782, representatives of no fewer than 80 000 Volunteers demanded greater political freedom for Ireland. In 1782 Rockingham repealed both Poynings Law and the Declaratory Act of 1720, thus achieving legislative independence for Ireland. The Williamite Settlement was at an end.

'Ireland is now a nation,' rejoiced Grattan, but she was not an independent nation. In fact, the new Parliament, 'Grattan's Parliament', as it is usually termed, was a great disappointment to the Irish. A third of its members were pensioners or placemen; only half were returned by anything resembling a free election. The Parliament still did not represent the Roman Catholic and Presbyterian populations, who together made up over 90 per cent of the population. Nor could members of these denominations become MPs. Indeed, it was not Grattan's Parliament at all, dominated as it was by the Anglo-Irish oligarchy. It was helpless to weaken the traditional English monopoly of political, ecclesiastical and judicial power. Yet it was just powerful enough to unsettle relations with England on major issues. It forced Pitt to drop his trade proposals of 1785. Furthermore, and potentially even more dangerously, it chose in 1789 to follow Fox's line and to install the Prince of Wales as regent. By then, the minority had developed what Marianne Elliot has termed a 'constitutional nationalism' – an awareness of themselves as the leaders of Irish opinion, an alternative ruling elite.[15]

It was at just this moment that the French Revolution worked upon the situation in Ireland, both to agitate and to transform it. It created enormous pressure to reform established institutions and to change prevailing relationships. More significantly, however, it played upon the provincial nationalism of the Protestant Dissenters of Ulster and, most dangerously of all, it generated reform ambitions among sections of the Catholic population. It was these newer political objectives which, in the end, led to the rising of 1798. The rising was not the culmination of decades of exploitation and intolerance but the consequence of the politics of the 1790s and new ideologies of republicanism and separatism.

These were at first distant and unlikely goals. Wolfe Tone and a group of middle-class reformers founded the society of United Irishmen in Belfast in October 1791, whose initial objectives included greater independence for Ireland and religious toleration. The Belfast society was originally largely Protestant; that in Dublin, founded in November 1791 by Napper Tandy, was predominantly Catholic. Even in its early stage the Dublin society expressed social as well as political objectives. 'Give the poor a country,' it warned the rich in 1793 'or you will lose one yourselves.'[16] In the background, too, the ominous threat of peasant violence was intensifying. Pitt was forced to make concessions. Under his influence, in 1792 the British administration at Dublin Castle passed an Irish Catholic Relief Act, which lifted some of the more important restrictions on Catholics: to hold legal and judicial positions, to carry arms, to own property, to serve on juries and to enter universities. In 1793 another Relief Act gave Catholics the vote in municipal and parliamentary elections. This was as far as Pitt was prepared to go in wartime. When Earl Fitzwilliam, who became Lord Lieutenant in 1795 as a consequence of the Pitt–Portland coalition, dismissed some of the existing ministers at the Castle and indicated his willingness to discuss proposals for Catholic emancipation he was immediately removed by London. Dublin, politicized by the United Irishmen and driven by local rural secret societies such as the Defenders, exploded into violence. The British government now threw its weight solidly behind the Ascendancy.

The Catholic majority now had nothing to hope for from the British government, but they were open to the appeal of the United Irishmen. By the end of 1795 the Ulster middle-class Dissenters who had been at the heart of the United Irishmen in its early years were being challenged by lower-middle-class Catholics, angered by the recall of Fitzwilliam, with an agenda of conspiracy and revolution. The Catholic church itself was seriously divided; the hierarchy, impressed with the concession by the government of the establishment of a seminary at Maynooth in 1795, was inclined to be cautious about the call for further reform.

Catholic grievances were influenced by economic hardship, which culminated in systematic rural violence. Among the Catholic majority, groups of Defenders emerged, secret, oath-taking societies which invested in conspiratorial, sectarian violence against Protestants, who retaliated by forming 'Peep O'Day' societies. Defenderism enabled large numbers of local grievances to be welded together within a national format. As early as 1792 the Defenders had been contemplating a rising with French support and had even made overtures to the French. This was going much too far for the United Irishmen. Moreover, horrified Protestants were outraged by Defenderism. They were already concerned at the relief legislation of 1792–93, indeed, by the general drift of concessions to Catholics made since the 1770s. As religious divisions worsened the traditional social and religious controls began to break down. In September 1795 the 'Peep O'Day' boys inaugurated the Orange Society to commemorate William III's victories. The brutality and violence with which the Orange lodges and the government put down Defenderism and other forms of Catholic protest was, perhaps, to be explained by the fears and needs of wartime. To the Catholics, however, together with the fact that an exclusively Protestant yeomanry was formed to suppress these disturbances, this was final proof that the Protestant Ascendancy and the British government were at one in their wish to exploit the masses and to subjugate the old faith.

By 1796 the United Irishmen had committed themselves to a platform of republican independence with French assistance. Tone went to France in that year to plan and coordinate the coming insurrection. The United Irishmen were strong in the Dublin and Belfast areas; elsewhere they had to coordinate their actions with groups of Defenders. The only prospect of success for the United Irishmen and the Defenders lay in a rising occurring simultaneously with a French invasion. In December 1796 a French fleet with 14 000 troops under Hoche reached Bantry Bay but was unable to effect a landing. Had the French landed there would have been little to stop them: there were very few regular soldiers in Ireland. If the French had marched on Dublin, how much support would they have attracted as liberators of the Irish nation? If a republic had been proclaimed, could it have survived? Such questions make for fascinating speculation. What matters is that the failure of the French to land gave the British forces of order time to organize. Ulster was disarmed in 1797 with ruthless violence and torture, while the more moderate leaders of the United Irishmen were seized. In the south a government spy network penetrated the organization of the rebels. Moreover, the Catholic church came out against the United Irishmen (only 70 priests out of 1800 were ultimately to be involved in the rising). Consequently there was little support among the peasantry for the rising when it came in May 1798. The rebels did not wait for the French. In the north, the Presbyterian farmers of Antrim and Down rose without much coordination with the Catholic rebels south of Dublin, the small farmers and labourers of Carlow, Wexford and Wicklow. But the west, where a small French force ultimately appeared in 1798, remained quiet. Most important of all, Dublin had been secured by the authorities in a series of pre-emptive strikes. The rising was ended by the bitter defeat of the rebels at Vinegar Hill and by subsequent savage military reprisals. Altogether the rising cost 12 000 Irish lives.

It was clear to Pitt and his cabinet colleagues that the Protestant Ascendancy was no longer a reliable basis for keeping Ireland both politically and militarily secure during the Napoleonic Wars. Sizeable measures of parliamentary reform might just have satisfied the Catholic majority, but they would only have horrified the Protestants, and might even have led to a Catholic-dominated Irish Parliament opting for independence, and to a violent Protestant backlash. The Protestant minority and the Catholic majority could only be reconciled, and the interests of Great Britain preserved, through a policy of Union. In 1800 the Act of Union passed the British Parliament with no difficulty, but more persuasion was needed in Ireland. Pitt held out hopes of some measure of further emancipation for the Catholics, and promised that compensation would be paid for those who suffered by the Act. But it was not so much financial persuasion as a growing political recognition that there was no alternative to Union which convinced enough members of the Ascendancy to vote for it. Few individuals changed their stated opinions on Union in 1799–1800. On the other hand, the prospect of compensation must have convinced many fence-sitters. One and a quarter million pounds were spent on compensating borough proprietors. Underlying such persuasions was the feeling among the Ascendancy that their position could best be guaranteed through incorporation with Britain. Many Catholics, too, supported Union because it promised reform and an administration which would treat them with less brutality than they had recently endured.

In 1800 the Irish Parliament voted for its own extinction by passing the Act of Union of the two Parliaments, to take effect from 1 January 1801. By the Act 100 Irish MPs were to be added to the British House of Commons and 28 Irish peers and four bishops to the House of Lords. The two Anglican churches of England and Ireland were to be amalgamated and the legal administrations of the two countries unified. Ireland received considerable economic benefits: free trade with Britain, 20 years of protection for the Irish textile industry and an independent exchequer until 1817. Ireland, however, had to pay 12 per cent of the costs of the British budget.

The Act of Union had serious consequences for the Irish. Pitt was unable to persuade either the King or the majority of his cabinet of the necessity for Catholic emancipation, and on this issue he resigned in February 1801. Had Pitt been able to pass emancipation, perhaps accompanied by other measures of economic and social reform, the history of Ireland in the nineteenth and twentieth centuries might have been very different. On the other hand, if emancipation had been a condition for Union then Union would probably not have passed the English Parliament. Pitt's hope was that Union might be followed by some degree of emancipation, by commercial development, by prosperity and by the subsequent softening of denominational tensions. His resignation put an end to all these possibilities. Later historical tradition that Pitt deliberately misled the Irish over emancipation have little validity in fact, but the Irish Catholics had every reason to feel cheated.

With the benefit of hindsight, the Union established a framework for the development of Ireland in the nineteenth century which was to have tragic consequences, but these could not possibly have been anticipated in 1800. Nevertheless, the introduction of free trade in the nineteenth century weakened Irish industry and devastated the rural scene at a time of rapid population increase. After the Union the Irish gentry began to leave their estates, and even their country. In the long term, too, the Irish Catholic Church, with the final discrediting of the United Irishmen, emerged as the sole and uncontested champion of Catholic Ireland, a fact that was to have enormous repercussions for Ireland in and after the 1820s. Such development lay decades in the future. When George IV visited Dublin in 1821 he received the sort of welcome that he was to receive on his royal visit to Scotland a year later. There was, even then, some reason to believe that Ireland would not be a nation lost to Britain.

Economy and empire

The second half of the long eighteenth century is remarkable for the speed of its economic growth and the mounting effect of economic change in many areas of British life. There is not space to do justice here to these developments in a work more specifically directed to political themes and their background, but they clearly should not be ignored. It will be useful at least to identify some of these changes and to indicate their relationship to the imperial, and to some extent to the political, circumstances of the period.

One of the primary causes of economic growth was the extraordinary population increase, outlined in Table 11.1, which was steady in the first half of the eighteenth century, rapid in the second half of the eighteenth century and positively explosive in the early decades of the nineteenth century. Scotland's population grew rather more slowly than that of England and Wales in the long eighteenth century, Ireland's much more quickly.[17] The existence of more mouths to feed encouraged agricultural producers to grow food more efficiently. The development, moreover, of a steadily expanding consumer market stimulated British manufacturers to increase their levels of production and exerted pressure on them to improve their efficiency. In general a growing population, increasingly concentrated in urban centres – between 1700 and 1850 the percentage of the population of England and Wales living in towns increased from about one quarter to about one half – made it immensely profitable for people to improve production and services. These developments prompted the most extensive changes in transport which Britain had experienced since Roman times.

There can be little question that these changes were demand-led because the construction of turnpikes and canals involved few great technical difficulties: they could have been built 50 years earlier had the demand for them existed. Similarly, they could have been financed much earlier because the financial institutions and the capital surpluses which their construction required already existed. When they came, the changes in transport were monumental in their significance. They linked areas and regions hitherto remote and separate, they facilitated contact and communications of all types, they cheapened the transportation of goods and they thus encouraged agriculture, commerce and industry. What is often forgotten is that they assisted the frequent transmission of news, information and postal communications which went far towards unifying the political nation. In 1751 it took two days to travel by coach from London to Oxford. In 1828 it took six hours. In 1740 one coach a week travelled between Birmingham and London; in

Table 11.1 Population of Britain 1701–1851

Year	England and Wales	Scotland	Ireland	England (less Monmouth)*	Compound annual rate of growth over preceding decade*
1701	5.30	1.04	2.54	5.058	–
1751	6.50	1.25	3.12	5.772	–
1761	6.70	–	–	6.147	0.6
1771	7.20	–	–	6.448	0.5
1781	7.50	–	–	7.042	0.9
1791	8.25	1.50	4.75	7.740	0.9
1801	9.20	1.60	5.22	8.664	1.1
1811	10.20	1.80	6.00	9.886	1.3
1821	12.00	2.10	6.80	11.492	1.5
1831	13.90	2.40	7.80	–	–
1841	15.90	2.60	8.20	–	–
1851	17.90	2.90	6.50	–	–

* Data from E.A. Wrigley and R.S. Schofield, *The Population History of England, 1541–1871* (1981)

1783 that single coach had become 30; by 1829 there were 34 *a day*. By the 1820s no fewer than 55 coaches were leaving Cheltenham *each day* not only for local destinations but also for London, Exeter, Liverpool and even Holyhead. Such examples could be multiplied indefinitely.

Transport by road was improved by the establishment of turnpike trusts, which financed and maintained improvements to particular routes. The number of turnpike trusts grew slowly in the first half of the eighteenth century; on average, eight Acts of Parliament per year established trusts. Between 1750 and 1770 the number shot up to 40, and after a relaxation in growth between 1770 and 1790 the annual average figure rose to 55 and, from 1800 to 1830, to over 80. By the 1830s there were over 1100 trusts responsible for over 22 000 miles of road. (This compared with over 100 000 miles of parish highways.) By 1830 the principal networks of roads had been built, not only in England but also in Scotland and Ireland. Turnpike Acts are an excellent example of the facilitating role that Parliament played in response to local economic initiatives. So long as local sponsors could agree on the establishment of a turnpike, its approval by Parliament was normally a matter of course. Moreover, if in England road-building was left to private initiative, in Scotland and Ireland the state took a much more prominent role. The earlier network of military roads built in the Highlands under General Wade between 1725 and 1737 and after the '45 by Major Caulfield was modernized by Telford in the early years of the nineteenth century under the auspices of the Commissioners for Highland Roads and Bridges in 1803. Under its terms the state paid half the cost of road-building and maintenance. Elsewhere in Scotland, turnpikes connected the major centres, particularly after 1790; by the 1840s a modern network of roads was in place. In Ireland in 1822 parliamentary grants aided road-building and in 1831 a Board of Works was established which assumed responsibility for roads, canals and public works. Without such political approval and state sponsorship, road improvements would have been much less comprehensive.

Political sponsorship was somewhat less in evidence in the case of the canal-building of the eighteenth century, but political endorsement was no less essential. Canal-building proceeded steadily throughout the century but with particular rapidity during two periods of low interest rates, the early 1750s and the late 1780s and early 1790s. In the earlier period many canals were cut in the north west and the Midlands, of which the Manchester Ship Canal was the most notable example. Later cuts linked the emerging canal system to the great rivers: for example, in 1772 the Mersey was linked to the Severn at Stourport and in 1778 to the Trent; in 1790 it was joined up to the Trent and the Thames. The Grand Junction, started in 1793, finally linked the Midlands with London in 1805. Most canal-building was privately initiated and funded; occasionally, however, the government might step in, as it did with the financing of the Caledonian Canal, which rendered unnecessary the dangerous and unpleasant sea journey around the north of Scotland. Canal building petered out in the 1830s. By then the canal mania was over and 4000 miles of navigable waterway were in existence.

The importance of canals has perhaps been exaggerated. They are best treated as a regional phenomenon. They were of the first importance to the opening up of the north west and the Midlands but somewhat less important elsewhere. There were relatively few canals in much of southern and eastern England, and their number and function in the north east was limited. In general, their superiority to roads was limited to the transportation of bulky and heavy loads at reliable, if low, speeds. They also tended to be slow to navigate in hilly districts and in poor weather conditions. Nevertheless, they transported coal and iron and certain other heavy manufactured products not only more cheaply but over much greater distances than had ever been the case before. British civil engineers were confronted with large-scale engineering problems. Their skills in solving them and the accumulation of experience which they acquired were to be of considerable importance in the railway age of the 1840s.

Improvements in communications stimulated the movement of goods, whether agricultural or industrial, and thus promoted trade, external but particularly, internal. It was not domestic markets alone which drove and sustained the demand for manufactured goods; new markets abroad also created demand. Indeed, foreign demand for British goods was always well ahead both of population growth and of output. At the start of the eighteenth century exports represented about 7 per cent of national output, about 17 per cent at the end. One historian has estimated that over the century as a whole exports were responsible for as much as 40 per cent of the increase in industrial output.[18] Furthermore, by 1800 about one-third of all manufactured goods were exported compared to one-fifth at the beginning of the century. Although the Continental System served for a time to depress British trade with Europe, it focused British interest upon new markets in South America. After the war British exports to Europe quickly recovered, until in 1830 they accounted for 40 per cent of all exports. As for trade with North America, in spite of the pessimism which overcame commercial circles at the end of the American war, the older patterns of commerce with that continent rapidly re-established themselves in the 1780s. Indeed, by 1785 British trade with America had recovered, and the new nation proceeded to supply raw cotton in ever-increasing quantities for the British market. In return, British manufactures satisfied rapidly rising consumer demand in America.

Commercial expansion stimulated industrial development in Britain but its importance should not be exaggerated. It is not clear, for example, that commercial expansion did much directly to stimulate technological change. Down to the 1780s most of the growth in exports was in traditional sectors such as wool and metals. The important inventions in cotton occurred when exports were still small, not when they were leaping ahead. Similarly, it cannot be maintained that it was profits from the commercial sector which fuelled the drive to invest in industry. It has been estimated that reinvested profits amounted at most to 15 per cent of total investment in the British economy. Nevertheless, commerce familiarized people with credit transactions and bills of exchange, and stimulated profit-making and profit-seeking values. In some towns, especially the west-coast ports of Bristol, Glasgow and Liverpool, local accumulations of capital led to industrial investment in the textile industries in their respective regions, but their extent was limited. Finally, commerce did not automatically create a surplus in the balance of trade. After 1800, indeed, the price of exports fell steeply and Britain carried a mounting trade deficit, not a surplus. By 1815, therefore, the City of London was playing a vital part in financing investment and trade with new markets in Africa, Asia and Latin America.

The enlargement of the British empire was a natural extension of steadily mounting commercial activity. Here, once more, political considerations played their part. This is not to say that rational programmes of imperial expansion and government existed. They did not. Even in the years after the loss of the American colonies there are few signs of a systematic rethinking of imperial relationships. Consciously motivated policies of imperial expansion were conspicuous by their absence. Although there was much reflective theorizing about the British empire, precious little of it seems to have penetrated ministerial circles. Imperial questions were dealt with as they arose. Some historians have even doubted whether anything like an 'imperial policy' existed at all. What may politely be termed administrative pluralism reigned. Between 1768 and 1782 a third or Colonial Secretary existed, but thereafter colonial policy was transferred to the Home Secretary. In 1784 a replacement for the old Board of Trade came into existence and it exercised some responsibility for the colonies. The new Indian territories remained outside this structure. Until 1784 they were ruled by an army of officials from the East India Company. In 1784 Pitt's India Bill established a Board of Control which exercised indirect supervision over British territorial possessions in India. Significantly, the same bill extended the powers of the governor-general over the council. In most places the old ways and the old structures continued. The empire remained an untidy mixture of colonies and settlements, and it was still governed according to the old prescriptions.

Yet it would be absurd to deny that in the later eighteenth century a remorseless and strategic policy of imperial *acquisition* was pursued by the British state. It was not undertaken according to any blueprint and it was not achieved on any preconceived timetable. It amounted, however, to a coherent pattern of commercially valuable acquisitions. The loss of the American colonies was compensated for by the consolidation of the empire in Canada and by a flood of new acquisitions, most of them in commercially and strategically vital locations. Britain acquired New South Wales (1788) and the Cape (1806). In Africa she occupied Sierra Leone (1808), Mauritius (1810), The Gambia (1816) and the Gold Coast (1821). In Asia she obtained Penang (1785), Ceylon (1795), Singapore (1819), Malacca (1824) and Western Burma (1824). In India the empire was extended by the acquisition of Bengal (1793) and Poona (1802). In the Caribbean Britain won Trinidad (1797), Tobago and St Lucia (1803) and Demerara (1814). In the government of these numerous and widely distributed colonies, British policymakers were anxious to maintain colonies as outlets for exports and as sources of materials. At the same time they sought to foster the loyalty of local elites whose respect for the principles of hierarchy and property – to say nothing of Evangelical Christianity – reflected the dominant patterns of civilized life in Britain itself. In many parts of the empire after 1783 imperial government struck a firm note, as though Britain had learned the lessons of 'salutary neglect' which had lost her the American colonies. Both the Cape and New South Wales received authoritarian governors. Canada received in 1791 a constitution in which a governor-general, assisted by an appointed legislative council in the two provinces of Upper (Ontario) and Lower (Quebec), more than balanced the powers of elected provincial assemblies. The government of India was the subject of many changes which owed much to political considerations but little to systematic thought and planning. After 1784 the subcontinent was governed by a succession of strong governor-generals who were in theory responsible to a council of Indian and English officials.

In the second half of the period covered by this book, then, the British empire became a truly global empire ruled by the British crown in Parliament, an empire which made Britain the greatest power on earth. It was an intoxicating vision, the object of immense pride and burgeoning patriotism. Such an imperial consciousness emphasized and confirmed a powerful Protestant triumphalism. Emigrants took with them to the colonies a strong British cultural nationalism which was to have a long and enduring history.

The British still assumed that the world trading role of her empire brought economic benefits to the mother country which were indispensable to her great-power status. Consequently, they never doubted that colonial trade should be reserved for British shipping and colonial markets retained for British manufactured goods. Britain had always been determined to retain her empire in North America and the West Indies; indeed, her inflexible determination to retain the North American colonies had driven her into one of the most disastrous wars in her history. Until the 1770s the British had assumed that American colonists, like the Welsh and the Scots, were part of the British nation. Defeat plunged Britain into a mood of intense pessimism. The loss of the colonies, it was widely believed, presaged economic ruin and national decline. Yet this mood soon passed; national resilience restored British pride and optimism. Finally, earlier uncertainty about the value of India was quickly overcome; before the end of the century the subcontinent was well on the way to becoming a jewel in the imperial crown.

Yet there can be no doubting the changing orientation of Britain's geopolitical role as she underwent the transition from European to world power. In 1700 82 per cent of Britain's home produced exports went to Europe; in 1772 it was only 40 per cent. In 1700 68 per cent of her imports came from Europe; in 1772 only 47 per cent did. In 1713–17 Europe's share of Britain's overseas trade was 74 per cent; by 1803–07 it was down to 33 per cent. There are at least two economic explanations for this fundamental shift in the pattern of British commerce. First, there is some evidence that down to the third quarter of the century it was import-led demand, especially for the new colonial products, silk and tobacco, which determined the changing pattern of British trade. Second, Britain needed to find new markets for her wares in view of the difficulty of expanding markets for the old – largely woollen – products. This she did particularly in British North America. The percentage of British domestic exports going to North America, in fact, steadily increased from 10 per cent in 1700 to 37 per cent in 1772 and to no less than 57 per cent in 1800. Britain was already becoming the warehouse as well as the shop window of the world.[19]

This she achieved in spite of, perhaps in some ways because of, her involvement in the Revolutionary and Napoleonic wars. Although it has been argued that the wars in fact inhibited rather than stimulated the economy, the real position is hugely complex. The evidence available suggests that the wars did slow down the levels of growth of the British economy achieved during the exceptional period of recovery after the American war, 1783–92. Some British industries were damaged by the war, including building, brewing, malt, salt and spirits, but others surged ahead, including shipbuilding, metallurgy, textiles, silk and paper. In general, the average rate of growth of industrial production was more rapid in the 1780s and 1820s than in the intervening decades, but not by an enormous margin. In fact trade continued to increase strongly in that period, even compared to the levels of 1783–92. Exports to America boomed and, thanks to the superiority achieved by the British navy, trade with mainland Europe continued to increase until the Peace of Amiens. The closure of European ports to British ships during 1806–14 had a serious effect but in the long term the integration of Ireland, the transfer to Britain of enemy colonies in 1815 and the opening up of the South American trade were to be of far greater significance.

Of course, the war damaged industry in some ways, erecting obstacles to imports and exports and intensifying competition for scarce resources of raw materials and skills. Yet it created new demands, stimulated production, gave rise to rapid improvements in the banking system and, in the end, led to the capture of new markets. To all this, the policies of the government contributed hugely.

> Pitt's policies liberalized credit, depressed real interest rates, and contained the accumulation of public debt by squeezing current consumption ... That great administrator has not received anything like the praise he deserves for keeping the Industrial Revolution on course during a major war.[20]

Successive British governments were able to sustain existing levels of private capital formation while raising sufficient public capital with which to conduct the wars against France. (What suffered during the war was not private capital but private *consumption*, which declined from an estimated 83 per cent of national expenditure in 1788–92 to 64 per cent in the closing years of the war.) At the same time, successive governments did everything they could to reassure investors in government stock of the security of their investments and of their regular redemption both during and after the war. In short, the confidence of the investing community was maintained. Perhaps even more important, in the long term, Britain had achieved – and was demonstrating that she could sustain – great-power status. Military expenditure *after* the wars was 2.7 times higher at constant prices than it had been before the war and at those levels it stayed.[21] Britain survived the years of war with great success. Indeed, the wars had more than paid for themselves, while Britain remained on course for further expansion and growth. Finally, she had come close to eliminating her nearest neighbour as a serious competitor for military, imperial and economic predominance in Europe.[22]

The social order

A transfiguring aristocracy

To what extent had a 'class society' emerged in Britain by the end of the long eighteenth century? Historians have devoted a remarkable amount of energy to this issue, trying to prove or disprove the importance of class relationships in the long eighteenth century. Here, I can do little more than summarize the outlines of the debate. In brief, I shall argue that the old model of a hierarchical society of orders, resting upon foundations of deference and reciprocal obligation, was remarkably resilient, continuing until the end of the eighteenth century to dominate contemporary thought and practice. By then class perspectives were gaining in currency. By 1830 they were well on the way to rivalling – but had not yet displaced – the traditional language of a society of orders. Furthermore, I shall argue that, with some exceptions, discussions of society in class terms, while tending to be dismissive of capitalist society, were essentially moderate, collaborative and peaceful.

Nobody could seriously deny that during the long eighteenth century Britain displayed serious social tensions and experienced bitter economic divisions. Conflict was everywhere, but it was not the conflict of classes. Some of the most bitter conflicts were between religious denominations; others took place between privileged bodies such as corporations and those who were excluded from them. A further axis of frequent conflict was that between government employees, such as excise officers or press gangs and the population at large. Nor should we ignore the possibilities of conflict within the *same* social group. Internal disputes among artisans, for example, might be almost as serious as disputes between artisans and their suppliers or customers. In such a society, the idea of *conflict* between 'classes' was unfamiliar. The sources of conflict in the long eighteenth century were usually anything other than the extremely vague and indeterminate divisions of 'class'. Mutual dependence was the order of the day, not systematic social conflict. Most challenges to established authority, moreover, could normally be contained and controlled by existing mechanisms such as the Poor Law, Petty and Quarter Sessions and, at times, by the militia.

In the literature of the time there are many criticisms of existing society, but they do not normally or directly dispute the principle of hierarchy.[23] They drew attention to its abuse and excesses, they condemned the selfish restriction of privileges to the few and they advocated the widening of access to those privileges, not the abolition of the privileges themselves. The language of class conflict had not yet arrived. Earlier in the eighteenth century, when contemporaries tried to conflate the complex gradations of their society of orders into larger and more manageable groups they usually employed the language of 'ranks' and 'orders', suggesting that wealth and status were conferred by birth. But as the century wore on, and as the static, traditional language of orders became less useful to a mobile and acquisitive society, other words began to be used: 'sorts', 'parts', 'interests' and, of course, 'classes'. It is not clear which of these was the most common. Furthermore, the language of orders and the newer language of social description could coexist. Guy Miege, for example, in the early eighteenth century was an exponent of both, writing about 'orders and degrees' on some occasions but adopting the language of 'sorts' on others. Interestingly, as the eighteenth century wore on it became increasingly common for observers to describe the society around them in tripartite terms. Defoe singled out the 'gentry', the 'tradesman' and the 'labouring people'. David Hume wrote of 'the great', 'the middle station of life' and 'the poor'.[24] Even Gregory King had admitted that he sometimes used the word 'classes' to describe people and adopted the usage of 'the better sort', 'the middle sort' and 'the poorest sort'. In the second half of the century, the tendency to simplify the social structure into three classes became even more pronounced. Although it remained possible to divide it into five or seven, the social structure was usually divided neatly into triads, as was the case for so many other institutions such as 'King, Lords and Commons'. One social triad employed the distinction between 'gentlemen', 'the people' (the most respectable among the propertied element who believed themselves to be part of the political order) and 'the mob' (those who either excluded themselves or were excluded). More familiar, however, were 'higher, middling and lower', which began to reshape themselves into 'upper, middle and industrious' and, eventually, 'upper, middle and working'. The terminology 'working class' first appears in 1789. Until then 'industrious' or 'lower' or, more commonly, 'labouring' class or classes were to be found. By the end of the eighteenth century the language of class – 'the upper class', 'the middle class', 'the working class' – was being employed with some frequency, as also was the language of classes 'the upper classes', 'the middle or middling classes' and 'the working or labouring classes'.

It is likely that contemporaries were inhibited from developing a fully-fledged three-class model of their society by the close and overlapping relations between many members of the 'upper' and 'middle' classes. In an earlier chapter we described the ruling order of Hanoverian Britain as a flexible and limited aristocracy, driven by economic acquisition and commercial ambition as well as by the desire to maintain its landed status. As the eighteenth century wore on, social power was increasingly coming to rest upon the ready cooperation of many members of the middling orders, who were charged with ever-expanding spheres of administration. After the middle of the eighteenth century these tendencies intensified. By the end of the eighteenth century the middling orders were identifying their fortunes with those of the landed aristocracy more strongly than ever before. It was clearly in the interests of many of them to support and sustain the model of a benevolent, hierarchical society.

The aristocracy continued to occupy positions of rarely questioned pre-eminence in national life in the second half of the long eighteenth century. Some historians have been tempted to describe Hanoverian society as 'classless', in view of the overwhelming ascendancy of the aristocracy.[25] Indeed, such a description matches the social beliefs of the aristocracy itself, who never doubted their right to speak for the interests of those beneath them, thus 'virtually' representing their interests. Indeed, the landed estate itself united masters and servants, owners and tenants, into groupings of men and women of socially dissimilar status by the vertical bonds of loyalty. Nevertheless, the landed elite had a very highly developed sense of its own economic self-interest. It was an acquisitive and capitalistically inclined elite which had thoroughly incorporated the profit motive and the rest of free-market ideology into its ideas and practices. Although its members complained throughout this period of the burden of taxation, the available evidence suggests that they got off extremely lightly. As the eighteenth century wore on, the weight of taxation was shifting steadily away from direct taxes on wealth and income, which included land, on the one hand to customs and excise duties on consumption on the other. At the end of the seventeenth century the former claimed 36.3 per cent of tax income; by the early 1830s this figure had shrunk to only 10 per cent. Correspondingly, the latter contributed 52.6 per cent of tax income at the end of the seventeenth century but had risen to no less than 71.3 per cent in the early 1830s.[26]

The landed elite, moreover, was heavily involved in what used to be termed 'the Agricultural Revolution'. More recently, historians have extended the period of improvement in agriculture back into the seventeenth century and have persuaded us that the process was more gradual than used to be thought.[27] Nevertheless, between 1700 and 1800 while the population of England, Scotland and Wales almost doubled the number of those working in agriculture rose hardly at all. The pattern of British, not just English, land-holding was unusually conducive to agricultural development. The great estates were securely in the hands of a small capitalist, rentier group commit-ted to profits. Furthermore, there is ample evidence that landowners acted as agencies of agricultural improvement by diffusing information, by experi-menting with new crops and new methods of breeding and by patronizing agricultural societies. A well-run estate heightened the landowner's prestige and underscored his role in promoting and diffusing, rather than personally undertaking, agricultural improvement. Improvements in livestock, horses and cattle were one of the characteristic obsessions of the eighteenth-century aristocratic and gentry classes. Robert Bakewell's experiments with livestock received much publicity and no little imitation. There can be no question that the size and shape of English farming animals improved immeasurably dur-ing the long eighteenth century. Of course, not every member of the aristoc-racy was interested in farming techniques, but even those uninterested in such matters could recognize the desirability of higher rents and more effi-cient methods of production. There were many ways in which landowners could assist their tenants to improve their farming methods. The landlord might withhold rent and sponsor schemes of drainage and building; for his part the tenant would lay out for stock, fertilizer and seed.

The landed elite was intimately and actively involved in the enclosure and consolidation of open, cultivable land into larger units, which accelerated in the later eighteenth century. Historians now take a view of enclosures which contradicts the interpretation of them as the heartless expropriation of the English peasantry, depicted in generations of works since the Hammonds's *The Village Labourer*, published in 1911.[28] Historians are now inclined to treat the enclosure 'movement' of the eighteenth century as the culmination of a long process of agricultural change and one that served a number of social as well as economic functions. There was certainly nothing new about enclo-sures. A combination of private agreement among local proprietors and the passage of parliamentary statutes had already enclosed around 70 per cent of the land area of England by 1700, around 50 per cent of the cultivable land area, less in Wales and Scotland. As late as 1760, there were only some 130 enclosure Acts on the statute book. The pace of enclosure by statute was at first gradual. Between 1730 and 1789 about 2.5 millions of acres were enclosed, much of it in the period 1760–80, when the heavy clay areas of the Midlands were enclosed. In a second burst stimulated by high wheat prices, no less than 3 million acres of land were enclosed by Parliament between 1789 and 1815. About one third of it was hitherto uncultivated land, especially in the north, where some of the unlikely and uneconomic land was then cultivated for the first time, because of increased levels of wartime demand and high prices. No less than 7 million acres of land were enclosed between 1760 and 1815. One thousand Acts were passed between 1760 and 1800 and a further 800 between 1800 and 1815. By 1830 about 90 per cent of the land of England and Wales was enclosed.

The ruling elite did far more, however, than maintain its unity and advance its wealth during this period. It experienced significant changes both in its sense of purpose and in its self-image. The context within which this occurred was a long-term challenge to the ruling elite between 1780 and 1815.[29] The loss of the American colonies, the anti-aristocratic example of France in the 1790s, Britain's early setback in the Revolutionary wars and the pressures and strains of over two decades of warfare proved stern and formidable tests of the stamina of the British aristocratic oligarchy. Furthermore, the devastating criticisms of the theory and practice of hereditary monarchy and aristocracy, set out in Tom Paine's *The Rights of Man*, were popularized by Spence and Cobbett and carried by them into the nineteenth century. They were developed into encyclopaedic and detailed criticisms of the role of the aristocracy in Thomas Oldfield's *History of the Boroughs* (1797) and *Representative History of Great Britain and Ireland* (1816) which outlined the influence of aristocratic families in elections. John Wade's *Extraordinary Red Book* (1816) and *Black Book: or Corruption Unmasked* (1819) listed in embarrassing detail the state offices which such families enjoyed. George Wade argued in the *Black Book* that no fewer than 487 out of 658 MPs were 'returned by nomination' while at least one third of MPs owed their return to the influence of members of the House of Lords. Such a comprehensive indictment of 'old corruption' had never been produced before. Radical reformers and, increasingly, a wider public began to challenge the basic premises upon which aristocratic power rested. Unthinking acceptance of the right of the aristocracy to rule began to give way to accusations of nepotism and corruption. Far from being a check upon the executive, Parliament itself appeared to be a site for aristocratic greed and jobbery.

In the face of these dangers, the aristocracy stiffened the sinews of its unity. In the eighteenth century many boys had been educated at home on their estates by tutors. By the early nineteenth century the vast majority of sons of the peerage and gentry were being educated collectively in the public schools. Here they acquired habits of ostentatious patriotism and personal service. Aggressive masculinity, individual heroism and the gospel of patriotism were instilled by an unceasing diet of classical, particularly Roman, literature (Livy turned out to be an exceptionally useful source of wisdom on the subject of patriotism). It was a selective diet. Much, for example, was heard about Greek art and culture, but precious little about Greek democratic traditions. Public schools boasted that they inculcated habits of physical toughness. These were exemplified in the customs of the fox hunt, which grew massively in popularity in the last few decades of the eighteenth century. The hunt, with its emphasis on male bonding and physical rigour, advertised the tough-minded values of the British ruling order. It was not merely, however, in its education and leisure pursuits that the nature of the ruling order was being transformed. The Evangelical revival commended a more sober and less ostentatious style of life, encouraging increased attention to family responsibilities and discouraging gambling, swearing and fornication. How many members of the ruling elite were influenced in this manner is impossible to establish. Nevertheless, the arrival of a new ideal of personal behaviour is significant; it is quietly recalled in the numerous conduct books published in these decades. By 1815 a more coherent landed elite had materialized, and was taking care to present a more acceptable face to the world.

But it was the French Revolutionary and Napoleonic wars which revived the confidence and the reputation of the British ruling class, enabling them to serve the state and to be seen to do so. It gave them a stage on which to enact the theatre of personal heroism and collective chivalry. It provided them with an opportunity to proclaim the power, as well as the future destiny, of the British empire. Without any substantial alteration in its institutions, Britain was victorious in the battles against Napoleon, against the Irish rebels, against domestic radicals. Without any substantial concessions to those beneath them on the social ladder, the ruling classes had protected their property, vindicated their influence and reaffirmed their right to govern. Their code of honour had been upheld, and thus renewed. These sentiments were symbolized in the figure of Horatio Nelson, the tragic victor of Trafalgar. His patriotism, his leadership, his concern for hierarchy yet his indifference to money summed it all up. And after his death, the cult of the great man preserved and perpetuated the timeless values of a selfless elite.

A cohering middle class

In the second half of the eighteenth century the middling orders and the landed elite continued to coexist with every sign of mutual respect, yet with occasional outbursts of mutual aversion. The landed classes had a traditional distaste for wealth unalloyed by manners. Their hackles might rise at the pretensions of some of the richer sections of the middling orders who rose to rival their own social pre-eminence. A modest flow of industrialists, merchants, bankers, lawyers, soldiers and sailors leavened the mass of hereditary peers, attracted a considerable amount of attention and provided enough of a continuing spur to encourage the ambitious and the aspiring. For their part, many members of the middling orders had little time for the values of the ruling class – their flashiness, their snobbery, their immorality and, not least, their reluctance to pay their bills.

Too much should not be made of such social strains. Rural and urban elites may have differed in many of their social habits, but they adopted a common code of manners and professed a common code of honour. They revelled in the routines of gentility and courtesy and shared strikingly similar leisure habits. There was no cultural divide here. Social tensions between the ruling classes and the middling orders were less the origins of a new class hostility than the continuing discomforts of incorporating new money and new men into traditional social structures. 'Charity, benevolence, and the responsible values of a sadly missed antique age, legitimized the retention of riches.'[30]

Even the wealthiest members of the middle classes showed little inclination to rock the aristocratic boat. The City of London was the traditional home of an old commercial elite which revelled in imperial acquisition, commercial expansion and hostility to Britain's Bourbon competitors. The London aldermen, in particular, included some of the richest commoners in Britain. The great merchants of London began to marry their sons and daughters into the gentry. The growth, in particular, of the London 'season' enabled vitally important social contacts to develop between the middle and upper classes. By the middle of the eighteenth century both the London residences and rural retreats of the big bourgeoisie were beginning to emulate those of their landed counterparts. Provincial merchants, however, were much less concerned to acquire landed estates. They enjoyed a secure social status and felt little need to defer to the provincial gentry. On the whole, however, merchants and professional men found general acceptance in polite society. They did not wish to upset it nor did they wish seriously to amend or alter it; they wished to join it and to turn it to their own advantage.

Such patterns of mutual acceptance were the culmination of decades of collaboration and cooperation in activities as varied as philanthropy, the founding of charity and Sunday schools and the establishment of hospitals and clinics. Furthermore, many of the progressive causes in social reform such as the abolition of the slave trade (1807) and of slavery (1833) enabled men of these middling and upper ranks to cooperate. Most of all, it was in the patronage of science and technology that men of the middling orders found support and sponsorship from their social superiors.

At the political level such collaboration may be seen in their fading interest in constitutional change, epitomized in the attitudes of the government of the Younger Pitt and the gradual abandonment of its earlier reformism. The architect of parliamentary reform in 1782, 1783 and 1785 became unwilling to extend further religious toleration to Protestant Dissenters in 1787 and 1790. In the 1790s, indeed, the government became hostile to most politically liberal measures. After their flirtation with reform in the early 1790s, the middle classes largely abandoned it; indeed, the aristocracy and the middling orders joined together against the radical threat of the 1790s. The collaboration continued unabated into the new century, even intensifying during the threat of invasion of 1803 to 1806 amidst constant demonstrations of patriotic loyalty. Indeed, the middling orders endorsed the reconstruction of the social image of the aristocracy and even participated in it, flocking into the militia regiments, sporting the colourful uniforms of the Volunteers and thus rallying to the defence of the existing social structure. The growth and the rising importance of the middling orders was not restricted to England. In Wales, however, an urban middle class remained weak during much of the eighteenth century, still dependent on occupations which were based on services to agriculture and to the landed elite. An autonomous urban middle class did not appear until the early years of the nineteenth century. The Scottish middle class was much more like the English. The professions, especially the law, advanced rapidly after 1750, while commercial interests prospered with new imperial opportunities not only in European markets but in India, North America and, eventually, in China. The movement of the Edinburgh middle classes into the new town typified these developments and symbolized their physical segregation. Even in Ireland a Catholic middle class, largely based on the textile trade, had emerged by the end of the century. Furthermore, there was a visible influx of Irish entrepreneurs into commerce and industry around the time of the Revolutionary and Napoleonic wars.

Not surprisingly, the middling orders of Britain were capable of flexing their political muscles when the occasion demanded. As early as 1765–66 they maintained a formidable nationwide protest against the damaging economic consequences of the Stamp Act disorders in America. Even more serious and better organized were their protests against Pitt's government in the mid-1780s. In 1784 Pitt imposed an excise tax on fustian and in 1785 attempted to establish free trade with Ireland. The first of these measures aroused opposition within the textile industry, the second provoked more general consternation. They aroused a strong reaction among provincial merchant and manufacturing communities and led to the establishment of the General Chamber of Manufacturers. Many provincial urban elites displayed a marked Nonconformist consciousness, and they were now prepared to combine in peaceful political agitation against the measures. Petitioning campaigns were launched, local committees of correspondence were established and a nationwide organization was established to coordinate opposition. Faced with such hostility, not least 60 petitions against his policy, Pitt relented: the measures were heavily amended.

It is tempting to see in these economic debates of the mid-1780s an important watershed in the rise of a self-conscious middle class, but we should not place undue emphasis on them. Although the agitation was successful, it was not to be the immediate harbinger of a united middle-class consciousness. The Chamber of Manufacturers disbanded in 1786. Many of those who supported it were at once divided over the issue of free trade, provoked by the Eden Treaty of 1786, which liberalized trade with France. During the next two decades, indeed, the middling orders were divided by a series of issues: by the attempt of the Protestant Dissenters to secure the repeal of the Test and Corporation Acts between 1787 and 1790, by the Regency Crisis of 1788–89, by the impact of the French Revolution on Britain, by the issue of parliamentary reform in the 1790s and, after 1793, by the question of war against France. It was not before the campaigns against the Orders in Council in 1808–12 that the old unity of 1786 was to be recaptured. The success of the campaign in 1812 encouraged the middling orders to establish permanent local chambers of commerce. These developments coincided with the gradual spread of free-trade ideology. The renewal of the charter of the East India Company and its alleged monopoly of trade to China in 1812–13 aroused the middling orders yet again and provoked them to argue the case for free markets with the East. These vitally important economic issues in the early years of the nineteenth century indicated clearly that the middling orders were prepared to use political agitation to protect their economic interests.

Many years ago, Asa Briggs set out four factors which encouraged 'the development of a sense of class unity' among the middling orders.[31] Of the four factors which he singled out, two – the imposition of Pitt's income tax in 1798 and the inequality of the tax burdens borne by the middling orders compared to the landed classes in wartime – appear to have had little more than a minor effect. It was the other two, the struggle for parliamentary reform and the Corn Law of 1815, which deserve closer attention. The campaign for parliamentary reform was not, of course, confined to the middling orders, but in

1807–12 and again in 1815–19 it generated massive anti-aristocratic propaganda which popularized the case against 'old corruption' in church and state and familiarized hundreds of thousands of people with the case for a more representative political system. The number of members of the mercantile and manufacturing middle classes in unenfranchised towns like Manchester and Sheffield active in, and often leading, the raising of petitions in favour of parliamentary reform should not be underestimated.

More than any other factor, however, as Professor Perkin has argued,[32] a sense of middle-class outrage was generated by the Corn Law of 1815. The Corn Law allowed the import of foreign corn free of duty when the price of wheat had risen to 80s. a quarter. The arguments on both sides of the case were well balanced. Clearly the interests of farmers, and of those they employed, demanded some measure of protection. Yet the Corn Law kept the price of bread up. More controversially, the selfishness of a landed Parliament in protecting the exclusive interests of agriculturalists disgusted the middling orders and gave rise to an indignant campaign against landed privilege, aristocratic self-interest and agricultural protectionism. But it was not merely the disgust and anger aroused by the Corn Law which deserves attention but the fact that it gave widespread credibility to the intellectual case against the aristocratic oligarchy. Indeed, the persistence of the postwar economic depression made the years 1815–21 of supreme significance in converting many sections of the middling orders into severe critics of the prevailing economic and political establishment. By 1820 the rhetoric of middle-class hostility to a corrupt oligarchy had certainly caught the mood of hundreds of thousands in the provincial and metropolitan mercantile communities. By then, many of them were ready to adopt the opinions of Jeremy Bentham and his friends. Bentham gave them a utilitarian, as opposed to a prescriptive, criterion against which to test the value of actions and the usefulness of institutions. At the social and economic level Ricardo taught them that the landlord class were profiteering parasites, while James Mill brought up to date Tom Paine's attack on the theory and practice of hereditary, aristocratic government and his defence of universal suffrage.[33]

After the Corn Law of 1815 the middling orders, particularly in the provinces, were increasingly inclined to leap to the defence of their economic interests by attacking what they were coming to perceive as a corrupt government. Many of them became involved in the parliamentary reform groups of 1815–20 and took an interest in the case of Queen Caroline. These agitations went far towards creating a self-consciousness within the middling ranks of society of their own interests and an awareness of their own separateness – from the ruling elite above and the labouring classes below – as a social group. There is even evidence of a growing recognition of the superiority of their own values, as against those of other sections of society. Yet perceptions, self-consciousness and a growing awareness of identity, while important in the evolution of a British middle class, are arguably less important than the experiences in which this class participated in the new and growing towns of the early nineteenth century.

The process of urbanization was quickening towards the end of the long eighteenth century and was being increasingly driven by industrialization. As early as 1775 five of the largest ten towns were manufacturing towns:

Leeds (24 000), Sheffield (27 000), Manchester (30 000), Norwich (38 000) and Birmingham (40 000). By 1801, four of the top five after London were; the fifth, Bristol, was partly industrialized. Manchester (with Salford) had a population of 89 000, Liverpool 83 000, Birmingham 74 000, Bristol 60 000 and Leeds 53 000. Indeed, so clearly was England distinct from her continental neighbours that on one estimate no less than 70 per cent of the urban growth of Europe in the second half of the eighteenth century took place in England.[34] Further, at this stage of their development the early industrial towns had not been overcome by congestion, smoke and disease. Their energy and wealth combined to effect genuine cultural growth, manifested in the Manchester Literary and Philosophic Society (1781) and the Lunar Society of Birmingham (1775). Such bodies brought together manufacturers and gentlemen, often of Dissenting faith, to share in philosophic and artistic pursuits. Other societies were more exclusively devoted to particular activities such as science and music, but these could adopt a remarkably wide definition of their activities. Yet others, such as the rapidly spreading Gentlemen's Societies, were by definition notably catholic in their interests. Whatever the case, such societies tended to become larger and better organized as the long eighteenth century proceeded. Many, indeed, even acquired their own premises.

It is not just the great industrializing towns which demand attention. In 1700 only one provincial town, Norwich, had a population over 25 000. By 1820 there were 15 of them. In 1700 about 22–23 per cent of the inhabitants of England and Wales were town-dwellers. By 1800 the figure had increased to around 30 per cent and by 1820 perhaps to 35 per cent. Indeed, the most important agency of middle-class formation was not so much any dramatic political breakthrough at national level as a steady and almost unquestioned assertion of their influence over civic society in the provinces. At this level the middle classes were capable of manifesting a considerable degree of cohesion. Many of them were happy to act as local officers, aldermen and even mayors. Through the growth of taverns, clubs and lodges their commercial networking was enhanced by social intercourse. Their contribution to the life of local institutions such as schools, hospitals, prisons and, not least, societies for moral improvement was prodigious. They came to fashion the culture of the provincial towns of the industrial revolution. The huge increase in the number of civic, voluntary societies and groups of all kinds – political, religious, charitable, medical – acted as a vehicle for members of rising urban elites to assert their social eminence and political power over rapidly developing industrial communities.[35] These elites frequently included members of the Nonconformist chapels, which themselves often acted as the organizational cores of such voluntary societies and local institutions. Several of them, the Poor Laws and the Sunday schools, for example, acted as means of disciplining and improving the behaviour of children of the working classes. Others, such as the Society for the Suppression of Vice, were less concerned with sexual licence than with curbing rude, rebellious and disorderly behaviour on the part of the lower classes more generally. The extent of poverty in a society with a rapidly increasing population could not be ignored by the middling orders. An Act of 1723 legalized the establishment of workhouses by parishes or groups of parishes, and within 50 years around 2000 workhouses had been established. Not only did the workhouses offer a last resort to the starving, the infirm and the aged. They set their standards sufficiently rigorously to deter the idle and to set them to work. Typically, the workhouses were to be profit-making concerns, but their activities had to be supplemented by countless acts of private and personal charity.

The foundation of hospitals was also a popular arena for charitable activity. The hospitals movement of the eighteenth century saw the foundation of many of the great London hospitals: the Westminster in 1720, St George's in 1733, the London in 1740 and the Middlesex in 1745. These were all founded by public subscription, deriving over half their income from such sources. The provincial hospital movement gathered pace in the 1730s: between 1735 and 1760 12 provincial hospitals were founded, followed by another 12 by 1783. Those who subscribed no doubt did so with a mixture of Christian morality and civic spirit, but they can hardly have been unaware of the privileges which their position conferred, including the right to nominate a certain number of patients and, of course, the right of treatment for themselves and their families. Given the development of medical specialization and – not least – the complexity of administering such lumbering giants, the second half of the century was to be a period of more specialized foundations, such as lying-in hospitals, smallpox hospitals, hospitals for venereal diseases and lunatic asylums. Even here, the provision of appropriate moral instruction and instructions concerning behaviour, meals and dress accompanied medical treatment.

The organization of these forms of philanthropy are of the very greatest interest. They were based on the principle and practice of subscription, sometimes private but often public, through which a group of individuals could further some sort of charitable activity. Such organized charity was open to all men (and women) regardless of social standing. It was a method of involving quite humble individuals in the administration of schools, hospitals and workhouses and, as a consequence, in the complex world of local systems of patronage, Significantly, the subscription lists were usually headed by local notables followed by merchants and their inferiors. The terms of such charitable bequests often included regulations as to behaviour, and even concerning dress and language and such contentious matters as the mixing of the sexes. The modern student is likely to leap to the conclusion that the principal motive of these involved must be social control, but distinctions between charity, social control and ostentatious philanthropy are always difficult to draw. However, it would be churlish to assume that social control was always uppermost. In a society preoccupied with moral issues it would have been unthinkable for such charitable activity to have gone unaccompanied by some form of moral commitment. What assumes greater importance, however, by the end of the eighteenth century is the repeatedly declared social intention of those administering such institutions that they were working for a patriotic purpose and seeking to regenerate the nation. These worthy badges of middle-class endeavour became, therefore, less the signs of class warfare than the symbols of the peaceful incorporation into the patriotic community of the middling orders of Hanoverian Britain. In the end, it was a common patriotic political outlook rather than any common economic or social position which was serving to consolidate the growing cohesion of the middle class.

A self-conscious working class

The emergence of the English working class has been much more thoroughly investigated than that of the middle class, but the subject remains open to discussion because of the scale of the numbers involved and the problem of local variation. Here, of all places, it becomes difficult to reach precise definitions of 'class' and of what constitutes shared 'class' experience. Historians have long since moved away from a simple, economic version of the emergence of the working class (which roots economic interests such as capital and labour at the centre of class) towards a broader and more flexible concept which incorporates popular culture and religion and which admits something of the autonomy of political traditions and political experience. Modern accounts of the origins of the working class in Britain usually begin with an eighteenth-century traditional popular culture that was imbued with the ethics of a 'moral economy', sensitive to abuses of the paternalist ideal. As the century advanced, according to this view, the state gradually abandoned the regulation of wages, prices and the quality of goods, all of which had been prominent features of economic organization in early modern England. Their abandonment left individuals increasingly vulnerable to market conditions. The seeds of class were not, then, to be found either in the early factories or in any possible identification of a person's lifestyle with his place in the productive process, but in the social and economic tensions created by the abandonment of paternalism. 'Class', in this sense, then is a social reflex rather than a progressive social ideal, open to rural as much as to urban groups and arising within the skilled as much as within the unskilled occupational groups. (The isolation of such industrial communities as did exist in the eighteenth century, mining and fishing, for example, prevented the emergence of a nationally based class sentiment.)

In his famous account of *The Making of the English Working Class*, E.P. Thompson located the effective origins of working-class thought and action in the 1790s, in the euphoria generated by the reception of the French Revolution in England and in the temporary popularity of reform societies, inspired by the ideas of Tom Paine. These early signs of working-class activity were reinforced by both state repression and economic hardship during wartime, by the fostering of an underground tradition of proletarian political, and often violent, activity. By 1815 a coherent and identifiable working class had acquired its own ideology and organization and, not least, its own traditions, myths and martyrs with which to fire the imagination of a new generation of recruits in the bitter years after 1815.

No one could deny the existence of widespread and often very bitter social conflict and popular hardship in Britain in the 1790s, but it is not clear to what extent they should be interpreted as 'class' activity leading to class conflict. Certainly, the combination of political repression, subsistence crisis and the general privations of wartime gave rise to a widespread sense of alienation from, at times even hostility to, the rulers and institutions of Hanoverian Britain which by 1815 had gone quite far.[36] Whereas in Ireland and, to a lesser extent, in Scotland such alienation had religious overtones and nationalist elements, in England and Wales such resentments were focused upon politicians and the political system. Only towards the end of the war, however, did such sentiments acquire powerful class overtones. The Combination Acts of 1799 and 1800 could certainly be construed as an affront to labouring men; and, indeed, the grim economic conditions of the turn of the century, the hardship provoked by the Orders in Council and the never-ending hardships of the war all aggravated social tension. Further, the Luddite protests of 1811–12, coinciding with a subsistence crisis in many ways as severe as that of 1800–01, together with the government's harsh response, marked a further stage in the emergence of a working-class self-consciousness. On top of all this, Parliament in 1814 deprived JPs of their powers to regulate wages to a just level, a significant gain for the forces of a free-market economy. This abandonment of regulation, what Perkin has termed 'the abdication of responsibility',[37] turned many artisans and labouring men against an economic system which had hitherto offered them some protection. How quickly, and by what processes, this abandonment gave rise to class consciousness, however, still needs careful analysis.

The emergence of class consciousness by 1815 was still incomplete and the processes involved in it intermittent. It is not enough to emphasize the factors working in its favour. Some trends worked against it. The voice of the working classes was dependent upon economic circumstances and upon the political leadership and social networks of men from higher social ranks, such as Burdett, Cartwright, Hunt and Cobbett. Furthermore, many factory workers, sometimes a majority, were woman and children whose labours were unlikely to feed directly into streams of class hostility. Much activity which, at one level, may be identified as 'class' activity may in fact have had a restraining effect on the emergence of class consciousness. The early trade unions and friendly societies were moderate bodies who willingly worked within the existing economic structure and established habits of negotiation. Such men, usually craftsmen, who enjoyed the support of traditional organizations and practices, were conscious of their own status and skill. While they would jealously protect their standards of work and life, they did not yet conceive of themselves as members of a working class locked in combat with a middle class. If there was want and hardship in the war years there were, too, massive economic opportunities generated by wartime needs and demands. 'Unprecedented mobilization acted as a safety valve against the full expression of the over-supply of labour, which was delayed until the immediate post-war years.'[38] The terrible hardship of the subsistence crisis of 1799–1800 persuaded JPs to treat law-breakers with sympathy. It also evoked an immense amount of local philanthropy which, as the most trenchant critic of the ruling orders has put it, 'enabled the magistracy and the courts to retain some popular credibility ... permitting the ruling class to relegitimise itself'.[39]

Even with these reservations, however, there can be little doubt that in the years immediately after the war, with the disappearance of the most powerful patriotic restraints, the forceful expression of lower-class hostility to government repression can no longer be denied. Among certain of the old artisan trades, especially in the textile industry, among the domestic weavers and frame knitters and among the early factory workers, congregated into the demographically exploding towns of Lancashire, the West Riding and the north Midlands, political protest movements appeared on an extraordinary scale. Certainly the scale of the vast meetings, with their fiery rhetoric and mass proletarian audiences, impressed contemporaries and continue to impress historians. In particular, the government repression in 1817 created a wave of very real, perhaps unprecedented, proletarian resentment. Although the radical platform still proclaimed the creed of traditional, popular constutionalism, the mood of the meetings was increasingly one of social bitterness. During 1818 the brief economic upturn led to strikes which sought the restoration of former pay scales. When political agitation resumed in 1819 it was with clear class overtones. From the great series of political meetings which marked the summer months, of which Peterloo was one, the middle classes largely absented themselves. These became vast rallies of working people. The upper classes shuddered, many of them believing that revolution was close at hand. This mass, nationally organized demand for universal suffrage encompassed not only the traditional geographical areas from which radicals had drawn support – the metropolitan areas, East Anglia and the north east – but now, unquestionably, the newer industrial districts and newer factory occupations as well.

By this time powerful elements of class organization were entering into industrial disputes. Combinations of workers were to be found, for example, among the Wiltshire woollen towns as early as 1802. In the same year the Yorkshire shearmen went on strike in the Leeds area and with the aid of a strike fund forced their employers to meet their demands. Strike funds also aided the efforts of the Lancashire and Cheshire cotton spinners in a three-month strike in 1810. In this dispute around 10 000 workers were locked out in Stalybridge alone. Two years later nearly 40 000 cotton workers went on strike in Cumberland and Scotland. In 1818 there were strikes in many parts of the country, but particularly in the north west. The Lancashire weavers and calico printers both went on strike, as did the Manchester cotton spinners. There were even attempts to organize them into a national movement. Spinners' delegates from the Manchester strike made contact with the 'Philanthropic Hercules', a would-be national body of all unions led by the leader of the shipwrights, John Gast.

Whether all these agitations were overwhelmingly *class* agitations is, however, still not entirely clear. There are several reasons for this. First, even some of the most militant of class warriors; the Luddites, were seeking to maintain their own skills, their own differentials and their own exclusiveness. It is a mistake to see Luddism, however compelling the cause and however tragic the condition of the men and their families, as a class movement. Furthermore, much trade union activity was of an exclusive character, particular rather than general. The early trade unions were anxious to protect their own skills and the wages of their own members; such unions would restrict apprenticeships and operate closed shops. So much for class solidarity. Second, the idea of a homogeneous 'factory proletariat' may, in part at least, be a myth. When historians have examined the work that workers actually did they find a great variety of specialized trades and processes and minute distinctions of skill and differentials of pay which, in their way, are reminiscent of the subtle gradations of a society of orders.

Third, much of the class hostility to be found in the postwar years was locally generated by a dispute in a particular industry or, as in 1820 at Swansea, by an attempt to suppress a union combination of copper smelters, which led to violence and injuries. At Coalbrookdale in 1821 3000 miners, who had been trying to close the pits as a protest against reduced wages, fought a body of yeomen calvary who had been brought in to break the strike. Two people died and dozens were injured. There can be no question that these were serious, sometimes violent and certainly militant disputes. What is less certain is whether such disputes were consciously part of a broader class struggle. Much of this union activity was bread-and-butter business far removed from the utopian schemes of the early Co-operative societies of the 1820s, whose objective was peacefully to transform capitalist society into a socialist commonwealth. Robert Owen's appeals to the masses to adopt a cooperative and unionized solution to social ills for long evoked little response. For a while in the late 1820s and early 1830s some union leaders dreamed of national unions which would unite both the skilled and the unskilled, but they all floundered on the usual obstacles of geography and indifference. The great factories of Lancashire, Yorkshire and Glasgow and the coal mines of the north east were still untypical of the working environments of most workers. Even in the textile industry, only cotton was produced in large factories. Elsewhere in the industry the domestic system still survived. Finally, although class consciousness could certainly be stirred up on certain occasions, for example in 1817 and in 1819, it is not clear that it could maintain itself in 'normal' times. Class tension and class conflict appeared on occasions of particular stress and difficulty. Certain occupations may for a time have conceived themselves to be a part of a provincial, even a national movement, with an awareness of shared class identity, as in 1819 and 1831. However, working people often lacked the literacy and the leisure, and their communities sometimes lacked the institutions – libraries, clubs and newspapers – which might have sustained class feeling over a period of years.

Yet by about 1820 the concept of a 'working class' was in wide circulation, as any examination of radical speeches at events like Peterloo and the march of the Blanketeers will confirm. Ricardo had popularized the argument that landlords, capitalists and workers had conflicting class interests, and it received considerable attention in the 1820s. The *Economist*, founded in 1821, and the London Co-operative Society, established in 1824, were among the most important propaganda organs of the emerging working class in the 1820s. In their pages Tom Paine's political 'rights of men' became the 'rights of labour' of the early socialists. Working men were taught that parliamentary reform, in the shape of universal suffrage, would guarantee to the worker the fruits of his labours. In 1823 Thomas Hodgkin and Joseph Robertson founded *The Mechanics* magazine which, together with a number of successors, sought to instil a sense of common identity among its readers. In 1830 John Doherty established yet another grandly titled body, the National Association of the Protection of Labour, with its newspaper, *The Voice of the People*. It was a magnificent aspiration to unite all trades and crafts in a peaceful, united struggle against the capitalists. Like all such bodies, however, it swiftly collapsed. The force of its rhetorical message, however, was not forgotten. In this way social and economic antagonisms were constantly being redefined in class terms.

No less important than the circulation of class ideology and class language in the making of the working class were the residential realities of the new industrial towns. Because of their rapid growth, they did not manifest the delicate social hierarchies of older towns; they were created on the basis of a sometimes quite drastic social segregation. In established communities the old language of orders survived because such residential segregation was uncommon, a fact which promoted status consciousness and fine gradations of social awareness. In the new industrial towns skilled workers tended to live in the same streets as other skilled workers, rarely marrying their sons and daughters into the ranks of other social groups. It was these quite sharp patterns of residence and marriage, as well as common patterns of work and, sometimes, political experience, which betokened the unmistakable and continuous existence of a working-class culture. Because of residential segregation, furthermore, there developed common patterns of leisure, often of religious observance and even of education. The historian of class, therefore, should be as alive to the less frequently researched patterns of lower-class housing as to the much more familiar territory of class ideology and language.

It remains to include the rural labouring classes in this discussion. As late as the census of 1831 there were still twice as many agricultural labourers as labourers in manufacturing industry. With the disappearance of the peasantry, Britain became a country of rural landless labourers whose dependence on the landlord class for employment and housing was considerable. With enclosure and the loss of common rights and, after 1780, with the decline of in-service and the prospect of reasonably secure employment on the great estates, there was a noticeable loosening of the bonds of deference in the countryside. As a result, there were many scattered acts of violence and vandalism and even some regional patterns of disaffection, as in East Anglia in the years immediately after 1815. The demobilization of soldiers and seamen crowded the labour market at exactly the same time as the appearance of threshing machines reduced the demand for labour on the land. Before the Swing Riots of 1830–31, however, there was little sign of organized, nationally based action, although a resentful culture of protest, arson and violence was developing. In spite of the existence of considerable social bitterness in the countryside, a coherent rural working class had not yet emerged because of physical isolation, the hegemonic presence of the great estate and the fragility of political awareness. Furthermore, the harsh operation of the Poor Law maintained efficient surveillance and superintendence over the lives of many sections of the rural poor. Although many of the features of English and Welsh rural life were to be found in the lowlands of Scotland and in Ireland, rural society in these nations was characterized by the survival of the rural peasantry. In these places, alternatives to agricultural employment which might have mopped up surplus population did not exist. Harsh conditions prevailed and considerable suffering was the consequence. Such obstacles powerfully hindered the emergence of a rural working class.

Distinctions of class were, nevertheless, developing with some speed in the early nineteenth century. Historians, while recognizing this, should resist the temptation to leap to conclusions about inevitable conflict between the classes. They should at the very least consider the ubiquity of collaboration between members of the middle and working classes in their joint crusade against 'old corruption' and in favour of reform. Many members of the working class were prepared to accept the capitalist system but to work peacefully for its reform. Furthermore, trade unions were specialized bodies which negotiated with their employers, and thus within the framework of the capitalist system, over bread-and-butter issues like pay, hours and conditions of work. Such attitudes were particularly prominent during periods of relative prosperity, suggesting strongly that while class resentment could be unleashed at moments of economic stress and political bitterness, at other periods there was no inevitable or rational hostility between the working and middle classes. If they were to be successful, working-class political movements needed sustained support from other powerful social groups. By the same token, middle-class reform obviously needed popular support to become effective. Without that collaboration, reform movements failed in the 1790s; with some measure of collaboration, reform became a possibility in the immediate postwar years. With consistent, nationally organized and well coordinated class collaboration between 1830 and 1832 the reform of Parliament was ultimately to be achieved.

Constructions of gender in later Hanoverian Britain

In almost all areas of life, national and local, eighteenth-century society was dominated by men. Men wrote, and male historians subsequently wrote up, the historical record to emphasize that domination, but it was in some ways an anxious domination. Women had power in many situations and circumstances, but such power was usually deemed to be irregular and thus unwarranted. Eighteenth-century men were always looking over their shoulders for 'petticoat power', whether royal mistresses toying with helpless politicians or cuckold wives henpecking their husbands. Yet the stubborn survival of patriarchy during the long eighteenth century does not mean that gender roles remained unchanged. Indeed, there was constant tension between the orthodox, biblical constructions of gender and newer forms of gender, which was perhaps typical of a complex and rapidly changing society and culture. Eighteenth-century ideas of femininity and masculinity were social constructs, reflecting a stable yet dynamic social consensus which was at the same time religious, ideological and legal. They were not fixed, they were not monolithic and they were capable of almost infinite refinement and variation.

Much has been made in the recent literature of an alleged gender division of labour according to which men after the middle of the century increasingly inhabited the 'public' sphere of business and politics, leaving the 'private' sphere of domesticity to women.[40] The construction of masculinity was based, of course, upon biblical precepts about the male role as head of the household with duties as well as powers, but thereafter constructs of masculinity followed social patterns. Upper-class masculinity was moulded by codes of chivalric honour and by physical, usually military courage. Under the twin pressures of Evangelicalism and of the demand of polite social conformity, middle-class masculinity followed a more sedentary pattern, involving Christian love, moral earnestness, personal sincerity and the performance of paternal duties. However, the masculine identity of the middle-class Christian father arose as much from his commercial occupation as from his Christian paternalism. He was literate, numerate and a responsible employer. In this world of Christian commercialism, sexual restraint, not sexual indulgence, was the mark of mature masculinity. On the other hand, lower-class men had a different construction of masculinity to do with physical strength and endurance, stoical reliability and sexual indulgence. Indeed, the alarming growth of unmarried pregnancies during the eighteenth century was probably a response to the increase in the number of unemployed and landless labourers who had little or no conception of restraint, planning and patience.

Left to become 'angels in the home', women commanded the family and the children, maintaining overall responsibility for the moral welfare of its members. The construction of femininity operated around the dependence of women upon men as constrained in countless biblical and customary precepts. The moral and social inferiority of women was re-emphasized by Evangelicals at the end of the century who insisted upon the traditional roles of women as wives and mothers. To the Evangelicals the home and the hearth was the sphere of upper- and middle-class women. They should organize it, adorn it and bring culture and learning to it. Women might help informally in the world of work, but that was not their prime responsibility. Similarly, they might enhance civic occasions and political celebrations with their presence, but it was the men whom they were enhancing and their achievements that were being celebrated. Feminine values embraced the ideals of passive acceptance, calculated restraint and the avoidance of violence and harshness. These ideals of femininity were universally recycled during the century and were powerfully endorsed by writers like Hannah More and by scores of lesser-known, usually female writers, who painstakingly set out how women might apply these precepts to daily life.

Some voices were raised against patriarchy and the idea of 'separate spheres' for men and women during the late eighteenth century. When Mary Wollstonecraft did so in the 1790s, she stood in a long line of writers and pamphleteers who had asserted the right of women to education, to a freer choice of marriage partner and, in general, to a more equal relationship with men. Many writers, including male authors such as Steele, Defoe and Richardson, offered literary portraits of women in their writings which were far removed from the shrinking violets who inhabited the manuals of formal etiquette. In the second half of the century the number of women writers leaped ahead. Wollstonecraft's *Vindication of the Rights of Women* (1792), however, was a rational critique of the basis of patriarchy. Refuting the theory of the natural subordination of women, Wollstonecraft affirmed the natural autonomy of women, arguing that women had a right to equality with men and, indeed, the right to pursue their own careers. What she wished to do was to combine and to unite the qualities seen hitherto as female and male, i.e. feeling and rationality. While shocking to many contemporaries in her rejection of biblical precepts, Wollstonecraft was much less radical than might at first appear. The measures of education which she claimed for women were reserved to the upper and middle classes. She was writing for women in those social groups who enjoyed leisure and comfort. She deplored the fact that too many women from the middling orders had been seduced by fashion and by their love of externals to neglect their rationality. She had little to say to poor women who might have benefited from greater social equality. Furthermore, she was vague about the ability of women to establish and to realize their claims to greater equality, in practice looking to men to release women from their bondage. Nevertheless, she gave an historic impetus to the cause of women's rights. Many women were shaken out of their torpor by the fresh, radical language which she employed. Just when Evangelicals were energetically reworking the old hierarchical ideas about the place of women, Wollstonecraft launched an important intellectual challenge to patriarchal ideas which was to act both as an intellectual example to others and as a symbolic repudiation of the subordination of women.

The place of women in society during the long eighteenth century, however, may best be illuminated from their actual conduct, not from theoretical discussions about it. While there was a massive corpus of prescriptive literature exhorting women to cling to their domestic sphere, it is always dangerous to argue from the precept to the reality. Why was there so much exhortation if women were obediently keeping to their sphere? Why were eighteenth-century women, many of them well read and well educated, prepared to submit to patriarchy? The beginnings of an answer to such questions may be found in the fact that most careers in political, commercial and professional life were still closed to them. Consequently, women in the second half of the eighteenth century increasingly centred their identities on their domestic role. Yet it would be a mistake to conclude from this that women's lives were consequently of little account. After all, the family was of vital significance in commerce, in farming, in production and in retailing. Women may have occupied a domestic role but their very domesticity might well have enabled even quite humble women to run small enterprises such as shops and taverns either before or, frequently, after the death of a husband or father. Such considerations applied to all orders in society. Their birth and rank and their relationships as daughter, wife and mother enabled many women to expand their sphere beyond that laid down in the prescriptive literature of the time. There are many examples of women energetically expressing themselves by skilfully operating their domestic roles to their own advantage.

Their preoccupation with domesticity should not, however, be exaggerated. Many women enjoyed a social life which was punctuated at many points, charitable, educational, philanthropic and even political, with essentially non-domestic concerns. Women's periodicals exemplify a breadth of such concerns, not least political interests, which do not obligingly fall into a 'separate spheres' theory. Furthermore, there are a remarkable number of instances where women chose to occupy spheres traditionally male, such as writing. Women were closely involved in the explosion of print culture which occurred during the later eighteenth and early nineteenth century. As writers, subscribers and readers, women involved themselves in the newer cultural ferments of the age. Debating societies had existed in London since the 1720s; by the 1780s many women attended them and over half of the societies regularly debated women's issues. Consequently, although the formal roles of women in political and commercial bodies were confined to supporting activity they could not – in case of abolitionism, for example – be ignored. How can the thousands of women who took part in the abolitionist campaign in the 1780s, organizing female anti-slavery societies, be consigned to a private sphere? The remarkable influence of women within the Methodist movement is a further case in point. The movement gave women positive roles to play within a nationwide extended family. They were able to do so because of the organizing experiences which both middle- and lower-class women derived from their domestic and in many cases their working lives.

The social horizons of upper- and middle-class women widened still further during the years of war against Revolutionary France: 'war work took women out of the house and taught them how to lobby, run committees and organise ... allowing them to demonstrate that they enjoyed a measure of economic power.'[41] Women were in evidence among reforming societies, but they were also extremely active in the loyalist societies and played a considerable role in the literary counter-revolution. Women were the authors of no fewer than over 50 anti-Jacobin novels written before 1804 which flooded the circulating libraries. Although women could not become full members of the literary and philosophical societies, nor even full members of reading-rooms, they played a formidable role in the world of print culture in the 1790s. The loyalist cause owed much to the tireless and unceasing activity of middle- and upper-class women, of whom Hannah More and Sarah Trimmer were role models.[42] The increasing scope for the participation of women in literary, religious, philanthropic and reformist activity in this period was a social development of far-reaching significance, but it must be qualified in two ways. First, while women did much of the work in these religious, charitable and reform bodies, men took most of the decisions and did most of the organizing.[43] Second, women were welcomed into these areas of activity but only so long as social constraints of femininity did not threaten the superior position of men in the power relationship between the sexes. Indeed, these activities may even have strengthened the prevalence of traditional perceptions of the female sex.[44] Of considerable significance here is the extraordinary mass outpouring of female support for Queen Caroline in 1820. Arguably, popular female sympathy for Caroline was a symptom of the simmering hostility of many women to the restricted public roles in which they continually found themselves. These gestures of female independence certainly alarmed the powerful loyalist societies which the Caroline agitations instigated. They set themselves to re-establish female obedience to patriarchal authority. The agitation is important, however, for politicizing countless thousands of poor women and awakening them to the humiliations of patriarchal restrictions and male misogyny in their own lives. The craft unions and radical societies of the early nineteenth century may have been the heroes of traditional narratives of the history of the working class, but in the history of gender they were unsympathetic to the interests of women. Many battles lay ahead for women from the middle and working classes.

Within the overall context of feminine acceptance of patriarchy, however, there can be little doubt that some women experienced a widening of social opportunities during the long eighteenth century. This was related not only to their participation in religious and charitable activity but to the general phenomenon of urbanization. In most towns by the end of the eighteenth century women were in a numerical majority because of male military service and the currency of itinerant male occupations. Indeed, female emigration out of the more patriarchal countryside, where there might be few outlets for female skills and ambitions, into the more socially diverse and economically dynamic towns was a feature of eighteenth-century life. In manufacturing, in retailing and even in service there were more opportunities for women in the towns than in the countryside. Furthermore, women may well have benefited from the social climate of the towns that was receptive to novelty, fashion and innovations. For example, a more enlightened procedure for the delivery of babies, with a trained doctor replacing the traditional midwife, with the use of surgical instruments in place of old wives' tales and with a delivery room open to air and light in place of the darkened and womb-like chamber of past practice, all signified a more humane and civilized attitude both to childbirth and to women. At the same time, the greater value placed upon children – what Plumb termed the 'new world of children' – betckened a softening of traditional patriarchal attitudes.[45]

Yet the experience of women in the long eighteenth century was very far from being uniformly fortunate. Many women, for example, were adversely affected – sometimes disastrously so – by developments in the labour market during the long eighteenth century. For talented women from the middle classes, careers in commerce had been possible in earlier periods: according to one estimate, in early eighteenth-century London no fewer than a third of all women of property ran some sort of business.[46] That figure declined quite steeply in subsequent decades. In the eighteenth century many of the increasingly specialized managerial skills associated with running a business came to be redefined. Increasingly, women were found to lack the professional training and other forms of specialized knowledge required, and they took refuge in domesticity. Prospering merchants and retailers tended to move their homes away from their place of work, leaving their wives (and often their daughters) to play domestic roles. Lower down the social scale women fared no better. In the artisan trades, women did particularly badly. After the middle of the eighteenth century fewer women entered apprenticeships. From a maximum of around a third of all apprenticeships in early modern England, female apprentices became quite rare by the end of the eighteenth century, surviving in any numbers only in occupations like bookbinding. Where mechanization led to changes in work practices, women were badly hit. As the century advanced the job prospects for women in the countryside, especially for full-time permanent work, sharply deteriorated because of improved farming methods. Moreover, demographic changes worked to the disadvantage of women. An increasing surplus of male labourers put pressure on women's work. As a consequence, many women became domestic servants, where they remained subject to patriarchal control. Colquhoun estimated that there were 200 000 domestic servants in London in the early nineteenth century and 900 000 in the country as a whole, 800 000 of them women. By this time, domestic service was the most common form of female employment outside the home, many times more common than factory employment. However, while domestic service clearly redefined social relations, with its formalities, courtesies and, in larger households, intricate hierarchies, it did offer employment, respectability and some prospect of modest social mobility, especially for girls from charity schools, workhouses and orphanages. To these women their place was in the home, even if the home belonged to somebody else.

Not all girls, however, ended up in service. Others, especially young, unmarried girls, moved into the newer manufacturing industries. Here, however, they fared little better. Rigid sexual segregation accompanied mechanization, and women were reduced to menial tasks in the putting-out system or consigned to repetitive factory labour. As most women did not form trade unions their power of resistance to exploitation was minimal. On the other hand, the wages for factory work were superior to those on the land or in service. Factory work, while exhausting and even dangerous, gave a certain independence, a little surplus money and the prospect of an early marriage. As the head of her own household a young working-class mother would have greater status and independence than in service. On the whole, however, there was little improvement in women's working conditions nor any closing of differentials by the end of the long eighteenth century. Consequently, early socialist thinkers like Robert Owen became early champions of the rights of women. In their critique of capitalism they noted the degradation of women and the disastrous effects of capitalism upon family life. Only in a cooperative society marked by harmony would sexual discrimination disappear.

During the course of the long eighteenth century, then, there were few changes in the separate legal and formal spheres inhabited by the sexes. In spite of a number of developments which emphasized the subservience of women, it is arguable that they enjoyed a somewhat broader range of social opportunities and acquired a greater consciousness of their status and their potential. Because of the endeavours of female writers and because of the Methodist and Evangelical movements, men at least came under greater pressure to respect women as people and to treat their wives and daughters less like servants and more like companions. Much of the literature of the century, particularly novels, focused upon the position of women in society and celebrated their virtues and their capabilities, arguably providing viable role models with which literate women, at least, could identify. Such literature both popularized and vindicated the importance of feminine values. Whether modern scholars choose to focus upon the intellectual nonconformity and political radicalism of Mary Wollstonecraft or the non-political feminism of Hannah More, the literary and social developments of the long eighteenth century enabled many women to become more clearly aware of their own situations, even if the real struggles towards greater equality lay in the future.

Notes

1. L. Colley, *Britons: Forging the Nation, 1707–1837* (1992), p. 7.
2. See above, pp. ix–xii.
3. I am indebted to Professor John Cookson of Canterbury University, Christchurch, New Zealand, for permitting me to see a typescript of his forthcoming book, *Citizen Armies*. See also the interesting figures assembled by Professor B. Lenman, 'Scotland and Ireland, 1742–89' in J. Black, ed., *British Politics and Society from Walpole to Pitt* (1990). Of new appointments to the rank of colonel between 1715 and 1739, only 19 out of 94 were Scots (20 per cent). Between 1739 and 1763, 47 out of 199 (24 per cent) were. In view of the strength of anti-Scottish and anti-Jacobite prejudices, these figures are remarkable.

4. Colley, *Britons*, pp. 201, 218, 233.
5. *Op. cit.*, p. 370.
6. *Op. cit.*, p. 129.
7. J.A. Cannon, *Aristocratic Century: The Peerage of Eighteenth Century England* (1984), p. 21.
8. J. Lucas, *England and Englishness: Ideas of Nationhood in English Poetry, 1688–1900* (1990).
9. And, indeed, in England. There was 'near unanimous support for coercion' in Scotland; J. Bradley, *Popular Politics and the American Revolution in England* (1986), p. 59.
10. Colley, *Britons*, p. 123.
11. H. Kearney, *The British Isles: A History of the Four Nations* (1989), p. 146.
12. R. Houston, *Scottish Literacy and Scottish Identity: Literacy and Society in Scotland and Northern England, 1600–1800* (1988), p. 257.
13. J. Robertson, *The Scottish Enlightenment and the Militia Issue* (1985) p. 7.
14. Henry Grattan (1746–1820), a lawyer, was elected to the Irish Parliament in 1775 and through his oratorical brilliance rapidly became the spokesman for the 'Patriots', advocating legislative independence and the liberalization of Irish trade. Henry Flood (1732–91) had been in the Irish Parliament since 1759, organizing and leading the opposition.
15. M. Elliot, *Partners in Revolution* (1982), p. 72.
16. See J. Smyth, *Men of No Property* (1992), p. 142.
17. The table of population growth is taken from R. Brown, *Society and Economy in Modern Britain, 1700–1850* (1991), p. 33.
18. W.A. Cole, 'Factors in Demand', in R. Floud and D. McCloskey, eds, *Economic History of England*, 1 (1981), pp. 38–39; J.C. Rule, *The Vital Century: England, Developing Economy, 1714–1815* (1992), pp. 38, 97.
19. P.J. Cain and A.G. Hopkins, *British Imperialism: Innovation and Expansion, 1688–1914* (1993), pp. 88–89.
20. P. O'Brien, 'The Impact of the Revolutionary and Napoleonic Wars, 1793–1815 on the Long-term Growth of the British Economy', *Review* (Fernand Braudel Centre), 12 (3) (1989), p. 381.
21. J.G. Williamson has suggested that the need for government borrowing on such a massive scale crowded out investment in industry. Such an argument, however, rests on the dubious assumption that the increase in government debt of £954m which accumulated between 1789 and 1820 would have been otherwise directed into industry. Williamson, *Did British Capitalism Breed Inequality?* (1985); 'Why Was British Growth So Slow During the Industrial Revolution?', *Economic History Review*, 44 (1984).
22. O'Brien, 'The Impact of the Revolutionary and Napoleonic Wars', p. 379.
23. I find it difficult to accept Harold Perkin's argument that the divisions employed by King and Colquhoun 'leads to broad horizontal layers which approximate to classes' *(The Origins of Modern English Society* (1969), p. 27). The examples he gives of Adam Smith's 'famous asides and forthright comments' on the subject of class amount to little more than traditional anti-landlordism and fashionable hostility to the middling orders.
24. W.A. Speck, *Stability and Strife: England 1714–60* (1977), p. 31.
25. See e.g. E.P. Thompson, 'Eighteenth Century English Society: Class Struggle Without Class', *Social History*, 3 (1978); P. Laslett, *The World We Have Lost*, 3rd edn (1983).
26. M. Daunton, *Progress and Poverty: An Economic and Social History of Britain, 1700–1850* (1995), p. 593. Furthermore, in one of the most remarkable and sustained rearguard actions in the history of the long eighteenth century, the landed interest successfully resisted any reassessment of the Land Tax burden.

27. For a convenient overview of 'the agricultural revolution', see Daunton, *Progress and Poverty*, pp. 35–52; J. Rule, *The Vital Century* (1992), ch. 3.
28. See e.g. J.A. Yelling, *Common Field and Enclosure in England* (1977); J.M. Neeson, *Commoners: Common Right, Enclosure and Social Change in England, 1700–1820* (1993); M.E. Turner, *Enclosures in Britain, 1750–1830* (1984).
29 Colley, *Britons*, ch. 4. See also the unjustly neglected chapter 'The Revival of the Aristocratic Ideal' in Perkin, *The Origins of Modern English Society*, pp. 337–52.
30. J. Raven, *Judging New Wealth* (1992), p. 257.
31. A. Briggs, 'The Language of Class in Early Nineteenth Century England', in A. Briggs and J. Savile, eds, *Essays in Labour History* (1967).
32. Perkin, *The Origins of Modern English Society*, pp. 165, 192, 214.
33. For this literature see *op. cit.*, chs. 6 and 7.
34. D. Wahrman, *Imagining the Middle Class: The Political Representation of Class* (1995), p. 403.
35. E.A. Wrigley, *Continuity, Chance and Change* (1988), p. 15.
36. E.P. Thompson, *The Making of the English Working Class* (1963), chs. 14–16.
37. Perkin, *The Origins of Modern English Society*, pp. 214–15.
38. R. Wells, *Wretched Faces: Famine in War-time England, 1793–1803* (1988), p. 333.
39. *Op. cit*, p. 323.
40. Notably L. Davidoff and C. Hall, *Family Fortunes: Men and Women of the English Middle Class, 1780–1850* (1992).
41. Colley, *Britons*, p. 261.
42. Sarah Trimmer had 12 children whom she educated herself, on the basis of which she proceeded to write popular works of educational theory, such as *Reflections Upon the Education of Children in Charity Schools* (1792) and *The Œconomy of Charity* (1801). Hannah More's position is rarely understood. She did not believe that women were intellectually inferior to men but, in view of the different social roles they were called upon to play, that they required a different type of education.
43. F. Prochaske, ed., *Women in English Philanthropy, 1790–1830* (1974).
44. B. Kanner, ed., *Women of England: Interpretive Biographical Essays* (1980), p. 199.
45. J.H. Plumb, 'The New World of Children in Eighteenth Century England', in N. McKendrick, J. Brewer and J.H. Plumb, *The Birth Of a Consumer Society: The Commercialization of Eighteenth Century England* (1982), pp. 286–315.
46. P. Earle, *The Making of the English Middle Class* (1989), p. 173.

12

The renewal of the regime, 1820–1832

The coming of reform, 1820–1830

The Reform Crisis of 1828–32 was one of the greatest challenges to the Hanoverian political and religious order. Although there was less of a military threat than had been the case in 1715 and 1745, and while the international scene was less menacing than during the crisis of the 1790s, the sheer strength of reform sentiment, the dramatic loss of public confidence in the regime and the near-collapse of its legitimacy should not be underestimated. The regime was in serious trouble, and it was fortunate to be able to extricate itself in the manner in which it eventually proved capable of doing. Paradoxically, the strengthening power and legitimacy of the ruling orders of Hanoverian Britain had been one of the most prominent themes of the 50 years before the Reform era. Why did the British political and religious establishments experience a crisis of confidence towards the end of the 1820s? Jonathan Clark has written bitterly of 'a final and sudden betrayal from within' the regime when liberal politicians acquiesced in the repeal of the Test and Corporation Acts (1828) and the passage of Catholic emancipation (1829).[1] For Clark it was not the 'radical tide' of enthusiasm for parliamentary reform which swept away the *ancien régime* but the inability of the ruling elite of that regime to stand up to its religious enemies. Critics have fastened on the idea of a 'sudden betrayal' and subjected Clark's interpretation to severe criticism. They have tended to ignore his recognition that long-term factors did play an important part in undermining the foundations of the *ancien régime*. 'What changed was not the theoretical validity or potential success of Anglicanism in an urban and industrial society, but the emergence of that society very largely beyond the pale of the traditional Anglican parochial structure.'[2] It was not that the Anglican church became either unpopular or irrelevant or unacceptable; it was simply unable to establish hegemonic presence within the new industrial towns.

Nevertheless, there are still some serious problems with this revisionist interpretation of the fall of the *ancien régime*. The first is the insistence that the *ancien régime* was still as overwhelmingly monarchical, Anglican and aristocratic in the 1820s as it had been half a century earlier. As we have seen, the decline of monarchical authority and the wilting of Anglican supremacy was proceeding apace by the early nineteenth century. The second is the judge-ment that those responsible for the legislation of 1828 and 1829 were involved in a 'betrayal' rather than a restructuring of the regime. As we shall see, those involved in the 'betrayal' were in fact endeavouring to save the regime, not to destroy it. The third problem is the revisionist argument that the demand for parliamentary reform was less a coherent campaign than a varied collection of popularist grievances that played on every prejudice – that it was not exclusively or rationally a parliamentary reform agitation. We shall certainly examine the agitation, but suggest that parliamentary reform was indeed the predominant aspiration of those involved. The fourth problem with the revi-sionist view is its neglect of divisions within the Tory party after 1827 in enabling reform legislation to pass. For the Tories, the passage of reform was more an act of political suicide than an act of betrayal.

In contrast to Clark's revisionist interpretation, Professor Cannon has advanced a socially based explanation. Cannon argues that 'the old system came to be dismantled [because] the excluded grew stronger, better organ-ised and less divided, while the conviction of the governing classes that those exclusions were justifiable grew correspondingly weaker'. The excluded groups he identifies are the Protestant Dissenters, the Roman Catholics, the lower classes and the middle classes. 'The root cause of the overthrow of the old order,' according to Cannon, 'seems to have been the growing political awareness of large sections of the nation.'[3] The Reform Crisis was not a col-lapse or a betrayal of the old order but the growth of powerful, external dis-content with it. The old problems which the Revolution Settlement of the late seventeenth century had been designed to solve had been those of a revived Catholic threat and royal despotism, neither of them exactly imminent in the 1820s. The problems of the 1820s required different solutions and thus differ-ent political machinery.

Such an approach offers a comprehensive interpretation, even if it totters on the verge of a Whiggish type of social inevitability. Nevertheless, it does not explain the occurrence of reform, merely the background to it. Reform could only come when those excluded from the regime joined together to achieve it, as they did between 1830 and 1832. But reform could only come when one at least of the two great parties in the state was convinced both of its necessity and of its urgency. Reform could also only come when the obstacles to its passing had weakened to such an extent that they could be overcome.

Common to both these interpretations is the assumption that the old order was destroyed in 1832 – something which would have astonished those who framed the Reform Act, who were determined to save as much as they could of the old electoral (to say nothing of the political) structure more generally. Indeed, almost all historians who have investigated these issues have reported that continuity rather than change was the intention of the men who had to wrestle with the Reform Crisis. To what extent this was indeed the case will be considered later in this chapter.

For several years, however, the *ancien régime* appeared to be alive and well. The later years of Lord Liverpool's administration represented an Indian summer of the old regime, a continuation of an aristocratic, propertied style of government and one based upon political consensus around which patriotic men could rally. This was a Tory government dedicated to the preservation of the constitution, the maintenance of the Union, the defence of the social hierarchy and the protection of property. It exploited and defended the existing political structure but it was also committed to its administrative reform.

There is no clear dividing line in the history of Lord Liverpool's administration, no general dawning of a policy of 'Liberal-Toryism', as historians once believed. Canning resigned in December 1820 at the start of the reign of George IV, a deed which left Castlereagh secure in the posts of Foreign Secretary and Leader of the House of Commons. His suicide in August 1822 enabled Liverpool to bring Canning in for both posts and made possible an extensive ministerial reshuffle. By early 1823 Huskisson had become President of the Board of Trade and Robinson had replaced Vansittart as Chancellor of the Exchequer.[4] But no new departures in economic policy occurred. It was the economic prosperity of the 1820s which marked the difference from the earlier decade, not any serious shift in policy. By the mid-1820s free trade was regarded not merely as an economic strategy but as a force for moral advantage. Huskisson, in particular, caught the mood of optimism in stripping away many obstacles to internal trade within the British empire. Following the Corn Law of 1815, however, the protection of agriculture remained a high government priority. Prices and production settled down, but a further collapse in prices during a renewed agricultural depression triggered further government action. In 1822, when the price had slipped to as little as 40s. a quarter, the government imposed a sliding scale starting at 80s.

The government pursued a policy of prudent finance, but in economic terms it was far from reactionary. It had already committed itself to a policy of free trade and commercial expansion in 1819, based upon tariff reductions and sound money. This it proceeded to implement pragmatically and cautiously. In 1820 Liverpool celebrated the policy as an attempt to unite the agricultural, manufacturing and commercial interests. While it stood for the protection of agriculture, the government was also determined to permit industry to prosper and expand by lowering taxes and customs duties and by ending the Navigation Laws. Liverpool thus saw government as an honest broker, aloof from contending interests but acting as an impartial, conciliating agency between them. At the same time, a mass of statutes and regulations restricting trade, especially tariffs on imports, were rescinded. In spite of a financial crisis in 1825, exports, and thus government income, soared. Against this optimistic background, the government agreed with a parliamentary committee which, on Benthamite lines, argued that repression in the 1790s had created trade associations and trade unions. Against the background of prosperity it was hoped that the repeal of the Combination Acts in 1824 would end, once and for all, the persistence of strikes and sedition. In the event the repeal was followed by a wave of strikes, and the government had to pass a further bill in 1825 imposing penalties for intimidation.

Even if there was no new 'Liberal-Tory' policy in the 1820s, ominous divisions existed within the government of Lord Liverpool. Men like the Duke of Wellington, who had been a cabinet minister since 1818, deplored Canning's liberal foreign policy, especially his refusal to send troops to defend the King of Portugal from his subjects in the summer of 1823. More serious were the tensions produced by the growing sympathy of Lord Grenville and his friends, Huskisson and, not least, Canning, in favour of Catholic claims in Ireland. Wellington and Peel were horrified. The last four years of the Liverpool government thus witnessed a cabinet divided between the Tory Ultras, Wellington, Bathurst, Eldon and Westmorland, on the one hand, and those adopting more progressive diplomatic and religious policies, Liverpool, Canning, Robinson and Huskisson on the other. These were not merely theoretical differences; on some occasions they could be extremely damaging. The government's response to the distress in the manufacturing districts which followed the financial crisis of 1825 was to claim the right to admit foreign corn as it thought necessary during the parliamentary recess. Moreover, it allowed corn stored in bonded warehouses on to the market at the extremely low price of 10s. a quarter. These decisions diverted the demand for the repeal of the Corn Laws, but the agricultural lobby was horrified. As a consequence, the government had to rely upon opposition votes to get its way. As Robert Stewart remarks, 'Liverpool's coalition was disintegrating'.[5]

The fragile unity of the Tory party could not survive the paralytic stroke which caused Lord Liverpool's retirement in February 1827. The departure of a long-serving prime minister frequently ushered in a period of political confusion. On this occasion, the confusion was to be particularly intense. Liverpool's reputation in recent years has improved, and deservedly so, but his undoubted political skills had simply postponed, not settled, a number of vital issues, including Catholic emancipation, parliamentary reform and the question of a Corn Bill. These in the end were to destroy his Tory successors.

Much to George IV's disgust, Canning, the clear choice of the cabinet (except Peel), became Prime Minister. Canning enjoyed the backing of the majority of his party in the Commons, but Wellington, Peel, Eldon and four other members of the old cabinet resigned. Furthermore, no fewer than 35 resignations occurred among the minor office-holders, many of them Ultras. They were afraid that Canning would bring in Catholic emancipation even though he denied that he had any intention of doing so. Furthermore, four Whigs, including Tierney and Lansdowne, who had accepted places in the government, promised not to raise the issue. The formation of Canning's ministry advertised the serious divisions within the Tory party. In particular it demonstrated the numerical strength and the passionate sincerity of the Ultras in the Tory party, those who stood out against concessions either to Protestant Dissenters, Catholics, parliamentary reformers or free traders. Their resignations somewhat ominously implied that their fears for the Protestant constitution were stronger than their loyalty to the monarch and the minister of the monarch's choice.

The unexpected death of Canning in August 1827 threw everything into confusion. His successor, Lord Goderich, was too weak either to deal with the King – he accepted George IV's nomination of Herries as Chancellor of the Exchequer – or to settle divisions within his cabinet. An issue of confidence soon arose when Herries quarrelled with Huskisson over the appointment of the Whig, Lord Althorp, to the chairmanship of a parliamentary finance committee. Huskisson refused to give up Althorp but Goderich was determined to stand by Huskisson. Certain to be weakened by the loss either of Herries or of Huskisson, Goderich chose to resign in January 1828.

In this situation the King turned to Wellington, who proceeded to attempt to reunite the fractured elements of the Tory party. Wellington had a number of advantages. The victor of Waterloo was still a national hero and a symbol of unity. Not least, he could be relied upon to hold the Protestant line against Catholic emancipation. In early 1827, on the death of the heir to the throne, the Duke of York, Wellington assumed the mantle of the champion of the 'Protestants'. The Duke of York had been a fervent anti-Catholic and his successor, William, Duke of Clarence, was more moderate in his opinions. Those fearful of Catholic emancipation now looked to Wellington to protect them from 'Catholics'. Furthermore, Wellington had considerable political and diplomatic experience, having been a member of Liverpool's cabinet between 1818 and 1827. In constructing his cabinet he retained Huskisson and some of the Canningites, while Peel trooped back into office. Although Wellington was desperately trying to balance his cabinet, his political instincts were the very opposite of Lord Liverpool's. He was not by nature a conciliator. He had a 'social contempt for his intellectual equals, and an intellectual contempt for his social equals'.[6] Indifferent to the feelings of his political subordinates and ignorant of the sensitivities of public opinion, he was not the man to heal the wounds in the Tory party.

It did not take long for the divisions in the government to show themselves. The Huskissonites wanted to demonstrate their liberal credentials by disfranchising the two constituencies most evidently guilty of electoral corruption at the general election of 1826, the boroughs of East Retford and Penryn, and transfer their seats to Birmingham and Manchester. In May 1828, however, Peel proposed to transfer the representation of East Retford to the neighbouring hundred of Bassetlaw, where the ultra-Tory Duke of Newcastle would be able to dominate it. Huskisson voted against Peel and thereupon resigned from the government, taking his followers with him.

Yet the history of the Wellington government deserves a better reputation than its divisions, and its later collapse, have normally earned. It weathered yet another Corn Law crisis and effected some useful Home Office reforms. In 1828 a new Corn Bill excluded foreign wheat until the domestic price was 73s. For a time this settled the bitter dispute both inside and outside the ranks of the Tory party between the free traders and the agricultural protectionists. Whilst maintaining protection, it was a modest retreat from the high protective tariff of 1815. At the same time, Wellington's government enacted a steady stream of home office reforms which went back to the early 1820s. Peel had himself got rid of dozens of trivial offences which had carried the death penalty while he was Home Secretary under Liverpool (1822–27). Back in office as Home Secretary under Wellington, his Metropolitan Police Bill of 1829 established a police force for the capital. Although similar forces were not established for provincial towns until after the Reform Act, the model was now in place and the precedent had been created.

But well-meaning and well-prepared Home Office reforms, while adding to the reputation of Peel and the reputation of Wellington's government, were not likely to relieve it of its most acute embarrassments, centred on religion and reform. In February 1828 Lord John Russell[7] introduced a bill for the repeal of the Test and Corporation Acts. He was supported by a powerful Nonconformist pressure group, the United Committee (of Baptists,

Congregationalists and Unitarians) and by the militant Protestant Society. The Protestant Dissenters, fully conscious of their wealth, influence and rising social prestige, were no longer prepared to tolerate the insulting symbols of Anglican supremacy. It was not enough for Anglicans to argue that the indemnity acts protected them from the full force of the legislation. The Dissenters were prominent citizens, loyal, successful, prestigious. In the previous decade three lord mayors of London had been Dissenters. At first Peel and Wellington resisted the Bill but it clearly had the support of the Commons, where it passed its crucial division on 26 February by 237 to 193. They tried to compromise but in the end were compelled to give way.

Russell was overjoyed that the Tories, the great defenders of the confessional state, had surrendered so meekly the first of their two great principles, 'that none but Churchmen are worthy to serve the State', and he looked forward to the surrender of the second, 'that none but Protestants are'. He added, significantly in famous words, 'Peel is a very pretty hand at hauling down his colours'. So, of course, was Wellington. As the Annual Register put it, repeal was 'the first successful blow that had aimed at the supremacy of the Established Church since the Revolution'. It is significant that even the government of the Duke of Wellington put up so little resistance. Ministers realized that it would not have been in their interests to have totally alienated one of the richest, most numerous and most influential groups in British society. Parliament was ready to pass repeal and public opinion was decisively in its favour. Even more surprising, and of much more significance, was the supine acceptance of repeal by the leaders of the Anglican church. Not a single bishop voted against repeal. Now that the church had become partially complicit in the dismantling of the confessional state – according to Wellington the repeal legislation could have been stopped in the House of Lords but the bishops were against doing so – it would be very much more difficult in the future to resist the claims of the Catholics. The reluctance of the church to defend itself seriously drained the enthusiasm of the laity to leap to its defence. What sort of confessional state was it whose clergy, at the crucial moment, surrendered without a fight on a cardinal point of both principle and practice? True, repeal had passed on the understanding that it did not imply an open door to Catholic emancipation but much would depend on events.[8] Ominously, indeed, there was a majority of six on an emancipation vote in the Commons in May 1828. Repeal did not lead directly to emancipation, but politically it made it much more likely.

Emancipation was a much more complex and, in many ways a more difficult issue than repeal. Privately, Liverpool believed that emancipation would come in time but he treated it as an 'open' question in cabinet. After all, two governments had fallen – in 1801 and 1807 – on the issue. George III's veto on emancipation was continued by his successor, and royal intransigence on the issue was strongly supported by public opinion in England and Scotland. In fact, fear of Catholicism was not as virulent in many quarters as it had been in earlier decades. Catholics and Protestants had formed a common front during the war against France after 1793. Thereafter, Catholics could not by any stretch of the imagination be treated as a subversive force. After the Relief Act of 1791 there was no demand on their part for further concessions before 1808. They accepted quite placidly their status as one of a number of churches peacefully coexisting outside the framework of an Anglican establishment. Popular prejudices could be whipped up against them, but the old antagonisms were in general cooling. Natural prejudice against Irish immigrants into some of the manufacturing towns of the north west could not be ignored, but they remained as yet only a small proportion of a Catholic community which numbered no more than 250 000 in the early nineteenth century.

It was to be one of the most important developments in the unfolding of Catholic emancipation that in the years after 1807 parliamentary opinion began to change, and change decisively. On the occasional motions moved by Irish members or radicals the majority against emancipation steadily diminished. An emancipation motion had passed the Commons as early as 1813, failing to clear the Lords by only one vote, another motion in 1819 failed there by only two votes. In 1821 there was a majority, albeit only of six, in the Commons for emancipation. This bill had to be defeated in the Lords. A similar fate met a motion moved by Burdett in 1825. A permanent, if tiny, majority for emancipation now existed in the Commons. After 1812 emancipation motions were usually opposed by under 250 MPs, less than 40 per cent of the House, and of those only 170 MPs were determinedly and persistently opposed to it. Although there was a small majority against emancipation in the upper House, the Lords could not for ever defy the will of the elected lower House.

When emancipation came, however, it was as a result of events in Ireland. Since Union the island had been deceptively peaceful. The Catholic bishops had accepted Union on condition that Catholics should be allowed to become MPs. Pitt's inability to carry the point rankled with Catholic opinion but for the moment did not embarrass the British government, which was intent on making a reality of Union. The Act of 1800 provided for the tightly drawn incorporation of Ireland with England. Where possible, any duplication of institutions was to be eliminated. On this basis the two Exchequers were united in 1816. Moreover, Ireland was drawn more closely under the administrative control of Dublin Castle. In 1814 special police powers for disturbed areas were given to the Lord Lieutenant. In 1822 a Constabulary Act established a chief constable in each locality, supported by local constables appointed by local magistrates. Beneath the surface, however, the grounds for discontent in Ireland had not disappeared. The detested Protestant Ascendancy remained securely in power. Furthermore, serious famine conditions – the result not of shortage but of the export of grain to England and consequent high prices in Ireland – caused immense suffering in 1817 and again in 1821–22. The old problems of agricultural backwardness, short tenures, overpopulation and a land shortage resulted in poverty, insecurity and lawlessness. It seemed that Ireland had gained nothing from Union. Against this background, in 1823 Daniel O'Connell launched the Catholic Association, a moderate, middle-class body, dedicated to the repeal of all discriminatory legislation against Catholics and committed to the repeal of the Act of Union.[9] The Catholic Association caught the mood of Catholic Ireland. The combination of religious and nationalist resentment was irresistible. Supported by the Catholic church and by the people's 1*d*. a month (the 'Catholic rent'), the movement rapidly grew in size and confidence. Its suppression in 1825 only worsened the situation. By 1828 Ireland was lapsing into anarchy. Widespread violence, the destruction of property, the spread of secret societies and the breakdown of law and order suggested that the country was drifting into a state of civil war.

At this point British domestic politics intersected dramatically with the gathering crisis in Ireland. It is clear that the Act of Union had drawn the affairs of Ireland dangerously close to the centre of British politics. Responsibility could no longer be shuffled off onto Dublin. British and Irish politics became fatally intertwined when the resignation of the Canningites from Wellington's government in May 1828 caused by-elections in the constituencies of their replacements, one of them an Irish county seat at Clare. O'Connell, who had held back from confrontation, hoping for concessions from Canning and his friends, now concluded that he could hope for nothing from Wellington. He contested and won the Clare by-election. As a Catholic he would not be able to take his seat; but if he were not allowed to do so, Ireland might descend into civil disorder. Had Wellington's government tried to hold Ireland by military force, it is doubtful if a House of Commons which had already consistently revealed a majority, however slight, for emancipation would have supported it. The only obvious political alternative was to dissolve Parliament. But another general election would simply inflame Catholic and thus Protestant feeling and, almost certainly, lead to the return of more Catholics in Irish seats. Wellington now saw that the national interest demanded the huge concession of Catholic emancipation if civil war were not to consume Ireland.[10] Peel's decision not only to accept emancipation but also to pilot the measure through Parliament was equally decisive. In March–April 1829 he rushed emancipation Bills through both Houses. The government's arguments were irresistible. To try to maintain discrimination against Catholics on the business of 140 years ago would plunge the nation into civil war now. To make timely concessions would pave the way for the peaceful incorporation of the mass of Roman Catholics into the state. The Emancipation Act of 1829 enabled Catholics to hold offices (with the exception of some minor offices close to the throne) and to take their seats in Parliament. In a desperate attempt to dilute O'Connell's electoral base, the Act altered the county franchise in Ireland from the 40s. freeholder, as it was in English counties, to the £10 householder. The meaning was clear. Catholics were to be full members of the political nation.

Catholic emancipation was greeted with horror by the Protestant population of Britain. After 1801, the right-wing press had been swinging uniformly against emancipation; to its readers, 1829 was presented as a betrayal of the people and as a violation of the proud ancestry of Protestant Britons. It was not just Anglicans but the mass of Protestant Dissenters, including many Methodists, who were appalled. The prejudices of the humble and uneducated were whipped up. Angry Protestants in Ireland as well as England flocked into the Brunswick clubs, which had begun to form in the summer of 1828 and which numbered around 200 at their height, and the Orange lodges, at least 300 of which were organized in England alone. Between 2000 and 3000 petitions were presented to Parliament in 1828–29 from such organizations, protesting against a policy of emancipation, some of them signed by over 20 000 people. As in 1828, however, resistance to a religious reform measure was not sufficiently well organized to impose itself upon a course of political events which had their own inexorable logic. Furthermore, this out-pouring of anti-Catholic opinion remained peaceful. Although hundreds of thousands of people reacted against emancipation with fury, on this occasion there was no violence, no mobbing and no Gordon Riots. The confessional state had been dismantled without a civil war.

The bitterness within the Tory party generated by emancipation was extra-ordinary. Most of the 202 MPs and 118 peers who voted against emancipation were Tories. Having lost the Huskissonites, Wellington now lost the Protestants or 'Ultras'. The crises of 1828–29 had given birth to nothing less than a party within a party. The Ultras threatened to transform the broad and inclusive Toryism of Liverpool, Peel and Canning into a narrow, well-financed and well organized reactionary body. It was an extremely powerful force, including most Tory peers, a growing number of Tory MPs, the press, the Brunswick clubs and the Orange lodges, together with powerful support at court. In Parliament, there was a core of about 40 Ultras in the Commons, capable of calling on a further 30–40. They were led publicly by Sir Edward Knatchbull but behind the scenes by Sir Richard Vyvyan. They simmered with resentment that they had been defeated on such a vital issue. They had been betrayed by their own party and by two of its staunchest 'Protestants', Wellington and Peel, and in the teeth of public opinion.[11] Even worse, many of them found it difficult to stomach the argument repeated during the 1829 debates, that the Anglican church shared many fundamental doctrines with the Roman church and that it stood closer to Rome than it did to the Dissenters. To understand the passions and resentments generated in 1829, we need to remember that emancipation was not merely a matter of religious toleration but a grave political issue involving Ireland and the future of the Union. Some of the 'Ultras' even feared that emancipation might be the pre-lude to attacks upon Protestant property in Ireland.

The passage of Catholic emancipation had important consequences for the reform of Parliament. Although there was no immediate demand for parlia-mentary reform in the country, the issue leapt to the top of the political agenda. It could no longer be evaded or postponed on the grounds that eman-cipation had first to be settled. Within a year political unions were springing up in many parts of the country which emulated many of the organizational features of the Catholic Association. Reformers had noted, too, that the changes to the Irish electorate contained in the Emancipation Act undermined the basis of one of the most compelling arguments against reform: that a tradi-tional propertied electoral system should never be tampered with. Furthermore, the traditional bulwarks against reform, the House of Lords and the monarchy, suddenly looked much less insurmountable. In short, Catholic emancipation was a triumph of organization, a precedent for reformers and a political breakthrough of the first order. Ironically, it also attracted a certain amount of Ultra support. On the argument that a parliamentary system that fairly represented public opinion could not have passed emancipation, some of the Ultras now dropped their previous hostility and proved to be adamant supporters of parliamentary reform between 1830 and 1832.[12]

After the passage of emancipation the government staggered on for a further year. By now it had alienated both the liberal wing of the Tory party, the Canningites, and the reactionary wing, the Ultras. Indeed, its prosecution of the extreme Protestant newspaper, the *Morning Journal*, for its libellous attacks on ministers worsened the rift with the Ultras. The government, on the other hand, failed to impress liberals, Whigs and reformers with the East Retford Bill, which transferred the seats of the notoriously corrupt Nottinghamshire borough into the neighbouring hundreds rather than to Birmingham. Peel had to work hard to drive it through the cabinet and through the Lords. To make matters worse, the government's position was weakened by the economic depression which spread over both rural and urban areas of the country alike from late 1829. Wellington lacked a strategy and seemed to be waiting on events. Sensing the growing paralysis in the Tory party, the Whigs began to revive their commitment to reform. In February 1830 Lord John Russell moved a motion to enfranchise Birmingham, Leeds and Manchester. He lost, but by the very respectable division figures of 188 to 140.

To complicate a complex political situation even more, in June 1830 George IV died. At once the longstanding royal veto against taking in the Whigs as a party disappeared; in particular, George IV's detestation of Grey would no longer be a barrier to the formation of a Whig government. His successor, William IV, was an elderly man without much political passion. If anything, he had Whiggish tendencies, and he had supported Catholic emancipation. At the general election which legally had to follow a monarch's death, moreover, public opinion – especially among the middling classes – was clearly sympathetic to parliamentary reform. In those constituencies where opinion could make itself felt, in the summer of 1830 it was clear that the government was bitterly unpopular. More ominously, reform candidates were speaking a language of bitter class resentment not only against aristocratic influence in elections but against landed power in general. Interestingly, Ultras friendly to parliamentary reform were in evidence, but they were thin on the ground at these elections. It was not sections *of* the landed interest which were prompting reform; it was dissatisfaction *with* the landed interest which was proposing it.[13]

As a result of the election, the Whigs increased their strength by 25 to 30 seats. Reforming opinion, however, was goaded beyond endurance by Wellington's extraordinary speech in the Lords on 2 November 1830 which claimed not only that parliamentary reform was unnecessary at that juncture but that it would not be forthcoming while his government was in power. The speech roused both Whigs and radicals in the Commons and alienated the Ultras as well. Wellington's motives in delivering such a massive rebuff to reforming hopes at the beginning of a new Parliament have never been satisfactorily explained. Perhaps, with characteristic vigour and frankness, he was simply making a response to Lord Grey's speech, which had urged the ministers to introduce a moderate measure of parliamentary reform. But it was the consequences rather than the motives of his speech which gave it such high historical significance. On 15 November, on a motion for a select committee to investigate the Civil List accounts, the ministry was defeated by 233 to 204. Of the 17 new county members who voted, only two supported Wellington. The English county members as a group voted 47 to 15 against him. The Ultras, indeed, voted 33 to 8 against their own government. There was now little alternative to resignation. Several of the outgoing cabinet ministers, but not

Wellington, advised William IV that some measures of parliamentary reform were now inevitable. On that basis, William IV invited the Whigs to form a government.

The passage of reform, 1830–1832

The Whigs had come to power, but rather through the self-destruction of the Wellington ministry than through any exertions of their own. Indeed, their prime asset was the fact that they were the only realistic alternative to Wellington. It was not the parliamentary strength nor the ideological radicalism of the Whigs which commended them to the public in November 1830, but the universal unpopularity of the Tory party. In this sense the political changes of November 1830 were not a victory for party. Indeed, the government formed by Grey was not exclusively a party ministry, its cabinet containing as it did four Canningites and one ultra-Tory.

The Whig party had been less than zealous in its support of parliamentary reform in recent years. For a while, in the early 1820s there were some signs of enthusiasm. In 1822 Russell moved to disfranchise 100 rotten boroughs and transfer their representation to the counties and unenfranchised towns. Russell lost, but by the very respectable margin of 269–164. However, his subsequent motions did not fare so well. In 1824 and 1825 he moved none at all. In 1826 he was defeated by 247 to 124. After that not a single parliamentary reform petition was presented to the House of Commons until 1829. Even now, in late 1830, the impetus to parliamentary reform was coming from out of doors, not from the Whig party. Furthermore, the Whigs had never systematically enlarged upon the old reform schemes of the 1790s which included a householder franchise, an attack on the rotten boroughs and triennial Parliaments. Because Grey did not believe that parliamentary reform would come in his lifetime, he had no prepared programme of reform in 1830.

The party that Grey took into government was not distinguished by its unity. In 1827, indeed, four of its leaders had served in the Canning and Goderich cabinets. Nevertheless they continued to regard themselves as Whigs. Whilst in office they continued to receive the Whig whip; they were never absorbed into the ranks of the government and they returned to the opposition benches in January 1828. Yet even in late 1830 the party was not united on parliamentary reform. Durham and Brougham stood on the radical wing, Holland and Lansdowne in an older, Foxite tradition.[14] Grey and Russell would have an unenviable task in keeping the party united. It says something for the uncertainty of Grey's position in late 1830 that he felt it necessary to find junior offices for a handful of Tories. Yet this was to be emphatically a Whig administration, with Whig leaders in both Houses and with the vast majority of office-holders toeing the Whig party line. Whether it would prove to be strong enough to surmount the obstacles standing in the way of the passage of a Reform Act was by no means certain.

The reform drama of 1830–32 was to be played out against a background of economic depression, grinding economic hardship and widespread popular excitement. Already when Grey came to office a rising tide of reform sentiment was sweeping the country on a scale that had not been experienced for over a decade. Led by Henry Hunt and William Cobbett, a national agitation was already rousing the poorer classes. The harvests of 1829 and 1830 were poor. The resulting distress led to rural rioting which racked the country from August 1830 to December 1831, starting in Kent and spreading across the south of England as far west as Dorset. In what are usually termed the 'Swing Riots', after the mythical Captain Swing, the agricultural labourers were responding to conditions of want and distress which intensified their depressed status and conditions as machine farming and market forces took their toll. The new Whig government showed little mercy to the rioters. The Home Secretary, Melbourne, set up special commissions to try suspects, who were treated to a stern range of punishments including imprisonment (644), transportation (481) and execution (19). The sense of national crisis was, moreover, heightened by a cholera outbreak in October 1831.

This grim background should be borne in mind when considering the passage of reform in 1830–32. Indeed, the Reform Act would almost certainly not have passed had it not been for the extraordinarily powerful popular demand for reform in general. Those who wished to reform Parliament were part of a broad coalition including currency reformers, like the Birmingham radical Thomas Attwood, who blamed the current economic crisis on financial mismanagement, those who demanded the repeal of the Corn Laws, others who agitated for factory reform and yet others campaigning for the abolition of slavery. Many people anticipated, indeed, demanded, that the reform of Parliament should not be an end in itself but that it should be a preliminary to reform in other areas of national life. The Wigan reformers, for example, celebrated 'Potter and Purity of Election: Food, Knowledge and Justice Without Taxation'. Universally, it was assumed that reform would attack corruption in central as well as in local government and lead to a more just and humane society.

The demand for reform was exceptionally well organized and maintained. Three features require comment. The first is the role of the press in politicizing the lower classes. Since the first decade of the century Cobbett had taught the poor to agitate peacefully. In the years of peace after 1815 his *Poor Man's Guardian* sold 40–50 000 copies per issue. Newspapers like the *Gorgon* and the *Poor Man's Guardian* were aimed directly at them, the latter selling around 15 000 copies per issue. Now, however, it was the provincial press which came into its own. Important newspapers like the *Leeds Mercury* and the *Manchester Guardian* (founded in 1821) advocated class cooperation and peaceful agitation. Significantly, they were even joined by some Tory newspapers, including the influential *Nottingham Journal*. Second, the sheer scale of petitioning was almost unprecedented. Three thousand reform petitions were sent to parliament. Some of the petitions were signed by tens of thousands of people – one from Kent by 81 000 – a fact which renders unlikely the possibility of people being intimidated into signing. The third feature of the reform agitation was the massive involvement of the middling orders, especially those from the newer manufacturing centres. The 'big bourgeoisie' of the City of London and the south east already enjoyed political influence. Now the great manufacturing bourgeoisie of the north and Midlands, hitherto content with the indirect influence which they enjoyed through their entitlement to vote in county elections, demanded direct representation in the electoral system. It was not just the Nonconformist Dissenters of the north and Midlands but also, in many places, the Anglican middle classes and – it needs to be underlined – the rural middle classes, too, who supported reform in 1830–32. In addition, hundreds of thousands of unenfranchised artisans now demanded the franchise as a right and as a means of securing further improvements in their economic and social position. Such men had always been capable intermittently of directing criticism at the political and economic systems under which they lived; now that potential for agitation was to be exploited as never before.

The organizational thrust of middle-class radicalism was provided by the political unions. In December 1829 Thomas Attwood established the Birmingham Political Union which was the inspiration for, but never became the prototype of, many such reform unions throughout the country. There were slightly under 100 political unions, a third of them in the north, a third in the Midlands, a sixth in the south west and the rest dispersed throughout the rest of England. About half of them were established in towns which were already represented in Parliament, the other half in those which were not. Their objectives varied, but in general they campaigned for male universal suffrage, annual Parliaments and the secret ballot. Their main functions were to politicize the public, to organize meetings and to petition Parliament. The objects of the 3000 petitions which showered upon Parliament between October 1830 and April 1831 alone were overwhelmingly focused on parliamentary reform. Only a small minority, in the end, included such demands as the abolition of tithe and the reduction of taxes. The unions were peaceful bodies – the motto of the Birmingham Political Union was 'Peace, Law and Order' – and preached the gospel of patriotic cooperation between the working and middle classes. Indeed, this was no mere fiction. Working-class individuals, including trade unionists, appeared on the lists of union councils and committees, bringing workers and their bosses under the same banner of collaboration. Dissenters of all types were very well represented. Agricultural labourers and women appeared very rarely. Whatever their social background, millions of people awaited Lord Grey's Reform Bill.

Because the Whigs had no detailed plan of reform when they came into office, Grey appointed a subcommittee of the cabinet, consisting of Lord Durham, Lord John Russell, Sir James Graham and J.W. Ponsonby,[15] to draw up a scheme 'of such a scope and description as to satisfy reasonable demands, and remove at once, and for ever, all rational grounds for complaint from the minds of the intelligent and independent portion of the community'. This scheme was presented by Lord John Russell on 1 March 1831 to a House of Commons which quickly showed itself to be astonished at the extent of the proposed reform. Modern scholars like to emphasize the extent of continuity and moderation in the proposals,[16] but many contemporaries thought them dangerous, even revolutionary. They rested upon two simple basic principles. First, an extensive redistribution of seats was to take place: the abolition of small boroughs with populations of fewer than 2000, the partial disfranchisement (i.e. the loss of one of the existing two seats) of small boroughs with populations of 2000–4000 and the roughly equal distribution of the new seats thus created to new county and new urban constituencies.

Second, a uniform £10 householder franchise was to be established in the boroughs, while the 40s. freeholder franchise was to be retained in the counties. These proposals were well calculated to test the opinion of the House, and it was clear that Grey had gone as far as he could. To have eliminated more than a quarter of the seats in the House of Commons was as much as its members could stomach. On the second reading on 2 March the Bill had a majority of only one (302–301) in the largest house in the history of the unreformed Parliament. When the Bill ran into difficulties during the committee stage, the ministers asked the King for a dissolution. Parliament was dissolved on 22 April. As a result of the subsequent general election Grey secured a majority of well over 100. No fewer than 76 out of 82 English county members were now in favour of the Bill. Scarcely a single anti-reform Tory survived in an open seat. When the new House met it was clear that the electoral verdict was strongly in favour of the ministers. Russell introduced a slightly modified Bill which easily passed its second reading by 367 to 231 on 24 June. On 22 September the Bill finally passed the Commons by 345 to 236. During the committee stage, the ministry was forced to accept the Chandos amendment which increased the county electorate by enfranchising tenants-at-will paying rent of over £50 a year. This consolidation of landlord influence was unquestionably the price that the ministers had, in the end, to pay to persuade the Lords to pass it.

The drama now switched to the upper House, where the Tory peers mustered in a final trial of strength. Thanks to their efforts the Lords threw the Bill out on 8 October 1831, by 199 to 158, an action which provoked popular indignation. The government rethought the Bill and made a number of changes, the most important of which retained the votes of existing freemen voters during their lifetimes. Thus amended, the Bill sailed through the Commons by a majority of 324 to 162 in December 1831. With the threat of creating additional peers hanging over their heads, the Lords passed the Bill on the second reading by 184 to 175 on 13 April 1832. Even then, the excitement was not finished. On 7 May the peers voted by a majority of 35 to postpone the disfranchising clauses, thus virtually rejecting the entire Bill. The government asked the King either to create 50 peers or to accept the government's resignation. William IV, wavering, accepted Grey's resignation and invited Wellington to form an alternative administration which might carry a more moderate reform measure, for a reform measure there must be. But there was nothing he could do to assuage public opinion which during May 1832 showed by mass meetings, demonstrations and petitions that only a Whig Bill would be tolerated. Fortunately for the peace and security of the country, Wellington had to confess failure, especially once Peel had refused to serve. The Whigs returned to office, and the reform Bill eventually received the royal assent on 7 June 1832.

The role of public opinion during the Reform Crisis can hardly be overestimated. At the beginning the favourable result of the general election in the spring of 1831 had been absolutely essential to Grey's prospects of success. At the end, it was fear of the likely public consequences of the Bill's rejection which finally persuaded hostile peers to absent themselves from the final stages of the bill's passage in May and June 1832. Throughout the crisis, the role of the political unions was of the first importance in persuading the King and the House of Lords that public opinion would not be cheated of reform. The unions were able to frighten the politicians with the threat of uncontrolled popular anger if the Bill failed. Certainly both Attwood and Place continually told ministers of the dangerous mood of public opinion. Both of them were prepared to mobilize the streets and risk the possibility of disorder. In point of fact, the importance of violence during the Reform Crisis should not be underestimated. In October 1831 rioters swept through Bristol, protesting against the Tory recorder, while at Nottingham the castle of the Ultra-Tory Duke of Newcastle was set alight. These October demonstrations had a distinctly anti-clerical tone. Out of the bench of 26 bishops, no fewer than 21 had voted against reform. At Bristol, in fact, the bishop's palace was burned down. With the public mood angry and unsettled, disorder was never far away. Consequently the unions had to keep the peace in 1831–32, while taking their supporters to the very limit of peaceful protest. The implied threat of violence, however, was enough to stiffen Grey's resolve to fight on and to persist with reform. Moreover, during the May Days of 1832 some petitions, including one from the Common Council of the City of London, demanded that the Commons should stop supplies if a Tory government were formed. In Birmingham 500 wealthy merchants and professionals self-consciously and publicly joined the Birmingham Political Union, while notices appeared in many shops threatening to withhold taxes if the Tories came in. It is well known that Francis Place theatrically advocated a run on the banks, but it is often forgotten that such a run did in fact take place. Within a few days almost half the banks' reserves were withdrawn. Massive public meetings and the threat – or bluff – of violence did much to dissuade Wellington and the Tories from forming a government in May 1832.

The political unions represented collaboration between the middle and the working classes. Yet the Reform Crisis also fostered the stirrings of a much more radical form of proletarian radicalism, especially in the factory towns. The Reform Crisis is an event of historic significance in the history of the working class. The crisis marks the moment when vast sections of the working class came to political consciousness: when they began to relate their own personal experiences to the broader context of national politics. There can be no mistaking the currency of the language of class. Richard Carlile preached regularly to enthusiastic audiences the gospel of class conflict in London in 1830. In the same year Cobbett toured the country lecturing to labourers in rural as well as urban areas. In April 1831 the National Union of the Working Classes was established, led by William Lovett, Henry Hetherington (the editor of the *Poor Man's Guardian*) and John Cleave. This was a body based on the Blackfriars Rotunda and reflected a mixture of ideas derived from Robert Owen and William Cobbett. The virulent class language of this body outraged middle class reformers, some of whom, including Francis Place, established the rival National Political Union, which aimed at cooperation, not conflict, between the classes. Such bodies were perhaps at the height of their influence in the Days of May in 1832, when reports of their revolutionary inclinations, however exaggerated, probably did much to concentrate the minds of the propertied classes. In general, most working-class radicals were willing to support the Bill even though it would not have enfranchised the poorer classes. They seem to have reasoned that the present Bill was only the start of a process which would eventually enfranchise them. Despite these divisions, an impression of unity between the classes was given out during the Reform Crisis which was never really justified. Indeed, as soon as the Bill was passed, the Political Unions, having unleashed sections of the working class in order to widen a propertied, middle class franchise, suddenly ceased their agitation, leaving working-class radicals isolated and frustrated. Henry Hunt, who had opposed the Bill as a liberal and middle class measure, now once more came into his own. The scene was set for the Chartist movement.

The background of national discontent had a further bearing on the nature of the Reform Act itself. It did much to fashion the intentions of Whig ministers. As a primarily landed party, the Whigs represented the terrors of a ruling order which had feared for its security during the 1790s and again, in the disturbed period after the war. Grey's government was anxious to settle the state of the country and, if possible, to remove not merely the symptoms but the causes of disorder. Yet the ministry was not united over the purposes of a Reform Act. The old Canningites, Melbourne and Palmerston, were the least optimistic, prepared reluctantly to enact reform in order to settle the country. Grey, too, was now convinced that a Reform Act was necessary to preserve the peace of the country, 'to satisfy all reasonable demands, and remove at once, and for ever, all rational grounds for complaint from the minds of the intelligent and independent portion of the community'. To do so would strengthen the constitution, reinforce the power of the ruling classes, detach the middling orders from the dangerous radical demands of the working classes and make them junior partners in a rejuvenated electoral system. To delay reform and to defy public opinion might be dangerous.[17] Others, such as Althorp and Durham, were much more positive about the prospects for change and renewal. To such men there was little danger in extending the franchise among the propertied middle class who would become the best guarantors of the constitution. Althorp actually liked to talk about strengthening the power of the industrial and commercial middle classes, but such opinions were not common among ministers. Consequently, the Whig case for reform was not democratic, it was not theoretical and it had everything to do with political realities. Lord Grey told the House of Lords at the outset of his ministry that he wished to 'stand as much as I can upon the fixed and settled institutions of the country' while 'doing as much as is necessary to secure to the people a due influence' in Parliament. Grey understood that in the new electoral system aristocratic influence would have to be exercised in a much less arbitrary fashion. He told the Lords on 24 March 1831 that the future influence of the aristocracy

> must depend on their cultivating a good understanding with the people; becoming known for their good offices, supporting the principles of the Constitution, and the rights of the people, and by the performance of these duties for which alone the public trust and confidence, and all the privileges they enjoyed were given them.

He and his ministerial colleagues did not expect the new electors to be unduly deferential. What Lord Durham, at least, wanted was 'an independent and excellent constituency', not a servile electorate. Even Lord Grey predicted that after the Bill had passed the aristocracy would not 'retain the power of dictating to the electors'. The new system, in short, would be a combination of continuity but with a well calculated measure of change.

The Reform Act of 1832

How did the stated intentions of Lord Grey's government over reform translate into practical electoral measures? The Reform Act of 1832 was based upon a number of strategic principles which gave rise to the detailed measures contained in the Bill. The first requirement was the elimination of the more scandalous abuses which had discredited the electoral system. This entailed the abolition of the rotten boroughs and the corresponding enfranchisement of the greatest of the hitherto unrepresented towns. It is difficult to believe that the Whigs were ignorant of the fact that most of the existing members for the rotten boroughs were more sympathetic to the Tories than to the Whigs. Their removal, and their replacement by members elected from places which were more sympathetic to old Whiggism than to old Toryism, might well give the Whig party a built-in political advantage in subsequent decades. The second requirement was that the Whig party would have to present itself as the party of property, not merely aristocratic nor merely landed property, but property in general. By enfranchising property they would ensure that electoral reform would strengthen the legitimate influence of property in the constitution and draw a clear distinction between an electoral system based on property and one based on individual rights. Third, a Reform Bill would have to include some improvement in the method of polling. Many reformers had criticized the lengthy and often disreputable polling period, which gave many opportunities for the coercion and intimidation of voters. If the idea of a secret ballot was still much too adventurous for those who sought to defend a propertied electoral system, it was still imperative to improve the method of taking the poll. Fourth, at the level of future policy it would mean a series of concessions to middle class demands while maintaining the fabric of aristocratic government. How extensive the concessions might have to be, and on what particular topics, remained to be determined.

If these were the strategic principles of the Reform Bill, what were the grounds of the Tories' opposition? These were four in number. First, the Tories argued that the Bill was an attack on the property rights of those who were threatened by it, especially in the disfranchised boroughs. This, they argued, was not merely wrong in itself but a dangerous precedent. Second, they attacked the proposed Bill which, while claiming to reform the existing franchise, maintained old anomalies and introduced new ones. For example, some of the proposed constituencies with one seat had a bigger population than some of those with two. Third, they attacked the likely political consequences of the Bill. Deprived of the reliable votes of members for the small boroughs, governments would find it increasingly difficult to maintain their majorities in the House of Commons. Fourth, they argued that the Bill would not be a permanent settlement of the electoral system. In spite of all their protestations about the sanctity of property, the Whigs had already conceded the principle that political power should, in part at least, be related to population. The Bill was full of calculations about the population of boroughs. Ultimately, the Tories argued, reform would lead to the destruction of the existing balance of the constitution by reducing the importance of the non-elective elements, the monarchy and the House of Lords. Politicians would inevitably compete with each other for popular support until in the end the existing propertied electoral system would be replaced by a democratic system.

These hostile arguments should not be dismissed as groundless alarmism. They had formed the systematic basis for Tory hostility to reform over many decades, and represented a perfectly coherent and legitimate political position. Tories in 1831–32 were, of course, capable of exaggerated alarmism as when, for example, they denounced the Bill as leading to the overthrow of hierarchy and the destruction of property; but many of their criticisms of Grey's Bill were less excessive. The problem with Tory attitudes was not the accuracy or inaccuracy of their doom-laden predictions but their inability to produce an alternative strategy to that of Lord Grey. Some kind of reform Bill was necessary. Peel hinted that a minor Bill might have been acceptable to him, but he and Wellington had not been willing to countenance reform in 1830 and refused to pass a reform measure in May 1832. In any case, a minor reform measure would not have been acceptable to public opinion in 1831–32.

I must now briefly summarize the changes effected by the Bill. First, as to the *franchise*, a standard householder franchise in the boroughs of England and Wales of £10 per annum replaced the varied traditional franchises. To lend continuity, however, existing voters were allowed to retain the franchise as long as they lived (the 'ancient rights' voters). In the English and Welsh counties the franchise went to adult males owning property worth at least 40s. per annum, or those with a copyhold worth at least £10 per annum and – the famous Chandos Clause – those leasing or renting land worth £50 per annum. Second, as to the *redistribution of seats*, 56 English boroughs lost both their members, 30 lost one of their two seats, Weymouth and Melcombe Regis lost two of its four seats. No fewer than 144 seats were thus abolished, 22 per cent of the total. To replace them, 22 new double-member borough seats were created and 19 single-seat boroughs. This total of 63 new borough seats was almost evenly matched by the creation of 65 new English and Welsh county seats. (The balance of new seats went to Scotland and Ireland.) Twenty-six counties were split into two divisions of two seats each, thus doubling their representation; Yorkshire obtained two new members; seven counties received a third MP. It is worth noting that the Reform Act of 1832 actually *reduced* the number of borough seats from 465 to 399 and *increased* the number of country seats from 188 to 253. Although it may be true that some of the new counties (South East Lancashire, for example) were really industrial seats, it is still the case that many newly enfranchised market towns looked to the countryside for their economic prosperity and their social leadership. Third, as to *the method of election*, the 1832 reform remedied some of the worst abuses. The polling period was restricted to two days (from two weeks) and by the provision of more polling places and polling booths. A register of electors was to be compiled in each constituency.

English historians often ignore the fact that the Reform Act had the most dramatic consequences outside England. For example, at the general election of 1826, owing to the scarcity of election contests, only 500 out of more than 25 000 Welsh voters had been able to use their suffrages. Even worse, in the absence of a contest, not a single Welsh voter had voted in 1830.[18] That simply could not happen after 1832 because of the increased number of electors and the increased uncertainty as to their loyalties. In Scotland the position was the same. In 1826 not a single Scottish elector had voted; in 1830 only 239 had done so. In 1832 the Scottish electorate leapt up from 4000 to 65 000, making many Scottish seats unpredictable and election contests thus much more likely. Indeed, the operation of the £10 franchise and the continued grouping of burghs resulted in average burgh electorates of around 1300. These, including eight new burgh seats, would be difficult to control. On the other hand, the average Scottish county electorate, 1100, was not large enough to prevent landed property from influencing the representation of the Scottish counties. The Irish electoral system had recently been reformed in 1800 and again in 1829, when the extensive franchise of 1800 had been modified by raising the county franchise. The 1832 legislation opened up the Irish electoral system, adding £10 leaseholders to the county franchise. Indeed, the new uniform borough franchise, the £10 householder, succeeded in unsettling the old proprietorial system in about half the boroughs.[19] The Act increased the number of Irish county voters from 26 000 to 61 000 and the number of borough voters, less spectacularly, from 23 000 to 29 000.

Before 1832 about 440 000 voters had the right to vote (although in practice the turnout was normally about 340 000). After the Reform Act the potential electorate was about 656 000, an increase of about 45 per cent. In England and Wales after 1832, indeed, something like 18.4 per cent of adult males could vote, far fewer in Scotland and Ireland.[20] Every historian who has ever written about the consequences of the Reform Act of 1832 has drawn attention to powerful continuities in electoral and political history before and after 1832. After all, in many places the new electoral system was operated by the men who had operated the old one. Although the excitement generated by the political drama of 1831–32 and the widely shared sense of expectation led many contemporaries to expect a new political world, they were in many ways to be disappointed, once the dust had settled. In view of both the personalities and the motivations of the ministers, it would have been astonishing if change had been more pronounced than continuity. Because the 'continuity' interpretation is so well established, it is worth considering in some detail.

First, and most important, the politics of influence was still of enormous importance in many of the counties and smaller and medium-sized boroughs. Family and proprietorial interest continued unhindered, much to the disappointment of many reformers, and as a consequence electoral abuses continued. The Reform Act of 1832 made no effective attack upon electoral malpractice; in other words, the landed interest continued to reign supreme over the electoral, and thus the political, system. Lord Grey's early decision not to propose a secret ballot was a sensible recognition that any attempt to subvert landed influence would have been futile. As has often been pointed out, the addition of 65 new county seats and the operation of the Chandos

Clause served, if anything, to strengthen it. There remained after 1832 no fewer than 73 borough seats with electorates of fewer than 500. Most of these were highly vulnerable to local landed influence. Some writers have argued that the government tried to ring-fence landed influence, separating it from that of industry and commerce, by redrawing constituency boundaries. Of the boroughs that survived the 1832 Act one-third had their boundaries changed, in many cases quite substantially. This may have been a subsidiary motive, but it does not seem to have influenced the major provisions of the Act. It was impossible, in most places, to separate rural from urban influences. Many 40s. freeholders lived in towns, and many boroughs were enlarged in 1832 by extending their boundaries into the rural hinterland. Nevertheless, the landed interest knew that it had done very well out of the Act. Althorp fully understood that the Corn Laws had been given another lease of life. As Russell said in 1837, 'we overdid it'.

Second, many anomalies remained within the electoral system. The south was still over-represented, to the detriment of the industrial north and Midlands. The Reform Act had not removed the very considerable disparities in the size of constituencies which had been such a feature of the electoral system before 1832. No fewer than 31 boroughs after 1832 had electorates of 300 or less. Many small towns were represented, while several large towns, including Croydon, Doncaster and Loughborough, were not. In some ways this should occasion no surprise. It can hardly be said too often that this was a *propertied* electorate. Population has to be taken into account but it was never regarded as the principal consideration in the electoral calculations made in 1831–32. Property, in its various forms as land, wealth, commerce and industry, was. Thus some small towns were given the representation in 1832 not because of their population but because, for example, Whitby was an important centre of the shipping industry and, in another example, because Frome was an important town in the West Country cloth trade. Furthermore, although the urban electorate was newly standardized with the enfranchisement of the £10 householder, there was still enormous variation in practice. Everything depended upon the level of rentals. Where house values were high, as in London and Bristol, many skilled workers would qualify. Where they were low, however, as in many industrial towns and in rural areas like Cornwall and Wales, relatively few householders achieved the £10 qualification. In Leeds only 5000 out of a population of 125 000 did so, in Birmingham only 7000 out of 144 000. Over the longer term, inflation raised the number of voters. On the other hand, in some constituencies, indeed, where the pre-1832 franchise had been unusually wide, the operation of the Reform Act actually reduced the size of the electorate. These included some towns where working-class voters were virtually eliminated either through the new franchise or through the dying out of the old 'ancient rights' voters – at Coventry, Preston, Westminster and, most of all, Lancaster, where the electorate steadily declined from 4000 in 1832 to 1000 by the 1860s.

Third, there was no change in the type of person representing the new constituencies, no sudden appearance of middle-class radicals and Nonconformists, no sudden increase in the number of merchants and manufacturers. There was some talk of giving salaries to MPs but nothing came of it. They remained a wealthy and leisured group. As was revealed in the first general election on the new franchise in December 1832, men of the landed interest still made up between 70 per cent and 80 per cent of the House of Commons. They also monopolized positions in the government. Of the 103 persons who served in the cabinet between 1830 and 1866 it has been calculated that only 14 represented new wealth. The number of middle-class MPs began slowly to increase in the 1840s but they did not constitute a majority until the end of the century. Until then, the middle classes were happy for members of the landed interest to represent them in Parliament.[21]

Fourth, there was little change in the status of the act of voting. Voting was still viewed as the public action of voters, who were thus accountable to the rest of the inhabitants of the constituency. It was not a right to which everyone had access. Voters were thus a privileged group with grave civic responsibilities. The secret ballot would have introduced a concept of the act of voting as a private, individual action. To men like Lord Grey who rejected the secret ballot, selfishness and secrecy would have devalued electoral politics. Without the secret ballot money might change hands and bribery and intimidation might be attempted, but these at least were usually public actions.

Fifth, there was only a limited change in the structure of the electorate after 1832. Even on the new franchises, the electorate was still dominated by small men from the middling orders. Both before and after 1832 such men – artisans and retailers – constituted about 60 per cent of the electorate. The Reform Act did not usher in a middle-class electorate, it effected a change of balance within an existing middle class electorate, increasing the number of retailers from one-fifth to one-quarter, and reducing the number of craftsmen from 40 per cent to 30 per cent. It was still an electorate of small men of property. What the Reform Act did ensure was that voters would reside in their constituency. One of its most underestimated features was its elimination of non-resident voters. These had formed a significant minority in the freeman boroughs. The Reform Act required householders to have resided at the address in which they lived for one year. The new electorate was therefore a resident, and thus a stable, electorate.

Yet it is still too easy for historians, who have been privileged with the benefit of hindsight, to emphasize the elements of continuity after 1832. The supremacy of the landed interest, the operation of electoral influence and property all survived 1832. Yet the struggle for the Reform Act had been a politicizing experience. The old days could never be recaptured, and if continuity had been a deliberate policy in 1832 it was impossible to put the clock back. Contemporaries tended to be impressed with the elements of novelty, innovation and risk in the provisions of the Reform Act. These, especially to a remarkably conservative people, were formidable. Lord Grey may have not attempted to uproot existing institutions, but one-quarter of the existing parliamentary seats were eliminated; the franchise was drastically changed, with many old franchises being completely eliminated; the size of the electorate was increased by almost half, potentially by much more; the method of taking the poll was changed, especially in the counties. Although the landed interest was still supreme in politics, urban centres had assumed a much more prominent place in British politics than they had enjoyed before 1832. The reform door had been opened and, it would never again be in the power of the politicians to close it.

The effects of the Reform Act on political parties were particularly far-reaching, more so at local than at national level. It is often claimed that with the formation of the great party clubs, the Carlton Club for the Tories in 1832 and the Reform Club for the Whigs in 1836 – significantly, in response to electoral reverses for each party in the preceding year – Britain entered a period of 'Club government'. But it is not clear that these Clubs were the first examples of formal central party organizations. London clubs like Brooks's for the Whigs and White's for the Tories, and in some ways the Pitt and Fox clubs, had performed similar functions earlier. Such bodies had acted as wining and dining houses for the party elite, and as clearing-houses for information and instruction. Election campaigns had been planned and executed in them and candidates matched with constituen-cies. The 'Club government' of the 1830s was built upon solid foundations of earlier practice and experience.

Parties acquired permanent and continuous functions of the highest importance on account of the registration clauses of the 1832 Reform Act. Registration was not automatic and it was not straightforward. Electors needed the parties to assist with the complex processes that led to their enfranchisement. Here was vital work for parties to do, sponsoring and assisting voters to get onto the register and pleading disputed cases in the revising barrister's court. Hence the registration clauses accelerated the formation of *permanent* local party associations and the appointment of *permanent* local agents in the place of the older, ad hoc party organizations which usually sprang into life only when an election was looming. These indispensable functions rooted local parties into the politics of their com-munities. The impetus to party formation, therefore, came less from high politicians at the centre than from the logic of the provisions of the Reform Act and from the enthusiasm of local party supporters in the constituencies. Furthermore, the financing of registration, the payment of agents and – still to a large extent – the selection of candidates remained in the hands of local enthusiasts.

At the political level, the Reform Act registered the steady diminution of the powers and prestige of the House of Lords and of the monarchy. The Act did not, as was claimed at the time, upset the balance of the constitution of King, Lords and Commons. For many decades that balance had already been tilting steadily towards the Commons and, more recently, away from the crown. The 1832 Reform Act was a further accession to the prestige of the lower House, and, not least, its ability to respond to the popular will. The obduracy of the House of Lords and its long rearguard offensive against the Reform Bill did not go unnoticed. The Reform Act also marked a further stage in the steady decline of royal power: William IV did not play a positive role during the Reform Crisis, and he showed himself to be vulnerable to the tac-tics and strategies of his Whig ministers.

The provisions of the Reform Act, moreover, did much to party-politicize electoral politics. This was to some extent the case because the Reform Act came in the middle of a series of remarkable political campaigns, for Catholic emancipation and for the abolition of slavery, which could not fail to have consequences for party politics. At the electoral level, the Reform Act seems to have been responsible for a dramatic increase in voter partisanship. After

1832 the overwhelming majority of voters were much more willing to give both their votes to candidates of the same party than they had been earlier.[22] Furthermore, the Reform Act created new voters and new constituencies, neither of which had earlier had an opportunity of declaring their party loyalties. In many of the new constituencies the balance of party advantage was not known, and for some years did not become evident. Consequently, the percentage of seats contested at general elections (no more than 30 per cent before 1832) increased sharply. At the general elections of 1832, 1835, 1837 and 1841 around two-thirds of seats were contested. By the 1850s, however, when the political complexion of many of the seats had become clearer, the rate sank back to below half.

The passing of the Reform Act marked one of the lowest points in the history of the Tory party. It had been less the strength of the Whigs than the internal fragmentation of the Tories which had led to the passing of Catholic emancipation, which had paved the way for the Whig triumph on parliamentary reform and thus to the great election defeat which the Tories suffered in December 1832. The results could not have been worse. The old party of government was down to 150 MPs and thrown back upon the proprietary boroughs. Only one county – Shropshire – returned two Tories in 1832 and only one of the Tory borough seats won in 1832 had over 600 voters.[23] Of the newly enfranchised boroughs the Tories took only two out of 65. Having dominated the representation of Scotland for decades the Tories were now virtually obliterated there, winning only eight out of the 53 Scottish seats. These dire results only highlighted the ideological ambivalence of the Tory party. Were the Tories a free-trade party or a party of agricultural protection? Were they an Ultra party or a party of liberal Toryism? How strongly would they continue to protect the remaining privileges of the Anglican church? What would be their attitude to Whig reforms? They might, with the aid of the monarch and perhaps the House of Lords, be able to veto or to arrest the momentum of Whig reform, but such tactics would hardly impress public opinion. Furthermore, having deployed royal patronage in the interests of successive Tory governments, were Tories now to oppose ministers of the monarch's choice? Although the political fortunes of the Tories revived after 1832, these problems were not effectively confronted and the continuing tensions within the Tory party were left to sharpen.

As for the Whigs, they held the immediate political future in their hands. The great heroes of public opinion in 1831–1832, they had a massive parliamentary majority and they now proceeded to enact a series of measures which have well merited the 'age of reform' epithet, including the abolition of slavery (1833), the reform of the Poor Law (1834) and the reform of municipal government (1835). Few nineteenth-century governments can rival the sheer range and amount of their legislative achievement. Significantly, none of this battery of legislation was reversed by Peel after 1841. Further, it is not obvious that these measures can be dismissed as a simple desire to maintain aristocratic power and to reinforce hierarchy.[24] The Whigs may not have been an entirely united or coherent party – which parties in British history have been? – and they may have turned to these issues piecemeal. Moreover, it is doubtful if they had a systematic manifesto of reform in 1830. Yet many of the measures did not directly impinge upon aristocratic power, and many of the younger Whigs displayed genuine social concern.

The social consequences of the Bill are much more controversial. It is one of the most persistent of all historical generalizations that the working classes were cheated out of representation in 1832. The truth is that they were. It is difficult to see what, if anything, they gained from the Bill. A smattering of respectable working men came in under the £10 franchise, but they were outnumbered by their counterparts in places like Lancaster and Preston who lost the vote. It is difficult to defend either the Grey government or the middle classes from the charge of deserting the working classes. The government can hardly have been unaware of the consequences of its own legislation; they had no desire to enfranchise voters whom they believed to be vulnerable to Tory beer and bribery. The middle classes had employed the threat of mass unrest to frighten the government, but once they had secured their objectives they dropped even the pretence of being seriously concerned with the political objectives of working-class reformers. Nevertheless, it would be unwise to exaggerate the degree of frustration among the working classes. Many of them were uninterested in parliamentary reform, preferring to agitate peacefully for trade union rights. Other working-class reformers were more interested in factory reform and cooperatives or, in many cases, the campaign to abolish slavery. It is difficult to estimate the precise extent to which the radical tide of 1831–32 intensified immediate working-class political consciousness, but there can be no doubting the long-term politicizing effect of the agitation. Certainly, the resentment caused by the unwillingness of the government to concede a working-class franchise swelled over the years and contributed powerfully to a widely felt sense of betrayal.

The middle classes were content with the enhanced electoral and political power which they had seized, particularly at the local level. It was to be in vestry and municipal politics that the middle classes were able to exert political control and to manage political parties. They had no immediate desire to replace the landed elite as a ruling class at national and parliamentary level. They lacked the leisure, the traditions and the patterns of unearned capital enjoyed by the landed classes which might have enabled them to do so. But most of all they lacked the will. They were determined to contain and to control working-class agitation and to defend the political gains they had made, but they lacked a strategy for transforming the *ancien régime* into a middle-class body politic. In any case, there was no need to. The Whigs, abetted by the Tories, were anxious to conciliate the middle classes. Neither of the parliamentary parties had an interest in creating a resentful and hostile middle-class radical party. After 1832 both Whig and Tory governments were forced to show themselves sensitive to public opinion in order to earn middle-class electoral support. This, together with the political reforms being hatched by civil servants and others at the centre, created an impetus for reform measures which continued the transformation of the *ancien régime* which had been proceeding since 1828. The stream of Whig reforms, followed by Peel's repeal of agricultural protection in 1846, completed the dismantling of the major political and religious structures that had dominated Britain since the Glorious Revolution.

Notes

1. J.C.D. Clark, *English Society, 1688–1832* (1985) p. 409.
2. *Op. cit.*, pp. 372–73.
3. J.A. Cannon, 'New Lamps for Old: The End of Hanoverian England' in J.A. Cannon, ed., *The Whig Ascendancy: Colloquies on Hanoverian England* (1981), p. 103.
4. William Huskisson (1770–1830), a Canningite and specialist in economic affairs. He was Minister of Woods and Forests, 1814–23, and President of the Board of Trade, 1823–27. He joined the Wellington government as Colonial Secretary and Leader of the House of Commons, but resigned within a few months. F.J. Robinson (1782–1859), became Viscount Goderich in 1827. His two nicknames 'Prosperity Robinson' and 'Goody Goderich', were provided by Cobbett. Nicholas Vansittart (1766–1851), was Chancellor of the Exchequer, 1812–23 and Chancellor of the Duchy of Lancaster (1823–28).
5. R. Stewart, *The Foundation of the Tory Party, 1830–67* (1978), p. 33.
6. See C.P. Cuttwell, *Wellington* (1936), p. 105.
7. Lord John Russell (1792–1878), a Whig MP since 1823 and the most notable reformer in the party. It was his initiative in 1828 that did so much to secure the repeal of the Test and Corporation Acts in 1828. Russell became a prominent Whig cabinet minister in the 1830s and later Prime Minister 1846–52 and 1865–66.
8. Catholic emancipation is the phrase usually applied to the demand that Catholics be allowed to hold office, to vote and to sit in Parliament. Since 1793 Catholics had been allowed to vote and even stand for election but the law required them to take two oaths, one of them renouncing transubstantiation, the other affirming their loyalty to the Church of England. These in effect made it impossible for them to take their seats.
9. Daniel O'Connell (1775–1847), an Irish lawyer and champion of Irish nationalism, known as 'the liberator'. An early advocate of Catholic emancipation in 1805.
10. Wellington was more statesmanlike and even more moderate than several of his cabinet colleagues. Indeed, during the political crisis that followed the success of Burdett's Bill in 1825 he had advocated a settlement of the Catholic question which would have included a concordat with Rome, which would have limited the papacy's influence in Ireland, and a scheme which would have brought the Catholic church in Ireland more closely under the control of the British government. Although these precedents were not to be followed in 1829, their existence indicates that Wellington was not the extreme reactionary on the issue that he is usually portrayed.
11. Both Liverpool and Peel had supported bills presented in 1823 and 1824 to give Roman Catholics the vote. Moreover, they would have been willing to admit Catholics to office on the same basis as that enjoyed by Protestant Dissenters down to 1828, i.e. by annual Indemnity Acts.
12. The point is a valid one but it can be exaggerated. In practice, only about half (29) of Ultra county MPs were to support the reform of Parliament.
13. The Revolution of July 1830 in France came too late to have much effect upon the outcome of the election, although it was to be much discussed by reformers in the months that followed. See N. Gash, 'English Reform and French Revolution in the General Election of 1830', in R. Pares and A.J.P. Taylor, eds, *Essays Presented to Sir Lewis Namier* (1956).
14. George Lambton, 1st Lord Durham (1799–1840), was a Whig county MP for Durham (1813–28) before his elevation to the peerage in 1828. He was Lord Grey's son-in-law and was Lord Privy Seal from 1830. The 3rd Marquis of Lansdowne (1780–1863), chancellor of the exchequer in the Talents ministry (1806–07) and a fervent advocate of the abolition of the slave trade. He was instrumental in the coalition between the Whigs and Canning and became Lord President of the

Council under Grey. Lord Holland (1773–1840), nephew of Charles James Fox, was Lord Privy Seal in the Talents ministry and became Chancellor of the Duchy of Lancaster under Lord Grey in 1830.

15. Sir James Graham (1792–1861) became a Whig MP in 1818 and First Lord of the Admiralty (1830–34). Later crossed the floor of the House and became Home Secretary under Peel in 1841–46. F.W. Ponsonby (1781–1847), a Whig MP from 1805, became Viscount Duncannon in 1834.
16. See J.A. Cannon, *Parliamentary Reform* (1972), particularly the discussion on pp. 254–59; N. Gash, *Politics in the Age of Peel* (1953), pp. 2–4.
17. See the argument by R. Quinault in 'The French Revolution of 1830 and Parliamentary Reform', *History*, 257, (Oct. 1994). Quinault underlines the very real fears of revolution in England at a time of revolution in Europe.
18. D. Beales, 'The Electorate Before and After 1832: The Right to Vote and the Opportunity', *Parliamentary History*, II (1992) pp. 139–50.
19. On Ireland, see T. Hoppen, *Elections, Politics and Society in Ireland, 1832–85* (1984).
20. For a detailed discussion of the size of the electorate, see F. O'Gorman, *Voters, Patrons and Parties: The Unreformed Electorate of Hanoverian England, 1734–1832* (1989), pp.178–82. See also the figures in M. Brock, *The Great Reform Act* (1973), pp. 312–13. In brief, of a population of slightly less than 2.4 million the Scottish electorate increased from 4500 to 65 000. Of a population of slightly less than 7.8 million the Irish electorate increased from 49 000 to 90 000.
21. W.L. Guttsman, *The British Political Elite* (1963), pp. 38–40
22. J.A. Phillips and C. Wetherill, 'The Great Reform Bill of 1832 and the Rise of Partisanship', *Journal of Modern History*, 4 (1991).
23. *Op. Cit.*, pp. 298–99.
24. As is argued rather unsympathetically in I. Newbold, *Whiggery and Reform, 1830–41: The Politics of Government* (1990).

Conclusion

In the century and a half since the Glorious Revolution Britain had experienced a number of the most important transformations in her history. These may be conveniently treated by recalling the themes which were outlined in the Introduction to this book and which have constantly recurred in these pages.

The first theme concerned the development of the internal structure of Great Britain. The Acts of Union with Scotland (1707) and Ireland (1800) occurred in different circumstances. The Union with Scotland had been negotiated in a controversial political climate and had led to armed rebellion. A century later, however, Scotland had become reconciled to Union and had become a particularly enthusiastic participant in the life of the British empire. Scottish society was, moreover, considerably more prosperous and harmonious. The Scottish Enlightenment of the second half of the eighteenth century established Scotland's cultural place in Europe and emphasized her continuing distinctiveness within the framework of the British empire. Although the important decisions affecting Scotland were now taken in London, the northern kingdom was far from becoming a servile dependency of England. Political integration had not led to economic stagnation nor to the weakening of the social and cultural identity of Scotland, even if the more militant displays of Scottish national feeling were a thing of the past. Indeed, as the political incorporation of Scotland into England proceeded so a romantic and nostalgic, and, in many respects, mythological version of the Scottish past was fashioned by writers like Robert Burns and Sir Walter Scott.

There was some prospect, too, that the future of Ireland within the British state might yet be auspicious. Without the benefit of hindsight into the tragic experiences of Ireland later in the nineteenth century, it is at least arguable that Ireland might have followed the example of Scotland. The domestic problems of Ireland remained intractable, but Union had at last been accompanied by emancipation in 1829, and in the 1830s and 1840s British ministers, both Whig and Tory, made some attempts to deal constructively with Irish social and economic problems. Posterity was to learn that these attempts were to be unavailing. Even well-meaning initiatives were incapable of surmounting the formidable religious division between England and Ireland. They were, moreover, much too modest even to contest the overwhelming power of Protestant property and its rights. Yet this did not seem inevitable in 1829. For much of the eighteenth century Ireland had been more secure within the Hanoverian political system than Scotland had been. If the '98 rising had changed all that, Ireland had been conspicuously quiet for two decades after Union. It still seemed possible to contemporaries after 1829 that peace, and even some prosperity, might come Ireland's way. Yet emancipation had not been accompanied by the establishment of the Roman Catholic church in its institutional aspects. Peel had argued, in many ways understandably, that if a Protestant state like England imposed the Roman Catholic church upon Ireland it would have led to serious political trouble with Protestant Ireland. Yet again, it was the internal contradictions of the confessional state which caused damaging and disruptive difficulties to the welfare and future prospects for Britain.

This brings us naturally to the second theme, the role of religion in the life of the British state and people. It is likely that by the end of our period religion was no less important in politics and in the life of the people than it had been at the beginning. The dramatic expansion of evangelical religion within the Church of England and the revival of Protestant Dissent outside it suggest that organized religion filled important needs during a period of unprecedented social and economic change, albeit of a religiously diverse character. As we have argued, the confessional state could not be sustained in such a period. Indeed, the attempt to re-establish the civil as well as the ecclesiastic power of the Church of England after the Restoration had been threatened from the outset even by the Stuart monarchy and its policies of religious indulgence. The ideal of a comprehensive, established church was not, in the end, to be achieved. Although Bishop Hoadley's vision of a church which permitted the flowering of private religious beliefs, contained in his famous sermon in 1717, was many decades ahead of its time, it is significant that Convocation, the voice of the militantly aggressive high-church Anglicanism, was suspended in the same year and in 1719 both the Occasional Conformity and Schism Acts were repealed. By the end of the eighteenth century religious diversity was almost taken for granted, leaving only an Anglican monopoly of civil offices. (Even that was challenged, however, by the Catholic Relief Acts of 1778 and 1791 and in effect wrecked by the legislation of 1828 and 1829.) If the Church of England survived the long eighteenth century intact and without the internal schismatic divisions that might have fragmented its structure, it remains true that it proved itself incapable of adjusting to the needs of a new urban society. Yet its resources, property and wealth were, and still looked, impressive. Between the Reform Act and 1851 the church was to show itself capable of an astonishing rehabilitation. Within 20 years the number of beneficed Anglican clergy was to rise from 11 000 to 18 000, while the besetting ills of pluralism and non-residence were virtually eliminated. In the first half of the nineteenth century, moreover, over 2000 Anglican churches were built, most of them in the new industrial towns, and another 1000 were built between 1851 and 1865. That the Anglican church was weakened by serious structural weaknesses in the eighteenth century can scarcely be denied. However, once its confessional status had been breached, it showed itself capable of a comprehensive renaissance.

The third theme introduced earlier in this volume was that of the cohesion of the social order. During the long eighteenth century the British state completed many stages in the journey by which a hierarchic society of orders became a class society. The protracted nature of this process has frequently been remarked upon and it was by no means complete by 1832. Indeed, it was not until the last three decades of the long eighteenth century that the finely graded hierarchies of pre-industrial society finally transformed themselves into nationally organized, horizontally formed classes. Even then, however, lingering residues of the old formations were to be found in rural areas; religion and the power of the churches could mobilize people politically just as powerfully as the agencies of class.

Nevertheless, class had arrived by 1832. The middle and working classes had forged their respective identities in their mutual interaction, sometimes in conflict, sometimes in cooperation. Whether the formation of classes inevitably led to class conflict is a topic of perennial fascination. That it *could* do is unquestionably the case; whether it inevitable *would* is much less obvious. Much depended on circumstances rather than upon any iron logic of class. Much depended, too, on the divisions within classes and the possibility either of healing or of containing them. The middle class in the 1820s, for example, was fissured by internal divisions between Anglican and Dissenter, between Whig and Tory and by yet further divisions of wealth and status, to say nothing of geography. Such divisions could be overcome in a variety of ways – by propaganda, by a common political or economic objective, by the operation of voluntary and charitable societies which brought them together and, not least, by the swelling patriotic sense of Britishness which was such a powerful feature of the latter half of the long eighteenth century. Such divisions, and such strategies for their management, must be regarded as integral features of class in general, and of class in politics in particular.

If it is the case that British society displayed a notable, and in some respects a growing, social cohesion then one set of reasons must be the ability of the English elite to incorporate the Welsh, Scottish and Irish elites, to maintain their property, power and political position and, in the end, to make their supremacy acceptable to a sufficient number of their fellow countrymen. Their association with the throne, their involvement in the armed services, their rural, landed power, their identification of themselves with the growing ideology of Britishness and their involvement – often personal, philanthropic and charitable – in local life did much to make their leadership acceptable to society in general. Their role in the administration of the Poor Law and their continuing importance in the administration of law and order, not least the deployment of troops, preserved their hegemonic position in local communities. Only when levels of recorded crime soared and when Captain Swing made his ominous appearance was the rural elite tempted to consider alternative methods of governing the countryside. The Rural Police Act of 1839 was the tardy consequence. Nevertheless, the local magistracy continued to enjoy an Indian summer of prestige in rural areas in the middle of the nineteenth century. County government was not expensive and it was not inefficient; it was locally based and locally manned and thus capable of responding to local – especially ratepayers' – opinion. In these and similar ways the ruling elite maintained its hold on power, national and local, partly by making timely concessions and partly by rendering its control acceptable to so many sections of the nation. Yet the economic basis of landed supremacy was gradually ebbing as Britain became a more urbanized country and, in its social as well as in its economic life, more preoccupied with the town, its institutions, its facilities and its lifestyle.

The fourth theme raised in the Introduction was the commercial and imperial expansion which had such a momentous effect on the people of Britain. During the long eighteenth century Britain maintained her record of agricultural improvement whilst entering a period of sustained technological change and industrial development. This occurred during, and to some extent because of, an increase in the population of Britain from 6.3 million in 1701 to 16.4 million in 1831. The scale of this increase had dramatic consequences for demand and – combined with improvements in agricultural techniques and methods of breeding, with changes in industrial technology and production – conspired with yet further developments in communications to effect historic transformations in British society by the end of the long eighteenth century. It is possible to exaggerate their force and it may be true, as Jonathan Clark remarks, that 'In 1832 Britain was still essentially horse drawn and sail driven' and that it was not until the 1830s and 1840s, 'when the railway and steamship arrived', that the output of iron and coal surged ahead. As he comments, the British economy 'was dominated by its traditional sectors and by traditional technologies, slowly evolving'.[1] Many industries, indeed, had undergone little substantial change by 1832; yet others had been accelerating since the 1780s: cotton, iron and engineering. The British economy that entered the Victorian era was already an economy based on coal. In the 1830s, moreover, cotton employed almost half a million people; it was in cotton that the most dramatic gains were secured, it was cotton which made up no less than 40 per cent of Britain's export trade. By 1801 agriculture accounted for only 33 per cent of national income, a figure which declined steadily to 20 per cent by 1851. In the same period, the dominant place in the economy was taken by manufactures, increasing from 23 per cent to 34 per cent.

Perhaps the most obvious and least disputed aspect of Britain's growing economic weight lay in the extent of her commercial expansion. Already by 1714 Britain had become the major European commercial power, outstripping the Dutch, and London had become the centre of world – not merely European – trade. Already by then the ports of the west coast were heavily engaged in colonial trade. Professor Coleman has estimated that the annual value of all Britain's commerce (imports, exports and re-exports) rose from £5.5 million in 1640 to an annual average of £7.9 million in the years 1663–69, but then grew remorselessly to over £20 million in 1752–54 and continued upwards to almost £28 million twenty years later. By 1789–90 their annual value was over £38 million.[2] In other words, in the century after the Glorious Revolution the annual value of Britain's commerce roughly doubled.

The fifth theme with which this book is concerned is the place of Britain in Europe and its status as an *ancien régime*. We noted constantly Britain's involvement in six major wars and their repercussions on politics and society. It is not too much to say that warfare changed the nature of the British state. Britain became a major European and, after 1800, a major world power by becoming, as Professor Brewer, has termed it, a 'fiscal-military' state. Britain become capable of financing her large military involvement in Europe from the 1690s onwards by means of deficit finance, long-term loans and the development of an elaborate system of capitalist institutions. Britain may not have been alone in Europe in expanding her armed services, her bureaucracy and her tax base. Nor was she alone in her agricultural, commercial and imperial development. Where she *was* arguably alone in Europe was in her ability to sustain these developments, indeed accelerating them during the Revolutionary and Napoleonic period. By that date, she believed herself to be pursuing an independent and unique course of development as an urbanized, industrial and imperial society. As a consequence, she believed herself to be aloof from the interests, experiences and values of her European neighbours.

In many respects, as we noted in Chapter 6, the structure of British society and politics was not altogether different from that of her neighbours. By the early nineteenth century, however, the trajectory of British history was beginning to depart from theirs. Britain was in the forefront of technological and scientific innovation; she had become a great land *and* sea power, a commercial as well as a liberal society. In these respects, Britain was growing out of the paradigm of an *ancien régime* society and was well on the way to the establishment of a pluralist, representative and imperial power. Far from being a corrupt and effete *ancien régime*, Britain had established an efficient and financially prudent, and bureaucratically professional, government machine. In the late eighteenth and early nineteenth centuries 'Economical Reform' trimmed the size of the 'fiscal-military state', rendering it more respectable and less prone to accusations of corruption levelled at it by country politicians, radical reformers and even by Evangelicals.

The final theme set out in the Introduction was the development of constitutional government, and of liberal conventions, habits and institutions. This may be defined as the transition from a body politic deriving both its legitimacy and its momentum from monarchy to one which was coming to rest upon a parliamentary basis, and to be accountable to extraparliamentary elements in the electorate and in public opinion. During the long eighteenth century Parliament became a permanent and indispensable element within the political system; and if it was slow to develop its potential during the eighteenth century it nevertheless acted as a defence against any revival of royal autocracy. When such a revival became unlikely, Parliament could still act in a variety of capacities, as a sounding-board for opinion, as a legislative agency and as a focus for party conflict. In general, Parliament became a flexible institution which, subdued as it so frequently was by ministerial majorities in both Houses, was nevertheless capable of fulfilling a series of invaluable functions. More particularly, executive government based on the royal prerogative of appointing ministers was in terminal decline in the early decades of the nineteenth century. The pattern of politics which had replaced the old Whig–Tory polarity in the early 1760s could not indefinitely survive the popular forces which came to the surface of politics in the 1820s and whose legislative consequences in the same decade created fatal tensions in the Tory party. Because of this circumstance favoured the Whig party, which took full advantage of the possibilities presented by the rising demand for parliamentary reform. Naturally, the Whigs became the beneficiaries of their own Reform Act and justly became the principal party of government between 1832 and 1867.

The old dynastic and 'composite' state of the later seventeenth century had become the more ordered and more coherent body politic of the early nineteenth. The dynastic, Anglican state had become a rich and powerful capitalist society with a reasonably stable and adaptable political system. Much of the old order still existed: the church, the monarchy, the House of Lords and a propertied electoral system. But the leaders of the regime had been prepared to collaborate with men from the middling orders, to incorporate men and ideas and to adopt their political ideologies and organizational techniques.

Britain at the end of the long eighteenth century was no perfect state, no perfect society. There were many imperfections and many targets for criticism. (Indeed, these seem to have excited some historians almost as much as they infuriated contemporaries.[3]) Inequalities were increasing: many people lived on the edge of poverty and some even on the brink of destitution. Relations between the social orders, outwardly ordered, were rarely close. The governing classes were always liable to panic at the first sign of threat, the first hint of disorder. This was in many ways an uneasy society. The rather exaggerated sense of British patriotism which streamed through all levels of British society has to be treated as much as a response to insecurity as a mark of healthy and well-founded pride.

Yet if it is legitimate for the historian to criticize through analysis, it must be equally legitimate to mark some of the features of the more civilized order that was emerging. The treatment of religious minorities, not least Protestant Dissenters and Roman Catholics, was infinitely more tolerant and more humane than it had been in the late seventeenth century. A more flexible, more representative and more responsive political system had been fashioned since the Glorious Revolution. This had shown itself capable of being used by the reform groups and humanitarian campaigns, such as the Abolitionists, which had become such an inescapable feature of the life of Britain throughout the long eighteenth century. If such campaigns had been pushed into the political background during the war years after 1793 they acted a forceful and aggressive part after 1815. As the legislation of 1828–32 demonstrated, reform *could* be achieved, and when it came it could come quickly. That an 'Age of Reform' was at hand could not be denied. How it would unravel, how quickly, how thoroughly and with what consequence could not in 1832 be envisaged. In that 'Age of Reform', however, the long eighteenth century would, at last, expire.

Notes

1. J.C.D. Clark, *English Society, 1688–1832* (1985), p.65.
2. D.C. Coleman, *The Economy of England 1450–1750* (1977).
3. Especially Roy Porter, whose otherwise vivid and valuable volume, *English Society in the Eighteenth Century* (1982), is vitiated by his detestation of practically everything and everyone in authority.

Bibliography

General

There is no thoroughly satisfactory guide to the long eighteenth century. Excellent volumes which deal with aspects of it include J.R. Jones, *Country and Court: England 1658–1714* (1978), W.A. Speck, *Stability and Strife: England 1714–60* (1977), I.R. Christie, *Wars and Revolutions: Britain 1760–1815* (1982), and N. Gash, *Aristocracy and People: Britain 1815–1865* (1979). All four of these volumes were published by Edward Arnold in the New History of England series. Valuable textbooks in other series include R. Porter, *English Society in the Eighteenth Century* (1982); J. Owen, *The Eighteenth Century* (1974); J. Rule, *The Vital Century: England's Developing Economy, 1714–1815* (1992) and *Albion's People: English Society, 1714–1815* (1992). The most recent and in many ways the most valuable contributions to any series are G. Holmes, *The Making of a Great Power: Late Stuart and Early Georgian Britain, 1660–1792* (1993), G. Holmes and D. Szecki, *The Age of Oligarchy: Pre-Industrial Britain, 1722–1783* (1993) and E. Evans, *The Forging of the Modern State: Early Industrial Britain, 1783–1870* (1983), all published by Longman. At the time of going to press, only one volume in the Short Oxford History of the Modern World series relating to Britain had been published: N. McCord, *British History, 1815–1906* (1991).

Important, self-standing textbooks include G. Williams and J. Ramsden, *Ruling Britain: A Political History of England* (1990); M. Daunton, *Progress and Poverty: An Economic and Social History of Britain, 1700–1850* (1995); and P. Mathias, *The First Industrial Nation: An Economic History of Britain, 1700–1914*, 2nd edn (1983).

Chapter I. Britain in the later seventeenth century

This period is best covered in J.R. Jones, *Country and Court: England 1658–1714* (1993). Useful general surveys of Britain in the later seventeenth century may also be found in J. Sharpe, *Early Modern England: A Social History 1550–1760* (1987); C. Hill, *Reformation to Industrial Revolution: A Social and Economic History of Britain 1530–1780* (1991); K. Wrightson, *English Society, 1580–1680* (1982); R.W. Malcolmson, *Life and Labour in England, 1700–1780* (1981); R. Brown, *Society and Economy in Modern Britain, 1700–1850* (1991); and the same author's *Church and State in Modern Britain 1700–1850* (1991).

Place

Useful specialized works include D. Cressy, *Bonfires and Bells: National Memory and the Protestant Calendar in Elizabethan and Stuart England* (1989); B.A. Holderness, *Pre-Industrial England: Economy and Society, 1500–1750* (1976); H. Kearney, *The British Isles: A State of Four Nations* (1989); L. Stone, ed., *An Imperial State of War: Britain from 1689 to 1815* (1994); G.H. Jenkins, *The Foundation of Modern Wales, 1642–1780* (1987).

Belief

There is no single volume on this period of religious history but the following are useful. N. Sykes, *From Sheldon to Secker: Aspects of English Church History, 1660–1768* (1958); J.H. Pruett, *The Parish Clergy under the Later Stuarts: The Leicestershire Experience* (1978); R. O'Day and F. Heal, eds, *Princes and Paupers in the English Church, 1500–1800* (1981); T. Harris, P. Seaward and M. Goldie, *The Politics of Religion in Restoration England* (1990); J. Spurr, *The Restoration Church of England* (1991); J. Scott, *Algernon Sidney and the Restoration Crisis, 1677–83* (1991); E.G. Rupp, *Religion in England, 1688–1791* (1986).

Gender

In spite of many criticisms, Lawrence Stone's, *The Family, Sex and Marriage in England, 1500–1800* (1979) will deservedly attract many readers. See also R. Houlbrooke, *The English Family, 1450–1700* (1984); and R.B. Outhwaite, *Marriage and Society: Studies in the Social History of Marriage* (1981). See also L. Charles and L. Duffin, eds, *Women and Work in Pre-Industrial England* (1985); P. Mack, *Visionary Women: Ecstatic Prophecy in Seventeenth Century England* (1993); A. Erickson, *Women and Property in Early Modern England* (1993). On the raising of children, see A. Pollock, *Forgotten Children: Parent and Child Relations from 1500 to 1900* (1983).

Society

On this perennially attractive topic only a few titles can be mentioned in the space available: J.V. Beckett, *The Aristocracy in England, 1660–1914* (1986); P. Roebuck, *Yorkshire Baronets, 1640–1760* (1980); P. Earle, *The Making of the English Middle Class: Business, Society and Family Life, 1660–1730* (1989); J. Barry, *The Middling Sort of People* (1993); K. Snell, *Annals of the Labouring Poor: Social Change in Agrarian England, 1660–1900* (1985). See also the interesting introduction to A.J. Fletcher and J. Stevenson, eds, *Order and Disorder in Early Modern England* (1985).

Economy

Standard textbooks include D.C. Coleman, *The Economy of England, 1450–1750* (1977) and B.A. Holderness, *Pre-Industrial England: Economy and Society, 1500–1750* (1976). A more up to date account may be found in J. Rule, *The Vital Century: England's Developing Economy, 1714–1815* (1992). See also W.E. Minchinton, ed., *The Growth of English Overseas Trade in the Seventeenth and Eighteenth Centuries* (1969); C. Wilson, *England's Apprenticeship, 1603–1763* (1984); B. Coward, *The Stuart Age: A History of England, 1603–1714* (1980). Of the works listed in earlier sections, those by Beckett and Daunton will be found of value for the late-seventeenth-century economy.

Politics

Relevant discussions will be found in J.R. Jones, *Country and Court: England 1658–1714* and G. Holmes, *The Making of a Great Power*. See also R.M. Bliss, *Restoration England: The Reign of Charles II* (1985); J. Miller, *Popery and Politics in England, 1660–88* (1973); J. Miller, 'The Potential for "Absolutism" in Later Stuart England', *History*, 69 (1984); J.N. Figgis, *The Divine Rights of Kings* (1965)

Chapter 2. The Glorious Revolution in Britain, 1688–1714

The Glorious Revolution in England, 1688–1689

The literature on the Glorious Revolution is vast. Useful modern accounts may be found in B. Coward, *The Stuart Age: A History of England, 1603–1714* (1980); J.R. Jones,

Country and Court: England 1658–1714 (1978; J.R. Jones, *The Revolution of 1688 in England* (1972); J.R. Western, *Monarchy and Revolution: The English State in the 1680s* (1972); W.A. Speck, *Reluctant Revolutionaries: Englishmen and the Revolution of 1688* (1988); L. Schwoerer, *The Declaration of Rights, 1689* (1981); J. Miller, *The Seeds of Liberty: 1688 and the Shaping of Modern Britain* (1988). The European dimension is well treated in J. Carswell, *The Descent on England* (1969). Revisionist views are stimulatingly set out in J.C.D. Clark, *English Society, 1688–1832* (1985). The best introduction to the intellectual and ideological background to this period is H.T. Dickinson, *Liberty and Property: Political Ideology in Eighteenth Century Britain* (1979).

Crown and Parliament, 1689–1714

Many of the titles in the last section are relevant here. See also the general surveys in G. Holmes, *The Making of a Great Power*. Particular studies of specific themes and events of the 1689–1714 period include P.G.M. Dickson, *The Financial Revolution in England: A Study in the Development of Public Credit, 1688–1756* (1967); H. Roseveare, *The Treasury* (1969); G.V. Bennett, *The Tory Crisis in Church and State: The Career of Francis Atterbury, Bishop of Rochester* (1975); G. Holmes, *The Trial of Dr Sacheverell* (1973).

Politics and parties, 1689–1714

The literature on party is of exceptional quality. Anyone's selection would include J. Plumb, *The Growth of Political Stability in England, 1675–1725* (1967) ch 5; G. Holmes, *British Politics in the Reign of Anne*, rev. edn (1987); W.A. Speck, *Tory and Whig: The Struggle in the Constituencies, 1701–15* (1970); G. Holmes, ed., *Britain after the Glorious Revolution, 1689–1714* (1969); J.P. Kenyon, *Revolution Principles: The Politics of Party, 1689–1720* (1977); C. Jones, ed., *Britain in the First Age of Party: Essays Presented to Geoffrey Holmes* (1987); G.S. de Krey, *A Fractured Society: The Politics of London in the First Age of Party, 1688–1715* (1985); T. Harris, *Politics Under the Later Stuarts: Party Conflict in a Divided Society, 1660–1715* (1993).

Studies of individuals are legion. Useful recent works include: S.B. Baxter, *William III* (1966); H.T. Dickinson, *Bolingbroke* (1970); E. Gregg, *Queen Anne* (1980); B.W. Hill, *Robert Harley, Speaker, Secretary of State and Premier Minister* (1988); H.G. Horwitz, *Revolution Politicks: The Career of David Finch, 2nd Earl of Nottingham, 1647–1730* (1968); R.A. Sundstrom, *Sidney Godolphin: Servant of the State* (1992).

Britain and Europe, 1689–1713

Although this theme has always attracted a steady trickle of interest, its significance is such as to deserve greater attention. The best titles include J. Brewer, *The Sinews of Power: War, Money and the English State, 1688–1783* (1989); J. Childs, *The Army, James II and the Glorious Revolution* (1980); G.C. Gibbs, 'The Revolution in Foreign Policy,' in G. Holmes, ed., *Britain after the Glorious Revolution* (1969); J.B. Hattendorf, *England in the War of the Spanish Succession: A Study of the English View and Conduct of Grand Strategy* (1987); J.R. Jones, *Britain and Europe in the Seventeenth Century* (1966); J.R. Jones, *Britain and the World, 1649–1815* (1980); P. Langford, *The Eighteenth Century* (1976).

The Glorious Revolution and the unity of Britain, 1689–1714

In addition to the works of Kearney, Stone and Jenkins listed for Ch. 1 under 'Place' see L. Colley, *Britons: Forging the Nation, 1707–1837* (1992); A. Grant and K. Stringer, eds, *Uniting the Kingdom: The Making of British History* (1995); M. Hechter, *Internal Colonisation: The Celtic Fringe in British National Development, 1536–1966* (1975); and T.M. Devine and D. Dickson, eds, *Ireland and Scotland, 1600–1850: Parallels and Contrasts in Economic and Social Development* (1983). See also the contributions by D. Hayton, 'John Bull's Other Kingdoms: Ireland' and D. Szecki, 'John Bull's Other Kingdoms:

Scotland' in C. Jones, ed., *Britain in the First Age of Party: Essays Presented to Geoffrey Holmes* (1987). On Scotland, see B. Lenman, *The Jacobite Risings in Britain, 1689–1746* (1980); D. Szecki, *The Jacobites: Britain and Europe, 1688–1788* (1979). On the union with Scotland, see D. Szecki, *The English Ministers and Scotland, 1707–27* (1964); B. Galloway, *The Union of England and Scotland, 1603–1608* (1986); T.J. Rae, ed., *The Union of 1707: Its Impact on Scotland* (1974). Older, general works are still useful; see T.C. Smout, *A History of the Scottish People, 1560–1830* (1970); R. Mitchison, *Lordship to Patronage: Scotland 1603–1745* (1983); W. Ferguson, *Scotland's Relations with England to 1707* (1977); W. Ferguson, *Scotland: 1689 to the Present* (1968). On Ireland, see the relevant parts of R. Foster, *Modern Ireland, 1600–1972* (1988), although certain older works are still indispensable; J.C. Beckett, *The Making of Modern Ireland, 1603–1923* (1966); J. Simms, *Jacobite Ireland, 1685–91* (1969); *The Williamite Confiscation in Ireland, 1690–1703* (1956). See also the relevant parts of vols. III and IV of T.W. Moody and W.E. Vaughan, eds, *A New History of Ireland* (1986).

Chapter 3. Whiggism supreme, 1714–1757

The Hanoverian Succession, 1714–1721

The period of the Hanoverian Succession is reliably dealt with in some of the general books mentioned above, including those by Holmes, Speck, B.W. Hill, Williams and Ramsden, Owen and Dickson. More detailed accounts will be found in W. Michael's old-established but still authoritative volumes, *The Beginnings of the Hanoverian Dynasty* (1936–7) and *The Quadruple Alliance* (1939). More recent studies focus valuably on specific aspects of the period, including S. Biddle, *Bolingbroke and Harley* (1975); J.M. Beattie, *The English Court in the Reign of George I* (1967); J.F. Naylor, ed., *The British Aristocracy and the Peerage Bill of 1719* (1968); J. Carswell, *The South Sea Bubble* (1960). R. Hatton's biography of *George I* (1978) is easily the best biography in this period; other biographies include B. Williams, *Stanhope* (1932); B.W. Hill, *Robert Harley* (1988).

Useful general accounts of foreign policy may be found in D.B. Horn, *Great Britain and Europe in the Eighteenth Century* (1967); and P. Langford, *Great Britain, 1688–1815* (1976). On the foreign policy of the period, see J. Murray, *George I, the Baltic and the Whig Split of 1717* (1969); R. Hatton, *Diplomatic Relations Between Great Britain and the Dutch Republic, 1714–21* (1950); J. Black, *British Foreign Policy in the Age of Walpole* (1985).

The Walpolean regime, 1721–1742

The years of Walpole's supremacy are dealt with in several of the standard general accounts, not least those by Holmes, Holmes and Szecki, Speck, B.W. Hill, H. Dickinson and Owen. Important material on a number of issues will be found in J. Black, ed., *Britain in the Age of Walpole* (1984). See also L. Colley, *Britons, Forging the Nation, 1707–1837* (1992); P. Langford, *A Polite and Commercial People: England, 1727–1783* (1989); J. Black, *British Foreign Policy in the Age of Walpole* (1985); B.A. Goldgar, *Walpole and the Wits: The Relation of Politics to Literature, 1722–44* (1977); M. Harris, *London Newspapers in the Age of Walpole* (1987). The standard biographies of Walpole include those by J. Plumb, *Sir Robert Walpole*, 2 Vols (1956, 1960); B. Kemp, *Sir Robert Walpole* (1976); B. Hill, *Sir Robert Walpole: 'Sole and Prime Minister'* (1989). On George II, see 'George II Reconsidered', in A. Whiteman, J.S. Bromley and P.G.M. Dickson, eds, *Statesmen, Scholars and Merchants: Essays in Eighteenth Century History Presented to Dame Lucy Sutherland* (1973).

The opposition to Walpole is discussed in L. Colley, *In Defiance of Oligarchy: The Tory Party, 1714–60* (1982); A.S. Ford, *His Majesty's Opposition, 1714–1830* (1964); E.P. Thompson, *Whigs and Hunters: The Origins of the Black Act* (1975); P. Fritz, *The English Ministers and Jacobitism, 1714–45* (1975); G.V. Bennett, *The Tory Crisis in Church and State*

(1975); C.B. Realey, *The Early Opposition to Walpole* (1931); I. Krammick, *Bolingbroke and His Circle: The Politics of Nostalgia in the Age of Walpole* (1968); H.T. Dickinson, *Bolingbroke* (1970); P. Langford, *The Excise Crisis: Society and Politics in the Age of Walpole* (1975).

The Pelhams and patriotism, 1742–1757

The general works mentioned earlier in this section include the period 1742–57. More detailed studies cover particular aspects of the period, not least J.B. Owen, *The Rise of the Pelhams* (1956); T.W. Perry, *Public Opinion, Propaganda and Politics in Eighteenth Century England* (1962) (on the Jewish Naturalization Bill); R. Harris *A Patriot Press: National Politics and the London Press in the 1740s* (1993); J.C.D. Clark, *The Dynamics of Change: The Crisis of the 1750s and English Party Systems* (1982). Biographies of leading personalities are in general disappointing. See, however, R. Browning, *The Duke of Newcastle* (1975); J. Withs, *Henry Pelham: A Whig in Power* (1964); B. Williams, *Carteret and Newcastle* (1943); E. Eyck, *Pitt versus Fox, Father and Son* (1950); J. Black, *Pitt the Elder* (1992).

Chapter 4. The social foundations of the early Hanoverian regime, 1714–1757

The identity of Britain

Many of the titles listed for Chapter 2 under 'The Glorious Revolution and the Unity of Britain' will once more be helpful, especially Foster, Kearney, Grant and Stringer, and Stone. See also the essay by B. Lenman in J. Black, ed., *British Politics and Society in the Age of Walpole* (1990). More detailed general and comparative accounts include L. Colley, *Britons: Forging the Nation, 1707–1837* (1992); T. Wilson, *The Sense of People: Politics, Culture and Imperialism in England* (1995); T.M. Devine and D. Dickson, eds, *Ireland and Scotland 1600–1850: Parallels and Contrasts in Economic and Social Development* (1983). The two essays on Ireland and Scotland by H. Ayton and D. Szecki in C. Jones, ed., *Britain in the First Age of Party* (1987) are particularly illuminating.

On Ireland, see the relevant sections of J.C. Becket, *The Making of Modern Ireland* and T.W. Moody and W.E. Vaughan, *A New History of Ireland*, IV, (1986); L.M. Cullen, *Anglo-Irish Trade, 1600–1801* (1968); S.J. Connolly, *Religion, Law and Power: The Making of Protestant Ireland, 1660–1760* (1992); F.G. Jones, *Ireland in the Empire, 1866–1770* (1973); T. Bartlett, *The Fall and Rise of the Irish Nation: The Catholic Question, 1690–1830* (1992).

The situation in Scotland is dealt with in the relevant sections of T.C. Smout, *A History of the Scottish People, 1560–1830* (1970); R. Mitchison *Lordship to Patronage: Scotland 1603–1745* (1983); and W. Ferguson, *Scotland's Relations with England to 1707* (1977). See also R.H. Campbell, *Scotland Since 1707: The Rise of an Industrial Society* (1985); H. Hamilton, *An Economic History of Scotland in the Eighteenth Century* (1963); B. Lenman, *An Economic History of Modern Scotland, 1660–1976* (1977); J.S. Shaw, *The Management of Scottish Society, 1707–1764* (1983); B. Lenman, *The Jacobite Risings in Britain, 1689–1746* (1980). Finally, a book which has implications far beyond its somewhat daunting title is C. Kidd, *Subverting Scotland's Past: Scottish Whig Historians and the Creation of an Anglo-British Identity, 1689–1830* (1993). For Wales, see G.H. Jenkins, *The Foundations of Modern Wales, 1642–1780* (1987).

The ruling order: oligarchy and deference

Once again, volumes from an earlier section, Chapter 1, under 'Economy', will be found useful. There is a particularly fine chapter in Speck's *Stability and Strife* (ch. 6 'The Making of the English Ruling Class'). J.P. Jenkins provides a welcome shift of emphasis in his *The Making of a Ruling Class: The Glamorgan Gentry, 1640–1790* (1983). H. Habbakuk's thesis of the consolidation of landed estates was outlined in three papers: 'The Rise and Fall of English Landed Families, 1680–1800', *Transactions of the Royal*

Historical Society (1979, 1980 and 1981), as well as in 'English Landownership, 1680–1740', *Economic History Review*, 10 (1939–40). Reconsiderations of this interpretation can be found in J. Beckett's papers, 'English Landownership in the later Seventeenth and Eighteenth Centuries', *Economic History Review*, 30 (1977), and 'The Pattern of Landownership in England and Wales, 1660–1880', *Economic History Review*, 37 (1984). Other important contributions to this debate have issued from C. Clay, 'Marriage, Inheritance and the Rise of Large Estates in England, 1660–1815', *Economic History Review*, 21 (1968); C. Clay, 'Landlords and Estate Management', in J. Thirsk, ed., *Agricultural History of England and Wales, v*, 1640–1750 (1984); J.V. Beckett, 'The Decline of the Small Landowner in Eighteenth and Nineteenth Century England: Some Regional Considerations', *Agricultural History Review*, 30 (1982). More general treatments of the aristocracy include J. Beckett, *The Aristocracy of England, 1660–1914* (1986) and F.M.L. Thompson, 'Landownership and Economic Growth in England in the Eighteenth Century', in E.L. Jones and S.J. Woolf eds, *Agrarian Change and Economic Development* (1969).

The political aspects of aristocratic oligarchy are dealt with magisterially in J.A. Cannon, *Aristocratic Century: The Peerage in Eighteenth Century England* (1984); but see also P. Langford, *Public Life and the Propertied Englishman, 1689–1789* (1991); J.A. Cannon, 'The Isthmus Repaired: The Resurgence of the English Aristocracy, 1660–1716' *Proceedings of the British Academy*, 68 (1982).

The middling orders: enterprise and docility

The commercial background is provided in W.E. Minchinton, ed., *The Growth of Overseas Trade in the Seventeenth and Eighteenth Centuries* (1969); R. Davis, 'English Foreign Trade, 1700–1774', *Economic History Review*, 15 (1962); R.G. Wilson, *Gentlemen Merchants: The Merchant Community in Leeds, 1700–1830* (1971).

On the professions, see G. Holmes, *Augustan England: Professions, State and Society, 1680–1730* (1982); W. Prest, ed., *The Professions in Early Modern England* (1989). On London, see P. Earle, *The Making of the English Middle Class: Business, Society and Family Life in London, 1660–1730* (1989); G.S. de Krey, *A Fractured Society: The Politics of London in the First Age of Party, 1688–1715* (1985); and H. Horwitz, 'Party in a Civic Context: London from the Exclusion Crisis to the Fall of Walpole', in C. Jones, ed., *Britain in the First Age of Party* (1987). Much has been published on the growth of consumerism in recent years since N. McKendrick, J. Brewer and J.H. Plumb, *The Birth of a Consumer Society: The Commercialization of Eighteenth Century England* (1982). Among the best titles are J. Brewer and A. Bermingham, eds, *The Consumption of Culture* (1985); J. Brewer and S. Staves, eds, *Early Modern Conceptions of Property* (1995); C. Shamman, *The Pre-Industrial Consumer in England and America* (1993); J. Brewer and R. Porter, eds, *Consumption and the World of Goods* (1994); L. Weatherill, *Consumer Behaviour and Material Culture in Britain, 1660–1760* (1988); H.-C. Mui and L.H. Mui, *Shops and Shopkeeping in Eighteenth Century England* (1989); B. Lemire, *Fashion's Favourite: The Cotton Trade and the Consumer in Britain, 1660–1800* (1991).

Urban society: culture and elites

Students are advised to base their studies of urban history on P. Corfield, *The Impact of English Towns, 1700–1800* (1982); P. Clark and P. Slack, eds, *Crisis and Order in English Towns: Essays in Urban History* (1972); P. Clark, ed., *The Transformation of English Provincial Towns, 1600–1800* (1984); P.N. Borsay, *The English Urban Renaissance: Culture and Society in the Provincial Town, 1660–1700* (1989); P. Corfield et al., *Rise of the New Urban Society* (1975); C.W. Chalklin, *The Provincial Towns of Georgian England: A Study of Eighteenth Century England* (1984); M. Girouard, *The English Town: A History of Urban Life* (1990).

The common people: assertion, festivity and direct action

J.F.C. Harrison's *The Common People* (1984) is an unjustly neglected work. Chapters 5 and 6 provide an effective introduction to this topic as, incidentally, does K. Wrightson's *English Society, 1580–1680* (1982), although principally for an earlier period (esp. chs. 2 and 6). See also A. McInnes 'The Revolution and the People' in G. Holmes, ed., *Britain after the Glorious Revolution, 1689–1714* (1969). Edward Thompson's approach to popular culture is memorably outlined in 'The Moral Economy of the English Crowd in the Eighteenth Century', *Past and Present*, 50 (1971) and applied to the period of Walpole in *Whigs and Hunters: The Origins of the Black Act* (1975). It received vital reinforcement from K.D.M. Snell's *Annals of the Labouring Poor: Social Change and Agrarian England, 1660–1900* (1985); and R.W. Malcolmson, *Life and Labour in England, 1700–1780* (1981).

A different type of approach is provided in H. Dickinson's *The Politics of the People in Eighteenth Century Britain* (1995). J. Brewer, *Party Ideology and Popular Politics at the Accession of George III* (1976) has important perspectives which are relevant even earlier than 1760. Similarly the methods employed by those historians studying ritual celebrations can be more widely applied. See e.g. K. Wilson, 'Empire, Trade and Popular Politics in Mid-Hanoverian England: The Case of "Admiral Vernon"', *Past and Present*, 121 (1988). Her thesis is more fully outlined in *The Sense of the People: Urban Political Culture in England, 1715–85* (1995). See also G. Jordan and N. Rogers, 'Admirals as Heroes: Patriotisms and Liberty in Hanoverian England', *Journal of British Studies*, 28(3) (1989).

The vexed issue of 'popular politics' is assessed in N. Rogers, *Whigs and Cities: Popular Politics in the Age of Walpole and Pitt* (1989); and 'The Urban Opposition to Whig Oligarchy, 1720–60', in M. and M. Jacob, eds, *The Origins of Anglo-American Radicalism* (1984).

Chapter 5. The political foundation of the early Hanoverian regime, 1714–1757

Politics and print

Ruminations on the nature of politics in this period are none too common, but see J.C.D. Clark, *The Dynamics of Change: The Crisis of the 1750s and English Party Systems* (1982), pp.1–26; M. Bentley, *Politics Without Democracy, 1815–1916* (1984), pp. 19–30; J. Ehrman, *Pitt the Younger* (1989), vol. I, ch. 1; R. Porter, *English Society in the Eighteenth Century* (1982) ch. 3.

On the emergence of print culture, see M. Spufford, *Small Books and Pleasant Histories: Popular Fiction and Its Readership in the Seventeenth Century England* (1981); B. Capp, *Astrology and the Popular Press: English Almanacs, 1550–1800* (1989); M. Harris and A. Lee, *The Press in English Society* (1987); J. Black, *The English Press in the Eighteenth Century* (1987); M. Harris, *London Newspapers in the Age of Walpole: A Study in the Origins of the Modern English Press* (1987); R. Harris, *A Patriot Press: National Politics and the London Press in the 1740s* (1993); J. Feather, *The Provincial Book Trade in Eighteenth Century England* (1985); I. Rogers, ed., *Books and Their Readers in Eighteenth Century England* (1982); R.M. Wiles, *Freshest Advices: Early Provincial Newspapers in England* (1965).

Crown and Parliament

There is surprisingly little scholarly historical work on the first two Georges. The best works include R. Hatton, *George I: Elector and King* (1978); R. Hatton, 'New Light on George I of Great Britain', in S.B. Baxter, ed., *England's Rise to Greatness, 1660–1760* (1983); J.M. Beattie, *The English Court in the Reign of George I* (1967); J. Owen, 'George II Reconsidered', in A. Whiteman, J.S. Bromley and P.G.M. Dickson, eds, *Statesmen, Scholars and Merchants* (1973).

More general works include J. Owen, *The Pattern of Politics in Eighteenth Century England* (1962); E. Cruickshanks, 'The Political Management of Sir Robert Walpole', in J. Black, ed., *Britain in the Age of Walpole* (1984); S. Lambert, *Bills and Acts: Legislative Procedure in Eighteenth Century England* (1971); P.D.G. Thomas, *The House of Commons in the Eighteenth Century* (1971).

Sir Lewis Namier's commanding perspectives may be found in L.B. Namier, 'Monarchy and the Party System', in *Personalities and Power* (1962); 'Country Gentlemen in Parliament', in *Personalities and Powers* (1955); *The Structure of Politics at the Accession of George III*, 2nd edn (1982); *England in the Age of the American Revolution*, 2nd edn. (1961)

The state: central and local

On the links between central and local government, consult E.N. Williams, *The Eighteenth Century Constitution* (1970); J. Brewer, *The Sinews of Power* (1989); L.K. Glassey, *Politics and the Appointment of Justices of the Peace, 1675–1725* (1979); N. Landau, *The Justices of the Peace, 1679–1760* (1984); L.K. Glassey, 'Local Government', in C. Jones, ed., *Britain in the First Age of Party* (1987).

On the electoral system, see J. Cannon, *Parliamentary Reform, 1640–1832* (1973); F. O'Gorman, *Voters, Patrons and Parties: The Unreformed Electorate of Hanoverian England, 1734–1832* (1989); 'The Unreformed Electorate of Hanoverian England: The Mid-Eighteenth Century to 1832', *Social History*, 2(1) (1986); 'The Social Meaning of Elections, Campaign Rituals and Ceremonies in England in the Eighteenth and Nineteenth Centuries', *Past and Present*, 135 (May 1992); W.A. Speck, 'The Electorate in the First Age of Party', in C. Jones, ed., *Britain in the First Age of Party* (1987); P. Langford, 'Property and "Virtual Representation" in Eighteenth Century England', *Historical Journal*, 31 (1988); J.A. Phillips, 'The Structure of the Unreformed Electorate', *Journal of British Studies*, 19 (1979).

Whigs and Tories

General works on parties and the party system include R.R. Sedgwick, *The House of Commons, 1715–54*. (2 vols, 1970); B.W. Hill, *The Growth of Parliamentary Parties, 1689–1742* (1976); W.A. Speck, 'Whigs and Tories During Their Glories: English Political Parties Under the First Two Georges', in J.A. Cannon, ed., *The Whig Supremacy* (1981); J.C.D. Clark, *The Dynamics of Change: The Crisis of the 1750s and English Party Systems* (1982); J.C.D. Clark, 'The Decline of Party, 1740–60', *English Historical Review*, 93 (1978).

On the Whigs, consult H.T. Dickinson, *Walpole and the Whig Supremacy* (1973); 'Whiggism in the Eighteenth Century', in J.A. Cannon, ed., *The Whig Supremacy* (1981); J.B. Owen, *The Rise of the Pelhams* (1957); N. Rogers, *Whigs and Cities* (1989); B.W. Hill, *British Parliamentary Parties, 1742–1832* (1985); A.S. Foord, *His Majesty's Opposition, 1714–1832* (1964).

On the Tories, see G.V. Bennett, *The Tory Crisis in Church and State, 1688–1730* (1975); L. Colley, *In Defiance of Oligarchy: The Tory Party, 1714–60* (1982); H.T. Dickinson, *Bolingbroke* (1970); E. Cruickshanks, *Political Untouchables: The Tories and the '45* (1979); J.C.D. Clark, 'The Politics of the Excluded: Tories, Jacobites and Whig Patriots, 1715–60' *Parliamentary History*, 2 (1983); I.R. Christie, 'The Tory Party, Jacobitism and the '45', *Historical Journal*, 30 (4) (1987).

The Jacobites

The Jacobites have attracted an enormous literature in recent years. Among the most useful titles are J. Baynes, *The Jacobite Risings of 1715* (1970); E. Cruickshanks, ed., *Ideology and Conspiracy: Aspects of Jacobitism, 1689–1759* (1992); P.S. Fritz, *The English*

Ministers and Jacobitism Between the Rebellions of 1715 and 1745 (1975); J.S. Gibson, *Playing the Scottish Card: The Franco-Jacobite Invasion of 1708* (1988); R.C. Jarvis, *Collected Papers on the Jacobite Risings* (2 vols, 1972); B. Lenman, *The Jacobite Risings in Britain, 1689–1746* (1980); F. McLynn, *France and the Jacobite Rising of 1745* (1981); *The Jacobites* (1985); P.K. Monod, *The Invention of Scotland: The Stuart Myth and the Scottish Identity* (1991); W.A. Speck, *The Butcher: The Duke of Cumberland and the Suppression of the '45* (1981); D. Szecki, *Jacobitism and Tory Politics, 1710–14* (1984); *The Jacobites: Britain and Europe, 1688–1788* (1994).

Chapter 6. What kind of regime? (1714–1757)

A stable regime?

The two principle texts in the 'stability' debate have been J. Plumb, *The Growth of Political Stability in England, 1675–1725* (1967) and G. Holmes, 'The Achievement of Stability: The Social Context of Politics from the 1680s to the Age of Walpole', in J.A. Cannon, ed., *The Whig Supremacy: Colloquies on Hanoverian England* (1982). Further discussion may be found in J. Black's introductions to two of his own volumes: *Britain in the Age of Walpole* (1984) and *British Politics and Society from Walpole to Pitt* (1990). Half of *Albion*, 25 (2) (1993) was given over to a (rather disappointing) series of papers on the stability debate.

A confessional regime?

A most critical review of J.C.D. Clark's position as expressed in *English Society* will be found in *Enlightenment and Dissent*, 7 (1988), especially pp. 98–100. An interesting restatement of Clark's position is offered in his paper, 'England's Ancien Regime as a Confessional State', *Albion*, 21 (3) (1989).

On the Church of England in the first half of the long eighteenth century, see C.G. Brown, *The Social History of Religion in Scotland Since 1730* (1987); C. Clay, 'The Greed of Whig Bishops? Church Landlords and Their Lessees, 1660–1760', *Past and Present*, 87 (1980); R. Currie, A. Gilbert and L. Horsley, *Churches and Churchgoers: Patterns of Church Growth in the British Isles Since 1700* (1977); A.D. Gilbert, *Religion and Society in Industrial England* (1976); D.R. Hirschberg, 'Episcopal Incomes and Expenses, 1660–1760', in R. O'Day and F. Head, eds, *Princes and Paupers in the English Church, 1500–1800* (1981); E.G. Rupp, *Religion in England, 1688–1791* (1991); N. Sykes, *Edmund Gibson: Bishop of London* (1926); *Church and State in England in the Eighteenth Century* (1934); P. Virgin, *The Church in an Age of Negligence: Ecclesiastical Structure and Problems of Church Reform, 1700–1840* (1989); A. Warner, *Church and Society in Eighteenth Century Devon* (1969).

An ancien régime?

The case for an *ancien régime* was set out by J.C.D. Clark's *English Society* (1985), and in *Revolution and Rebellion* (1986). Among the most vigorous critiques of the thesis is R. Porter, 'English Society in the Eighteenth Century Revisited', in J. Black, ed., *British Politics and Society from Walpole to Pitt* (1990). See also J. Innes, 'Jonathan Clark, Social History and England's "Ancien Regime"', *Past and Present*, 181 (1987). Also valuable is G.S. Rousseau, 'Revisionist Polemics: J.C.D. Clark and the Collapse of Modernity in the Age of Johnson', in P. Korshin, ed., *The Age of Johnson*, III (1989). Shorter discussions may be found in J. Black, 'England's Ancien Regime', *History Today*, 38 (1988) and F. O'Gorman, 'Recent Historiography on the Hanoverian Regime', *Historical Journal*, 29 (1986). The whole of *Albion* 21 (3) (1989) was devoted to discussion of the 'ancien régime' thesis.

Chapter 7. Patriotism and empire, 1756–1789

Commerce and empire

Several of the studies listed for Chapter 4, under 'The Middling Orders,' especially Minchinton, Davis and Wilson, can profitably be consulted. The principal texts also include R. Davis, *The Industrial Revolution and Britain's Overseas Trade* (1979); P. O'Brien, *Power with Profit: The State and the Economy, 1688–1815* (1991); D. Baugh, 'Maritime Strength and the Atlantic Community: The Uses of Grand Marine Empire', in L. Stone, ed., *An Imperial State at War: Britain 1689–1815* (1946); R.F. Thomas and D.N. McLoskey, 'Overseas Trade and Empire, 1700–1860', in R.C. Flood and D.N. McLosky, eds, *The Economic History of Britain since 1700, I: 1700–1860* (1981); J.H. Parry, *Trade and Dominion: The European Overseas Empires in the Eighteenth Century* (1971).

William Pitt and the Seven Years War, 1756–1763

The best of the old biographies of Pitt is by A. von Ruville (1907), which is much less Whiggish than the more popular treatment by Basil Williams (1913). Of more modern works, that by S. Ayling, *The Elder Pitt* (1976), is less prone to hero worship than P. Brown, *William Pitt, Earl of Chatham* (1978). Recent biographies include *Pitt the Elder* by J. Black (1992) and the eagerly awaited volume by M. Peters (1997). Meanwhile, see M. Peters, *Pitt and Popularity: The Patriotic Minister and Public Opinion during the Seven Years War* (1980). See also P. Langford, 'William Pitt and Public Opinion, 1757', *English Historical Review*, 88 (1973); J.P. Greene, 'The Seven Years War and the American Revolution: The Causal Relationship Reconsidered', in P. Marshall and G. Williams, eds, *The British Atlantic Empire Before the American Revolution* (1980). On the conduct of the Seven Years War, see R. Middleton, *The Bells of Victory: The Pitt–Newcastle Ministry and the Conduct of the Seven Years War* (1985).

The origins of the American Revolution, 1756–1776

The best short introduction to this subject is still I.R. Christie, *Crisis of Empire: Great Britain and the American Colonies, 1754–83* (1984). See also I.R. Christie and B.W. Labarce, *Empire or Independence, 1760–1776* (1976); M. Jensen, *The Founding of a Nation: A History of the American Revolution, 1763–76* (1968). The most authoritative account of the British political context is the work of P.D.G. Thomas, *British Politics and the Stamp Act Crisis: The First Phase of the American Revolution, 1763–67* (1975) and *The Townshend Duties Crisis: The Second Phase of the American Revolution, 1767–77* (1987). See also P. Langford, *A Polite and Commercial People: England, 1727–1783* (1989); J.A. Henretta, *Salutary Neglect: Colonial Administration under the Duke of Newcastle* (1972). The British political context is also discussed in J. Derry, *British Politics and the American Revolution* (1976); K. Perry, *British Politics and the American Revolution* (1990). Two further vital texts are P. Lawson, *George Grenville: A Political Life* (1984); P.D.G. Thomas, 'George III and the American Revolution', *History*, 70 (1985).

The American War of Independence, 1776–1783

The best work remains P. Mackesy, *The War for America, 1775–83* (1965), but much has been added to the story of the war in the last three decades. See, e.g. P.D.G. Thomas, *Lord North* (1976); R.A. Bowler, *Logistics and the Failure of the British Army in America, 1773–83* (1975); G. Wills, *Inventing America: Jefferson's Declaration of Independence* (1978). Works by Christie, Derry and Perry will also be of value in this section. See also J.R. Alden, *The American Revolution, 1775–83* (1954); R.W. Von Alstyne, *The Rising American Empire* (1960); M. Beloff, ed., *The Debate on the American Revolution* (1949). For British opinion during the war, compare D.M. Clark, *British Opinion and the American Revolution* (1930) with J.E. Bradley, *Popular Politics and the American Revolution in*

England (1986). On the making of peace, P. Maier, *From Resistance to Revolution: Colonial Radicals and the Development of American Opposition to Britain, 1765–78* (1972), and R.B. Morris, *The Peacemakers: The Great Powers and American Independence* (1965) are still useful.

Chapter 8. The age of George III, 1760–1789

George III and the politicians, 1760–1770

The politics of the first half of the reign of George III has attracted a considerable literature. Convenient summaries will be found in textbooks such as those by Christie, Owen and in general works, such as those by Foord. The traditional, classic discussions of the politics of the new reign are those by L.B. Namier, *England in the Age of the American Revolution*, 2nd edn (1961) and *The Structure of Politics at the Accession of George III*, 2nd edn (1982), together with the critique of H. Butterfield, *George III and the Historians* (1957). See also R. Pares, *George III and the Politicians* (1953).

Useful modern surveys which build on these foundations include B.W. Hill, *British Parliamentary Parties, 1742–1832* (1985); J. Brewer, *Party Ideology and Popular Politics at the Accession of George III* (1976); G.H. Gutteridge, *English Whiggism and the American Revolution* (1966); J. Derry, *British Politics and the American Revolution* (1976); F. O'Gorman, *The Rise of Party in England, 1760–1832* (1982); *The Emergence of the British Two-Party System, 1760–1832* (1982); 'Party in the Late Eighteenth Century', in J.A. Cannon, ed., *The Whig Ascendancy* (1981); K.W. Schweizer, *Lord Bute: Essays in Re-interpretation* (1988); J. Brooke, *The Chatham Administration, 1766–68* (1956); P. Langford, *The First Rockingham Administration* (1973); B. Donoughue, *British Politics and the American Revolution (1773–75)* (1964); I.R. Christie, *The End of North's Ministry* (1958); P.D.G. Thomas, *British Politics and the Stamp Act Crisis, 1763–67* (1975); J.A. Cannon, *The Fox–North Coalition: Crisis of the Constitution* (1969); D. Ginter, *Whig Organization in the General Election of 1790* (1967); J. Derry, *The Regency Crisis and the Whigs* (1963); L.G. Mitchell, *Charles James Fox and the Disintegration of the Whig Party 1782–94* (1971); F. O'Gorman, *The Whig Party and the French Revolution* (1967); *Edmund Burke: His Political Philosophy* (1973); P. Brown, *The Chathamites* (1967); J. Bradley, *Popular Politics and the American Revolution in England* (1986); H. Bowen, *Revenge and Reform: The Indian Problem in British Politics, 1757–73* (1991).

Authoritative recent biographies are rather thin on the ground. The best of them are J. Brooke, *George III* (1972); P.D.G. Thomas, *Lord North* (1976); J. Ehrman, *The Younger Pitt: The Years of Acclaim* (1969); P. Lawson, *George Grenville: A Political Life* (1984).

Reform politics, 1763–1789

On the origins of reform, see H.T. Dickinson, 'The Precursors of Political Radicalism in Augustan Britain,' in C. Jones, ed., *Britain in the First Age of Party* (1987); L. Colley, 'Eighteenth Century Radicalism before Wilkes', *TRHS* 5th series, 31 (1981); R.E. Richey, 'The Origins of British Radicalism: The Changing Rationale for Dissent', *Eighteenth Century Studies*, 7 (1973–6). Seminal early works on the reform movement are still valuable. See G. Rudé, *Wilkes and Liberty* (1962); *Paris and London in the Eighteenth Century* (1973); I.R. Christie, *Wilkes, Wyvill and Reform* (1962); G. Nobb, *The North-Briton* (1939); J.A. Cannon, *Parliamentary Reform, 1660–1832* (1972); E.P. Thompson, *The Making of the English Working Class* (1963); I.R. Christie, 'The Yorkshire Association', *Historical Journal*, 3, 1960 and in I.R. Christie, ed., *Myth and Reality in Late Eighteenth Century British Politics* (1970); J. Norris, *Shelburne and Reform* (1963); E.C. Black, *The Association* (1963); J. Osborne, *John Cartwright* (1972).

More modern studies lack the pioneering perspectives of these early works. See, however, C. Bonwick, *English Radicals and the American Revolution* (1977); J. Brewer, *Party Ideology and Popular Politics at the Accession of George III* (1976); R.E. Toohey, *Liberty and Empire: British Radical Solutions to the American Problem* (1978); T.M. Parsinnen, 'Association, Convention and Anti-Parliament in British Radical Politics, 1771–1848', *English Historical Review, 88* (1973); P. Woodland and B. Heath, 'The Opposition to the 1763 Cider Excises', *Parliamentary History*, 4 (1985); E. Royle and J. Walvin, *English Radicals and Reformers, 1760–1848* (1982); D.G. Wright, *Popular Radicalism: The Working Class Experience, 1780–1880* (1988); H.T. Dickinson, 'Radicals and Reformers in the Age of Wilkes and Wyvill', in J. Black, ed., *British Politics and Society from Walpole to Pitt, 1742–89* (1990); C. Hay, *James Burgh: Spokesman for Reform in Hanoverian England* (1982); C. Haydon, *Anti-Catholicism in Eighteenth Century England, c.1714–80: A Political and Social Study* (1993); P.D.G. Thomas, *John Wilkes: A Friend to Liberty* (1996).

Chapter 9. The crisis of the Hanoverian regime, 1789–1820

The Revolutionary and Napoleonic Wars, 1789–1820

Useful material of an introductory character may be found in D.B. Horn, *Great Britain and Europe in the Eighteenth Century* (1967); E. Evans, *The Forging of the Modern State: Early Industrial Britain, 1783–1870* (1983); and I.R. Christie, *Wars and Revolutions: Britain 1789–1815* (1982); J. Erhman, *The Younger Pitt: The Reluctant Transition* (1983) is the standard work now, but it may be used with P. Mackesy, *The War in the Mediterranean, 1803–10* (1957); R. Glover, *Peninsular Preparations: The Reform of the British Army, 1795–1809* (1963); J. Weller, *Wellington in the Peninsula, 1808–14* (1962); P. Jupp, *Lord Grenville 1759–1834* (1985); P. Mackesy, *Statesmen at War: The Strategy of Overthrow, 1798–9* (1974).

The papers by M. Duffy ('British Diplomacy and the French Wars, 1789–1815') and P. Mackesy ('Strategic Problems of the British War Effort') in J. Black, ed., *Britain and the French Revolution, 1789–1815* (1989) are most valuable.

Radicalism and patriotism, 1789–1820

From the previous section, the works by Erhman, Evans and Christie are of value here. Other volumes mentioned in earlier sections include those by Cannon, Black, Cone, Wright and Royle and Walvin. The classic work remains E.P. Thompson, *The Making of the English Working Class* (1963). His interpretation may be contrasted with that of A. Goodwin, *The Friends of Liberty: The English Democratic Movement in the Age of the French Revolution* (1979). A more concise account, plainly in the Thompson mould, is G. Williams, *Artisans and Sans-Culottes* (1968). More balanced is the brief account in H. Dickinson, *British Radicalism and the French Revolution, 1789–1815* (1985). See also D.J. Jones, *Before Rebecca: Popular Protests in Wales, 1793–1935* (1973); J. Stevenson, *Popular Disturbances in England, 1700–1870* (1979); K.J. Logue, *Popular Disturbances in Scotland, 1780–1815* (1979); J.A. Hone, *For the Cause of Truth: Radicalism in London, 1796–1821* (1982); I. McCalman, *Radical Underworld: Prophets, Revolutionaries and Pornographers in London, 1795–1840* (1988); J. Belchem, *Henry Hunt and English Working Class Radicalism* (1985); M. Elliott, 'The Despard Conspiracy Reconsidered', *Past and Present*, 75 (1977).

On the political activities of loyalists, see E.C. Black, *The Association* (1963); R.B. Dozier, *For King, Constitution and Country: The English Loyalists and the French Revolution* (1983); H. Dickinson, 'Popular Conservatism and Militant Loyalism, 1789–1815', in J. Black, ed., *Britain and the French Revolution, 1789–1815* (1989); A. Booth, 'Popular Loyalism and Public Violence in the North West of England, 1799–1800', *Social History*, 8, (1983); J. Sack, *From Jacobite to Conservative* (1993).

The politics of wartime and after, 1789–1820

Volumes by the following authors mentioned in earlier sections of this bibliography will be useful here: Ehrman (1969), Mitchell (1971), Evans (1983), Christie (1982). Useful general introductions will be found in F. O'Gorman, *The Emergence of the British Two-Party System* (1982) and J.W. Derry, *Politics in the Age of Fox, Pitt and Liverpool* (1990). More specialized studies include J.E. Cookson, *Lord Liverpool's Administration, 1815–22* (1975); A.D. Harvey, *Britain in the Early Nineteenth Century* (1978); B. Hilton, *Cash, Corn and Commerce* (1977). The most useful biographies include C.J. Bartlett, *Castlereagh* (1966); J.W. Derry, *Castlereagh* (1976); P. Ziegler, *Addington* (1965); W. Hinde, *George Canning* (1973); N. Gash, *Lord Liverpool* (1984). On the Whig opposition, see F. O'Gorman, *The Whig Party and the French Revolution* (1967); E.A. Smith, *Whig Principles and Party Politics* (1975); L.Mitchell, *Holland House* (1980); A. Mitchell, *The Whigs in Opposition, 1815–30* (1967); M. Roberts, *The Whig Party, 1807–12* (1939); C. New, *Life of Henry Brougham* (1961).

The avoidance of revolution, 1789–1820

The most dramatic historiographical conflict on this topic is that between I.R. Christie, whose *Stress and Stability in Late Eighteenth Century England* (1984) provides an appreciative and optimistic version of the fortunes of the regime, and the works of Roger Wells: *Insurrection: The British Experience, 1795–1803* (1983) and *Wretched Faces; Famine in War-time England, 1793–1801* (1988), which set out an interpretation more sympathetic to the likelihood of revolution. See also H. Perkin, *The Origins of Modern English Society, 1780–1880* (1969); R. Dozier, 'Democratic Revolution in England: a Possibility?', *Albion*, 4 (4) (1972); C. Emsley, 'The London Insurrection of December, 1792: Fact or Fantasy?', *Journal of British Studies*, 17 (2) (1978). More general discussions include M.I. Thomas, *Threats of Revolution in Britain, 1789–1848* (1977). Useful background to other British preoccupations will be found in G. Rudé, *Revolutionary Europe, 1783–1815* (1964); R.R. Palmer, *The Age of the Democratic Revolution* (2 vols, 1959); D. Jarrett, *The Begetters of Revolution: England's Involvement with France, 1759–89* (1973).

Chapter 10. State and church in later Hanoverian Britain, 1757–1832

Monarchy and the party system, 1780–1832

Many of the books listed for Chapter 9, under 'The Politics of Wartime and After', will be of use in this section. See also H. Hanham, *The Nineteenth Century Constitution* (1969); J. Derry, *Politics in the Age of Fox, Pitt and Liverpool* (1990); W.R. Brock, *Lord Liverpool and Liberal Toryism*, 2nd edn (1967).

J.J. Sack, *The Grenvillites, 1801–29: Party Politics and Factionalism in the Age of Pitt and Liverpool* (1979); R.W. Davis, *Political Change and Continuity: A Buckinghamshire Study* (1972); D. Large, 'The Decline of the Party of the Crown and the Rise of Parties in the House of Lords, 1783–1837', *English Historical Review*, 77 (1963); F. O'Gorman, 'Pitt and the Tory Reaction to the French Revolution, 1789–1815' and J. Derry, 'The Opposition Whigs and the French Revolution' may both be found in H. Dickinson, ed., *Britain and the French Revolution, 1789–1815*, (1989); E.A. Smith, *Lord Grey, 1764–1845* (1990); B. Coleman, *Conservatism and the Conservative Party in Nineteenth Century Britain* (1988); R. Stewart, *British Politics, 1830–32* (1989).

The state and the law

Little has been written about the state in early nineteenth-century Britain. The standard works are H. Parris, *Constitutional Bureaucracy* (1969); H. Roseveare, *The Treasury: Evolution of a British Institution* (1969), which is of far more general significance than its title suggests; and D.M. Young, *The Colonial Office in the Early Nineteenth Century* (1961).

Two valuable recent monographs are P. Harling, *The Waning of Old Corruption: The Politics of Economical Reform in Britain, 1779–1846* (1996) and D. Eastwood, *Governing Rural England: Traditions and Transformation in Local Government, 1780–1840* (1994).

Crime and criminals have attracted far more attention. J. Beattie, *Crime and the Courts in England, 1660–1800* (1986); J. Beattie, 'The Pattern of Crime in England, 1660–1800', *Past and Present*, 62 (1974); A.R. Ekirch, *Bound for America: The Transportation of British Convicts to the Colonies, 1718–75* (1987); C. Emsley, *Crime and Society in England, 1750–1900* (1987); V. Gatrell, *The Hanging Tree: Execution and the English People, 1770–1868* (1994); D. Hay *et al.*, *Albion's Fatal Tree: Crime and Society in Eighteenth Century England* (1977); D. Hay, 'War, Dearth and Theft in the Eighteenth Century', *Past and Present*, 95 (1982); M. Ignatieff, *A Just Measure of Pain: The Penitentiary in the Industrial Revolution, 1750–1850* (1978); P. King, 'Decision Makers and Decision Making in the English Criminal Law, 1750–1800', *Historical Journal*, 27 (1984); P. Linebaugh, *The London Hanged: Crime and Civil Society in the Eighteenth Century* (1992); J. Styles and J. Brewer, *An Ungovernable People: The English and Their Law in the Seventeenth and Eighteenth Centuries* (1980); E.P. Thompson, *Whigs and Hunters: The Origins of the Black Act* (1975); M. de Lacy, *Prison Reform in Lancashire, 1700–1850: A Study in Local Administration* (1986).

The retreat from the confessional state, 1756–1820

Anglicans and Evangelicals

Many of the works listed for Chapter 6 under 'A Confessional Regime?' will continue to assist students in this period. See also, on the established church, E.R. Norman, *Church and Society in England, 1770–1970* (1976); A. Smith, *The Established Church and Popular Religion, 1750–1850* (1971); M. Smith, *Religion in Industrial Society: Oldham and Saddleworth, 1740–1865* (1994); W.R. Ward, *Religion and Society in England, 1790–1850* (1972).

The Evangelicals continue to attract historians. Recent works include M. Noll, D. Bebbington and G. Rawlyk, eds, *Evangelicalism: Comparative Studies of Popular Protestantism in North America, the British Isles and Beyond, 1700–1900* (1994); B. Hilton, *The Age of Atonement: The Influence of Evangelicalism on Social and Economic Thought, 1785–1865* (1988); D. Bebbington, *Evangelicalism in Modern Britain: A History from the 1730s to the 1980s* (1989); M.J. Crawford, 'Origins of the Eighteenth Century Evangelical Revival: England and New England Compared', *Journal of British Studies*, 26(4) (Oct. 1987); S. Drescher, *Capitalism and Anti-slavery: British Mobilization in Comparative Perspective* (1987); D. Eltis, *Economic Growth and the Ending of the Atlantic Slave Trade* (1987).

Abolitionism has attracted much attention recently: D. Turley, *The Culture of English Anti-Slavery, 1780–1860* (1991); J.R. Oldfield, *Popular Politics and British Anti-Slavery: The Mobilisation of Public Opinion against the Slave Trade, 1787–1807* (1995).

Methodists and Dissenters

Methodism has been rather better served than Dissent by the historical work of the last generation. See S. Andrews, *Methodism and Society* (1970); A. Armstrong, *The Church of England, the Methodists and Society* (1973); R. Currie, *Methodism Divided* (1968); R. Davies and E.G. Rupp, eds, *A History of the Methodist Church of Great Britain* (2 vols, 1965); F. Dreyer, 'A "Religious Society under Heaven": John Wesley and the Identity of Methodism', *Journal of British Studies*, 25(1) (1986); D. Hempton, *Methodism and Politics in British Society, 1750–1850* (1984); B. Semmel, *The Methodist Revolution* (1973); E.R. Taylor, *Methodism and Politics, 1791–1851* (1935).

Books on the Dissenters include C.G. Bolam, *The English Presbyterians* (1968); T. Laqueur, *Religion and Respectability: Sunday Schools and Working Class Culture* (1976); I.

Sellers, *Nineteenth Century Nonconformity* (1967); A.C. Underwood, *History of the English Baptists* (1947); M. Watts, *The Dissenters: From the Reformation to the French Revolution* (1978).

Chapter II. The social foundations of the later Hanoverian regime, 1757–1832

The United Kingdom

Many of the titles listed for Chapter 4, under 'The Identity of Britain', have relevance in this section, especially those by Colley, Lenman and Kearney. They should be supplemented, above all, by G. Newman, *The Rise of English Nationalism: A Cultural History, 1740–1830* (1987). Works on Scotland have poured from the presses in recent years. The following is a small selection: C. Camic, *Experience and Enlightenment: Socialization for Cultural Change in Eighteenth Century Scotland* (1983); M. Fry, *The Dundas Despotism* (1992); R. Houston, *Scottish Literacy and Scottish Identity: Literacy and Society in Scotland and Northern England, c. 1600–1800* (1988); C. Kidd, *Subverting Scotland's Past* (1993); J. Robertson, *The Scottish Enlightenment and the Militia Issue* (1985).

On Ireland, a veritable renaissance in the field of eighteenth-century studies has been taking place. See e.g. D. Dickson, *New Foundations: Ireland 1660–1800* (1987); N. Curtis, *The United Irishmen* (1994); M. Elliot, *Partners in Revolution* (1982); A.P. Malcolmson, *John Foster: The Politics of the Anglo-Irish Ascendancy* (1978); R.B. McDowell, *Ireland in the Age of Imperialism and Revolution, 1760–1801* (1979); J. Smyth, *Men of Property* (1992); G. O'Brien, *Anglo-Irish Politics in the Age of Grattan and Pitt* (1987).

Useful literature on the empire in the second half of the long eighteenth century is led by C.A. Bayly, *Imperial Meridian: The British Empire and the World, 1780–1830* (1989); P.N. Miller, *Defining the Common Good: Empire, Religion and Philosophy in Eighteenth Century Britain* (1994); B. Semmel, *The Rise of Free Trade Imperialism* (1970); V.T. Harlow and F. Madden, *British Colonial Developments, 1774–1834* (1953); P.J. Marshall, *Problems of Empire: Britain and India, 1757–1813* (1968).

Economy and empire

The literature on these topics is little less than mountainous. A very brief selection would include the following: **On Population**: M.W. Flinn, *British Population Growth, 1700–1850* (1970); E.A. Wrigley and R.S. Schofield, *The Population History of England, 1541–1871: A Reconstruction* (1981). **On Industry**: M. Berg, *The Age of Manufacture, 1700–1820* (1985); M.J. Daunton, *Progress and Poverty: An Economic and Social History of Britain, 1700–1850* (1995); P. Hudson, ed., *Regions and Industries: A Perspective on the Industrial Revolution in Britain* (1989); P. Matthias, *The First Industrial Nation* (1969); J. Rule, *The Vital Century: England's Developing Econnomy, 1714–1815* (1992). **On Commerce**: P.J. Cain, *Economic Foundations of British Overseas Expansion, 1815–1914* (1980); V.T. Harlow, *The Founding of the Second British Empire, 1763–93*, I (1952). On the cost of the French wars: P. O'Brien, 'Public Finance and the Wars with France, 1793–1815', in H. Dickinson, ed., *Britain and the French Revolution, 1789–1815* (1989).

The social order

A transfiguring aristocracy

Several of the titles listed for Chapter 4, under 'The Ruling Order', are equally relevant to this section, especially those by Beckett, Cannon, Clark and Stone. Further reading includes J. Bourne, *Patronage and Society in Nineteenth Century England* (1986); D. Cannadine, *Lords and Landlords: The Aristocracy and the Towns* (1980); L. Colley, *Britons: Forging the Nation, 1707–1837* (1992); D. Eastwood, *Governing Rural England: Traditions and Transformation in Local Government, 1780–1840* (1994); P. Horn, *The Rural*

World: Social Change in the English Countryside, 1780–1850 (1980); D.R. Mills, *Lord and Peasant in Nineteenth Centruy Britain* (1980); H. Perkin, *The Origins of Modern English Society, 1780–1880* (1969); M. Reed, *The Georgian Triumph, 1700–1830* (1984); F.M.L. Thompson, *English Landed Society in the Nineteenth Century* (1963).

A cohering middle class

The work of Bourne in the previous section gives a view of the aspirant members of the middling orders seeking political advancement. Langford's works listed for Chapter 4 are likewise relevant, as are those of Corfield, Clark, Chalklin, (J.) Raven and Wilson. In general, the middling orders may be rapidly recovering from their traditional neglect. See D.T. Andrew, *Philanthropy and Police: London Charity in the Eighteenth Century* (1989); L. Davidoff and C. Hall, *Family Fortunes: Men and Women of the English Middle Class, 1730–1850* (1987); T. Koditschek, *Class Formation and Urban Industrial Society: Bradford, 1750–1850* (1990); J. Money, *Experience and Identity: Birmingham and the West Midlands, 1760–1800* (1977); W.D. Rubinstein, *Elites and the Wealthy in Modern British History* (1987); G. Russell, *The Theatres of War: Performance, Politics and Society, 1793–1815* (1995); D. Wahrman, *Imagining the Middle Class: The Political Representation of Class* (1995); J. Walvin, *English Urban Life, 1776–1851* (1984); J. Wolff and J. Seed, eds, *The Culture of Capital: Art, Power and the Nineteenth Century Middle Class* (1988). The entire volume of *Journal of British Studies*, 32(4) (1993) is given over to essays on 'Making the English Middle Class, c. 1700–1850'.

A self-conscious working class

All discussions of this subject begin with E.P. Thompson, *The Making of the English Working Class* (1963; rev. edn 1968). Other books listed earlier (Chapter 4, under 'The Common People') may profitably be consulted in this section, especially that by Snell. Studies more particularly devoted to the period covered by this chapter include C. Behagg, *Politics and Production in the Early Nineteenth Century* (1990); R.W. Bushaway, *By Rite: Custom, Ceremony and Community in England, 1700–1800* (1982); D. Bythell, *The Sweated Trades* (1978); J. Foster, *Class Struggle in the Industrial Revolution* (1974); E.J. Hobsbawm, *Labouring Men* (1964); E.J. Hobsbawm and G. Rudé, *Captain Swing* (1969); E. Hopkins, *A Social History of the English Working Classes* (1979); T. Laquer, *Religion and Respectability: Sunday Schools and Working Class Culture, 1780–1850* (1976); J. Rule, *The Labouring Classes in Early Industrial England, 1750–1850* (1986); R. Wells, *Wretched Faces: Famine in War-time England, 1793–1801* (1988).

Constructions of gender in later Hanoverian Britain

From the dozens of titles which have poured from the presses, the following selection can be recommended: A. Clark, *Women's Silence, Men's Violence: Sexual Assault in England, 1770–1845* (1987); A. Clark, *The Struggle for the Breeches: Gender and the Making of the English Working Class* (1995); L. Davidoff and C. Hall, *Family Fortunes: Men and Women of the English Middle Class, 1780–1850* (1992); M. Ferguson, *Subject to Others: British Women Writers and Colonial Slavery, 1670–1834* (1992); B. Fowlkes-Tobin, ed., *History, Gender and Eighteenth Century Literature* (1994); B. Hill, *Women, Work and Sexual Politics in Eighteenth Century England* (1989); M. Jackson, *Newborn Child Murder: Women, Illegitimacy and the Courts in Eighteenth Century England* (1996); A. Laurence, *Women in England, 1500–1760: A Social History* (1994); G. Malmgreen, *Religion in the Lives of English Women, 1760–1930* (1986); M. Prior, ed., *Women in English Society, 1500–1800* (1985); K. Snell, *Annals of the Labouring Poor: Social Change and Agrarian England, 1660–1900* (1985); K. Straub, *Sexual Suspects: Eighteenth Century Players and Sexual Ideology* (1992); C. Turner, *Living by the Pen: Women Writers in the Eighteenth Century* (1992).

Chapter 12. The renewal of the regime, 1820–1832

The coming of reform, 1820–1830

The Reform Crisis is covered in a number of works listed for Chapter 10, including those by Davis, Stewart, Smith and Coleman. Relevant works listed in for Chapter 11 include Cannon, Colley, Eastwood, Thompson, Hobsbawm, Rudé and Foster. See also R. Brent, *Liberal-Anglican Politics: Whiggery, Religion and Reform, 1830–41* (1987); M. Brock, *The Great Reform Act* (1973).

The passage of reform, 1830–1832

Excellent accounts may be found in M. Brock, *The Great Reform Act* (1973) chs 4–9; J.R.M. Butler, *The Passing of the Reform Bill* (1914); J. Cannon, *Parliamentary Reform* (1972), ch. 10; P. Mandler, *Aristocratic Government in the Age of Reform: Whigs and Liberals, 1830–52* (1990); I. Newbold, *Whiggery and Reform, 1830–41: The Politics of Government* (1990).

The Reform Act of 1832

On the Act itself, see J. Cannon, *Parliamentary Reform*, ch. 11; F. O'Gorman, *Voters, Patrons and Parties: The Unreformed Electorate of Hanoverian England, 1714–1832* (1989). R. Blake, *The Conservative Party from Peel to Churchill* (1970); N. Gash, *Reaction and Reconstruction in English Politics, 1832–52* (1965); *Politics in the Age of Peel*, rev. edn (1977); T. Hoppen, *Elections, Politics and Society in Ireland, 1832–85* (1984); D.C. Moore, *The Politics of Deference* (1976); J.A. Phillips, *The Great Reform Bill in the Boroughs: English Electoral Behaviour, 1818–41* (1992); J. Prest, *Politics in the Age of Cobden* (1977); C. Seymour, *Electoral Reform in England and Wales* (1970 edn); J. Vernon, *Politics and the People: A Study in English Political Culture, c.1815–67* (1993).

Index